Etruscan Civilization

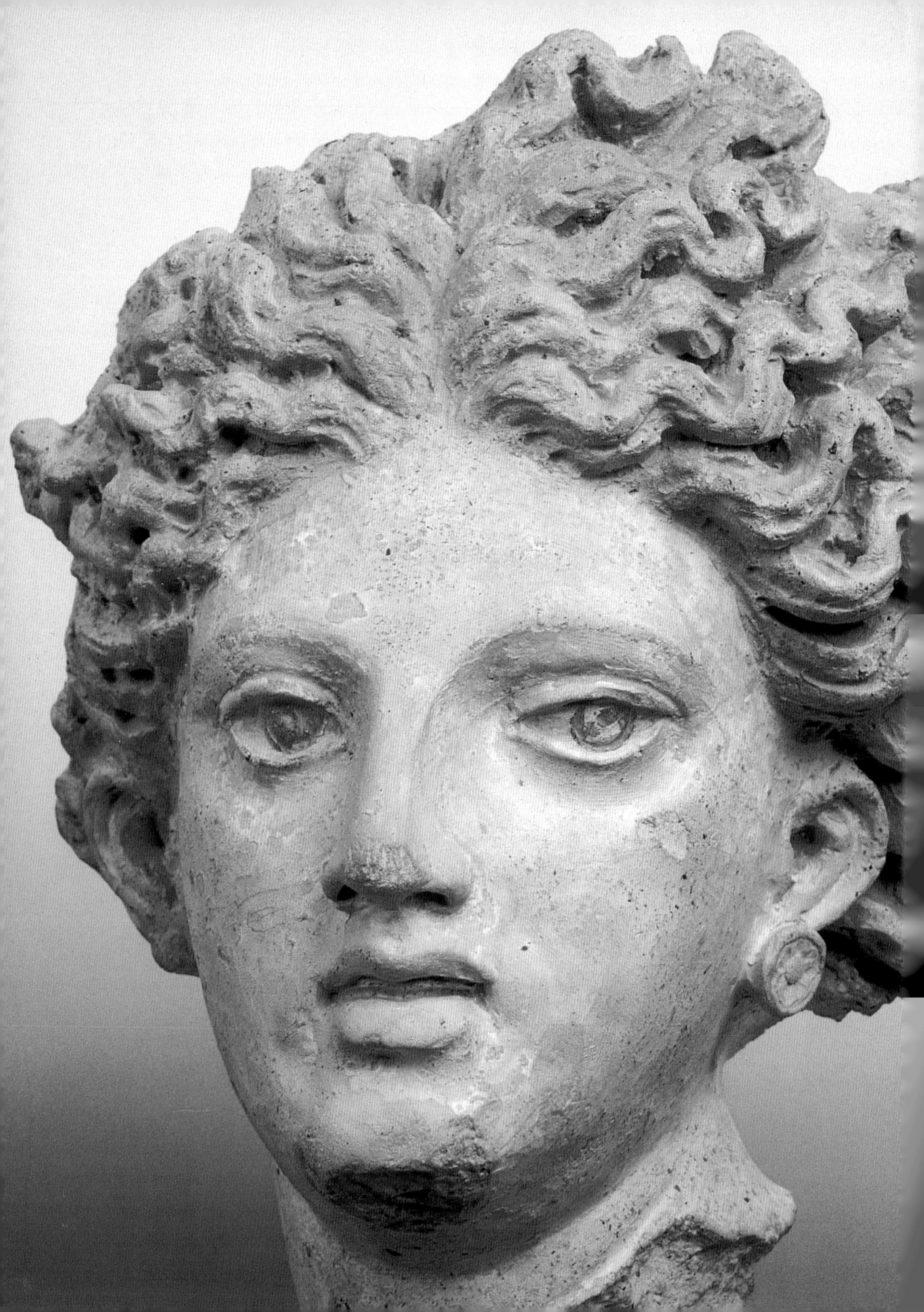

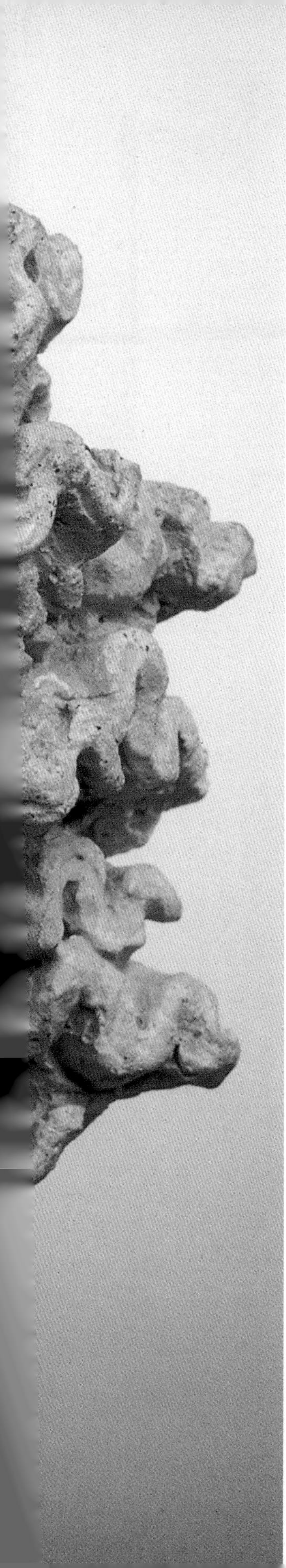

Etruscan Civilization

A Cultural History

Sybille Haynes

THE J. PAUL GETTY MUSEUM, LOS ANGELES

Thick as autumnal leaves that strew the brooks
in Vallombrosa, where the Etrurian shades
high overarched embower.

—Milton, *Paradise Lost*

1200 Getty Center Drive, Suite 400
Los Angeles, California 90049-1681

www.getty.edu/publications

Chris Hudson, *Publisher*
Mark Greenberg, *Managing Editor*

Benedicte Gilman, *Senior Editor*
Elizabeth Chapin Kahn, *Production Coordinator*
Pamela Patrusky Mass, *Designer*
David Fuller, *Cartographer*

Typography by G & S Typesetters
Printed in Hong Kong

FRONTISPIECE: Head of a young woman (Leukothea?). See figure 155.

Library of Congress Cataloging-in-Publication Data

Haynes, Sybille.
Etruscan civilization : a cultural history / Sybille Haynes.
p.cm.
Includes bibliographical references and index.
ISBN 0-89236-575-7 (cloth)
1. Etruscans. 2. Etruria–Civilization. 3. Italy–History–Etruscan influences. I. Title: Etruscan civilization. II. Title: Etruscan civilization. III. Title.

DG223.3 .H39 2000
937.5–dc21 00-025732

To the memory of my husband,
Denys Eyre Lankester Haynes (1913–1994), and
of our friend Kaoru Shepherd (1951–1993)

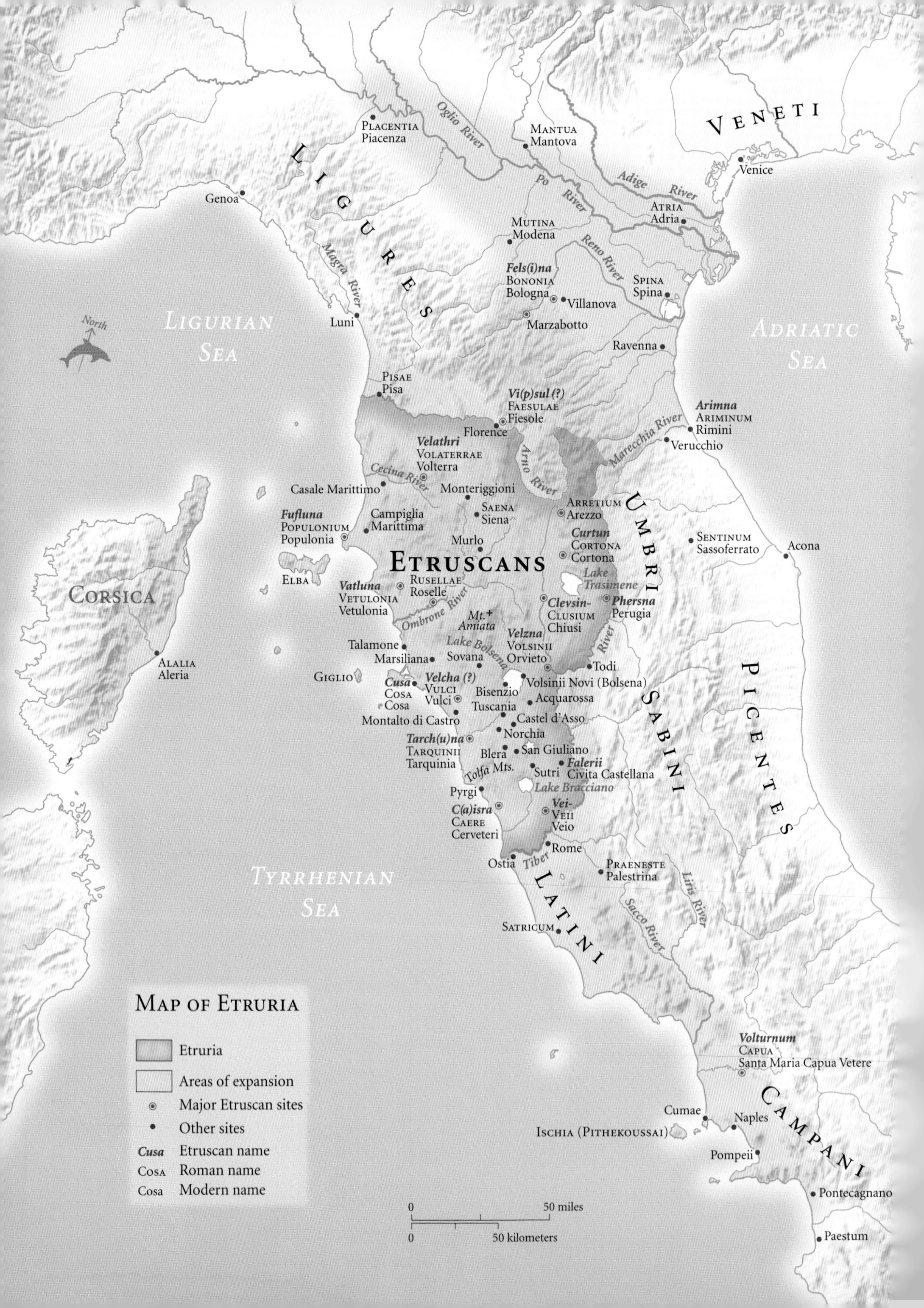

Map of Etruria
Etruria
Areas of expansion
Major Etruscan sites
Other sites
Cusa Etruscan name
Cosa Roman name
Cosa Modern name
0 50 miles
0 50 kilometers
North
Ligures
Veneti
Etruscans
Umbri
Sabini
Picentes
Latini
Campani
Ligurian Sea
Adriatic Sea
Tyrrhenian Sea
Corsica
Elba
Giglio
Ischia (Pithekoussai)
Placentia
Piacenza
Mantua
Mantova
Venice
Oglio River
Po River
Adige River
Atria
Adria
Genoa
Mutina
Modena
Reno River
Magra River
Fels(i)na
Bononia
Bologna
Villanova
Spina
Spina
Luni
Marzabotto
Ravenna
Pisae
Pisa
Vi(p)sul (?)
Faesulae
Fiesole
Arimna
Ariminum
Rimini
Florence
Marecchia River
Verucchio
Velathri
Volaterrae
Volterra
Arno River
Cecina River
Casale Marittimo
Monteriggioni
Arretium
Arezzo
Fufluna
Populonium
Populonia
Campiglia
Marittima
Saena
Siena
Murlo
Curtun
Cortona
Cortona
Sentinum
Sassoferrato
Acona
Lake Trasimene
Vatluna
Vetulonia
Vetulonia
Rusellae
Roselle
Ombrone River
Clevsin-
Clusium
Chiusi
Phersna
Perugia
Mt. Amiata
Velzna
Volsinii
Orvieto
Lake Bolsena
Talamone
Marsiliana
Sovana
Todi
Tiber River
Alalia
Aleria
Cusa
Cosa
Cosa
Velcha (?)
Vulci
Vulci
Bisenzio
Volsinii Novi (Bolsena)
Acquarossa
Tuscania
Montalto di Castro
Castel d'Asso
Norchia
Tarch(u)na
Tarquinii
Tarquinia
Blera
San Giuliano
Tolfa Mts.
Sutri
Falerii
Civita Castellana
Lake Bracciano
Pyrgi
C(a)isra
Caere
Cerveteri
Vei-
Veii
Veio
Rome
Ostia
Tiber
Praeneste
Palestrina
Liris River
Sacco River
Satricum
Volturnum
Capua
Santa Maria Capua Vetere
Cumae
Naples
Pompeii
Pontecagnano
Paestum

Contents

Foreword

Friendships and the valuable associations made through them offer many different dividends, often unexpected. It is only fair to say that this book is such a dividend, for it began with our working together with Sybille Haynes on the exhibition catalogue for the collection of Barbara and Lawrence Fleischman. Sybille and her husband Denys had enjoyed the close friendship of the Fleischmans for several years, as had many of us in the Museum, yet we had never had the opportunity to meet or to discuss our many overlapping interests. For the preparation of the Fleischman catalogue, however, we suddenly found ourselves in close and fairly constant contact, since Sybille was writing the entries for most of the Etruscan material in the collection.

To complement the exhibition's opening in Malibu, the Museum also organized a lecture series related to the various aspects of the collection, and Sybille came to speak about the Etruscans. Immediately impressed by her extraordinary familiarity with all aspects of Etruscan history and archaeology, the audience was captivated by her enthusiasm for this pre-Roman culture. They realized that they were hearing new information about recent discoveries, intelligently woven together with her discussions of the individual objects on view in the galleries—all in an effort to bring this highly developed civilization to life.

Following the lecture, we talked about the enduring public interest in the Etruscans, whose social values—especially their acceptance of a prominent position for women—have such an appeal for contemporary society, but whose complex culture remains little understood by all but the most committed scholars. Available publications on the subject have been few, and important results of ongoing excavations have often rendered those out of date fairly quickly. At the same time, classical scholarship has been slow to recognize that the Etruscans had a distinctive and unique civilization that did not offer easy parallels with the better-studied contemporary civilizations of ancient Rome, Greece, Turkey, and the Near East. The time therefore seemed propitious for a new book on the subject, and Sybille Haynes was clearly the person to write it.

For this study, the author has distilled her many years of experience working with the exceptional Etruscan collections in the British Museum—most the fruits of nineteenth-century excavations. In addition, her research has always been informed by close contact with the ongoing excavations in Italy, where she is a frequent scholar in residence, meeting with colleagues and seeking out every small regional museum and accessible Etruscan site to learn of the latest discoveries and their interpretations. The text covers more than nine centuries, making comprehensible the important transition from the early Iron Age cultures of the region to the fully developed Etruscan confederation of twelve cities. It explores in detail many of the changes in these urban areas and their related sanctuaries and ports following them to their decline and defeat by Rome. Modern finds and theories are often confirmed in references from ancient sources of which the author has a formidable command. Many of the material remains interpreted here come from tomb complexes, and as the author demonstrates again and again, they are critically important for our understanding of domestic architecture, social organization, cult practices, and international trade.

The preparation of this book, especially the identification and collection of the illustrations, was an arduous task that required the assistance of a number of collaborators, most notably Mary Louise Hart, who served as photo editor, and Benedicte Gilman, who served as text editor. Christopher Hudson, Head of Publications for the J. Paul Getty Museum, provided the much-needed administrative support to get the publication approved, since it fell somewhat outside the Museum's usual projects. It was, however, the unflagging commitment of Sybille Haynes that saw this book through to completion, in spite of great personal loss with the death of her beloved husband. Her fortitude is as inspiring as her scholarship, and we are indebted to her for her dedication.

MARION TRUE
Curator of Antiquities
The J. Paul Getty Museum

Acknowledgments

The present book could not have been written without the published original research of countless friends and colleagues who will, no doubt, recognize their own contributions, which I have incorporated into my text, selecting from the mass of material available what was relevant to my theme. In a general work of this nature it is impossible to acknowledge in detail all the sources I have made use of, for a complete bibliography, particularly of all articles consulted in periodicals, would exceed the limits possible and overburden the nonspecialist reader. The bibliography concentrates on the most recent publications and on such books, collective volumes, and articles that themselves provide bibliographical references to earlier literature.

I have received invaluable help and information for which I owe a debt of gratitude to the following: Benedetta Adembri, Luciana Aigner-Foresti, Anna Maria Bietti Sestieri, Fritzi Jurgeit Blanck, Horst Blanck, Piera Bocci Pacini, Francesca Boitani, Marisa Bonamici, Larissa Bonfante, Maria Bonghi Jovino, J. Rasmus Brandt, Stefano Bruni, Caroline Bruzelius, Friederike Bubenheimer, Francesco Buranelli, Cristina Cagianelli, Mirella Marini Calvani, Giovannangelo Camporeale, Maria Cataldi, Gabriele Cateni, Jette Christiansen, Edith Cicerchia, Giovanni Colonna, Elena Colonna di Paolo, Enzo Crea, the late Mauro Cristofani, Nancy Thomson De Grummond, Filippo Delpino, Richard De Puma, Carlo De Simone, Adriana Emiliozzi, Anna Maria Esposito, Anna Eugenia Feruglio, Edilberto Formigli, Bettina von Freytag, Françoise Gaultier, Fernando Gilotta, Jean Gran-Aymerich, Friedrich-Wilhelm von Hase, Eric Hostetter, Jean-René Jannot, Alan W. Johnston, Ines Jucker, Lars Karlsson, Ingrid Krauskopf, Irene S. Lemos, Fulvia Lo Schiavo, Claire L. Lyons, Ellen Macnamara, Guglielmo Maetzke, Elisabetta Mangani, Marina Martelli, Madeleine Mertens-Horn, Laura M. Michetti, Bryan Miller, Alessandra Minetti, Massimo Morandi, Cristiana Morigi Govi, Alessandro Naso, Jenifer Neils, Marjatta Nielsen, Benedetta Origo, the late Massimo Pallottino, Maristella Pandolfini Angeletti, Giulio Paolucci, Paola Pelagatti, Friedhelm Prayon, Tom Rasmussen, Annette Rathje, the late Emeline Hill Richardson, David Ridgway, Antonella Romualdi, Tracey Schuster, Anna Maria Sgubini Moretti, Stephan Steingräber, Simonetta Stopponi, Ingrid Strøm, Judith Swaddling, János G. Szilágyi, Peter Ward-Jackson, Cornelia Weber-Lehmann, Charlotte Wikander, Örjan Wikander, Dyfri Williams, Ingela M. B. Wiman, Nancy Winter, and Wim de Wit.

The hospitality of outstanding libraries and their staffs have greatly facilitated the research necessary; my thanks go in particular to the Deutsches Archäologisches Institut in Rome, the American Academy in Rome, the Greek and Roman Department of the British Museum, the Ashmolean Museum, and the Getty Research Institute for the History of Art and the Humanities.

I gratefully acknowledge the patient help received from James Vickers and the late Susan Vickers during my first faltering attempts to come to terms with a computer.

The writing of this book was most generously encouraged and fostered by Marion True of the Antiquities Department of the J. Paul Getty Museum, and Mary Louise Hart's tireless devotion to the complex collaborative task of illustrating it has made its completion possible. I am also extremely grateful to Susan Downey, Jean Turfa, and Francesca Serra Ridgway for expertly and helpfully reading the manuscript at an early stage.

S.H.

Introduction

In the English-speaking world Etruscan civilization has not always received the attention its importance merits. The decisive role the Etruscans played in receiving and adapting the cultural and artistic achievements of the Near Eastern civilizations and of Greece and transmitting them to the nascent Rome as well as to the neighboring Italic peoples and the inhabitants of Europe beyond the Alps is often overlooked; nor have the original contributions that Etruscan civilization made, either directly or indirectly, to the development of Europe been sufficiently emphasized.

The most recent of the many great Etruscan exhibitions shown during the last forty years in Italy, France, Germany, and Scandinavia took place in 1992–1993 and was specifically designed to demonstrate the importance of the Etruscans in the European context. Characteristically, the important exhibitions held in Paris in 1992 and Berlin in 1993 with their catalogues, *Les Étrusques et l'Europe* (Milan, 1992) and *Die Etrusker und Europa* (Milan, 1993), reached neither the United Kingdom nor the United States of America, though two exhibitions of objects from the Vatican did travel to the latter: *Antichità dall'Umbria a New York* (Perugia, 1991) and *The Etruscans: Legacy of a Lost Civilization from the Vatican Museums* (Memphis, 1992). Yet, continuous excavations in Italy, the study of new finds, and the reexamination of the material in museums have led to an ever deeper understanding of the Etruscans and their way of life.

It therefore seems opportune to attempt to provide a fresh general picture of the growth of Etruscan civilization, incorporating recent discoveries and discussing the many new insights and problems that have emerged. In order to make the book accessible to a wider public as well as to students, the use of technical jargon has been avoided as much as possible.

The second aim of the book is to survey the role played by Etruscan women. The last decades have seen a flood of studies dealing with various aspects of women in antiquity. But while almost no area in the life and death of Greek and Roman women has been left unexplored, the condition of Etruscan women has received less attention.

The first to occupy himself with this subject was J. J. Bachofen, whose influential ideas were published in *Das Mutterrecht: Eine Untersuchung über die Gynaikokratie der alten Welt nach ihrer religiösen und rechtlichen Natur* (Basel, 1861) and in *Die Sage von Tanaquil* (Heidelberg, 1870). Fresh impetus was provided a century later by a chapter on the Etruscan family in J. Heurgon's classic study, *La Vie quotidienne chez les Étrusques* (Paris, 1961). Since then the center of interest in the subject has been, not surprisingly, the United States, and it is from there that the majority of the important contributions in this field have come, most notably those of L. Bonfante: "The Women of Etruria," *Arethusa* 6 (1973): 91–101; "Etruscan Women: A Question of Interpretation," *Archaeology* 26 (1973): 242–56; "Etruscan Couples and Their Aristocratic Society," in *Reflections of*

Women in Antiquity, comp. H. P. Foley, pp. 323–42 (New York, 1981); "Dedicated Mothers," *Visible Religion: Annual for Religious Iconography* 3 (1981): 1–17; "Etruscan Women," in *Women in the Classical World*, E. Fantham et al., pp. 243–59 (New York, 1994); "Etruscan Sexuality and Funerary Art," in *Sexuality in Ancient Art*, ed. N. Boymel Kampen et al., pp. 155–69 (Cambridge, 1996); and "Nursing Mothers in Classical Art," in *Naked Truths: Women, Sexuality, and Gender in Classical Art and Archaeology*, ed. A. O. Koloski-Ostion and C. Lyons, pp. 174–96 (New York, 1997).

After M. Sordi's article "La donna etrusca," *Misoginia e maschilismo in Grecia e in Roma*, Pubblicazioni dell'Istituto di filologia classica e medievale 71 (Genoa, 1981), pp. 49–67, the first Italian book devoted entirely to Etruscan women appeared in Rome in 1989: *Le donne in Etruria*, ed. A. Rallo. A collaborative effort of eight female scholars—most, but not all, Italian—the volume deals with selected aspects of women's life and status in Etruria, as illuminated by works of art and other archaeological evidence and by the scanty references in Greek and Roman literature. Despite its distinguished authors, large bibliography, and numerous illustrations, *Le donne in Etruria* is a collection of essays of varying quality, which, perhaps inevitably given the number of different authors, suffers from a certain lack of focus. (For an exhaustive review of the book, see M. Martelli, in *Rivista di Filologia e di Istruzione Classica* 119 [1991], fasc. 3: 337–41.)

Etruscan civilization as a whole has hitherto tended to be seen through male eyes; but to see it through female eyes alone would be to invite a corresponding imbalance. As M. Nielsen has sagely remarked in "Women and Family in a Changing Society: A Quantitative Approach to Late Etruscan Burials," *Analecta Romana* 17–18 (1988–1989): 53–98, "Originally, my purpose had been to focus on women, but it proved impossible to separate the study of women from the study of their family, including men and children, as well as their society as a whole in its historical setting."

Any attempt to give a balanced account of what life appears to have been like for Etruscan women, as well as Etruscan men, in the long course of the people's history from the tenth to the first century B.C. is fraught with difficulties and uncertainties. Of these the greatest is the scarcity of passages concerning the Etruscans in ancient written sources. No Etruscan literature or historiography has survived; and when preserved texts by later Greek or Roman writers mention the Etruscans, their comments are often impaired by strong anti-Etruscan bias and inevitably affected by the spirit of their own times. Lost are works that might have been invaluable, such as the *Etruscarum rerum libri* (Books of Etruscan matters) by the Roman grammarian Verrius Flaccus and the twenty volumes of *Tyrrhenika*, written in Greek by the emperor Claudius. Surviving documents in Etruscan are mainly short funerary or votive inscriptions or fragmentary ritual texts that provide only scant information about the people's social and political institutions and cult practices.

Although we now dispose of an enormous amount of archaeological material, most of it derives from grave contexts and therefore gives us a somewhat lopsided picture, reflecting a way of death rather than of life. Furthermore, the majority of the excavated tombs belonged to aristocratic or well-to-do families and thus illuminate the economic and cultural setting of only the upper social strata, while the tombs of the poor have left few or no traces. In recent years, however, remains of a growing number of Etruscan settlements, farms, cities, fortifications, roads, and ports have been explored, and this has added greatly to our knowledge of secular activity: domestic and public architecture, agriculture and manufacture, commerce, transport, shipping, etc. But the sites of the most important Etruscan cities have been continuously inhabited until the present day, with the result that their remains are frequently inaccessible to archaeologists, overlaid as they are by the buildings of successive generations of inhabitants. Etruscan cemeteries, on the other hand, were always situated outside the cities and are thus often still in the open countryside, where they can be excavated more easily—unfortunately not only by scholars but also by clandestine diggers.

We know much more about certain periods of Etruscan history than about others. This is due partly to the somewhat haphazard process of excavation which, in the nature of things, cannot always follow a systematic plan, and partly to the large quantity of unpublished material kept in museum reserves and thus not yet available for the reconstruction of the Etruscans' past.

Lastly, Etruscan civilization is far from homogenous. There are strong geographical and cultural differences between the various regions of Etruria; moreover, as in most other civilizations, the lapse of time—here we shall be surveying nine centuries—inevitably brought change and development in the culture and art of the different cities and the more isolated rural areas.

The picture that emerges from these pages will necessarily be tentative and uneven, and the reader will have to bear in mind that conclusions drawn from the surviving material may need revision in light of as-yet-unpublished objects or future discoveries. Within the limits of these qualifications we shall try to give a coherent account of the development of Etruscan civilization, and for each period we shall discuss a selection of significant material remains that can tell us something about the life and status of women at that time. Such an approach inevitably leads to some chronological overlap, but it may serve to dispel widespread popular misconceptions about the "mystery" of the Etruscans and their uniqueness and isolation in the ancient world.

For reasons of space a detailed discussion of the Etruscan pantheon had to be excluded at the request of the publishers.

In order not to confuse the nonspecialist reader, footnotes in the text have been avoided. Instead, there is a classified bibliography at the end.

Abbreviations

Bibliographic abbreviations are listed on p. 390.

CLASSICAL REFERENCES

Ael. *NA* Claudius Aelianus *De natura animalium* (On the nature of animals)

Ael. *VH* Claudius Aelianus *Varia historia* (Miscellany)

Arist. *Pol.* Aristotle *Politika* (Politics)

Arn. Arnobius *Adversus nationes* (The case against the pagans)

Ath. Athenaeus *Deipnosophistai* (The learned banquet)

Cic. *Div.* Cicero *De divinatione* (On prophesy)

Cic. *Leg.* Cicero *De legibus* (Laws)

Diod. Sic. Diodorus Siculus *Bibliothēkē* (Library)

Dion. Hal. *Rom. Arch.* Dionysios of Halikarnassos *Romaikē Archaiologia* (Roman antiquities)

Festus Sextus Pompeius Festus, abridger of Marcus Verrius Flaccus *De verborum significatu* (On the meaning of words)

Hdt. Herodotos *Historiai* (The Histories)

Hom. *Il.* Homer *The Iliad*

Hom. *Od.* Homer *The Odyssey*

Livy Livy *Ab urbe condita libri* (History of Rome from its foundation)

Macrob. *Sat.* Macrobius *Saturnalia* (Saturnalia)

Mart. Cap. Martianus Capella *De nuptiis Philologiae et Mercurii* (On the marriage of Mercury and Philology)

Ov. *Am.* Ovid *Amores* (The Amores)

Ov. *Fast.* Ovid *Fasti* (Calendar)

Paus. Pausanias *Periegesis tes Ellados* (Description of Greece)

Pind. Pindar *Pythian Odes*

Plin. *NH* Pliny the Elder *Naturalis historia* (Natural history)

Plut. Plutarch *Vitae parallelae* (Parallel lives)

Poll. *Onom.* Pollux *Onomastichon* (Thesaurus of Greek terms)

Polyb. Polybius *Historiai* (The Histories)

Sen. *Q. nat.* Seneca the Younger *Quaestiones naturales* (Natural questions)

Servius *Aen.* Servius *Ad Aeneis* (On the Aeneid)

Sil. *Pun.* Silius Italicus *Punica* (On the second Punic war)

Strabo Strabo *Geographikon* (Geography)

Tac. *Ann.* Tacitus *Annales* (Annals)

Tac. *Hist.* Tacitus *Historiae* (The Histories)

Thuc. Thucydides *Historion* (History)

Varro Varro *De lingua latina* (On the Latin language)

Verg. *Aen.* Publius Virgilius Maro *Aeneis* (The Aeneid)

Vitr. Vitruvius *De architectura* (On architecture)

Zos. Zosimos *Historia nova* (New history)

OTHER ABBREVIATIONS

ca.	circa
cat.	catalogue
cf.	compare
cm	centimeter
diam.	diameter
e.g.	for instance
etc.	etcetera
Etr.	Etruscan
fig.	figure
Gr.	Greek
H.	height
i.e.	that is
inv.	inventory number
It.	Italian
kg	kilogram
km	kilometer
L.	length
Lat.	Latin
m	meter
Mus.	Museum
p.	page
pl.	plate
Umb.	Umbrian

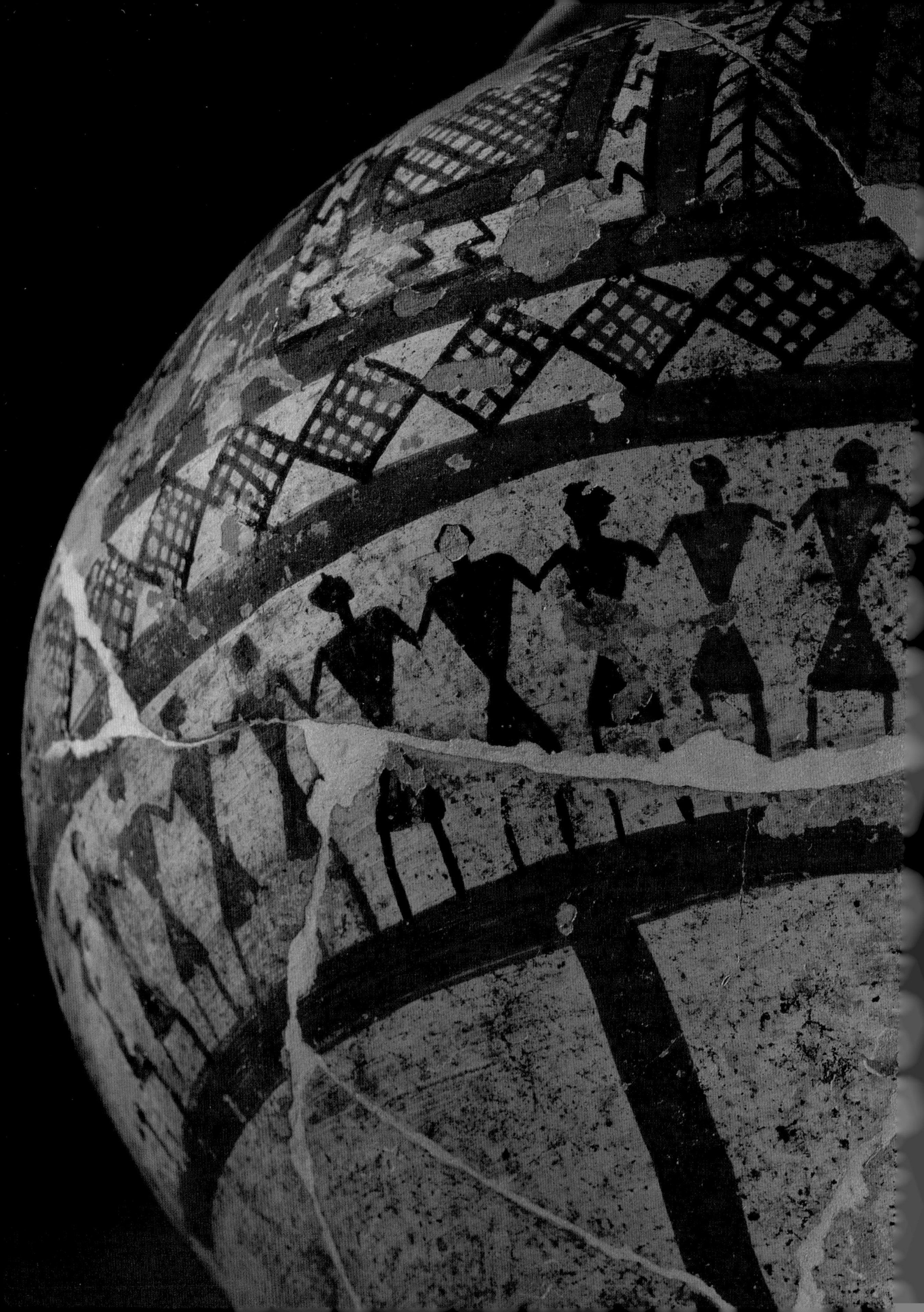

I

The Villanovan Civilization

ca. 900–720 B.C.

IDENTIFYING THE ETRUSCANS

The Etruscan people become linguistically (and thus historically) identifiable as such around 700 B.C., when the oldest Etruscan inscriptions appear on pottery found in Southern Etruria. For a considerable time literacy seems to have been confined to a wealthy aristocracy, but gradually writing became more widespread and, up to now, some thirteen thousand Etruscan texts are known. Although the inscriptions are often fragmentary and mostly very short, they show that the script is an alphabet and that the Etruscan language was unlike the others spoken in Italy at that time: Latin, Faliscan, Venetic, Osco-Umbrian, Greek, etc., which all belonged to the Indo-European family; the latter languages have, however, contributed loanwords to Etruscan. The only written texts from outside Italy that show affinities with Etruscan are from the island of Lemnos: an inscribed stela from Kaminia, some incised sherds of local pottery, and a little pyramid with the inscription *La(rthia) Tita* from the sanctuary of the Kabeiroi. The language documented by these monuments has been identified as a variant of Archaic Etruscan, and it has been suggested that it represents the language of Etruscan traders and sailors who settled on Lemnos between ca. 700 B.C. and the end of the sixth century B.C., when the Athenian Miltiades conquered Lemnos and drove out its inhabitants.

Detail of frieze of dancers, from figure 25a.

Ancient Greek writers often accused the Etruscans, whom they called Tyrrhenoi or Tyrsenoi, of piracy (Strabo 5.2.2). The historian Thucydides records that Lemnos was inhabited by Tyrrhenians in early times, and he equates them with the Pelasgians living in northern Greece in his own day (*History of the War between Athens and Sparta* 4.109). Herodotos states that the Pelasgians spoke a language that was not Greek (*The Histories* 1.57). Dionysios of Halikarnassos describes the Etruscans as a very ancient people that differed from all others in its language and its customs, and he held that they did not migrate from anywhere but were native to Italy (*Rom. Arch.* 1.30.1–3).

These ancient sources are not all reconcilable with the interpretation of the Lemnian inscriptions as those of Archaic Etruscan settlers, and divergent, less recent theories considered that the speakers of that language were remnants of a population originally more widely spread in the eastern Mediterranean. But the linguistic analysis of the epigraphic evidence from Lemnos, combined with the historical situation on the island at the end of the sixth century, support the suggestion that the inscriptions were those of Etruscan "pirates" who had lived there, separated from their people for several generations.

The script used by the Etruscans in Italy was an adaptation of the alphabetic script they had learned from their neighbors in Southern Italy, the Greek settlers from Chalkis and Eretria on the island of Euboea. During the second quarter of the eighth century these Euboeans had planted colonies on the island of Ischia (Gr. Pithekoussai) in the Gulf of Naples and, perhaps a little later, on the mainland shore opposite, at Cumae in Campania. The Greeks had elaborated for their own use the consonantic alphabet first invented by the Phoenicians of the Levant, a Semitic-speaking nation of craftsmen, merchants, and seafarers with whom the Greeks had been in commercial contact since the ninth century.

Having been adapted from the Greek model, the Etruscan alphabets (see FIG. 45) were eventually influential for the neighboring Italic peoples in all central and northern Italy and later, spreading beyond the Alps, for the Germanic peoples, whose runic script was derived via the Venetic alphabet from North Etruscan models.

The Beginnings of Etruscan History

The Etruscans must have lived in central Italy, in the area bordered by the Tyrrhenian Sea and the courses of the Arno and Tiber Rivers, for a long time before they became literate, for the mutual linguistic influence between Etruscan and neighboring Indo-European languages points to a lengthy period of proximity. But archaeology provides the main evidence for the Etruscans' long-established presence (MAP p. 3). The origin of most of the great Etruscan cities of historical times can be traced back to Early Iron Age villages located on the volcanic tufa plateaus of Southern Etruria and Lazio (Veii, Cerveteri, Tarquinia, Vulci, Orvieto, etc.) or on isolated hills dominating the sea or inland waterways in central and northern regions (Populonia, Vetulonia, Pisa, Volterra [FIG. 1], Chiusi, Cortona, Arezzo, etc.). Many of these places (for example, Veii, Cerveteri, Tarquinia, Bisenzio,

Villanovan, Etruscan, and Greek sites.

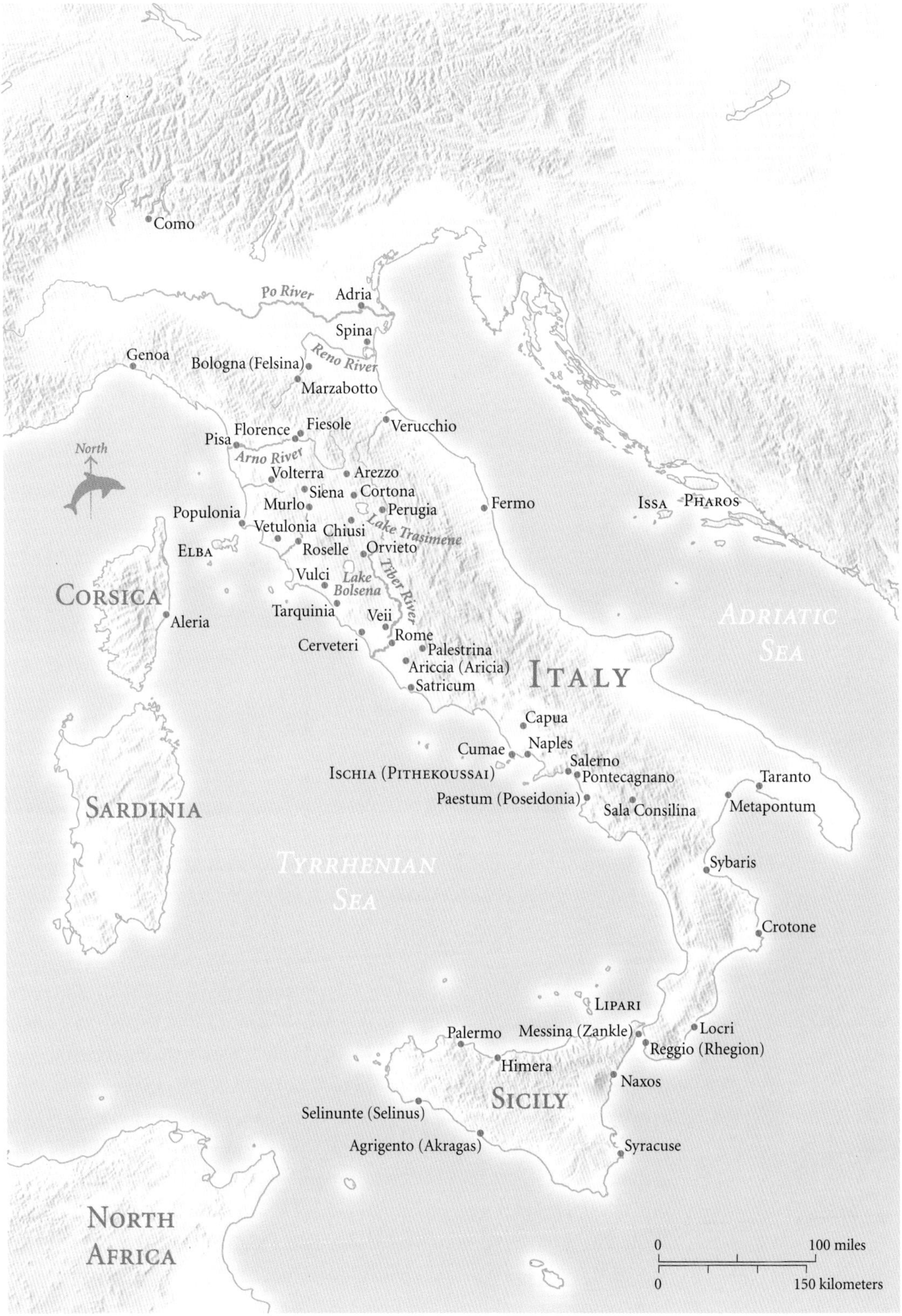
Como
Po River
Adria
Spina
Reno River
Genoa
Bologna (Felsina)
Marzabotto
Verucchio
Florence
Fiesole
Pisa
North
Arno River
Volterra
Arezzo
Siena
Cortona
Murlo
Perugia
Fermo
Issa
Pharos
Populonia
Vetulonia
Chiusi
Lake Trasimene
Roselle
Orvieto
Elba
Vulci
Lake Bolsena
Tiber River
Corsica
Tarquinia
Veii
Aleria
Adriatic Sea
Rome
Cerveteri
Palestrina
Ariccia (Aricia)
Satricum
Italy
Capua
Cumae
Naples
Ischia (Pithekoussai)
Salerno
Pontecagnano
Taranto
Paestum (Poseidonia)
Sala Consilina
Metapontum
Sardinia
Sybaris
Tyrrhenian Sea
Crotone
Lipari
Palermo
Messina (Zankle)
Locri
Reggio (Rhegion)
Himera
Naxos
Sicily
Selinunte (Selinus)
Agrigento (Akragas)
Syracuse
North Africa
0
100 miles
0
150 kilometers

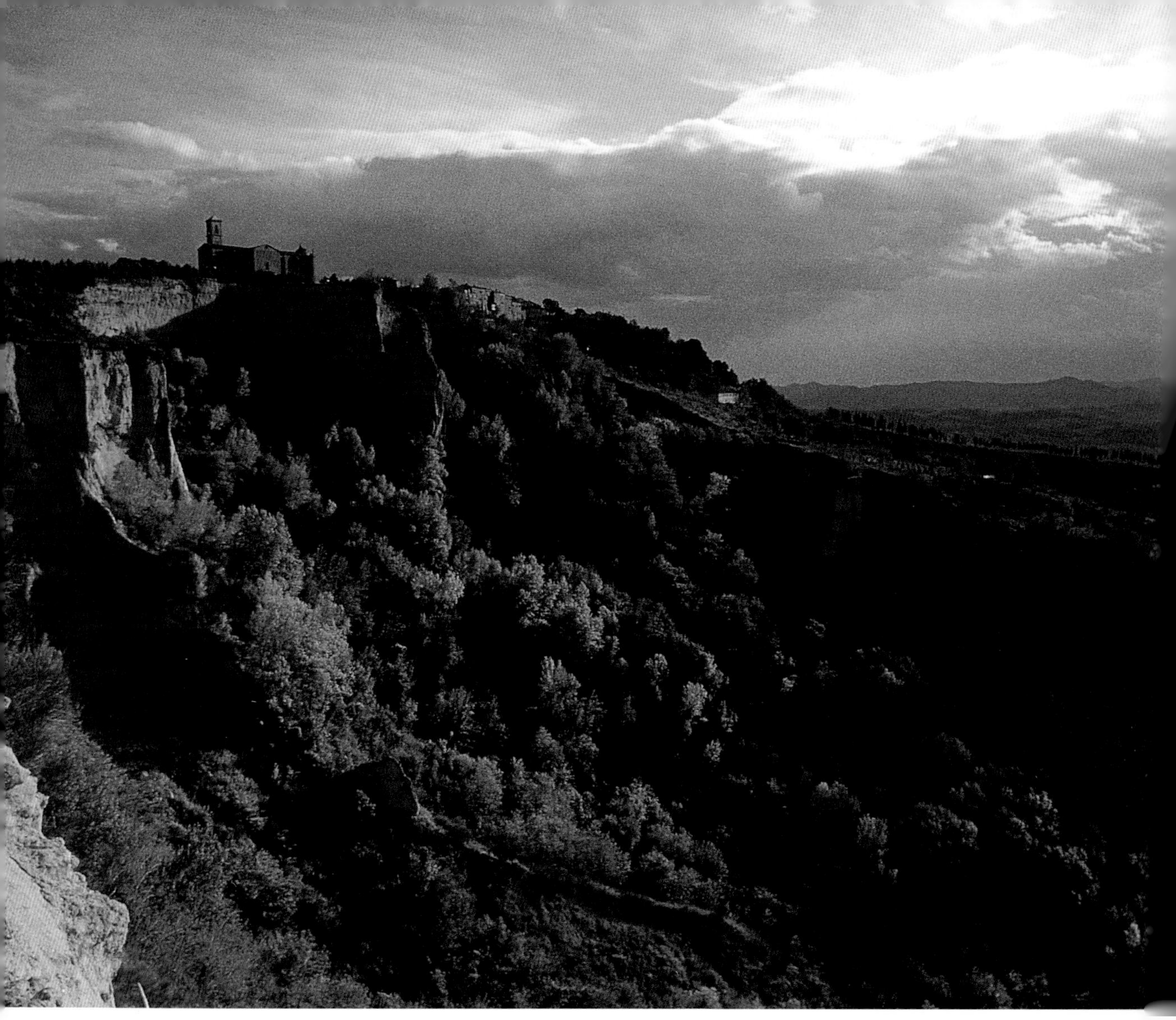

Fig. 1 View of Volterra.

Vulci, Luni sul Mignone, Sorgenti della Nova) have signs of occupation as early as the Late Bronze Age, a period also known as Protovillanovan.

The Iron Age

The Early Iron Age civilization of the villages from which the later Etruscan communities developed in an unbroken sequence is known as the Villanovan, a name derived from that of a site east of Bologna, Villanova di Castenaso, where this civilization was first identified through excavations in 1853. We can thus say that the Etruscans flourished at least from the tenth century onward and that—as is the case with most other nations—a great number of different ethnic, cultural, geographic, political, and linguistic factors contributed to the formation of their culture. The long and complex historical process of genesis may have begun as early as the Late Bronze Age, during the second millennium. In the absence of written sources from this early period, archaeology alone provides us with information on how the inhabitants of the Early Iron Age villages lived.

Traces of huts of the ninth and eighth centuries have been excavated, but so far only in a few sites. Among the best-explored remains are those of some twenty-five dwellings at Tarquinia in the Calvario area of the future necropolis of Monterozzi. Others have been identified at Veii, at Gran Carro on the shore of Lake Bolsena, at San Giovenale, Sorgenti della Nova, Acquarossa, and Campassini near Monteriggioni as well as at sites of the Latial culture: Satricum and on the Palatine in Rome. These huts, of circular, oval, or rectangular plan, are haphazardly arranged and loosely spaced out (FIG. 2). Rectangular or square huts may represent a slightly more recent stage. In most cases all that is preserved are shallow foundation trenches, cut into the soil or rock to receive wattle-and-daub walls and postholes for wooden uprights that supported a thatched roof with projecting eaves.

A small porch, again identifiable by postholes, sometimes protected the entrance, which was normally placed at one of the short sides of the hut and marked by a threshold. The large oval huts occasionally had a secondary door in one of the long sides and probably a window on the opposite side, and most huts would have had a centrally placed hearth. The rear part of the hut could form a separate room, divided off by a partition wall at the level of the last post supporting the roof. None of the structural parts of these huts have survived. In rare cases the perimeter of the hut is still outlined by low dry-stone walls that served to prop up the wooden posts of the wattle-and-daub elevation and by fragments of the covering layer of clay with impressions of the reeds and branches from which the walls were woven. Drainage channels to conduct rainwater from the steeply thatched roofs away from the hut and into pits or jars survive in some cases in the rocky ground.

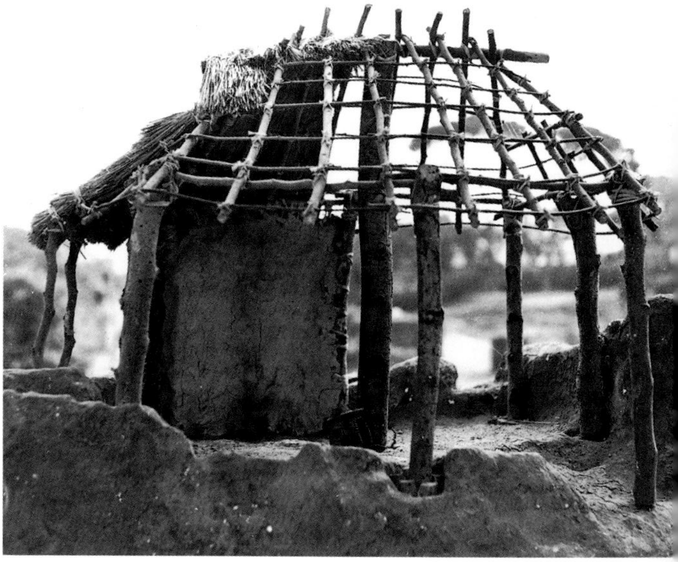

Fig. 2 Model of an Iron Age hut under construction. Based on Hut A on the Germalus Hill in Rome. Eighth century B.C. Rome, Museo Palatino 425531. Model by A. Davico.

Large storage jars for foodstuffs were sometimes sunk into the floor of a hut or immediately outside. Crevices in the rock, exhausted clay pits, and specially made holes in the soil served as refuse dumps.

Hut Urns

To get an idea of what the elevation and roof of such a hut looked like, we must turn to a special type of funerary ash urn, of which examples in pottery (exceptionally bronze) have been discovered in contemporary cemeteries in Southern Etruria at Veii, Tarquinia, Vulci, and Bisenzio and as far north as Vetulonia, as well as in Lazio (FIG. 3). Modeled in imitation of the houses of the living, these hut urns were buried in deep, well-like pits cut into the earth or rock and protected by stone containers or slabs or piles of stone. A number of comparatively well-preserved urns that have thus come down to us can tell us a good deal about the form and decoration of the prototypes.

Geometric patterns preserved on some of the hut urns suggest that the plastered walls of real huts may have been painted in some way. The ridge roof of the rectangular huts was supported internally by one longitudinally aligned row of posts, while the roof in the shape of a tortoiseshell that covered some of the larger oval huts rested on a framework carried by several pairs of strong internal posts. Externally the thatch was often held in place by ridge logs, which, when aligned and prolonged upward to project beyond the ridgepole, formed crossed pairs, whose top ends were sometimes carved in the form of birds or horns, symbols that may have been endowed with apotropaic properties. Small dormers in the thatch above the door and in the roof at the opposite end of the hut served for the escape of smoke from the central (or occasionally lateral) hearth. Doors and windows were rectangular or square.

Some hut urns from Vulci have an extended base in front of the door, suggesting that in the actual dwellings this was a level area where domestic work was carried out in good weather. Huts without any traces of internal hearths (recognizable by a shallow depression or by the remains of ashes in the center) probably used a portable hearth, or they served for storage only. The larger huts of oval or rectangular plan at Tarquinia, measuring roughly 13 x 7 m, could have housed family groups of up to ten people, while the smaller huts of about 5 x 4 m would have held no more than one couple and their children. The distance between the surviving hut foundations as well as their random location in relation to each

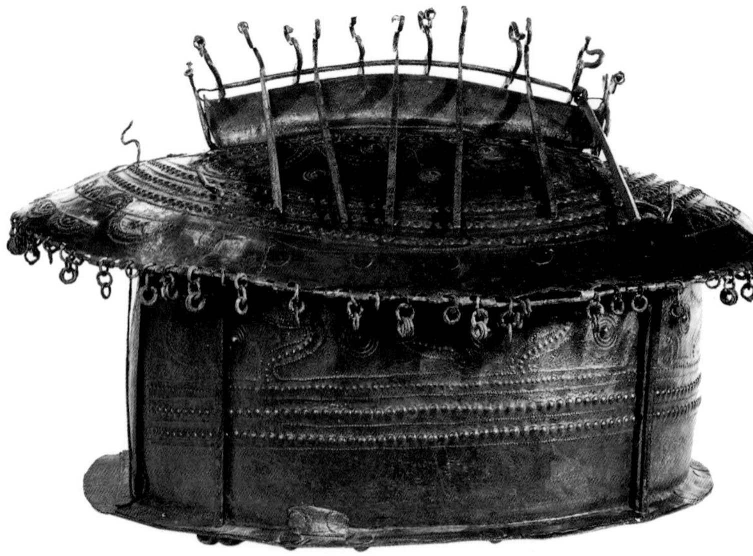

Fig. 3 Oval hut-shaped ash urn. From Vulci. Mid-eighth century B.C. Embossed sheet bronze with cast adjuncts. H. 26 cm. Rome, Museo Etrusco di Villa Giulia 84900.

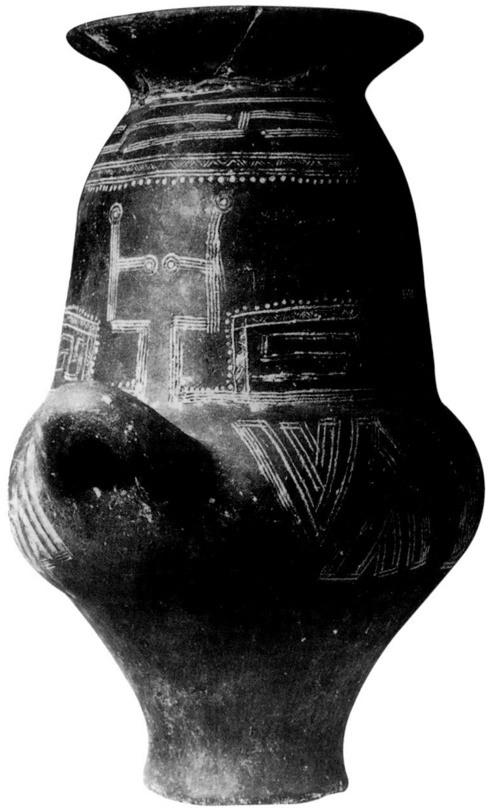

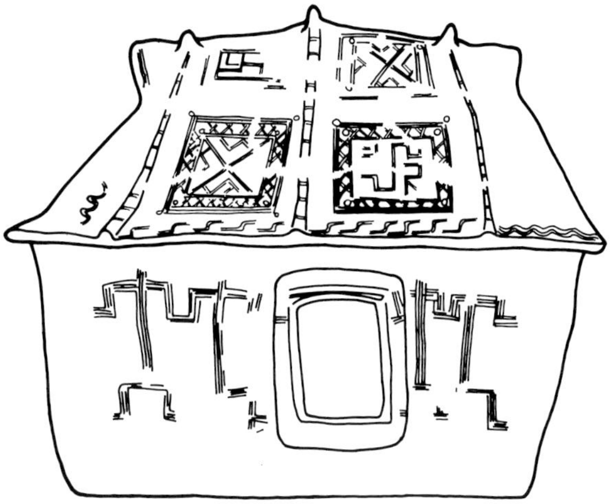

other (distances vary from 4 to 20 m) imply that the areas surrounding the individual huts were used for keeping animals and poultry or for the cultivation of small plots.

Fig. 4 Biconical ash urn. The incised geometric decoration includes seated human figures. Ninth century B.C. Impasto. H. 39 cm. Tarquinia, Museo Nazionale Archeologico.

Fig. 5 Rectangular hut-shaped ash urn with incised geometric decoration, including standing human figures holding hands. From Tomb 45, Poggio Selciatello, Tarquinia. Ninth century B.C. Impasto. Tarquinia, Museo Nazionale Archeologico.

THE REPRESENTATION OF HUMAN FIGURES

During this early period of the Iron Age the representation of human figures is rare and schematic. On a number of the pottery hut urns or on the more common biconic ash urns of the ninth century, particularly from Veii, Tarquinia, and Vulci, incised geometric designs are occasionally interspersed with "matchstick figures," which can be interpreted as sitting human beings, perhaps at a banquet (FIG. 4); some of the standing ones holding hands may symbolize a round dance (FIG. 5). The abstract conception of these figures does not distinguish between males and females.

On the roof of a hut urn from Bisenzio(?) (Rome, Museo Pigorini 105755), the small figure of a man is modeled in high relief just above the door and below the first pair of ridge logs. The suggestion that this is the image of a heroized ancestor protecting the hut at its most vulnerable point, the entrance, is very persuasive. At a later stage a comparable practice is attested in an actual building complex of the subsequent Orientalizing period at Murlo; in this aristocratic residence nearly life-size statues that probably represented ancestors were placed on the ridge of the roof (see p. 119).

For more everyday signs of family life we have to rely on surviving fragments of household pottery and tools, as well as vegetable remains and animal bones from refuse dumps to help us fill in a picture of how the Etruscans lived and worked. Funerary gifts deposited with the ash urns in the burial sites will tell us something about the personal possessions they owned.

FOOD PRODUCTION, DIET, AND DISEASE

The elevated sites chosen for the Villanovan villages were normally surrounded by well-watered land suitable for farming and by natural pasture and woods for grazing and hunting. The villagers subsisted on an economy in which everything that was produced in the community was consumed by it. Farming consisted of cereal and legume cultivation. Sheep and goats were kept for milk, cheese, meat, and wool; pigs for meat; cattle for milk, meat, and leather. Oxen served mainly as draft animals, especially for ploughing, and their meat was probably reserved for special occasions such as sacrifices and feasts. This diet was supplemented by hunting, fishing, and the collection of edible shellfish, tortoises, and birds' eggs.

Analysis of human bones is increasingly being used to discover what foodstuffs the population ate. However, the poor survival rate of skeletal remains due to soil acidity in inhumation tombs and fracture and destruction by fire in cremation tombs often inhibits such studies. Zinc in meat, milk, and dried fruit makes for strong bones. A study of skeletons from the seventh-century settlement of Ferrone in the Tolfa Mountains has shown that both men and women there ate a diet that contained more vegetables than meat. The average age for women at Ferrone was 27–34 years, with very few individuals reaching 45–50. Male life expectancy was somewhat higher—37–44 years—and a few reached 50+ years. The lower average life expectancy for women is probably due to the high mortality rate in childbirth.

Human bones from many different sites show the presence of anemia, both congenital and nutritional. The latter is due to low intake or poor absorption of iron in protein-poor diets. While anemia does not affect a person's height, children born to anemic women have a higher rate of infant mortality. Investigations at Pontecagnano (Salerno) have shown that in the seventh and sixth centuries the incidence of anemia was 8.7%, while in the fifth and fourth centuries it was 3.3%; this would suggest an improved diet in the later period, though none of these measurements can be assumed to be valid elsewhere.

Thalassemia, a form of genetically inherited anemia that stems from an abnormal form of hemoglobin in the blood, was widespread in ancient Greece and Italy, but it apparently protected against malaria. In central Italy malaria is thought to have appeared about the sixth century B.C.; improved drainage of marshy countryside by ancient Etruscans eventually reduced the incidence of the disease, and with that the higher survival rate due to thalassemia.

A number of skeletons from diverse sites show signs of arthritis, spondylitis, osteoporosis, and polio, as well as tuberculosis.

Palaeobotanic studies of plant remains from recently excavated central Italian sites show that beside fruit, nuts, broad beans, peas, and vetches, the vegetable diet included barley, emmer, and einkorn, or small spelt—resistant species of grain that are easy to cultivate even in poor soils. From emmer was made *puls*, the basic national meal of early Rome, which probably formed a staple diet of contemporary Etruria, too. Its preparation was laborious. The grain had to be roasted and pounded before it could be ground and boiled into a kind of pottage. We may assume that the preliminary work as well as the cooking was carried out by women (cf. Plin. *NH* 18.28.107). Large wooden pestles would have been used for pounding the roasted grain. Although no actual examples of these essential but perishable implements have survived, a pestle of the required size is illustrated on an Attic red-figured cup from Vulci, signed by the potter Brygos (Louvre G 152). On it a Trojan woman has raised her pestle with both hands to club a Greek warrior.

WOMEN'S WORK

Carrying Water and Cooking

Water for drinking and cooking is a daily need in every household. Fetching water from a spring or river in a vessel carried on the head or shoulder has been the task of women from time immemorial. Until the 1960s, village women in the south of Italy could still be seen drawing water from the communal fountain and carrying it home in typical conical copper vessels. We shall discuss the earliest Etruscan representations of this occupation in due course.

Recent excavations at Campassini (Monteriggioni) have produced evidence for a pond that served as a kind of cistern in the middle of a settlement of huts of the second half of the eighth century. Developments elsewhere (San Giovenale, Veii, Satricum) show that reservoirs of rainwater were an important part of the water supply.

Cooking was done on a hearth, either inside the hut or in the open air on small portable pottery hearths. Household and cooking vessels as well as ash urns were made of impasto, an unpurified clay modeled by hand, burnished, and fired at low temperatures. As in many other traditional societies, this pottery was not produced by craft specialists but may have been made by the women of the household for use by their own families.

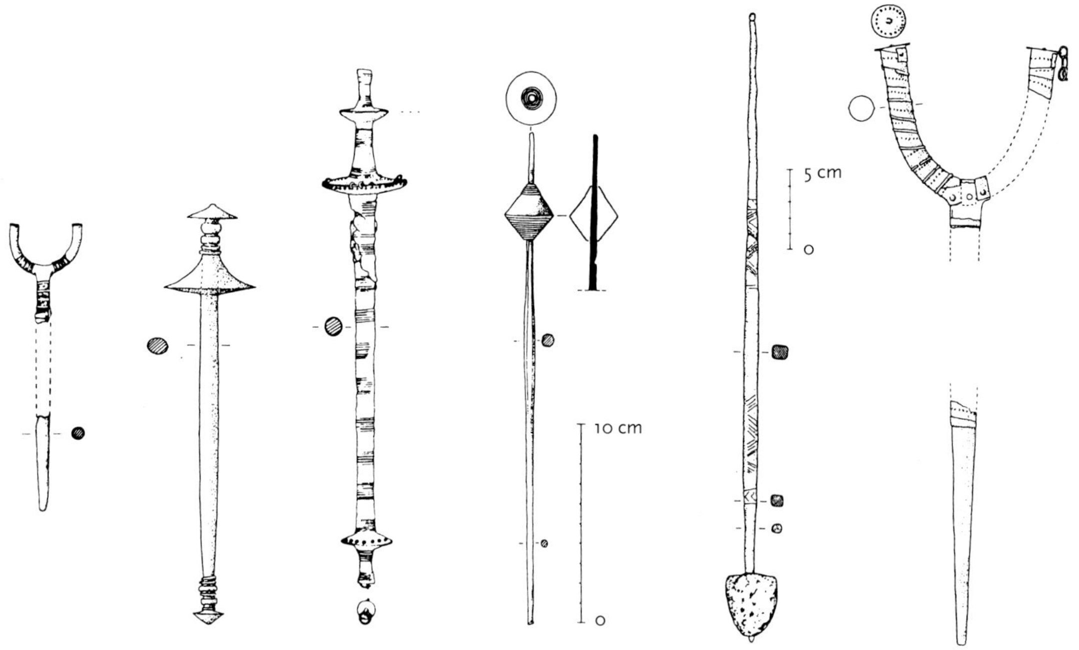

Fig. 6 Villanovan spindles and distaffs of bronze, wood, and impasto. No. 5 is a spindle from the submerged lakeside village of Gran Carro, Bolsena. Ninth century B.C. Wood and impasto. L. 40 cm. Bolsena, Museo Territoriale del Lago di Bolsena 2080–2081.

Woolworking

The main crafts practiced by women were spinning, dyeing, and weaving of the wool of both sheep and goats and sewing clothes from the cloth. A large number of burials defined as female by their grave goods, excavated in the Quattro Fontanili necropolis of Veii and in tombs at Tarquinia, Cerveteri, Populonia, and elsewhere, contained, either singly or in association with each other, spindle whorls, spindles, distaffs, loom weights, and pottery spools for thread—that is, implements connected with woolworking. In a submerged lakeside settlement at Gran Carro near Bolsena a wooden spindle with a pottery whorl has survived in the waterlogged site (FIG. 6). Normally only the whorls, made of imperishable pottery or, more rarely, of bronze, are preserved in the tombs, while the wooden parts of spindles and distaffs have disintegrated. Bronze or amber spindles are found in tombs with particularly rich grave goods (see p. 43). Occasionally bronze sewing needles are preserved in women's graves, showing that sewing was part of female activities. Etruscan painting and sculpture of the subsequent centuries prove that, in contrast to the simple rectangular garments worn by Greeks, the Etruscans preferred clothes of a more varied and complicated type, many of them cut in separate pieces and sewn together.

All necessary tools, utensils, and household goods as well as clothes were made in the households for their own use.

CEMETERIES AND ASH URNS

Cemeteries were usually located outside the villages, most commonly on surrounding hillsides, but occasionally also in valley bottoms. The tombs were simple cylindrical pits cut into the soil or rock, in which the ash urns, with a modest number of grave goods, were buried. It appears that the graves of a family group were concentrated in a given area, which was extended as more space was needed.

In the typical Villanovan burial, comparable to those of the Urnfield Culture of Central Europe, the dead were cremated and their ashes placed in biconic pottery urns with a flared everted lip, covered usually by an inverted bowl with a single handle (FIG. 7) or occasionally by a lid in the shape of a helmet (in the case of a warrior). As we have seen, the ashes of both men and women were sometimes interred in hut-shaped urns. Such urns seem to have been used first in graves in Lazio, where these urns were, however, seemingly reserved for males of high social standing. We may assume that the use of a house-shaped urn represents the wish of the survivors to restore to the cremated family member a semblance of his or her erstwhile home among the living; but it may have been equally important for showing the links between the house, the family, and the forebears and thus to emphasize the social rank of the deceased.

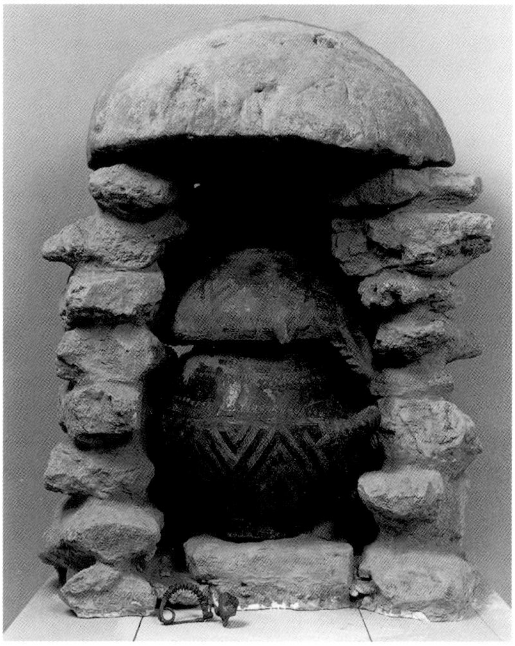

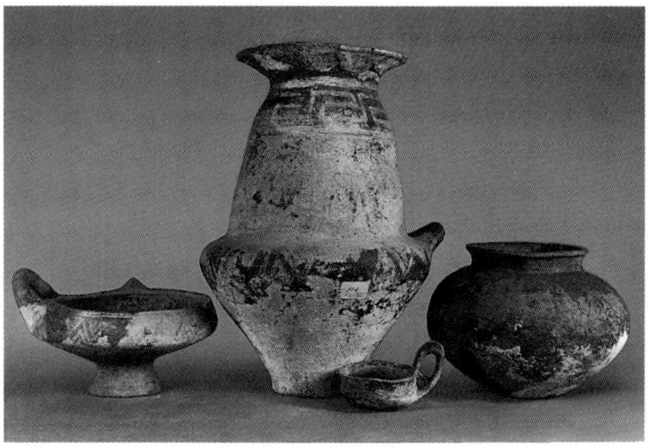

Before being fired, biconic urns and house urns were usually incised with a comblike tool with geometric forms such as squares, meanders, swastikas, and triangles, or impressed in a ropelike pattern and with circular stamps (sometimes the point of a snail shell) in single or multiple circles. A rarer form of decoration consisted of applied strips of metal (lead or tin), which were glued to the vessel in various angular patterns and have, in most cases, disappeared, leaving behind scarcely visible traces of the adhesive or the grooves that originally contained them. Occasionally there was modeled decoration. One urn from Vulci has breasts below the neck, suggesting an analogy between the vessel and the female body.

The one horizontal handle of the biconic ash urn is usually located at the widest expanse (the hip, as it were) of the vessel, where the two cone shapes merge with a slight bulge of the lower one (FIG. 8). If the vessel was originally made with

Fig. 7 Biconical ash urn covered with an inverted bowl in situ in burial pit. Tomb C, Ripaie necropolis, Volterra. Ninth century B.C. Impasto. H. of vase 31 cm. Volterra, Museo Etrusco Guarnacci, museum display.

Fig. 8 Grave goods. Cover bowl, biconic urn, cup, jar. From Tomb 34, Selciatello Sopra, Tarquinia. Late ninth–early eighth century B.C. Impasto. Florence, Museo Archeologico.

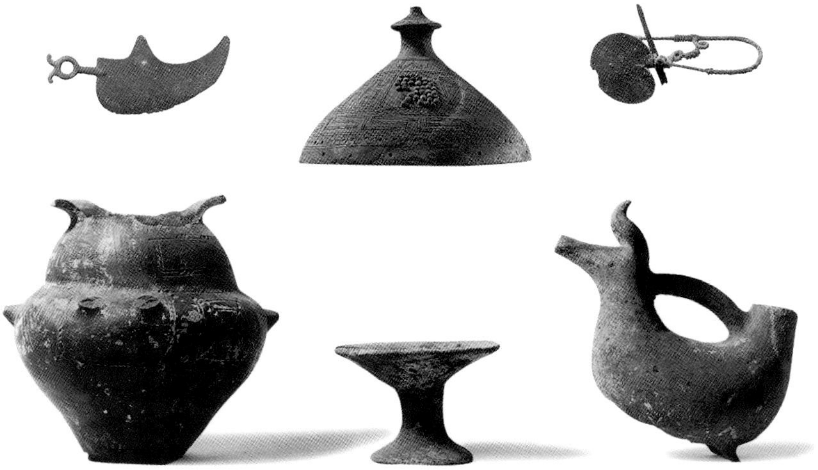

Fig. 9 Male grave goods. Helmet, jar, stand, and bull-shaped askos (impasto), disk fibula and razor (bronze). From Tomb 179, Selciatello Sopra, Tarquinia. Late ninth century B.C. Florence, Museo Archeologico.

two such handles opposite each other, one of them was deliberately broken off to adapt the urn for funerary use. The characteristic biconic shape is that of the traditional water vessel, which could be carried on head or shoulder using one hand only. It has been seen as significant that the funeral ritual required that the ashes be buried in a pottery shape developed to contain one of the most vital elements for life and perhaps in a generalized way derived from the female body.

Grave Goods

The artifacts deposited with the ash urns during most of the ninth century were few and modest, and, to judge from their relative uniformity, there seems to have been little distinction in funerary practice within the village population, though rank may be expressed by certain types of ash urns and by impasto grave goods such as cups, jugs, amphorae, sets of small plates, and occasionally vessels in the shape of animals (FIG. 9). The main difference is that between the sexes: Each was usually accompanied by its typical posessions, and these hardly ever occur together. We should remember, however, that gifts of food, wood, cloth, and leather that have usually decayed without a trace may have held particular personal or symbolic significance.

Apart from helmet-shaped lids on urns (see FIGS. 9, 10), male burials are recognizable by rectangular, double-bladed and later semilunate and lunate bronze razors, fibulae of serpentine bow form, and a few weapons (see FIGS. 9, 10). Occasionally a "staff of command"—a bronze rod with a round or pyramidal piece of bone or amber at either end—suggests that the deceased had a leading position. Female burials contain grave goods or ornaments such as bronze hair spirals, chains, little rings, bracelets, several fibulae of arch-bow type and pendants (FIG. 11), and, above all, the woolworking implements that we have already mentioned.

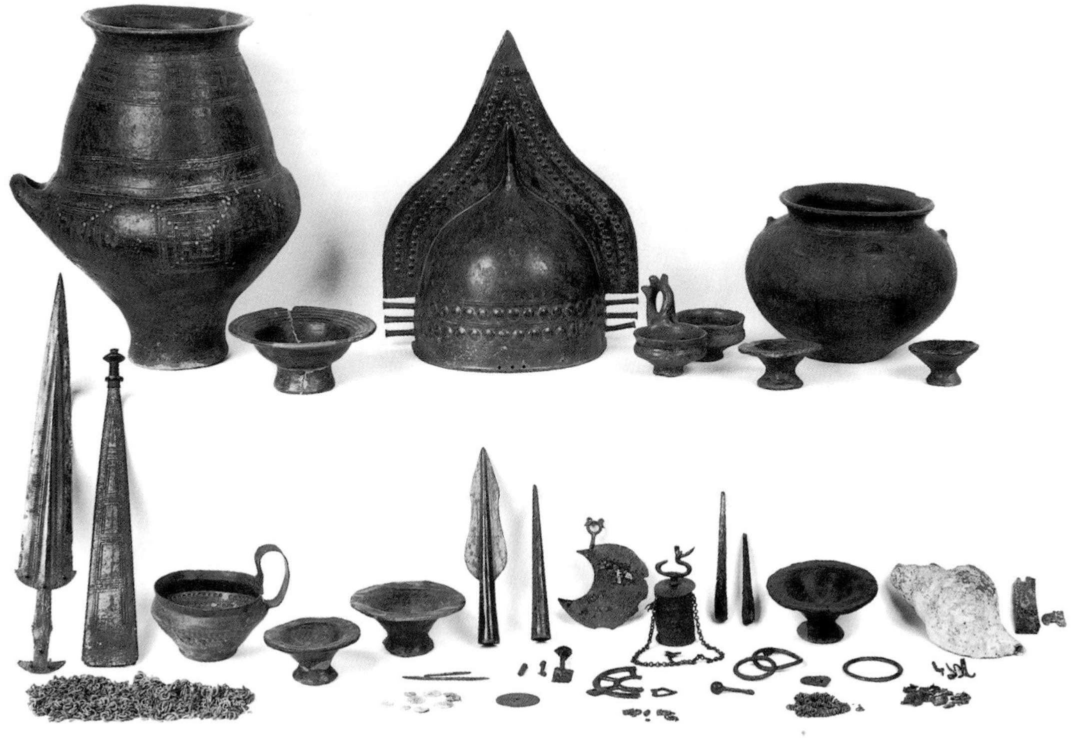

THE BEGINNING OF SOCIAL STRATIFICATION

Fig. 10 Male grave goods. From Tomb I, Impiccato, Tarquinia. Late ninth–early eighth century B.C. Cast and hammered bronze and impasto. Florence, Museo Archeologico.

Gradually, from the end of the ninth century throughout the eighth, the more or less uniform aspect of the Early Villanovan burials changed. More and richer sheet-bronze vessels and weapons and armor, as well as objects of iron appear in some tombs, indicating the prestige of the deceased (see FIG. 10). The finely hammered sheet-bronze vessels, crested helmets, and women's lozenge-shaped belts are embossed and incised with motifs, a number of which are of Central European Bronze Age origin (FIG. 12). This points to contacts with metalworkers from the north and from the Balkans. Frequent among such decorative elements are the foreparts of water birds and addorsed birds, combined with a circle or boss (thought to represent the sun) forming a so-called solar boat, and cast-bronze ducks' heads decorate the handles of razors and other objects. Female burials include necklaces with beads of bone, faience, and striped blue-and-white glass paste and occasionally gold hair spirals. There is a sequential development of bronze fibula types: in male burials the serpentine form develops into the dragon (It. *drago*) type; the (predominantly) female arch-bow fibula develops into swollen leech (It. *sanguisuga*) and boat (It. *navicella*) types.

While the custom of cremation continued, there arose a new practice of individual inhumation in trench tombs with wooden or sometimes stone sarcophagi,

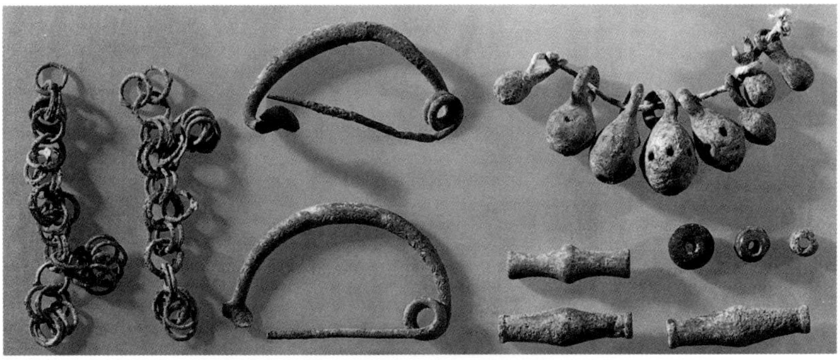

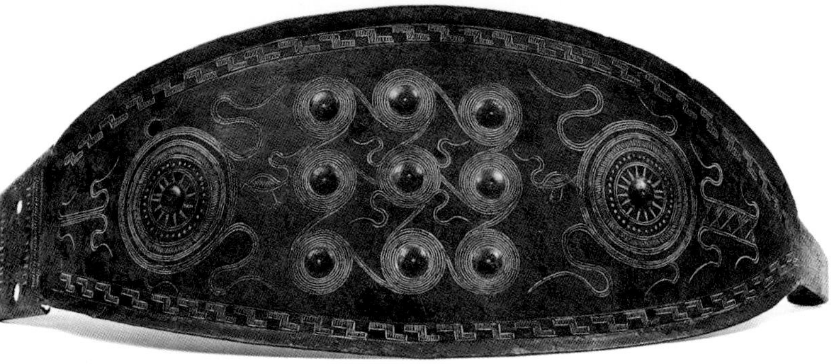

Fig. 11 Female grave goods. Bronze chains, bow fibulae, hollow pendants, biconical beads, three circular glass beads. From Tomb 82, Impiccato, Tarquinia. Eighth century B.C. Florence, Museo Archeologico.

Fig. 12 Belt. From Benacci necropolis, Bologna. First half of eighth century B.C. Embossed and incised sheet bronze. H. 11.9 cm. Bologna, Museo Civico Archeologico.

accompanied by a notable increase in grave goods. The earliest Villanovan inhumations are found at Veii, perhaps because of its proximity to Lazio, where the custom seems to go back to the beginning of the ninth century; but at Cerveteri, too, inhumation is practiced early. The change from cremation to inhumation led to the gradual disappearance of the biconic ash urn with its symbolic implications, but occasionally an ash urn was placed lying in a trench as if it were a body.

Beside the individual trench tombs, usual at most sites, at Populonia there are numerous trench tombs containing bodies of both a man and a woman.

In the second half of the ninth century an early form of chamber tomb of rectangular or circular plan with a false vault of limestone slabs also appeared exclusively at Populonia, in the cemeteries of Poggio and Piano delle Granate (perhaps as a result of contacts with the nuraghic architecture of Sardinia; FIG. 13). This type of tomb, accessible by a short, stone-lined corridor (dromos), contained inhumations accompanied by a wealth of bronze objects but hardly any pottery. The appearance of chamber tombs used for no more than a few bodies of a nuclear family marks the transition from the individual burial to collective funerary monuments used by a group of close relatives. These collective burials probably express the wish of individual families to distinguish themselves from the rest of the community.

At Vetulonia (Poggio alla Guardia necropolis) up to fifteen closely grouped cinerary urns are sometimes contained within a circle of rough stones set some distance from each other in a "circle of interrupted stones" (It. *circolo di pietre interrotte*). These are presumably the graves of family groups of "warriors" who wanted to emphasize their eminence and coherence. The wealth of such families may come from their exploitation of the local metal ores and the production and barter of metal goods.

An indication of early connections with the Near East is provided by Tomb 7 in the First Circle of Interrupted Stones (*Primo Circolo di Pietre Interrotte*), which, besides locally produced objects, contained an imported, probably Phoenician, bowl of hammered bronze decorated with rows of animals and floral elements (Florence, Museo Archeologico 6097), as well as glass beads and a scarab of amber. The tomb dates from about 730–720.

The changes in funerary practices and the deposition of richer and more varied grave goods in particularly prominent tombs mirror a growing social differentiation, with certain individuals and families—an emerging warrior aristocracy—assuming leadership over larger groups of dependants. With this more complex society went a division of labor in which specialized craftsmen took over many of the tasks originally performed at the household level.

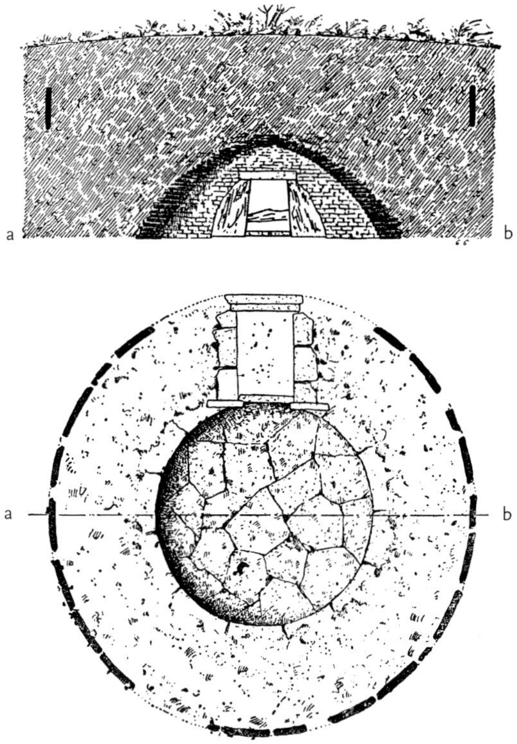

Fig. 13 Plan and section of the early chamber tomb. Tomb of the Bronze Lunate Razor, necropolis delle Granate, Populonia. End of ninth century B.C.

GROWTH OF POPULATION AND MIGRATION

Rapidly expanding cemeteries point to a considerable increase in the population of the existing villages. The need for more land to cultivate must have led to constant conflict between neighboring communities and the consequent subjugation of weaker parties. This probably contributed to more widespread occupation of the territory and to migrations of groups of people under the command of local leaders to new "colonial" regions in both the north and the south. Settlements in such fertile regions as the Po valley (Emilia-Romagna), the Adriatic region near Rimini (Lat. Ariminum), and Fermo, Campania (Capua), Sala Consilina, and the Salernitan coast (Pontecagnano, Fratte)—probably reached by sea—testify to such expansion. These movements of population groups can be traced in the cemeteries, where distinct regional pecularities of funerary urns and grave goods are transplanted to new areas.

The phenomenon of the Villanovan culture is, however, far from being homogenous or unified, and it comprised a variety of local groups of different ethnic composition.

EXCHANGE OF GOODS

A growing exchange of goods is evident from the appearance in tombs of artifacts, such as bronze fibulae or specific patterns on pots, typical of one particular group of communities in a number of widely distributed other settlements. From a tomb at Tarquinia (SS 140) thus come a vase made in South Italy as well as a fibula imported from Bologna and another of a type frequent at Veii. Besides by simple exchange, bronze objects were probably diffused by itinerant craftsmen who set up workshops in different places.

The coastal settlements of Populonia and Vetulonia (near the metal-rich Campigliese and the Catena Metallifera of Tuscany and the island of Elba), as well as the southern communities of Tarquinia and Cerveteri (near the mineral resources of the Tolfa Mountains), seem to have been particularly active in such exchanges. But Veii, which controlled the important waterway of the Tiber, and, in the north, Bologna, an entrepôt of both trans-Apennine and trans-Alpine traffic, were also considerable centers of distribution. Objects of non-Italian manufacture, such as bronzes of the European Hallstatt Culture from the Carpathian and Danube regions and others of Sardinian origin, as well as Baltic amber, attest to the long-distance range of such exchanges, some of which must have been seaborne. Two tombs at Tarquinia each contained a skyphos of Greek Late Geometric type.

BRONZEWORKING

Horse-Trappings and Vehicles

In rich male tombs of eighth- and seventh-century date, and in a smaller number of female ones, have been found horse bits of bronze or iron and, more rarely, harnesses and metal parts of carriages and chariots. Horse bits point to the growing importance of artistocratic cavalry, while the use of horses and mules and of two- or four-wheeled vehicles drawn by them must have been the privilege of wealthy families who thus demonstrated their high social (and perhaps priestly) status in death as in life. A good example is the burial of a lady in a trench (It. *fossa*) tomb in the necropolis of Casal del Fosso at Veii. The square burial trench was extended on one side by two niches (loculi) for the deposition of the numerous grave goods, including a carriage. Externally the tomb was distinguished by a large grave marker, a so-called stone cippus, of elliptical shape with a crested top. The concept of a vehicle as a sign of prestige is probably likewise expressed by grave goods such as miniature pottery models of carts with pairs of horses.

Of the large number of surviving bronze horse bits many have open-worked cheek pieces cast in the form of stylized horses and foals, often combined in an intricate pattern with ducks and small quadrupeds. The figure of a horse as a decorative but integral part of the bit goes back to Assyrian prototypes.

Simple human or apelike figures appear comparatively rarely, but are found on horse trappings from Vetulonia and Marsiliana d'Albegna. Small geometric figures of helmeted Villanovan horsemen form the openwork decoration of the cast legs of hammered bronze tripod bowls from Vetulonia, Tarquinia, Veii, and Lazio dated from the late eighth to the early seventh century (FIG. 14). The motif of a "horse tamer"—a frontal male figure between heraldically flanking pairs of horses—is found on bronze reliefs and on impasto vessels in aristocratic tombs from the Faliscan area (Narce) and in Campania (Capua).

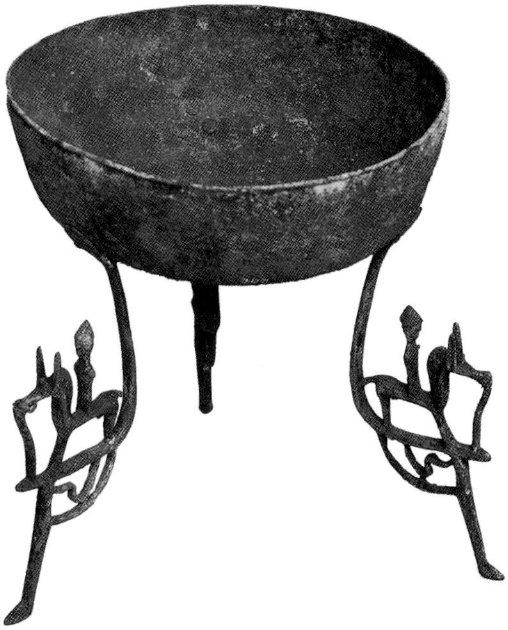

Early Bronze Figurines

Among the earliest bronze figurines cast in the round by the lost-wax process is a pendant (amulet?) in the form of a nude woman excavated from a trench tomb at Tarquinia (FIG. 15). A large suspension ring passes through the figure's bald oval head, whose main features are a crudely shaped broad nose and a horizontal gash for the mouth. Her protruding ears are pierced by earrings, and a chain encircles her neck. Standing with her sturdy legs apart, she supports a wiry arm on the left hip of her tubular body; the right arm is broken off. The geometric style of this figure is reminiscent of Greek Geometric bronzes of the eighth century, but it also has close affinities with the simple small pottery figures that decorate a number of Villanovan and Italic hut urns and vessels of various shapes.

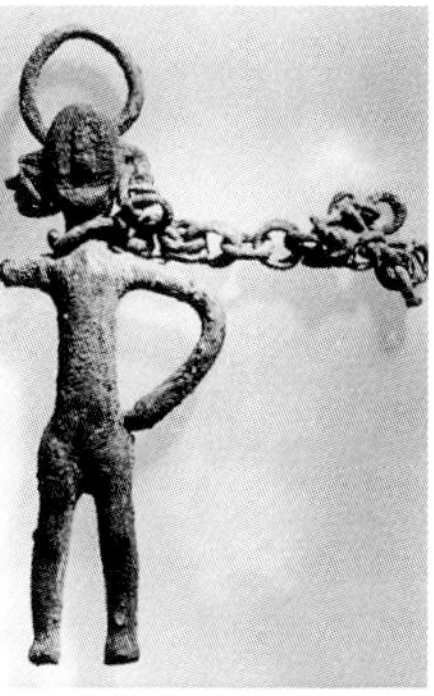

The introduction into cremation burials in Etruria of miniature objects may be due to influence from neighboring Lazio, where occasionally the dead were accompanied by human figurines of pottery and by small versions of objects of daily life. In some tombs (at Bisenzio and Tarquinia) miniature bronze tables were discovered; they probably represent the table of the funeral banquet.

Fig. 14 Tripod bowl of sheet bronze, each leg decorated with the geometrically stylized figure of a helmeted rider and a duck cast in openwork. From Capua. First half of seventh century B.C. H. 20.5 cm. London, The British Museum GR 73.8-20.210.

Fig. 15 Pendant in the form of a nude woman. From Tomb 9, Poggio Gallinaro, Tarquinia. Late eighth–early seventh century B.C. Cast bronze. H. 5.9 cm. Florence, Museo Archeologico 21187.

CONTACTS WITH SARDINIA

Ships: Coastal and River Traffic

Small, simple pottery models of flat-bottomed canoes and boats have been found in rich male burials from the ninth to the early eighth century in Southern coastal as well as in central inner Etruria. They point to the importance of river navigation but may also have a symbolic significance. Communications and exchange by sea with the island of Sardinia flourished mainly in the settlements of Populonia

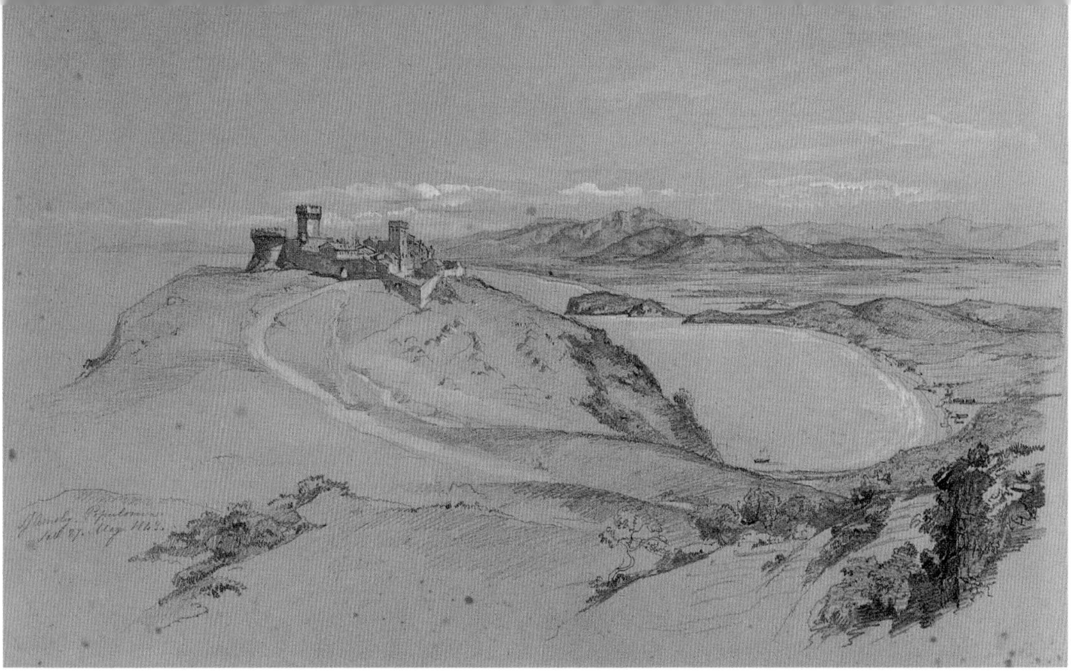

Fig. 16 S. J. Ainsley, *View at Populonia*. Signed and dated May 27, 1843. Pencil on drab paper, heightened with white. 27.6 x 44.1 cm. London, The British Museum, Department of Prints and Drawings, cat. LB 71.

(FIG. 16) and Vetulonia, both economically privileged by their proximity to mining areas (MAP p. 19).

Sardinia itself was rich in metals, such as iron, copper, tin, lead, and silver. The island enjoyed a long tradition of bronzeworking going back to close contacts with Cyprus during the Bronze Age. This contact is seen in the increasing number of finds in Sardinia of Cypriote artifacts and smithing tools, as well as of copper ingots in the shape of oxhides, common in the Eastern Mediterranean and perhaps of Cypriote origin. Prestige objects, such as bronze mirrors, handle attachments, and tripods of Late Cypriote type were first traded to and then imitated in Sardinia, and some of the nuraghic bronze objects and statuettes, cast by the lost-wax technique, date from before 900.

Small askos-shaped pottery jugs with oblique neck and mouth of ninth- and eighth-century Sardinian manufacture have been discovered in Etruria, from Volterra in the north to Cerveteri in the south, with the largest number at Vetulonia, where they were often imitated. Sardinia's contact with a far larger Mediterranean area is proved by the discovery of such typical jugs on the island of Lipari, in Sicily, and as far east as Crete.

Import of Sardinian Bronze Objects

From the second half of the ninth century the regions of Populonia and Vetulonia in particular, but also Vulci, Tarquinia, and Pontecagnano, saw the import of small Sardinian bronze votive objects; various types of "buttons" and pendants; and models of baskets, boats, quivers, and daggers, while bronze utensils of Northern Etruscan manufacture, such as fibulae, razors, and axes, have been found at Sardinian nuraghic sites. It seems that the northern coastal settlements were centers of distribution through which Sardinian bronze objects reached not only the great Southern Etruscan settlements but also Umbria and Bologna. From the latter, in turn, characteristic types of fibulae were exported to Populonia and Sardinia. The

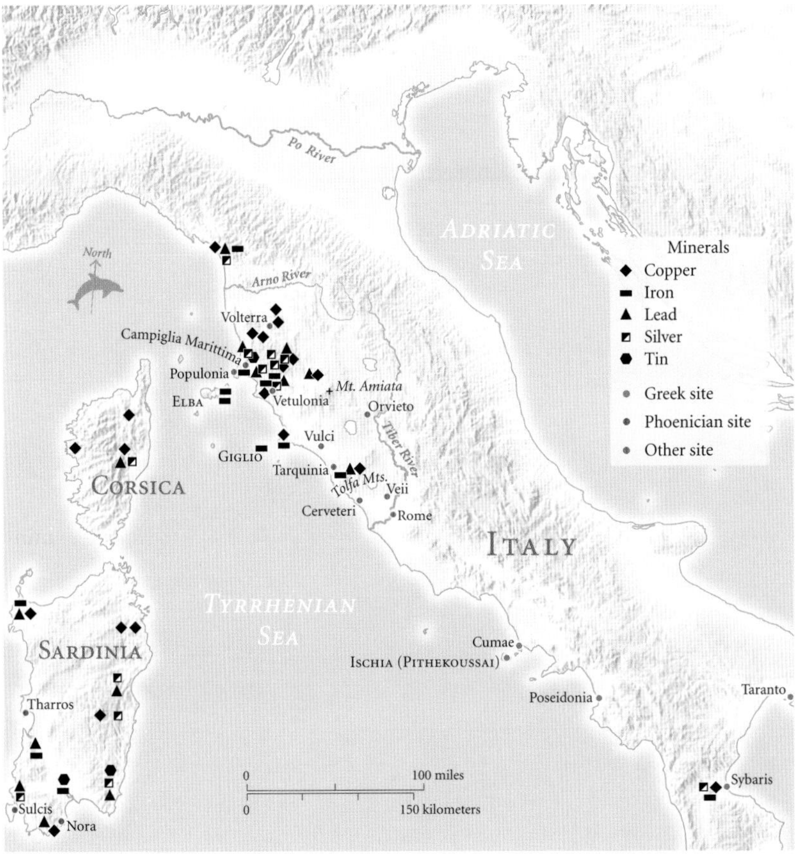

Mineral deposits in Italy, Sardinia, and Corsica.

majority of the votive objects of nuraghic manufacture in Etruria appear to come from female burials, and some of them, such as small boats, seem to have been kept for several generations before being interred.

The most striking example of such imports from the island is a group of three bronzes discovered inside the cinerary urn of a woman's tomb in the Mandrione di Cavalupo necropolis at Vulci. They consist of a miniature model of a two-handled wicker basket with a lid (FIG. 17), a stool-shaped object (perhaps part of a rattle, FIG. 18), and a statuette of a human being (FIG. 19). This figure stands with sandaled feet well apart. Dressed in a belted skirt and a tall pointed hat, the statuette has long plaited hair, which hangs over the chest and back in four thick tresses. The left hand holds a large shieldlike object of some pliable material, such as leather, and from the right wrist hangs a globular vessel; the right hand is raised, palm outward, in a gesture of greeting or prayer. The face is dominated by huge staring eyes. We cannot be sure whether this enigmatic little figure represents a priest or a warrior, nor is it certain that the richly furnished cremation burial was that of a Sardinian lady married to an Etruscan, as has been claimed by some. Deposited within a tufa container, the cinerary urn, covered by an inverted bowl, is typical of the Vulcian Villanovan—both vessels had a decoration of metal strips.

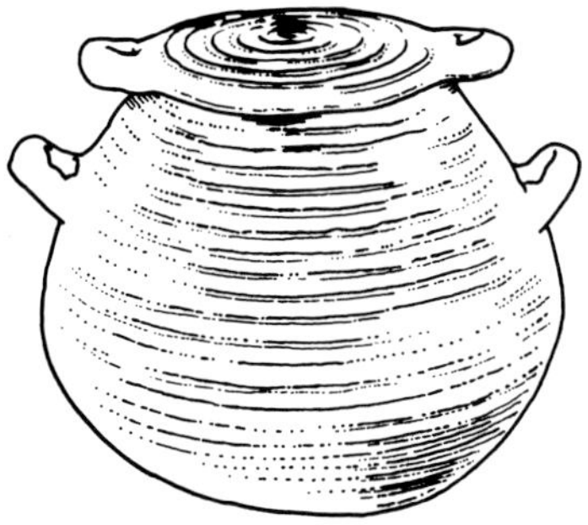

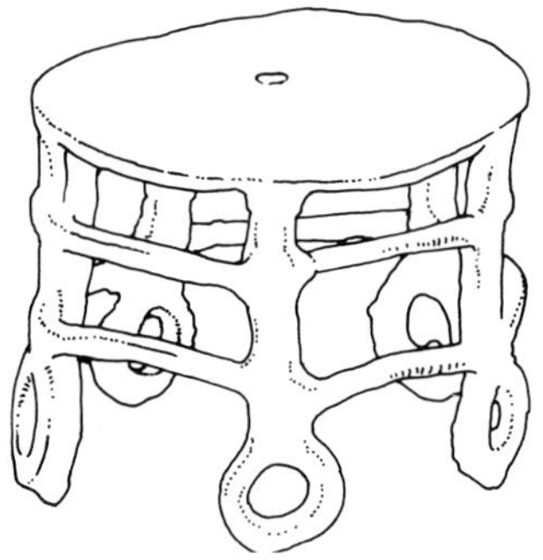

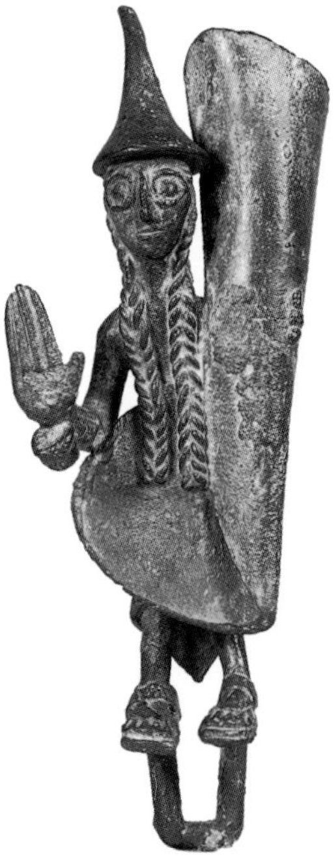

Fig. 17 Miniature model of Sardinian basket. From a woman's tomb in the Mandrione di Cavalupo necropolis, Vulci. Second half of ninth century B.C. Cast bronze. H. 3.3 cm. Rome, Museo Etrusco di Villa Giulia 59919.

Fig. 18 Miniature model of Sardinian stool. From a woman's tomb in the Mandrione di Cavalupo necropolis, Vulci. Second half of ninth century B.C. Cast bronze. H. 3.0 cm. Rome, Museo Etrusco di Villa Giulia 59918.

Fig. 19 Sardinian statuette. From a woman's tomb in the Mandrione di Cavalupo necropolis, Vulci. Second half of ninth century B.C. Cast bronze. H. 13.5 cm. Rome, Museo Etrusco di Villa Giulia 59917.

A bronze chain was suspended around the neck of the urn, suggesting that the urn was considered a substitute for the dead woman's body. The ashes were mixed with a quantity of bronze fibulae, rings, and hair spirals, as well as glass beads—the remains of her personal ornaments. The tomb also contained a bronze lozenge-shaped belt incised with linked spirals and a "solar boat" (all are now in the Museo Etrusco di Villa Giulia, Rome).

It is not unlikely that marriage between Etruscans and foreigners of high social standing influenced local traditions and products. The importance of marriage links and the ceremonial exchange of gifts played a large part in Homeric aristocratic society, as the *Iliad* and *Odyssey* attest, and comparable practices will have existed in Italy. Not only did foreign artifacts travel with their owners, but their makers also moved about, and it is probable that the stimulus that led to fresh developments in techniques and motifs in the Late Villanovan culture of coastal Etruria is due to foreign craftsmen.

BRONZE FIGURINES OF WOMEN

One of the most interesting features for our purpose is the emergence of small cast-bronze human figures that clearly distinguish beween the sexes. Such figurines make their appearance in the region of Vulci and Bisenzio and at Vetulonia in the second half of the eighth century. These figures, used as decoration of weapons, utensils, and ritual objects, give us, for the first time, a glimpse of the status of women.

The scabbard of a sword found at Vulci ends at the top in a projecting ledge, on either end of which stands a human figure facing outward and joined at the back to concentric circles decorating the sheath (FIG. 20). The highly stylized man and woman have strongly marked sexual characteristics. The man wears a flat cap and touches his genitals. Of equal height and perfectly balanced in their respective positions, the man and woman are clearly meant as equals—seemingly the guardians of the warrior's weapon and family.

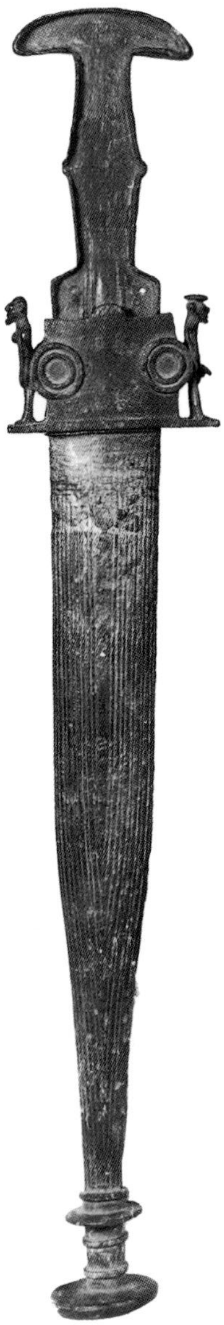

Fig. 20 "Italic" sword. The top of the scabbard is decorated with a nude man and woman in the round. From the Cavalupo necropolis, Vulci. Third quarter of eighth century B.C. Cast bronze. Rome, Museo Etrusco di Villa Giulia, Massimo collection, 64487.

Olmo Bello Necropolis, Tomb 2

From the same period as the sword comes a ritual object of cast bronze found in a woman's richly furnished trench tomb at Bisenzio on Lake Bolsena (FIG. 21a). It is an incense burner in the form of a wheeled, four-sided open-worked stand, whose circular collar rests on a frame of four upright rods connected by four arched ones. The stand supports a lipped bronze bowl, which contained the remains of resin.

On the horizontal connecting bars just above the wheels perch lively if cursorily modeled groups of figurines representing various activities of daily rural life and of hunting and warfare. On one side, next to each other and of the same size, stand a nude woman carrying a biconic water vessel on her head and an ithyphallic warrior with a crested helmet and a spear (FIG. 21b). With her right hand the woman touches the man's genitals, while he puts his left hand on her right breast. Next to them is a smaller figure (their son?) with a loincloth and a shield. A second side of the stand is filled with the figures of an armed warrior and a woman steadying a water vessel on her head and pressing a cup to her breast; beside them a stag is attacked from behind by a dog. On the third side, a man is ploughing with two long-horned oxen, while on the fourth side there are two hunters: one—armed with a bow, quiver, and arrows—aims at a boar(?), and the other raises his javelin and restrains his leashed dog. Further animals and human figures are distributed on the inner connecting rods of the stand: a goat, a wolf, a ram, and a wolf carrying off a lamb in its mouth. There are also two men with belts, caps, swords, and small shields fighting each other. Monkeys and birds swing from rings attached to the collar of the stand.

These complex groups of figures illustrate not only the main aspects and preoccupations of a warlike agricultural society devoted to hunting but also that beside the man/warrior/hunter/paterfamilias stands the wife/child rearer/head of household tasks as an equal, a fact expressed by the equal heights of the couple and by the gestures signifying fertility and procreation that unite them. The values of a socially dominant group are here expressed in a concentrated form.

Closely related in style to the figurines on the censer are those on a cinerary urn of hammered sheet bronze with embossed decoration, also found at Bisenzio

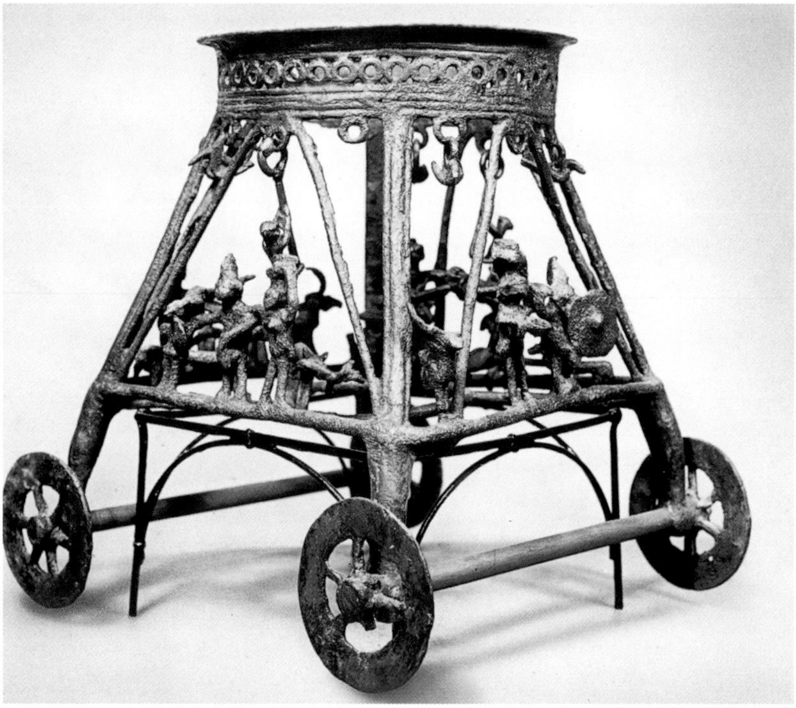

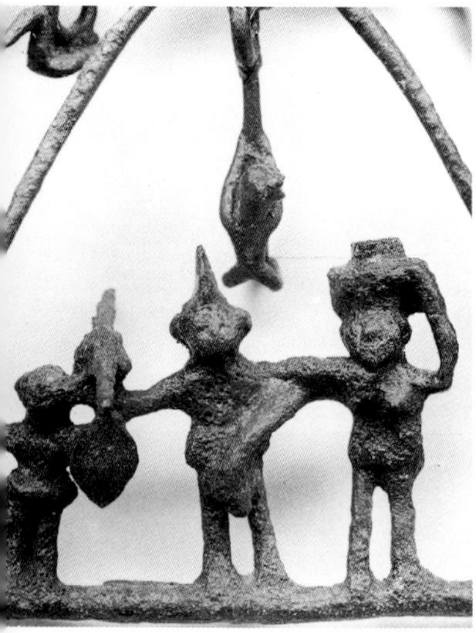

(FIG. 22). On the shoulder and lid of this vessel are cast figurines of ithyphallic men and warriors dancing around a monstrous chained animal (perhaps a divinity of death). One man is holding an ox, perhaps for sacrifice.

The local Etruscan craftsmen who made these two figured utensils may have been inspired by contact with foreign artisans or by imported prototypes (some details of the wheeled stand recall Sardinian and, more remotely, Cypriote models), but they transformed these influences into works reflecting the customs and ideologies of their own aristocratic society.

Fig. 21a Wheeled incense burner from a female burial. Tomb 2, Olmo Bello necropolis, Bisenzio. Second half of eighth century B.C. Cast bronze. H. 30.5 cm. Rome, Museo Etrusco di Villa Giulia 57022/2.

Fig. 21b Detail of incense burner, figure 21a. Statuettes of (from right) wife, husband, and son.

STATUS OF THE WOMAN BURIED IN TOMB 2 AT OLMO BELLO The lady in whose tomb the incense burner was discovered must have belonged to a high-ranking family, and she was presumably an important person in her own right, to judge from the opulence and variety of her grave goods. Deposited in a wooden sarcophagus, which was carefully surrounded by a protective layer of rocks, the body was covered with personal ornaments in bronze, amber, and gold. There were the bronze fibulae for fastening her clothes; gold hair spirals for her tresses; a pair of bronze fibulae decorated with alternating discs of amber and carved wood, the latter covered with incised gold foil; and a necklace of oblong amber beads with three disc-shaped gold pendants embossed with geometric patterns.

On the right side of the dead woman were a number of bronze objects: two bracelets decorated with incised triangles and hatched bands, a shuttle for weaving, a spindle, and a sheet-bronze cup with a decorative handle (FIG. 23). The lat-

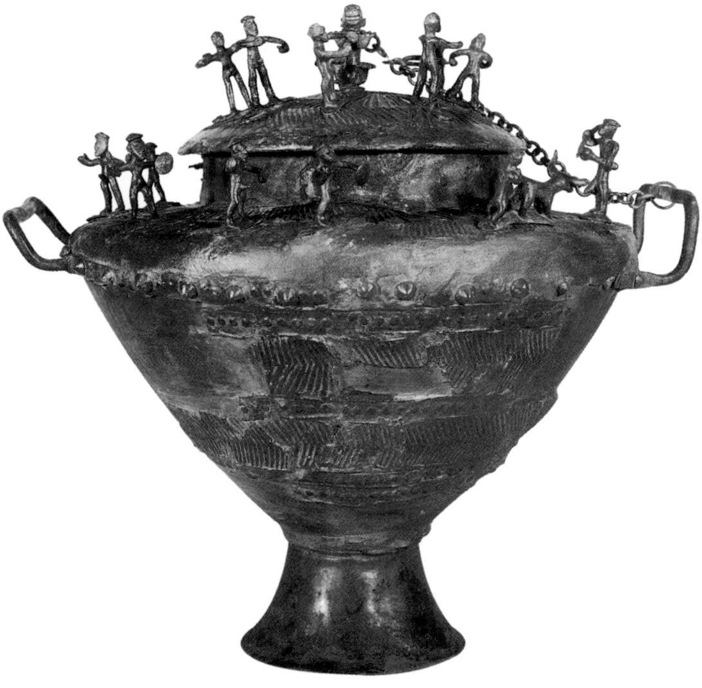

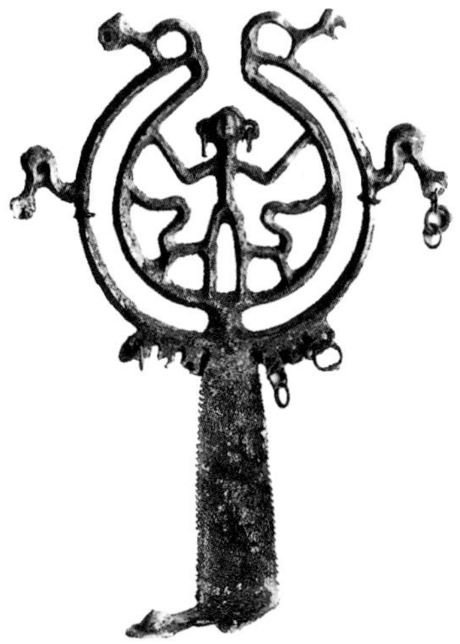

ter was cast in openwork in the form of a nude female figure wearing earrings. She stands, arms spread out and flanked by two ducks, in the center of a double circle on a tapering support. The outer circumference of the circle is decorated with figures of quadrupeds and duck's heads. This frontal female figure dominating animals (known as *potnia theron* = Mistress of the Animals) probably has a religious significance (see p. 45). A large number of comparable open-worked handles have been excavated in tombs of Vetulonia, where they were likely manufactured, and one particularly fine example, supported by a human figure in the round, was found as far afield as Spadarolo near Rimini.

On the left side of the body of the dead woman were a number of impasto vessels. Outside the sarcophagus, in addition to the incense burner described above, were several containers of hammered and riveted sheet bronze—one vessel with embossed decoration and cast handles with ornamental figures of ducks, and two containers for liquid (Lat. *situlae*) with twisted handles. An unusual ritual vessel consisted of a footed bowl with a strap handle across it and two trapezoidal lateral extensions on which small offerings could be deposited. Also outside the sarcophagus were long-necked jugs, large globular vessels, and a three-legged spouted cup, all of impasto, as well as vessels of purified clay with painted decoration of Etrusco-Geometric style, imitating Euboean Greek pottery.

The contents of this tomb not only show the wide range of locally made and imported goods available at Bisenzio in the third quarter of the eighth century but they also tell us something about the social position of the woman buried there.

ABOVE LEFT
Fig. 22 Two-handled urn. Lid and shoulder decorated with statuettes of men dancing around a monstrous animal. From Tomb 22, Olmo Bello necropolis, Bisenzio. Second half of eighth century B.C. Embossed sheet bronze with cast-bronze statuettes. H. 28 cm. Rome, Museo Etrusco di Villa Giulia 57066.

ABOVE RIGHT
Fig. 23 Handle of a cup in the form of a female divinity(?) framed by birds and quadrupeds. Sheet bronze with cast open-worked handle. Inv. 57021. Cast bronze. From Tomb 2, Olmo Bello necropolis, Bisenzio. Second half of eighth century B.C. Rome, Museo Etrusco di Villa Giulia.

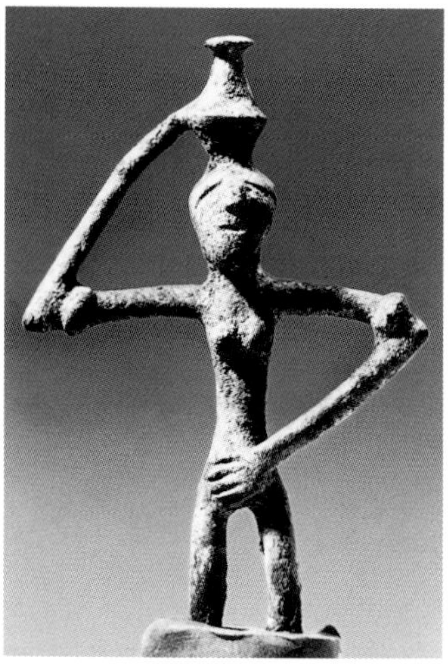

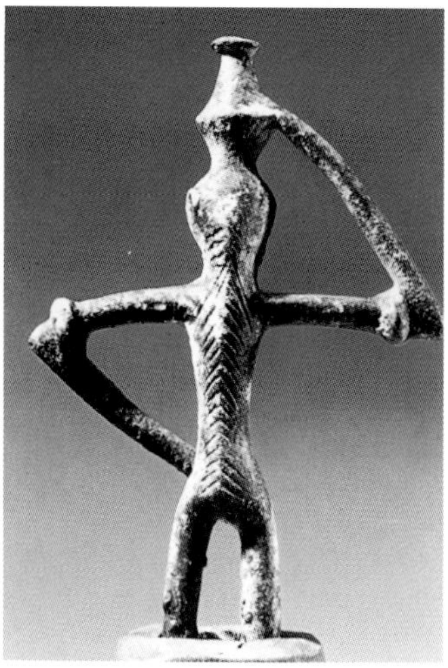

Fig. 24a Statuette of a woman carrying a biconical vessel. Top of a branched bronze stand for the suspension of cups. Front. From the Second Circle of Furs, Vetulonia. Mid-seventh century B.C. Cast bronze. H. 12 cm. Florence, Museo Archeologico 6830.

Fig. 24b Back of statuette, figure 24a.

Her jewelry and implements for woolworking are traditional female grave goods, but the rare bronze incense burner suggests that she may have had some priestly function. Though incense could have been used in either a domestic or a religious context, the added presence of the offering vessel indicates that both these utensils were employed in rituals rather than in ordinary daily tasks.

The Water Carrier from Vetulonia

Another early Etruscan bronze figure illustrating the activities of women is a statuette from a tomb in Vetulonia (FIGS. 24a, b); it decorated the top of a branched bronze stand for the suspension of cups. The young woman is nude except for a massive bracelet above each elbow. She stands with her legs spread and her sticklike arms bent at an acute angle. Her right hand steadies a biconic water vessel on her head while her left hand covers her pubes. Over her back hangs a long single plait of hair incised with a herringbone pattern, a Near-Eastern hair fashion that was adopted by Etruscan women during the Orientalizing period. For all its gawky angularity, this figure captures an emblematic female occupation and gesture with startling vividness. A water carrier is an eminently suitable decoration for a utensil designed for the suspension of drinking vessels.

We must not, of course, imagine that the bronze statuettes that we have been looking at represent reality in the sense that Etruscan women at this period went about in the nude—the Italian climate alone would rule this out, even if we did not have the testimony in Villanovan tombs of quantities of fibulae of different types and decoration, lying on the skeletons of both men and women in positions that show they were used to hold clothes in place.

PAINTED POTTERY

The introduction in the second half of the eighth century of new techniques and motifs in pottery contributed to a somewhat less abstract representation of the human figure than that first found on incised Villanovan cinerary urns. From an early seventh-century woman's tomb at Bisenzio comes a globular vase on a high foot (FIGS. 25a, b); it is made of purified impasto and painted in black and red on a cream-colored ground in a technique perhaps derived from Cyprus. The body of the vase is decorated with superposed bands of geometric designs familiar from Italo-Geometric pottery, but the lowest band shows a row of forty-eight clothed human figures in silhouette. Their heads are in profile, their bodies frontal, with an inverted triangle for the thorax joined to another triangle below for a short skirt, from which emerge sticklike legs, set well apart. The figures all hold hands in what looks like a dance, three black-painted silhouettes regularly alternating with three red ones. This change of color may be no more than a rhythmic device to enliven the design, but it is possible that it represents an attempt to distinguish

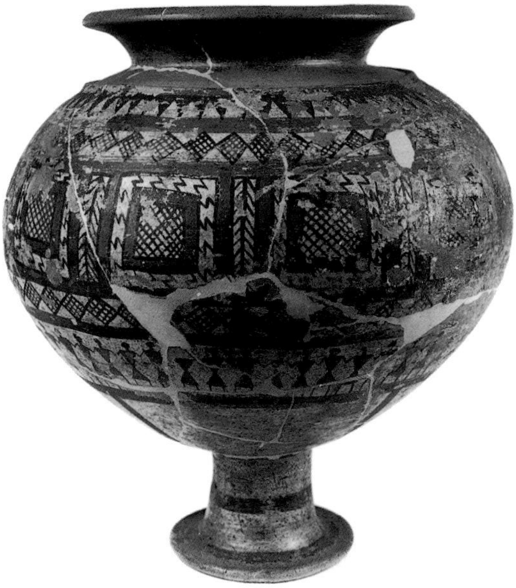

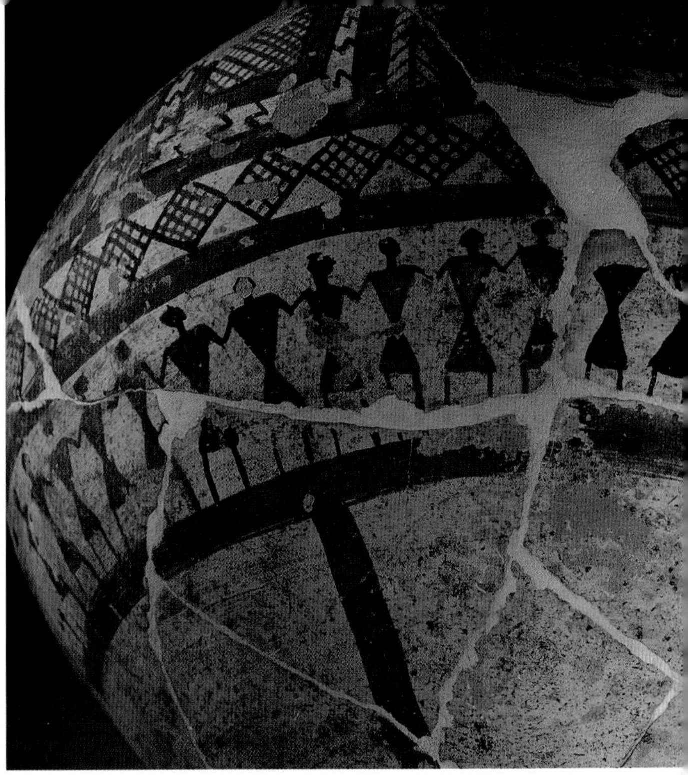

the sexes by different colors. In later Etruscan tomb-paintings women are always depicted with lighter skins than men. The red figures on the vase may represent the female participants in a dance, whereas the black figures could be men. Funerary and other round dances are frequent subjects on Greek Geometric pottery, but there the sexes are usually clearly distinguished by the physical attributes of their gender or by dress, and they dance in segregated groups, even if it is a dance of both youths and maidens, a fact also attested in Homeric poetry. If we are right in assuming that the Bisenzio vase shows an integrated dance of both sexes, it would be an early example of Etruscan women participating in a (funerary?) ceremony on an equal footing and in close proximity with men.

Fig. 25a Globular vase on a high foot. From Tomb 3, Bucacce necropolis, Bisenzio. About 700 B.C. Painted pottery. H. 31.5 cm. Florence, Museo Archeologico 85629.

Fig. 25b Detail of frieze of dancers, from figure 25a.

The burial from which this vase came was a rich one. The dead woman was placed in a wooden coffin in a trench, with impasto and bronze vessels and utensils—including a spool for woolworking—assembled at her feet and gold, silver, and amber jewelry and personal ornaments at her head. There were faience amulets and egyptianizing steatite scarabs of Saite date (664–525 B.C.)—imports brought to Etruria by Phoenician and Greek sailor-traders during the early stages of the Orientalizing period. Tombs of this type point to the growing wealth of aristocratic families through profitable contact with foreigners.

EVIDENCE OF EARLY RELIGIOUS PRACTICE

Recent excavations near modern Tarquinia on the Pian di Civita (the western part of the plateau on which the ancient city was situated) are of particular interest for the light they shed on the as yet little-documented religious beliefs and

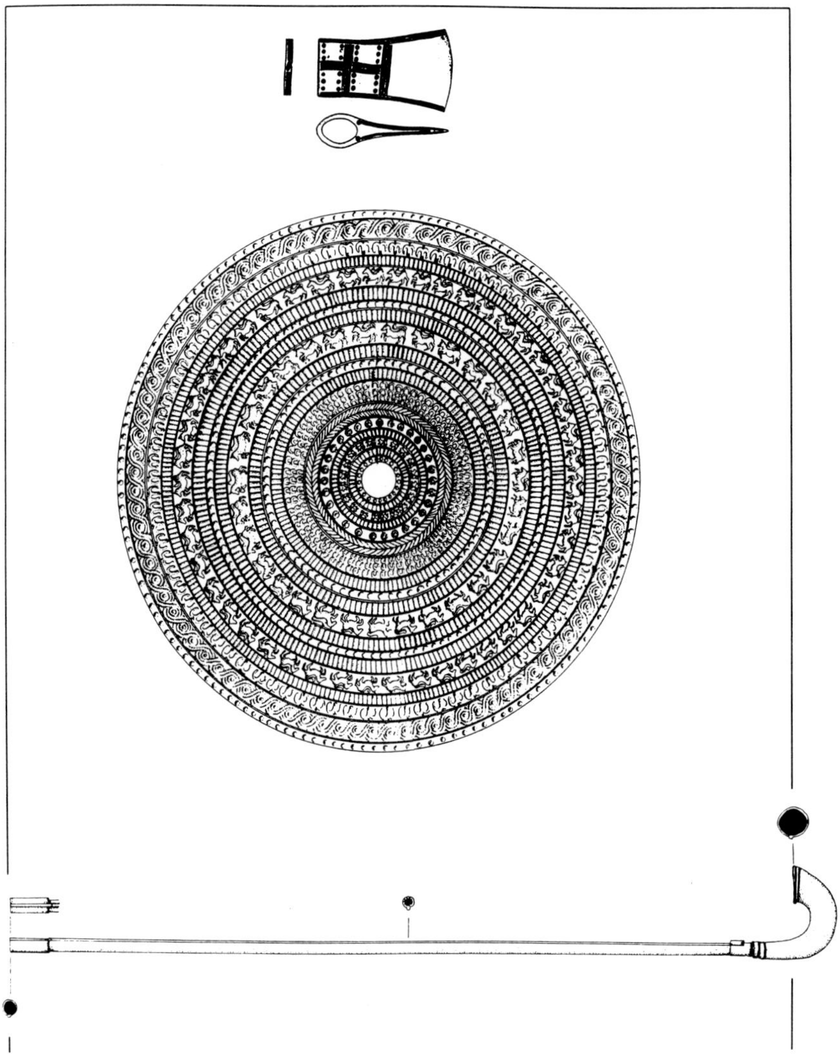

Fig. 26 Three votive bronzes. *Top* Axe head, L. 16 cm, inv. C 176/A/22. *Middle* Shield, Diam. ca. 96 cm, inv. C 176/A/21. *Bottom* Trumpet (*lituus*), L. 1.35 m, inv. C 176/A/20. From the Pian di Civita, Tarquinia. First quarter of seventh century B.C. Tarquinia, Museo Nazionale Archeologico.

practices of the Villanovan civilization and their continuation into the historical periods of Etruria.

The first evidence of settlement on this part of the Pian di Civita is an elliptical hut (of which postholes survive) and an oven from the late tenth century, that is, the Late Bronze Age (the period also known as the Protovillanovan), as well as a small trench containing fragments of impasto pottery, remains of animal sacrifices, the pips of a deposit of cultivated vine (*Vitis vinifera*), and emmer (*Triticum dicoccum*).

The excavation revealed a "sacred area" centered on a natural cavity in the rock, where from this early time onward a cult was carried on that has left successive layers of charcoal and ashes from sacrificial fires, mixed with pottery sherds and tips or sections of deer antlers. This primitive site received added significance during the ninth century by the ritual burial of a boy about eight years old, oriented with his head to the east. On his chest was a bronze pin, which probably once fastened a garment, and beside his head lay a bronze pendant. He seems to have been placed on the bare ground, without any grave goods, covered only by clay grit and ashes mixed with pieces of deer antlers. A conspicuous malformation of the boy's skull indicates that he must have suffered from epileptic fits.

During the second half of the eighth century, burials near the boy of three newborn infants likewise followed the then unusual practice of inhumation without a trench or grave goods, the dead covered only with gritty soil mixed with the remains of sacrificial fires and tips and sections of antlers. The area to the west was soon surrounded by a stone enclosure. During the third quarter of the eighth century a man was buried in a shallow ditch just north of this site with his head covered by a large fragment of a Euboean water jug. He died from a fatal blow to the right side of the head, and it has been suggested that he was a Euboean Greek sailor.

During the first quarter of the seventh century a rectangular stone building (6.50 x 11 m), oriented east-west, was erected to the east of and aligned with the subterranean cavity and the boy's grave. The walls were built in a mixture of ashlar blocks placed upright at intervals and stretches of irregular stones, reminiscent of the "pier-and-rubble" technique used in seventh-century buildings in the Levant. Evidence of a foundation ritual was discovered under the north wall of this sanctuary, where another newborn baby had been buried together with impasto vessels. An inner room contained an altar platform and a channel—probably for the blood of sacrificial animals—which communicated with the underground cavity. Just in front of the building's entrance were unearthed two irregularly shaped trenches with votive deposits. In the first were three bronze objects superposed on each other (FIG. 26): a cast-bronze axe head finely decorated with lines and punched circles—motifs of Villanovan derivation; a shield of sheet bronze, stamped with a variety of geometric and figural designs (quadrupeds, lotus buds, etc.) arranged in concentric circles, carefully folded over several times; and, bent into three sections, a long bronze trumpet (*lituus*) with a curved flared mouth. All these objects had thus intentionally been rendered useless. In the second trench were the deliberately broken pieces of at least ten simple pottery plates and two impasto drinking vessels, which were probably used during a sacrificial meal or dedicatory rite. A monumental enclosure was added to the building shortly afterward, and in the sixth century it was given a tiled roof. Drastic alterations that changed the nature of the site took place in the fifth century. A newly laid-out road system and drainage passed through the ancient sanctuary, which must by then have lost its original significance.

To sum up, the cult practiced from prehistoric times onward on the highest point of what was to become one of the most important Etruscan cities involved animal sacrifices around a rock cavity; deposition of votive offerings in the form of tips and sections of deer antlers; burial (not in a necropolis!) and veneration of the remains of an epileptic boy; and the nearby sacrifices of pigs, sheep, and bovines, as well as sixteen carapaces of tortoises during the eighth and seventh centuries. Three subsequently deposited newborn infants may have been human sacrifices. Three particularly fine bronzes (axe, shield, and trumpet), convincingly interpreted as symbols of authority, were deposited in the early seventh century by a high-ranking person, presumably a king, responsible for the erection of a stone temple. Offerings of pottery, bronze, a banqueting service, and miniature vessels in bucchero during the following centuries point to the continuation of the cult at this site, which had probably become a social and political center, as well as a religious one.

The Divinity of the Cult at Pian di Civita (Tarquinia)

The main goddess of the cult on the Pian di Civita is thought to have been Uni; the inscription on a fragment of a bucchero cup of the second half of the seventh century has been read as her name. Uni, the equivalent of the Italic Juno and the Greek Hera, was an Etruscan goddess of outstanding importance. In the harbor sanctuary of Santa Severa (Lat. Pyrgi) near Cerveteri she was worshiped at the end of the sixth century as Uni-Astarte and associated with Eileithyia, the goddess of birth (see p. 174). Sacrifices of goats were associated with the Juno of Lanuvium, known as Sospita, a warlike Latin fertility goddess and protectress of cities, represented with a shield and a lance and wearing a goat skin with horns on her head.

The tips of deer antlers found so plentifully in the excavation are thought to represent votive offerings in the form of small aniconic images (Lat. *baetyli*) of the goddess. It is uncertain whether the epileptic boy and the newborn infants buried near the cavity were sacrificial victims, but that cannot be ruled out, for human sacrifices were recorded, for example, for the period of the Etruscan monarchy at Rome during the sixth century (Macrob. *Sat.* 1.7.35). The habit of sacrificing infants as burnt offerings to ensure health and fertility for other offspring or to avert grave peril, is widely attested in the cult of Semitic deities in the burial places (tophets) of Phoenician and Punic cities. The identification of Uni with the Phoenician Astarte at Santa Severa/Pyrgi makes it possible that child sacrifices were practiced in Etruria as well. A further connection between Astarte—by the Greeks called Aphrodite Ourania—and the cult carried on in the "sacred area" of Tarquinia is the use of the tortoise as a sacrificial animal. The tortoise is associated in Greece with Aphrodite and other goddesses; it was highly regarded for religious, medicinal, and prophylactic reasons. Among its many therapeutic properties was its blood for the treatment of epilepsy.

The boy afflicted with epilepsy must have appeared to his contemporaries of the ninth century as a supernatural being, periodically possessed by hallucinations, a prodigy who during his attacks was able to communicate with hidden powers. His ritual burial near a natural underground cavity suggests a connection between him and the mythical Etruscan figure of Tages.

The legend of Tages, known only from Roman authors, tells of the revelation of the *disciplina etrusca*, the Etruscan ritual books (see p. 270). A peasant of Tarquinia is said to have been ploughing a field when he turned up in his furrow a miraculous being who looked like a newborn boy but with signs of old age and full of wisdom. The peasant cried out in astonishment, upon which "all Etruria" ran to the spot where Tages—such was the boy's name—had begun to utter the words that were written down as the *disciplina etrusca*. The sources vary as to who the writer was: According to some it was Tarchon, the founder of Tarquinia, but others say that it was the princes of the twelve Etruscan cities or their sons who listened to Tages' teachings and wrote them down. Having revealed the sacred texts, the miraculous boy disappeared again or died.

The questions raised by the excavations of the Pian di Civita at Tarquinia are almost as many as the new insights they produced; but it has certainly been established that since prehistoric times religious practices centered on the female divinity Uni were carried on in a settlement that became one of the grandest Etruscan cities. We shall discuss Uni's sanctuaries elsewhere in Etruria later.

A Water Cult at Banditella (Canino)

Recent discoveries at Banditella, about 5 km from Vulci, have produced copious evidence of votive offerings at a spring and in the associated swampy area, from the Middle Bronze Age (seventeenth century B.C.) to the Archaic period. The earliest offerings deposited on the edge of the swamp consisted mainly of pottery vessels, of which fragments survive, as well as of carved bone discs and glass beads. In the Villanovan period the watery area was tidied up by the erection of a straight dry wall of large stones in front of the spring, which created a small triangular lake. Beside the main spring were found deposits of one bronze vessel and about 150 miniature impasto vessels, some of them biconic, as well as rings of silver and bronze, a leech-fibula, and a small bronze horse with finely incised musculature and trappings(?). This little sculpture may have formed part of a group decorating the domed lid of a bronze vessel (perhaps a "horse tamer").

In contrast to the findings at Tarquinia, the votive gifts at Banditella were made in a rural spot, not in the center of a future city. When great urban sanctuaries arose in nearby Vulci in the Archaic period, the cult in the outlying area of Banditella seems to have lost its importance, and it was abandoned.

From the evidence we have considered, it appears that early cult practices were carried on near natural features such as caves and springs that were endowed with a special sanctity.

VILLANOVAN CIVILIZATION IN NORTHERN ETRURIA

Fiesole

On a hill north of the Arno, Fiesole dominated a ford across the river frequented as early as the Bronze Age, in the place where Florence was to arise. Small Villanovan settlements must have existed near this important crossing, for tombs with cinerary urns of men, women, and children have been excavated in the center of the city (the tombs of the Gambrinus). The deposition of the urns in large impasto jars (It. *dolii*) resembles the funerary customs of Chiusi and Volterra, but the grave goods, such as fibulae, have affinities with finds at Bologna. Recent discoveries in Piazza della Signoria in Florence include sherds of locally made pottery and others with Geometric decoration of eighth-century date. A cult area was located between Orsanmichele and Piazza della Signoria, as attested by small votive bronzes of nude men and women of the second half of the seventh century, and by a sixth-century statuette of an armed warrior with raised spear.

In the territory northwest of Florence the drainage of the river plain allowed minor centers such as Quinto and Sesto Fiorentino to flourish on agriculture. Aristocratic family groups settled here were to erect imposing circular tombs with vaulted ceilings (Gr. *tholos* tombs). Similar developments took place to the west, where at Artimino and Comeana settlements on the northern bank of the Arno with important cemeteries were to enjoy a prolonged existence.

Remains of an Iron Age settlement have been identified on the highest, western part of the hill of Fiesole (San Francesco), an easily defended position from which to control the river traffic, the ford of the Arno, and the agricultural plain below. Little is known about the conditions of Fiesole during the seventh century, but excavations have produced evidence at the place of the later temple for a cult that goes back to the seventh century: Three votive bronze statuettes of nude worshipers, one male and two female, of Geometric style have been found there. The importance of Fiesole was to increase after about 600 with the political and commercial expansion northward of Etruscans from Volsinii, Volterra, and Chiusi.

Volterra

The oldest Villanovan settlement at Volterra (see FIG. 1) was situated on the south side of the hill above the vast Le Ripaie necropolis. Fragments of Late Bronze Age pottery found here point to an earlier occupation of the site. The highest point of the hill, the Piano di Castello, where a Late Villanovan village existed, developed into the future acropolis of Volterra. It overlooked the Cecina valley, which connected it with the west and the Tyrrhenian coast and, via the Cornia valley, with the region of Populonia and Vetulonia. On the northwestern side of the plateau of Volterra, Villanovan villages have been identified at Guerruccia and Badia. They dominated the Era valley, which afforded communications to the north with the course of the Arno and the coastal region of Pisa. The extensive hill of Volterra underwent continuous erosion, particularly at its northern and western spurs. Entire sections have collapsed into the ravines below, taking with them parts of the cemeteries, spectacularly so at Le Balze. This may explain the comparative scarcity of finds from the Orientalizing and Archaic periods.

Servius (commentary on Verg. *Aen.* 10.172) credits Volterra with having founded Populonia, but despite undoubted cultural connections between the two cities, the comparative modesty of the finds from Villanovan Volterra—an inland agricultural settlement—makes it unlikely that the flourishing maritime and mining center of Populonia with its far-flung early trade connections owed its existence to Volterra.

The Volterran cemeteries of Ripaie, Guerruccia, and Badia contained cremation burials in ovoid and biconic ash urns covered with bowls and set in pits or, later, placed inside large jars, the latter often protected by a box constructed from six large stone slabs (It. *cassetta* tomb). The grave goods, at first few and simple, later included weapons and bronze fibulae, razors and horse trappings, as well as pottery.

An aristocratic warrior's splendid possessions, excavated in 1996 at Poggio alle Croci and dated to the last quarter of the eighth century, point to cultural links with Southern Etruria: the crested bronze helmet, a double flask of lentoid shape, a shallow bowl, a goblet, a horse bit, as well as the weapons—sword, javelin, and lance head—are all of typically Tarquinian manufacture.

The Villanovan period of Volterra covers the ninth and eighth centuries. In the Orientalizing phase of the seventh century there is some evidence of greater wealth, however, without numerous imported luxury goods as in Southern Etruria. At the end of the seventh century a sanctuary seems to have been established on the castle hill.

In the region west of Volterra, at Casale Marittimo near the mouth of the Cecina River, new light has been thrown on the here hitherto little-known Late Villanovan and Orientalizing periods. A rich necropolis at Casa Nocera belonged to an aristocratic family group. Ranging in date from the late eighth to the early sixth century, nine tombs of different types have been excavated: rectangular tombs lined with stone slabs (It. *cassone* tombs), trench tombs, and underground chamber tombs. The sophisticated funerary customs of these warrior princes are documented in particular by the oldest *cassone* tomb; it contained a panoply of axe, lance, and helmet, a scepter, personal ornaments, bronze banqueting vessels, a large clay jar covered by an incised bronze shield, and the ash urn within with the bones wrapped in a piece of purple linen (a rite for the burial of heroes described by Homer). In addition there was such food as a honeycomb, nuts, grapes, and a pomegranate, as well as the iron remains of two chariots burnt on the pyre with the dead. Other male tombs contained bronze axes, whose curved wooden handles were sheathed with bronze and decorated with a row of cast figurines of ducks. The modestly furnished female tombs yielded only fibulae, amber, spindles, and a little knife. Displaced by grave robbers were found two almost life-size male stone statues wearing a broad belt and *perizoma* tentatively dated to the first half of the seventh century B.C. Among the earliest sculptures in Etruria, both wear a belt, lozenge shaped in front and at the back. One held his arms across the chest, the other clasped his neck with his left hand, perhaps a gesture of mourning.

Pisa

Recent excavations at Pisa and in the coastal region to the south have revealed the existence of small Late Bronze Age (Protovillanovan) villages on the islands and sand dunes at the mouth of the Arno River.

In the ninth century a Villanovan settlement and a necropolis seem to have occupied the Area Scheibler, west and north of the medieval city. The fragment of a biconic vessel, decorated with a comb-incised meander and circular depressions, found in Via Pietrasanta in Pisa, shows a close relationship with a cinerary urn from Tomb D1 of the Ripaie necropolis at Volterra and points to Volterra's cultural influence on the Pisa region, while sporadic fragmentary bronze razors belong to types attested at Bologna and Populonia.

Traces of a settlement of the mid-eighth century have been identified in Via Buonarroti, and remains of curvilinear buildings dating from the end of the eighth century have been discovered both in Piazza Dante and in the northeastern corner of Piazza del Duomo. Material from elsewhere in the area of the city points to a concentration of different nuclei in strategic positions. Cultural and trade relations with Populonia are confirmed by a bucchero pyxis lid closely resembling a specimen from the Tumulus of the Cylindrical Pyxides (*Tumulo delle Pissidi Cilindriche*) at Populonia and by the discovery of slag from Elban iron ore in workshop remains datable to the second half of the seventh century. Fragments of vessels for the consumption of wine indicate the emergence of an aristocratic class in contact with coastal Etruria further south, where Greek drinking rituals were being adopted.

At the end of the eighth century a monumental cenotaph tomb (recently excavated and still being analyzed) was erected for an important member of that elite in a large necropolis extending northwest of the Piazza del Duomo beyond the medieval city walls in Via San Jacopo. A tumulus (30 m in diameter) was confined by a circle of closely set, upright, thin stone slabs, outside of which pairs of monoliths, placed 7 m apart, and a stela marked the limits of this monumental area. In a large square trench inside the circle was buried a wooden box containing only fragments of vases and some ovine bones, presumably the remains of a funerary ceremony. On a level above was deposited a big iron trident, whose handle had been ritually broken. Above the trident had been constructed a large stone altar on which were found a big knife, four iron spits, and the jawbone of a horse that had probably been sacrificed. In a large sealed pottery jar beside the altar were ash from a pyre of oakwood, many small bronze nails, and a thin piece of gold wire. It has been suggested that these were the remains of a burnt image of the deceased. The altar had been intentionally broken after the funerary ceremony, and the tumulus was finally heaped on top of it.

The absence of human remains indicates that this monumental tomb was a cenotaph, erected for the head of an aristocratic family who had died abroad. The trident was a weapon used by Greek heroes for hunting (for example, the Kalydonian Boar), but in the Mediterranean especially for harpooning big fish, such as tuna. The trident was the attribute of the ruler of the sea, Poseidon/Neptune, and thus a symbol of power. Such an interpretation of this weapon is confirmed by similar tridents found in aristocratic tombs at Vetulonia (Circle of the Trident, *Circolo del Tridente*) and Marsiliana d'Albegna (Circle of the Fibula, *Circulo della Fibula*). The Pisan prince who was commemorated by elaborate funerary rites, including the deposition of a trident below an altar, was probably not only a great landowner but also a seafarer, and he may have died in pursuit of sea-trading or piracy. Subsequently he seems to have been worshiped as a hero, for in the third quarter of the seventh century two male and two female cremation burials were made in the tumulus above the area of the altar. These presumably contained the remains of members of the same family. Outside the stone circle of the tumulus were discovered two large stone blocks that must have served as rudimentary altars in a cult of the dead, for animal bones were found still lying on top of one of them.

VILLANOVAN CIVILIZATION NORTH OF THE APENNINES

Bologna

As we have already noted, the Villanovan civilization flourished not only in Tuscany, parts of present-day Lazio, and in the areas of Capua, Salerno, and Sala Consilina but also in the Po valley and in the Adriatic region near Rimini and Fermo. One of the most important northern centers was Bologna (Etr. Felsina), a group of villages probably settled from Etruria via the Apennine passes and the valleys of the Reno and Savena early in the ninth century. The nucleus of the future Etruscan city of Felsina seems to have been the area of Villa Cassarini-Villa Bosi, where one of the oldest Villanovan villages was located. Situated at the foot of the Apennines between the rivers Apona and Ravone, these settlements profited from rich agricultural land and from a position in command of ancient trade routes.

A thriving bronze industry is attested by a foundry in a hut of eighth-century date and by typical local grave goods in bronze, such as bow-fibulae with rhomboid section and lowered bow; the so-called palettes in male tombs; and flat, bell-shaped bronze rattles (Lat. *tintinnabula*) in female ones. The hoard of San Francesco (*Ripostiglio di S. Francesco*)—an enormous deposit consisting of 14,838 finished objects, rejects, and fragments of bronze—was collected for re-use in a foundry in the beginning of the seventh century B.C. Many of these pieces of bronze were marked with Etruscan letters, which may represent number values. The tools and utensils in this deposit—saws, files, hammers, anvils, burins, axes, chisels, borers, gouges, sickles and scythes, fishhooks, harpoons, blades, and fibulae—give a far more comprehensive idea of the hunting, fishing, agricultural, building, metallurgical, and woodworking activities carried out in the community in the eighth and seventh centuries than is provided by the few surviving remains of huts and vegetable matter (such as wood, fruit kernels, seeds, and pollen).

In male tombs there is a notable absence of defensive weapons, such as helmets and shields, but evidence for the use of horses (bits), goads, and chariots, reflecting the rise of a local aristocracy.

The development of the Villanovan civilization of Bologna between the ninth and sixth centuries has been subdivided into four phases designated by the names of specific cemeteries of the area: I, Savena, San Vitale (ca. 900–800); II, Benacci I, Caprara (ca. 800–750); III, Benacci II (ca. 750–680); and IV, Arnoaldi (ca. 680–530). The latter phases are strongly permeated by orientalizing elements, but they adhere to the traditional rite of cremation; however, instead of being deposited in biconic urns with incised geometric ornaments, the ashes of the dead were buried in situla-shaped urns with a wealth of stamped decoration.

A recent detailed study of eighth-century grave goods found in 621 tombs from eleven cemeteries of Villanovan Bologna has shown stratification of social roles and ranks for both men and women. Analysis of the finds in individual burials suggests clear distinctions in occupation, wealth, and rank. In female tombs three different types of sets of objects have been found:

1) The first and simplest type consists of only bronze fibulae.
2) The second includes a spindle besides the fibulae.
3) The third comprises fibulae as well as various personal ornaments.

This last type has again been subdivided into three different groups:

a) Burial with jewelry consisting of amber and paste, as well as bronze chains, pendants, bracelets, and rings.
b) The same type of jewelry as a) with the addition of a bronze belt.
c) Jewelry of type a) plus spools and distaff.

Women buried with bronze belts represent only 12% of all those accompanied by jewelry, and they seem to have belonged to an elevated class, whereas the women buried only with fibulae probably belonged to the lower social stratum. Spinning and weaving, as represented by distaffs and spools beside many personal ornaments, appear to have been a prerogative of the upper strata.

FUNERARY STELAE In the north the Villanovan civilization lasted longer than in the south, and it had strongly marked local features that were rare in the rest of Etruria. Among the most striking of these are the monumental stone stelae of Bologna, carved with low reliefs and originally painted. They served as markers on Villanovan cremation tombs and are known as *pietre protofelsinee*, that is, they belong to the period before the foundation of Etruscan Felsina.

Beginning with Phase I, the tombs are often marked by upright oblong stones or slabs. The earliest examples, which seem to be in the tradition of the menhirs of France and of the alpine region, probably represent a stylized human figure. They consist of a rectangular slab for the body, ending on top in a roughly oval disc for the head. The flat surface is carved with circles, double spirals, solar symbols, geometric patterns, and animals; the undecorated, tapering lower part of the stela was inserted into the soil.

A stela from Saletto di Bentivoglio adheres to this anthropomorphizing shape, but it is carved in low relief with a sphinx on the circular top part, while the rectangular "body" shows two rampant goats, heraldically flanking a tree—motifs of Near Eastern inspiration (FIG. 27).

Another group of stelae, also from the seventh century, shows a more elongated form, pointed at the top and carved on the front and back with orientalizing motifs in high relief (flowers, palmettes, sphinxes, trees of life, and human figures, armed, mounted on horses, or on a biga). Other fragmentary specimens approach three-dimensional form.

Beside stelae, elongated cippi were used; round or oval in section, they recall phallic rather than anthropomorphic shapes. Few of the tombs that these monuments surmounted have been scientifically excavated, so the scarcity of datable contexts and the astonishing diversity of the models from which the carvers took their inspiration make it difficult to arrive at a reliable chronological development. The monuments range in date from the eighth to the late sixth century and suggest that Bologna received, directly or indirectly, artistic impulses from regions as far apart as western Europe and Northern Syria.

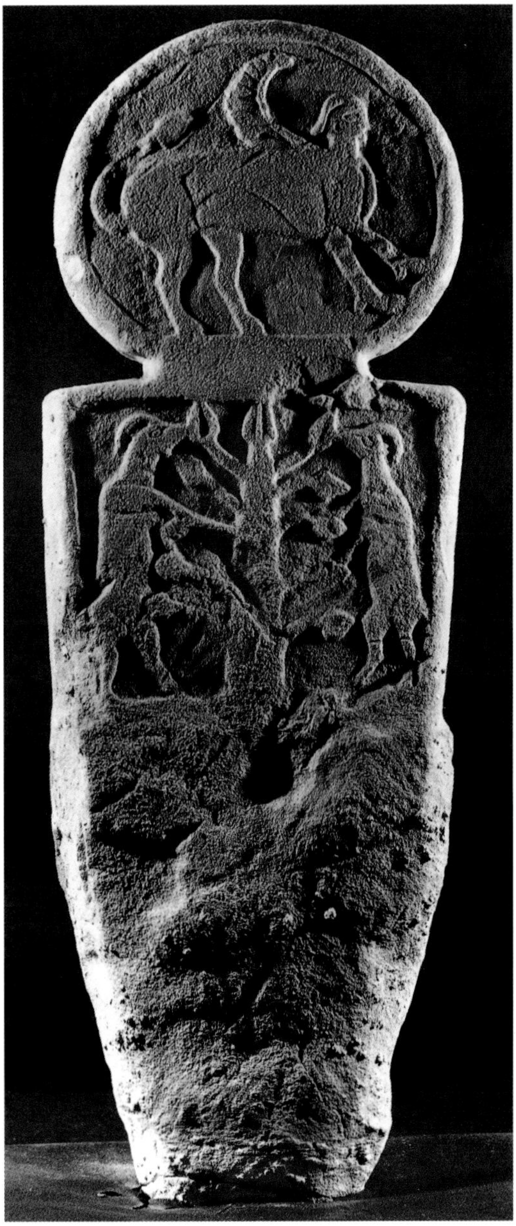

Fig. 27 Funerary stela carved in low relief with a sphinx and goats grazing off a tree. From Saletto di Bentivoglio (Bologna). Second half of seventh century B.C. Sandstone. H. 72 cm. Bologna, Museo Civico Archeologico 25677.

TOMB OF THE GOLD, NO. 5 The contents of a rich woman's tomb in the Villanovan necropolis of the Arsenal at Bologna, the Tomb of the Gold (*Tomba degli Ori*), no. 5, likewise show the wide range over which goods were traded and craftsmen moved. The ash urn was deposited in a large impasto jar (*dolio*), and the grave goods comprised personal ornaments of amber and glass paste, an egyptianizing amulet in the shape of the god Bes, and fine gold jewelry: gold hairbands of filigree and a leech-fibula with an applied animal pattern in a particularly fine form of granulation called *al pulviscolo* in Italian. This sophisticated technique is often seen on jewelry from seventh-century tombs at Vetulonia, where gold decorated *al pulviscolo* was probably manufactured. But granulation is ultimately an invention of Near Eastern craftsmen, who must have taught their skills in the west.

The most fascinating find in the Tomb of the Gold is a tintinnabulum (FIGS. 28a, b). Made from two pieces of sheet bronze joined together and provided with a cast open-worked handle, it was chased on each of its two surfaces with two superposed figured scenes. On the lower half of one side of the rattle two women are seated facing each other over a large basket of carded wool. Each of them pulls up a thick strand of wool to put on her distaff. Both are draped in heavy mantles of diagonally striped material that leave only their faces and forearms exposed. Their cylindrical chairs with splayed, rounded backrests are decorated with bosses and hatched bands; the rectangular footstools are plain. On the wall between the women hangs an inverted semicircular fan. Behind each chair a flower bud serves as space filler.

On the upper half of this side of the rattle stands a tall woman in profile to the right, spinning. She, too, wears a diagonally striped mantle of probably triangular cut. Her striped dress, which reaches to her ankles, is trimmed at the bottom with a triple border. Raising her distaff in her left hand, she twirls with her right hand the thread of wool with the spindle attached. A rosette and vegetal forms fill the surrounding space.

The other side of the tintinnabulum has suffered damage at the bottom, hampering the interpretation of a complex scene that probably represents a subsequent stage in the manufacture of cloth—the preparation of the warp threads for the loom. It has been suggested that the woman seated on the left, who works facing an upright support, is weaving the heading band from which, once the band has been fastened to the top beam of the loom, the warp threads will hang down, weighted at the bottom. On the right, a second woman pulls out the loops of thread that will become the warp. The measuring pegs on a lozenge-shaped stand are behind her. On the floor stand two widemouthed containers.

In the space above this scene is depicted a tall, elaborately turned and carved, warp-weighted loom on whose cagelike upper platform another woman sits on a chair with a curved backrest. She handles the warp threads suspended from the top beam in front of her; they are kept taut by two sets of weights at the bottom. At the foot of the loom stands another draped woman, who reaches up to hand her

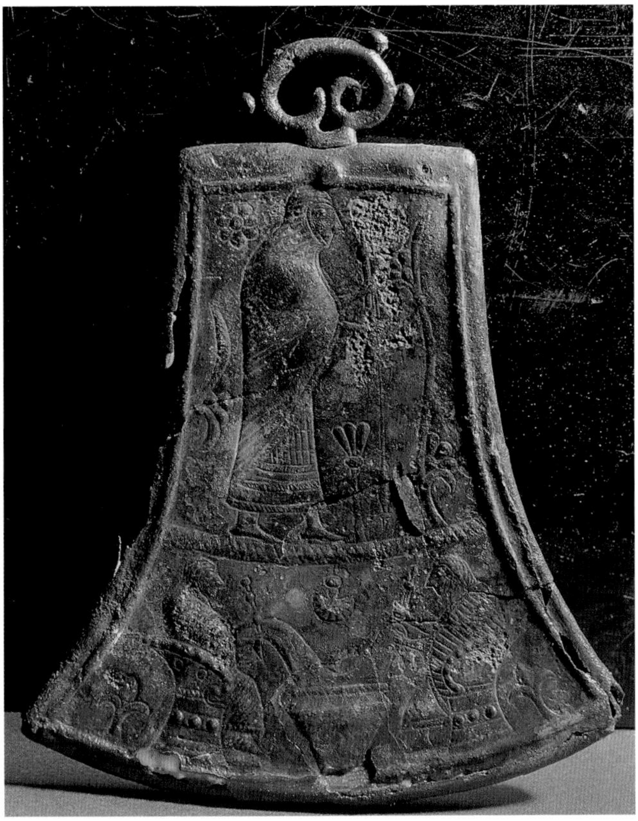

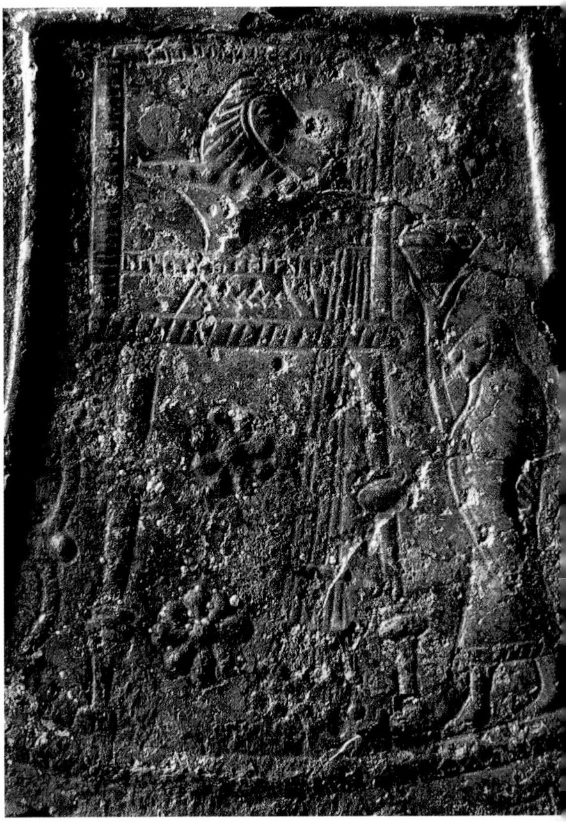

companion a container, probably a supply of weft yarn. Rosettes and a flower bud fill the empty spaces.

The representation of this type of loom, which enables particularly long pieces of material to be woven, is, so far, unique. Its ingenious construction and elegant decoration attest to the high level of technical skill and aesthetic sense of the local population. The women are all represented in the same kind of dress, they occupy seats of identical form (characteristic for aristocratic dwellings and tombs, see FIGS. 29a and 300), and the difference in size between the figures on the first side of the rattle is clearly dictated by formal and decorative considerations rather than by any intention to characterize different social rank. The fan suspended between the smaller seated women is also a symbol of their high status; we shall find actual fans used in this sense, deposited in tombs of the Orientalizing period or depicted in later tomb-paintings (see FIGS. 88 and 184). Instead of interpreting the tall, spinning figure as a mistress, aided by maids or slaves, we should perhaps see the women as equal members of an extended family group, working together in a complex enterprise that will benefit them all.

The style of the figures and their garments are typical for the orientalizing art of Northern Etruria (Volterra, Chiusi). Rattles are known from other Villanovan tombs of Bologna, but none of them has such an accomplished and informative

Fig. 28a Tintinnabulum from a woman's grave. Side A. Women spinning. From Tomb 5, Tomb of the Gold, Arsenal necropolis, Bologna. Late seventh–early sixth century B.C. Embossed sheet bronze. H. 11.5 cm. Bologna, Museo Civico Archeologico 25676.

Fig. 28b Side B of tintinnabulum, figure 28a. Woman weaving.

decoration. It has been conjectured that the able artist who chased this rattle may have stimulated bronzeworkers in the northern region of Este to develop the so-called situla art of the late seventh and sixth centuries. On these bronze situlae, scenes of the life of the local aristocracy are represented in a lively style. A fine example of this type of vessel, re-used as an ash urn for a woman buried in Tomb 68 of the Certosa necropolis of Bologna, depicts a military parade, the preparation of a sacrifice and banquet, a musical contest, and scenes of hunting and ploughing. It was probably made during the first half of the sixth century.

The discovery of an Etruscan inscription on a vessel of the Late Villanovan Arnoaldi phase proves that Etruscan was spoken in Villanovan Bologna as early as about 600. Recent anthropological studies of human bones have produced evidence that the populations of the Bologna area during the Villanovan and Etruscan periods were remarkably similar, with both Dinaric (from the eastern shore of the Adriatic) and Mediterranean types present.

The analysis of DNA material from ancient Etruscan bones is as yet too problematical to allow any valid conclusions about human continuity in Central Italy when compared with the sample of genetic data collected from a small number of modern inhabitants of the Tuscan village of Murlo near Siena.

Verucchio (Romagna)

Roughly contemporary with the rise of Villanovan Bologna, Verucchio, another important though smaller center, grew up on the lower course of the river Marecchia, which flows into the Adriatic near Rimini. The Marecchia valley and Verucchio seem to have been settled from Southern Etruria via the upper Tiber valley and the Casentino. The contents of some local tombs show cultural and chronological parallels with finds from eighth-century Tarquinia and Veii, and contacts with Chiusi are noticeable until the end of the seventh century. South of Verucchio, in the Piceno area at Fermo, there was another small Villanovan enclave.

The well-watered and wooded land surrounding Verucchio must have been particularly suitable for agriculture and animal pasture; but Verucchio's greatest source of wealth was probably the trade in amber and its manufacture into personal ornaments. From about the middle of the twelfth to the early ninth century B.C., the plentiful amber from the Baltic was traded over long distances to Frattesina (Fratta Polesine, Rovigo). This port near the mouth of the river Adige was a center for locally manufactured blue glass beads and Baltic amber as well as ivory and ostrich eggshell imported from North Africa. From Frattesina these works were redistributed, not only throughout Italy, but also to the Aegean. Verucchio seems to have taken over the role of amber importer and -carver from Frattesina.

Perched on an easily defended height some 17 km from the mouth of the river Marecchia, Verucchio controlled the traffic in the valley and access to the Adriatic. The period of the settlement's greatest prosperity covers the ninth to the second half of the sixth century. The Villanovan civilization of this region of the Romagna has been called Verucchiese; it is subdivided into three phases: I, ca. 900–750; II, ca. 750–670; and III, ca. 670–550.

The huts of the settlement occupied the top of the hill, while the cemeteries lay in various locations on the lower slopes, indicating that originally there may have been a number of different nuclei of habitation. An artisans' quarter with potters' kilns existed as early as the ninth century. Three sheet-bronze shields with embossed geometric decoration, comparable to shields discovered in Southern Etruria, were found with the remains of a fire; it is uncertain whether this context indicates a workshop or whether the shields formed a votive deposit. Among about twelve hut foundations on the Pian del Monte was a central one, in which pottery loom weights and spools have turned up.

The earliest pit- or trench tombs were marked with a stone of a size commensurate with the importance of the dead person. These burials, in biconic ash urns of impasto with geometric comb decoration covered with an inverted bowl, are accompanied by grave goods of pottery, bronze, and iron. Male tombs are richer in weapons than at Bologna, and there are many horse bits and goads, as well as the remains of a number of chariots. From the ninth century onward, ornaments of amber, glass paste, and bone were included, particularly in female tombs.

Two burial pits discovered in 1972 had fortuitously been sealed and thus protected from decay by an air-free mixture of water and clay. They yielded perishable objects not usually preserved in burials elsewhere in Etruria, such as wooden articles, basketwork, and dyed woolen materials. Beside the customary bronze vessels, weapons, and armor—all badly corroded—these opulently furnished tombs of the mid-seventh-century warrior aristocracy of Verucchio contained special ceremonial furniture and utensils made of wood: thrones, footstools, coffers, boxes, fans, vessels, etc., which were carved with intricate geometric ornaments and adorned with bronze studs. Fibulae of complex design and even impasto vessels were often inlaid with amber.

PODERE LIPPI, TOMB 89 Of outstanding interest is a cylindrical wooden throne from the first half of the seventh century that was discovered in Tomb 89 in the Podere Lippi in Verucchio (FIGS. 29a, b). In shape it resembles those depicted on the tintinnabulum from the Tomb of the Gold at Bologna (see FIGS. 28a, b). Placed on top of the large wooden box in which the ash urn of the deceased was found, wrapped in cloth and surrounded by grave goods of bronze and wood, the throne was itself protected by a layer of wood above it. Carved from a single tree trunk, the throne's tambour and flared, curved backrest are decorated all over with meander and volute patterns and with figured scenes, as well as with bronze-studded solar wheels in openwork. On the inside of the backrest are two superposed bands of narrative scenes, divided by bronze studs and arranged as a series of symmetrical images. In all probability they illustrate the various stages of the wool and textile production in which the entire community seems to have been engaged.

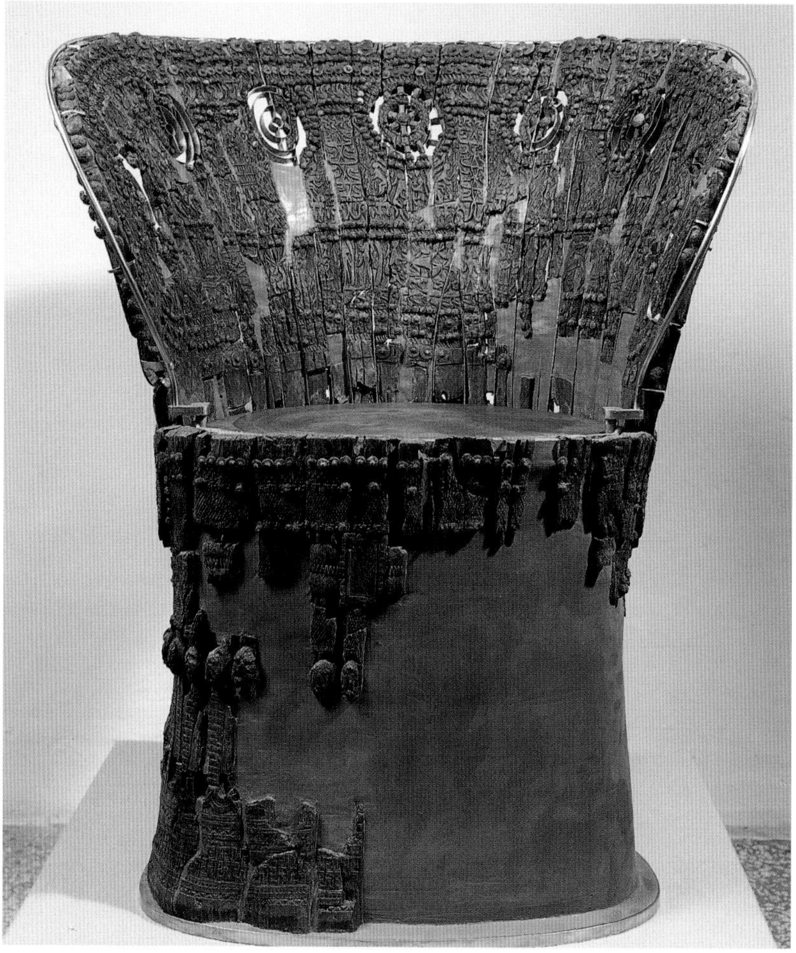

Fig. 29a Cylindrical throne. From Tomb 89, Podere Lippi, Verucchio. First half of seventh century B.C. Wood with bronze adjuncts. Bologna, Museo Civico Archeologico.

Fig. 29b Drawing of the carvings on the back rest of the throne, figure 29a.

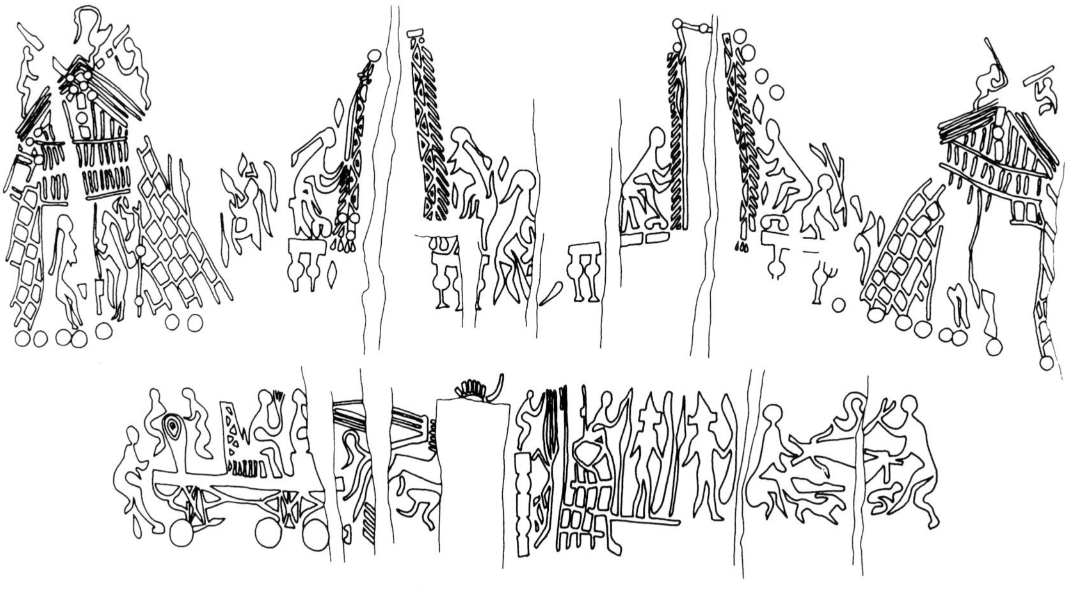

In the center of the lower frieze the intial woolworking tasks are performed by men, who are shown on a platform or bridge, shearing goats and perhaps washing the wool and combing it with long-handled combs. These operations take place in the open, as suggested by a row of ducks below and flanking figures of stags. Warriors with crested helmets, lances, and shields protect the workers. A long, four-wheeled, horse-drawn wagon approaches this scene on either side. In front sits the driver holding the reins. Behind him, holding an object in his hand, is a person whose high social standing is signified by his elaborately carved, high-backed seat. At the rear end of the wagon two men busy themselves with a load standing between them. Innumerable cracks in the wood prevent us from identifying the sex of the enthroned person, and divergent interpretations of the scene have been offered: transport of wool, supervised by an aristocrat; his journey to the beyond; the bridal journey of his wife.

In the frieze above, the subsequent stages of the manufacture of wool cloth are shown as women's work. The women are distinguished from the silhouettes of the male figures by a long plait of hair hanging from the backs of their heads. In two huts that show the appearance of contemporary dwellings—a pitched roof, ridge logs carved with birds and monkeys, walls clad with wood, and a trelissed courtyard—we see two women stirring the contents of a conical vat; this may represent the dyeing of the wool. Between the huts women are spinning with distaffs and spindles, while other women weave pieces of richly patterned material on tall carved looms. They are seated on chairs placed on tables with turned legs, and they have footstools with volute-shaped feet that recall the actual footstool found in the tomb with the throne.

Despite its imperfect state of preservation, the throne is an invaluable cultural document. Its characteristic shape was hitherto known to us only from fragmentary examples made of sheet bronze, terra-cotta, or stone from tombs of the seventh and sixth centuries in Northern Etruria (Chiusi) and in the south (Cerveteri, Ceri, Palestrina). The throne depicts in detail the activities of a community in which labor was sex segregated: men, guarded by warriors, attended to the work outside the village—the shearing, cleaning, and combing of the wool—while women were engaged in the house-centered tasks of dyeing, spinning, and weaving, which allowed them to supervise and care for babies and children too young to leave the house and its immediate neighborhood.

The warrior-prince who once sat on this splendid piece of furniture probably owed some of his wealth to the activities represented on it. As part of his treasured possessions the throne and footstool followed him into his grave, where they assumed the symbolic function of expressing their owner's high social position and heroization. Inside the wooden *cassone*, which contained the ash urn, were placed other signs of his dignity: scepter, axe, chariot, horse bits, arms, shield, and helmets, as well as a wooden fan handle carved in openwork and a large golden dragon-type fibula decorated with triangles in granulation. His wool tunic and the silver clasp of his belt are preserved as well.

A parade shield of hammered sheet bronze and a helmet with a tall bronze crest are of the typical form found in Central Italy, but a second helmet of conical form with the remains of a crest of hog's bristles belongs to a type characteristic for the areas of Novilara (near Pesaro), Istria, and Slovenia. It seems that the ceremonial armor here was modeled on that from Tyrrhenian Italy, while the arms for actual use find their nearest parallels in the region of the Upper Adriatic and show cultural exchange with the population of neighboring Piceno. The military character of the local rulers probably allowed them to control the traffic from the coast to the Tiber valley and may have included piracy on the Adriatic.

PODERE LIPPI, TOMB 85 Of the same date as Tomb 89 (mid-seventh century) is another warrior tomb, Tomb 85. It was formed by cutting a deep square trench into the soil and covering it with wooden boards supported by a horizontal beam that rested in the forks of upright tree trunks. Here, too, a wealth of wooden furniture was preserved. On three elegant, round, wooden tables, each with three curved legs ending below in an open-worked, harp-shaped foot, were placed impasto vessels stamped with a variety of dense geometric patterns: cups with a high foot, plates, and situla-shaped containers with lids. Hazelnuts and remains of fish and hare in cups and covered bowls represented the foodstuffs of the funerary banquet. One cup contained grape pips, showing that some vines must have been cultivated at Verucchio; but the comparative rarity of banqueting vessels in these northern regions suggests that wine production was not widespread.

A throne of the same form as that from Tomb 89 is decorated simply with two great carved volutes where the curved backrest meets the seat. The remnants of this aristocrat's woolen clothes were wrapped around his ash urn and found associated with two dragon-type fibulae and one of serpentine form threaded with amber, as well as with a wooden container for a curved knife and bronze horse bits. The warrior's domed helmet is so far unique in Italy in being made of wickerwork ornamented with large and small bronze discs and surrounded with closely set bronze studs. This type of helmet is, however, common in the area of the Hallstatt Culture, particularly in Slovenia. The grave goods in this tomb emphasize the convivial and priestly (the sacrifical knife) activities of the chief rather than his high military rank.

Amber jewelry, presumably manufactured at Verucchio itself, reached its greatest perfection during the seventh century. It is particularly common in the cemeteries of the Podere Lippi and Moroni-Semprini. Such is the quantity of amber ornaments found in female burials there (and its relative rarity in male ones) that it has rightly been assumed that the presence of amber qualifies a tomb as female, just as weapons characterize a tomb as male. The combination, typical for this jewelry, of intricately carved bone platelets with inlays of different shades

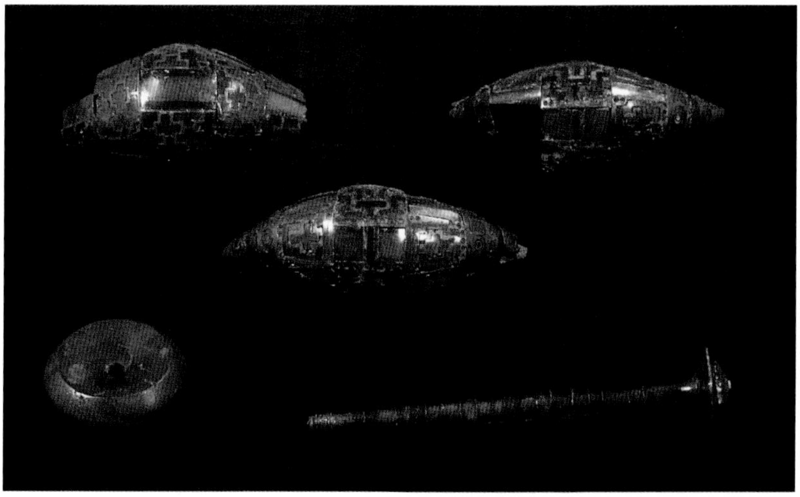

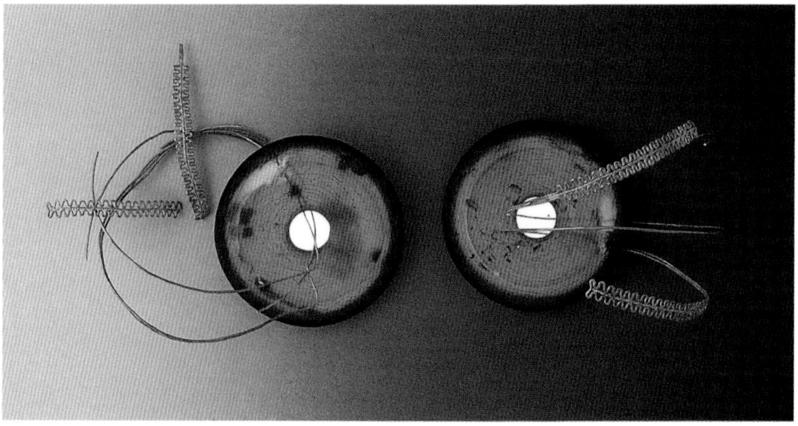

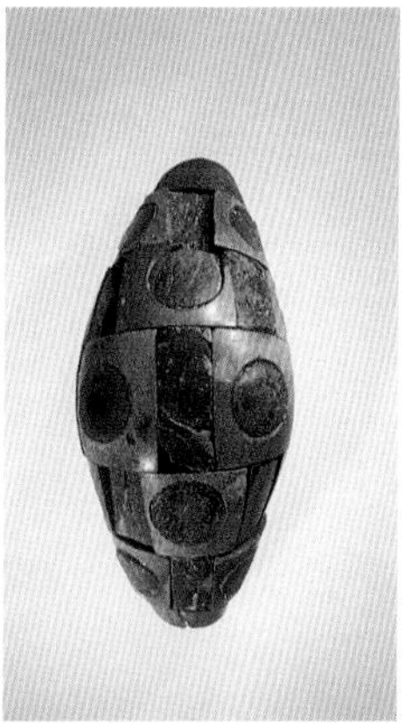

UPPER LEFT

Fig. 30 Spindle and leech-fibulae. From Tomb 47, Podere Lippi, Verucchio. First half of seventh century B.C. Spindle: Amber and bronze, L. 18 cm, Verucchio, Museo Civico Archeologico 11675.

LOWER LEFT

Fig. 31 Earrings. From Tomb 23, Podere Lippi, Verucchio. First half of seventh century B.C. Amber and gold. Diam. of amber disk 6 cm. Verucchio, Museo Civico Archeologico 8410-850.

ABOVE

Fig. 32 Leech-fibula. From Tomb 27, Podere Lippi, Verucchio. First half of seventh century B.C. Bronze, bone, and amber. L. 6.5 cm. Verucchio, Museo Civico Archeologico 11385.

of amber occurs above all in *sanguisuga*-fibulae and belt clasps, while amber discs with a central hole were used for earrings and on bronze fibulae. Variously shaped amber beads and spacers were threaded as necklaces or sewn as ornaments on the hems of dresses. An especially prestigious amber spindle consists of individually carved pieces threaded on a bronze shaft (FIG. 30). Occasionally, as an alternative to amber, striped, colored glass-paste beads occur as pendants or on fibulae. Carved amber roundels as well as carved bone and ivory studs were used as inlays on impasto tableware, in particular on two-handled cups.

Gold is comparatively rare in the tombs of Verucchio, but it was used in thin sheets for cut-out, stamped dress ornaments and for a few dragon- and serpentine-fibulae. One pair of large earrings consists of an amber disc threaded with gold wire, part of which is fashioned into open-worked bands of two serpentine wires soldered to a central twisted wire (FIG. 31).

A number of the inlaid patterns of the amber and bone fibulae (FIG. 32) recall the overall geometric decoration stamped on pottery vessels or carved on wooden furniture; they are perhaps all originally textile patterns. These unusual works of skilled artisans suggest that there were important workshops at Verucchio, where such prestigious objects were manufactured for the local aristocracy and their ceremonial gift exchanges. Highly competent weaving of complex designs was carried out by the women of Verucchio as we see in the weaving scene carved on the throne from Tomb 89.

This stage of the Verucchiese (the seventh century) was certainly influenced by the orientalizing culture of Southern Etruria, but the people of Verucchio retained their traditional local burial ritual and displayed an astonishing virtuosity in the carving of a variety of materials. However, from the sixth century onward, Verucchio declined and became a provincial backwater, while Rimini and Covignano assumed greater importance.

THE STATUS OF WOMEN DURING THE VILLANOVAN PERIOD

We have been looking at the very last stage of the Villanovan civilization in the Northern Etruscan regions, when the traditional way of life was being transformed by external influences. Before turning back to the Southern coastal parts of Etruria to examine the momentous developments that had taken place there, we may try to sum up what has emerged from our survey of the Villanovan phase about the status of women.

It appears that women were regarded as the equals of men during their lives, each sex performing the tasks that nature and tradition had allotted to it. In families of high social position, marriageable women and their rich jewelry and other possessions may have been an important means of ensuring favorable relations and durable links with other local clans or foreign notables.

After death women were given the same type of burial as men, accompanied by grave goods characteristic for their sex. These were, on the whole, less spectacular than those of warriors, though with increasing social stratification, the contents of the tombs of aristocratic women, too, were often remarkably opulent. The fact that biconic ash urns as well as the comparatively rare hut urns were used for both men and women proves that the sexes were essentially thought of as being of equal status. A similar conclusion may be drawn from the cases where horse trappings or carriages were found in richly furnished female tombs.

The representations of communal dances on painted pottery found in tombs and of dancing male figurines of cast bronze on an ossuary from Bisenzio suggest the performance of dance rituals connected with fertility, death, and burial. The monstrous animal figure in the center of the lid of the Bisenzio urn may represent a demon of death. The presence of an elaborate bronze incense burner and offering vessel in a rich woman's burial at Bisenzio shows that some women played a part in certain cults.

Spinning and weaving are depicted on the bronze rattle from Bologna as work carried out by well-to-do women; the amber spindle from Verucchio and the bronze shuttle from Olmo Bello, Tomb 2, indicate the same high social status of these crafts. It is therefore significant that the poorest women's graves in the cemeteries of Bologna never contain woolworking tools, but only fibulae, which had an essential function in female clothing. Amber appears to have had some special, probably amuletic, appeal, apart from its natural beauty.

EVIDENCE OF RELIGIOUS BELIEFS

Solid evidence that a cult focused on the natural feature of a cavity in the rock existed as early as the Late Bronze Age in the center of the community that was to become Tarquinia points to the long-lived worship here of a sacred spot. Inscriptions prove that a great female divinity, whose name we know to have been Uni, was connected with the site in the historical period. This is an early indication of the outstanding role played in Etruscan religion by goddesses. It is likely that a nature goddess, a Mistress of the Animals, is represented by the nude female figure flanked by ducks and quadrupeds that decorates the open-worked handle of a bronze cup found in the female burial at Bisenzio and on similar adjuncts.

Even earlier, during the Middle Bronze Age, evidence for cult practices connected with a spring was discovered in the rural territory of the future city of Vulci at Banditella. The veneration of the site continued until the Archaic period and testifies to the persistence of human belief in the sanctity of water.

Exceptional monuments indicative of religious cult were discovered in Via Fondazza in Bologna in 1985. Two large cylindrical stone cippi, richly molded and carved in an accomplished style with orientalizing vegetation motifs, such as rosettes and double spirals ending in palmettes and lotus buds, as well as a row of walking sphinxes, were found ritually buried in a trench in an area outside the settlement of Villanovan Bologna. Stylistically related to some of the local orientalizing grave stelae, these monuments are perhaps products of a workshop for which Near Eastern craftsmen could have provided the models. The weight, size, and quality of the monuments indicate that about 600 B.C. the local population was well on the way to urbanization since they were able to commission and organize the moving and erection of such monumental objects. No architectural remains were discovered in the vicinity, so the cult with which these objects were connected probably took place in the open air, perhaps within a sacred enclosure or in a flimsy wooden shelter. We do not know what form the cult took. Some votive terra-cottas, shaped like miniature parts of the human body, were found in more recent levels of this excavation, suggesting that a healing cult was practiced here in the fourth century.

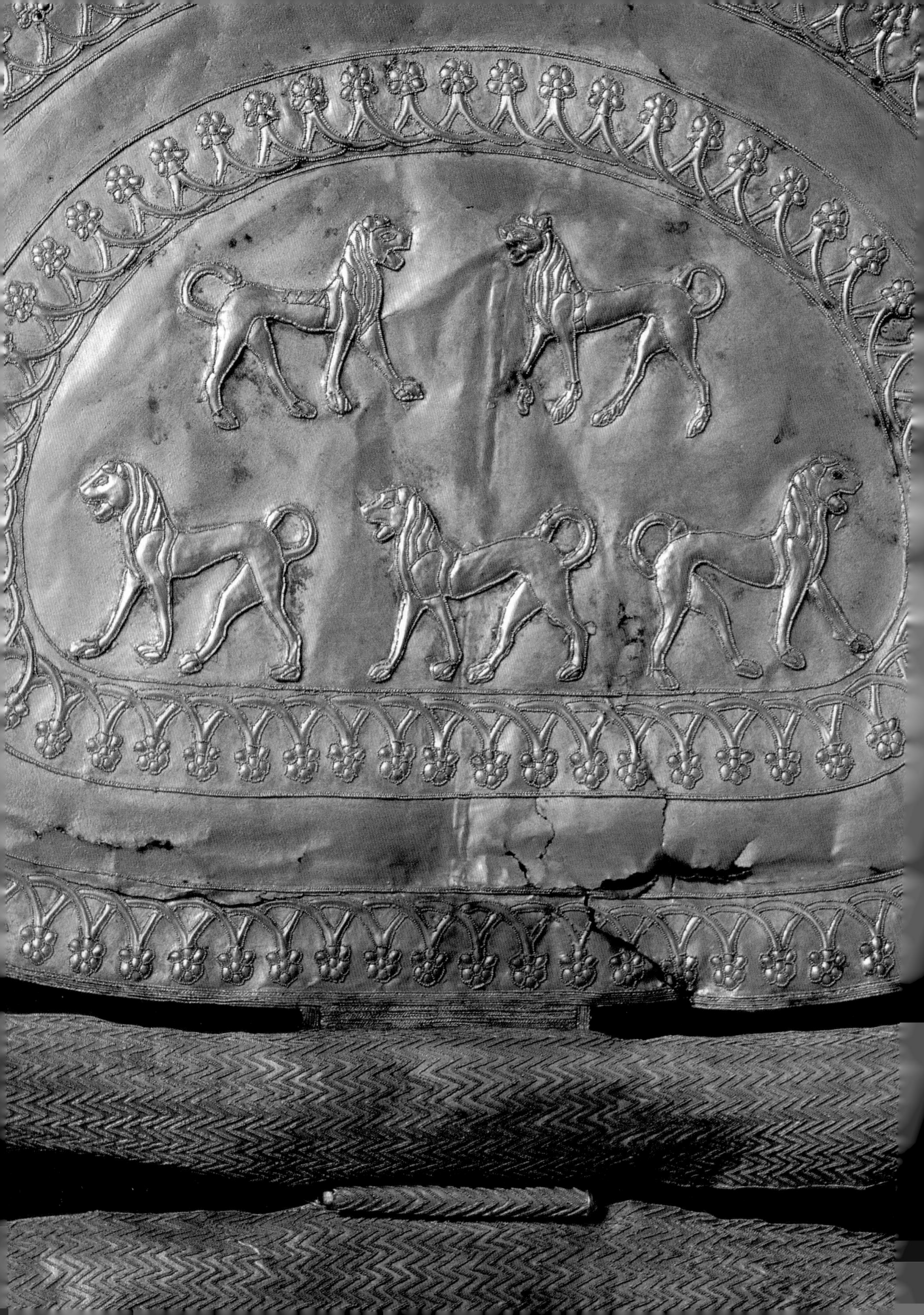

II

The Orientalizing Period and the Emergence of the Etruscan Cities

720–575 B.C.

BRONZE AGE ANTECEDENTS

Traders, sailors, and craftsmen from the Aegean and the Levant had been in cultural and commercial contact with Italy, Sicily, and Sardinia during the Late Bronze Age. The collapse of the Mycenaean civilization in the twelfth century—with the concomitant destruction of existing settlements and loss of architectural and handicraft traditions and ability to write down records in the syllabic Linear B script—had disrupted these former links, but they were never entirely broken. After the impoverished eleventh and tenth centuries, the gradual economic and cultural recovery of mainland Greece brought with it a renewal of the earlier maritime network that was to prove of fundamental importance for Italy and Etruscan civilization in the succeeding centuries.

Detail of a disk fibula with decoration in the form of lions, griffins, and floral and geometric patterns, from figure 57.

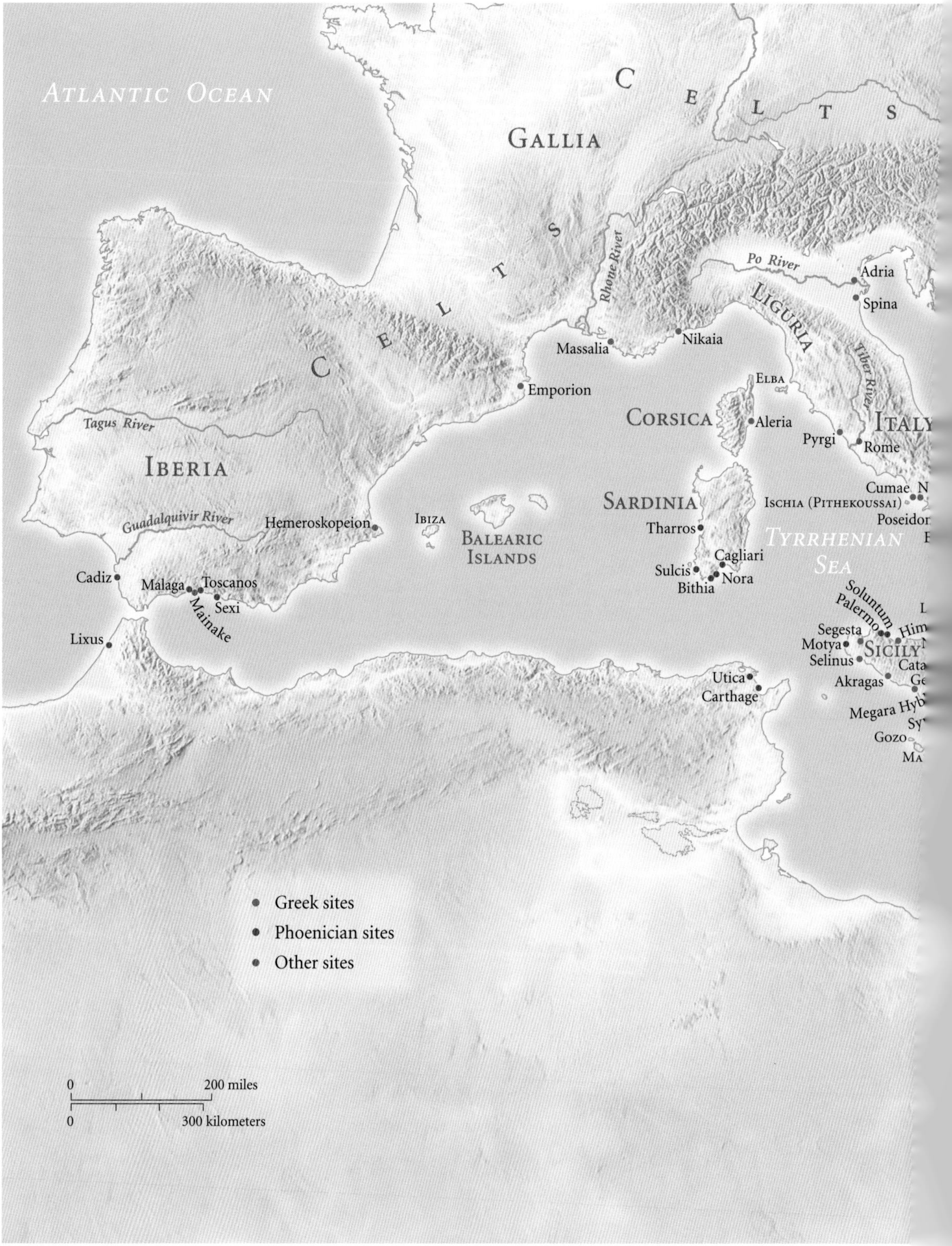
Atlantic Ocean
Celts
Gallia
Celts
Rhone River
Po River
Adria
Spina
Liguria
Tiber River
Nikaia
Massalia
Emporion
Elba
Corsica
Aleria
Pyrgi
Rome
Tagus River
Iberia
Sardinia
Cumae
Ischia (Pithekoussai)
Poseido
Guadalquivir River
Hemeroskopeion
Ibiza
Balearic Islands
Tharros
Tyrrhenian Sea
Cagliari
Sulcis
Nora
Bithia
Cadiz
Malaga
Toscanos
Sexi
Mainake
Lixus
Soluntum
Palermo
Segesta
Motya
Selinus
Sicily
Akragas
Utica
Carthage
Megara Hyb
Gozo
Greek sites
Phoenician sites
Other sites
0
200 miles
0
300 kilometers

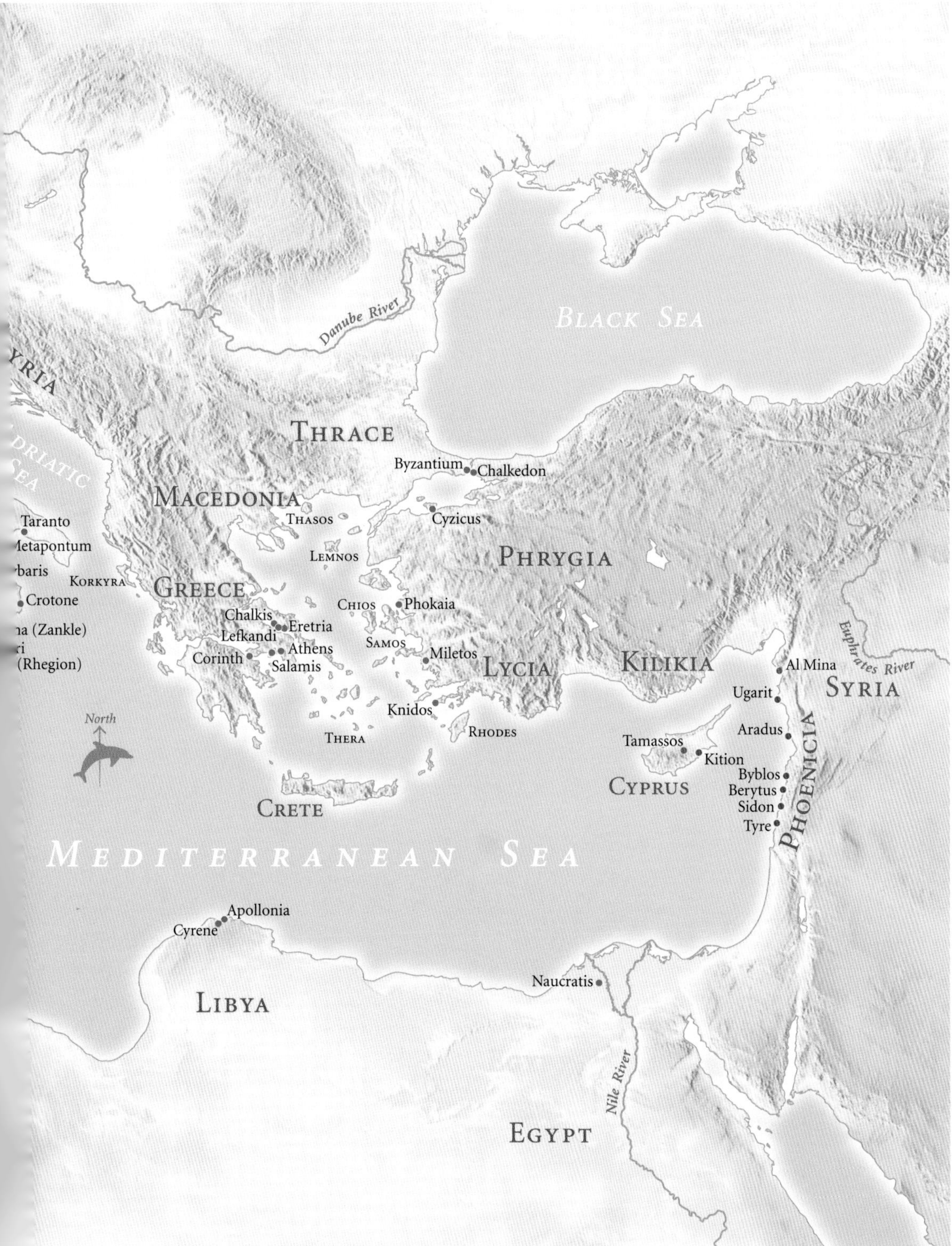
Black Sea
Danube River
Thrace
Macedonia
Greece
Byzantium
Chalkedon
Cyzicus
Phrygia
Thasos
Lemnos
Korkyra
Taranto
Metapontum
baris
Crotone
na (Zankle)
ri
(Rhegion)
Adriatic Sea
Chalkis
Eretria
Lefkandi
Athens
Corinth
Salamis
Chios
Phokaia
Samos
Miletos
Lycia
Kilikia
Knidos
Rhodes
Thera
North
Crete
Al Mina
Euphrates River
Syria
Ugarit
Aradus
Tamassos
Kition
Cyprus
Byblos
Berytus
Sidon
Tyre
Phoenicia
Mediterranean Sea
Apollonia
Cyrene
Naucratis
Libya
Nile River
Egypt

The Euboean Contribution

Among the most adventurous Greek sailors of the Iron Age were the inhabitants of the island of Euboea off the east coast of Attica and Boeotia (MAP pp. 48–49). Excavations at Lefkandi on the island's west coast and elsewhere have produced evidence that Euboean ships must have traveled the Aegean, from the Chalkidike in the north to Cyprus and the Levant in the south.

Sherds of Euboean pottery decorated with concentric circles and dated to the late tenth century have been excavated at Tyre, while the ninth- and eighth-century aristocratic tombs at Lefkandi abound in imported exotic grave goods, such as egyptianizing faience beads, seals, and bowls; Egyptian bronze vessels; North Syrian bronze bowls; an amphora of Cypriote manufacture; and Syrian gold jewelry. It is still a matter of some debate who the carriers of these luxury goods were. The Phoenicians were certainly involved in this maritime trade, and by the late ninth century the influence of Oriental jewelers and craftsmen is seen on Euboea, at Athens, on Crete, and in the Dodecanese. The Cypriote port of Kition was settled by Phoenicians in the middle of the ninth century, giving them access to the rich copper mines of Tamassos. A characteristic type of Euboean drinking cup, the skyphos, decorated with a geometric design of hanging semicircles, has turned up at Amathous on Cyprus. In the later part of the ninth century Euboean trading contacts had been established at various points in the Levant, the most important one at Al Mina on the mouth of the Orontes, where Euboeans exchanged goods. During the second quarter of the eighth century the Greek imports at Al Mina seem to have increased notably, as the quantity of Euboean pottery found there and in the hinterland suggests. Thus stimulated by direct as well as indirect contact with the Levant, Greece began to absorb a whole new world of Oriental imagery and techniques.

Euboean Settlements in the Gulf of Naples

Euboean Greeks settled on Ischia (Gr. Pithekoussai) in the middle of the eighth century. Intensive excavation of the site and its cemeteries has demonstrated that they engaged in trade, metalworking, and pottery production; they also farmed and practiced viticulture. The discovery of a piece of iron ore (hematite) from Elba in a dump on the acropolis of Pithekoussai implies that the island was involved in metal trade with Etruria.

TRADE CONNECTIONS BETWEEN THE EASTERN AND WESTERN MEDITERRANEAN

PREVIOUS PAGES
Greek and Phoenician expansion in the Mediterranean, eighth to fifth century B.C.

Both Greeks and Phoenicians were attracted to the Tyrrhenian coast by abundant deposits of metal ores, especially copper and iron, in Etruria and on Elba and Sardinia. Sporadic finds of imported Euboean and Phoenician pottery show foreign contact at the end of the ninth and the early eighth centuries on Sardinia (in the nuraghic village of Sant'Imbenia near Alghero), on Sicily at Villasmundo, and in Italy at Pontecagnano and Veii.

Besides the Greeks, Levantine merchants and craftsmen whose residence and burial on Ischia are attested by inscriptions on pottery and numerous scarab-shaped sealstones ("Lyre Player" type) played their part in these exchanges. Included in this trading circuit was Sardinia, which had profited from close contacts with Cyprus during the Late Bronze Age. Occasional Near Eastern visits to the island had taken place from the late fourteenth century onward, but direct imports and exchanges were interrupted by the general upheaval that affected the eastern Mediterranean around 1200 B.C. The search for new sources of metal, particularly tin, which is essential for the manufacture of bronze, had brought the ancient prospectors to the west, where they must have obtained knowledge of tin mines in Cornwall. Silver was another metal in demand; rich deposits were found in the lower Guadalquivir region of Spain, in Sardinia, and, to a lesser extent, in Northern Etruria, in the mountainous area between the rivers Ombrone and Cecina.

By the second quarter of the eighth century there is evidence of a Phoenician presence at Cadiz; as of the end of the eighth century the earlier transitory commercial contacts with the West were replaced by real Phoenician colonization there from the cities of the Lebanese coast and Cyprus. A contributing reason for this movement was the westward pressure on that area by the Assyrians under the kings Tiglathpileser III (745–727) and Sargon II (722–705). Tyre founded the city of Carthage; other settlements established on the North African coast were Utica and Lixus. In Spain, Almuñecar (ancient Sexi), Toscanos, and Malaga were founded after Cadiz. On the west and north coasts of Sicily, the Phoenicians founded Motya, Palermo, and Solunto, while on Sardinia the colonies of Nora, Bitia, Sulcis, and Tharros on the south and west coasts of the island were among the earliest. Nora has yielded an inscribed stela, dated by most scholars to the eighth century. In the Phoenician tophet of Sulcis on a small island off the Sardinian coast a child was buried in a Greek pot manufactured at Pithekoussai at the end of the eighth century. Recently, Phoenician sherds of the early eighth century have even been discovered in Portugal at Lisbon and at Santarém, 50 km up the river Tagus.

Early Conflicts at Sea

It is likely that the far-flung, seaborne enterprises of foreign prospectors, merchants, and settlers did not always have a peaceful character. It is highly significant that neither the Greeks nor the Phoenicians were able to found colonies on Italian soil north of the Bay of Naples, and it suggests that this region must have been jealously guarded by its inhabitants. We know that the Etruscans themselves had long been engaged in maritime traffic, particularly with Sardinia, and we may assume that hostile encounters between their ships and those of the newcomers occurred frequently.

The seas flanking the area of Italy settled by Etruscans received Etruscan names: the Tyrrhenian Sea to the west (the Greek name for the Etruscans was *Tyrrhenoi* or *Tyrsenoi*) and the Adriatic to the east (after the town of Adria, which ancient writers held to be Etruscan). According to Dionysios of Halikarnassos (*Rom. Arch.* 1.30.3–4), the Etruscans called themselves *Rasenna* "after one of their leaders." The Romans called them *Etrusci* or *Tusci*.

The emergence of what was to be known as a thalassocracy, that is, a maritime supremacy of Etruscan ships (Dion. Hal. 1.11; Diod. Sic. 5.40), is recognizable during the seventh century, a period when Etruscan pottery turned up in Sicily, and ships and battles at sea were first represented on Etruscan vases and on Greek vases made in Etruria. But the fourth-century Greek historian Ephoros (in Strabo 6.2.2) relates in connection with the foundation date of the city of Naxos (734), the oldest Greek colony in Sicily, that previously the Greeks had avoided these waters for fear of meeting with Tyrrhenian pirates. This comparatively late source thus suggests that Etruscan ships sailed in the region of the Straits of Messina as early as the eighth century, and the finds of Italic fibulae of late eighth-century date in eastern Sicily seem to confirm such early contacts.

GREEK INFLUENCE ON ETRURIA

The influence on the expanding and amalgamating preurban Etruscan (and Latial) communities of the Greek settlements planted on their southern flank contributed to profound social and economic changes in central Italy. This dynamic development can be traced in the process of increasing urbanization, but it is reflected above all in the abundance of precious imported objects accumulated in the splendid aristocratic tombs of Etruria and Lazio. In the seventh century, Etruscan society was dominated by chief-priests (Lat. *lucumones*), whose symbols of power were, in addition to those already established—double-axe, throne, scepter, and chariot—the often gigantic, architecturally conceived burial mounds built by important families. Their luxurious lifestyle, inspired by Oriental and East Greek models, eventually became that of a large part of a prosperous population, whose economic power was based on mineral and agricultural resources, barter, trade, and piracy.

Fine Painted Pottery for Banqueting

From the last decades of the eighth century individual Greek potters from the new colonies or from their Euboean mother cities and the Cycladic islands seem to have settled in Campania and Southern Etruria and introduced fresh ideas and new technologies that transformed local traditions and crafts. Among the most

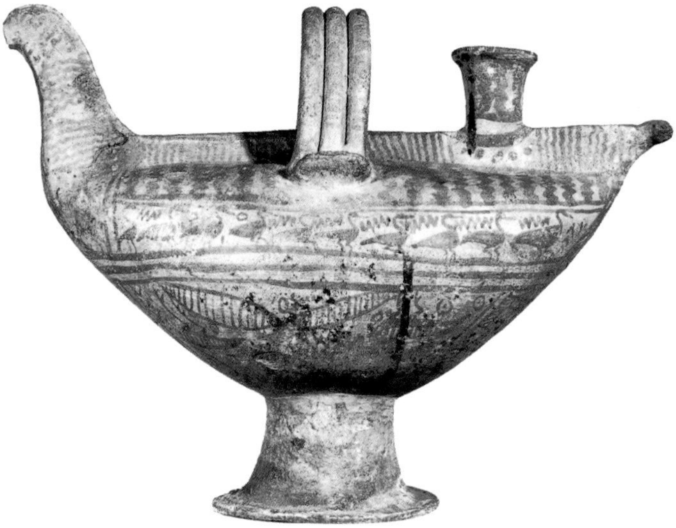

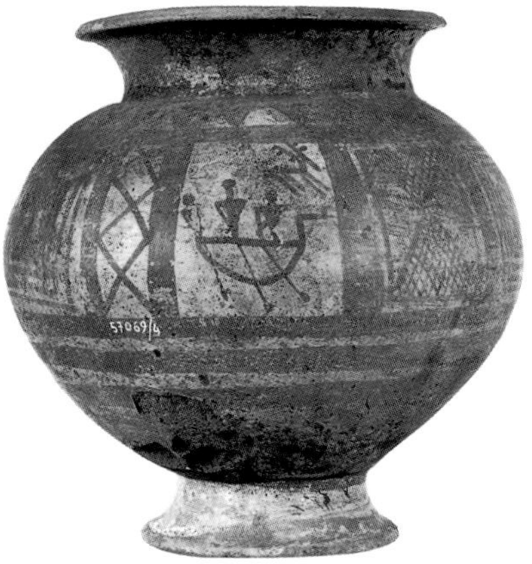

important innovations Greek potters taught their Etruscan apprentices was the use of purified clay and of the fast potter's wheel for the production of fine vases painted with motifs in Late Geometric style and fired at high temperatures in closed kilns (FIGS. 33, 34). These new skills seem to have been established first in Southern Etruria (Veii, Tarquinia, Vulci, Bisenzio).

Figures of birds, quadrupeds, fish, and occasional human beings began to invade the painted geometric repertoire of pots made by Greek craftsmen in Etruria and on Etruscan imitations of this pottery from the last quarter of the eighth century. These were often vases of large format, destined for use during banquets: stands and kraters for wine and water, as well as jugs and cups.

Ceremonial wine drinking while reclining goes back to Assyrian royal usage, as does the form of some of the vessels connected with it. The custom is illustrated, for example, on a stone relief from the palace of Assurpanipal (668–627 B.C.) at Nineveh (now in the British Museum) and on silver-gilt Cypro-Phoenician bowls of the early seventh century. This Oriental model of banqueting, taken over by the Greeks, gradually established itself among the aristocracy of Lazio and Etruria, too, along with the use of containers and stands of the appropriate shape. Some of these imitated in pottery the spectacularly decorated cone-shaped supports of embossed bronze and the big bronze cauldrons with cast attachments surmounting them that were imported from North Syria and found in princely tombs of Vetulonia (Circle of the Cauldrons, *Circolo dei Lebeti*) and Palestrina (Bernardini Tomb, *Tomba Bernardini*). Other vessels were modeled on purely Greek prototypes.

Besides these newly adopted banqueting vessels, pots with a long local tradition, such as biconic vases, were potted and decorated in the new techniques, and soon most of the wares for use at the aristocratic table and for special ceremonies were wheelmade. Coarse impasto kitchenware may still have been made in indi-

Fig. 33 Etrusco-geometric bird-shaped askos. From Tomb x, Olmo Bello necropolis, Bisenzio. Last quarter of eighth century B.C. Painted impasto. H. 28 cm. Rome, Museo Etrusco di Villa Giulia 57033/6.

Fig. 34 Etrusco-geometric vase. From Tomb 24, Olmo Bello necropolis, Bisenzio. Second half of eighth century B.C. Painted impasto. H. 22.5 cm. Rome, Museo Etrusco di Villa Giulia 57069/4.

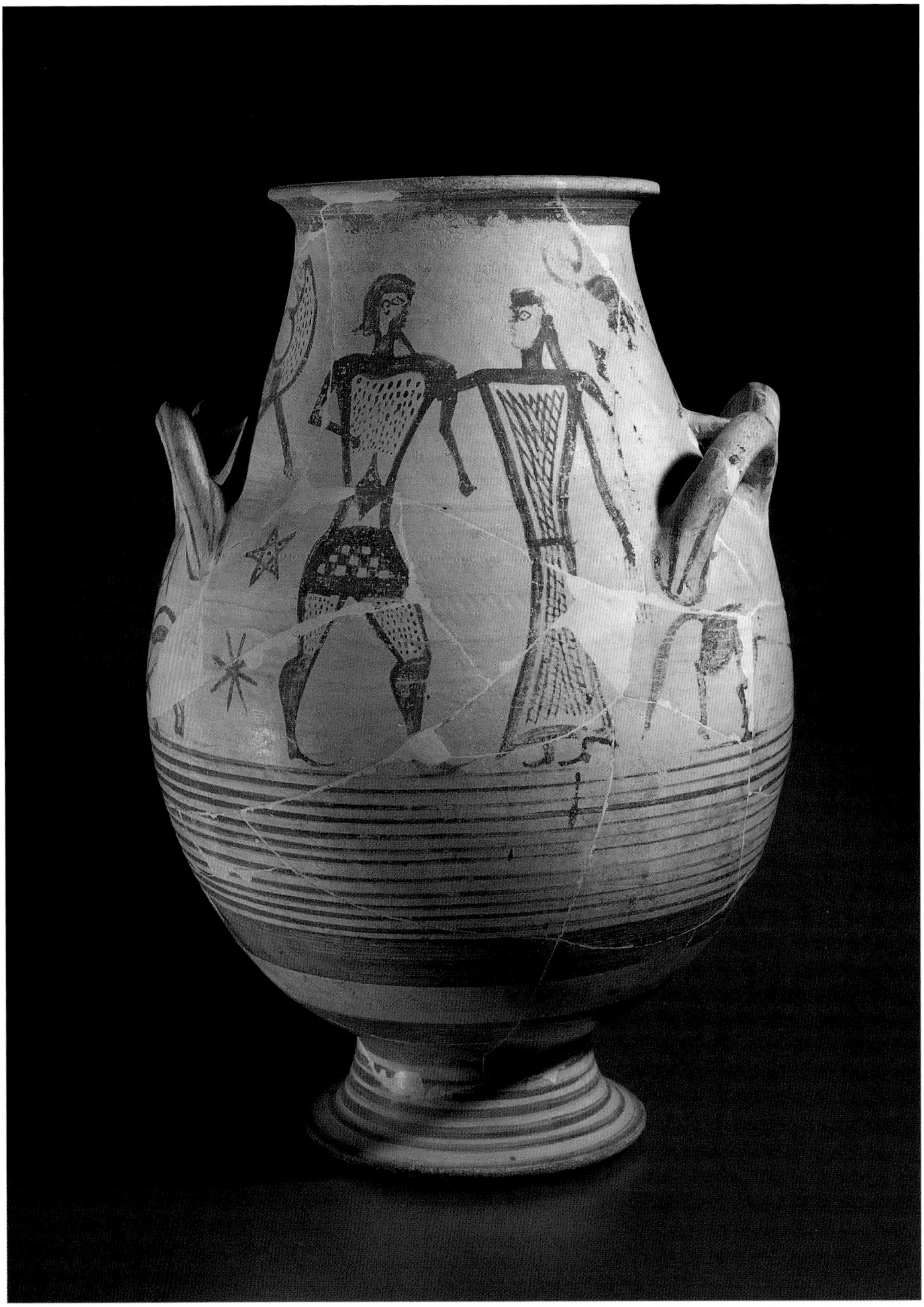

vidual households. Vessels in the Greek Geometric tradition are conventionally known as Etrusco-Geometric, while those routinely produced well into the seventh century are called Subgeometric. However, from the end of the eighth century the large quantity of Greek pottery imports reaching Southern Etruria came increasingly from Corinth, and local imitations of such wares were produced from the third quarter of the seventh century, principally in Veii, Cerveteri, and Vulci.

EARLY ORIENTALIZING VASE-PAINTING AT CERVETERI

By the last quarter of the eighth century Euboean influence in Etruria had begun to be replaced by that from Corinth. Sailors, merchants, and craftsmen from other Greek cities and islands now competed on the long-established trade routes between east and west, a traffic that was greatly increased by the founding of new Greek colonies in South Italy and Sicily. Commercial and other interests as well as rapidly growing numbers of inhabitants caused many land-hungry city-states of the Greek motherland to send their surplus population to new homes overseas, and fresh waves of settlers brought different ideas and pictorial styles to the Italian mainland.

One of the most interesting examples of the Early Orientalizing ceramic production of the second quarter of the seventh century B.C. at Cerveteri is a biconic krater with double-loop handles, decorated by an innovative craftsman called the Painter of the Heptachord (FIG. 35). This name is derived from the seven-stringed kithara played by a musician who accompanies the somersaults of a troupe of sword-bearing acrobats, painted by this master on another vase (an amphora in Würzburg). The krater preserves only vestiges of the traditional angular biconic form, which has been softened into a pear shape. The upper part shows on one side a narrative scene with large-scale figures of a couple painted in outline. The man, who must be a warrior, wears greaves, a checkered kilt, and a lozenge-shaped belt. He strides aggressively to the right with bent arms and clenched fists. The woman stands timidly facing him, reaching out with her right hand to touch his chin in a gesture that we know from Greek art and literature to represent a plea for mercy (Hom. *Il.* 1.500–502). Her belted dress with a rhomboid pattern swings out just above her ankles, and her hair hangs in a single long plait over her back, a fashion typical for Etruscan women during the Orientalizing period. However Etruscan their appearance, the couple probably represents a scene from the *Iliad*. The woman may be Helen appealing to her husband, Menelaos, who threatens her life after recovering her in the Sack of Troy. The other side of the vase is decorated with sinuous lions, grazing horses, stars, leaf shapes, and a pentagram. The tentative and awkward design of the human figures does not detract from the painting's clear narrative intent, and both the monumentality of the representation and the

Fig. 35 Vessel with decoration by the Painter of the Heptachord. From Tomb 297, Monte Abetone necropolis, Cerveteri. Second quarter of seventh century B.C. Painted pottery. H. 45 cm. Cerveteri, Museo Archeologico.

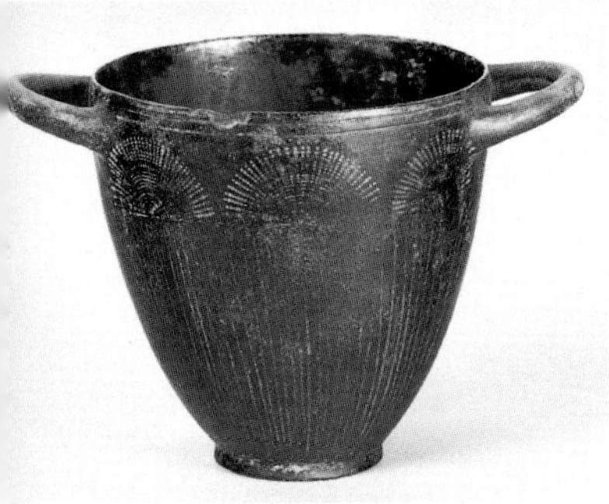

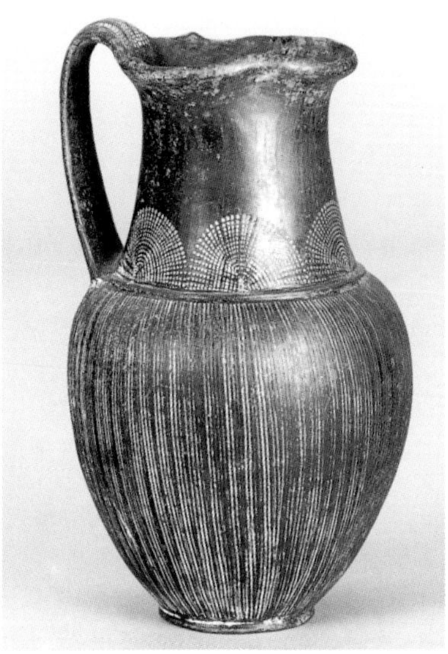

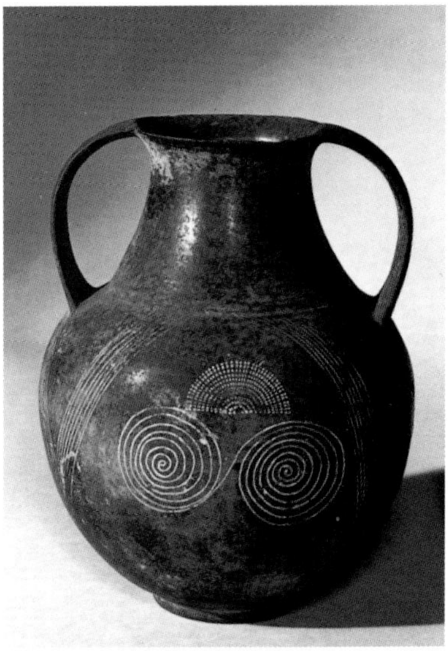

ABOVE LEFT
Fig. 36 Cup with incised lines and dotted fans. About 675–625 B.C. Bucchero. London, The British Museum GR 1839.2-14.89.

ABOVE CENTER
Fig. 37 Jug with incised vertical lines and dotted fans. About 675–625 B.C. Bucchero. London, The British Museum GR 1839.2-14.105.

ABOVE RIGHT
Fig. 38 Amphora with incised spirals. About 675–625 B.C. Bucchero. London, The British Museum GR 1839.2-14.96.

pictorial details in the treatment of the animals are owed to fresh impulses from Athens and from the Cycladic islands.

LOCAL POTTERY: BUCCHERO, IMPASTO, AND SUBGEOMETRIC

Beside the traditional impasto ware (increasingly refined during the eighth century), important new types of pottery for domestic and funeral use were developed locally by Etruscan artisans. The most successful—subsequently widely exported all over the Mediterranean—is called bucchero. This ware, characterized by a shiny blackish surface and fired throughout to a dark gray, was produced from the second quarter of the seventh to the fourth century (FIGS. 36–38). The technique of firing these at first exquisitely thin-walled, wheel-thrown pots involved reducing the supply of oxygen in the kiln, thus turning the red ferric oxide in the clay into black ferrous oxide. Production appears to have started in the first half of the seventh century at Cerveteri and spread quickly to other Etruscan cities (Veii, Tarquinia, Vulci, Vetulonia, and eventually Orvieto and Chiusi). Shapes and surface effects of bucchero vessels usually imitate prestigious metal prototypes, and isolated pieces show remains of an original covering with gold foil or tin. Decoration on bucchero vases could be incised and filled with red ocher, which has, however, rarely survived; or some vases could be painted. Stamped or molded figure decoration was applied to the carefully smoothed surface before firing (FIG. 39). Such designs were executed mechanically by repeatedly impressing a figured stamp or using a carved roller on the unfired pot, and modeled adjuncts could be added. Geometric and animal decoration of local tradition was increasingly enriched with figures inspired by Oriental or Greek models.

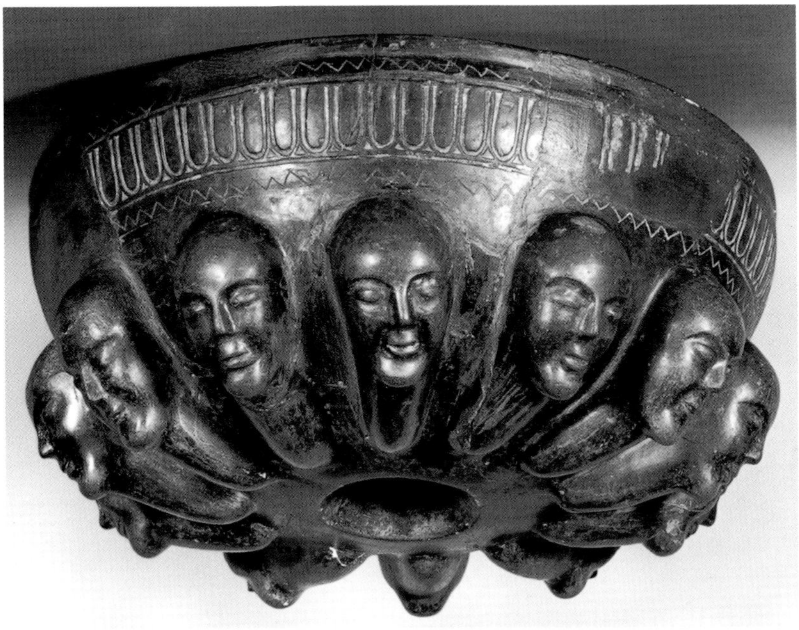

LEFT

Fig. 39 Bowl with relief decoration of twelve human heads. From the Tomb of the Painted Lions, Cerveteri. Third quarter of seventh century B.C. Bucchero. Diam. 17.8 cm. Rome, Museo Etrusco di Villa Giulia.

BELOW LEFT

Fig. 40 Pair of plates decorated with Subgeometric bird motifs (Heron Class). 680–670 B.C. White slip on red impasto. Diam. 27.6–28.4 cm. Malibu, J. Paul Getty Museum 96.AE.138.1–.2.

BELOW RIGHT

Fig. 41 Lidded pithos painted with geometric motifs. Third quarter of seventh century B.C. White slip on red impasto. H. 70 cm. Malibu, J. Paul Getty Museum 96.AE.136.

From the late eighth through the seventh century potters at Cerveteri also produced a smooth red-surfaced ware, probably based on Phoenician prototypes. Impasto pottery painted with a Subgeometric "heron" motif in red on a white slip applied to the pottery (FIG. 40) was made from the end of the eighth to the late seventh century, not only at Cerveteri, but also at Veii, while large storage vessels (Gr. *pithoi*) with both geometric and figure and floral decoration in white on red impasto appear from about 650 (FIG. 41). Impasto storage vessels (*dolii*) and braziers with stamped decoration were manufactured at Cerveteri from the late seventh to the fifth century.

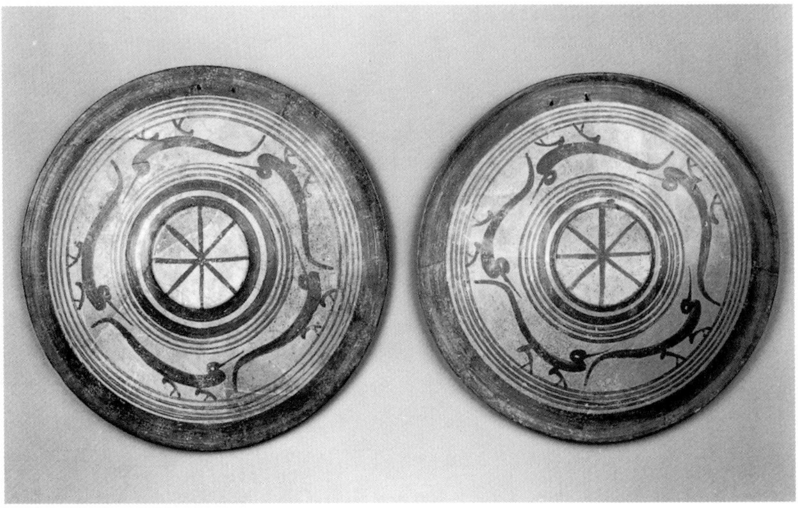

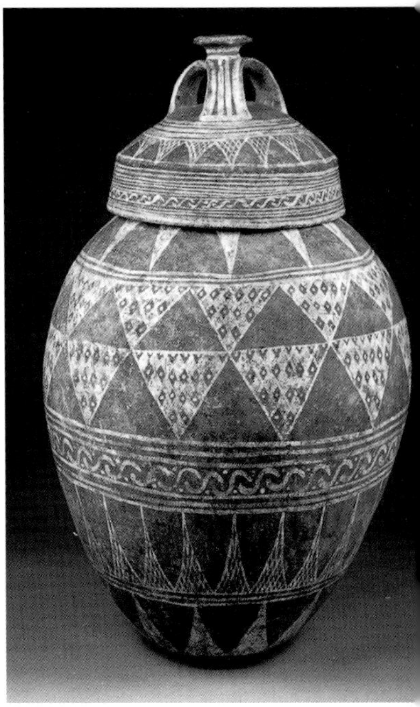

JEWELRY

It seems likely that Syro-Phoenician jewelers settled in Southern Etruria (probably at Tarquinia and Cerveteri) taught local apprentices the intricate techniques of gold granulation and filigree (decoration with fine spiral gold and silver wire). Granulation—the art of decorating smooth surfaces of gold jewelry with patterns composed of minute granules of gold—was originally invented in Mesopotamia in the third millennium and subsequently introduced to Anatolia, Syria, Egypt, Cyprus, and Mycenaean Greece. The collapse of the Bronze Age civilization in the Aegean brought with it the disappearance of such sophisticated arts in Greece, but they survived in the Near East and from there were reintroduced to Greece in the ninth century and transferred to Italy during the second half of the eighth. With these techniques came new motifs. Syro-Phoenician sacred emblems, such as the solar disc and the half moon, were incorporated into the traditional Etruscan geometric repertoire, but soon floral and figurative elements of Oriental inspiration dominated. Beside the older method of stamping and incising designs into hammered gold and silver sheet, which continued in use, jewelers in the service of rich aristocratic patrons also used filigree and granulation to embellish precious-metal ornaments of inherited forms known in bronze, such as fibulae, hair spirals, pinheads, beads, rings, bracelets, earrings, and large pectorals, with ever more exuberant decoration. The same artisans seem to have made the banqueting vessels of gold and silver that have been found in the princely tombs of Etruria and Lazio. Cerveteri, Tarquinia, and Vetulonia were probably the main centers for the production of this exquisite jewelry.

OBJECTS OF IVORY AND OSTRICH EGGSHELL

Among the more spectacular grave goods were objects made of imported exotic materials, such as ostrich eggshell and ivory. The former was fashioned into carved or painted ornamental containers (FIG. 42), the latter was carved into figured chalices and utensils or applied to or inlaid into wooden furniture, boxes, and jewelry. Ivory carving was a long-established art in the Levant (FIG. 43). But immigrant Eastern craftsmen practicing their craft in Italy and teaching Etruscan apprentices began to produce carvings inspired by foreign models while developing a style of their own and also, beside imported ivory, using more easily available bone and horn.

A large number of carved spoons of bone and a few of ivory come from Etruscan sites, but rarely from recorded contexts. These spoons, of Phoenician inspiration, usually have a rhomboid, drop-shaped, or oval relief handle—sometimes open-worked and covered with gold foil—and end in a decorative palmette or in a miniature human hand. In a tomb at Montalto di Castro near Vulci such a spoon

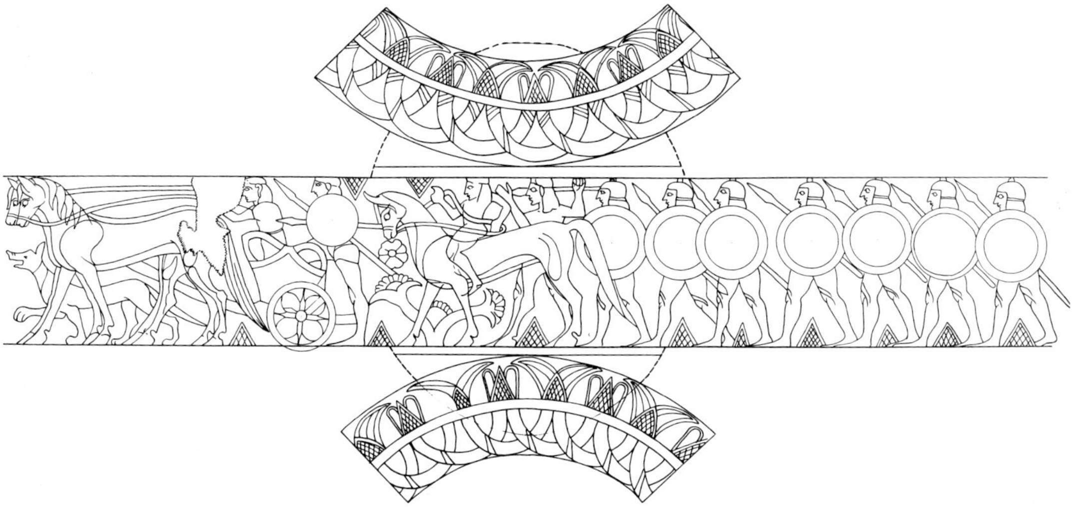

was found in association with jewelry, remains of a wooden casket, and alabaster pyxides and unguent bottles, which suggests that the spoon was used by a woman to spread cosmetic ointments or pastes. The majority of such spoons date from the seventh and sixth centuries and may have been made at Vulci.

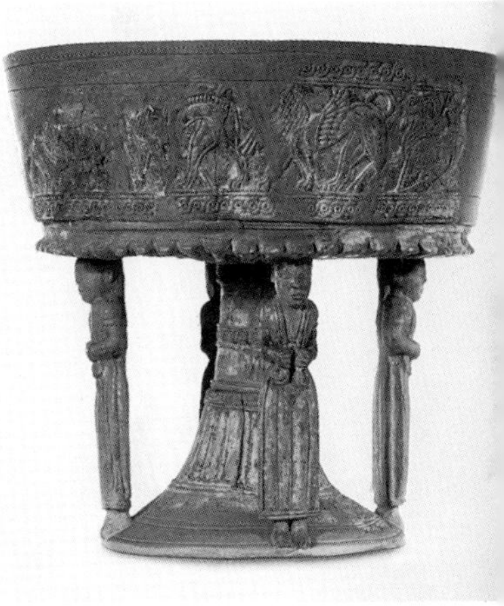

Fig. 42 Carved relief decoration on ostrich eggshell. From the Tomb of "Isis," Vulci. Early sixth century B.C. London, The British Museum GR 1850.2-27.9.

Fig. 43 Carved chalice with four supports in the form of standing women. From the Barberini Tomb, Palestrina. Mid-seventh century B.C. Ivory. H. 14 cm. Rome, Museo Etrusco di Villa Giulia 13234.

ETRUSCAN ORIENTALIZING BRONZES

After a long tradition of native bronzeworking Etruscan craftsmen now used their proven skills to enrich the familiar repertory of embossed geometric patterns with Orientalizing motifs for the decoration of a vast range of hammered bronze objects: vessels, utensils, armor, furniture, chariots, and carriages sheathed in bronze, many of which have been preserved as grave goods. The new ornaments decorating such bronzes—stars; rosettes; palmettes and other vegetal forms; animals, real and mythical; and human and divine figures—were inspired by a variety of imported foreign prototypes, among them an Assyrian bronze rhyton, reliefs embossed on North Syrian bronze bowls, stands and cauldrons with cast siren-shaped handle attachments, and Cypro-Phoenician silver-gilt bowls with figured friezes in repoussé. Perishable objects, such as woven and embroidered fabrics (for which the Sidonians were famous, cf. Hom. *Il.* 6.288–95) and patterned leather goods, may also have served as models.

Export of Etruscan Bronzes

Much fine Villanovan and Etruscan metalwork was transported abroad, as shown by the discovery of bronze razors, fibulae, helmets, shields, weapons, belts, horse bits, etc., in Sardinia, Central Europe, Gaul, and in the great Greek sanctuaries of the Samian Heraion, Olympia, Delphi, Perachora, and Dodona. In the latter sites objects such as armor and weapons were probably dedicated mainly by Greeks, who had acquired them by exchange, as gifts, or as booty, but some Etruscans, too, may have visited these sanctuaries and left modest gifts of personal ornaments. The second-century-A.D. traveler Pausanias relates (5.12.5) that the first "barbarian" (i.e., non-Greek) to make a dedication to Zeus at Olympia was Arimnestos, "who reigned among the Tyrrhenians"; he had offered up a bronze throne that was still there in Pausanias's day. It was perhaps of the form known to us from specimens found at Verucchio, Chiusi, etc.

ETRUSCAN AGRICULTURE

According to the ancient writer Diodorus Siculus (5.40), the Etruscan soil was naturally fertile, but it was due to the effort that the inhabitants put into cultivating it that it yielded an abundance of produce, beyond what was required locally.

Surviving rock-cut underground tunnels (It. *cuniculi*) accessible by vertical inspection shafts still testify to the skillful drainage system established by the Etruscans to improve waterlogged land and irrigate dry soils. Cultivation with more efficient agricultural implements of iron (such as iron-shod wooden ploughshares and iron-covered fellies of carts) led to surplus production, particularly of cereals. Pulses of various kinds, grown in rotation with cereals, provided invaluable protein for human nourishment, forage for cattle, and enrichment for the soil. It has been suggested that this agricultural method implies a division of land, a system of boundary demarcation, and the concept of private property, in contrast to the conditions that had prevailed in the self-sufficient Iron Age villages. Agricultural work must now have been carried out by serfs, comparable to the Latin *servi*, who labored for the urban noble families. Aristocratic groups of landowners may have created the many small satellite settlements accessible by ancient roads and watercourses that grew up on arable land in the territory of the big cities.

The polarization of Etruscan society between masters (Lat. *domini*) and slaves (*servi*), without any intermediate social strata, prevails in Roman sources; but it has been pointed out that the Greek historian Dionysios of Halikarnassos (2.44.7) compared these subject classes, perhaps more fittingly, to the *penestai* of Thessaly (according to Poll. *Onom.* 3.83), who were "half way between free men and slaves."

Most important among the new crops first systematically grown in Etruria at this period were olives (*Olea sativa*) and grapes (*Vitis vinifera*), products that served the aristocratic demands for oil and wine. Both plants are indigenous to Italy: Olive pits were excavated in a settlement dated to the second millennium at Vicarello on Lake Bracciano, and grape seeds were found in the submerged ninth-century village at Gran Carro on Lake Bolsena and at Tarquinia; but the cultivation of olives and grapes for large-scale production from the second half of the seventh century onward is probably due to contacts with Greek settlers in Campania. Greeks had practiced a polyculture of these crops together with cereals and legumes since the Bronze Age.

The Etruscan word for wine, *vinum*, first occurs on an inscribed jar, found at Gravisca (*CIE* 10390); the word does not appear to be connected with the Greek *oinos*, but comes from Latin, whereas the Etruscan word for olive oil (*eleiva*), which is incised on a late seventh-century spherical bucchero container for scented oil (Gr. *aryballos*)—*aska mi eleivana*—seems derived from Greek.

Oil and Wine

During the first half of the seventh century the storage amphorae for oil and wine found among the luxury goods in the aristocratic tombs of Etruria and Lazio mostly originated overseas, in Euboea, Corinth, Athens, Chios, Ionia, and Phoenicia, as did their contents.

Among the oldest tombs at Cerveteri that yielded commercial Greek amphorae is the left-hand side chamber of Tomb IV of the necropolis of Monte Abetone, dated by its rich ceramic finds to about 650–640. A lady was buried here, accompanied by her faience spindle whorl, a necklace with five Egyptian scarab-shaped faience amulets of the period of the pharaoh Psammetichus II (595–589 B.C.), an Etruscan unguent bottle of blue glass, and a Protocorinthian aryballos. The ceramic tableware consisted of two Rhodian cups, thin-walled bucchero cups decorated with a fan ornament, and three bucchero chalices with detachable tall foot. The Greek storage amphorae were from Athens, Corinth, and Chios.

Fine painted pottery aryballoi and alabastra for perfumed oil were imported originally from Miletos, Rhodes, Samos, and Corinth. But in the seventh century a flourishing local production of Subgeometric and Etrusco-Corinthian unguent containers grew up in Cerveteri, Tarquinia, and Vulci. Small containers of painted pottery with flower-scented oil or liquid pastes mixed with animal fat for exfoliation were widely distributed in Etruria and in the western Mediterranean. Blue and brown glass unguent bottles decorated with spiky protuberances appear in tombs from the middle of the seventh century onward; they were probably made at Cerveteri by Near Eastern craftsmen.

Export of Etruscan Wine and Drinking Vessels

The evidence from excavations and from cargoes from ancient shipwrecks in the Mediterranean shows that Southern Etruscan transport amphorae and wine, accompanied by bucchero and Etrusco-Corinthian drinking vessels and jugs, were exported widely. Bucchero vessels have been found in Provence, Spain, Corsica, Sardinia, South Italy, Sicily, Carthage, Syria, Asia Minor, and on the Black Sea, whereas Etrusco-Corinthian pottery is largely confined to the western Mediterranean. The consumption of wine and the pottery associated with it were introduced to the south of France, for example, well before 600, when Marseilles (Gr. Massalia), the first Greek colony in the area, was founded. It has been surmised that, in exchange for cargoes of wine, bronze vessels, and pottery brought to Gaul, the Etruscan merchant-sailors carried back, besides slaves and hides, metals not found in Italy but abundant in France, including gold and tin, some of the latter probably shipped from Cornish mines.

The trade routes between the Mediterranean and the Atlantic in Gaul largely followed the rivers Rhone, Soane, and Loire, with an important nodal point in the region of Bourges. Long-distance exchanges must always have been indirect, that is, goods were passed on in stages, carried by many different persons.

Celtic imitations in gray pottery of Etruscan bucchero jugs seem to have been produced in southern France during the second half of the sixth century, while Etruscan bronze vessels for banqueting have turned up in aristocratic tombs and residences in Gaul and in the Rhine and Danube regions, where they inspired local bronzeworkers. Exotic luxury vessels had become status symbols for the Celtic princes, who appreciated wine in addition to native mead and beer.

TRADE BY SEA

Some of the shipwrecks that have been excavated by underwater archaeologists carried mixed cargoes, suggesting that these boats operated over long distances, loading and unloading a variety of goods in many harbors along the way. Such must have been the case with a ship that sank near the island of Giglio, off the coast of Tuscany, early in the sixth century. The vessel must have started out from Phokaia on the west coast of Asia Minor or from the island of Samos, loaded with East Greek oil and wine amphorae and Ionian cups. Subsequently it took on Corinthian and Laconian unguent bottles, bars of iron and lead, and round copper ingots marked with Greek letters. Before putting in at Giglio, the ship had probably sailed via Corinth and through the Straits of Messina to Southern Etruria, taking on a cargo of Etruscan bucchero vessels and about 130 transport amphorae filled with the remains of resin, pine kernels, and preserved olives. A finely engraved Corinthian bronze helmet and arrowheads, wood and ivory pipes, a wooden diptych and stylus, a wooden bedstead with inlaid decoration, a small wooden box with a lid carved with a floral ornament, as well as East Greek lamps and fishing utensils were presumably the property of the ship's wealthy, literate, and musical owner. She went down, perhaps struck by a storm, while leaving the island, where anchor stocks made from local stone had been taken on board. Divers have raised part of the keel and hull of the ship; it had a sewn construction, that is, its planks had been lashed together with cords.

Other shipwrecks, notably some found off the south coast of France, contained more homogenous cargoes of wine amphorae, bucchero cups, etc. Such

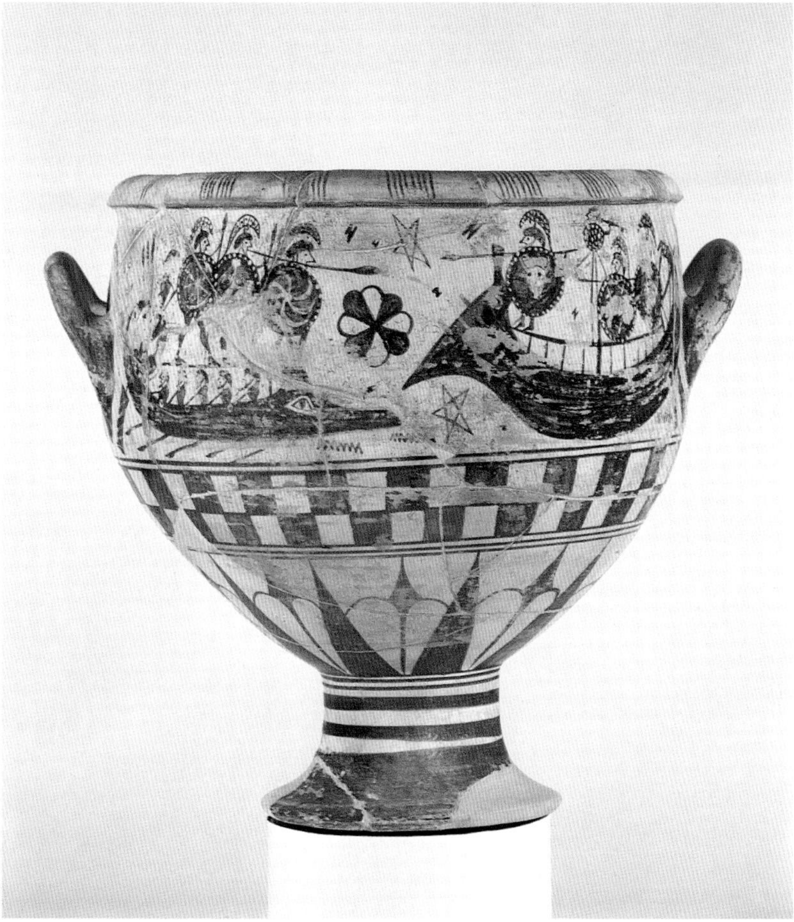

Fig. 44 Krater signed by the Greek Aristonothos. Side A. A sea battle. From Cerveteri. Mid-seventh century B.C. Painted pottery. H. 36.3 cm. Rome, Musei Capitolini 172.

ships will have served in the traffic between Etruscan merchants and native settlements there. We cannot be certain of the nationality of the owners and crews, but it is reasonable to assume that both Greeks and Etruscans carried on profitable seaborne trade (as well as piracy) in Tyrrhenian waters.

The increasing number of finds in the coastal regions of Pisa, the Versilia (north of Pisa), and Liguria show that in the sixth century there must have been a number of small Etruscan landfalls or ports on that coast, where traders had points of support and discharged part of their goods.

REPRESENTATION OF A SEA BATTLE An encounter between a heavy merchantman with a high defensive prow and a slim, oared warship with a sharp waterline spur for ramming, both with fully armed warriors on deck, is represented on one side of a krater discovered at Cerveteri (FIG. 44). The scene may be one the painter, a Greek immigrant called Aristonothos, had seen with his own eyes. On the other side is a mythical encounter between hostile opponents: the blinding of Polyphemos by Odysseus and his companions.

This krater is an instructive example of the manifold cultural influences that flowed together in the Southern Etruscan coastal cities in the vital stages of their formation. We have already mentioned the introduction of new techniques and styles in the potting and painting of vases. The subjects represented on the krater reflect both actual economic-political conditions and the growing familiarity of Etruria with Greek myth and poetry. The sea battle depicts naval and commercial rivalry between individual Greek and Etruscan ships and the gradual adoption of hoplite tactics (files of warriors, identically armed with round shields, spears, and helmets, who occupy the decks of both ships). We cannot tell who are Greek and who are Etruscan. Both ships are fitted with a ram spur, obviously to deal with piratical attacks. (According to Plin. *NH* 7.56.209, the ram spur was invented by an Etruscan named Pisaios = from Pisa.)

The artist's signature on the krater stands for the art of writing, acquired by the Etruscan aristocracy from the Campanian Greeks for social prestige as well as for practical and perhaps religious purposes. Lastly, the krater embodies the new way of life adopted by the ruling class, an important part of which is the use of fine painted pots for wine during banquets.

ETRUSCAN WRITING

Several Etruscan vase inscriptions document the fact that in the seventh century Greek settlers in Southern Etruscan cities became absorbed into the local communities. On a globular bucchero aryballos of the second half of the century we read: *mi larthaia telicles lechtumuza* = I (am) the (oil) flask of Larth Telikles (*TLE* 761). The word *lechtum* is derived from the Greek *lekythos*, a small flask for cosmetic oil. Larth is a common Etruscan personal name, while Telekles is a Greek one. The naturalized Greek (or offspring of intermarriage between Greek and Etruscan parents) who inscribed the vase could have been its owner or, perhaps, the producer, bottler, or retailer of such aryballoi filled with oil.

Under the foot of a jug of Corinthian type of the same date, found in the Doganaccia tumulus of Tarquinia, is painted in red: *achapri rutile hipucrates*. Rutile is a first name (related to Lat. *Rutilus*), and Hipukrates is the etruscanized form of the Greek name Hippokrates.

Such archaeological evidence for Greek immigrants establishing themselves in Etruscan cities illuminates a tradition, transmitted by Livy (1.34), Dionysios of Halikarnassos (3.46), Strabo (5.2.2; 8.6.20), and Pliny (35.43.152), which relates the story of Demaratos, an aristocratic Corinthian of the clan of the Bacchiadae, who had traded extensively with Etruria. In 657, fearing for his life and fortune when the tyrant Kypselos seized power at Corinth, Demaratos fled to Tarquinia with his retinue, including three artists named Eucheir (of the skillful hand), Diopos (keen-eyed), and Eugrammos (good designer), who are said to have taught their skills to the Etruscans. Demaratos married an Etruscan noblewoman, and their son, Lucumo, married the Etruscan lady Tanaquil, a powerful and ambitious woman with a gift for interpreting omens. Tanaquil persuaded her husband to move from Tarquinia to Rome, hoping that he would receive greater honor there than he did at home as the son of a Greek refugee. Thanks to his wealth and military gifts, Lucumo gained the friendship of King Ancus Martius and became one of his commanders. Succeeding Ancus Martius in 616, Lucumo ascended the throne as Lucius Tarquinius Priscus and founded the Etruscan dynasty of the Tarquins, who ruled Rome for much of the sixth century.

We may regard the Greek artists in Demaratos's employ with their "speaking" names as personifications of the different coroplasts and architectural painters from Corinth or from Sicilian or South Italian colonial cities who helped to transform the arts and architecture of Etruria during the second half of the seventh century.

Inscriptions

Inscriptions on pottery by Etruscans are naturally far more numerous than those by etruscanized Greeks. Among the earliest Etruscan letters known are those incised on five spools of impasto found in trench tomb 870 in the necropolis of Casal del Fosso at Veii; the context dates them to the late eighth–early seventh century. The rounded ends of the spools are quartered with crossed impressions of a cord, and in one sector of each the letter *A* was incised after firing, probably the mark of the woman who used the spools for her woolworking. The major part of the known inscriptions of the seventh century (about 120, so far) come from Southern Etruria: Veii, Cerveteri, Tarquinia, and Vulci; but it seems that Tarquinia may have been the first to introduce writing.

The discovery of writing utensils of precious material in an aristocratic tomb of the Orientalizing period suggests that literacy was largely restricted to the aristocracy. Among the grave goods, datable to about 670, in the rich Circle of the Ivories (*Circolo degli Avori*) at Marsiliana d'Albegna, was a rectangular ivory tablet with a double lion's head as handle and traces of gold-foil covering. Within a frame, the tablet had a sunken area, once spread with a layer of wax on which writing could be practiced with a stylus. To help the writer learn the new skill, a model alphabet was incised on the frame from which the twenty-seven letters in a Euboean Greek hand could be copied. Ivory-handled styluses and two blades for erasing the letters on the wax completed this elegant writing set.

The Etruscans probably learned the alphabet from their nearest Greek neighbors, the Euboean settlers in the Gulf of Naples. Some Etruscans may have moved south to Pithekoussai, as suggested by the discovery there of small, typically Etruscan impasto amphorae with spiral decoration of late eighth-century date and of characteristic great hammered bronze shields in cremation tombs at Cumae, as well as by a small number of inscriptions on pots with possibly Etruscan names.

Transcription/ phonetic value	Seventh century South Etruscan (Cerveteri)	Seventh century North Etruscan	Hellenistic South Etruscan	Hellenistic North Etruscan
a	𐌀	𐌀	𐌀	𐌀
c (k)	𐌂		𐌂	𐌂
e	𐌄	𐌄	𐌄	𐌄
v	𐌅	𐌅	𐌅	𐌅
z	𐌆	𐌆	𐌆	𐌆
h	𐌇	𐌇	𐌇	𐌇 ⊘
θ (th)	⊗ ⊕	⊕ ○	○	○
i	𐌉	𐌉	𐌉	𐌉
k	𐌊	𐌊		𐌊
l	𐌋	𐌋	𐌋	𐌋
m	𐌌	𐌌	𐌌	𐌌 Λ
n	𐌍	𐌍	𐌍	𐌍
p	𐌐	𐌐	𐌐	𐌐
q	𐌒			
ś		𐌑		𐌑
r	𐌓 ᗡ	𐌓	𐌓	ᗡ 𐌓
s	𐌔	𐌔	𐌔	𐌔
s̓	𐌔		𐌔	
t	𐌕	𐌕	𐌕	𐌕
u	𐌖 V Y	V	V	V
φ (ph)	𐌘	𐌘	𐌘	𐌘
χ (kh)	𐌙	𐌙	↓	↓
ṡ	+			
f			8	8

The adaptation of a system of writing created to reproduce the sounds of one language (Greek) to those of a completely different language (Etruscan) involved problems that required a number of changes at an early stage (FIG. 45). Thus several Greek sounds (expressed by the letters beta, gamma, delta, and omikron, the Greek *b*, *g*, *d*, and *o*) were dropped from the alphabet, evidently because the Etruscans had no need for them, making no distinction between the vowels *o* and *u* and pronouncing *b*, *d*, and *g* as *p*, *t*, and *k*. To designate an Etruscan *f* sound not present in Greek, an extra letter 𐌚 was introduced. Two different signs for an *s* sound were used: in Southern Etruria *S* was written 𐌔, but in Northern Etruria it was written 𐌑. In modern transcriptions the latter is written *Ś*. As a result of a number of changes that had occurred in the course of time, the simplified, neo-Etruscan alphabet was created about 400 B.C. Several letters were dropped, but in the Northern Etruscan cities the use of 𐌊 for *K* and the sibilant 𐌑 continued. It is thus possible to distinguish both regional and chronological differences in inscriptions.

Model alphabets and syllabaries incised on bucchero (ink?) pots of the mid-seventh century have been found in some aristocratic tombs (Cerveteri, Regolini-Galassi Tomb [*Tomba Regolini-Galassi*]; Veii, Tomb of Monte Aguzzo [*Tomba di Monte Aguzzo*]). They are probably status symbols that enhance the cultural (and magical?) value of the object and indicate that the paterfamilias was able to write and teach his family the letters. Women, too, used such alphabets, as proved by a shortened version in Northern Etruscan script incised on a spindle whorl from chamber tomb 21 of the necropolis of the Osteria at Vulci, dated to the first quarter of the sixth century. The lady buried here may have been of northern descent and married to a man from Vulci.

From about 500 onward, the first syllable of Etruscan words seems to have become particularly accented; this led to a weakening of the following vowels, their subsequent disappearance, and a resulting cluster of consonants. The phenomenon, known as syncope, appears most clearly in neo-Etruscan writing. Examples of such abbreviations are names that are contracted from *Rasenna* to *Rasna*, *Ramutha* to *Ramtha*, *Aranth* to *Arnth*, etc.

Inscriptions are usually written from right to left in a continuous chain of letters or, when the text is so long that it requires several lines, it is written as a boustrophedon, that is, alternately from right to left and left to right.

During the early phase writing appears mostly on pottery vessels (FIG. 46) and occasionally on objects of precious metal. The text normally gives the name of the owner in the genitive, while the object bearing it appears to speak. For example, on two oinochoai from Cerveteri, dating from about 675, we read: *mi qutun karkanas* = I (am) the jug of Karkana (*TLE* 63); *qutun* is derived from the Greek word *kothon*, a drinking vessel.

An impasto chalice in the Louvre of about 675–650 has a much damaged inscription that has been read plausibly as: *mi laucie mezenties* = I (belong to)

Fig. 45 Archaic seventh-century and later Etruscan alphabets and transcriptions with phonetic values.

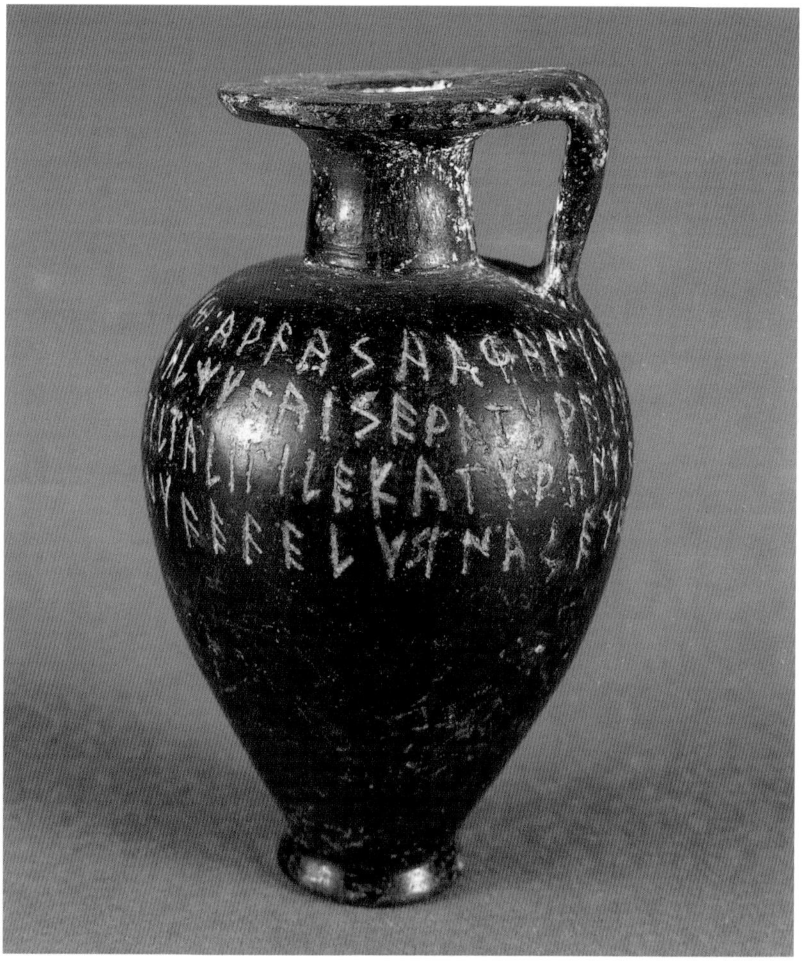

Fig. 46 Aryballos with incised inscription. Probably from Cerveteri. About 630 B.C. Bucchero. Rome, Museo Etrusco di Villa Giulia.

Fig. 47 Fibula with decoration and inscription in granulation. From Castelluccio di Pienza. Last quarter of seventh century B.C. Gold. L. 11 cm. Paris, Musée du Louvre Bj 816.

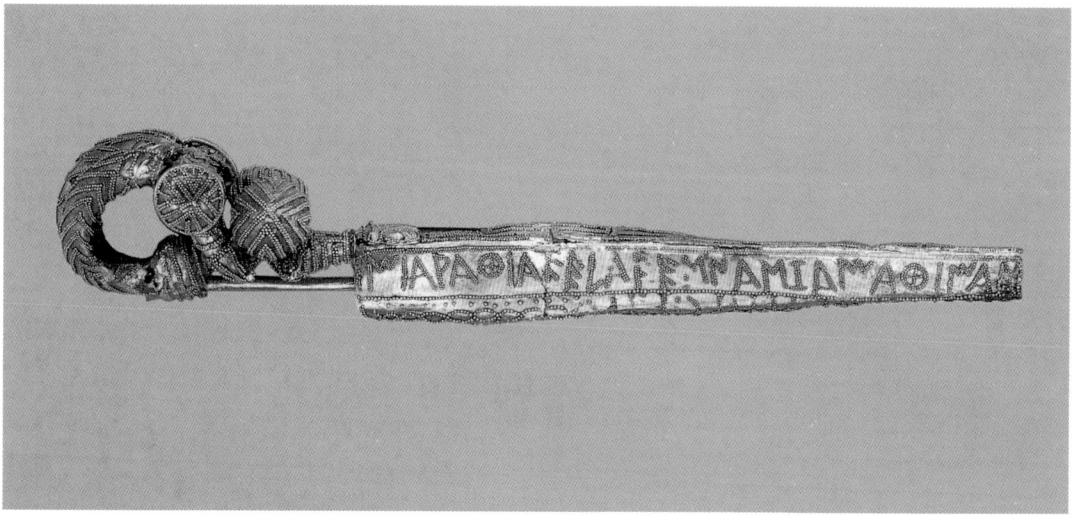

Laucie Mezentie. In the Latin form, Mezentius, the family name Mezentie is known from Roman literature (e.g., Verg. 7.692, 8.479; Livy 1.2.3), where Mezentius appears as an impious king of Cerveteri. The Laucie Mezentie of the inscription was a member of the Mezentie family, which thus indirectly confirms that the memory of real personalities is often preserved in semilegendary form by Roman authors of a later period.

Occasionally inscriptions give the names of both the recipient and the donor, as on the catchplate of a gold fibula decorated with geometric patterns in granulation, now in the Dallas Museum of Art: *mi mulu arathiale thanachvilus prasanaia* = I, given by Arath, belong to Tanaquil Prasanai; or in an inscription from Veii (*TLE* 34): *mini muluvanice mamarce apuniie venala* = Mamarce Apuniie gave me to Venai; here the verb *muluvanice* (from the root *mul-* = to give) is used. Another gold fibula of about 630 has a partially damaged inscription in granulation technique, which has been read as: *mi arathia velaveśnaś zamathi mamurke mulvenike tursikina* = I (am) of Arath Velavesna (of) gold. Mamurke tursikina gave (me) (FIG. 47).

Sometimes it appears from the context of a tomb in which an inscribed object has been found that the last person to own the object was not identical with the original owner and that the object had been passed on from one person to another. Such is probably the case with silver vessels deposited about 660 B.C. with an aristocratic lady in the Regolini-Galassi Tomb at Cerveteri; they are incised with: *mi larthia* = I (belong) to Larth. Larth being a male name (here in an archaic genitive), it appears that these luxury objects first belonged to a man, presumably the husband of the noble lady, who subsequently gave them to her, and they were buried with her.

Etruscan artists and artisans also occasionally signed their work. On the neck of a bucchero aryballos from Grotte Santo Stefano incised with lions and birds and dated to the second half of the seventh century is the inscription: *mi arathiale zichuche* = I was written (or incised or drawn) by Arath (*TLE* 278).

THE ETRUSCAN DOUBLE-NAME SYSTEM

The double-name system that established itself in Etruria and in Italic-speaking Italy seems to have developed from an earlier stage when each person had only an individual name. This became a first name when an inherited family name (the gentilicial name) was added. The Etruscan name system was quite distinct from that of the Greeks and other peoples in antiquity. The latter all used only an individual name and a patronymic (father's name). Thus, in Greece *Alexandros Philippou* = Alexander (the son) of Philip, does not express the concept of family continuity by using a family name.

The Etruscans, by contrast, used an individual first name (Lat. *praenomen*), such as those cited above: Laucie, Larth, Arath, Tanaquil, etc., followed by the name (Lat. *nomen*) of the family (Lat. *gens*, hence: gentilicial name), such as Mezentie, Prasanai, etc., which refers to an ancestral founder. The introduction of the double-name system instead of the simple patronymic has been recognized as the sign of a profound change from a tribal society, in which all members of the clan believed themselves to be descended from a common ancestor, to a more differentiated society with a class system based on division of labor and private ownership of land. Probably during the eighth century the high social status of the hereditary landowning class found its expression in the gentilicial double names, ensuring the new system of production and the continuity of the privileges of the aristocrats. With the subsequent growth of the cities in the second half of the seventh century, the number of double names increased greatly, which points to the development of a "middle class" of citizens. In inner and Northern Etruria this process was apparently somewhat delayed. In the colonial areas of Campania and in Corsica, with small towns such as Aleria, it seems that single names were often sufficient to distinguish the smaller number of Etruscans settled there.

In addition to the double onomastic form, Etruscan male funerary inscriptions usually give the father's and, more rarely, the mother's name of the dead person and, at a later period (third–first century), often a *cognomen*, that is, a separate name, chosen to distinguish one branch of a large family from another. The same formula is used for women, but a married woman also added the name of her husband. However, this full complement of names is relatively rare, particularly in Southern Etruria, sometimes perhaps because of limited space for the inscriptions.

The gentilicial system may originally have comprised all free citizens of the newly emerging Etruscan cities, but it did not include slaves or foreigners or people such as actors and jugglers, who were known by a personal name only. While the number of praenomina for both men and women is relatively limited, an extremely large number of gentilicial names have come down to us; it has been suggested that this rules out the possibility that the people excluded from the system represented the mass of the population, with only a limited number of families forming an oligarchy.

In a number of funerary inscriptions from the fourth century onward the term *lautni/lautnitha* occurs beside the name. It seems to designate a social condition, probably corresponding to the Latin *libertus, liberta* = freedman, freedwoman. Those released from slavery who had risen to modest prosperity often gave their patron's gentilicial name or cognomen after their own individual name. Only the second generation after manumission acquired the full status and nomenclature of a citizen.

The Etruscan term *etera/eteri* seems mainly connected with male names in funerary inscriptions; it is usually thought to refer to persons of low social status, such as foreigners or dependents, corresponding to the Latin *clientes*. But such an interpretation does not make sense in all cases, and it may mean juveniles.

The earliest inscription so far known giving the Etruscan title of magistrate, *zilath*, occurs on one of two cylindrical stone cippi found in a gravel pit by the river Secchia at Rubiera (Reggio, Emilia). These funerary monuments are of exceptional interest, not only as documents for the precocious development here of a system of magistratures, but also for the westward expansion of the Etruscans into the Po valley in the second half of the seventh century. The tapering lower part of the cippi was inserted into the soil. Carved in low relief, the cippi were originally painted with decoration consisting of friezes in the Orientalizing style with sphinxes, winged lions, and interlaced semicircles ending in lotus buds, divided by bands of inscription. On the least well-preserved cippus one can still clearly read the words: *mi avile(s) amthuras*, the possessive form of the male praenomen Avile and of the gentilicial name Amthura.

On the second cippus a longer text mentions a couple. First comes the name of a woman, *kuvei puleisnai*, then, after some gaps, the words *zilath mi salalati amake*, which have been translated, "I was zilath (magistrate or chief) of Misala (or Misa)," or as "zilath I was at Sala." The name of the magistrate is no longer legible. The script of this text is of the Northern Etruscan type characteristic for Chiusi, a city whose northward expansion is thought to have contributed to the foundation of Marzabotto (Misa?) on the Reno River in the northern foothills of the Apennines.

Of particular relevance for our interest in the status of women is the fact that Kuvei Puleisnai, the lady who must have been the wife or mother of the magistrate, is clearly making an individual statement in this inscription, followed by one made by the male, both obviously being equally important.

BURIALS

Tumuli

The profound changes that took place during the Orientalizing period also affected the traditional forms of burial. Inhumation in trenches in addition to cremation and burial in ash urns had begun to be practiced in the late ninth century. By now burial in trenches was widespread in Southern Etruria, where it remained in use for people belonging to the lower social strata (for example, in the necropolis of the sector of the Laghetto at Cerveteri). But aristocratic families tried to distinguish themselves by erecting ever more elaborate chamber tombs, covered by tumuli, in conspicuous places. At first the simple trench tombs were made more spacious and visible by being covered with a false vault formed by progressively inward-projecting layers of stone slabs, the final top layer joining the two converging sides above the center of the trench. Such tombs could be covered by a low mound.

In Southern Etruria the new chamber tombs for the socially prominent and wealthy were hollowed out from the local volcanic rock (FIG. 48), an easily carved material, absent in the northern regions; here, by contrast, the internal chambers of the tumuli had to be constructed entirely with stone slabs or blocks (Vetulonia [FIG. 49], Cortona, Comeana, Quinto Fiorentino, etc.). The often gigantic mounds (up to 30–40 m in diameter and 12–15 m high), rising above the tombs and confined at the foot by a cylindrical stone drum with elaborate moldings, served to protect the burial chambers, but they were also expressions of the pride and power of the leading aristocrats (FIG. 50). The inspiration for such monuments was perhaps provided by the imposing dynastic funerary mounds of western Anatolia of the first half of the seventh century in Phrygia and Lydia.

Building activities of this ambitious kind required large numbers of workers, many presumably slaves, who were acquired by warfare and piracy. Slaves also performed domestic and industrial work, and they may have served as rowers in ships.

BELOW LEFT
Fig. 48 Arched entrance to left dromos chamber with rock-carved bedstead and rafters. Tomb of the Ship 1, Banditaccia necropolis, Cerveteri. Second half of seventh century B.C.

BELOW RIGHT
Fig. 49 Interior of lower chamber of tumulus. Pietrera Tomb 1, Vetulonia. Second half of seventh century B.C.

Domestic Architecture Imitated in Chamber Tombs

In contrast to their monumental funerary architecture, Etruscan families, including aristocratic ones, seem to have continued living in ephemeral thatched huts or wooden houses with clay-covered roofs until well into the seventh century. The building materials of these dwellings have left few traces, but information on the shape of their walls, doors, windows, and roofs, as well as the increasing number and complexity of the rooms, comes from the interiors of grave mounds carved from the rock in imitation of such huts (particularly at Cerveteri).

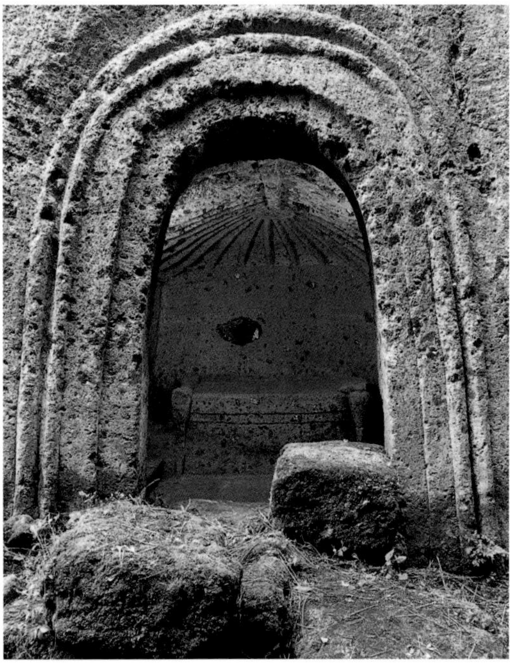

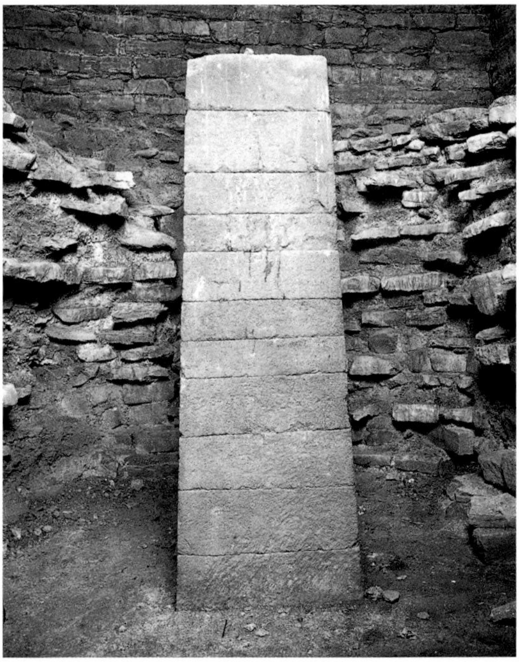

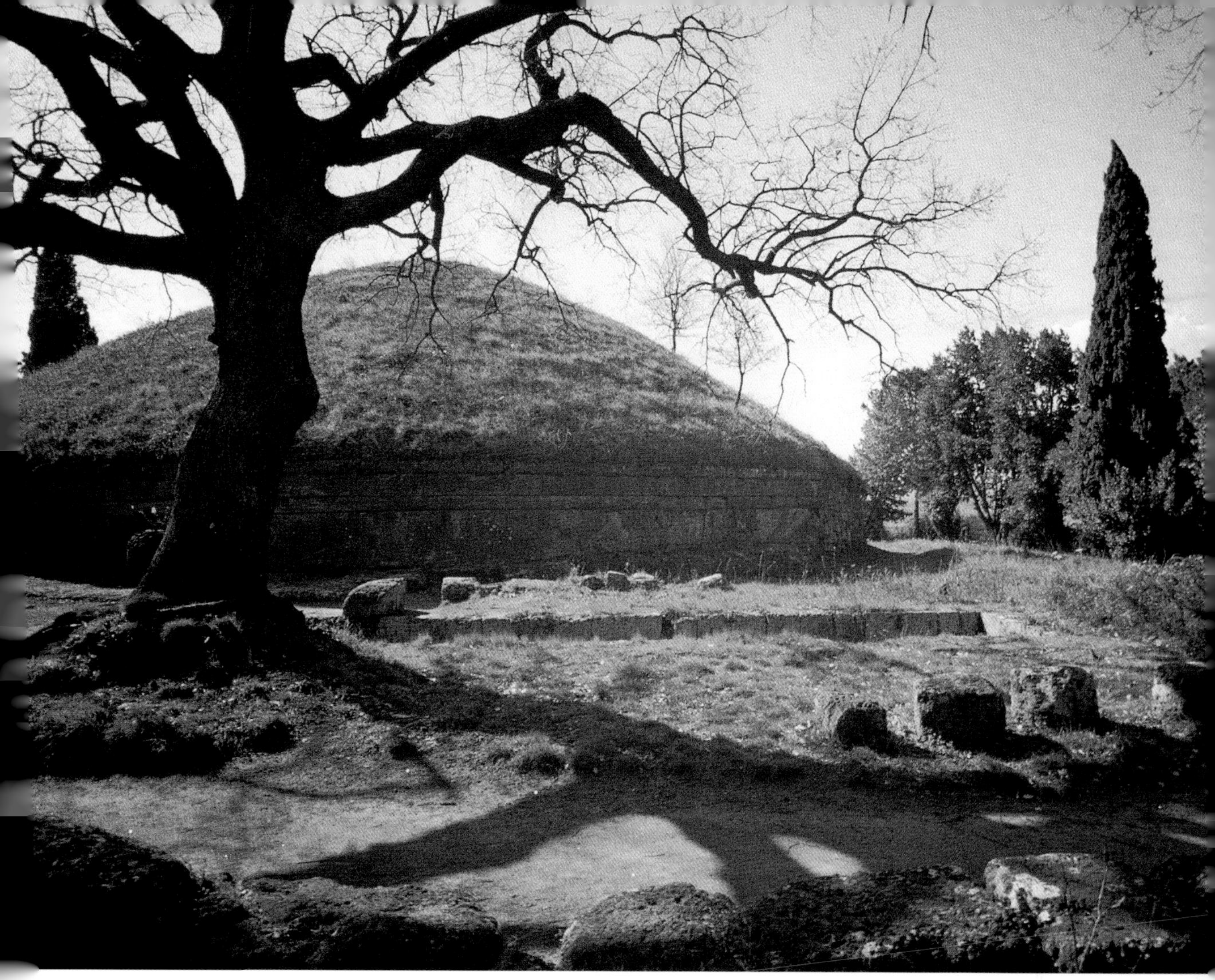

The idea of the tomb chamber as the house of the dead, which found its earliest expression in the hut urns of the Villanovan period, is here realized on a large scale. One of the oldest chamber tombs (early seventh century), situated in Tumulus 2 of the Banditaccia necropolis of Cerveteri, is the Tomb of the Hut (*Tomba della Capanna*), so called because it reproduces in its two innermost aligned chambers the simple forms of the inside of a rectangular hut with a high, thatched ridge roof (FIG. 51); there are low lateral benches in the front room, while in the second, inner chamber a bed of river pebbles runs around the side and back walls (FIG. 52).

Fig. 50 Tumulus, Banditaccia necropolis, Cerveteri. First half of sixth century B.C.

At first only a single person or the pater- and materfamilias seems to have occupied the comparatively small tombs prepared for them, but with the development of larger chamber tombs of more complex plan, unmarried children or siblings of the original couple were also buried there, and eventually entire generations of families found their last resting place in the vast burial chambers of the late period.

The earliest tomb chambers in the large tumuli were orientated to the north/west, the region of the Etruscan underworld. A stepped dromos ended at a stone slab or blocks, which could be removed when subsequent burials took place. Out-

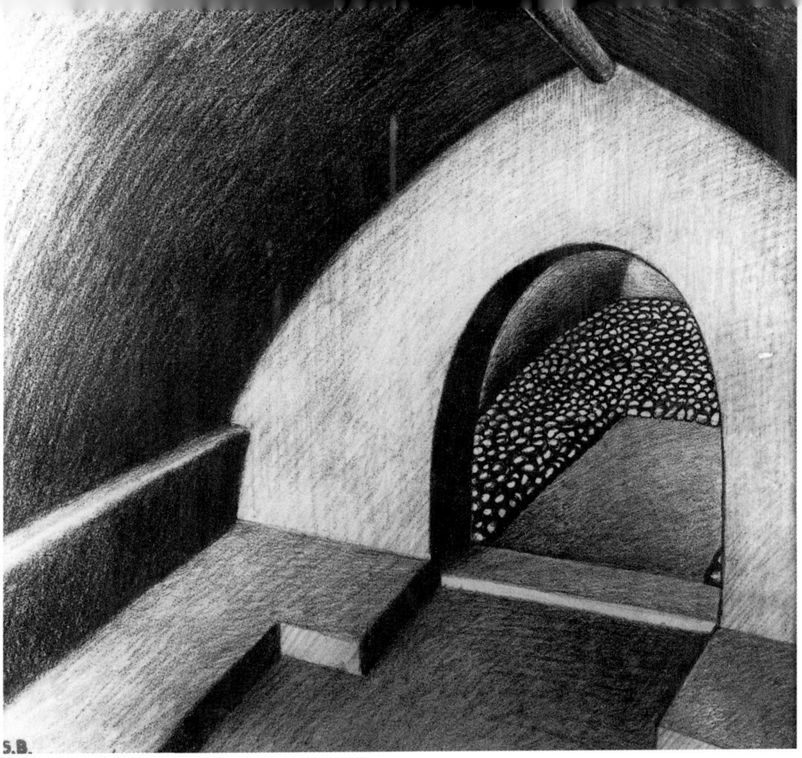

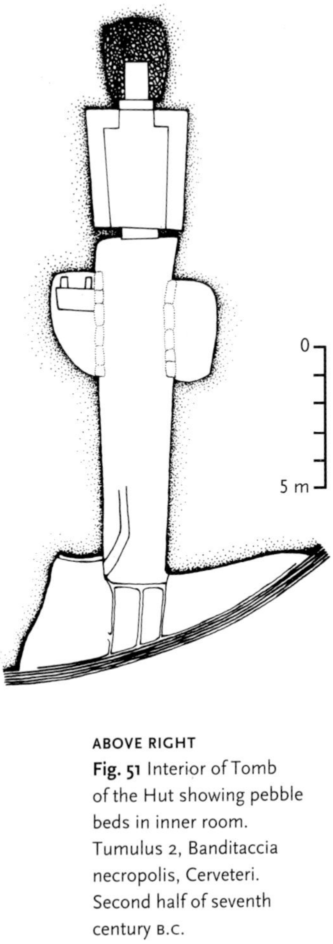

ABOVE RIGHT
Fig. 51 Interior of Tomb of the Hut showing pebble beds in inner room. Tumulus 2, Banditaccia necropolis, Cerveteri. Second half of seventh century B.C.

ABOVE
Fig. 52 Plan of the Tomb of the Hut.

side the stone drum of the tumulus, joined by a vaulted bridge, there was usually a platform or altar, accessible by a ramp or steps, from which one could reach the top of the mound to perform rituals there. In some cases rock-cut steps in a particularly wide dromos suggest by their layout and position that they were meant to accommodate spectators of funerary rites or ritual games held at the entrance to the tomb. Such spacious dromoi may be derived from Cypriote prototypes.

Early Funerary Sculpture

The importance attached to the gens and the veneration of its heads and founders led, as we shall see, to the rise of monumental sculpture in stone and, a little later, terra-cotta, connected with an ancestor cult practiced in the tomb.

The fragmentary torso of a human figure with arms folded across the chest, roughly carved from gray tufa, was found in the entrance corridor of the Tomb of the Hut. It was probably the image of an ancestor of the couple buried there.

This is presumably also the significance of two almost life-size figures of bearded and enthroned men that are carved in high relief from the rock of the lateral walls in the vestibule of the Tomb of the Statues (*Tomba delle Statue*) at Ceri near Cerveteri (FIG. 53). The two figures sit facing each other on either side of the inner door leading to the tomb chamber itself. Inside the tomb the married couple for whom it was built, was laid to rest on two stone benches—the man on the left, the woman on the right, as was the custom in Cerveteri. The statues in the vestibule are thought to represent the forefather of the husband on the left and that of the wife on the right. The closest stylistic and iconographic parallels for these early examples of monumental stone sculpture in Etruria (ca. 680–660) are found in North Syria and in late Hittite sites of Asia Minor. The men's blocklike form, with short thighs, almost neckless heads, smooth, ankle-length tunics, obliquely draped

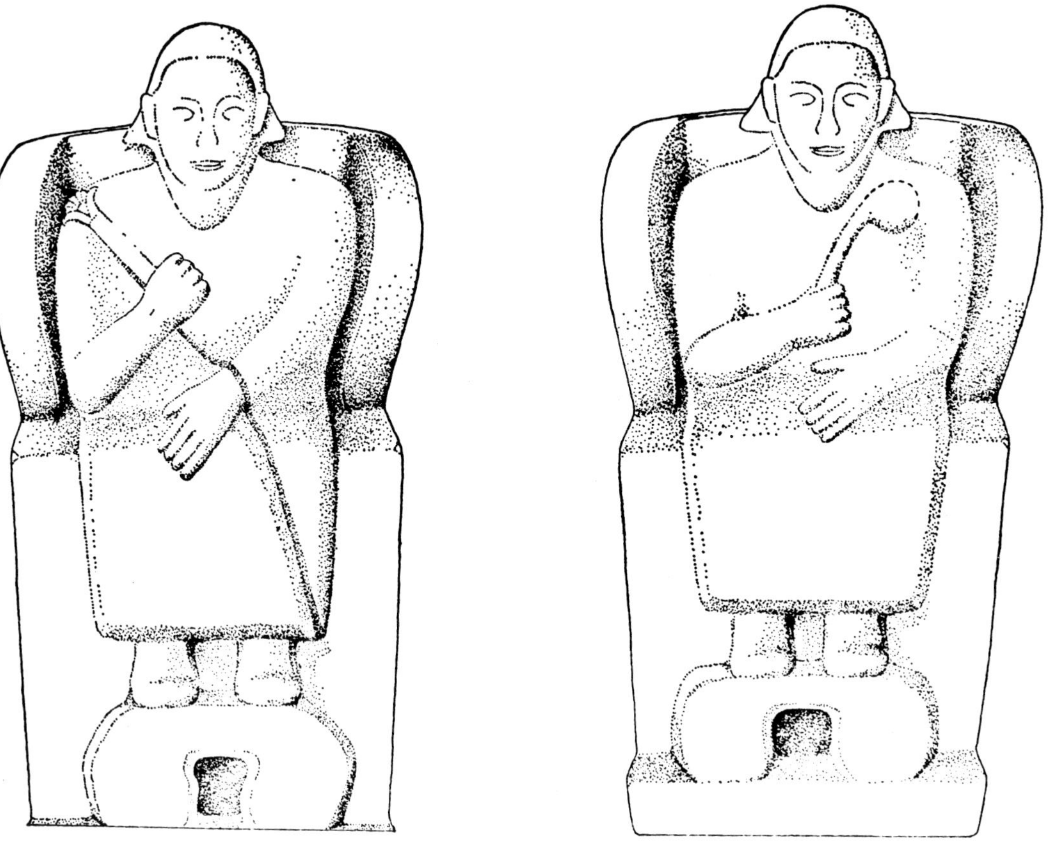

Fig. 53 Reconstruction of rock-carved statues in the vestibule of the Tomb of the Statues. Ceri, near Cerveteri. Second quarter of seventh century B.C.

mantles, sandals, and the palmette-tipped scepter one of them holds against his chest, strongly suggest that the Ceri statues were inspired by Syrian sculpture. A number of monumental stelae and cippi in Villanovan Bologna show close affinities with North Syrian architectural sculpture.

Cerveteri: The Regolini-Galassi Tomb

An intermediate stage between the older trench tomb and the early form of chamber tomb just discussed is represented by tombs only partially excavated from a bank of rock—long rectangular spaces, whose upper elevation is usually constructed with rows of superposed blocks converging in a kind of false vault. The most famous example of this type, discovered in 1836 in Cerveteri and named after its excavators, is the Regolini-Galassi Tomb in the Sorbo necropolis. Recent re-examination of eyewitness accounts of the discovery proves that only two—not three—people were buried in the tomb. It consists of a long narrow anteroom leading to an axially aligned corridorlike chamber. Near its junction with the latter, the anteroom is flanked on either side by an oval chamber hollowed out from the rock. The long inner chamber (corresponding to the bedroom of the houses of the living) had been occupied by the body of a woman of eminent social

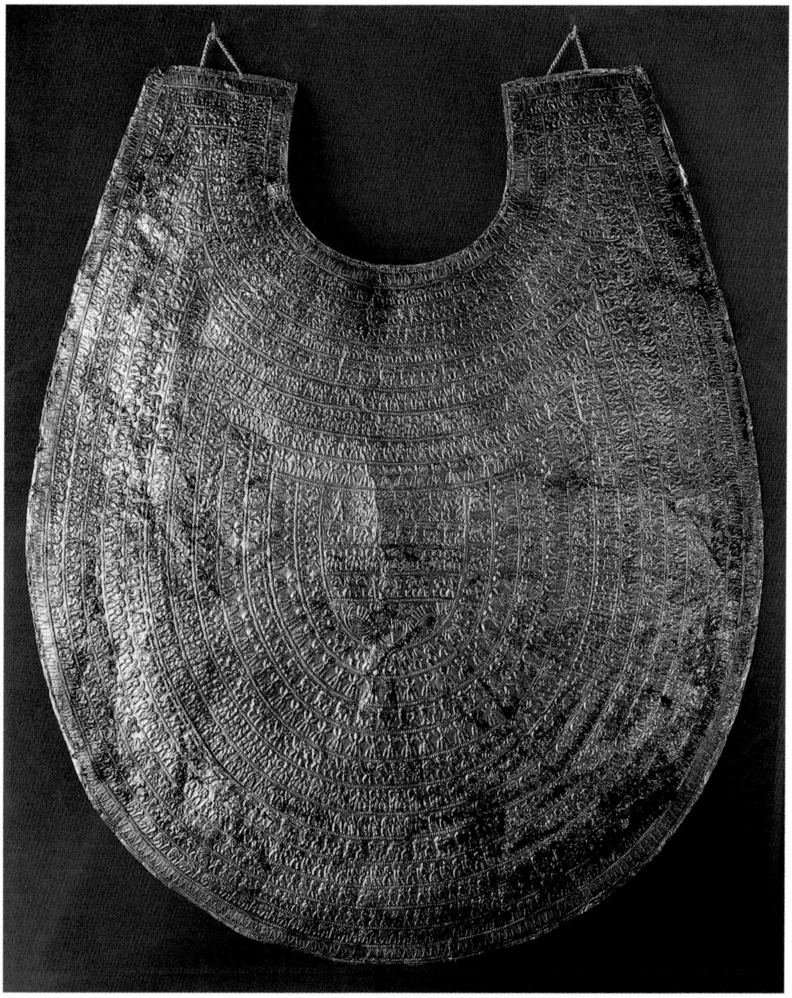

Fig. 54 Pectoral decorated with sixteen bands of different orientalizing motifs. From the Regolini-Galassi Tomb, Sorbo necropolis, Cerveteri. Second quarter of seventh century B.C. Embossed sheet gold on a support of copper sheet. H. 42 cm. Vatican, Museo Gregoriano Etrusco 20553.

Fig. 55 Pair of bracelets with orientalizing human figures outlined in granulation and framed by geometric patterns. From the Regolini-Galassi Tomb, Sorbo necropolis, Cerveteri. Second quarter of seventh century B.C. Embossed sheet gold. Diam. 10 cm. Vatican, Museo Gregoriano Etrusco 20562–63.

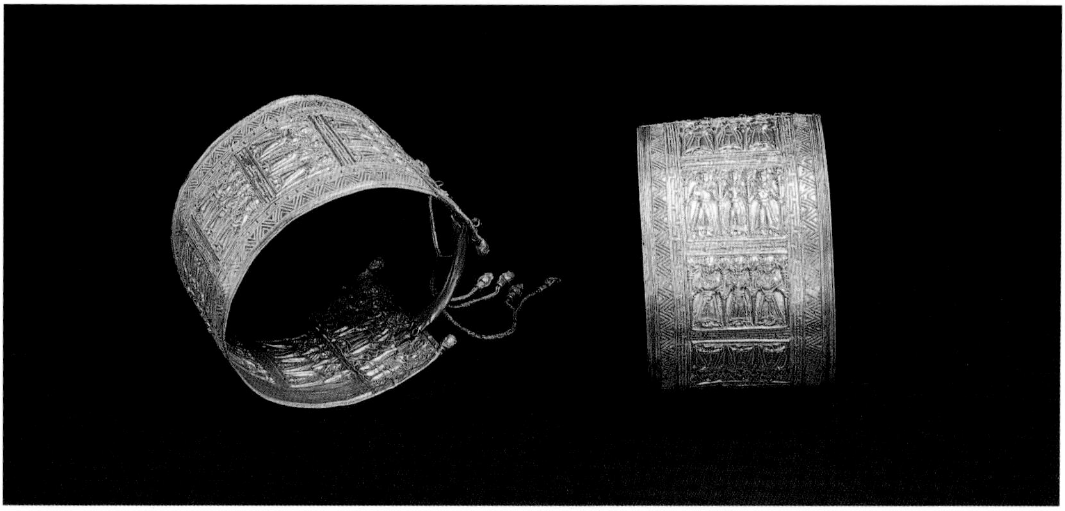

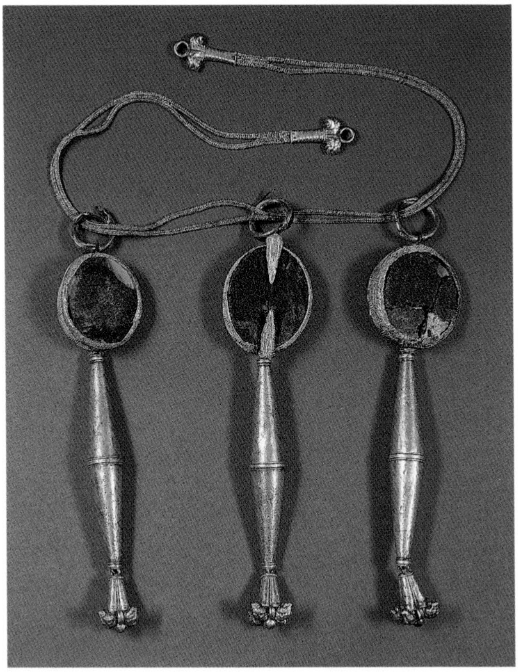

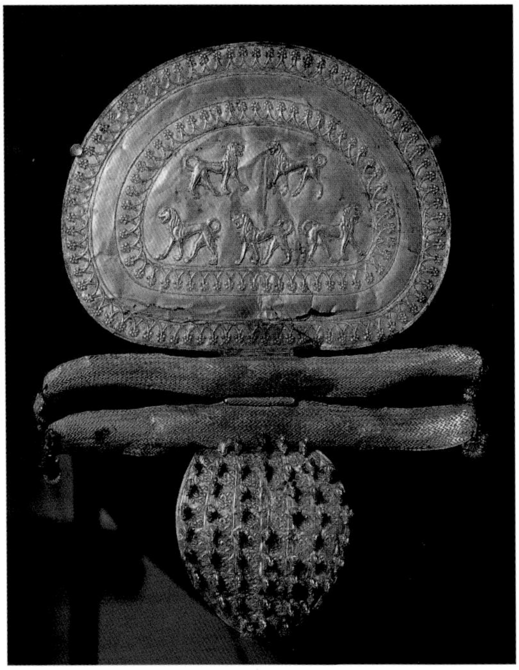

Fig. 56 Chain necklace with three pendants. From the Regolini-Galassi Tomb, Sorbo necropolis, Cerveteri. About 650 B.C. Gold and amber discs. L. of chain 68.5 cm, of pendants 24 cm. Vatican, Museo Gregoriano Etrusco 20557.

Fig. 57 Disk fibula with decoration in the form of lions, griffins, and floral and geometric patterns. From the Regolini-Galassi Tomb, Sorbo necropolis, Cerveteri. Second quarter of seventh century B.C. Sheet gold and granulation. H. 31.5 cm. Vatican, Museo Gregoriano Etrusco 20552.

status. Placed on the floor, her garments had been covered with a dazzling array of gold and amber jewelry. A number of these pieces were of local type and solid enough to have been worn during her lifetime. But a big pectoral (FIG. 54); a pair of bracelets or earrings (FIG. 55); a necklace with three pendants (FIG. 56); and a fibula with a large catchplate (FIG. 57), embossed and covered with the finest vegetal and figure ornaments formed by minute gold granules, were of such large size and such very thin gold sheet that they must have been made for burial purposes only. There were also a silver spindle and inscribed silver vessels, as well as two large bronze cauldrons adorned with the foreparts of griffins and lions and placed on iron tripods (FIG. 58). The latter are clearly based on Oriental prototypes from North Syria. This inner chamber was partially walled off after the deposition of the corpse, as was the right-hand lateral chamber, in which were found the cremated remains of a man in a pottery urn. The left-hand chamber contained no burial but silver-gilt bowls with embossed friezes of Cypro-Phoenician manufacture.

The high rank of the dead is documented by a large number of splendidly decorated bronze objects and iron utensils deposited in the anteroom. They comprise bronze shields, originally suspended from the walls; fluted shallow bowls (Lat. *paterae*); a wheeled incense burner; a bronze bedstead (FIG. 59); and the four-wheeled, bronze-sheathed carriage used to transport the corpse to the tomb. Other pieces of furniture, also covered with embossed bronze sheet, were likewise deposited here. The grave goods (which cannot all be precisely apportioned to their owners because of the displacement caused during excavation by the collapse of the upper part of the tomb) also included luxury items of carved ivory (dice, cir-

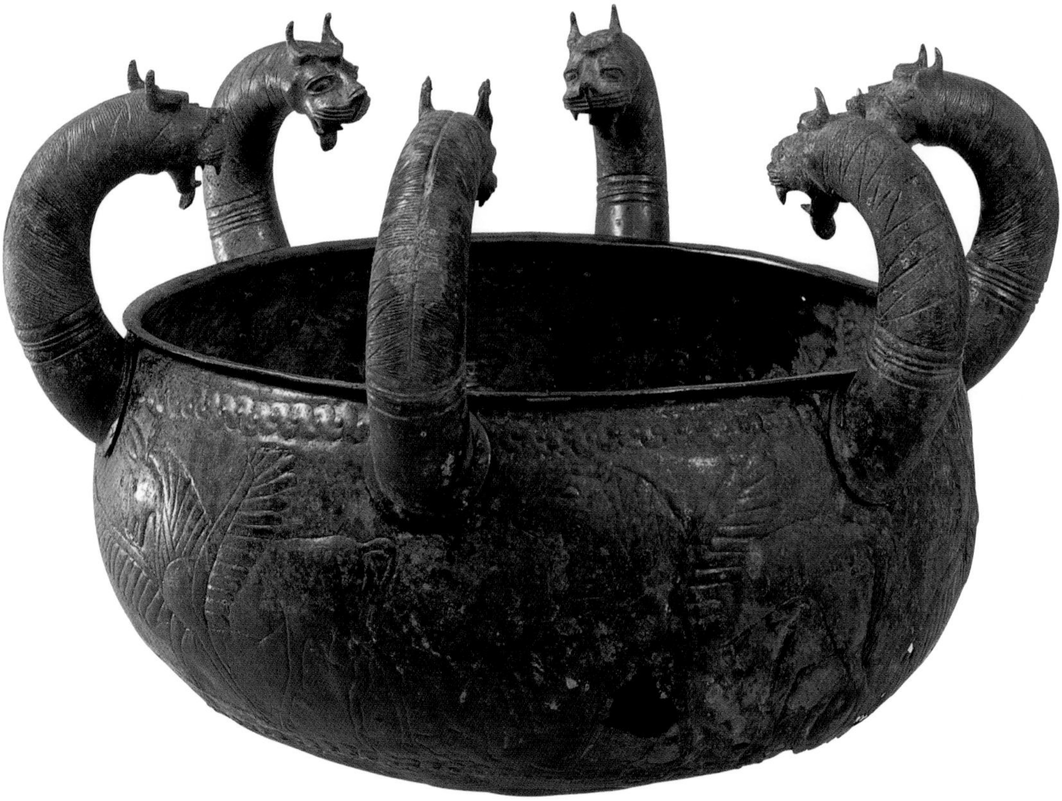

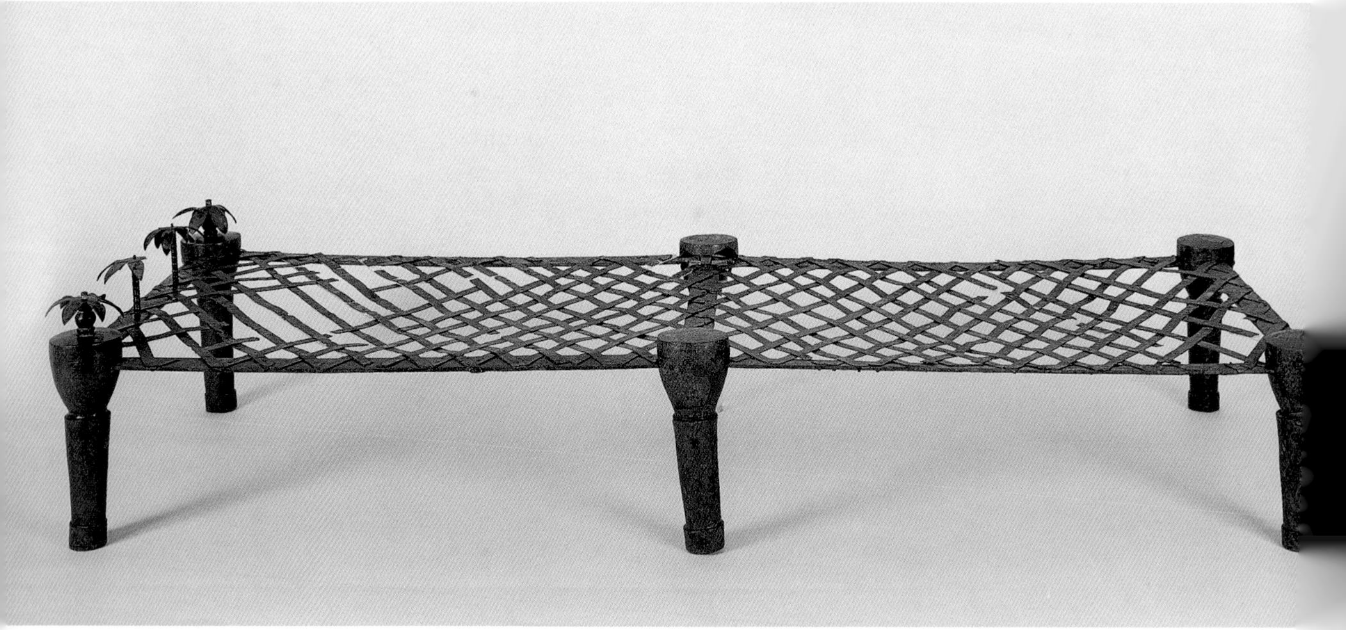

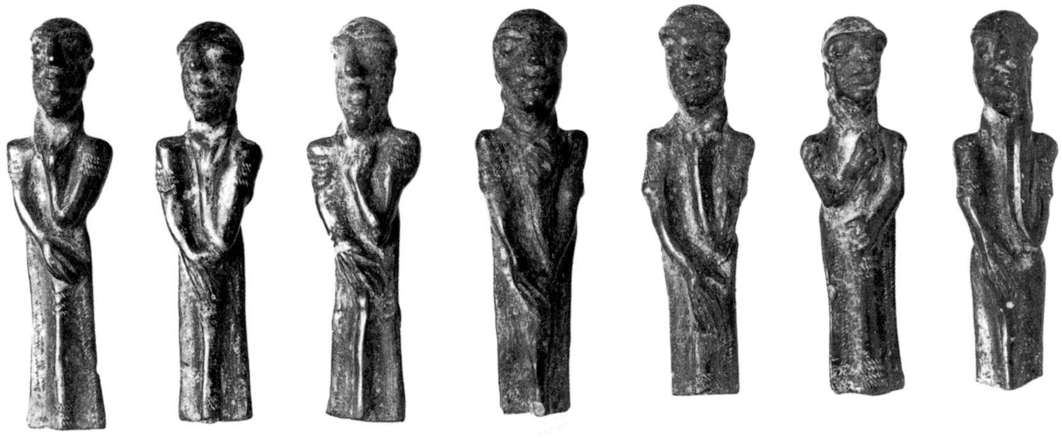

cular boxes, lion-shaped handles), amber, and bone, as well as large storage vessels of stamped impasto and fine bucchero pottery. Of the same material were thirty-three small standing figurines in long dresses, probably representing wailing women, their hands placed in various attitudes expressing grief (FIG. 60). These statuettes were found in the anteroom of the tomb around the empty bronze bedstead, on which the dead lady had presumably been lying in state in the vestibule of her house, surrounded by keening female relations, before being transferred to the tomb; the figurines thus eternalize the ritual mourning. This splendid tomb, which was built about 680–660, was later incorporated with its original tumulus into a much larger mound containing five further tombs, the most recent of which dates from the fifth century, when the eminent family to whom the site belonged probably died out.

Tarquinia: Monumental Tombs

A number of monumental chamber tombs related in plan to the Regolini-Galassi Tomb at Cerveteri were built in the first and second quarters of the seventh century at Tarquinia. Among the most significant for the chronology of the Early Orientalizing period is the Tomb of Bocchoris (*Tomba di Bocchoris*, FIG. 61), so called after an egyptianizing faience situla decorated with figures in relief (FIG. 62), including a hieroglyphic cartouche with the name of a pharaoh of the twenty-fourth dynasty, Bokenranf (Gr. Bokchoris), who ruled from 720 to 715 B.C. This imported (probably Phoenician) luxury vessel is regarded as a *terminus post quem*, not only for the other material discovered together with it, but for the whole cultural history of this period in Etruria. It is worth remembering, though, that such moldmade faience vessels in the Egyptian manner were probably reproduced over a number of years. The rock-cut tomb chamber, which was rectangular with a ridged roof and a bench along its left wall, had already been plundered when it was excavated in 1895, and there is some doubt about what was actually recovered. The remains of the rich grave goods seem to have belonged to an aristocratic lady with a pronounced taste for exotic imports, such as the egyptianizing situla,

OPPOSITE
Fig. 58 Cauldron with six attachments in the form of heads of long-necked beasts of prey. From the Regolini-Galassi Tomb, Sorbo necropolis, Cerveteri. About 650 B.C. Embossed bronze sheet with cast-bronze attachments. Diam. 45 cm. Vatican, Museo Gregoriano Etrusco 20207.

Fig. 59 Bedstead with raised headpiece. From the Regolini-Galassi Tomb, Sorbo necropolis, Cerveteri. About 650 B.C. Bronze. L. 1.87 m. Vatican, Museo Gregoriano Etrusco 15052.

ABOVE
Fig. 60 Statuettes of mourners. From the Regolini-Galassi Tomb, Sorbo necropolis, Cerveteri. About 650 B.C. Impasto. H. 9.5–10.8 cm. Vatican, Museo Gregoriano Etrusco 20374–75, 20381–82, 20402–404.

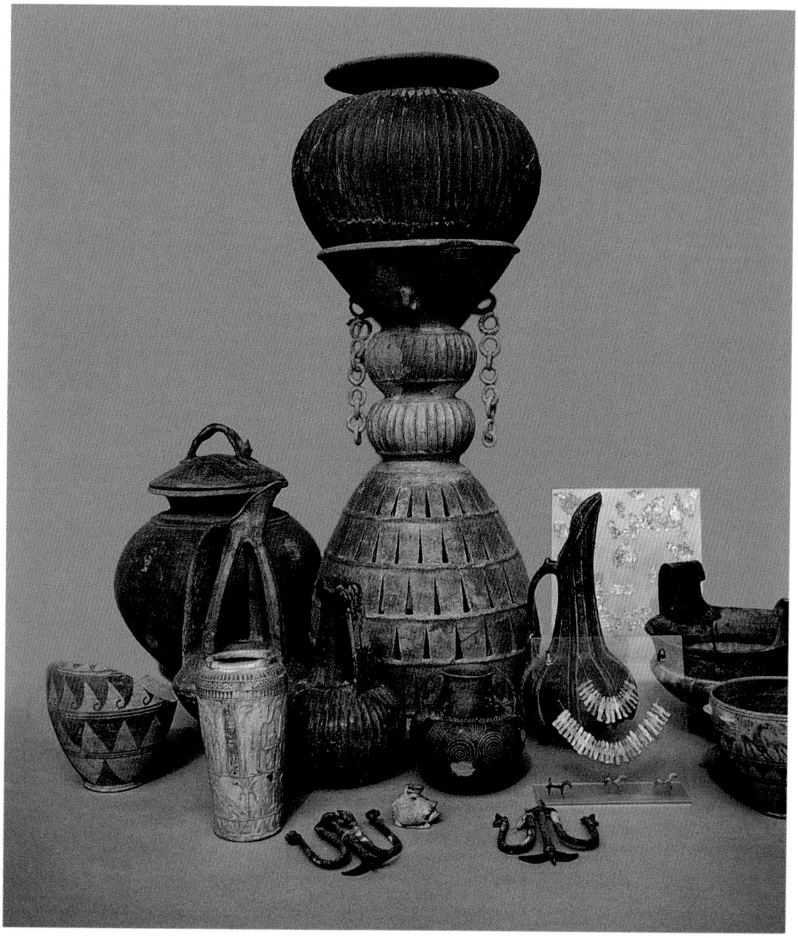

RIGHT
Fig. 61 Grave goods from the Tomb of Bocchoris, Tarquinia. Ca. 700–675 B.C.

BELOW
Fig. 62 Egyptian-style situla with molded relief decoration, including a cartouche with the name of the pharaoh Bokenranf (Bocchoris), in hieroglyphs. From the Tomb of Bocchoris, Tarquinia. Late eighth century B.C. Faience. Tarquinia, Museo Nazionale Archeologico.

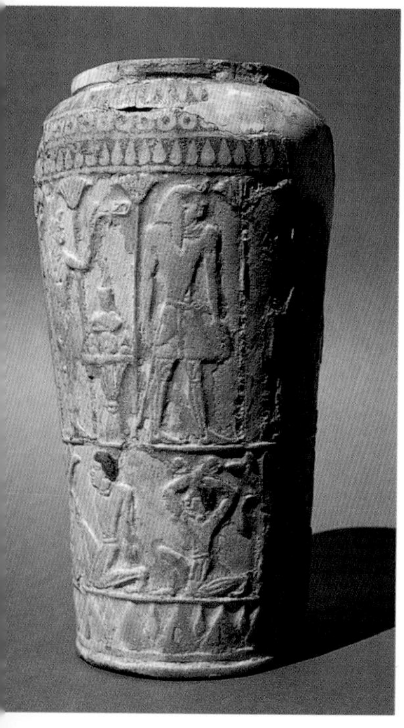

faience unguent bottles, and numerous Phoenician faience figurines that probably formed a necklace. There were two splendid tall, open-worked stands of local impasto that once supported two jars, presumably used during banquets for mixing water and wine; one of these jars is ribbed, like parts of the stands, while the second jar has a lid with a handle in the shape of a nude girl acrobat in a backward bend. Faint traces of white painted geometric ornaments and figures of helmeted warriors with round shields and three spears each survive on the latter jar. A little amphora incised with a double spiral belongs to the local pottery tradition, while a jug and cup painted in dark brown in the Etrusco-Geometric style are clearly inspired by Protocorinthian vases produced in the Euboean colony of Cumae. The lady's dress had been covered with stamped ornaments cut out from gold foil, and fragments of a pectoral and necklace have also survived. There were remains of wooden containers decorated with bronze studs, fibulae in the shape of horses, a hairpin, bronze vessels with lotus-bud handles, and ivory plaques. This splendid aristocratic burial probably dates from the first quarter of the seventh century.

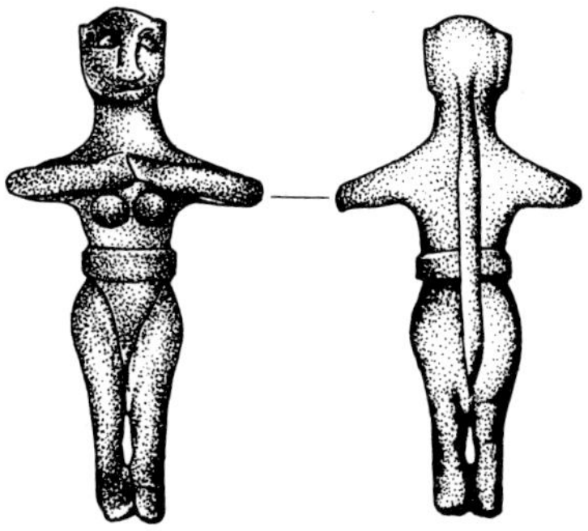

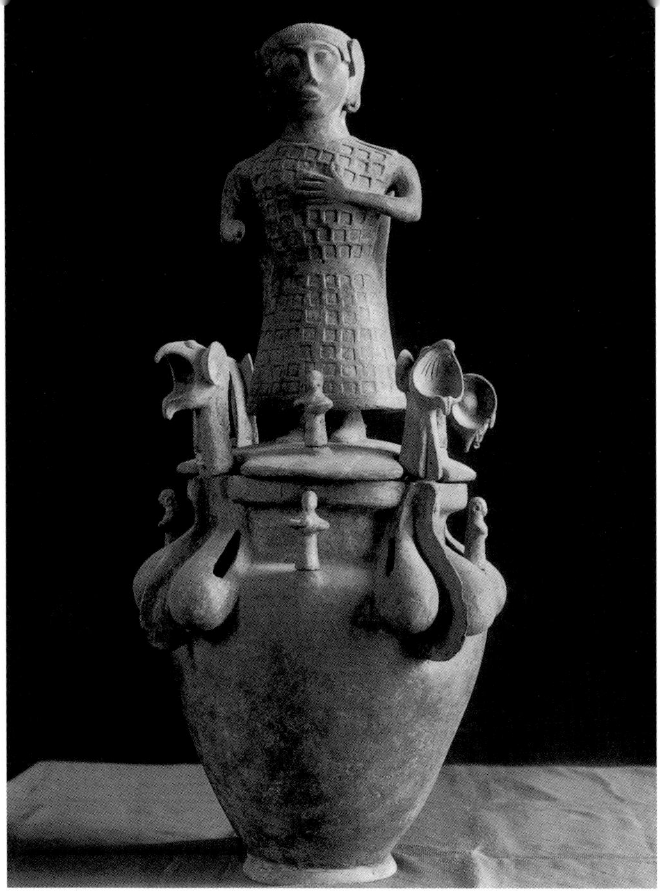

Another important tomb, discovered in 1971, is in the tumulus of Poggio Gallinaro. Its long, rectangular chamber was internally constructed of finely cut blocks of masonry with an ogival false vault supported by an axially placed row of pilasters with beveled edges. As in several other tumuli at Tarquinia (e.g., the restored Doganaccia tumulus), the exceptionally wide rock-cut dromos probably served as a kind of piazza for the performance of funerary ceremonies in front of the assembled family. The tomb had been plundered before its excavation, but interesting remains of the grave goods ranging in date from the second to the fourth quarter of the seventh century could be salvaged: besides vases of impasto, bucchero, and painted Italo-Geometric pottery, there were two models of double axes made of bucchero. As we have seen, axes were symbols of authority, and the owner of the tomb was further identified as a person of high rank by the remains of ivory spoons or plectra and of a chariot, of which iron fragments of two wheels were preserved.

ABOVE LEFT
Fig. 63 Front and back of statuette of wailing woman. From the Poggio Gallinaro tumulus, Tarquinia. Mid-seventh century B.C. Impasto. H. 7.3 cm. Tarquinia, Museo Nazionale Archeologico 101225.

ABOVE RIGHT
Fig. 64 Funerary vase with the image of the deceased on the lid surrounded by smaller figures of mourners and griffins' heads. Mid-seventh century B.C. Terracotta. Formerly Chiusi, Museo Archeologico Nazionale 63092.

Representations of Wailing Women

Among the most fascinating of the grave goods from the Poggio Gallinaro tumulus are five small, individually modeled impasto statuettes of women found at the end of the dromos in front of the walled-up entrance to the tomb's chamber (FIG. 63). They are nude but for a loincloth and belt, and they wear their long hair in a plait at the back. The women's hands are placed just above their

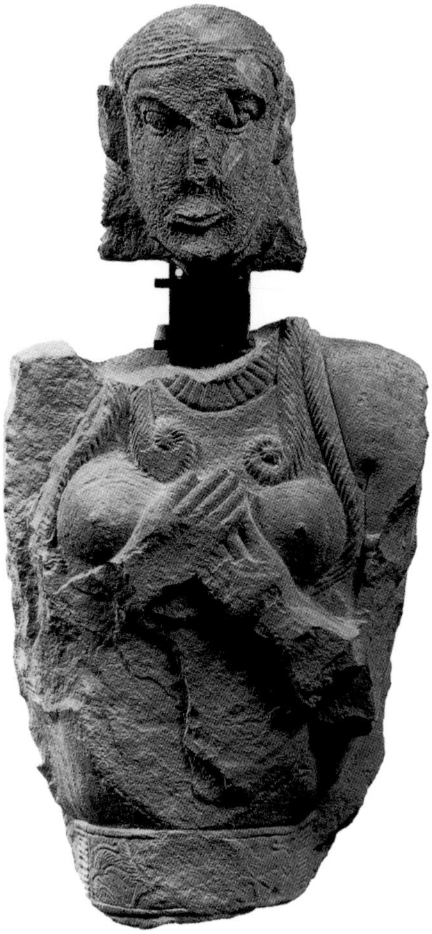

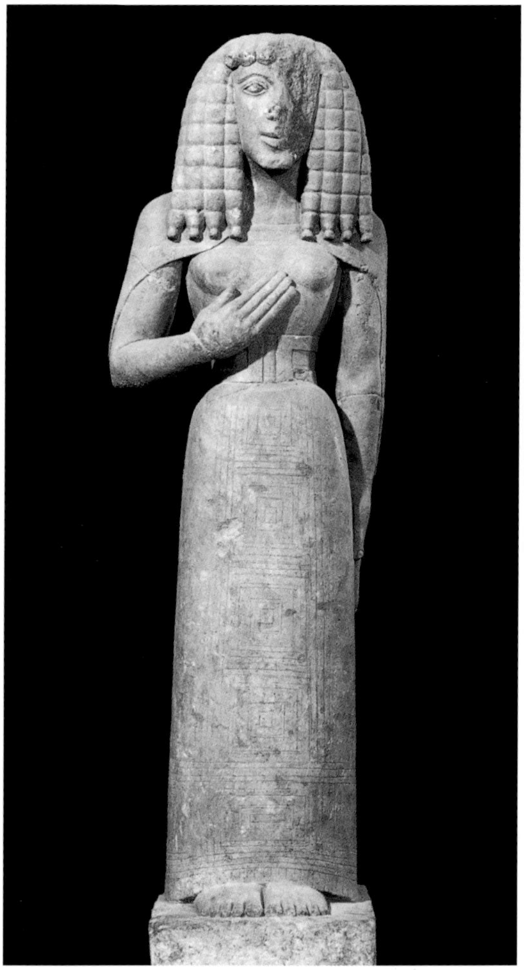

Fig. 65 Fragmentary sculpture of a woman. From the Pietrera tumulus, Vetulonia. Third quarter of seventh century B.C. Limestone. H. of head 27 cm, of bust 64 cm. Florence, Museo Archeologico 8514, 8553.

Fig. 66 Greek statuette of a woman. From Auxerre, France. Third quarter of seventh century B.C. Marble. H. 75 cm. Paris, Musée du Louvre Ma 3098.

pointed breasts with elbows out, an attitude suggesting they are beating their chests in mourning.

This gesture recurs in the small, clothed terra-cotta figurines of what must be mourners that encircle the shoulder and lid of funerary vases from tombs around Chiusi (such as the Paolozzi urn, FIG. 64). The heads of griffins that alternate with these figurines probably had apotropaic significance, while the male genitals in which their necks end below betoken regeneration. The lid is surmounted by a much larger statuette of the heroized deceased, who is characterized as a woman by her long back braid, earrings, checkered and belted dress, and rectangular back mantle.

Vetulonia: The Pietrera Tumulus

The idea of providing the dead with a perpetual chorus of male and female mourners or of ancestors received its most monumental expression in the gigantic Pietrera tumulus at Vetulonia.

This tumulus on a stone drum had a diameter of about 70 m. The main chamber, reached via a dromos flanked by side chambers, was audaciously planned (see FIG. 49). It was covered by a pseudocupola of flattish stones on corbeled corner brackets and supported by a central pillar of sandstone blocks; but the vault seems to have collapsed during its construction, for a new tomb chamber was built above the first one, which was filled in. Fragments have survived of stone bedsteads for the dead and of eight near life-size limestone sculptures of standing men and women, whose original positions in the tomb can no longer be ascertained. It has been suggested that they were placed in the dromos of the upper tomb chamber; the statues' relieflike flatness would certainly suit their placement against a wall. We cannot be certain whether they are meant to represent mourners or ancestors of the aristocrats buried here. They were probably carved in the third quarter of the seventh century.

The two best-preserved fragments, which probably belong to the same figure, are the head and torso of a woman pressing her crossed hands between her breasts (FIG. 65). Her elongated, oval face with a low forehead, large almond-shaped eyes, and a pinched mouth is framed by evenly striated hair, parted in the center. Four long, obliquely hatched tresses frame her breasts, curling up at their lower end, reminiscent of an Egyptian scheme known as "Hathor locks." Her torso appears nude but for a wide belt decorated in low relief with two heraldically opposed winged felines; but the raised edge of a short sleeve is preserved on her left upper arm, showing that she wore an almost transparent, clinging tunic, which was once distinguished by paint. A necklace of closely set, long, drop-shaped pendants adorns her neck.

In height and detailed finish the monumental mourning figures from Vetulonia surpass the earlier stone sculptures from the tomb at Ceri. The Oriental elements in their dress, jewelry, and hairstyle are unmistakable: similar necklaces and Hathor locks occur on the female heads embossed on a pair of sheet-gold and filigree bracelets from one of the peripheral tombs (Tomb IV) in the Pietrera Tumulus. There heraldically opposed winged felines are also represented, a motif that goes back to the iconographic repertory of the Early Orientalizing period.

INFLUENCE OF GREEK DAIDALIC SCULPTURE The sculptures from the Pietrera tumulus also show the first influence in Etruria of Greek Daidalic (i.e., post-Geometric monumental) art. The flatness of the statues and the women's slim, though well-proportioned bodies can be compared with the (probably Cretan) marble statuette of a woman found at Auxerre (FIG. 66). This fine work dates from the third quarter of the seventh century and represents a woman in a long skirt, a wide belt, a seemingly nude torso, her shoulders and back covered by a cape. Her right hand is placed between her breasts, the left one touches her side.

Clear evidence of Greek models also appears in an inscribed funerary stela of sandstone found at Vetulonia in the Tomb of the Warrior (*Tomba del Guerriero*),

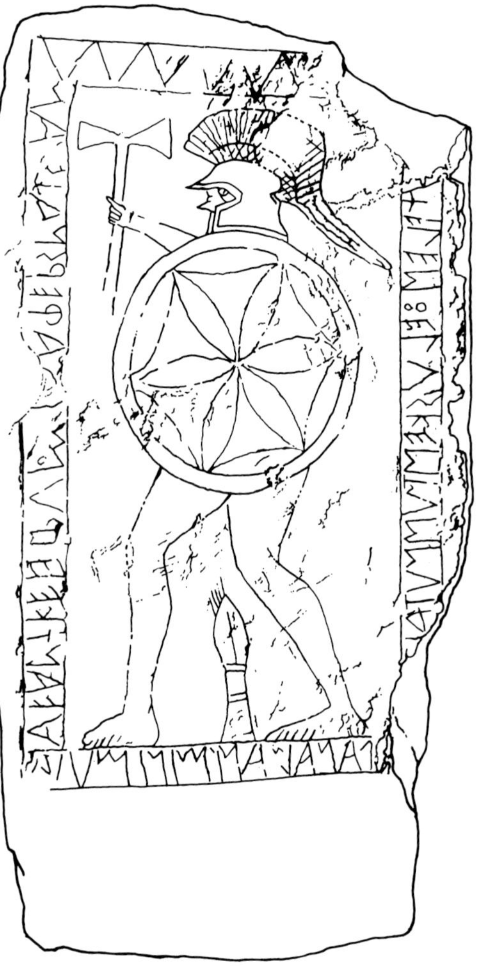

Fig. 67 Funerary stela of Avele Feluske. From the Tomb of the Warrior, Vetulonia. End of seventh century B.C. Sandstone. H. 1.07 m. Florence, Museo Archeologico 8620.

a circle grave at Le Costaccie that it presumably once surmounted (FIG. 67). Incised on the slab's rectangular surface is the figure of an aristocratic warrior striding to the left. He wears a Corinthian helmet, brandishes a double axe in his right hand, and covers his body with a round shield incised with a rosette emblem. The framing inscription (damaged in part) mentions his name, *Avele Feluske*, that of his father, *Tusnutaie*, and of his mother, . . *panai*(?), a well as that of the donor, *Hirumina* of Perugia(?). This is one of the earliest funerary inscriptions and the first known example (late seventh century) in which the name of the deceased is followed by those of both his parents. The double axe characterizes Avele Feluske as a person of great importance. It is interesting to note that from another Vetulonian burial of that period, the Tomb of the Lictor (*Tomba del Littore*), comes a miniature iron model of the fasces, the bundle of rods strapped around the shaft of a double axe. This combination of objects became the symbol of authority carried by the lictors of the consuls in Rome and, according to the ancient writer Silius Italicus (*Pun.* 8.485–87), it was from Vetulonia that Rome took over these insignia of power (also the curule chair of ivory, the purple-bordered toga, and the war trumpet, see Diod. Sic. 5.40.1).

CHANGES IN DOMESTIC ARCHITECTURE

Greek influence began to be reflected in building techniques as well as in sculpture. A significant change in the domestic architecture took place from the second quarter of the seventh century onward, when houses with a larger ground plan were erected on rectangular foundations of squared blocks of tufa; on these rested plastered walls of sun-dried bricks or of a wooden framework with rubble filling. The roofs were constructed of timber, covered with thatch or, eventually (from the third quarter of the seventh century), with terra-cotta tiles.

This stage, the transition from village to town, is accompanied by signs of urban planning and public works, such as streets, drainage channels, reservoirs, and retaining walls for terracing. Simple hut-type houses continued in use for lesser inhabitants, while the ruling families displayed their wealth and power in new architectural forms and in the use of ashlar masonry.

Such developments can be traced particularly well in the excavations of rural settlements, which have not been overlaid by subsequent building activities (as happened in big cities such as Cerveteri). They mirror, on a modest scale, phenomena that transformed the great coastal centers at that period. A good example is the settlement of San Giovenale in the hinterland of Cerveteri, where a number of aligned, rectangular buildings on the acropolis (Houses I, II, III) were excavated between 1961 and 1965. Recent reinvestigation of the site has produced a more complex architectural history of House I than was originally suspected. In its first phase the building's foundations were cut directly into the tufa rock; postholes along them suggest that the house had wattle-and-daub walls with a thatched ridge roof, as well as a frontal portico with four wooden supports at the short western end. In the inner room were pebble banks recalling those in the Tomb of the Hut. The pebbles kept rising damp—inevitable with floors of stone or beaten earth—from reaching those sitting or sleeping on the banks.

In the next phase (about 600) the walls were rebuilt with ashlar tufa blocks, the side walls being carried up to the western front. Heavy posts supporting a tiled ridge roof were placed in the main room and in the center of the western entrance.

About 550 an earthquake seems to have struck the settlement, after which House I was again altered: The western end was closed, and a new door on the north side led from a courtyard (with a well) into an anteroom.

The animal bones found on the site comprised sheep, goat, pig, cattle, horse, donkey, roe deer, dog, and turtle. It is significant that pigs were slaughtered at an early age, pointing to a pronounced taste for suckling pig, wasteful in terms of food production. Sheep and goats were more numerous than pigs, and cattle and were kept until the animals were fully grown, obviously for rational production of milk, wool, and meat. Remains of six horses and the evidence of the culinary preference for piglets indicate an aristocratic household, a conclusion already suggested by the architecture and position of these buildings on the acropolis of San Giovenale.

Six other rectangular buildings in the Borgo region of the settlement were more modest. They were likewise constructed of tufa blocks, some standing up to a height of 2 m, and there were signs of windows and doors. This was an area of artisans' dwellings with workshops, including iron- and bronzeworking.

What was perhaps a public building or sanctuary is being excavated at a bridge on the north side of the river Pietrisco. It, too, was reconstructed after the earthquake of about 550. The material from this rectangular, tufa-built structure dates from about 625–500 and includes local pottery as well as imports from other Etruscan centers and from Attica. Etruscan inscriptions and graffiti were preserved on a few bowls and cups, one naming the gods Maris and Laran. Other finds of terra-cotta consisted of braziers, cooking stands, loom weights, spindle whorls, and roof tiles. The building was equipped for dining and drinking and had a deep well and two water/wine basins.

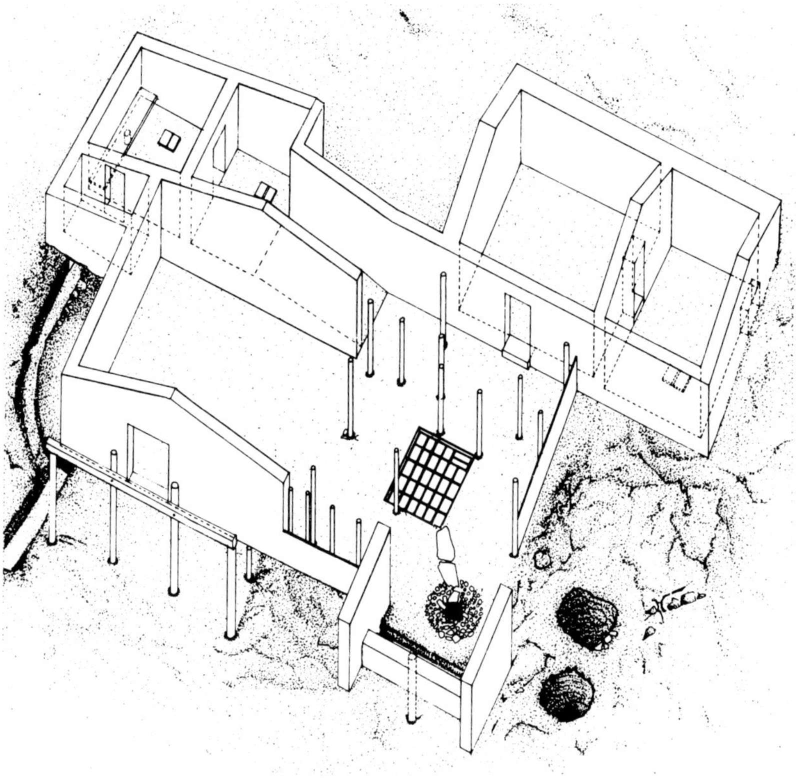

Fig. 68 Reconstruction of the House of the Impluvium at Roselle. Late seventh and second half of sixth centuries B.C.

At Roselle near Grosseto, a house of two rooms set side by side has come to light. Dating from the end of the seventh century, this small house was incorporated in the Archaic period (second half of the sixth century) into a much larger one of complex and innovative plan, mentioned here for continuity's sake (FIG. 68). In the new house the two rooms of the preexisting house became the dining room and kitchen (identified as such by fragments of Greek and local pottery from banqueting vessels in the former and a hearth and a millstone in the latter). As reconstructed by the excavators, the new house included an atrium communicating on the west with a courtyard that was open to the sky and surrounded by wooden columns. These supported the four inward-sloping sides of the roof (Lat. *compluvium*), designed so that rainwater would run into the central, shallow rectangular pool (Lat. *impluvium*) lined with terra-cotta slabs. From there the water drained into a cistern. One entered the atrium on the north through a columnar porch that was flanked on the south by a ramp/corridor leading to three small rooms forming the southeast corner of the house. Two of these rooms had a hearth of terra-cotta slabs and one also had a bench, presumably for a bed. A curved drainage channel covered with stone slabs ran underneath these rooms. In the northwestern corner of the house was a covered room containing a well with a circular wellhead of impasto. When excavated, this yielded a mass of pottery that allowed the building complex to be dated. The house, destroyed by fire in the early fifth century, contained a self-sufficient aristocratic household with its own water supply. Surrounded by fields, the household lived off its agrarian products, including plenty of meat: the bones of young bovines, pigs, goats, sheep, and deer have been identified.

The discovery of this domestic building of the second half of the sixth century that seems to incorporate an atrium and an *impluvium*, architectural features hitherto known in Italy only in Rome on the Palatine and the Via Sacra (late sixth to early fifth century), throws fresh light on the early development of the Roman house and on our scanty information on aristocratic Etruscan dwellings of the Archaic period; this reconstruction of the house is, however, not universally accepted.

Around the middle of the seventh century the entire settlement of Roselle was fortified with curving mud-brick walls. An equally impressive architectural feature in the center of Roselle is a large, rectangular mud-brick precinct, in the middle of which was an oval or apsidal building; this enclosed circular structure (tholos) was perhaps covered by a false brick vault under a thatched roof. Such an ambitious structure of unusual plan must have been a public building, probably destined for a special cult, as is suggested by the numerous fragments of pottery (one with an inscribed dedication), loom weights, spools, animal bones, and traces of a hearth found in the rear courtyard. A parallel has been drawn between this building and the circular Temple of Vesta in Rome, which was connected with the ancient residence of the king, the *regia*.

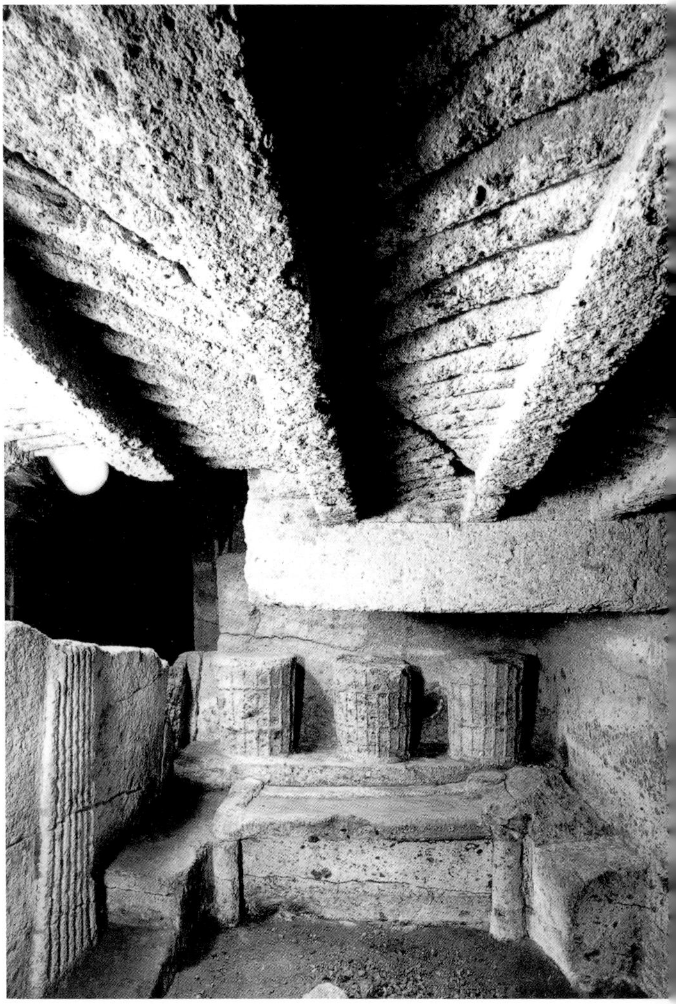

Fig. 69 Rock-carved left dromos chamber showing bed and three baskets. Campana Tomb 1, Monte Abetone necropolis, Cerveteri. Second half of seventh century B.C.

Complex Domestic Interiors Reflected in Chamber Tombs

Various types of more elaborate private dwellings, of which no actual examples have survived, are reproduced with all the intricate details of their wooden roof construction as well as with their interior fittings of pilasters, benches, beds, baskets, and other furniture in the rock-carved tomb chambers of a new series of huge grave mounds at Cerveteri—Tomb of the Painted Animals (*Tomba degli Animali Dipinti*), Campana Tomb 1 (FIG. 69)—and also at Vulci, Tomb of the Sun and the Moon (*Tomba del Sole e della Luna*, now lost), and at San Giuliano, Cima Tomb (*Tomba Cima*), dating from the second half of the seventh century. Some of the tombs at Cerveteri with their axially aligned dromos and chamber have a pavilion-like oval or round anteroom with apsidal or circular roof of fan-shaped rafters: Tomb of the Painted Animals (FIGS. 70, 71), Mengarelli Tomb, Tomb of the Crosses, Tomb of the Ship (*Tomba Mengarelli, Tomba delle Croci, Tomba della Nave*).

WALL-PAINTINGS IN TOMBS

Veii

At Cerveteri and elsewhere traces of painted decoration on the interior surfaces are preserved in a number of such tombs—Tomb of the Ship, Tomb of the Painted Lions (*Tomba dei Leoni Dipinti*), and Tomb of the Painted Animals. It is clear that wall-painting along with monumental sculpture arose in Southern Etruria in connection with the development of the rock-carved chamber tombs, whose smooth interior walls were suitable for painting.

The earliest wall-paintings to have survived are those in the Tomb of the Ducks (*Tomba delle Anatre*) at Veii (ca. 680–660), so called because of a row of five ducks (of a type known from contemporary Subgeometric painted pottery and incised impasto vessels and also referred to as "herons"). The birds appear above a frieze

Fig. 70 Plan of tomb showing the circular anteroom. Tomb of the Painted Animals 1, Cerveteri.

Fig. 71 Drawing of interior of tomb showing main chamber. Tomb of the Painted Animals 1, Cerveteri.

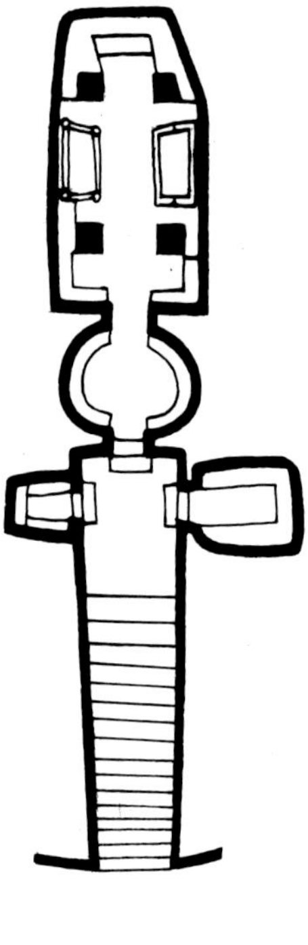

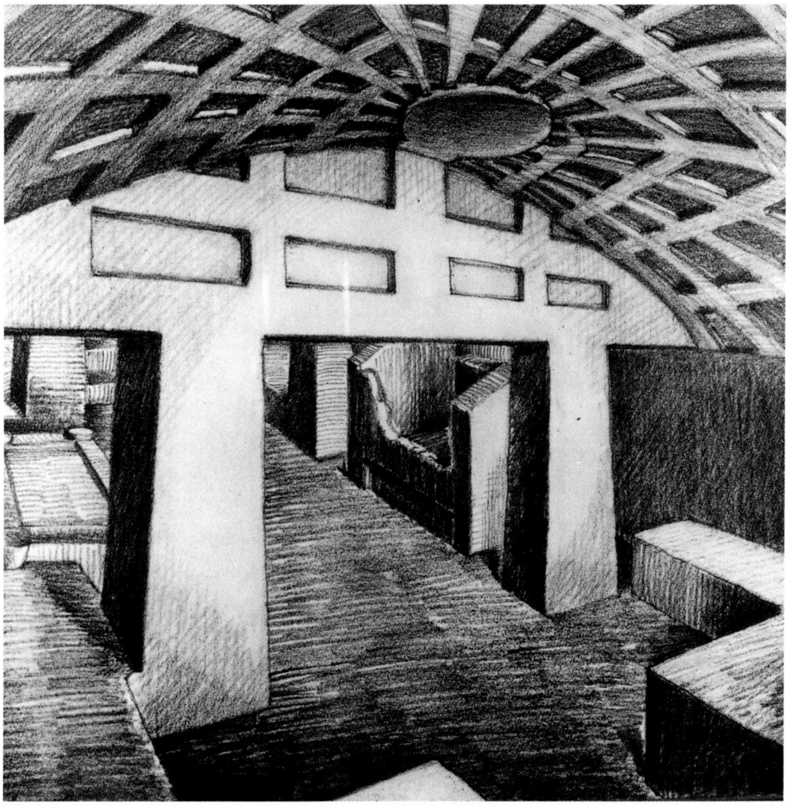

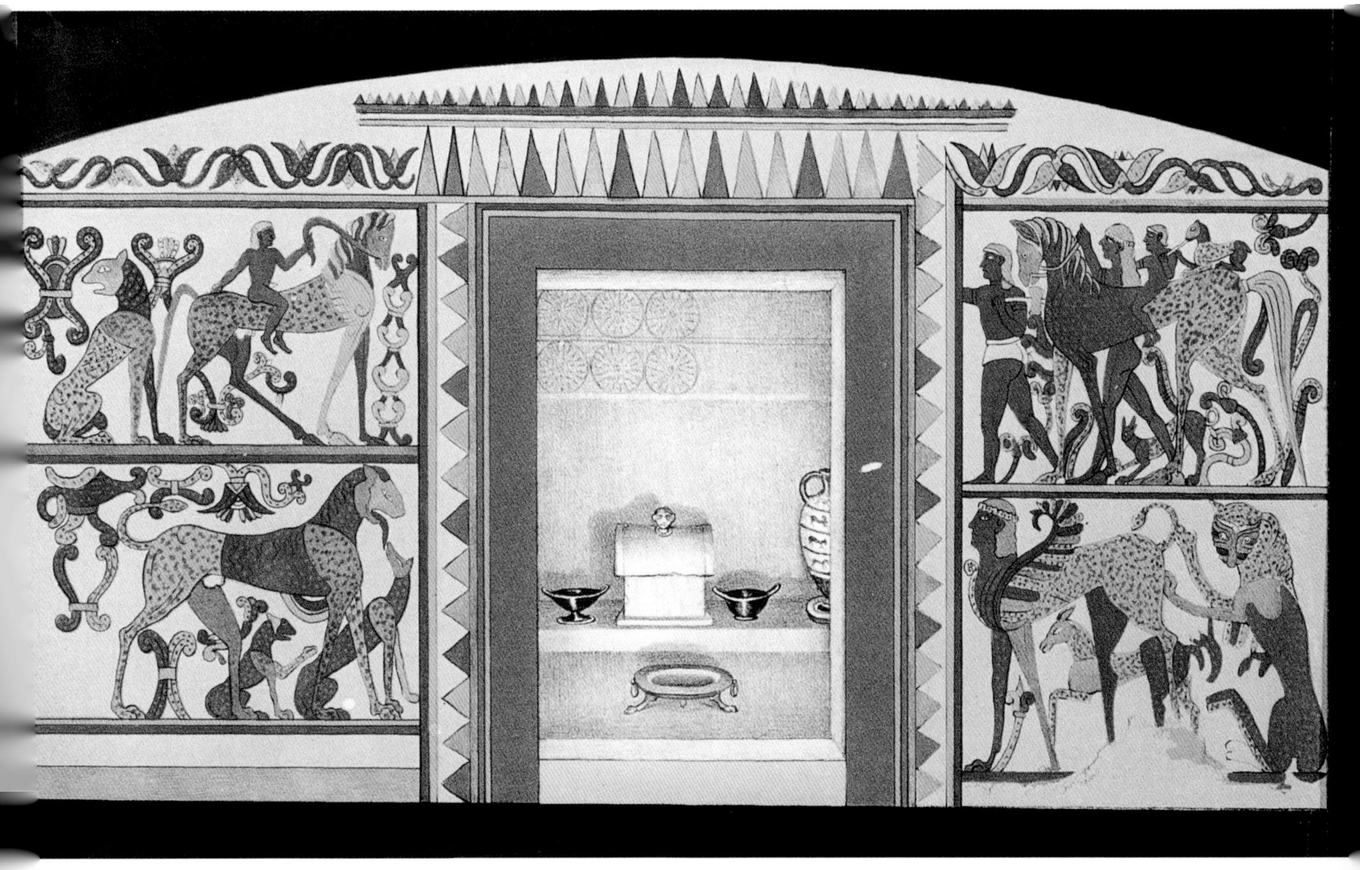

Fig. 72 Watercolor of the wall-paintings on the interior dividing wall of the Campana Tomb, Monte Michele, Veii. Date of wall-paintings about 600 B.C. (The material in the inner chamber does not belong to the tomb.)

of black, yellow, and red stripes, while the whole tomb is decorated to resemble the inside of a tent; this may reflect the custom of placing the deceased in a tent-like temporary structure for special preburial rites.

The other important painted chamber tomb in Veii is the Campana Tomb (*Tomba Campana*), at Monte Michele, which has deteriorated almost beyond recognition. Dated to about 600, the paintings decorated two axially aligned main chambers in a tumulus accessible through an open dromos with lateral chambers that led to a built facade with an arched entrance door into the first chamber. Colored drawings made after the alleged "discovery" of the tomb by the marchese Campana show two inhumations and assorted grave goods in the first room and a further array of vases and urns in the inner one. The pertinence of these objects to the tomb has, however, been doubted with good reason. But the paintings were certainly part of this aristocratic tomb and showed, on the rear wall of the first chamber, flanking the door to the inner one, two superposed rows of a tapestry-like design with geometric, animal, and floral elements and with narrative scenes (FIG. 72): horsemen, walking grooms, dogs, felines, a deer, and a sphinx. Men and long-legged beasts are of unequal size and move in a jungle of fantastic vegetation. The scene may represent the aristocratic pursuit of hunting, or perhaps the journey to the beyond of the tomb's owner. The person leading the horse carries a double axe. In some of the motifs and in style the paintings are a mixture of Cretan sculptural models and Corinthian and Etrusco-Corinthian vase-painting. The inner chamber was decorated on the rear wall only with two superposed rows of three shields, each painted with concentric circles of colored trapezoids. They undoubtedly represented the real bronze shields hung on the walls of earlier Orientalizing tombs, such as the Regolini-Galassi Tomb at Cerveteri.

Cerveteri

Cerveteri seems to have been another center where tomb-painting flourished, particularly in the middle of the Orientalizing period (670–640), though the state of preservation of the surviving tombs is very poor, the paint having been applied directly to the stone without any undercoat. Here the motifs—apart from color emphasizing the rock-carved architectural features—consist mainly of rows of lions, felines, and other quadrupeds, striding, fighting each other, or subdued by a human (or divine?) being, all perhaps endowed with apotropaic powers. Related motifs appear at Cerveteri on contemporary vases, painted in white on large red impasto vessels, and it is possible that some painters were active both on walls and on pottery.

The Tomb of the Painted Lions displays on the back wall of the right-hand chamber the image of the Master of the Animals: the Oriental motif of a god or hero holding by the mane two lions flanking him heraldically.

Among the oldest painted tombs at Cerveteri is the Tomb of the Painted Animals, decorated with two rows of fighting animals and men, inspired by Syro-Phoenician figurative prototypes, which had been adopted as early as the second quarter of the seventh century for the adornment of luxury goods of gold, ivory, and bronze. The rock-carved sarcophagus, painted with a lion and a deer, of the

Fig. 73 Funerary beds of male (left) and female (right). Tomb of the Crosses, Cerveteri. Late seventh to mid-sixth century B.C.

Fig. 74 Funerary beds of woman and child. Tomb 286 (Tomb of the Oak), Cerveteri. Late seventh to mid-sixth century B.C.

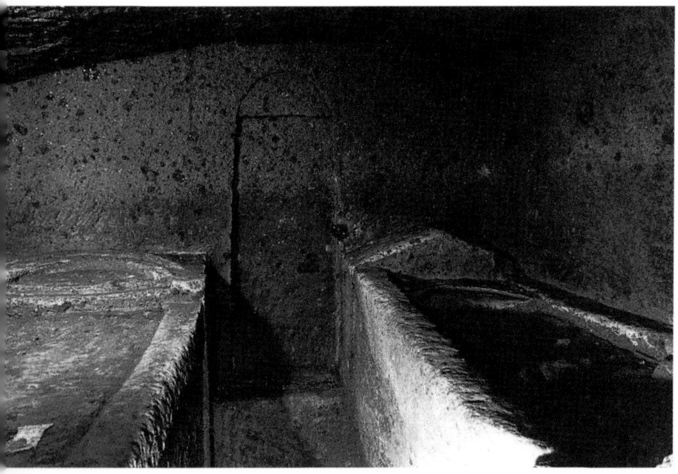

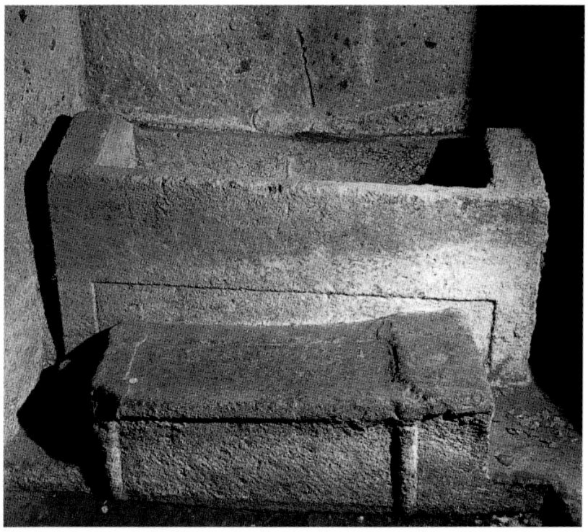

aristocratic lady buried in this tomb differs strikingly from the stone bed of the male occupant of the tomb (see FIG. 71). This important distinction in shape is characteristic for a considerable number of tombs of the Banditaccia necropolis at Cerveteri from the mid-seventh to the mid-fifth century: Whereas males were usually deposited on the left side of the tomb chamber, on a bedstead carved to simulate a real wooden bed with turned cylindrical legs, women were placed on the right side, with their beds enclosed, as it were, in a rock-carved house- or ark-shaped casing, whose short ends rise up in the form of gables (FIG. 73). The explanation of this elaborate differentiation between male beds and female "sarcophagus beds" (usually those belonging to the founder generation, located in the innermost chambers) has been sought by some in the perception of the wife and materfamilias as the mistress of the house and the guardian of the family's treasures, by others in a particular veneration of women. Occasionally a small carved bed is found beside the woman's, probably destined for a child (FIG. 74).

It seems that in the relatively few house- or ark-shaped terra-cotta urns for cremation burials of that period (the finest is the Calabresi Urn in the Vatican, Museo Gregoriano Etrusco 20825/26, of the third quarter of the seventh century) that have been excavated at Cerveteri, the associated grave goods can in some cases be ascribed to women. A number of later pottery ash chests of this type emphatically proclaim the female sex of their occupants by having a row of pendant women's breasts modeled along the lower edge of the chest, between the feet (FIG. 75).

The association of women's burials with a house-shape continued at Cerveteri even into the fourth–second century, when small, rock-carved cippi with inscriptions were placed outside some of the chamber tombs to indicate the number and sex of the people buried inside. For men, they take the form of a short column, and these far outnumber those for women, who are represented by a small house with a ridge roof.

Fig. 75 Ash urn in the form of a female sarcophagus bed. From a tomb in the Banditaccia necropolis, Cerveteri. Sixth century B.C. Terra-cotta. L. 34.5 cm. Rome, Museo Etrusco di Villa Giulia.

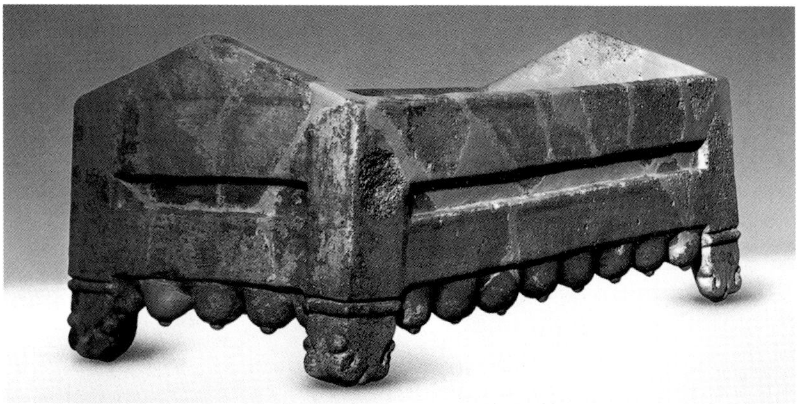

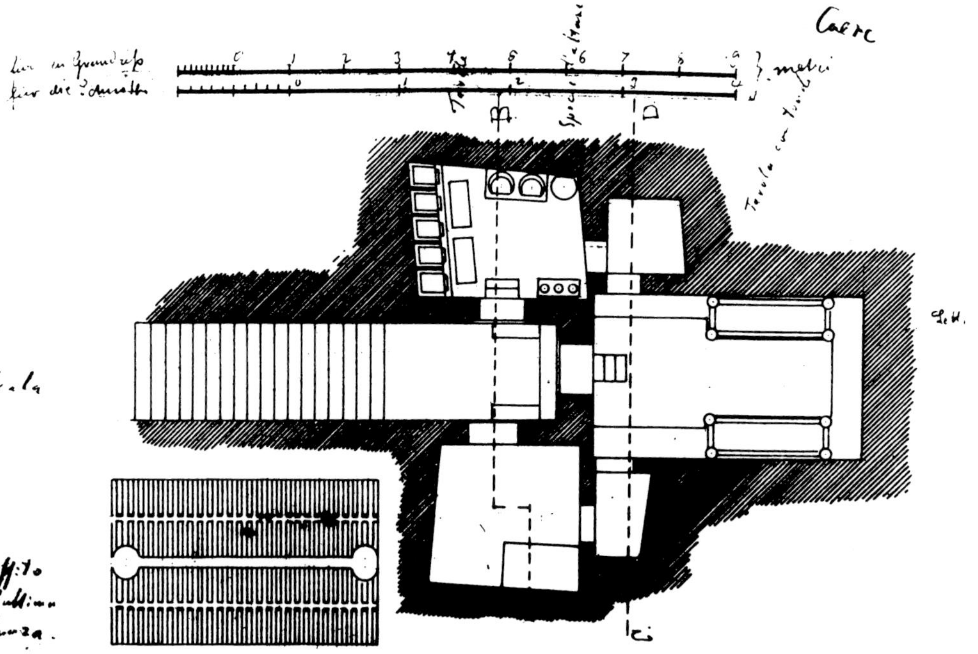

Fig. 76 Plan of the Tomb of the Five Chairs, Cerveteri. Original drawing in the Deutsches Archäologisches Institut, Rome.

THE TOMB OF THE FIVE CHAIRS Of particular interest among the rock-carved tombs of the second half of the seventh century at Cerveteri is the Tomb of the Five Chairs (*Tomba delle Cinque Sedie*), for it gives us a fascinating glimpse of the ancestor cult that was practiced in one of the chambers; this perhaps mirrors arrangements for a domestic cult of the forefathers in the vestibules of the actual houses of the great families.

Axially aligned with the main chamber, which was designed for two bodies, the entrance corridor of the tomb is flanked by lateral rooms that communicate with both the dromos and the burial chamber (FIG. 76). The left-hand wall of the side chamber on the left of the dromos is occupied by a row of five rock-carved, rectangular miniature chairs with straight backs, sloping armrests, and footstools (FIGS. 77, 78). On these seats were once enthroned five painted terra-cotta statuettes (ca. 50 cm high), of which three, those of one man (FIG. 79) and two women (FIG. 80), could be reconstituted from fragments. The surviving bodies are probably all of male figures, but two of them have been incorrectly joined to the fragmentary heads of the women.

All three statuettes are barefoot, and they wear ankle-length, short-sleeved, "plaid" tunics and diagonally draped heavy mantles of checkered material with remains of red paint. On the right shoulders the mantles are fastened by elaborate comb-fibulae, of which actual examples in gold, patterned with granulation, have been found in tombs of the second quarter of the seventh century. The women are distinguished by large hoop-earrings, which likewise have parallels in surviving gold specimens. All three figures wear wide bracelets rendered in red paint. The

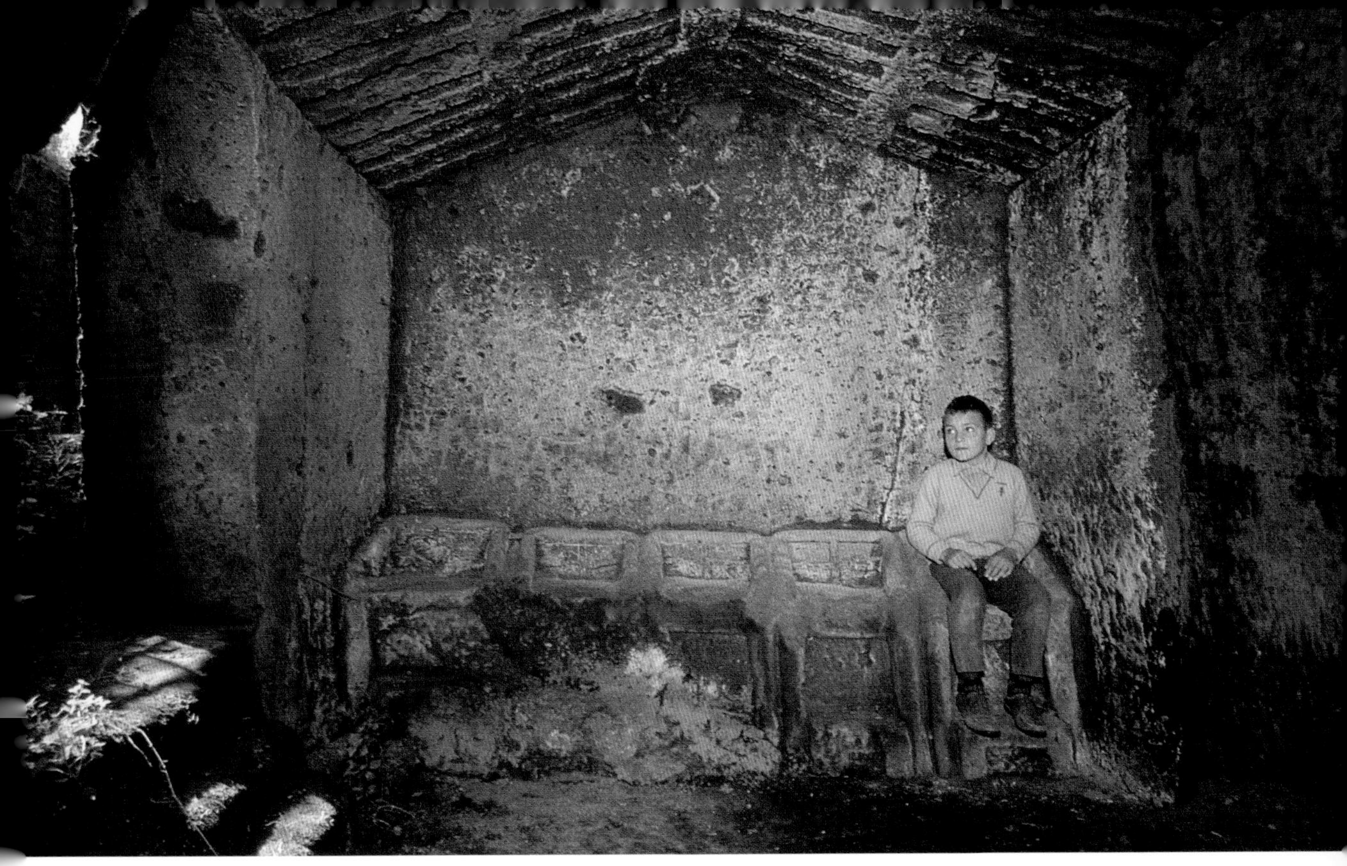

man's hair is combed back behind his ears and cut off straight at the nape; the rears of the heads of both women are missing, but their centrally parted front hair is brushed back and may have been tied or plaited in a single braid. Each statuette's left hand lies flat on the lap; the right hand—palm up—is stretched forward in a gesture as if to receive food at a banquet.

Fig. 77 View of interior of the left side chamber off the dromos showing five rock-carved seats. Tomb of the Five Chairs, Cerveteri.

The stocky, neckless bodies, the clothes, and the positions of the left arms strongly resemble the earlier stone sculptures in the Tomb of the Statues at Ceri, but unlike those, the terra-cotta statues in the Tomb of the Five Chairs convey a strong sense of vitality. Their rounded heads and features are disproportionately large, their bodies are softly modeled with virtually jointless limbs—stylistic elements that are evident in other small Etruscan terra-cotta and bronze statuettes of the second half of the seventh century.

In front of the seated figures once stood two rock-carved tables for food offerings. At the far end of the long sides of the room, opposite each other, were a cylindrical, fluted basket and a low, rectangular altar with three circular hollows for liquid libations. Side by side on a base next to the basket were two more seats with curved backrests of the same type as the wooden throne from Verucchio; these seats are thought to have been meant for the two occupants of the actual tomb chamber. The dead couple could thus, like their ancestors represented by the terra-cotta statuettes, participate in the repeated offerings made in the small cult room. This group of five male and female dining statuettes, all of the same size and sitting together in front of a table, is the earliest example so far known of a ceremonial banquet in which both sexes participate on equal terms. Dining and drinking

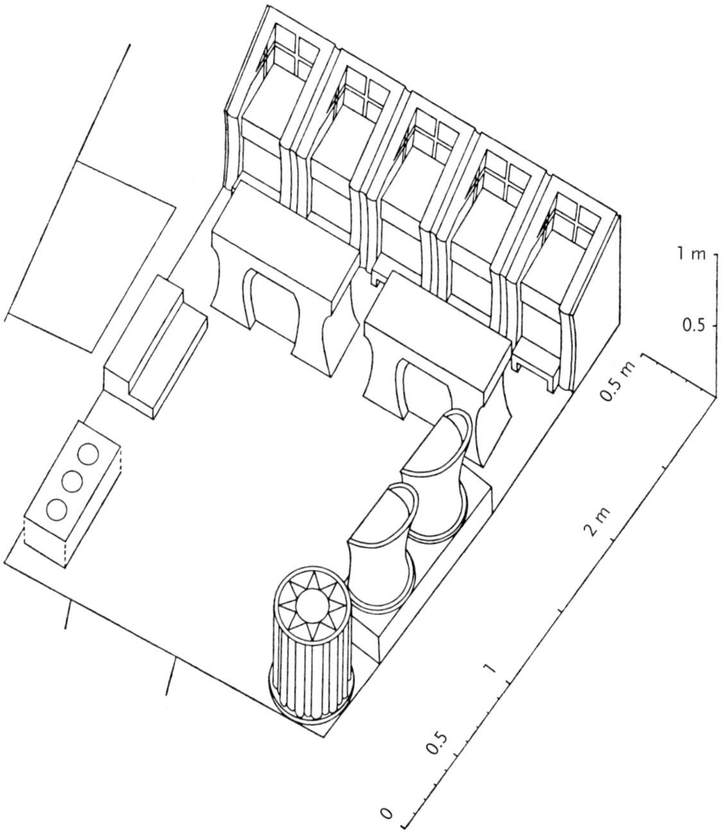

RIGHT
Fig. 78 Reconstruction drawing of the side chamber with all the features needed for the cult ceremonies: tables, basket, altar, and seats. Tomb of the Five Chairs, Cerveteri. 650–600 B.C.

BELOW LEFT
Fig. 79 Seated male figure from the Tomb of the Five Chairs, Cerveteri. 650–600 B.C. Painted terra-cotta. Rome, Musei Capitolini.

BELOW RIGHT
Fig. 80 Seated female figure from the Tomb of the Five Chairs, Cerveteri. 650–600 B.C. Painted terra-cotta. H. 58 cm. London, The British Museum D 219.

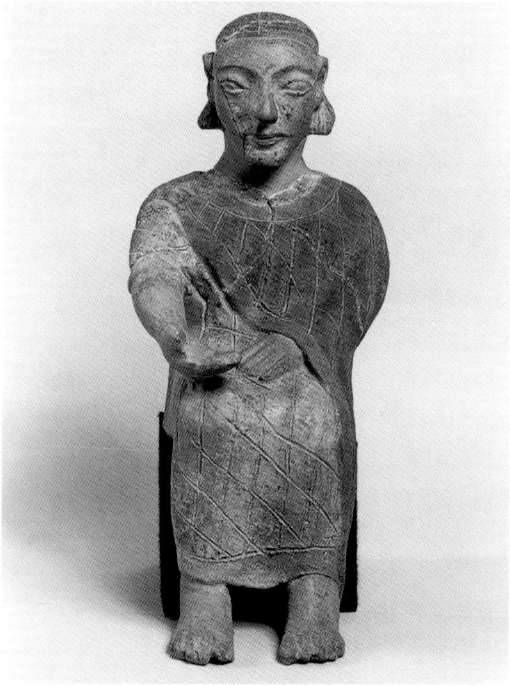

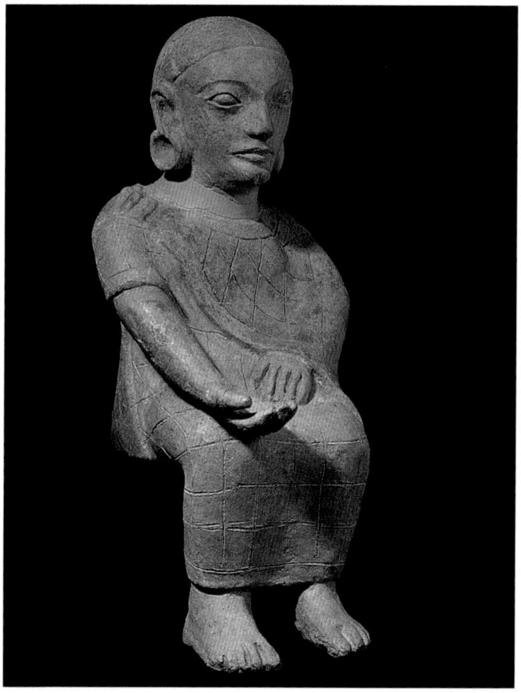

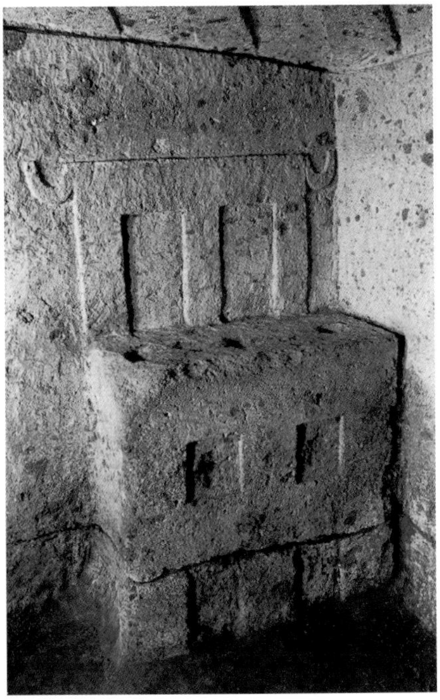

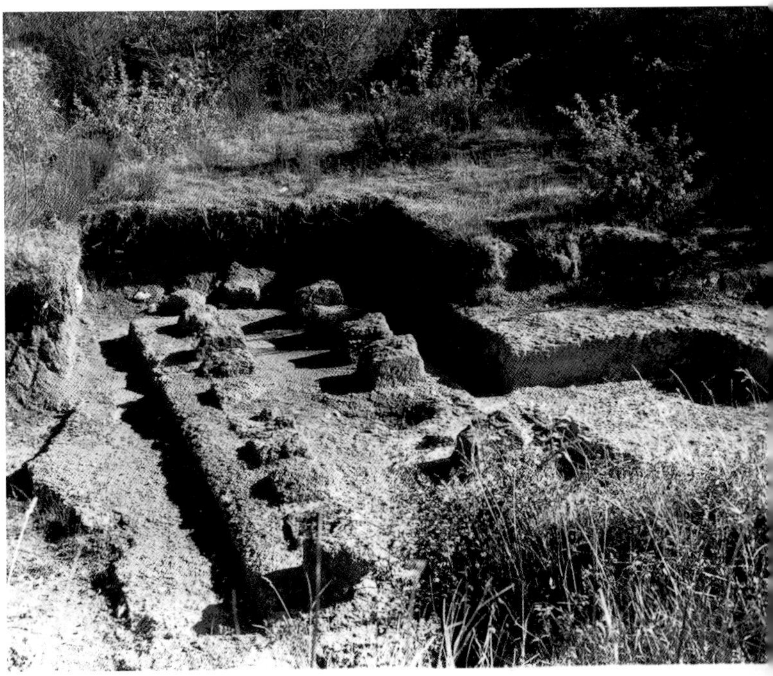

in a reclining position on beds is, as we have seen, a Near Eastern custom, adopted during the seventh century, that became widespread in Greece and, at a slightly later stage, in Etruria, largely replacing the custom of eating in a sitting position.

Fig. 81 Rock-carved altar with tall open-worked back and three hollows for offerings. From the main chamber of Campana Tomb 1, Monte Abetone necropolis, Cerveteri. Second half of seventh century B.C.

Fig. 82 Rock-carved rectangular platform with stumps of cippi outside the Cima Tomb, San Giuliano. Second half of seventh century B.C.

ALTARS

An altar with hollows to receive libations, resembling that in the Tomb of the Five Chairs but with an additional tall, open-worked back, has survived in the Campana Tomb 1, at Cerveteri (FIG. 81). Similar indications of cult practices connected with the tomb are found in the splendidly carved and partially painted interior of the tumulus of the Cima Tomb at San Giuliano. Beside an altar table for offerings in a big room off the dromos, there is, outside the tumulus, a long rectangular platform, carved from the rock (FIG. 82). Surmounted by the square stumps of seventeen (originally obelisk-shaped?) cippi arranged in two parallel rows, this platform has a large circular depression in the center, which probably once contained a separately carved round cippus, perhaps connected with the founder of the gens. Whether this monumental cult place dates to the last third of the seventh century, like the Cima Tomb itself, is not easy to establish, but it is an impressive document for the performance of religious practices next to a tumulus that must have been the center of the ancestor cult of an important local family. Complete obelisk-shaped cippi are preserved in the museum at Barbarano Romano and in the Palazzo della Corgna at Città della Pieve above the Chiana valley. Such cippi are represented surmounting funerary monuments of the Hellenistic period on ash urns from Volterra and have actually survived on the Tomb of the Horatii and Curiatii (*Tomba degli Orazi e Curiazi*), erected in the Late Republican period at Albano near Rome. These examples show the long life of such symbolic features. The Roman author Pliny describes a monumental tomb with obelisks belonging to the Chiusine king Porsenna (*NH* 36.19.91–93).

WOMEN AND WINE

Along with the other forms of banqueting borrowed from the Greeks, the Etruscans may have taken over the Greek custom of mixing wine with water for drinking parties, but we do not know this for sure. Significant information on the types of pottery used by aristocratic women during the third quarter of the seventh century was gained in the excavation of a rock-carved chamber tomb at Cerveteri, named after its painted decoration the Tomb of the Dogtooth Frieze (*Tomba dei Denti di Lupo*). Prominent architectural features of the eastern chamber, such as its corners and the flat ridge plank of the roof (Lat. *columen*), had been picked out in paint with bands of red and black triangles (the dogtooth frieze); on the ornamental discs at each end of the *columen* appeared the figure of a rampant lion. Although the whole tomb had been extensively plundered, the room contained one funerary bed and a great deal of pottery, both imported and locally made. Two specimens of the latter were incised with the name of the owner, which identified this chamber as the tomb of a woman.

The inscriptions are on the shoulders of two widemouthed vessels of red impasto with two horizontal handles. One of them reads: *mi pupai(a)s thina karkanas*, the other: (*mi*) *pupaias karkanas thina*. The praenomen and nomen of the aristocratic lady are in the genitive, while the "speaking" object is in the nominative: I (am) the thina of Pupaia Karkana. The word *thina* is from the Greek *dinos*, which describes a large bowl for wine, usually placed on a tall stand. The vessel called a *thina* seems typically to have been associated with women in Etruria and in the Faliscan area; perhaps it was the successor of the traditional biconic water container. When put on a conical stand (Gr. *holmos*) for the banquet, the *thina* probably became the krater for mixing wine and water. The word *dinos* appears to have been taken over by the Etruscans in the second half of the seventh century, together with the habit of lying on couches when dining and drinking. It is of great interest to find that an Etruscan lady owned two vessels used for dispensing wine.

This is not an isolated case as proved by a similar vessel of red impasto from a tomb in the Laghetto necropolis of Cerveteri, dated to about 630; a graffito on its shoulder reads: *mi squrias thina mlach mlakas*. The *dinos* belonged to a lady called Squria. We may remember, too, that the lady buried in the Bocchoris Tomb in

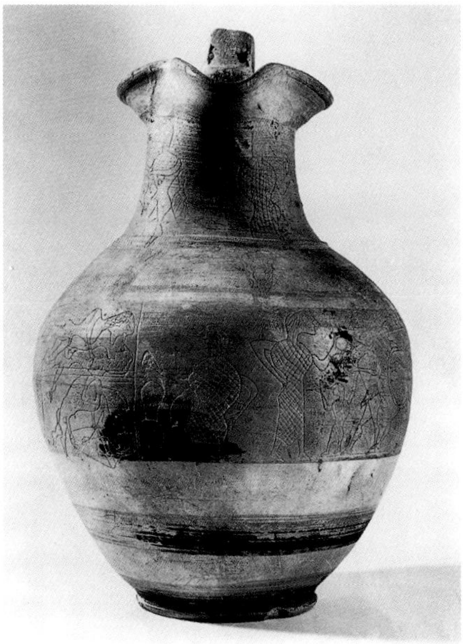

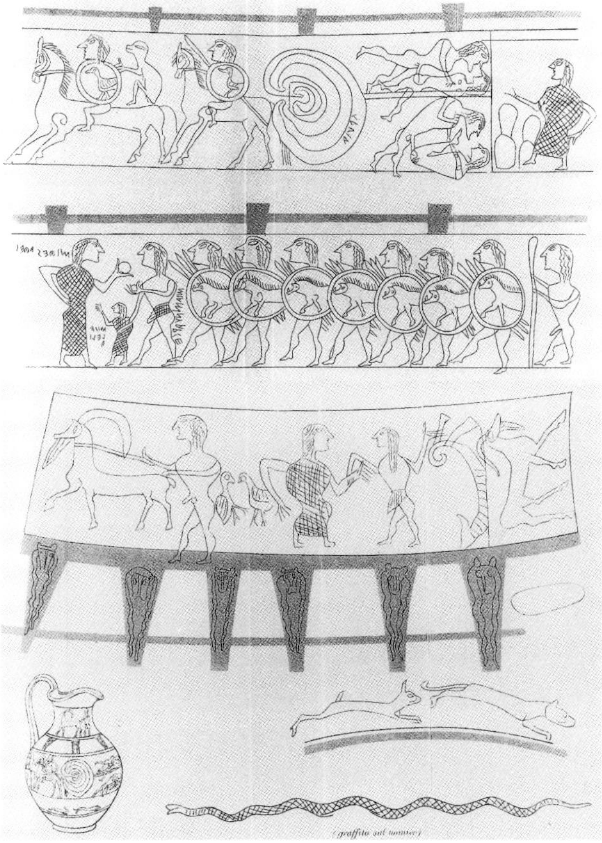

Fig. 83a Etrusco-Corinthian jug with incised friezes. From Tragliatella, near Cerveteri. 630–600 B.C. Painted pottery. H. 24 cm. Rome, Musei Capitolini 358.

Fig. 83b Incised friezes on jug, figure 83a.

Tarquinia was accompanied by two globular vessels on tall stands. As we shall see, Etruscan wives (in marked contrast to the custom at Athens and early Rome) participated in banquets together with men and enjoyed wine, a practice that incurred the strong opprobrium of later Greek and Latin writers. For lack of pictorial evidence it is difficult to decide whether, during the Orientalizing period here under discussion, Etruscan ladies were already equal drinking partners of men, but the fact that they could own the vessels in which wine and water were mixed must imply that they were intimately connected with the occasions on which wine was consumed. We may reach the same conclusion about the grave gifts that accompanied the lady buried in Tomb IV of the Monte Abetone necropolis at Cerveteri (see p. 61), among which were three transport amphorae as well as East Greek and Etruscan drinking vessels.

THE JUG FROM TRAGLIATELLA

Fine painted pottery in Southern Etruria had by 630 B.C. developed a figurative repertory that mixed Greek (Corinthian) prototypes with local features. A striking example is a jug found in 1877/1878 in a chamber tomb at Tragliatella in the hinterland of Cerveteri (FIG. 83a). This oinochoe, which belongs to the Etrusco-Corinthian Polychrome group of vases of about 630–600, retains remnants of brown paint and is incised with two figured friezes in a crude, but vigorous style. The following figures appear on the neck of the jug (FIG. 83b): a nude man holding a large goat on a lead; two heraldically opposed birds; a couple facing each other; a ship that, perhaps for lack of space, has been drawn tipped up on its prow at a right angle to the groundline; and, finally, another goat in the same tilted position.

The longer frieze on the belly of the jug is divided by a vertical line. To the left of this line lie two nude couples in amorous embraces, one pair incised above the other as if in bunk beds. Next to them on the left is a circular maze drawn in plan and inscribed in the outermost of its seven convolutions with the word *Truia* = Troia. Seemingly emerging from this labyrinth are two horsemen, both carrying round shields with the emblem of a bird; the hindmost rider is armed with a spear, the front one has a monkey crouching on the croup of his horse. They are preceded by a file of seven hoplites, each stepping out rhythmically, armed with three javelins and with the forepart of a boar as shield emblem. The rear is brought up by a nude man holding a stout staff with both hands. Beyond the detachment of warriors stands a couple facing each other with a small girl between them. Behind the man's back is his name written in a vertical line: *mi ammarce* = I (am) Ammarce. (It is likely that the name is a misspelling for the well-known Etruscan name Mamarce.) In his raised left hand he holds out a fruit or an egg to the woman, while his other hand rests on the shoulder of the girl in front of him. The girl's name appears in three horizontal lines in front of her: *mi velelia* = I (am) Velelia. The woman, whose name, *mi thesathei* = I (am) Thesathei, is written behind the nape of her neck, was probably called Thesanthei (after Thesan, the Etruscan goddess of Dawn). She proffers a large round object to the man. The frieze concludes with a woman facing to the left, away from this group; with her right hand raised, she approaches two objects, each consisting of two superposed irregular ovals, perhaps indicating high-backed chairs. On the foot of the vase are a running hare and hound.

Widely diverging interpretations have been suggested for these singular and enigmatic scenes, none of them wholly consistent or convincing. There is a certain amount of agreement in taking the couple next to the ship as illustrating the Greek myth of Theseus and Ariadne: After slaying the Minotaur in the Cretan labyrinth and thus rescuing his Athenian companions from death with the help of the thread of Ariadne, the daughter of King Minos, Theseus fled with her and the other youths and maidens by ship to Naxos. Here he abandoned Ariadne and sailed with his companions to Delos, where they performed a complex dance in memory of the labyrinth of Minos. Recent studies likewise explain the main frieze of the jug by this myth, which, it is claimed, is here ritually reenacted by an Etruscan aristocrat identifying himself with Theseus.

The careful naming of the figures of Ammarce (who puts his hand protectively on the shoulder of the small Velelia) and of Thesa(n)thei, who offers a gift to Ammarce, suggests that the protagonists of the whole design are a family group.

It has been proposed that like the Plikaśna "situla" (see FIG. 90) the design of the jug was commissioned by a client, probably Ammarce, the head of an aristocratic local family, who wanted the main interests and episodes of his life depicted on the frieze. The representation of lovemaking is relatively rare in Etruscan vase-painting, and the double symplegma here is puzzling. As a tentative explanation I would suggest that Ammarce was married twice and wanted to record his union with both his wives. The maze named Truia, rather than standing for Homer's city of Troy with its circuit of seven walls and the myths associated with it, may allude to the *lusus Troiae*, the game of horsemanship performed by young men and described in Vergil's *Aeneid* (5.545ff.). The two riders may be sons of Ammarce engaged in this (initiation?) ceremony. The scene of the couple beside a ship and a goat probably depicts Ammarce as a wealthy sea trader dealing in livestock, taking leave of or being greeted by his wife. Ships transporting animals are found on other vases of this period. The exchange of gifts between the couple in the main frieze forms part of the aristocratic way of life, as do horsemanship and the display of armed followers for warlike raids. Hunting, hinted at by hare and hound, is another traditional aristocratic pursuit. The snake on the jug's handle is connected with the underworld and death (chthonic) and thus points to the funerary destination of the vessel.

Such an interpretation of the friezes relies more on known Etruscan usage than on purely Greek mythological or modern structuralist concepts. We shall see that throughout Etruscan history, when artistic models were taken over from Greece, they were often endowed with a significance subtly different from their original meaning and, in the absence of any surviving Etruscan literature, we cannot be certain about the precise semantic content that such scenes held for the Etruscan borrowers.

TOMBS IN NORTHERN ETRURIA

Vetulonia

In the necropolises of Vetulonia the characteristic form of aristocratic burials during the Early Orientalizing period was the trench tomb. Dug into the ground and lined with stone slabs, it contained inhumations or cremated remains. Groups of large trenches were often enclosed within continuous circles (It. *circoli continui*) of carefully worked stone slabs; the circles vary from 15 to 30 m in diameter. Such tombs frequently contained extremely rich grave goods of bronze, gold, silver, ivory, amber, etc., including many objects of Southern Etruscan, Near Eastern, Greek, Sardinian, and Central European origin.

From the seventh-century Circle of Bes (*Circolo di Bes*), so called after a faience amulet of the Egyptian and Phoenician divinity Bes discovered there, also came a faience figure of Ptah, scaraboids, and female figures carved in amber.

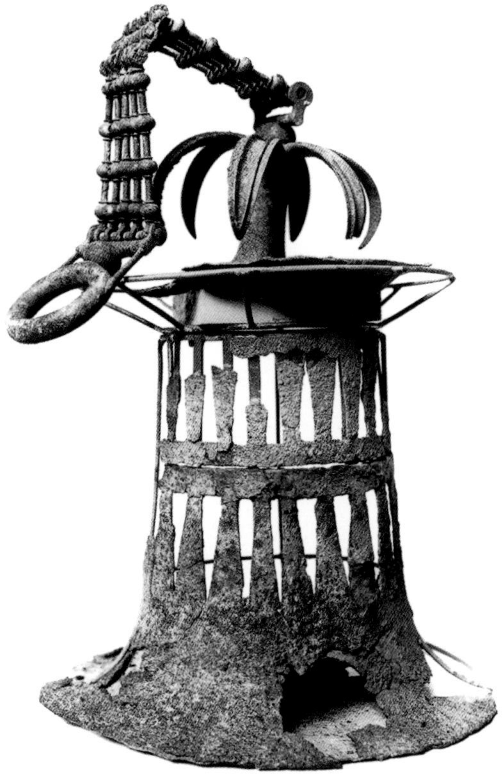

Fig. 84 Censer with mobile handle. From Vetulonia. Mid-seventh century B.C. Cast and hammered bronze. Florence, Museo Archeologico 8596.

Besides finished exotic goods, precious raw materials, such as ivory from the Near East and amber from the Baltic, were imported and carved at Vetulonia into beads and pendants (amulets?) for necklaces, as is proved by unworked lumps found there. The most conspicuous collection of carved amber was discovered in the Circle of the Jewelry (*Circolo dei Monili*) at Poggio alla Guardia, which yielded eleven female figurines with their hands placed on the abdomen, a seated women with a small figure between her legs (a child or a monkey?), several monkeys, a fish, and a scaraboid.

An interesting example of the diverse cultural influences that flowed together in Vetulonia is a cup from the second half of the seventh century found in the Tomb of the Leader (*Tomba del Duce*). The silver-gilt cup is shaped like the two-handled Greek drinking vessel, but it is decorated with incised friezes directly inspired by Oriental (Phoenician) prototypes.

The most prolific local industry was, however, metallurgy, based on the rich metal mines of the hinterland (FIG. 84). The tombs abound in bronze utensils, such as incense burners and household goods, often decorated with cast figurative adjuncts in the form of human beings and monkeys, comparable in style to the amber pendants.

During the later part of the seventh and the early sixth centuries monumental tumuli with tomb chambers covered by false vaults, such as the Pietrera and the Diavolino Tombs (*Tomba del Diavolino 1, 2*), became the fashion. The system of construction of the chamber of the Pietrera Tomb, with its central pillar of ashlar blocks supporting the false vault, is found also in the tholos tombs of Quinto Fiorentino, Casale Marittimo, and Casaglia in northern Tuscany, which belong to the early sixth century.

Populonia

Situated opposite the island of Elba, Populonia was favored by the only natural port, the Gulf of Baratti, on the whole of the Tyrrhenian coast. Like Vetulonia, Populonia flourished as a result of the exploitation of the rich copper mines in its own hinterland, the Campigliese, and—from the second half of the sixth century onward—also by smelting the iron ore from Elba, the island's native supply of wood having been exhausted. Huge slag mounds resulting from the relatively inefficient ancient extraction methods were in antiquity deposited on the shores of the Gulf of Baratti. During the first half of the twentieth century these mounds were removed by Italian metallurgists for reprocessing, which led to the discovery, beneath the ancient debris, of the comparatively well-preserved necropolises of the Orientalizing and Archaic periods belonging to the city of Populonia, which had once occupied the hill above the bay.

Here monumental chamber tombs with false vaults, constructed within a cylindrical masonry drum surmounted by a tumulus, had replaced the earlier trench tombs by the second quarter of the seventh century. In the latter type of tomb the drum rested on an outward-sloping stone pavement and was crowned by a projecting row of horizontal slabs that served as eaves to drain the rainwater away from the base of the drum. Occasionally a rectangular porch jutted out from the drum where the entrance to the dromos was situated, and in some cases upright stone stelae were erected outside. The dromos was roofed by horizontal stone slabs and was usually flanked by small side cells for grave goods. The tomb chamber was square or rectangular and had a false vault with corbeled corner brackets. Constructed from well-fitted stone slabs, the funerary beds sometimes had at their corners small molded stone columns imitating the turned wooden legs of actual bedsteads. There seems to have been no distinction in form between men's and women's beds, such as could be observed at Cerveteri.

These tombs at Populonia were in use over several generations, and many of the chambers were robbed of their grave goods already in antiquity. But treasures hidden in the side cells of the dromoi sometimes escaped depredation.

TOMB OF THE CHARIOTS Such was the case with the Tomb of the Chariots (*Tomba dei Carri*) in the necropolis of San Cerbone, dated by the finds to between the middle of the seventh and the early sixth centuries (FIG. 85). With a diameter of 28 m, it is one of the largest of the princely tombs of the mid-Orientalizing period at Populonia; it contained funerary beds for at least four occupants. Of women's objects only two spherical gold pendants and a gold leech-shaped fibula had survived, in the main chamber, while in the unplundered side cells off the dromos were discovered the possessions of the buried males, most important among them the remains of a chariot and a two-wheeled carriage.

The oak wheels of the carriage are unique in having two fellies, an outer one, covered with an iron hoop, and an inner one, halfway between the outer edge of the wheel and its bronze-and-iron hub. The wooden parts, including the spokes, have not survived, but they could be reconstructed because they were originally covered with well-preserved sheet-bronze pieces, cut to shape and fastened to the wood with nails.

The chariot (Lat. *currus*) had slightly smaller wheels with eight spokes and iron hoops (FIG. 86). Of the U-shaped wooden box, surviving fragments of decorative bronze plaques, originally attached to the leather-covered front and lateral parapets, are of particular interest for being inlaid with iron figures of files of walking animals and of hunters armed with lances; floral motifs recall Cypro-

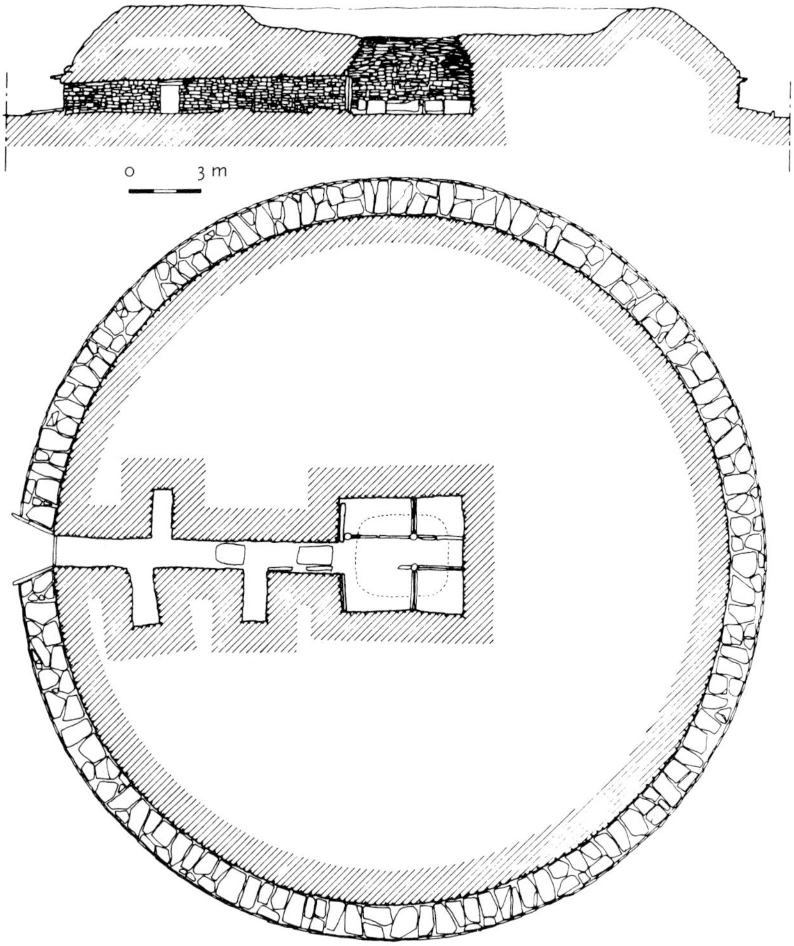

Fig. 85 Plan and section of the Tomb of the Chariots, Populonia.

Phoenician models. This rare combination of iron-and-bronze inlay is found also in a few ornamental cast-bronze buckles from Murlo, Castellina in Chianti, and Castelnuovo Berardenga; a workshop for bronzes thus decorated must have existed in Northern Etruria, probably in Populonia itself. The technique was used in the Caucasus region as early as the eighth century.

Taken over from the Near East by the aristocracy in Etruria for transport, warfare, and racing from the mid-eighth century B.C., chariots (bigas and, more rarely, trigas and quadrigas) as well as carriages became status symbols and eventually purely ceremonial vehicles: they served to parade the social rank of their owners in triumphal and other processions and were finally deposited in tombs. Of the surviving remains of over 250 chariots in Italy, Etruria has yielded far more examples than Piceno, Lazio, and Umbria. This proves the overwhelming importance attached to such vehicles by the Etruscans.

A further notable item found in the Tomb of the Chariots at Populonia was an ivory horn encircled by silver-gilt bands with a decoration of wild animals

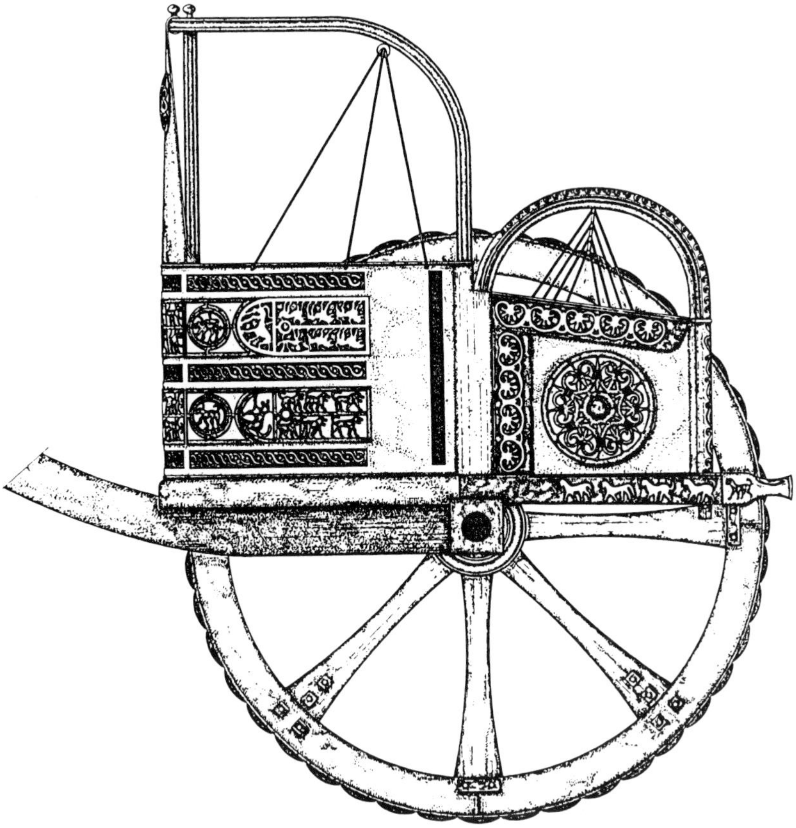

Fig. 86 Chariot from the Tomb of the Chariots, Populonia.

and human beings among floral elements—motifs inspired by the "Cypro-Phoenician" precious-metal cups found in contemporary Etruscan princely burials. A second horn, made of bronze, must have served as a war trumpet. There was also an ivory-handled knife, a belt clasp, horse bits, an axe, the iron points of javelins and arrows, and a Punic oil lamp of pottery.

TOMB OF THE BRONZE FANS A smaller, but extraordinarily richly furnished tomb of the same type, the Tomb of the Bronze Fans (*Tomba dei Flabelli di Bronzo*), was found intact (FIG. 87). Although it contained only two bedsteads (their headboards covered with sheet bronze), remains could be identified of four burials that took place between 630–620 and 570–560. To the latest phase must be ascribed that of a woman deposited on the left-hand bed, where gold jewelry and precious objects were discovered. These included a gold ring with an oval bezel embossed with a mythological scene (Herakles subduing Nereus?), probably of Vulcian workmanship; a gold leech-fibula of the same type as that found in the Tomb of the Chariots; hair spirals of gold wire; and earrings of *bauletto* type. The latter are made of rectangular plaques of sheet gold, bent to form a cylinder, open at the ends, and provided with wires for insertion through the earlobes; enriched with

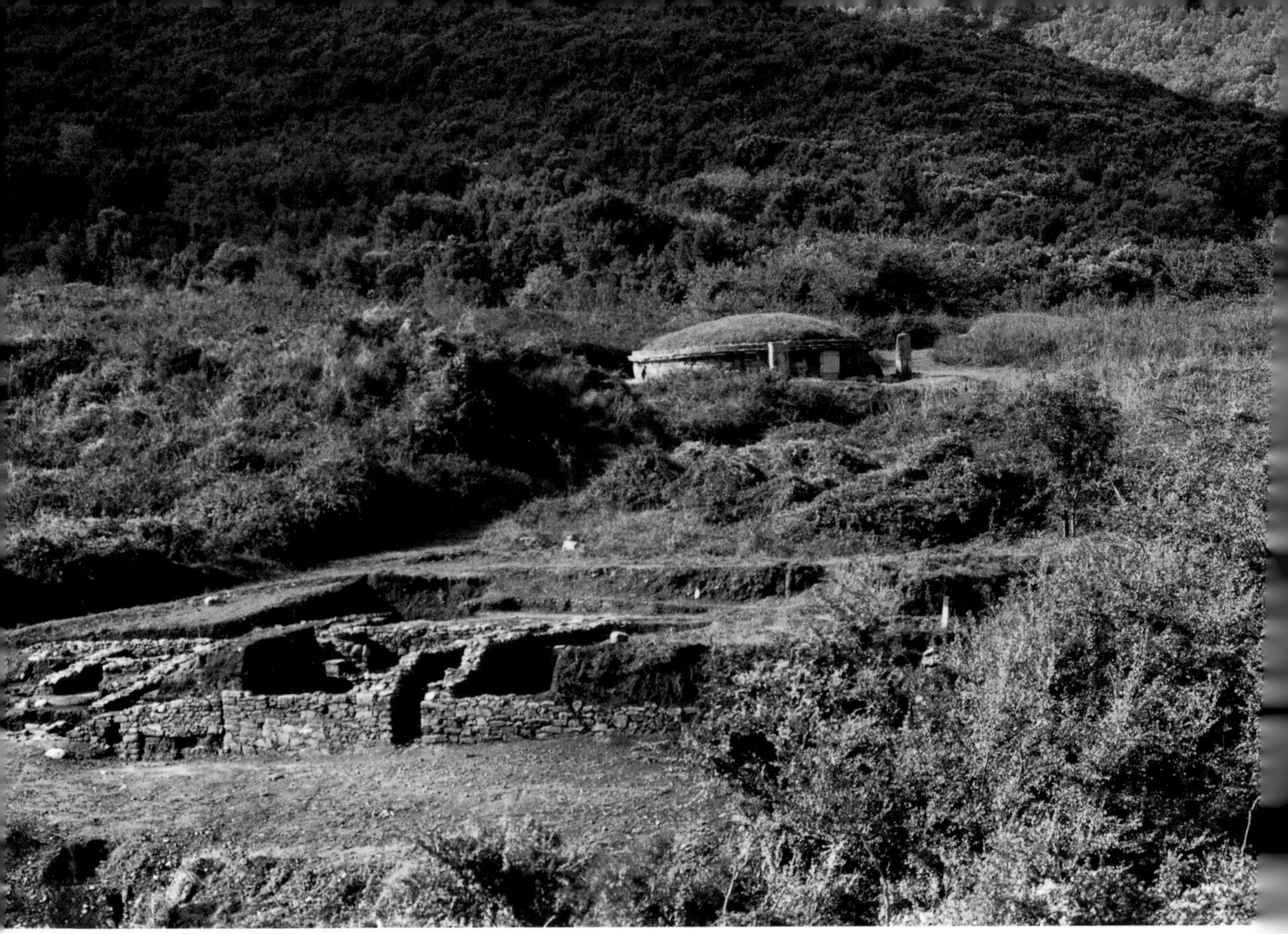

Fig. 87 Exterior view of the Tomb of the Bronze Fans, Populonia.

cut-out flower shapes and bordered by filigree and granulation, this type of earring became enormously popular during the Archaic period; the production probably started in workshops of Vulci; the specimens from the Tomb of the Bronze Fans belong to the earliest known examples.

A carved ivory comb and various pieces of carved bone ornaments for inlaying or nailing to wooden boxes or other objects formed part of the lady's toilet equipment, as did a number of fragmentary cylindrical alabaster unguent bottles whose upper parts are carved in the form of a bust of a long-haired woman; these were probably imported from some East Greek center (Rhodes or Samos), while a specimen of square section, ending on top in four roughly carved female heads, is of local manufacture.

The quantity of pottery, bronze utensils, weapons, and armor of high quality found in the tomb illuminates the extent of the trade that connected Populonia both with Greece and the Greek islands and with Southern Etruria, Vetulonia, Orvieto, and Bologna. There were bronze helmets, greaves, a shield, incense burners, basins, situlae, jugs, three cheese graters, and a strainer-funnel for dispensing wine without lees; three "Rhodian" oinochoai; iron spits, ferrules, and points of lances; painted pottery of Protocorinthian, Corinthian, Rhodian, and Etrusco-Corinthian style; and bucchero vessels of local and Southern Etruscan production.

Of the three fans of sheet bronze that have given the tomb its name, the best preserved is circular with a bronze-sheathed wooden handle (FIG. 88). It is decorated in repoussé with concentric rows of bosses, alternating with elongated tongue patterns, probably imitating feathers. The central medaillon shows two women in long checkered cloaks facing each other across a floral ornament, with one of them handing over a wreath or patera-like object. In style the figures are related to North Etruscan work. Fans, as we have seen, were status symbols associated with both male and female burials. They formed part of the furnishings of a princely tomb at Verucchio, and a fan was represented on the bronze tintinnabulum from a woman's grave at Bologna; rectangular bronze fans have also turned up in a rich tomb of the Orientalizing period at Veii, together with a carriage (Tomb 5 of Monte Michele), and at Trevignano (Tomb of the Fans, *Tomba dei Flabelli*). Later fans seem to belong exclusively to the female sphere, but in the Orientalizing period they express the high social standing of a person of either sex.

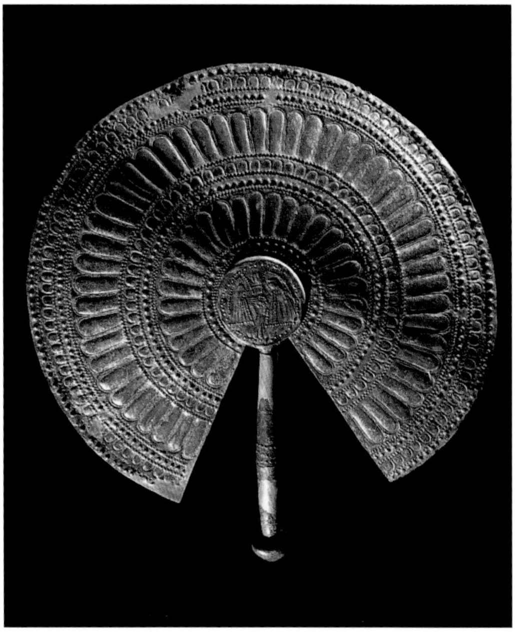

Fig. 88 Fan. From the Tomb of the Bronze Fans, Populonia. Second half of seventh century B.C. Embossed sheet bronze. L. including handle 21 cm. Florence, Museo Archeologico 89309.

The bronze and iron weapons and the roasting, dining, and drinking equipment all form part of the prestigious possessions of a warrior oligarchy of which the Tomb of the Bronze Fans at Populonia is such an outstanding example. Outwardly the tomb's importance was marked by two plain limestone stelae placed on either side of the entrance to the dromos and perhaps once painted.

Chiusi and Its Territory

CANOPIC URNS With a few exceptions, the inland region of Chiusi differed in the Orientalizing period from both Southern and coastal Northern Etruria in not adopting the custom of inhumation. Chiusi and its extensive fertile territory remained conservatively attached to cremation burials, which had prevailed in the Villanovan period.

The process of urbanization at Chiusi seems to have been somewhat delayed, and the large number of necropolises surrounding the center point to widely scattered habitation in the area of the future city of Chiusi. Other settlements, such as Cetona, Sarteano, Chianciano Terme, and Castelluccio di Pienza in the countryside west of Chiusi, have their own necropolises. The development of Chianciano Terme and Castelluccio di Pienza must be connected with their location on an important ancient road leading from the interior of Northern Etruria to the coastal cities over the pass of La Foce, controlled by the site of the Castelluccio di Pienza.

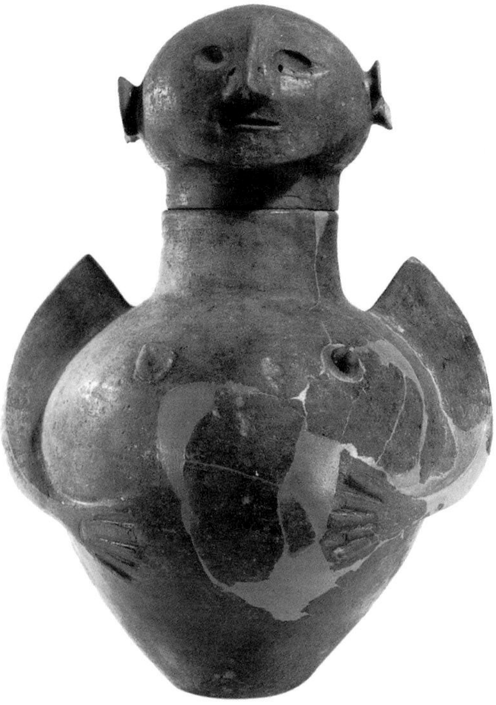

Fig. 89 Female "Canopic" ash urn. From Castiglione del Lago. Second half of seventh century B.C. Impasto. H. 50 cm. Florence, Museo Archeologico 72782.

During the first quarter of the seventh century, the *ziro* tombs gradually replaced the earlier burial pits containing biconic ash urns. A *ziro* (in modern Tuscan dialect) is a large terra-cotta storage jar that served to protect the urn and grave goods; it was usually set in a deep cut in the rock or clay and covered with a stone slab. Derived from the traditional biconic Villanovan urn with the lid formed by an inverted bowl or helmet, the globular lids of the ash urns found inside these *ziro* tombs (or set in little chambers) became by degrees more anthropomorphized and eventually assumed the characteristic form called "Canopic" by nineteenth-century antiquarians because of a superficial resemblance to the human-headed Canopic jars of Egypt. Though misleading, this term has been retained for the Chiusine urns for convenience's sake.

At first the lid of the ash urn was assimilated to a human head by a globular shape, roughly indicated facial features, or by attachment of a mask, which could be of hammered bronze sheet. In later examples, the whole cover of the urn was modeled in the shape of a human head with a face and hair (FIG. 89), while the ovoid body of the vessel could acquire a sternum furrow, or nipples, or rudimentary (occasionally separately modeled) arms besides or in place of the handles; the hands sometimes held objects, now missing. The same type of urn could also be made of hammered and riveted sheet bronze, and both pottery and bronze specimens were often placed on miniature thrones of stone, terra-cotta, or bronze and in some cases accompanied by small tables—furniture that recalls the rock-carved examples in the Tomb of the Five Chairs at Cerveteri and implies a banquet. On rare occasions, vestiges of textiles have been found still adhering to the urns, and sometimes fibulae or belts accompanied them; apparently some urns were clothed to make them as lifelike as possible, and the heads of female urns often had metal earrings.

Canopic urns were also found in early chamber tombs, some of them divided by a spur wall projecting from the rear, a form that became frequent in the Chiusine territory from the middle of the century.

An unusual example of an anthropomorphized ash urn was discovered in 1994 in a chamber tomb in a tumulus at Chianciano (località Morelli, now in the Museo delle Acque of Chianciano). In the left-hand partition stood a bronze urn on a stone base; the urn was covered with a red cloth fastened with a large iron leech-fibula, while a thin, square sheet of gold attached to the urn bore a pair of eyes carved from bone with pupils of amber. In front of the urn, on a four-legged bronze table embossed with animal friezes and geometric motifs, were placed ten drinking vessels of sheet bronze; behind the urn were fragments of a bronze shield and iron lance blades identifying this as the tomb of an aristocratic warrior. Among the other rich grave goods were bronze situlae and containers of pottery and glass paste for scented oil. Deposited in the right-hand partition of the chamber were pairs of bucchero vessels decorated with impressed friezes of walking men holding hands, as well as cups and jugs.

Clearly, in using anthropomorphized urns, the principal intention was to revitalize the deceased by restoring to the body, destroyed on the funeral pyre, an ash container in the form of an enduring image; and by placing the Canopic urn on a throne, the dead person was endowed with heightened dignity—he or she was heroized. This became a tradition in the Chiusine area, where, at a later stage (sixth–fourth century), ash containers and sarcophagi in stone took on monumental form, some representing the dead men and women on carved thrones, endowing them with an almost divine dignity.

Isolated early instances of the use of primitive anthropomorphic ash urns of impasto are known from Saturnia, Vulci, and Bisenzio (Olmo Bello Tomb 18, late eighth century). They confirm the early contacts between Chiusi and the settlements of the Fiora and Albegna valleys, though in these southern coastal regions the increasing practice of inhumation eventually eliminated the use of such ash urns.

Similar early attempts to heroize and eternalize the dead are found in a few tombs of the first half of the seventh century at Vulci (Tomb of the Bronze Chariot, *Tomba del Carro di Bronzo*) and at Marsiliana d'Albegna. Here the ash urns were sometimes associated with spherical lids and hands of hammered and cut-out pieces of bronze sheet, while simply constructed busts, made up from spherical and conical elements of hammered silver or bronze, represented the deceased.

THE NECROPOLIS OF TOLLE An extensive necropolis at Tolle belonging to an important settlement situated between the pass of La Foce and the Castelluccio di Pienza, west of Chiusi, has been excavated since 1996, so far yielding over a hundred burials, including *ziro* tombs in the hillside and small chambers with short dromoi, some constructed in the form of boxes from large stone slabs. An unusually high proportion of the Canopic urns recovered here come from female cremation tombs. Among the rich material from Tolle (preserved in the Museo Civico delle Acque at Chianciano) is that from Tomb 23, which was protected by such a box of stone slabs. This container enclosed both a male and a female cremation burial, each in a two-handled jar and accompanied by a variety of vessels in bucchero and impasto, as well as by an iron knife and personal ornaments, such as a bronze belt buckle, small silver rings, bronze and iron fibulae, and a hairpin of bone. The most fascinating object was the lid covering the husband's ash urn: It was surmounted by a small modeled figure of a man reclining on his left arm and draped in a light mantle, painted white; his head was not preserved. The wife's urn was simply covered by a bowl. Dating from the third quarter of the seventh century, the representation of the deceased, lying on his side as if at a banquet, is the earliest example hitherto known of a motif in Etruscan funerary art that was to become widespread and enormously influential; it seems to have been invented in the region of Chiusi.

Tomb 3 at Tolle was, unusually, a trench for inhumation containing the skeleton of a young woman. Her height was about 1.61 cm and her age between 20 and 25. The grave goods date from the last third of the seventh century and comprise spools and spindle whorls for woolworking, impasto pottery, and Etrusco-Corinthian ware: an askos, an *olpe* (jug), and an aryballos. There was also an elaborate rectangular open-worked metal object, probably part of the harness of a carriage horse, suggesting the elevated social position of the dead woman.

INDIVIDUAL FINDS FROM CHIUSINE TOMBS From Chiusi came an open-worked attachment modeled separately from an impasto vase or cup to which it was originally fastened (Copenhagen, National Museum 2041). It represents a nude frontal male figure, hands raised sideways and gripping the inner of two concentric rings within which he stands, with only his head projecting above. The position and frame of this figure recall the open-worked bronze handle from a woman's tomb at Bisenzio that shows a female figure surrounded by ducks and quadrupeds (see FIG. 23), possibly a representation of a Mistress of the Animals. Closely related in subject, style, and material to the attachment from Chiusi is the recently identified fragmentary attachment from Populonia (in Florence, Museo Archeologico) consisting of a nude, winged female figure with a long braid hanging down her back who stands within an open-worked ring, which she grips with hands raised sideways. Her wings proclaim her supernatural quality, and it is likely that she, too, represents a mistress- (*potnia*) type of divinity.

Ancient traffic routes connected the inland area of Chiusi with the territories adjoining it to the west and south (by way of the pass of La Foce and the Orcia and Ombrone valleys with Roselle, Vetulonia, and Populonia and, via the Fiora valley, with Vulci); the great south–north artery that made Chiusi a nodal point was formed by the courses of the Tiber, Paglia, Chiana, and Arno Rivers, which were largely navigable in antiquity. Cultural influences from Southern Etruria are documented by luxury objects of the Orientalizing period discovered at Chiusi.

One of the most striking of these is a small, silver-gilt vessel (falsely called a situla: the handles riveted to the everted lip are restored) dating from the middle of the seventh century (FIG. 90). Its decoration consists of two superposed figured friezes between cable patterns. The subject of the slightly damaged main frieze is still debated: two almost identical processions approach from either side a large cauldron on a tall tapering stand. Facing each other across the cauldron, two men in short kilts raise their arms in an aggressive attitude suggesting a boxing match.

A smaller, similarly attired young man advances behind each opponent, the one on the right side demonstratively holding out a small vessel of the same shape as the "situla" itself. Behind them on each side musicians play the double flutes (auloi). Then follow pairs of hoplites, each armed with two javelins, a round shield, greaves, and a crested helmet. The leading warrior on each side executes a leaping dance step. Next come two bearded and kilted men, the first bearing a sheep, the second a pig across his shoulders. They are followed by two women in short-sleeved, knee-length dresses with a herringbone pattern; each steadies with both raised hands a rectangular box on her head. Their hair is cut short, pageboy fashion. The procession is brought up at the rear by a horseman wielding a whip followed by a walking hoplite. The final warrior on the right side of the frieze wears a horned helmet instead of a crested one, as does the second warrior on the same side.

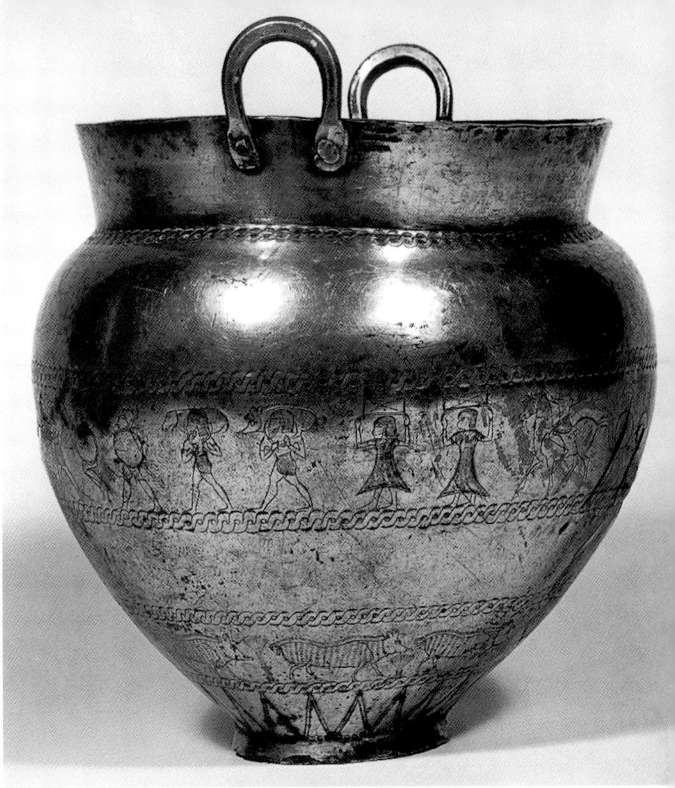

Fig. 90 Vessel with two incised figured friezes and inscription of owner's name, Plikaśna. From the vicinity of Chiusi. Mid-seventh century B.C. Silver gilt. H. 14.2 cm. Florence, Museo Archeologico 2594.

The lower frieze shows a herd of pigs walking to the right, each animal separated from the next by a small palm tree or papyrus plant and guided by a nude auloi player, who is followed by a large dog.

In both style and detail the friezes shows a mixture of motifs—Egyptian, Syro-Phoenician, Cypriote, and Greek—a mixture typical of a number of incised vessels in precious metal found in the princely tombs of Southern Etruria and Lazio. These vessels have been ascribed to Oriental craftsmen settled in Southern Etruria (probably Cerveteri) and working in an eclectic style. The present vessel differs from others of such type, both in the subject, which represents a local event, and in being inscribed twice—below the lip and underneath the foot—with the name Plikaśna (Plikaśnaś in the possessive), presumably that of the owner.

Some scholars have interpreted the main scene as a conciliatory sacrifice centered on a libation, but no clear parallels for such a represention can be adduced. Another, more persuasive explanation is that the upper frieze shows various events of funerary games. Boxing, horse racing, and footraces by hoplites, as well as armed dances are standard elements in many later depictions of games found in the tomb-paintings of Chiusi, Sarteano, and Tarquinia; carved in low relief on Chiusine funerary cippi; and impressed on bucchero vessels. The prizes for the winners of the games are also often shown, both in wall-paintings and on reliefs. Here the prize is clearly the large central cauldron, presumably of bronze, that stands between the boxers. Further prizes, destined for the other competitors, may be represented by the sheep and pigs and by the decorated chests carried by the servant girls in the procession, although the animals might equally well be intended for sacrifice.

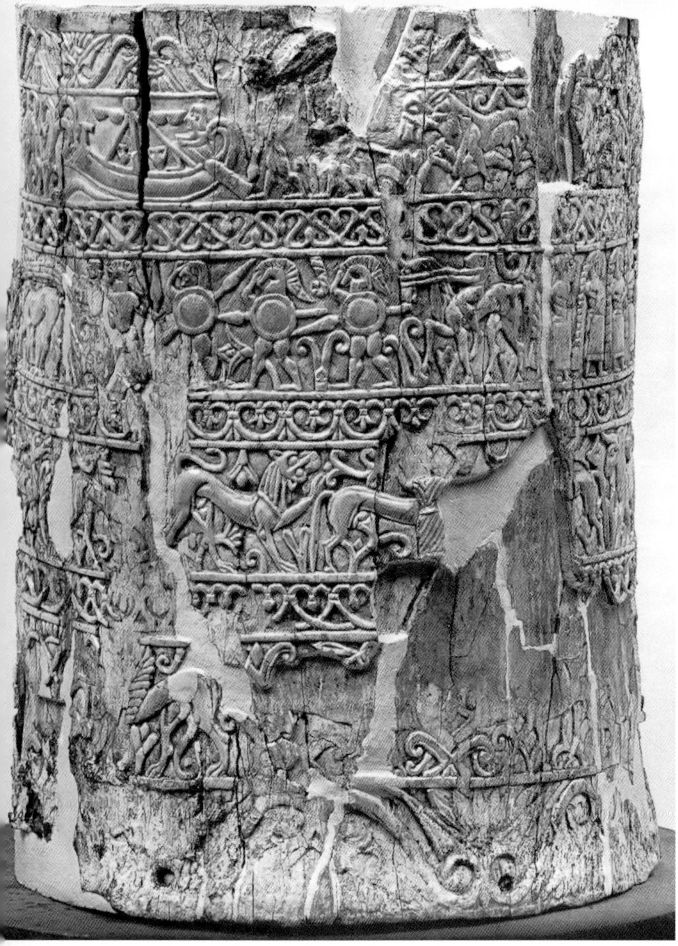

Despite the strong Eastern and Corinthian elements that characterize the friezes, their subjects have an unmistakably Etruscan flavor, which may be due to the wishes of the person who commissioned the work. He might be identical with the owner, who so proudly twice inscribed his name on the vessel. We know from ancient sources that it was the habit of the Etruscans to box to the sound of the auloi (Ath. 4.154; 12.518b), and, according to Aelian (*NA* 12.46), wild boar followed the Etruscan hunter's flute. This practice is seemingly adopted by the armed swineherd who plays the auloi on the lower frieze, leading an orderly file of five sows and two boars and escorted by his dog.

Another splendid luxury object of slightly later date (about 620–580)—a cylindrical ivory pyxis, probably imported from Southern Etruria—was discovered in a plundered chamber tomb in the Pania necropolis of Chiusi (FIG. 91). Carved from a section of an elephant's tusk, the pyxis is decorated with nine friezes in low relief: four bands with figured scenes alternating with five chains of vegetal motifs. Holes along the rim of the pyxis show that it was originally lined with an inner container of a different material. In the second frieze from the top can be identified episodes from the *Odyssey*: two warriors walking left are followed by three big rams; under the belly of each ram a companion of Odysseus clings to the fleece of the animal—the ruse by which the trapped Greeks escaped unnoticed from the cave of the blinded Polyphemos. To the left of this scene is Odysseus's ship with furled sails; it is loaded with two wine amphorae and watched over by the helmsman at the rudder. Beyond the ship's prow the Skylla, a snakelike sea monster with three canine heads, rears up menacingly.

Fig. 91 Pyxis carved with nine friezes in low relief. From the Pania necropolis, Chiusi. Late seventh–early sixth century B.C. Ivory. H. 22 cm. Florence, Museo Archeologico.

The fourth frieze shows a warrior setting out on a biga, guided by a charioteer and followed by three hoplites and a horseman. Facing the other way stands a row of four women in belted, tubular dresses with bordered hems, their hair worn in a long, ropelike plait down the back and their fists pressed to their stomachs in a gesture of mourning or despair. In front of this group dances a warrior wearing only a Corinthian helmet. Among the badly damaged figures behind him a flutist in a brief chiton plays the accompanying music. He is faced by armed warriors raising their right hands to their heads in salute or lament. This could be a generic scene of the departure of a heroic warrior for battle, but it is more likely to represent the dead aristocrat's last journey, mourned by his clansmen-soldiers and keening women, whose costume and hairstyle introduce a strong Etruscan flavor.

The two lower figure friezes show processions of real or mythical animals interspersed with vegetal forms suggesting a wood(?); a horseman may represent an aristocratic hunter, while a pair of centaurs wielding branches introduce a mythical element. The preserved front part of one of the centaurs shows him as a complete human figure in a long striated tunic; only his hindpart is horse shaped. It has been argued that he is thus characterized as Chiron, the wise centaur who initiated the young Achilles, and that the whole iconography of the pyxis represents examples of education, heroism, and wisdom of heroes from Greek myth and epic, virtues to be striven for by Etruscan aristocrats.

It is probable that the artist who carved the friezes drew for his models on Greek painted pottery, particularly Corinthian, which had been reaching Southern coastal cities of Etruria in great quantities. At this advanced stage of the Orientalizing period, Cerveteri was being overtaken by Vulci as the leading city for the reception, adaptation, and distribution of foreign models, either imported or produced by freshly arrived Greek immigrant artists, such as the East Greek Swallow Painter, active during the last decades of the seventh century, and the Etrusco-Corinthian Painter of the Bearded Sphinx. It has therefore been argued that the workshop of the Pania pyxis was located in Vulci rather than Cerveteri; but in view of the many carved ivory and bone luxury goods of comparable quality discovered in the princely tombs of Northern Etruria, we must consider the possibility of itinerant specialists who set up shop and carried out commissions in different far-flung places.

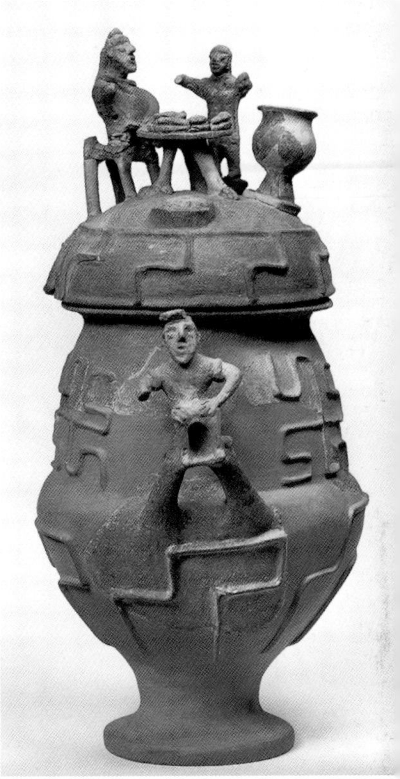

Fig. 92 Ash urn. From Montescudaio, near Volterra. Third quarter of seventh century B.C. Impasto. H. 63.6 cm. Florence, Museo Archeologico.

The most famous Greek vase found in Etruria is the François Vase (named after its discoverer), which was excavated in fragments in a sacked tumulus just north of Chiusi in the Fonte Rotella necropolis in 1844/1845. It is a large krater, made about 570 by the Athenian potter Ergotimos and painted in black-figure technique by the painter Kleitias. The inscribed figure scenes represent a veritable compendium of Greek mythology, some of them depicting the wedding of the goddess Thetis, mother of Achilles. This splendid vase, probably acquired via Vulci, is one of the heralds of the growing Attic imports that reached Northern Etruria. It is now in the Museo Archeologico of Florence (inv. 4209).

THE ASH URN FROM MONTESCUDAIO An interesting example of an impasto cinerary urn surmounted by small figurines on the lid that recall those on the Chiusine funerary vessels mentioned above (see FIG. 64) was discovered at Montescudaio, west of Volterra (FIG. 92). The tomb dates from the third quarter of the seventh century. The shape of this ash urn and its overall decoration with ridges in geometric patterns of stepped meanders and swastikas hark back to Villanovan biconic urns, but the small statuettes attached to it introduce the important theme of the funerary banquet.

On the lid a bearded man is enthroned on a chair with a backrest. In front of him is a circular table on three bovine legs; on the table are round and crescent-shaped loaves of bread or cake. A huge container of wine stands beside the table; a similar vessel on the other side of the table is broken off. On a footstool beside her feasting master stands a serving woman, who probably once held a fan; she wears a simple dress reaching to the knees, and down her back hangs a thick plait of hair. On the single handle of the urn itself sits another bearded man, palms on knees, wearing a flat cap like those of the bronze figurines from Vulci and Bisenzio (see FIGS. 20, 22). The modeling of the impasto figures is crude but lively and clearly expresses a message: the deceased feasts at a funerary banquet that eternalizes his cult and his high social position, symbolized by his throne and by the presence of a female attendant with a fan.

The Ombrone Region

We have already noted the fundamental importance of navigable rivers and passable valleys in spreading cultural influences. Northern inland Etruria (the Senese, the Chianti, and the Arno valley) is an instructive example of how very articulated geological conditions shape local developments. The region of the upper course of the Ombrone River and its tributaries and headwaters is particularly fertile; in addition, it is favored with deposits of metal ores; extensive woods for charcoal production, necessary for smelting ovens; and with quarries of excellent building stone (for example, travertine from Rapolano). During the Orientalizing period this agricultural and mineral wealth sustained the growth of a large number of small but flourishing rural centers under a local aristocracy in close contact with the cities of the coastal areas. They exchanged goods with and attracted craftsmen from Vetulonia, Populonia, as well as Chiusi, cities that also transmitted products from Southern Etruria (Cerveteri, Vulci, etc.). Via the rivers Chiani, Arbia, Elsa, Pesa, and Ambra, the Ombrone region communicated with settlements such as Castellina in Chianti, San Martino ai Colli, San Casciano Val di Pesa, and, in the middle Arno valley, with Quinto and Sesto Fiorentino, Comeana, and Artimino, a region that shows a remarkable cultural homogeneity.

Recent excavations have produced a number of richly furnished aristocratic chamber tombs dating from the second half of the seventh to well into the sixth century. These were constructed from large slabs of local stone, accessed by entrance corridors, and covered by tumuli; remains of the residences of such local potentates have also come to light. Among the most important of these sites are the Poggione necropolis at Castelnuovo Berardenga, with the neighboring settlement of Piano Tondo; the Molinello tumulus at Asciano; and the buildings on Poggio Civitate near Murlo.

THE MOLINELLO TUMULUS The large Molinello tumulus contained fifteen tombs. The oldest chambers are constructed from massive, vertically placed slabs of travertine and roofed with horizontal slabs (once supported by internal wooden posts) or with a ridge roof made of two inclined stone slabs. The disturbed material recovered in these chambers dates from the late seventh to the mid-sixth century. The most recent tombs, with contents datable from the end of the fourth to the late first century, contained travertine and pottery ash urns inscribed with the names of the Marcni family. It is tempting to think that the descendants of the same wealthy family who built this enormous tumulus still owned it six hundred years later and buried their dead in the still unused parts of it. In rural areas such as this, traditional forms of life and burial survived much longer than in the big cities.

Outside the entrance corridor of Tomb B, the oldest and grandest of the tombs in the Molinello tumulus, was found a fragmentary, three-quarters life-size stone statue of a man in a short-sleeved tunic and a mantle. He clasps a slightly curved *lituus* to his chest; extensive remains of yellow ocher and red paint are preserved on his clothes and staff. Found separately was a male head that perhaps belonged to the statue. Its roughly carved, massive face with huge bulbous, almond-shaped eyes is framed by a wiglike hairstyle comprising a flat cap of hair projecting from the forehead and horizontally waved tresses falling to the shoulders. Unworked at the back, the statue probably originally stood against a wall of the tomb; like the seated figures in the tomb at Ceri (see FIG. 53), it may represent an ancestor.

In an adjoining tomb was a second male head of more accomplished and more recent style. It has a cylindrical tenon below the neck, which enables it to be plugged into a hollowed-out cinerary statue that has not survived. These sculptures are carved from a friable white limestone known from Chiusine sculptures. Chiusine statues are closely related in style, in particular the statue of a male draped figure with smooth, centrally parted hair, discovered at Podere Casalta, Lucignano, in the Chiana valley (FIG. 93). Among the funerary sculpture preserved from the region of Chiusi the earliest appears to be the statue from the Molinello tumulus at Asciano, dated to the first quarter of the sixth century. It has been plausibly suggested that Peloponnesian artists must have introduced the strong Daidalic elements noticeable in the workshops of sculpture (and some minor arts) of the Chiusi and Ombrone area.

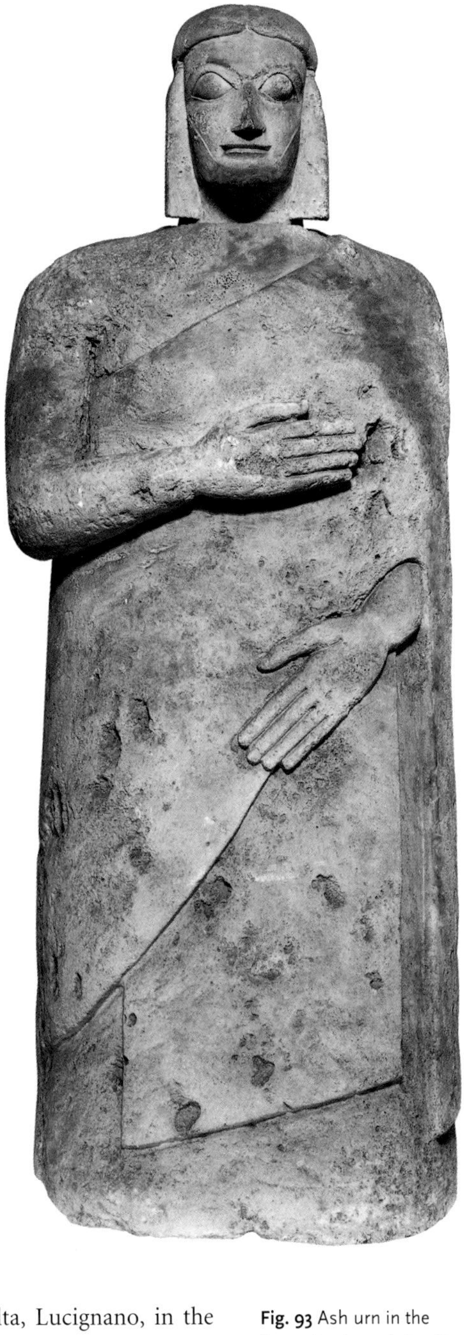

Fig. 93 Ash urn in the form of a draped standing man. From Podere Casalta, Lucignano. Mid-sixth century B.C. Limestone. H. 1.36 m. London, The British Museum GR 1884.6-14.61.

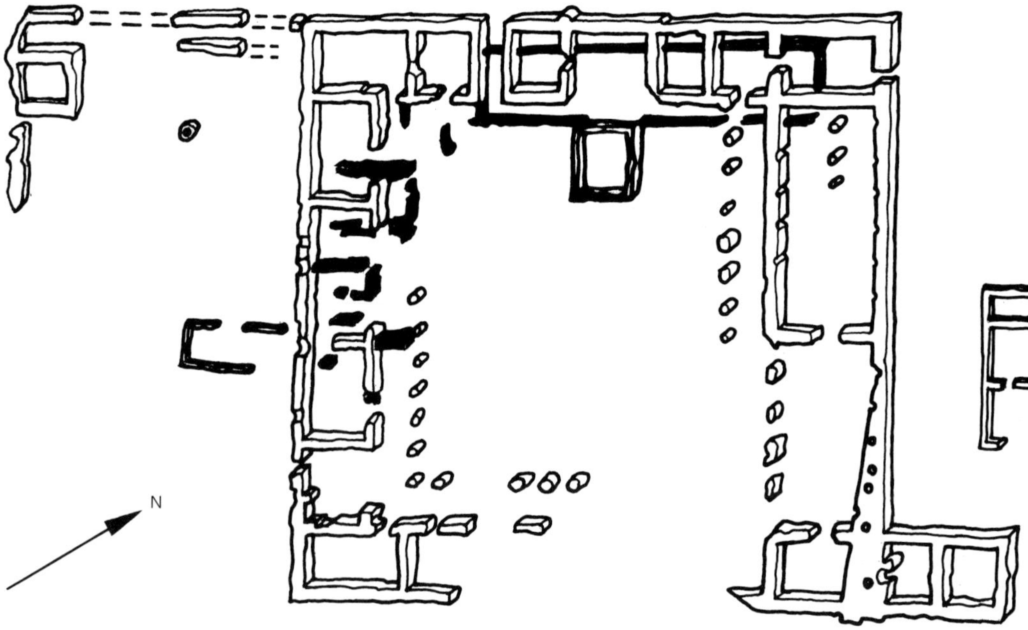

Fig. 94 Plan of the superimposed buildings from the Orientalizing and Archaic periods. Poggio Civitate (Murlo).

The gigantic mound also yielded fragments of a relief-decorated, rectangular stone ash urn belonging to the Archaic period. On its lid are effigies carved in the round of a husband and wife, semireclining beside each other propped up on the left elbow as if banqueting on a couch; enough of the stone chest is preserved to show that its front was carved to represent a wooden dining couch decorated with rosettes and lotus flowers and, in front of the couch, a low serving table and an incense burner. Dated to about 520–510, this ash urn is perhaps just a little younger than the two famous terra-cotta sarcophagi from Cerveteri with a similar subject. The Molinello ash urn represents the oldest example in stone to have come to light so far of a type of funerary monument invented by Etruscan artists and copied by both Roman and Renaissance sculptors: the sarcophagus bearing on the lid reclining effigies of the deceased, shown as if still alive.

ARCHITECTURE: POGGIO CIVITATE

Archaeological fortune has allowed us to learn where and how some of the aristocrats of this area actually lived. A site, significantly called Piano del Tesoro (treasure plateau), on the commanding hill of Poggio Civitate near Murlo was known already from an associated necropolis at nearby Poggio Aguzzo, where an impasto cup dated to the second quarter of the seventh century was found in a trench tomb. Later an extensive Archaic building complex arose at Poggio Civitate; it appears to have been a princely residence, though a politico-religious use of these imposing structures cannot be excluded (FIG. 94). Underlying buildings from the

Orientalizing period are still being investigated. They consist of three buildings that were damaged by fire toward the end of the seventh century and replaced, probably in the first quarter of the sixth century, on a monumental and more splendidly decorated scale. This Archaic building complex was, in its turn, destroyed in the third quarter of the sixth century. At this stage the remains of the buildings seem deliberately to have been completely dismantled and some of their terra-cotta revetments and acroteria scattered, with the majority carefully buried in a pit and in ditches on the site. The whole area was finally surrounded by an uninterrupted earth bank, thus making it ritually inaccessible; it was never subsequently inhabited.

The Orientalizing Buildings

The building techniques were the same in both periods: earthen walls, coated with lime plaster, on rubble foundations; the preserved floor levels were of beaten earth. The structures of the Orientalizing period (not yet completely excavated) consisted of a long building (8 x 35 m) on the west, which probably had two stories, and, at right angles to it in the southwest, a recently identified three-room building on massive foundations, within which was found a cup of the same date as the one just mentioned from a trench tomb at Poggio Aguzzo. A well lay just behind the three-room building. These buildings were presumably residential and formed two sides of a large open space or court. The ground floor of the long western building must have served as a magazine, for large storage jars were set into its floor. These were found covered with carbonized debris of the wooden beams that had supported the floor above. Tiles from the roof and household objects had collapsed onto this level during the conflagration. The ridge roof was covered with tiles, and fragments of terra-cotta acroteria, antefixes, and revetments are also preserved. These are among the earliest architectural terra-cottas known in Etruria.

At some distance from the Orientalizing buildings just described and aslant to the southeast stood a long, ridge-roofed building, which has been identified as a workshop (FIG. 95). It was open on all four sides and internally supported by rows of pillars, whose stone bases have survived. The lateral gutter (*sima*) of the roof was decorated with moldmade female-head antefixes and lion's-head waterspouts—probably apotropaic images of the Mistress of the Animals. To judge from the finds made in this building, all sorts of crafts were practiced here. The western half was dedicated to the manufacture of roof tiles and architectural terracottas, some of which have been found in situ in an unfired state. The eastern part seems to have been used for casting metal objects and carving bone, horn, and ivory ornaments, as well as making glass. This discovery shows that the residence included an industrial production center, whose surplus goods were probably a means of exchange. The fact that such a utilitarian building had the same type of terra-cotta decoration as other buildings of the Orientalizing residence is of great interest. Whereas in contemporary Greece only temples and shrines had molded

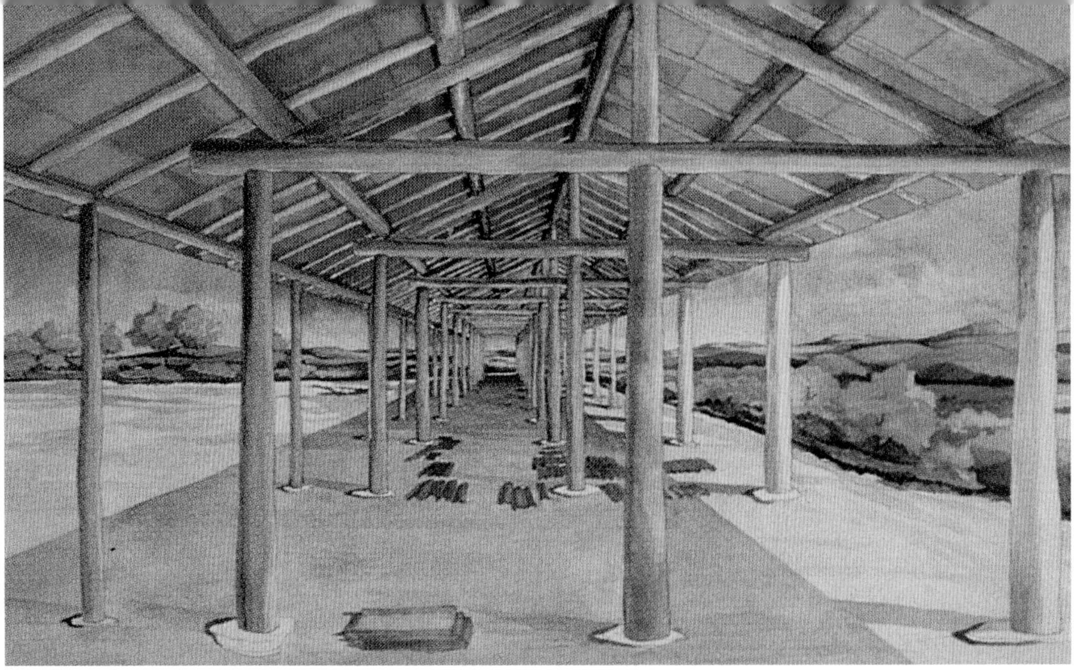

Fig. 95 Reconstruction of workshop from the Orientalizing period. Poggio Civitate (Murlo). Watercolor.

and painted terra-cotta decoration, in Etruria domestic and utilitarian architecture, too, was distinguished by such adornments. This large workshop seems to have gone up in flames (probably at the same time as the other Orientalizing buildings), as suggested by the discovery of highly vitrified tiles and quantities of carbon in the debris. Imprints of bare and small-shod (female?) feet left by fleeing workers on freshly molded tiles drying on the floor are a vivid testimonial of this unexpected conflagration.

The practice of decorating the roofs with architectural terra-cottas was not confined to aristocratic "palaces" and their workshops; such decoration is found also in more modest domestic architecture of the Etruscan settlement at Acquarossa near Viterbo. There the houses in Zones A, B, G, and L of the settlement displayed cut-out acroteria as well as terra-cotta revetments painted in white on red and designed for the protection of the wooden parts of the buildings. This custom remained characteristic of Etruscan domestic and public architecture throughout much of its history.

The tiled ridge roofs, acroteria, and antefixes on the Orientalizing buildings at Poggio Civitate and Acquarossa must be connected with the architectural techniques for terra-cotta roofing developed in Greece during the first half of the seventh century. But a decorative tradition that can be traced back to the Villanovan period, when the ridge roofs of huts in central Italy were surmounted by carved wooden ridge logs (see the hut urns, FIGS. 3, 5), may also have played a part in the creation of diverse types of acroteria in Etruria. The original position of a number of molded female-head antefixes from the Orientalizing building is still unclear, but they strongly resemble some terra-cotta masks on Chiusine Canopic urns and suggest a shared stylistic tendency; they are perhaps a symbolic representation of ancestors.

The Orientalizing acroteria of Poggio Civitate were cut out with a knife from thick slabs of preformed clay, and details of the open-worked designs were incised on some of them. They took various shapes: a triangle flanked by volutes, a horseman in profile (probably the self-representation of the local elite, FIG. 96); and fragments of a female figure flanked by felines (again probably the apotropaic Mistress of the Animals) were modeled in low relief. A raking *sima* perhaps belonged to the main building; the surface of the *sima* was probably painted white on red (like pieces from Acquarossa, where this technique may have been introduced from Cerveteri, which had a tradition of large pottery vessels and house-shaped terra-cotta ash urns decorated in this color scheme).

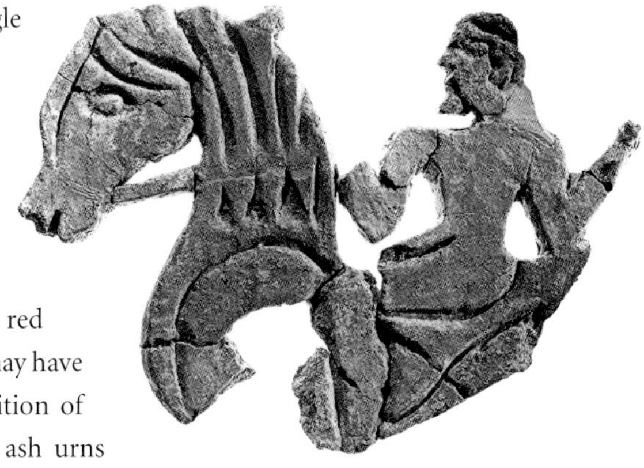

Fig. 96 Architectural terracotta of horse and rider. From the Orientalizing building, Poggio Civitate (Murlo). Seventh century B.C. H. 32 cm. Antiquarium di Poggio Civitate 69-284.

Large quantities of fragmentary plain, locally made impasto and bucchero pottery—plates, serving dishes, covered bowls, jugs, drinking cups, cooking stands, and braziers—found in the main building among the burnt debris prove that great banquets must have taken place on the site. More elaborate vessels with handles adorned with molded figures of winged female divinities (*potnia theron*) and helmeted heads will have served for special occasions, as did fine, imported Greek skyphoi and cups of Corinthian, Laconian, and Rhodian manufacture and Etrusco-Corinthian pottery, the latter probably made at Vulci.

Among the small finds were pottery spools, spindle whorls, and loom weights—evidence of woolworking in this building. There were many small luxury objects, such as tiny silver fibulae, fragments of a gold bracelet, engraved gemstones, and carvings in ivory and bone for inlaying, all ornaments of a type familiar from the aristocratic tombs of the period.

Particularly attractive are small carved figures of creatures such as a sphinx, a griffin, a hare, and a ram, which may have served as handles on the lids of ivory boxes. A fine fragmentary group in high relief of a standing couple embracing could also have been such an attachment. Several pieces appear to be works of the same hand and confirm the existence of a local workshop for bone- and ivory-carving at Poggio Civitate. On the flat back of a fragmentary ivory plaque in the form of a lion's head is an incised inscription: *mi avil*, the name of its owner; comparable plaques found elsewhere suggest that this was a means of identification for a guest with a right to hospitality. Stylistically related bone objects, such as plaques carved with lotus flowers and roundels, etc., have been discovered at other Northern Etruscan sites (e.g., Quinto Fiorentino in the Arno valley), showing that the occupants of Poggio Civitate were in contact with aristocratic families settled over a large area of Tuscany.

Metal objects such as the iron-inlaid bronze buckles found in the nearby necropolis of Murlo point to the importance of Poggio Civitate in an extensive network of trade (and political?) connections. The most interesting of the metal finds are fragments of three fire-damaged bronze figurines, perhaps originally

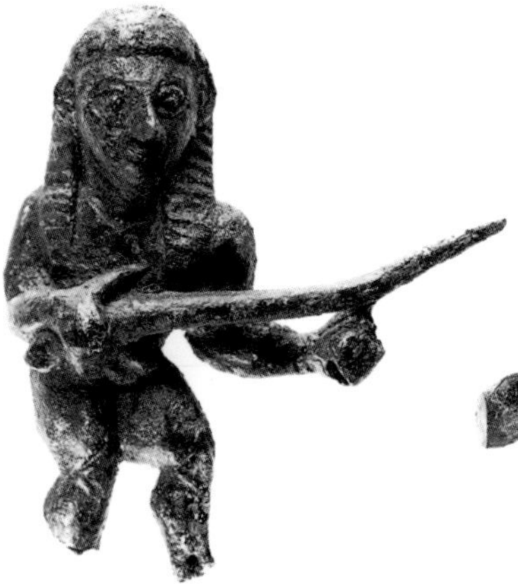

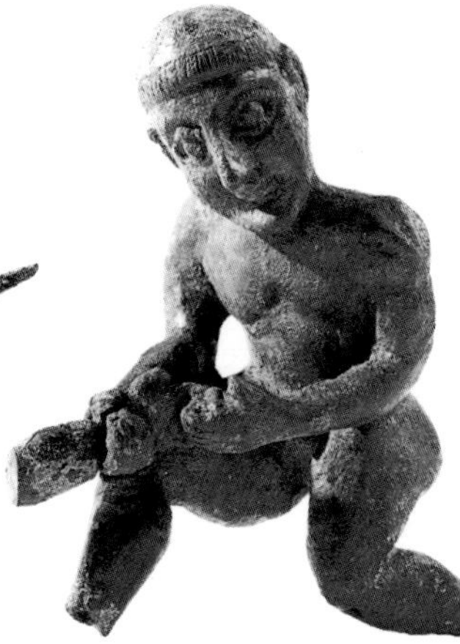

ABOVE LEFT
Fig. 97 Statuette of a referee. From the Orientalizing building, Poggio Civitate (Murlo). Seventh century B.C. Cast bronze. H. 6 cm. Antiquarium di Poggio Civitate 71-106.

ABOVE RIGHT
Fig. 98 Statuette of a wrestler. From the Orientalizing building, Poggio Civitate (Murlo). Seventh century B.C. Cast bronze. H. 9 cm. Antiquarium di Poggio Civitate 71-105.

BELOW
Fig. 99 Female head from lateral *sima*. From the Archaic building, Poggio Civitate (Murlo). 600–575 B.C. Terracotta. H. ca. 12 cm. Antiquarium di Poggio Civitate.

attached to an elaborate bronze cauldron (FIGS. 97, 98). They represent two nude wrestlers with short-cropped hair coming to grips with each other (of the second only one hand survives) and a smaller, long-haired male figure, perhaps an umpire, holding a staff. Lively attitudes and cheerful expressions make these small statuettes extremely attractive; they show the existence of Greek-style athletic contests in Etruria during the Orientalizing period, something also suggested by the boxers represented on the Plikaśna "situla" from Chiusi (see pp. 108f.). Bronzeworking was carried out at Poggio Civitate itself, as shown by the excavated remains of crucibles, slag, small furnaces, and the mouthpiece of bellows.

The Archaic Building Complex

The new residence, or Upper Building, is perhaps better referred to as the Archaic Building Complex. Built on the leveled site after the fire, the complex formed a monumental square (ca. 60 x 62 m) of four wings, with watchtowers projecting at the northeast and southwest corners, where slingshot were found. Subdivided into rooms of different sizes, and on the north side of greater height than the other wings, the buildings surrounded a central courtyard with covered colonnaded porches on the north, east, and south. On the west side of the court stood a lightly built, small, rectangular enclosure, perhaps a *templum*, open to the sky, or a thatched shrine. It was centrally aligned with a symmetrical group of three rooms in the west wing—an open-fronted large rectangular recess flanked by two slightly smaller rooms.

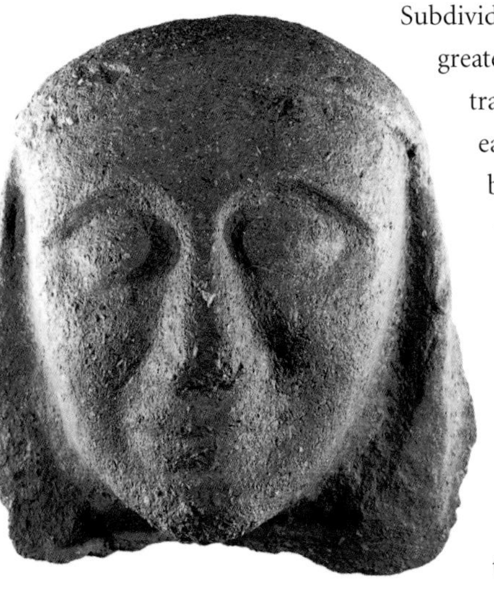

The first excavator suggested that this part of the structure had a religious function, and that the whole complex at Poggio Civitate was the meeting place of a Northern Etruscan League. Others see it as the residence of a local dynast and seek the prototypes of its elaborate plan in Oriental and East Greek

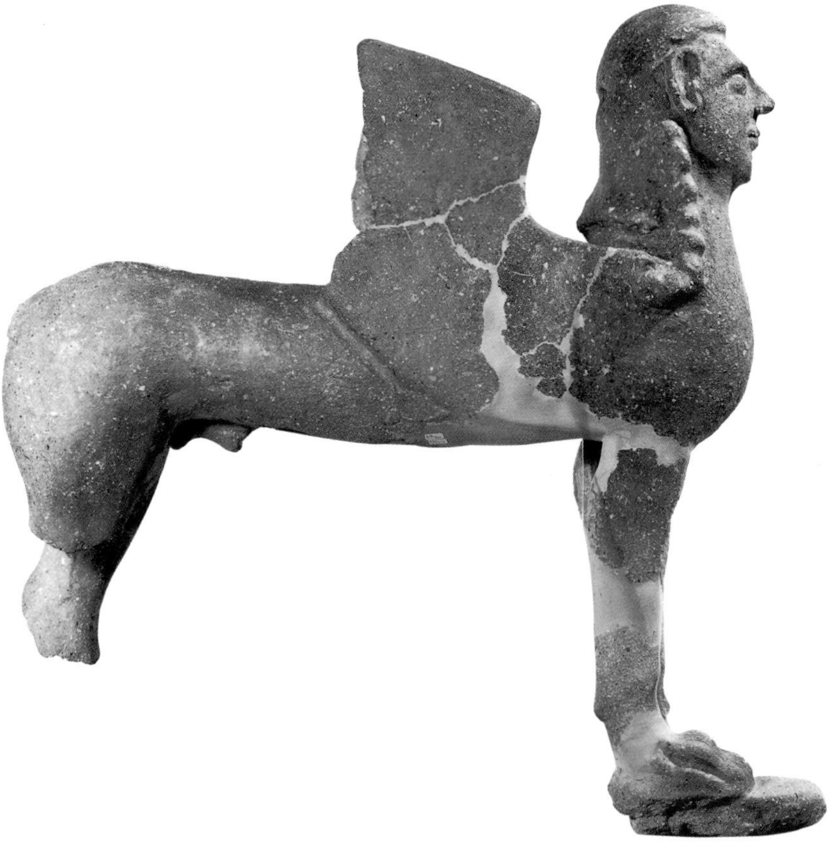

Fig. 100 Acroterial figure of a standing male sphinx. From the Archaic building, Poggio Civitate (Murlo). 600–575 B.C. Terra-cotta. H. 70 cm. Antiquarium di Poggio Civitate 68-500.

palaces (such as Vouni on Cyprus and Larissa on Hermos in western Asia Minor); yet others compare the arrangement of the triple rooms on the west side of the court with the Eastern architectural form of the *liwan*, an arrangement of two flanking rooms with a porch between them. Another interpretation of this particular group of rooms draws a parallel between them and the layout of the *tablinum* of the atrium house, the ceremonial center of the ancient Roman dwelling. What is certain is that external, probably Near Eastern, stimuli must have led to the creation of this unusual building complex, which was most carefully planned and provided with drainage.

The roofs were adorned with a complete system of locally made tiles and molded, painted terra-cotta revetments; lateral *sima*; antefixes of female heads (FIG. 99) alternating with rosettes and lion's-head waterspouts; and big, hand-modeled acroterial figures placed on the ridgepole of the roof on all sides of the courtyard. The fragments of acroterial figures have been identified as at least twenty-three male and female statues of different sizes, seated, standing, or kneeling. The larger human figures were placed across the ridgepole so as to look into the courtyard, while the smaller ones and a number of real and fantastic animals faced each other along the lines of the ridges (FIG. 100). Some of the male statues

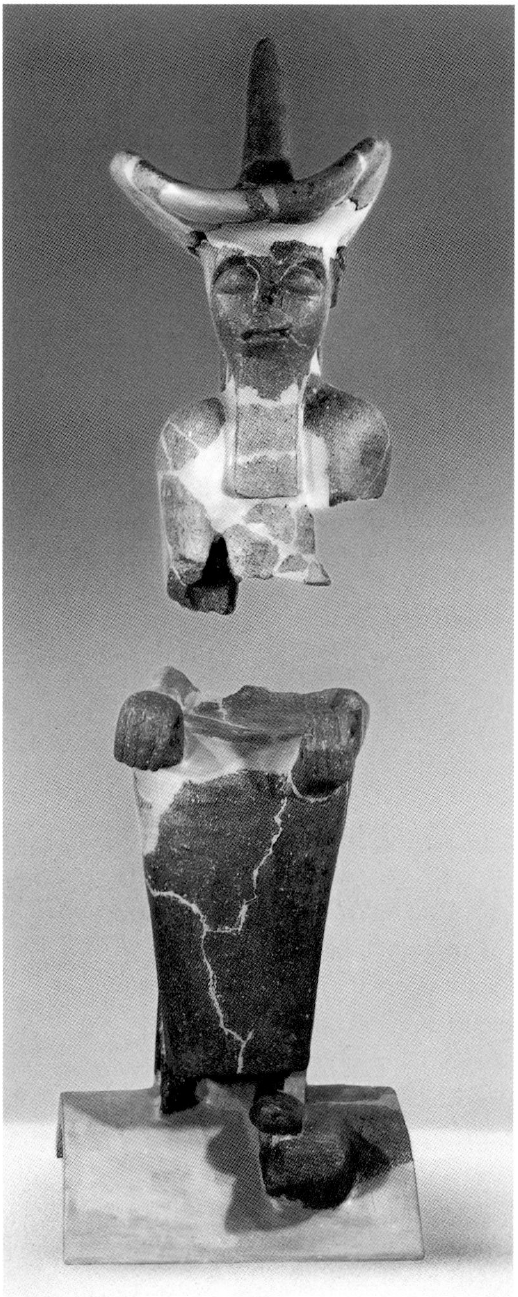

were bearded and wore broad-brimmed, high-peaked "cowboy" hats (FIG. 101); others wore close-fitting caps or helmets. The women were dressed in long skirts with a wide, painted lower border and were shod in soft, laced boots with up-turned toes. All the wooden or metal attributes the statues once held are lost, making interpretation of the figures difficult. It has been suggested that they were nameless divinities (Lat. *numina*), but a more likely explanation is that they depict heroized ancestors of the local rulers and were meant to glorify the importance of the family and protect the residence. Stylistically their faces have affinities with some Chiusine Canopic urns, though the inspiration for such monumental terra-cotta figures may have come from Cyprus or Asia Minor. The new and demandingly large scale of the figures at times strained the ability of the modelers. Apotropaic qualities may be ascribed to the Gorgon antefixes and the panther masks that decorated the roofs. A raking *sima* had a molded frieze of hounds pursuing hares; hare hunting, as we know from the frieze on the foot of the Tragliatella jug (see FIGS. 83a, b) and from later works, was a favorite aristocratic sport.

THE TERRA-COTTA FRIEZE PLAQUES Among the most interesting and informative pieces of the terra-cotta revetments are the numerous fragments of a long molded frieze showing four different types of figured scenes. They are influenced by a variety of prototypes: Oriental as well as South Italian Greek friezes and Corinthian painted pottery.

The easiest scene to understand depicts a horse race (FIG. 102). Each plaque shows three riders in short tunics and pointed caps, with hair flying and mantles (or quivers?) fluttering from their shoulders. Whip in hand, they gallop to the right toward the goal and the prize—a column with a large, two-handled cauldron on top, which appears as the first feature on each plaque. This probably represents a real sporting event (reminiscent of the annual Palio horse race that today takes place at nearby Siena). As early as the Villanovan period helmeted riders appear as decoration on cast-bronze feet of small tripod bowls (see FIG. 14); a similar aristocratic ideology probably informs later

Fig. 101 Acroterial figure of a bearded man with hat. From the Archaic building, Poggio Civitate (Murlo). 600–575 B.C. Terra-cotta. H. 1.70 m. Antiquarium di Poggio Civitate 68-200 and 67-411.

Etruscan representations of mounted horsemen. The motifs of riders and of bigas also occur on bucchero vases from Chiusi decorated with friezes impressed by a carved cylinder.

On another set of fragments is a procession led by two men in long tunics (FIG. 103). One of them carries what appears to be a large chopper, the other a spit or stick, while both hold the reins of two horses harnessed to a two-wheeled carriage with a seat on which two persons sit side by side. The near figure is a woman entirely wrapped in a cloak that even covers her hair. The far figure, whose sex cannot be determined, holds a large parasol shading them both. Behind the vehicle walk two servant girls in long belted dresses, each carrying a semicircular fan and a situla with vertical strap supports between foot and bowl. In addition, the first girl balances on her head a lidded container, the second girl two inverted stools.

It is difficult to be certain about the nature of this scene. If the figure holding the parasol is a man, the most likely interpretation is that of a marriage procession: led by his retainers, the bridegroom rides with the bride and her dowry (carried by her maidservants) to their future home. But the couple might equally well be local aristocrats proceeding to a religious ceremony or formal visit. If both are women, they might be the bride and her mother. Chopper and spit carried by the two men in front suggest sacrificial slaughter or roasting of meat for a banquet, and the fans allude to the high status of the pair in the carriage.

The model for the carriage procession was perhaps South Italian. On a painted terra-cotta relief plaque from a frieze that decorated a small shrine (named C) in the city sanctuary of Metapontum, two draped women are shown riding in a similar carriage drawn by mules and guided by a nude boy carrying a box (FIG. 104). The vehicle is followed by a procession of women holding flowers in one hand. This scene (examples of which, made from the same mold, have been discovered at Francavilla near Sybaris and at Siris) has been identified as priestesses in a carriage moving toward a sanctuary, followed by female worshipers holding floral gifts for the divinity and raising their hands in adoration; the plaque dates to the first quarter of the sixth century.

This Greek motif has been subtly adapted by the craftsmen at Poggio Civitate to demonstrate the high social standing of the people riding in the carriage. Instead of one nude boy leading the team of draft animals, we have here two male retainers dressed in the Oriental, clinging, unbelted tunic and carrying instruments of sacrifice or feasting. The big parasol—absent in the Metapontum plaque—is a typical status symbol imported from the Orient, as are the fans and stools. Riding in a carriage is the privilege of the Etruscan aristocracy and of only a few ladies of high rank in Tyrrhenian Italy. We have already noted the association of carriage and fans in aristocratic burials. The maids are characterized as servants by the fact that they carry objects on their heads (cf. the Plikaśna "situla," FIG. 90). The careful insistence here on all the familiar accoutrements of the aris-

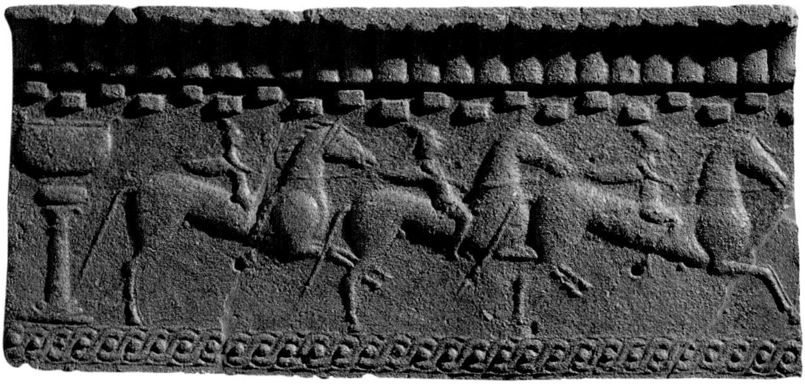

Fig. 102 Terra-cotta frieze plaque: horserace. From the Archaic building, Poggio Civitate (Murlo). 650–575 B.C.

tocracy suggests that the couple in the carriage are human beings rather than divinities (as some scholars think); the most persuasive explanation therefore seems to be that they are members of the great family who commissioned and lived in this splendid residence.

In connection with the carriage we are reminded of the Roman tradition, transmitted by Livy (1.34ff.), of the arrival in Rome from Tarquinia of the noble Etruscan lady Tanaquil and her husband, Lucumo, the son of the Corinthian Greek Demaratos. The couple is described as "sitting in their carriage" at a period corresponding to the date of the frieze in Poggio Civitate. In Rome the use of the carriage by women was reserved for the priestesses of Vesta, whereas Etruscan ladies of the royal family of Tarquin, traditionally descended from Tanaquil and Lucumo (who became the fifth king of Rome under the name of Lucius Tarquinius Priscus), continued to enjoy the privilege of all high-born Etruscan women to ride in a carriage, even in Rome. Two generations later the story of the younger Tullia, daughter of the sixth king of Rome, Servius Tullius, shows in Livy's tale (which is entirely seen through Roman eyes) the evil ambitions of such an Etruscan lady and the terrible use she made of her vehicle. Married to Arruns Tarquinius, she persuaded her brother-in-law, the future Tarquinius Superbus, to murder her own husband and after that her father, so that she could become the wife of Superbus and thus queen. To crown her atrocious crimes, Tullia ran over the body of her slaughtered father with her carriage, staining its wheels and her own clothes with his blood (Livy 1.48).

Returning to the frieze from Poggio Civitate, we assume that the remaining two themes represented on its plaques—a banquet and an assembly of seated figures with attendants—likewise belong to the human sphere and illustrate the great ceremonial moments in the life of the inhabitants of the residence.

The banquet with participants reclining on couches appears here for the first time in Etruria (FIG. 105). The Etruscan aristocracy originally dined sitting on chairs and thrones, and in some Etruscan regions ladies continued to do so, enthroned beside their reclining husbands. The banquet on couches for both sexes was to become one of the favorite subjects represented during the sixth cen-

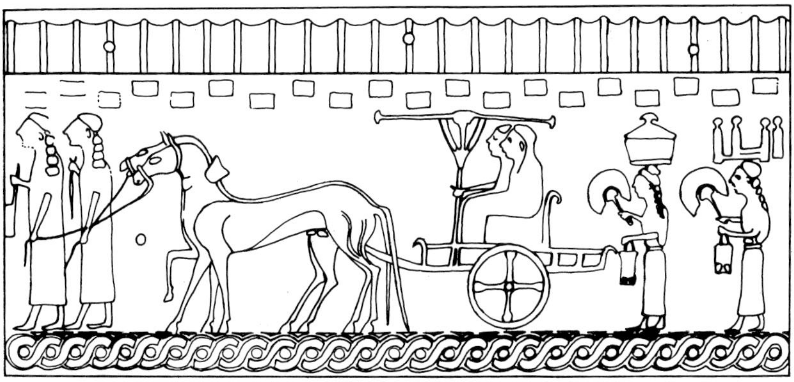

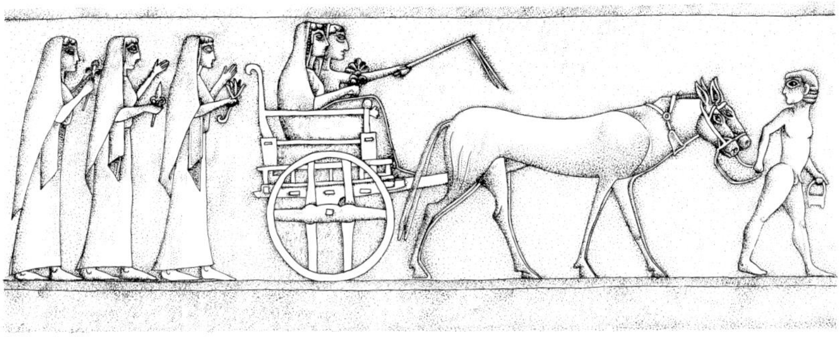

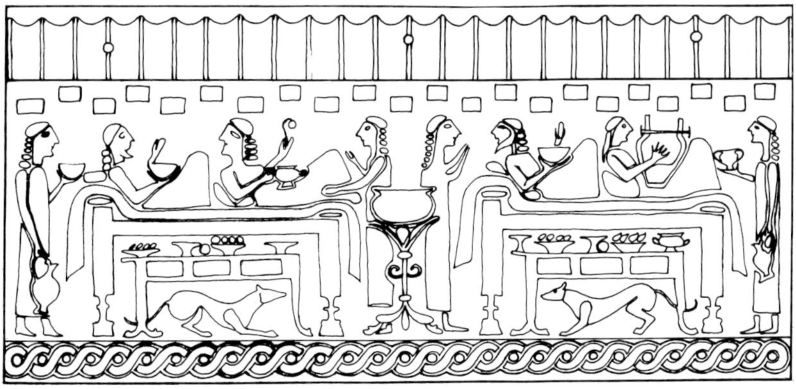

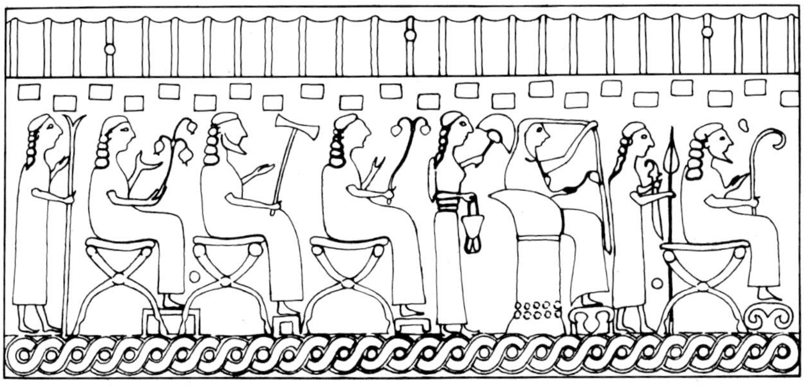

Fig. 103 Terra-cotta frieze plaque: procession. From the Archaic building, Poggio Civitate (Murlo).

Fig. 104 Terra-cotta frieze plaque: procession. From Metapontum, Temple C I.

Fig. 105 Terra-cotta frieze plaque: banquet. From the Archaic building, Poggio Civitate (Murlo).

Fig. 106 Terra-cotta frieze plaque: assembly of seated figures. From the Archaic building, Poggio Civitate (Murlo).

tury on architectural terra-cotta friezes in Etruria and Lazio; on Chiusine funerary sculpture as well as on wall-paintings of Etruscan tombs such representations continued well into the fourth century.

In Etruria (unlike in Greece) wives participated in feasts as equals of their husbands, as is demonstrated by the frieze plaques from Poggio Civitate. The second figure on the first of the two dining couches, symmetrically flanking a big wine container on a stand, must be a woman: her prominent bosom is clearly distinguished from the flatter chests of her three male companions, and she is the only one to hold a flower as well as a wine cup. A clear distinction between the sexes is made difficult by the uniformly worn, ankle-length garments for all the figures, as well as by their long hair, mostly dressed in the conventional wiglike style, which seems to have replaced the single back braid for women. Only the first banqueter on the second couch is shown as bearded. His beardless companion, supported by a large cushion, plays a lyre, whose strings must once have been indicated by paint. Singing and accompanying oneself on the lyre formed part of the training of an educated Greek citizen; this musical culture was taken over by the Etruscan aristocracy. As we have noted, the sound of the auloi played a large part in Etruscan daily and ritual life. The flute, however, seems to have been a less aristocratic instrument and one not used by the actual banqueters. Here the auloi are played by a man standing at the head of the couch of the lyre player, seemingly accompanying the second banqueter on it who turns to him, his mouth opened in song. At each end of the plaque stands a cupbearer, facing the couch in front of him with a cup in one raised hand and a wine jug in the other. Another servant, back to the flutist, gestures with both hands, seemingly trying to attract the attention of the banqueting lady, who has turned back her head to converse with the partner sharing her couch.

The whole atmosphere here is one of luxury and the leisurely enjoyment of aristocratic privilege. The couches with their elegantly fretted legs are covered with ample blankets and cushions of various sizes. On the long, low serving tables are dishes, fruit stands, and cups containing food and drink, while the central position of the large wine bowl with its ornate stand emphasizes the important role of wine drinking in the Etruscan banquet. The excavation at Poggio Civitate has yielded many fragments of pottery of the same shapes as the vessels represented on these plaques, strengthening the impression that what is shown here is a real event, eternalized on the frieze to proclaim to those visiting the residence, or meeting place, the wealth and status of the ruling family. Dogs crouching below the tables allude to the aristocratic pursuit of hunting. The artist who made the model created a lively and finely balanced composition, skillfully blending Oriental ideology with local elements and motifs of Greek inspiration.

The fourth group of frieze plaques—an assembly of five seated figures with three standing attendants—is more solemn, both in form and content; it has been interpreted by a number of scholars as a group of enthroned divinities (FIG. 106). Others see in this row of dignified figures, all facing to the right, eminent humans whose attributes exemplify the religious, political, juridical, and military powers wielded by the Etruscan princely families. The latter explanation seems more convincing in the general context of the frieze. The most important personages are undoubtedly the two seated figures on the right side of the plaque; they are distinguished by each having an attendant standing behind and by their elaborately decorated footstools, which recall the shape of an Ionian capital (similar footstools of wood were found in tombs at Verucchio). The man sits on a folding seat whose feet end in hooves, a piece of furniture that, carved from ivory and known as a *sella curulis*, was used as a sign of high office by Roman magistrates (Roman writers knew of the Etruscan origin of the *sella curulis*). Dressed in an ankle-length smooth tunic, this bearded dignitary holds a curved staff in his right hand. It is the *lituus*, carried by priests and magistrates as a symbol of their powers. A long-haired young man holding a lance and a sword attends the man. On an embossed, high-backed throne behind him sits a lady lifting the edge of the mantle covering her head in a gesture typical for brides or matrons; in her right hand is a flower identical to that of the banqueting lady. Next comes her maid in a long, belted dress; she fans her mistress and holds a situla of the same shape as that carried by the servant girls in the carriage procession. There follow three people sitting on identical folding chairs with simple, rectangular footstools. All wear the same dress and wiglike long hairstyle, but the central figure is bearded and holds a double axe, which, as we know, is also a symbol of power. The other two figures are presumably ladies, each holding a flowered stem (or pomegranates) in her right hand. The scene closes with a standing, beardless male with a tall staff, forked at the top; in later representations of athletic events on wall-paintings such a staff, with a somewhat longer fork, characterizes trainers or umpires.

It is tempting to interpret this scene as depicting members of the aristocracy, furbished with all the emblems of their power and dignity, assembled to watch games, perhaps the very horse race shown on another part of the frieze. The subject of both men and women seated and attending (funerary?) games appears in friezes on Chiusine bucchero vessels and in later wall-paintings in tombs such as the Tomb of the Monkey (*Tomba della Scimmia*) at Chiusi and the Tomb of the Bigas (*Tomba delle Bighe*) at Tarquinia; here it may be represented for the first time. However, we cannot identify the subject with certainty; the assembly could well be a ceremonial reunion of persons of rank, and the attendant with the forked staff might be a herald or a master of ceremonies.

What is beyond doubt is the important role played by women in the imagery of the frieze, either as equals of men, as in the banquet and assembly scenes, or as the most prominent figures, as in the carriage procession. Livy recounts the way the Etruscan wives of Tarquin's sons feasted in Rome, enjoying themselves at a dinner party in the greatest luxury together with a group of young friends (Livy 1.57.9), a description that could fittingly be applied to the banquet scene on the frieze plaques from Poggio Civitate.

An echo of how differently Roman ladies during the early period of the monarchy were expected to behave appears in Plutarch. In his life of Numa Pompilius, the second king of Rome, Plutarch tells us that Numa "forbade [women] all busy intermeddling, taught them sobriety, and accustomed them to be silent; wine they were to refrain from entirely, and were not to speak, even on the most necessary topics, unless their husbands were with them" (*Lycurgus and Numa* 3.5, Loeb translation).

Athenian ladies were certainly not allowed to participate in banquets or symposia held by their fathers, brothers, or husbands. They led supervised lives, shut away in the women's quarters. It is the prostitutes (Gr. *hetairai*) who appear as lightly clad flute players or as naked companions of men in the scenes of symposia and lovemaking depicted on Greek vases.

If we have discussed the frieze plaques from Poggio Civitate rather fully, it is because their themes clearly illustrate features that are characteristic for Etruscan aristocratic society at the end of the Orientalizing period. And while some aspects of this way of life, such as the high status of women, are found also during subsequent centuries, others are not. This is due not only to the passage of time but also to the different rates of development in different regions of Etruria. Thus a luxurious aristocracy that depended on the loyalty of blood ties and faithful clients and slaves continued to flourish in rural areas and family seats such as Poggio Civitate in the interior and northern parts of the country. The southern and coastal cities seem by this time to have reached an advanced state of urbanization with a more complex social stratification. This comprised a newly emerged "middle class" of property-owning artisans, craftsmen, and traders, a number of whom were settled foreigners. Eventually "tyrants" were to assume power in some cities, backed by classes no longer belonging to the old social order of the gentilician system.

RELIGIOUS BELIEFS: ALTARS—SACELLA—VOTIVE DEPOSITS

While considering the nature of the terra-cotta sculptures on the ridge roofs of the Archaic buildings at Poggio Civitate, we mentioned that they might represent divinities. But notions valid in the Near East and contemporary Greece, such as cult statues and their worship in temples built to shelter them, are not applicable in seventh-century Etruria (the stone building at Tarquinia, see p. 27, is exceptional). Instead, there will have been sacred groves and enclosures, open to the sky, in which the divinity was thought to reside, probably in the aniconic form of a stone, a piece of wood, or a weapon, and where sacrifices took place on altars of various types. Representation of the gods in human form seems not to have taken place until the end of the Orientalizing period.

The primary act in creating a sanctuary was to separate off a piece of land and define its boundaries (Etr. *tular*) and its entrance, either by a precinct or by stone cippi, thus marking the area as sacred in accordance with the divine laws of division that emanated from Tinia/Zeus. Animal sacrifices were made in different rituals, depending on the nature of the divinity to whom they were offered. If the animal was burnt, it was destined for celestial gods, and the act took place on a rectangular, molded stone altar either of single-block form or with lateral wings. If the animal was sacrificed to underworld divinities, its throat was cut and the blood made to flow through a channel carved into a drum- or cone-shaped altar that communicated with a subterranean hollow below. These altars differed from those destined for libations and bloodless sacrifices in the cult of ancestors within chamber tombs, such as those mentioned above (see FIG. 81).

Besides altars, a sanctuary could contain a rectangular podium constructed of blocks with complex moldings, which combined various cult functions and corresponded to what in Latin was called *sacellum* (a roofless space, sacred to the gods).

If the isolated square little building on the western side of the courtyard of Poggio Civitate (see FIG. 94) was a sacred enclosure (Lat. *templum*) from which to observe omens, it preserved in its structure the older form of domestic architecture, the thatched hut, rather than the new type of the solid surrounding complex with a heavy, tiled roof. The earliest temples may, in fact, have been buildings of ephemeral material.

The first solid structure in Etruria that can properly be called a temple has survived in traces at Veii. A rectangular building (ca. 8 x 15 m), it was erected about 600 B.C. on the Piazza d'Armi, the steep acropolis isolated from the main plateau of Veii. A Villanovan village had occupied this elevated spot, but at the end of the Orientalizing period the whole area underwent urban planning with the creation of a main street and four crossroads, a piazza, and a huge oval open cistern, an essential feature in case of a siege. Of the temple, which took the form of an exceptionally large house, the two lowest courses of squared stone blocks have remained in situ. Its ridge roof, supported internally by one or two pillars, was tiled and fitted along the eaves with moldmade terra-cotta antefixes in the form of female heads of Daidalic style. The frieze plaques of the revetments of the front pediment were decorated in low relief with a procession of warriors, on foot, riding, or on a biga; they were painted in white on red. Typologically these moldmade plaques, dated to the first half of the sixth century, derive from prototypes found in South Italian Greek architecture (Metapontum, etc.), but the theme of the heroic warrior on a biga and his armed followers became a standard one on friezes of temples and aristocratic residences.

The second temple, whose existence in an earlier form is proved by votive inscriptions, is the (probably oracular) sanctuary dedicated to Menerva at Portonaccio on the western flank of the plateau of Veii, outside the city walls. The

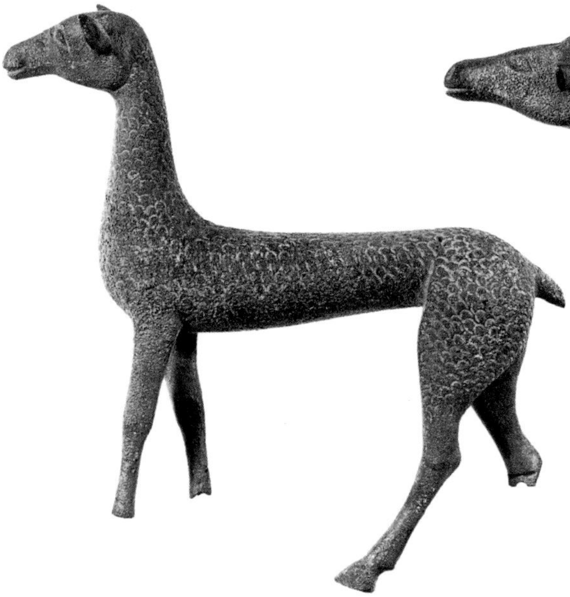

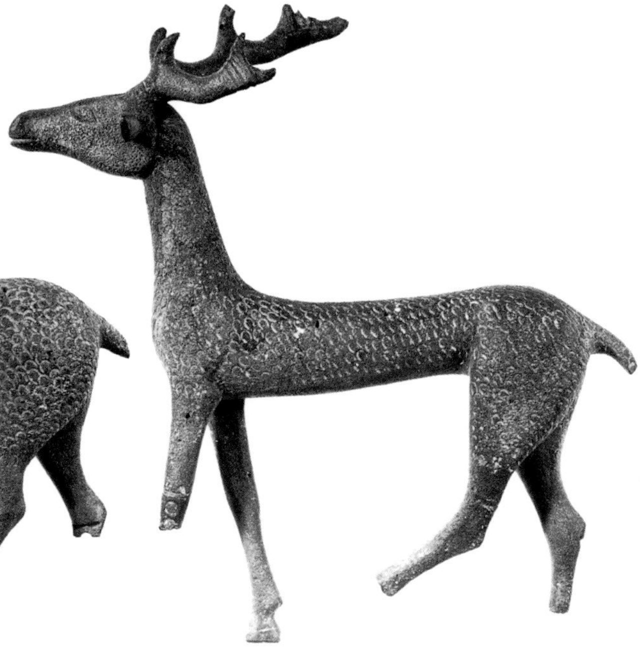

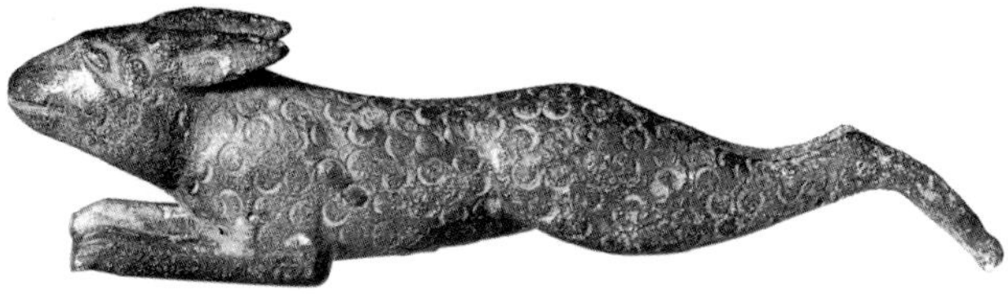

Fig. 107 Doe. From Brolio. First half of sixth century B.C. Cast bronze. H. 13.4 cm. Florence, Museo Archeologico 559.

Fig. 108 Stag. From Brolio. First half of sixth century B.C. Cast bronze. H. 15.1 cm. Florence, Museo Archeologico 558.

Fig. 109 Hare. From Brolio. First half of sixth century B.C. Cast bronze. L. 8.5 cm. Florence, Museo Archeologico 580.

present state of the building dates from a reconstruction in two phases at the end of the sixth century (see p. 205).

Further evidence for religious worship in Etruria during the later Orientalizing period is provided by the large number of bronze statuettes of men, women, and animals made as votive gifts to divinities whose names are unknown to us. Many of these figurines originated in Northern Etruria, particularly in the region of Arezzo and Volterra where they were found, but the circumstances of their dedication and their exact provenances are mostly obscure. Some of them have turned up in France in places that may have been stations along routes used by tin traders.

A votive deposit of a large quantity of bronze figurines, utensils, and pottery fragments was actually excavated and recorded in 1863 at Brolio in the Chiana valley. It comprised material dating from the early sixth to the fifth century, much of it subsequently lost. Among the most spectacular surviving bronze pieces were the foreparts of griffins, statuettes of deer (FIGS. 107, 108) and hares (FIG. 109) that once decorated the rims of bronze basins (inspired by Samian or East Greek prototypes), as well as four elongated statuettes—three armed warriors wearing a helmet and a loincloth, and one woman in a long, belted dress and necklace (FIG. 110). All four have identical studs on the crowns of their heads, by which they were originally attached to a utensil or a piece of furniture as supports. These fine bronzes were probably made at Chiusi and may have been part of a support for a prestigious object, such as a large cauldron, dedicated in a rural sanctuary by one of the aristocratic families in control of the traffic through the Chiana valley.

As we shall see, votive statuettes in bronze were to remain characteristic for Northern internal Etruria (from Orvieto and Chiusi to Arezzo, Volterra, and Bologna), whereas in Southern Etruria terra-cotta became the preferred material for votive offerings. We cannot be entirely certain that all the small bronze images of warriors, men, and women represent the dedicants themselves. By offering up a statuette of durable material in a sanctuary, the worshiper may have hoped to remind the presiding divinity of his or her perpetual presence there, thus ensuring personal well-being or expressing gratitude for favors received. Another possibility is to consider these statuettes substitutes for human sacrifices, a primitive practice, of which echoes survive in later Roman writers (Ov. *Fast.* 3.339–44; Macrob. 1.7.30 and 34; Festus 272 L). But the sheer quantity of votive statuettes preserved argues in favor of the former interpretation. A number of statuettes, however, are characterized by their attributes as small images of the divinities to whom the sanctuary was sacred.

Figurines of cattle may be either propitiatory substitutes for real sacrificial animals or indications of an agricultural rite to increase the fertility of the herds on which the prosperity of the rural population depended. Modest votive offerings of this type reflect the public devotion by a vast social class to collective divinities; this has nothing to do with the private ceremonies of the aristocracy dedicated to their deified ancestors.

Of exceptional interest for our inquiry into religious beliefs is a small carved ivory statuette of a nude woman found in the richly furnished male burial (FIGS. 111a, b). The statuette is well proportioned and stands (her lower legs and feet are broken off) with her arms bent, her left hand squeezing her left breast, while in her right hand she holds a cup below her right breast. Her hair is plaited in the familiar thick back braid. Originally the statuette was covered with a fragile layer of gold foil, traces of which were preserved on her upper body and back at the time of excavation. The rarity and durable nature of gold charged this metal with a supernatural quality. The statuette's nudity and gesture connect it with Mesopotamian and Syro-Phoenician prototypes representing Ishtar/Astarte, the great Oriental goddess of love, fertility, death, and rebirth. The precious material of the statuette and its deposition in a tomb suggest that it was highly valued and may have been thought of as ensuring life beyond death.

It is interesting to note that further Ishtarlike representations of nude women were discovered in the burial of an aristocratic lady, also at Marsiliana d'Albegna (Tomb II in the Banditella necropolis), dated to the first quarter of the seventh

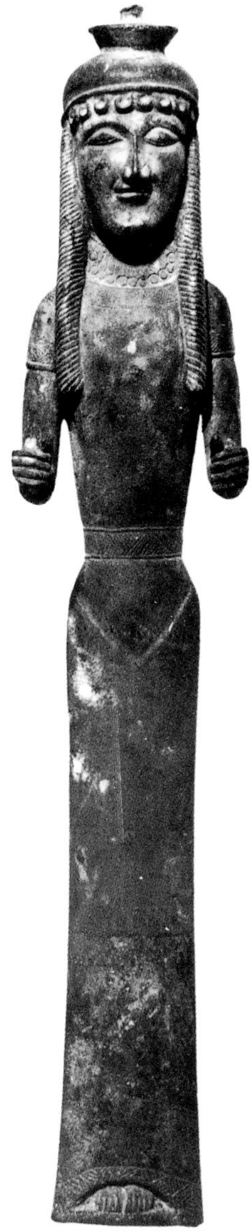

Fig. 110 Support in the form of a woman. From Brolio. Second quarter of sixth century B.C. Cast bronze. H. 36.1 cm. Florence, Museo Archeologico 561.

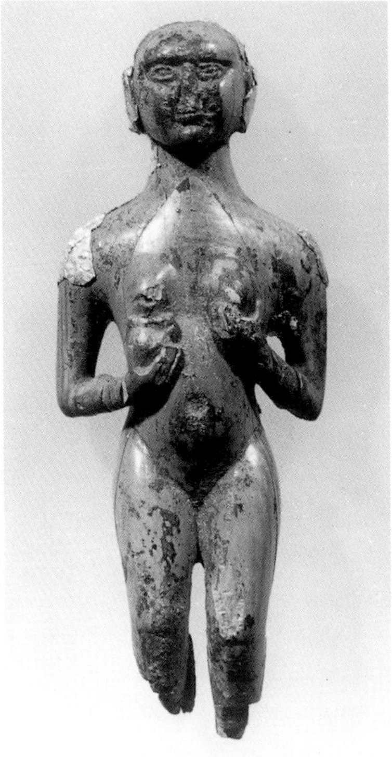

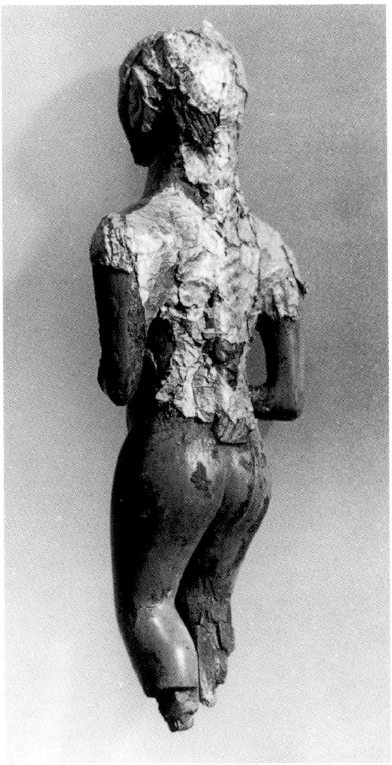

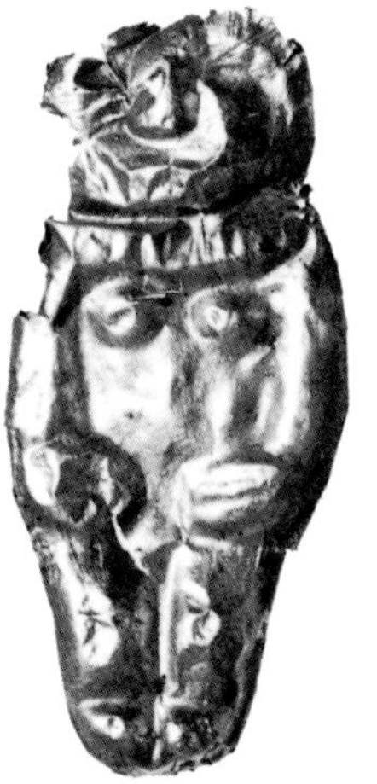

ABOVE LEFT
Fig. 111a Statuette of a nude woman. From Tomb XLI, Circle of the Fibula, Marsiliana d'Albegna. Second quarter of seventh century B.C. Ivory, originally covered with gold foil. H. 9.5 cm. Florence, Museo Archeologico.

ABOVE RIGHT
Fig. 111b Back view of woman, figure 111a.

RIGHT
Fig. 112 Pendant in the form of a woman touching her pubic parts. From Marsiliana d'Albegna. First quarter of seventh century B.C. Bronze covered with gold foil. Florence, Museo Archeologico 11139.

century. The tomb, a rectangular trench covered with river pebbles and marked by a shield-shaped stone, contained the remains of a carriage and an iron bed, on which the richly dressed lady rested. Her garments were decorated with ornaments of gold foil in the form of squares and meanders punched with geometric patterns. Her numerous jewels and personal ornaments of gold, silver, ivory, and amber included the bronze pendants of a necklace, covered with gold foil. Ten of these pendants take the form of frontal images of plump nude women wearing broad necklaces and holding their hands against their abdomens in a gesture of fertility (FIG. 112). They are comparable to the amber figurines of women in the same pose found in seventh-century tombs of Vetulonia (see p. 100). The other pendants also show Oriental motifs: anchorlike shapes and a circular medallion embossed with astral symbols. Such representations of nude women are, as we shall see, relatively rare in the Orientalizing and Archaic periods in Etruria and must have a special religious significance, most probably relating to death and rebirth. Further Near Eastern objects in this tomb were a faience scarab and a small bronze bell of Caucasian manufacture.

At Satricum in Lazio, where there was a temple of Mater Matuta, a goddess of growth, small seventh-century bronze images (pendants) of a nude woman combined with the sun disc or moon indicate similar Oriental inspiration.

FEMALE DIVINITIES

From the rare glimpses of Etruscan funerary and religious practice we may deduce that a female divinity, in nature not unlike the Oriental goddess Ishtar/Astarte and perhaps represented in the just-mentioned ivory statuette from Marsiliana d'Albegna (see FIGS. 111a, b), was connected with fertility, death, and rebirth. Similar ideas seem to be expressed by the gold pendants in the form of nude women touching their pubic parts found in a female tomb at the same site (see FIG. 112) and perhaps also the amber pendants from Vetulonian grave circles.

We cannot prove whether other images of Near Eastern inspiration, such as the Mistress of the Animals and the hero-subduing monsters that appear repeatedly stamped on the splendid funerary sheet-gold jewelry from the Regolini-Galassi tomb in Cerveteri and on related pieces, as well as on bucchero and bronze vessels, correspond to divine beings worshiped by the Etruscans. The goldsmiths who inspired much of this jewelry must originally have come from the Syro-Phoenician area, where such motifs with specific religious significance were widely used, but it is uncertain what they meant to the Etruscan aristocrats who commissioned such pieces. It is possible that these images corresponded to preexisting concepts of nature divinities flanked by birds and quadrupeds that figured in earlier representations on open-worked bronze handles found as far apart as Bisenzio, Bologna, and Spadarolo.

WOMEN'S CLOTHES

In contrast to the Geometric bronze figurines of the Villanovan civilization, which, as we have seen, mostly represented women in the nude, the votive statuettes of the Orientalizing period were usually clothed. The majority of the male figures wear a *perizoma* (FIG. 113) and a belt, or a tunic of varying length. Etruscan women assume a variety of garments: short unbelted dresses, either sleeveless or short sleeved; longer belted dresses of heavy material (FIG. 114); long belted dresses like the Greek chiton, the hem of which arches up over the feet; rectangular mantles hanging from the shoulders over the back to the hem of the dress; heavy cloaks covering head and body in the manner of a cape; rectangular cloaks hanging in one piece from the head over the back, but split up to the middle in front and thus forming two rectangular lappets reaching down to the breasts or to the knees (FIG. 115); and square head scarves worn over the head and shoulders. This diver-

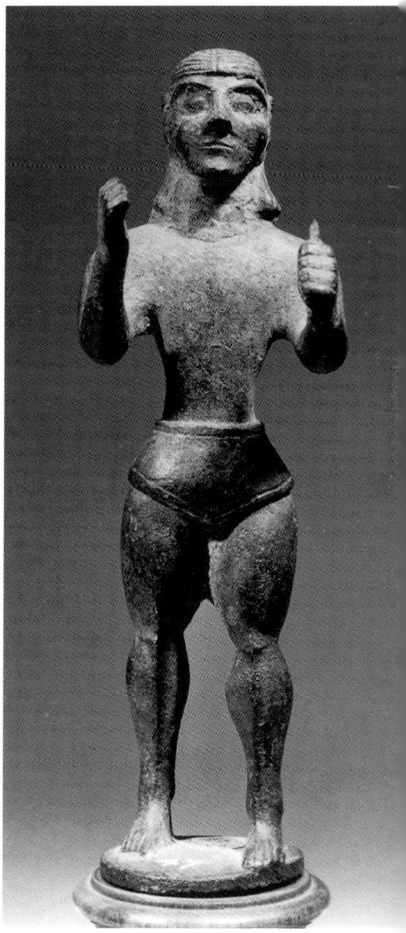

Fig. 113 Votive statuette of a man wearing a *perizoma*. Early sixth century B.C. Cast bronze. H. with base 12.4 cm. Florence, Museo Archeologico 47.

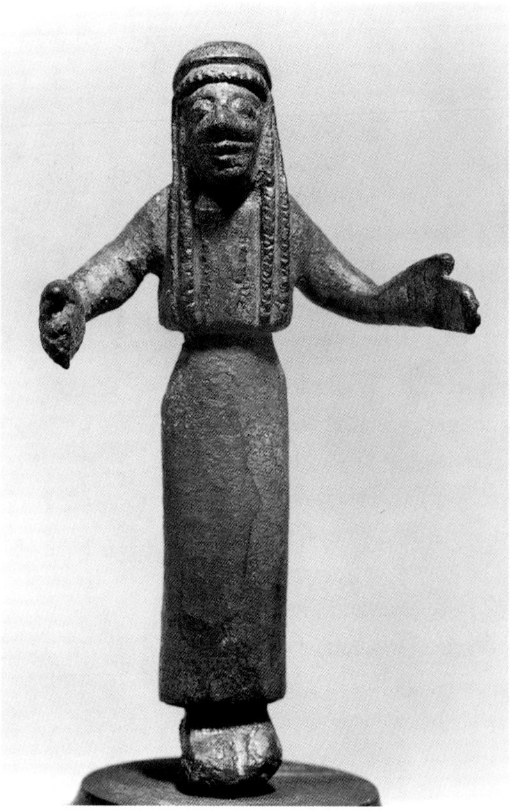

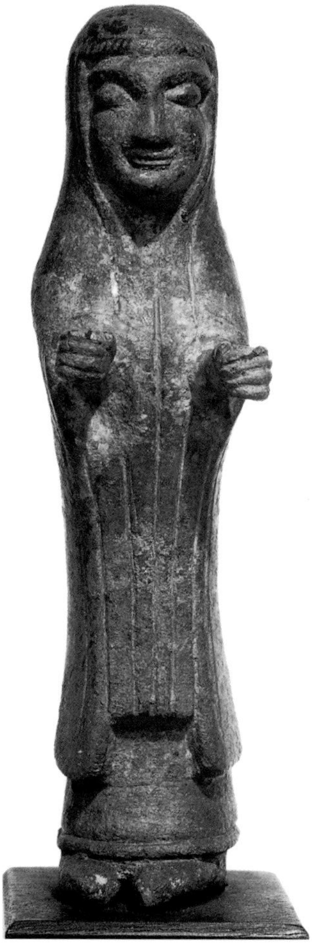

ABOVE LEFT
Fig. 114 Votive statuette of a woman wearing a belted dress. First half of sixth century B.C. Cast bronze. H. 7.5 cm. Perugia, Museo Archeologico Nazionale dell'Umbria 926.

ABOVE RIGHT
Fig. 115 Votive statuette of a woman wearing a heavy cloak. Early sixth century B.C. Cast bronze. H. 14.1 cm. London, The British Museum GR 1907.3-11.1.

sity in dress is probably partly regional costume, but it must also have something to do with the different climates in the various parts of Etruria.

The prevailing female hairstyle during the Orientalizing period—the long back plait—may in addition have sidelocks that hang forward from the temples and are sometimes grasped by the women at breast level, or their ends may be turned up (see FIGS. 43, 65). This gesture and the locks go back to Oriental prototypes.

The difference in dress between aristocratic ladies and servant girls is not always particularly marked at this time. We can, however, be certain that female figures carrying objects on their heads belong to the lower social strata. They usually wear a simple tunic, belted or unbelted, that ends well short of the ankles.

The fashion in clothes and hair changes over time, becoming more unified with the increasing adoption of Greek models. We shall draw attention to such new developments during the Archaic and Classical periods.

Reviewing the—necessarily very limited—evidence of the material remains chosen from a wide range of Etruscan sites of the Orientalizing period, we are led to conclude that the position of Etruscan women, at least of those belonging to the aristocracy, was one of evident equality with men.

The grave goods accompanying female burials in the monumental family tumuli are often luxurious and numerous, rivaling those of the males. The cult devoted to the ancestors in the tombs included both men and women, as we have learned from the terra-cotta statuettes of both sexes that originally occupied the five chairs in the tomb called after them (see FIGS. 79, 80).

Inscriptions on pottery and funerary monuments indicate that aristocratic women were literate and made and received gifts and dedicated objects, although the majority of the names preserved are those of men. All free women had their own individual name (praenomen) and family name (nomen), and these were not infrequently mentioned in funerary inscriptions of men who give both their father's and their mother's name. The double-name system survived until the first century and, at Cerveteri, even influenced some Latin inscriptions. This was in marked contrast to the Roman custom, where daughters were given no praenomina, but were simply called after their father, for example: Claudia (major and minor, in the case of an elder and younger daughter), Antonia, Tullia, Livia, etc. The funerary inscription of the Roman aristocratic lady Caecilia Metella on her famous tomb on the Via Appia, for example, defines her exclusively by her family relationship to the men in her life, her father and her husband: *Caecilia Metella Cretici f.* (from Quintus Caecilius Metellus, her father) *Crassi* . . . (from Marcus Crassus, her husband).

There are indications that in certain regions and contexts Etruscan women were accorded particular importance. A striking example is the protective house-shaped sarcophagi encasing the funerary beds of women in the tombs of Cerveteri from the seventh to the fifth century.

In general, it is clear that in a society dominated by the aristocracy, women of blood were accorded high respect because they were the guarantors of the continuation of the family. This vital fact, as well as the possibility of forming marriage alliances favorable to the family, must have played an important part, particularly at times when the aristocracy felt itself under threat politically or suffered from lack of legitimate descendants.

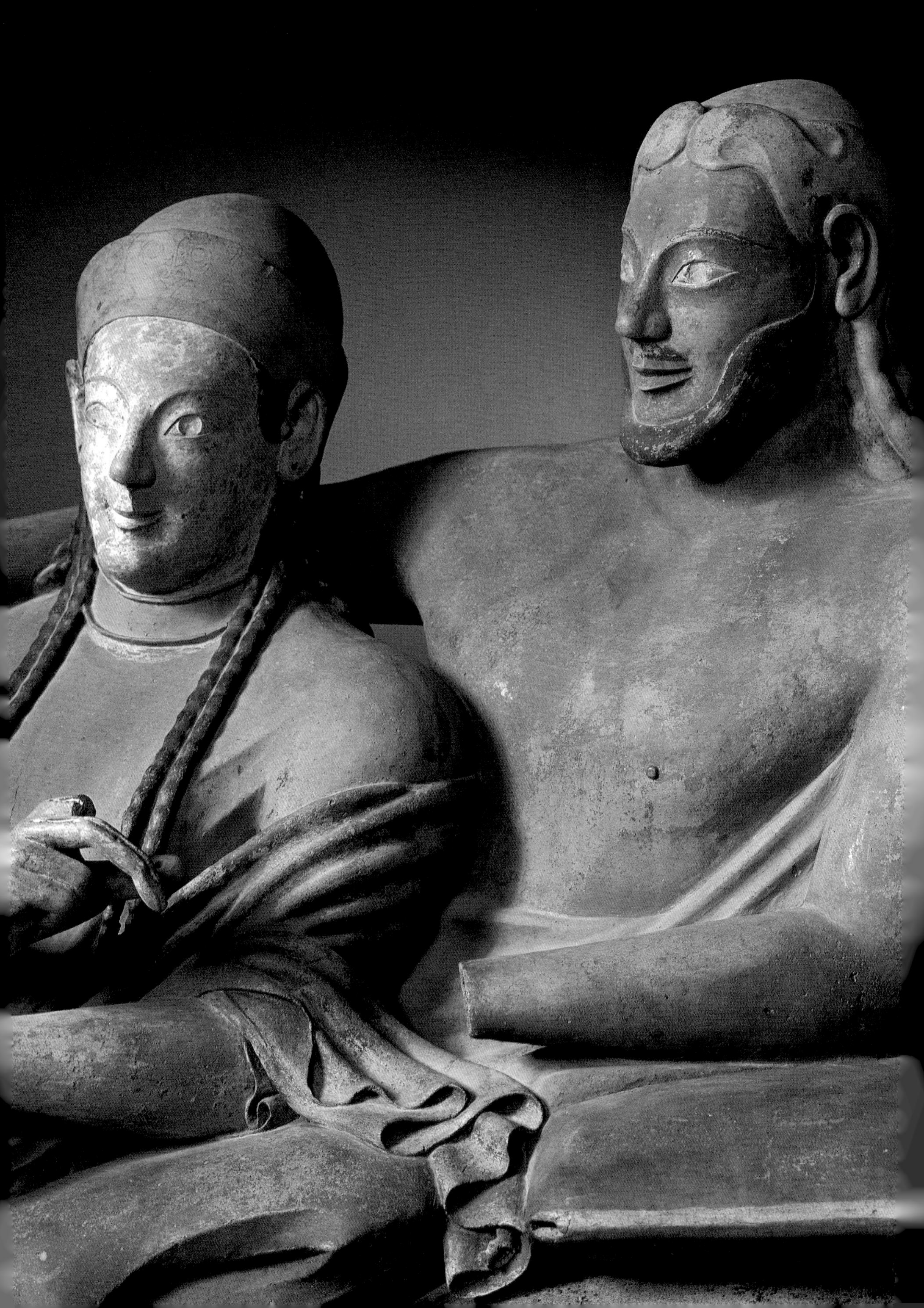

III

The Archaic Period

about 575–480 B.C.

THE FLOWERING OF THE ETRUSCAN CITIES

The principal Etruscan cities were autonomous and only loosely linked in a (religious) association. Separately they had developed their cultural identity and their political and economic institutions and spheres. We have seen how this diversity is reflected in the artistic individuality and varying funerary customs of the different cities. The most important and famous were, from south to north, Cerveteri (Etr. *Caisra*, *Cisra*; Lat. *Caere*; Gr. *Agylla*), Tarquinia (Etr. *Tarch*[*u*]*na*; Lat. *Tarquinii*), Vulci (Etr. *Velch-*, *Velc*[*a*]*l*; Lat. *Vulci*), Roselle (Lat. *Rusellae*), Vetulonia (Etr. *Vetluna*, *Vatluna*), and Populonia (Etr. *Fufluna*, *Pupluna*); and, in the interior of Etruria, Veii (Etr. *Vei-*), Volsinii (Etr. *Velsena*, *Velzna*), Chiusi (Etr. *Clevsin-*; Umb. *Camars*; Lat. *Clusium*), Perugia (Etr. *Per*[*u*]*sna*; Lat. *Perusia*), Cortona (Etr. *Curtun-*), Arezzo (Lat. *Arretium*), Fiesole (Etr. *Vipsul*; Lat. *Faesulae*), Volterra (Etr. *Velathri*; Lat. *Volaterrae*), and Pisa (Lat. *Pisae*).

Ancient authors mention the association of Etruscan cities as the twelve or fifteen peoples of Etruria (*duodecim* or *quindecim populi Etruriae*), or simply as *Etruria* or all of Etruria (*omnis Etruria*). The number twelve for the cities of Etruria proper (which was perhaps mirrored in those of the "colonial" areas of the Po valley and Campania) was probably of ritual nature. It is found also in western Asia Minor, where the Greek cities, with which Etruria was in close cultural contact, were organized into the twelve members of the Ionian League.

We know very little about the nature of the Etruscan "League." Livy mentions that the Etruscan cities under their leaders (Lat. *principes*) assembled annually for consultation at the Fanum Voltumnae, the federal sanctuary near Orvieto that is

Detail of sarcophagus, from figure 176b.

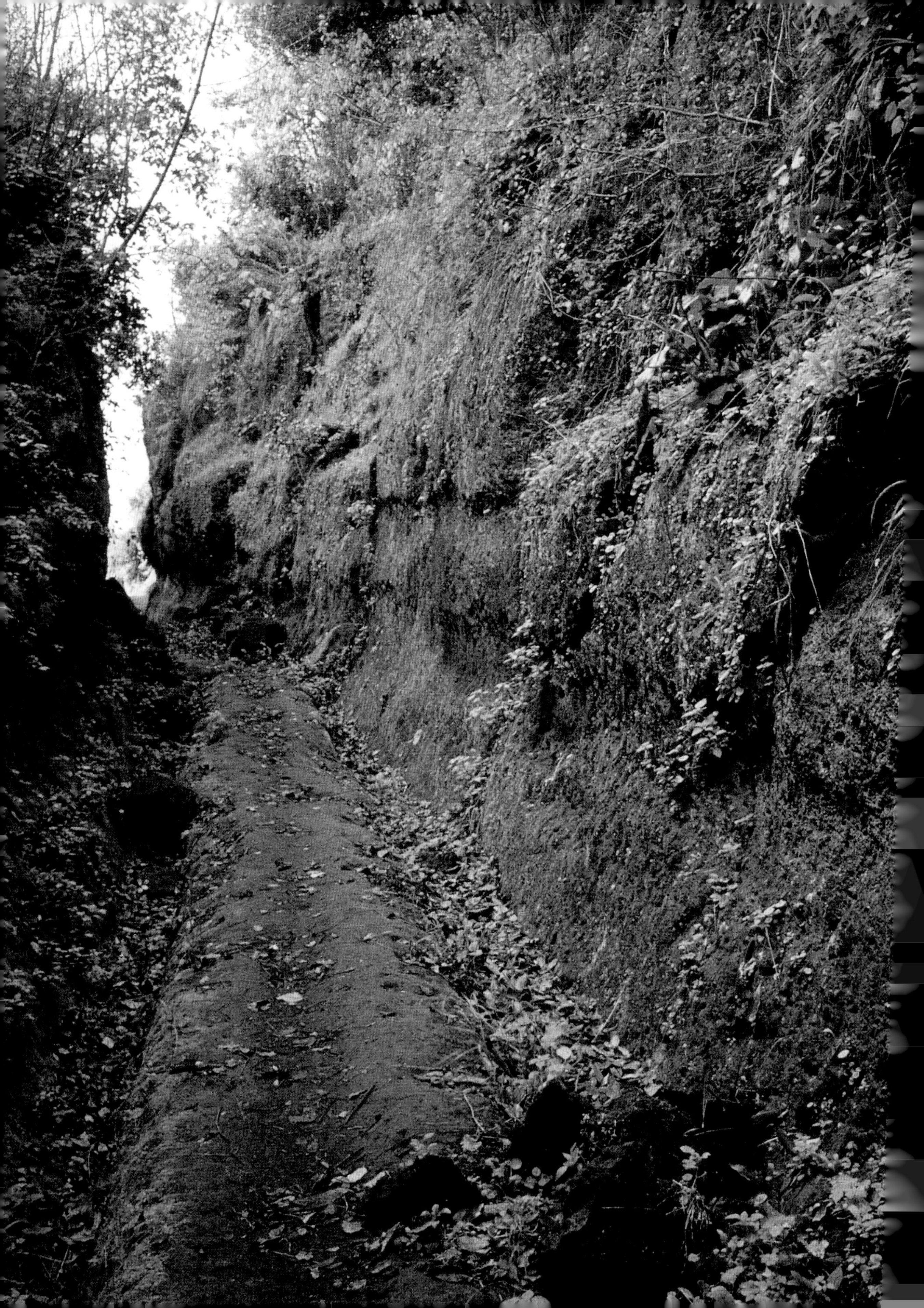

as yet undiscovered (Livy 4.23, 5.1, 10.16). Religious celebrations and games recalling the pan-Greek festivals held at Olympia took place at this sanctuary. A passage in Servius indicates that there were twelve Etruscan kings (Lat. *lucumones*), one of whom presided over these assemblies (*Aen.* 8.475). Livy refers to the election of a king by the twelve *populi*, each of whom contributed a lictor (1.8, 5.1). He also mentions the election of a priest by the periodic assembly. The description of this elected head of the Etruscan cities (at the end of the fifth century, when the conflict between Rome and Veii had started) as *sacerdos* points to his having extraordinary religious and temporal powers. It is likely that during the Archaic period the functions of king and priest were closely allied.

CHANGES IN MILITARY EQUIPMENT AND TACTICS

Among the many social and political consequences of urbanization in Etruria must have been the growing dependence of the *principes* on the military cooperation of a large number of male inhabitants of the cities. The partial introduction of the phalanx of heavily armed hoplites (foot soldiers) reflected on many painted pottery vases and on moldmade terra-cotta friezes from princely residences and temples probably indicates a move to a new form of warfare, away from the old aristocratic reliance on cavalry and lightly armed troops of clan members and clients. Each hoplite was armed with a round shield, short sword, and lances, and he wore a crested helmet and greaves; the similarly equipped chief is usually shown as mounting or standing in a war chariot driven by a charioteer. This emphasis on the biga, an aristocratic type of vehicle by now obsolete in battle, was perhaps an attempt by the heads of the great families to reaffirm their leading role; it may be regarded in the same light as the deposition of chariots in princely tombs in the sixth century (see FIG. 86). Proper hoplite tactics and the citizen ideology that characterized contemporary Greek warfare, were, however, alien to social conditions in Etruria and do not seem ever to have become the general rule.

We have noted the mud-brick city wall of the second half of the seventh century surrounding the hill of Roselle, and we may imagine that many of the surviving stone-built walls of Late Classical and Hellenistic date in other cities had earlier defenses of similar perishable type during the Archaic period. Roselle herself erected massive stone walls in the mid-sixth century to replace the earlier mud-brick ones. Vetulonia, Populonia, and Volterra have stone walls that in part go back to the sixth century.

ROADS AND BRIDGES

Besides using rivers and coastal waters for transport by boat, the Etruscans built roads and bridges connecting the main towns for wheeled traffic. Such roads were

Fig. 116 Rock-cut road with wheel ruts in Etruria.

skillfully adapted to existing geographical conditions and often entailed major feats of engineering. The volcanic tufa region of Southern Etruria provides many examples of a road passing through a deep trench, cut laboriously through the steep hillside so as to enable carts and wagons to follow a short and straight route rather than make their way in a long serpentine over the crest of the hill. These artificial ravines, often narrower at the top than at the bottom where the traffic passed, had to be drained to prevent flooding; some of them still preserve the channels for carrying off rainwater. The deep ruts worn into the surface of the road by the wheels of vehicles passing during centuries of use are also visible (FIG. 116). An impressive example of a major road connecting an important city with its harbor is that running through the coastal plain from Cerveteri to the sanctuary at the port of Pyrgi. Small branch roads served minor rural settlements.

Narrow rivers and torrents that could not be forded were crossed by wooden plank bridges, which often rested on massive abutments of ashlar masonry. Eventually, vaulted bridges, built entirely of specially cut tapering stone blocks, spanned the smaller rivers, while ferries will have served the larger ones.

HABITATIONS IN TOWNS: ACQUAROSSA

The limited possibilities of excavation in large Etruscan cities still inhabited nowadays have led to the exploration of smaller settlements not overlaid by later occupation. In one such minor urban center, Acquarossa near Ferento, various types of domestic buildings have been unearthed. Traces of foundations of round or oval huts show that an Iron Age village had earlier occupied the plateau.

Beginning in the third quarter of the seventh century Etruscan houses had rectangular foundations of tufa blocks; the walls above consisted either of tufa in a wooden framework or, more often, of sun-dried mud bricks covered with plaster. The roofs had cover- and pantiles, with terra-cotta revetments nailed to the ends of the wooden beams. The earliest tiles and revetments were painted white on red in a variety of motifs of Southern Etruscan and Faliscan ceramic inspiration—horses, birds, fish, and, in one case, a seated man with his feet on a footstool. Later a more unified decor of the revetments comprised single- and double-guilloche patterns as well as lotus-and-palmette chains, indebted to Magna Graecian and Greek prototypes. From the mid-sixth century private houses had simple undecorated roofs. A tile preserved from one roof had a circular hole in it to admit light or let smoke escape from the interior; attached to this tile was a separately made disc-shaped cover that from the inside could

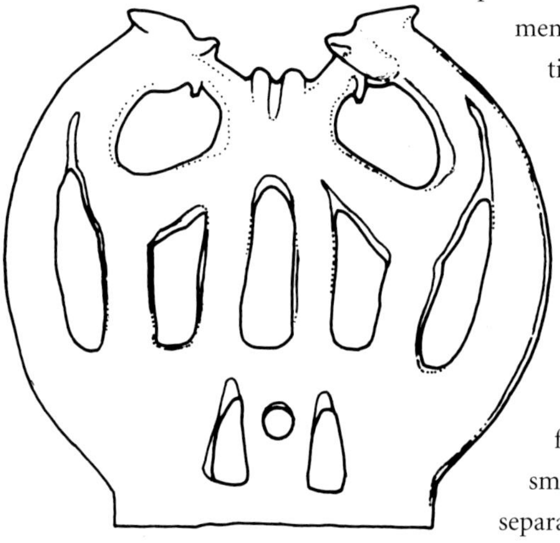

Fig. 117 Acroterion with heradically confronted figures of quadrupeds. From Zone B at Acquarossa. Third quarter of seventh century B.C. Terra-cotta. Viterbo, Museo Archeologico Nazionale.

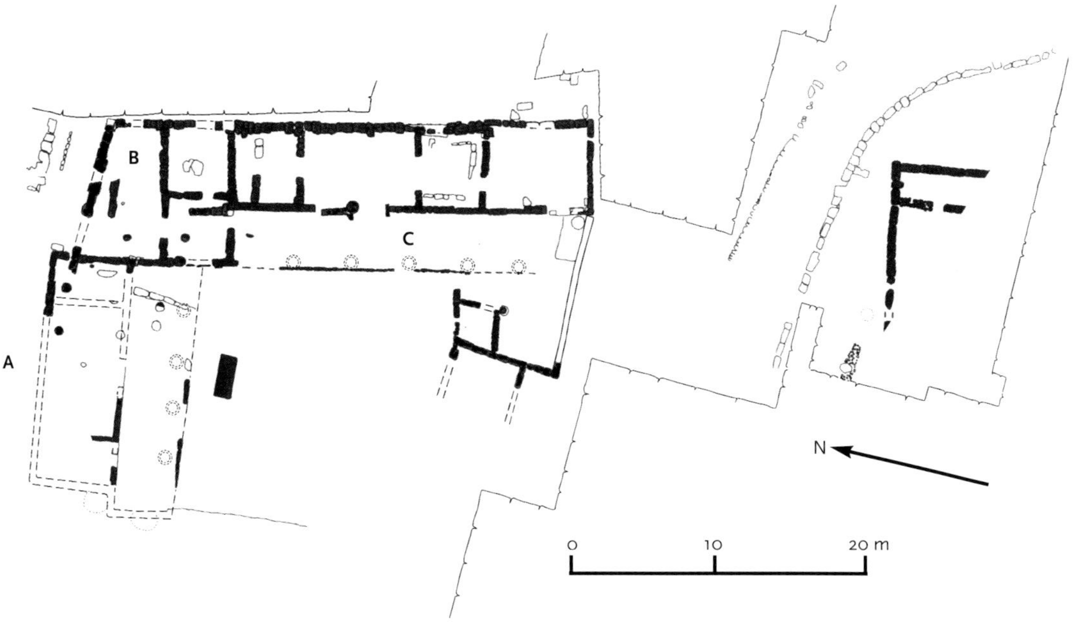

be moved with a stick to close the hole in case of rain. A group of tiles from another house was decorated with hand-modeled foreparts of griffins, recalling the animal protomes attached to bronze and pottery cauldrons of the Orientalizing period (see FIG. 58).

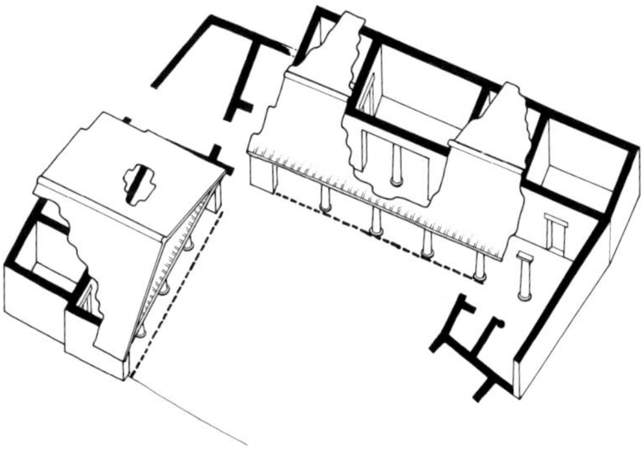

Acroteria in a variety of symmetrical patterns were cut out in openwork from thick slabs of clay. Volutes combined with a base triangle have parallels at Poggio Civitate, but the repertory at Acquarossa is richer, particularly in the use of addorsed quadrupeds, felines, and horses (FIG. 117).

The houses consisted of several intercommunicating rooms, often two or three side by side, accessible from the front through the central room and occasionally provided with a broad anteroom or porch. Many houses had a courtyard adjoining others where most of the activities of daily life, including woolworking, took place. Inside people slept, dined in bad weather, and kept their domestic and agricultural implements and big terra-cotta jars full of dried provisions; sometimes storage spaces and shelter for cattle, etc., were carved into rock outcrops adjacent to the houses.

After the middle of the sixth century a monumental residential building complex was constructed in Zone F (FIGS. 118, 119). It was distinguished by the L-shaped layout of two buildings (A and C) fronted by a portico of wooden columns forming two sides of a large forecourt. The columns' stone bases and some capitals were found in situ. In the center of the northern side of the court-

Fig. 118 Monumental residence complex in Zone F, Acquarossa. Mid-sixth century B.C.

Fig. 119 Isometric drawing of the monumental residence complex in Zone F, Acquarossa. Mid-sixth century B.C.

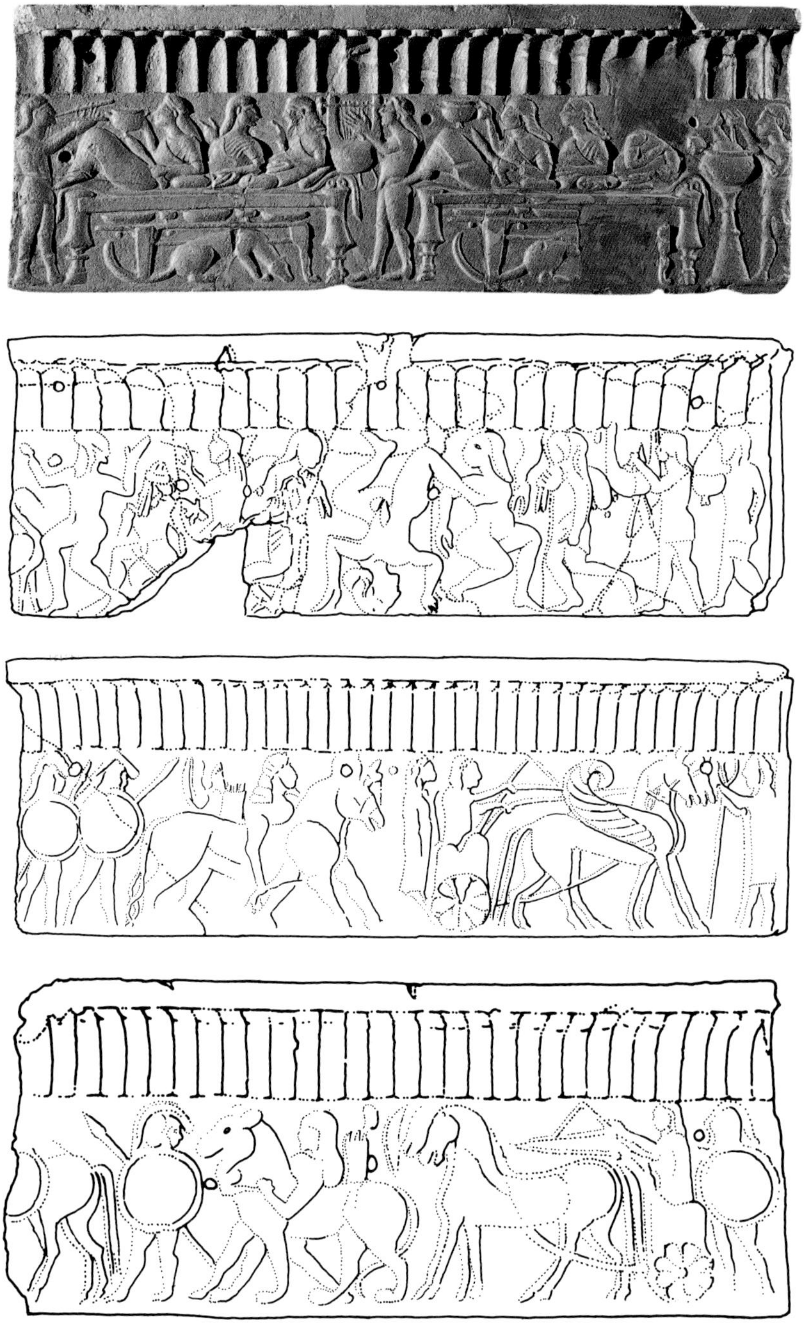

Figs. 120–23 Molded revetment plaques from Buildings A and C in Zone F, Acquarossa. Mid-sixth century B.C. Painted terracotta. H. (all) ca. 21 cm. Viterbo, Museo Archeologico Nazionale.

yard, aligned with the entrance to this symmetrical tripartite part of the complex, was a trench filled with remains of sacrifices, perhaps a family cult. The central room in the adjoining asymmetrical eastern building had a wide doorway supported by a single column in the center; this room communicated with two smaller ones flanking it, the door on the right opening into what was probably a dining space fitted with benches around three of its sides.

A series of finely molded and painted revetment plaques decorated the facades of this residence (FIGS. 120–23); they show banqueters on couches as well as dancers, including a somersaulting acrobat accompanied by musicians. Among the figures are winged horses drawing a chariot with a couple, Herakles subduing the Nemean lion, and the Cretan bull. These supernatural creatures may hint at the hero's apotheosis. It is possible that the aristocratic owners of this building complex—whose military power is alluded to by files of marching soldiers, horsemen, and chariots also represented on the plaques—identified themselves with the heroic figure of Herakles.

While these fine revetment plaques must have been made by specialist itinerant craftsmen, the majority of the undecorated roof tiles of the ordinary houses of Acquarossa were made in local workshops from local beds of clay, which also provided the material for household pottery. Only about forty houses have been excavated at Acquarossa, but it has been calculated that the settlement had about seven thousand inhabitants, a number that implies a highly organized manufacture of such necessities as roof tiles.

The finds recovered from domestic buildings and their courtyards include local pottery, portable cooking stoves, and hearths of various types. Female crafts were represented by spindle whorls, spools, and various sizes of terra-cotta loom weights. The lighter weights were for looms on which linen rather than wool was woven. Numerous wall-paintings at Tarquinia show women wearing light linen chitons of almost transparent or crinkled material (see, e.g., FIGS. 185, 188). Literary sources of a later period name Tarquinia as the source of linen sailcloth in quantities implying production on an industrial scale (Livy 28.15–19). Linen was used also as material on which to write (see FIG. 219).

Bronze and iron were worked at Acquarossa as early as the preurban phase of the seventh century, as documented by the remains of furnaces and slag from smelting the iron ore, which must have been mined nearby.

The monumental center of the acropolis of Acquarossa (Zone F) was laid out on an orthogonal plan, while the rest of the town with its irregularly scattered habitations did not follow any rules. However, some form of urban planning must have been used for the construction of rock-cut channels for the diversion of rainwater away from the bases of the houses and for filling cisterns as well as for retaining walls and a well-defined street.

For reasons that escape us, Acquarossa was destroyed and completely abandoned about 500 B.C. The most likely explanation is that its territory was annexed by one of the big cities (Orvieto/Volsinii?) and the inhabitants transferred to new homes there. The same fate seems to have overtaken a large number of minor settlements in other parts of inner Southern Etruria during the Late Archaic period (San Giovenale, San Giuliano, Blera, Bisenzio, Poggio Buco, etc.); this was perhaps due to a redistribution of the countryside demanded by the growing urban population of the larger cities. The destruction of Poggio Civitate (Murlo) about 525 is a slightly earlier example of this type of event and may have been due to the expansionists ambitions of a ruler of Chiusi, perhaps Lars Porsenna, who about 507 even occupied Rome.

ECONOMIC CHANGES AND EARLY CURRENCY

During the Orientalizing period the economy had been based on barter of agricultural and other products and on the reciprocal exchange of gifts of prestigious objects among the aristocracy, who were in control of the land, the mines, the ships, and the labor. The changed urban conditions brought to the fore new and more broadly based classes, who began to play an important role. Manufacturers, craftsmen, and merchants trading with the new Greek emporia established in coastal areas of Southern Etruria dealt with a large number of different and often highly successful foreign trading partners. These activities, no longer based on the static possession of hoarded treasure, land, or mines, probably led to the development of a primitive premonetary form of exchange. From between the first and second quarters of the sixth century onward, there were sporadic appearances in Lazio, Central Italy, Marzabotto, and Mantua of bronze ingots of a certain weight, marked with the emblem of a leafless or dry branch (It. *ramo secco*) that must have served as currency for long-distance trade. The archaeological evidence is perhaps illuminated by a passage in Pliny (*NH* 33.43), according to which the king of Rome, Servius Tullius, whose traditional dates (578–535) coincide with this period, was the first to countersign bronze (Lat. *aes signatum*).

CHANGES IN THE FORM OF TOMBS

The comparative wealth of the newly emerging classes found its expression in the necropolises of the Etruscan cities with the creation of smaller, simpler, and more unified tombs facing orthogonally planned streets. Where once the gigantic tumuli of the noble families, erected on their land without any overall plan, had dominated the roads and necropolises as visible signs of the economic and political power of their owners, these new, strictly aligned tombs of the "middle classes" heralded a more isonomic society, in which mobile wealth had a wider, more dynamic distribution.

The necropolis of the Nuovo Recinto della Banditaccia at Cerveteri with its street of cube tombs (see FIGS. 124, 125)—and, a little later, that of the Crocifisso del Tufo at Orvieto (see FIG. 126)—provide well-preserved examples of this new development.

Fig. 124 Aerial view of the necropolis of Nuovo Recinto della Banditaccia, Cerveteri. Mid-sixth century B.C.

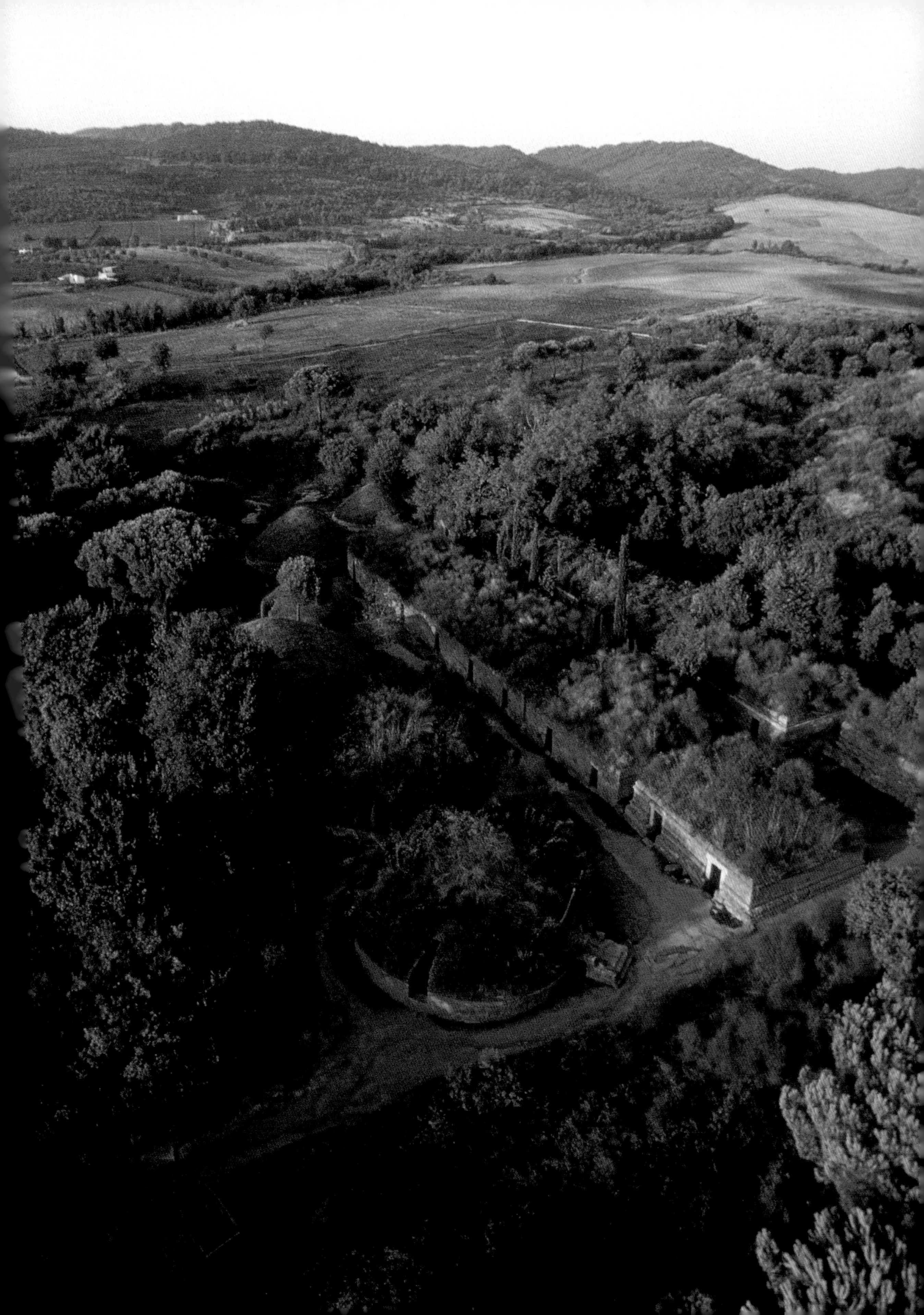

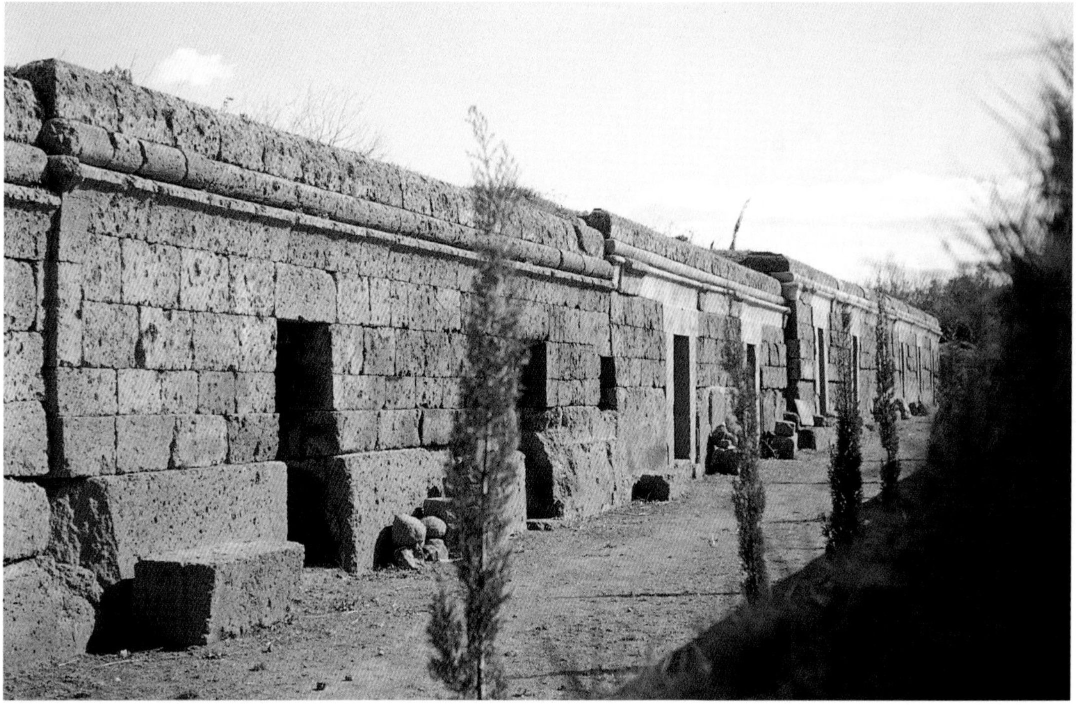

Fig. 125 Street of cube tombs in Banditaccia necropolis, Cerveteri.

Veii

In the sixth century, the earlier, richly furnished Orientalizing tombs at Veii were succeeded by austere burials containing only the cinerary urns of thick-walled bucchero, placed in loculi in open trenches sunk into the rock or buried in simple pits. It has been suggested that such restraint in funerary practice may have been due to new sumptuary laws, for which evidence exists in nearby Lazio.

An exception is a female cremation burial (at Pantanaccio) of the mid-sixth century that was accompanied by an array of gold jewelry: two hair spirals, nine leech-type fibulae, square gold-foil dress ornaments stamped with rosettes, and a ring with an oval bezel decorated with a recumbent sphinx of East Greek inspiration (now in the Villa Giulia Museum in Rome).

Cerveteri

During the first half of the sixth century, the large tumuli at Cerveteri were succeeded by uniformly aligned, rectangular cube tombs (It. *a dado*) in rows forming streets (FIG. 124). Partly cut from the living rock and partly constructed of regular tufa blocks, the cube tombs have an accessible platform roof and are marked by a series of distinct moldings both at the foot of the wall and below the top (FIG. 125). Access to the interior is through a tapering rectangular door and a short dromos. The interiors of the earliest cube tombs still reflect the plans of the chambers of the aristocratic tumuli with lateral chambers, an anteroom with several parallel burial chambers opening off the rear, all containing stone bedsteads or sarcophagi.

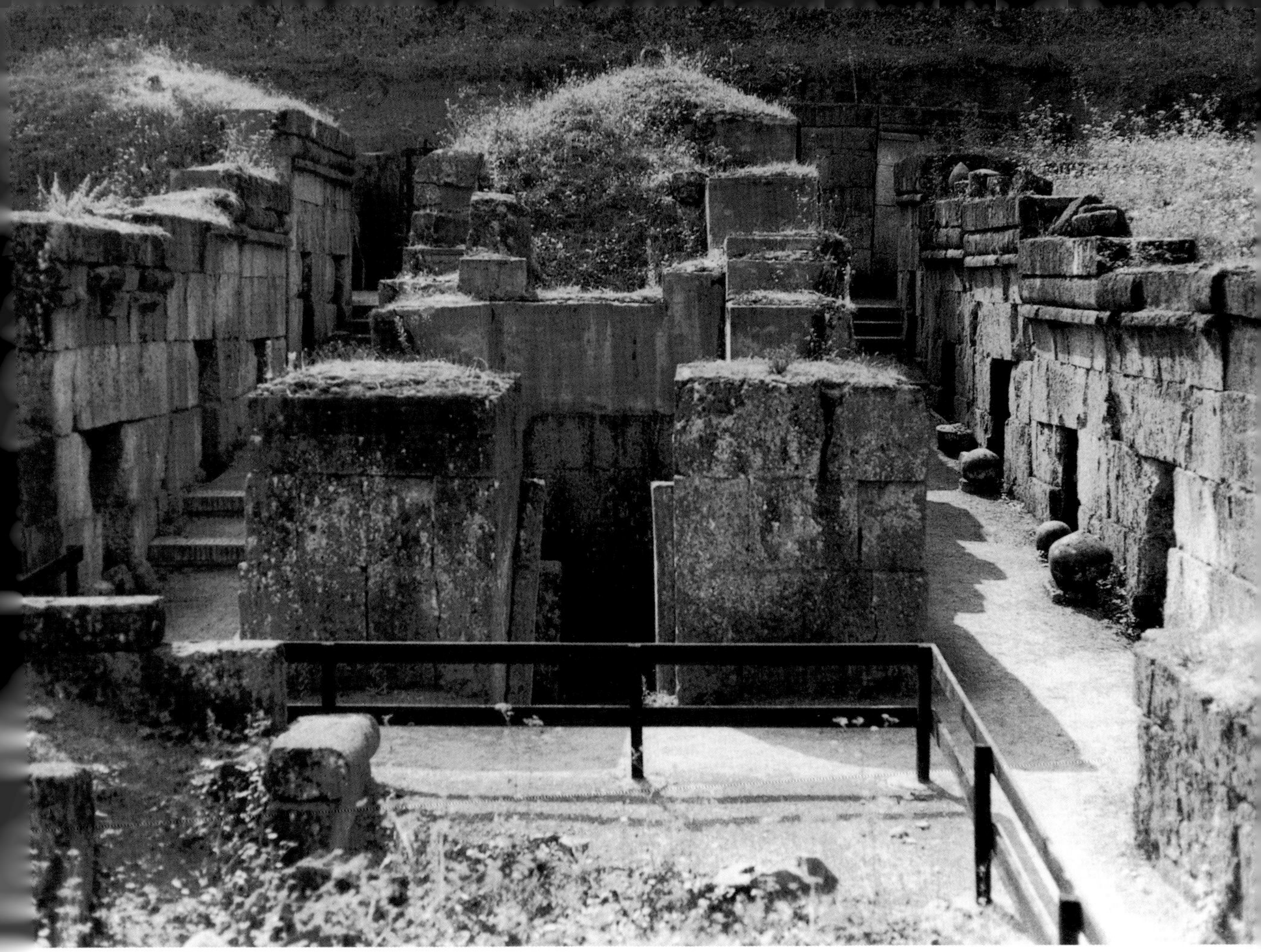

Later cube tombs have simpler plans with two consecutive or single chambers. The architectural layout of such cemetery streets serves as indirect evidence of a corresponding change in domestic architecture with a more rigorous approach to town planning, based on accurate land surveying and a more rational use of the common civic space. In tombs of the seventh century the orientation was toward the west or northwest (the region of the underworld in Etruscan belief), but in the sixth century the arrangement of tombs along predetermined streets no longer took such cult-inspired orientation into account.

Fig. 126 Crocifisso del Tufo necropolis, Orvieto. Late sixth–early fifth century B.C.

Orvieto

Although the steep tufa plateau of Orvieto was occupied during the eighth century, the Villanovan burial grounds surrounding the foot of the rock were probably destroyed when later necropolises were installed there, and today only sporadic sherds attest to their existence.

Burials ring the entire foot of the city plateau, with the densest concentration of tombs in the northwest and in the south. In the necropolis area of Crocifisso del Tufo, laid out in the second half of the sixth century B.C. and in use throughout the fifth, identical small rectangular tombs constructed from tufa blocks adjoin each other, flanking orthogonally aligned sepulchral streets (FIG. 126). The single (sometimes two consecutive) chambers usually contain two stone benches for the deposition of the dead. The roofs of the chambers are formed by longitudinal courses of stone slabs, each course overlapping the one below it until the gap between the two sides is small enough to be closed by keystones. Externally the tombs are surmounted by modest mounds and crowned by cippi with columnar, bulbous, spherical, or floral finials or by the over-life-size stone head of a helmeted warrior.

Inside one tomb was a small semicircular terra-cotta relief with two molded frontal heads of divinities close together: a bearded and wreathed god and a young goddess with a wreath in her thick hair parted in the middle. Dating from the late fifth century, the couple probably represent the rulers of the underworld, Hades/Aita and Persephone/Phersipnai.

On the facade above the entrance to each tomb was usually carved the name of its first owner and occupant. These names reveal that more than ninety different families were buried here in the course of the sixth and fifth centuries. There were 124 male names but only 6 female ones. Thus, only a very small proportion of women seem to have been independent heads of households. The comparative rarity of women owning tombs suggests that it happened only under unusual family circumstances; the norm was that a man was the head of the family.

The names on the lintels include individual names of people of non-Etruscan descent, such as Faliscans, Umbrians, Sabines, and even a Celt (*Katacina*), who all seem to have been well integrated into the local society. This shows Orvieto as one of the most important nodal points in a commercial traffic network that joined the Etruscan coastal cities with the Umbrian and Faliscan areas by ancient transit routes and rivers such as the then-navigable Fiora and Marta, while the Tiber, Chiana, and Paglia Rivers served as connections between south and north.

Recent excavations in the Cannicella necropolis have revealed a seventh-century woman's burial (Tomb 5) in a trench (It. *fossa*) marked above ground by a row of stones. The grave goods included one leech-type bronze fibula and a quantity of vessels for eating and drinking; these consisted of pairs of one bigger and one smaller specimen of each type, of a particularly finely burnished impasto that immediately preceded the production of bucchero.

Most of the subsequent burials in the Cannicella were in chamber tombs arranged on terraces that follow the contours of the sloping ground. Eventually lack of space led to tombs of the same type as in the Crocifisso del Tufo necropolis being superposed on existing ones; many are marked by cippi that often bear funerary inscriptions.

The most unusual feature in the Cannicella, however, is a sanctuary dedicated (according to an inscription on a small bronze plaque found there) to Vei, a divinity of death and fertility with affinities with the Greek Demeter and the Roman Ceres. Below the third terrace of the necropolis and sheltered by a retaining wall are architectural remains; water basins fed by conduits; a well; a votive deposit

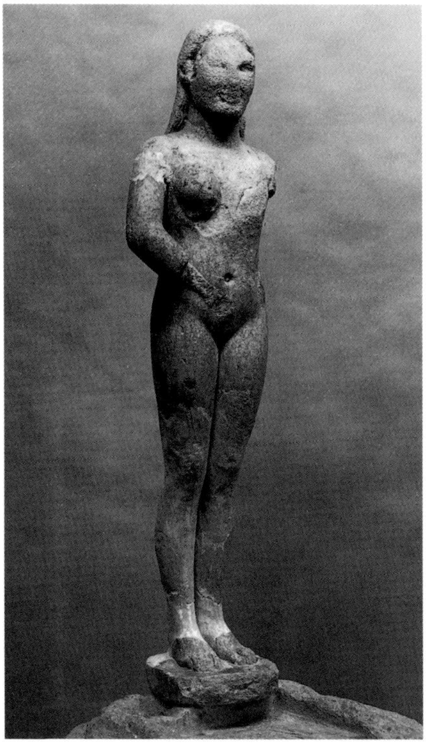

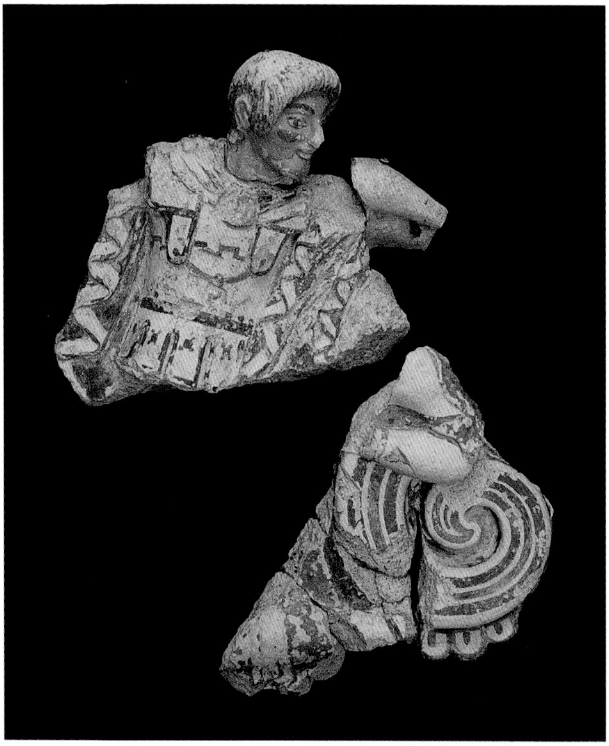

containing offerings of loom weights, spindles, and spools; and small bronzes and terra-cottas dating from the sixth to the early third century. The most important finds were a circular altar and a statuette of Greek island marble representing a nude goddess with her right hand placed over her pubes in a gesture of sexual fertility (FIG. 127). The image was carved during the second half of the sixth century; its sculptor, presumably an Ionian Greek, adapted the schema of the Greek kouros—the standing figure of a nude youth—to represent a female divinity. Such female nudity is unique in contemporary Greek marble sculpture and was probably demanded by the local cult. The front part of the statuette's hair was subsequently cut back crudely to fit it with a diadem, presumably of gold, which has not survived; neither have the necklace and earrings, for which holes are preserved. This embellishment with precious metal must represent Etruscan taste; it recalls the layer of leaf gold covering the ivory statuette of a naked goddess from Marsiliana d'Albegna (see FIGS. 111a, b).

The location of this sanctuary in the necropolis suggests that Vei, the presiding goddess (like the Greek Aphrodite Epitymbia and the Roman Venus Libitina), must have been closely connected with the underworld and funerary rites. Two terra-cotta acroteria from a small temple confirm the sepulchral nature of this cult place in the necropolis. The acroteria represent a warrior slaying a collapsing woman with one breast bared (FIG. 128), a subject that has been identified as the immolation of Polyxena by Neoptolemos on the tomb of Achilles, but it might

Fig. 127 Statuette of a nude goddess. From the Cannicella necropolis, Orvieto. Second half of sixth century B.C. Greek island marble. H. 73 cm. Orvieto, Museo Fondazione "Claudio Faina" e Museo Civico Palazzo Faina.

Fig. 128 Acroterion of warrior slaying a collapsing woman. From the sanctuary in the Cannicella necropolis, Orvieto. Early fifth century B.C. Painted terra-cotta. Max. reconstructed H. 63 cm. Orvieto, Museo Archeologico Nazionale.

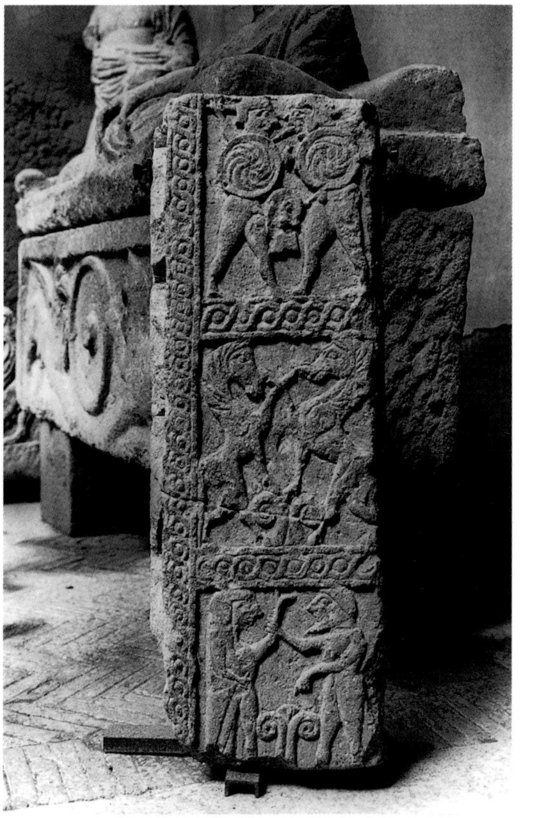

Fig. 129 Fragmentary relief slab from Tarquinia with a divine couple on the lowest panel. First half of sixth century B.C. *Nenfro*. Tarquinia, Museo Nazionale Archeologico.

also be the slaughter of Klytaimnestra by Orestes (often represented on ash urns from Volterra). Both themes are well suited to an area where sacrifices to the shades of the dead were a perpetual concern of the living. The water basins and conduits not only served the necessary purification rites but also created verdancy, a setting suitable for a divinity concerned with fertility and death. It is not without significance that among the many votive offerings by female donors (such as woolworking instruments) and terra-cotta statuettes of women, there were bronze and terra-cotta statuettes of Herakles—the Etruscan god Hercle—who was closely connected with springs, male fertility, and prosperity.

Tarquinia

During the sixth century the few large aristocratic tumuli at Tarquinia of the Orientalizing period were progressively being surrounded by countless minor mounds belonging to individual families, while the painted chamber tombs that began to appear in that period were of small scale and served nuclear families.

In the second half of the seventh century the architectural and artistic endeavors of Tarquinia seem temporarily to have been outshone by those of Cerveteri, but a particular class of carved and painted panels of tufa or *nenfro* is found in quantities only in the necropolis of Tarquinia (and in small numbers at Vulci). These so-called stepped slabs (*lastroni a scala*) may have served as doors marking the entrance into the dromoi of tumuli; alternatively they may have separated the end of the dromos from the tomb chamber proper; some were found walled into the drum of a tumulus.

The slabs were sculpted in flat relief (recalling embossed bronze sheets or wood carvings), with figured scenes or individual figures in squares arranged within a framework of zigzag-, cable-, and tongue patterns and incorporating parallel, vertical bands of small steps. The step motif, which seems to imitate originals made of stepped wooden slats, also occurs as the sole ornament. The pictorial inspiration of the reliefs is eclectic, some reflecting models found in (Oriental) textile patterns on Attic black-figured vases by Sophilos and Nearchos and on Tyrrhenian amphorae.

Besides Greek mythological subjects, the panels comprise the aristocratic themes of banqueting and hunting, as well as isolated figures of winged demons, griffins, sphinxes, centaurs, *hippocamps*, and sirens—creatures symbolizing the transition between life and death. An interesting fragment with three superposed

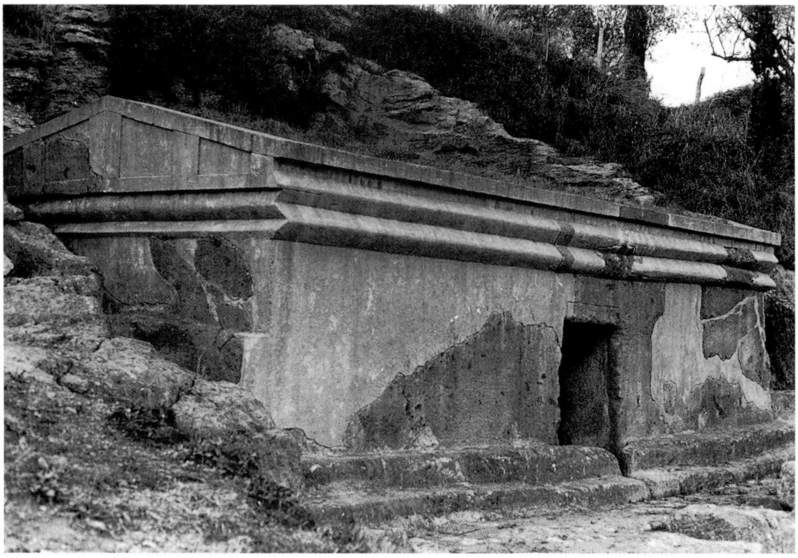

Fig. 130 Tomb in the shape of a house. From the Peschiera area, Tuscania (Viterbo). Sixth century B.C.

relief panels shows in the lowest field what may be the union of a divine couple (*hieros gamos*, FIG. 129). A naked man on the right has seized the arm of the woman opposite him; she is draped in a mantle, which covers her head and body; deliberately pulling up the garment, she has bared her legs and pubes with obvious erotic intent (cf. Turan/Aphrodite on the painted panel in the British Museum, FIG. 178). The man points to a flower springing up between them. In the panel above are two rearing, heraldically confronted horses, and in the topmost scene two warriors armed with round shields and spears fight over a crested helmet on the ground between them. Whether these motifs represent scenes from Homer's *Iliad* (lovemaking between Zeus and Hera and the fight over the arms of Achilles) or purely Etruscan subjects is difficult to decide. The effect of the carvings is rich and decorative and was originally enhanced by paint. The production of the *lastroni a scala* in several workshops at Tarquinia covered the later part of the seventh and much of the sixth century.

Tuscania

At Tuscania, situated halfway between Tarquinia and Lake Bolsena in the fertile agricultural region west of Viterbo, a series of exceptionally interesting rock tombs of the first half of the sixth century was carved entirely from banks of tufa flanking the valleys of the rivers Marta and Maschiolo. The tombs' exteriors reproduce the architecture of real houses. In the necropolises of Peschiera and Pian di Mola rows of rectangular, house-shaped tombs with adjoining short sides and entrances in the centers of the long facades faced a sepulchral street (FIG. 130). The shallow ridge roofs were crowned along the ridgepole by acroterial figures and cippi of stone. These wide-fronted houses give a good impression of what a real street in an Etruscan town must have looked like (cf. Marzabotto, pp. 189f.); the layout of

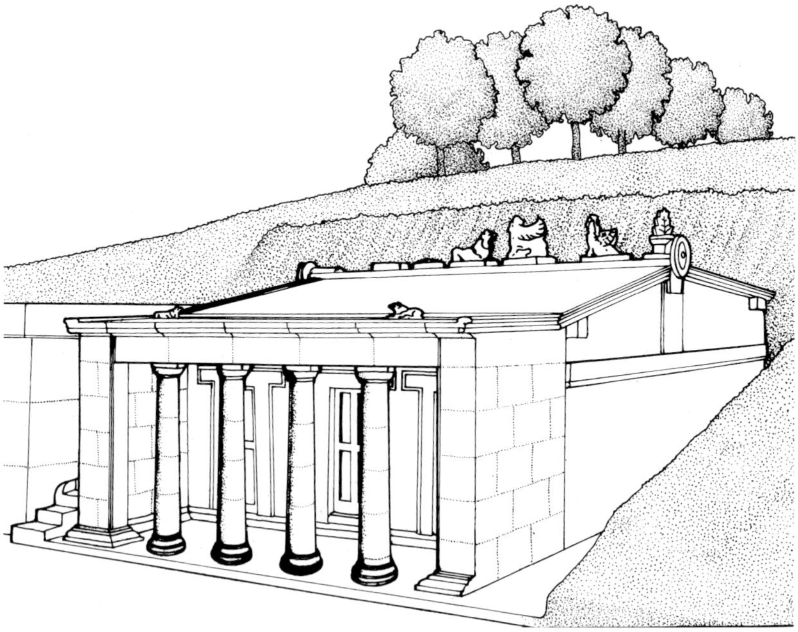

Fig. 131 Reconstruction of monumental tomb. Pian di Mola necropolis, Tuscania (Viterbo). Second quarter of sixth century B.C.

the interior with its transverse arrangement of three rooms side-by-side resembles the plans of some of the houses at Acquarossa (see p. 139).

At the highest point of the sepulchral road on the western slope of Pian di Mola, an opulent aristocratic tomb was partly carved from the rock and partly built with ashlar blocks and slabs of stone whose different colors were used for deliberate effect (FIG. 131). Again, the ridgepole was surmounted by sculptures of sphinxes and lions (which in their style recall Vulcian works) as well as by cippi. Each of the two pediments was crowned by a disc-shaped acroterion. The long side forming the facade of the tomb had a stone-built porch with four Tuscan columns between antae with Ionic moldings. The flat roof of this portico was used for funerary rites. From the porch one entered the tomb's central room through a single door, whose frame was carved to simulate a heavy wooden one of Doric type; the actual door of the tomb consisted of a removable stone slab. The two lateral rooms, accessible only from the central room, were marked externally by false doors within the porch. The funerary bed and the ceiling of the main room imitated wooden prototypes. This arrangement of three parallel rooms—the middle one largest—off a broad portico is frequently found in the chambers of tumuli at Cerveteri, such as the Tomb of the Shields and Seats (*Tomba degli Scudi e delle Sedie*, FIG. 132) the Tomb of the Cornice (*Tomba della Cornice*), etc. It prefigures the plan of the Classical Central Italian atrium house.

This impressive aristocratic tomb was in use for about three generations, about 570–500, as indicated by fragments of Greek and Etruscan pottery and faience and a small bronze statuette of a lion that probably once decorated the rim of a cauldron. The family buried there must have been among the leading ones of Tuscania.

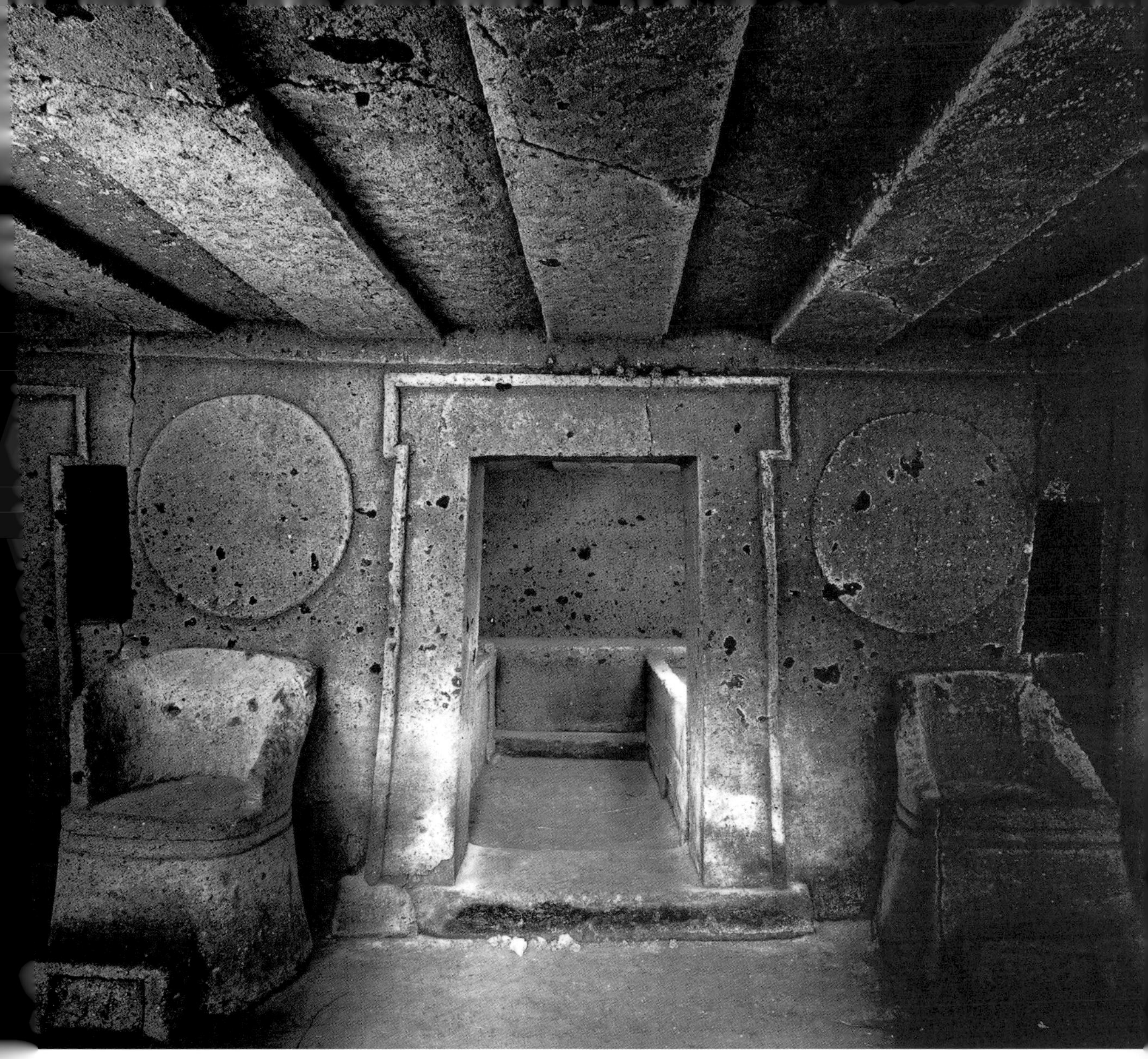

Fig. 132 Interior of rock-carved tomb. Tomb of the Shields and Seats, Cerveteri. Second half of sixth century B.C.

Vulci

At Vulci one of the most characteristic tomb forms was the *cassone* tomb. It consisted of a dromos leading to a sunken rectangular vestibule, open to the sky, off which opened several tomb chambers. Funerary sculptures of mythical beings of apotropaic or transcendental significance, such as sphinxes, winged lions, rams, centaurs, etc., carved from local tufa guarded these tombs. During the first half of the sixth century such sculptures reflected the style of Daidalic Greek models. A work of this type is the centaur carved in massive, stereometric volumes, his broad face framed by long, wavy, wiglike hair (FIG. 133). A little later Ionic prototypes predominated; this phase is exemplified by the sculpture of a boy riding on a fish or sea horse; he is carved in softly rounded, flattish shapes, his receding forehead and chin echoing an East Greek ideal. In recent years a number of more vigorously modeled sculptures of sphinxes exhibiting the same stylistic features and in all

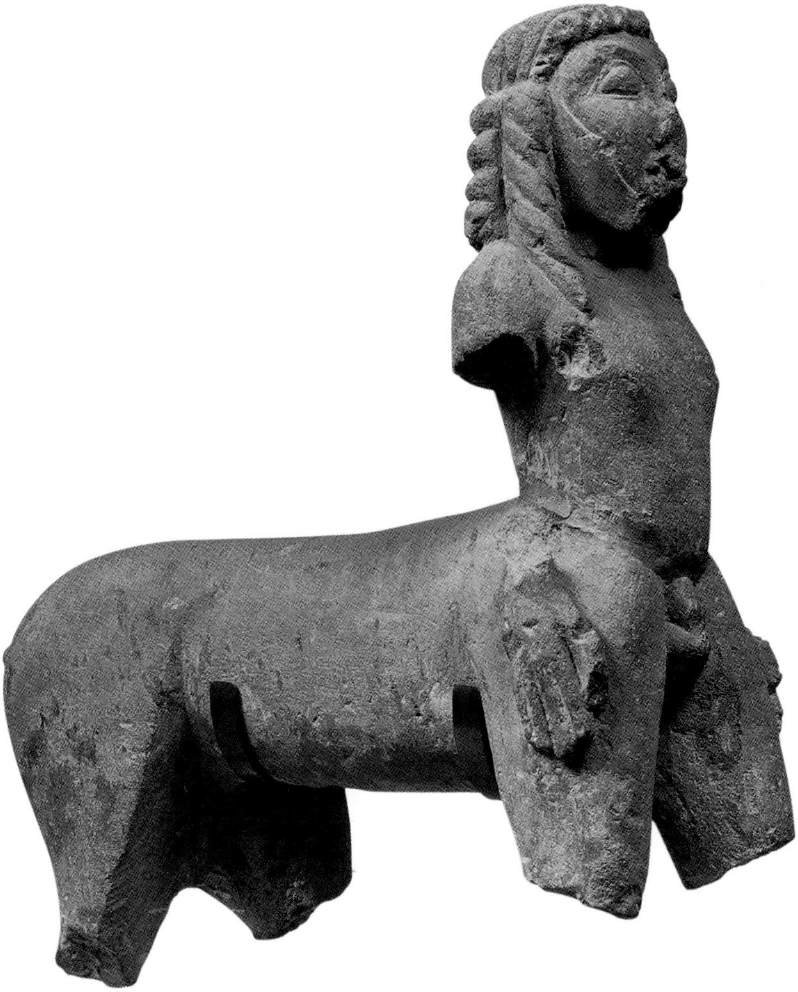

Fig. 133 Statue of a centaur. From a tomb at Vulci. Late seventh–early sixth century B.C. *Nenfro.* H. ca. 77 cm. Rome, Museo Etrusco di Villa Giulia.

OPPOSITE
Fig. 134 Statue of a crouching sphinx. Second half of sixth century B.C. *Nenfro.* H. 91 cm. Private collection.

probability made at Vulci have appeared on the art market (FIG. 134). This productive school of Vulcian sculptors exercised a strong influence on the workshops of other centers, such as Castro, Magliano, and Tuscania (cf. p. 150) and, further afield, Chiusi (p. 170).

THE CUCCUMELLA The most important Vulcian tumulus of the first half of the sixth century is the Cuccumella in the eastern necropolis. This type of tomb is relatively rare at Vulci and was presumably reserved for particularly illustrious families. One of the largest mounds in Etruria, with a drum of stone blocks measuring 65 m in diameter, the Cuccumella originally had a height of about 18 m. In its southern sector lay the two main chambers, aligned with the dromos and accessible through a rectangular vestibule surrounded on three sides by steps, probably to accommodate the spectators of funerary ceremonies. Two small lateral chambers were covered by false ogival vaults. Remains of two different sets of sculptures

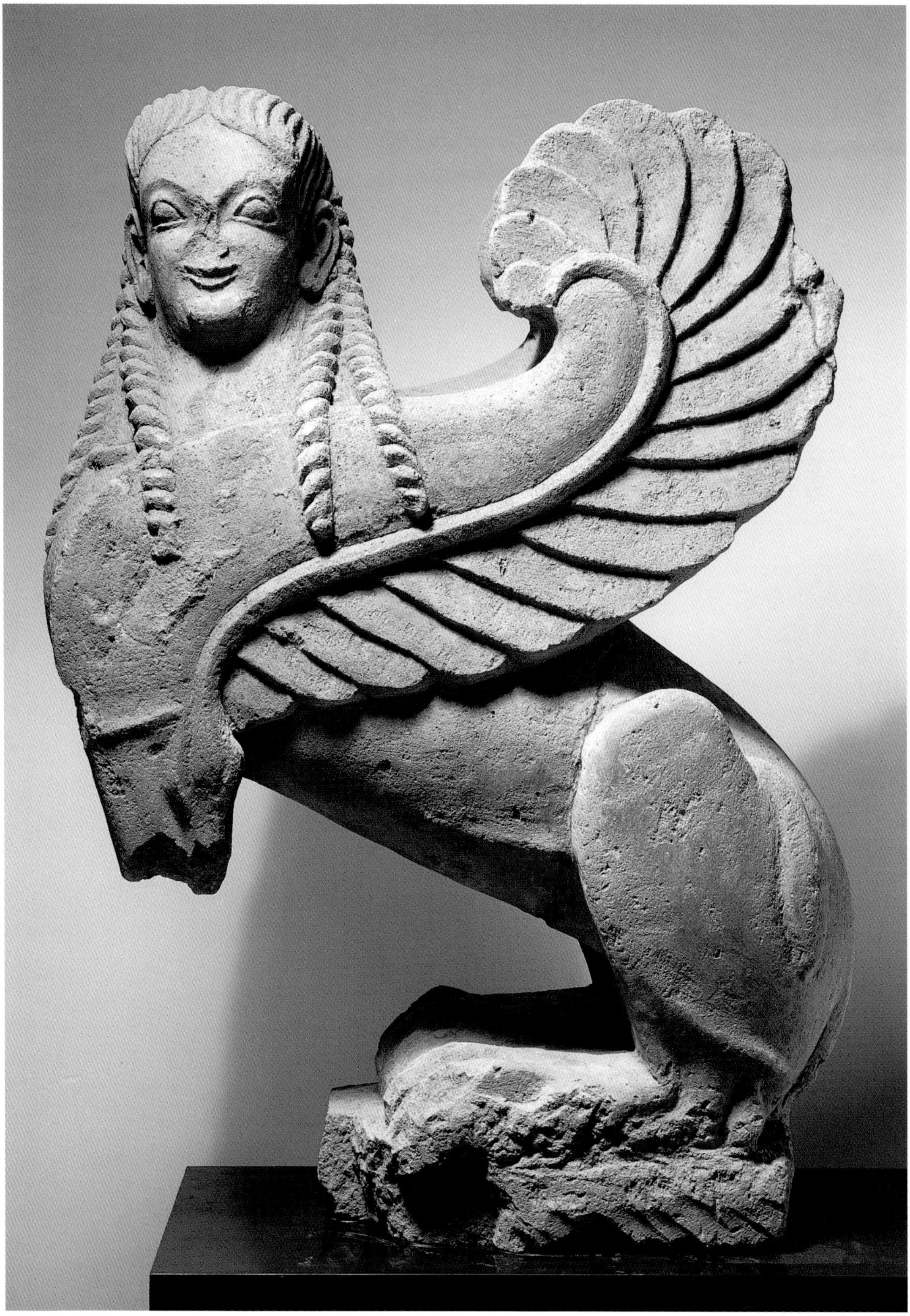

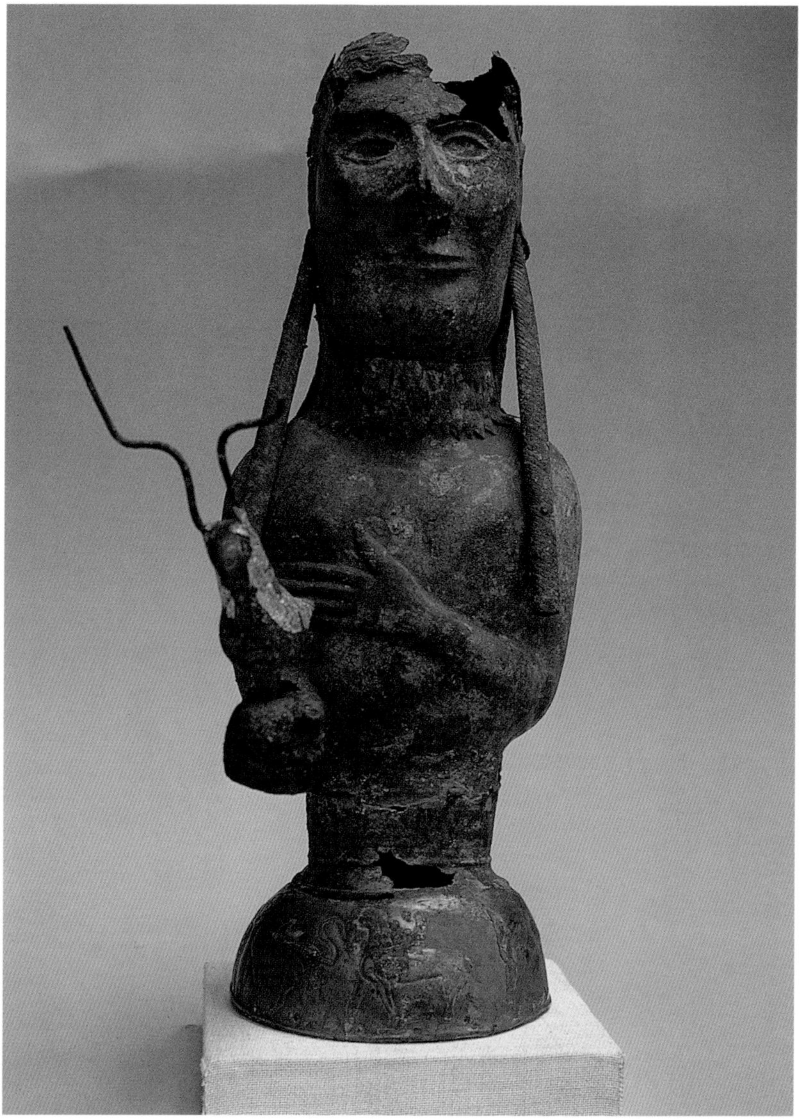

Fig. 135 Bust of a goddess holding a bird. From the Tomb of "Isis," Vulci. First quarter of sixth century B.C. Hammered and cast bronze with gold foil. H. 34 cm. London, The British Museum, BM *Bronze Cat.* 434.

representing human(?) beings, sphinxes, and lions, as well as two gigantic bases for tall cippi of conical and pyramidal shape, were discovered here; they probably originally surmounted the monument. There is archival evidence for a second, similar set of tomb chambers in the same southern sector of the mound, recorded in the nineteenth century but not preserved.

TOMB OF "ISIS" This chamber tomb (*Tomba d'Iside*), in the Polledrara necropolis of Vulci, was emptied in February 1839 of its unusual and varied grave goods by its "excavator," Napoleon's brother Lucien Bonaparte, Prince of nearby Canino. After his death the grave goods were sold and dispersed. The tomb, fancifully named the Tomb of "Isis" after supposedly Egyptian figures discovered in it, was filled in again immediately, but it seems to have comprised two chambers and to have contained a number of burials, among them those of a warrior and of an eminent lady. The majority of the objects were bought by the British Museum in 1850, but others are preserved in museums in Karlsruhe (bronzes) and Munich (mainly gold fibulae).

Among the most important pieces is the hammered bronze bust of a woman, naked from the waist up, who with her left hand supports her right breast, while holding in her cast right fist a horned bronze bird, whose cast body is covered with gold foil (FIG. 135). The woman's almond-shaped eyes were once inlaid with a different material, probably glass paste. Her hair hangs in a broad mass over her back, and two tubular tresses fall forward over her shoulders. She wears a wide choker necklace of three interlaced rows of rhomboid beads. A broad belt circles her waist, below which a spherical piece of bronze sheet, decorated with an animal frieze of Corinthian inspiration, probably represented the top of a skirt. Nail holes and two surviving ancient nails show that the bust is incomplete and was originally nailed to a support, presumably of wood.

The technique of the bust recalls seventh-century busts of bronze and silver sheet from Marsiliana d'Albegna (Circle of the Fibula, Circle of the Ivories) and sheet-bronze urns from Vulci and Chiusi, which represent early attempts to reconstitute an image of the deceased from a durable material. But the bust from the Tomb of "Isis" did not form part of an ash urn; it is probably one of the oldest surviving cult images of a goddess. Her seminudity and the gesture of supporting one breast relates her to the ivory statuette from Marsiliana d'Albegna (see FIGS. 111a, b) and suggest a divinity of fertility and rebirth. The horned, gold-covered bird is a supernatural creature with Villanovan antecedents (cf. a wheeled cult vessel of bronze in the form of two horned birds from a female *pozzo* tomb in the Monterozzi necropolis of Tarquinia). We have noted the possible religious significance of bronze cup handles with the image of a human figure flanked by birds and quadrupeds in tombs at Bisenzio and elsewhere (see FIG. 23, above). Birds associated with priestesses or goddesses (Atargatis, Artemis Ephesia, Artemis Orthia) are known from Syria, Ephesos, Dodona, and Sparta.

We do not know the Etruscan name of the divinity represented by the bust. A small bronze statuette in Cortona (Museo dell'Accademia Etrusca 1571) may be the same kind of goddess. She, too, is bare-breasted and wears a belted skirt; her wings proclaim her supernatural quality, and a bird perches on her head. A Laconian (or Tarentine) version of this goddess appears on a richly decorated bronze hydria found at Graechwil in Switzerland (Bern, Historisches Museum 11620); her headdress is surmounted by a bird, and she is surrounded by wild animals (*potnia theron*). The bronze bust from the Tomb of "Isis" was probably made in the first quarter of the sixth century, a date that corresponds with those of the statuette in Cortona and of the Graechwil hydria.

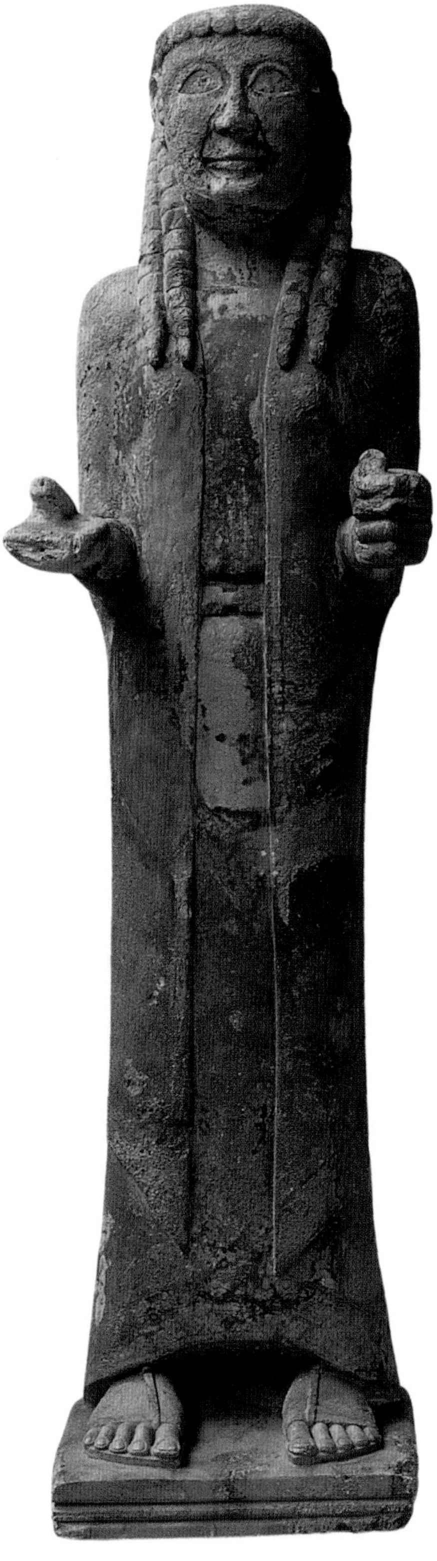

Fig. 136 Statuette of standing draped woman. From the Tomb of "Isis," Vulci. Second quarter of sixth century B.C. Painted gypsum. H. 89 cm. London, The British Museum GR 1850.2-27.1.

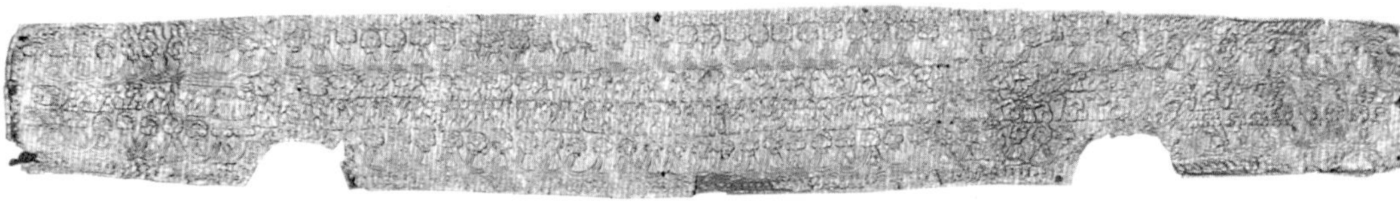

Fig. 137 Diadem. From the Tomb of "Isis," Vulci. Mid-seventh century B.C. Stamped gold sheet over bronze. L. 51 cm. London, The British Museum, BM *Jewellery Cat.* 1257.

The second outstanding work of sculpture from the Tomb of "Isis" is a half life-size gypsum statuette of a standing draped woman with her forearms held out horizontally, the left fist grasping a now-lost object, the right palm opened in a gesture of offering (FIG. 136). She stands with her sandaled feet on a low, molded plinth. Her smooth belted chiton has a painted lower border with an intricate chain of alternating pendant and upright lotus flowers, for which the closest parallels are in the work of the Attic vase-painter Sophilos. A mantle, also with a painted border, covers her back and hangs in two long lappets with slanting edges over the front of her body. This type of mantle is characteristically Etruscan, and so is the arrangement of her back hair in a series of plaits tied together at waist level and ending in a tassel. In front it hangs in two beaded tresses over her breasts. The flattish crown of her head is smooth, with the hair above the low forehead ending in a level wavy edge, a feature shared with a Vulcian sphinx in Vienna and with the centaur in the Villa Giulia (see FIG. 133). Her blocklike, square face has huge almond eyes, once inlaid, and a broad nose with deep folds running to the corners of her wide, thin-lipped mouth. The Peloponnesian models that inspired the considerable Vulcian artist who carved the statuette suggest that it was made in the second quarter of the sixth century. A complex work that combines Daidalic, Attic, and local Vulcian features, the statuette may represent a materfamilias or ancestress of the important family buried in the tomb, if not the deceased herself.

The extremely rich and varied grave goods from the Tomb of "Isis" included a rectangular gold-sheet diadem stamped all over with cable pattern, interlaced semicircles crowned by palmettes, and rows of walking lions and Chimairas; cut-out semicircles allowed the diadem to be neatly fitted over the ears of the wearer (FIG. 137). Technique and decoration connect it with the gold jewelry from the Regolini-Galassi Tomb (see FIGS. 54, 57) and point to a date for it in the middle of the seventh century; it is thus the oldest object from the Tomb of "Isis" and may have been buried with the earliest occupant of the tomb, or, as a precious heirloom handed down in the family, with a later descendant.

Exotic imports included ostrich eggs carved and painted by Vulcian artists; Egyptian faience flasks of the Saite period (664–525 B.C.); seven faience scarabs; about thirty-three thousand glazed faience beads in four different colors, probably once embroidered on a lady's splendid funerary dress; and alabaster vessels and stands. Of local manufacture were a large number of bronze utensils, among them two four-wheeled, rectangular containers (charcoal braziers) with the forepart of a horse at each corner; a lamp and a stand for it, inspired by Cypriote models; two biconic urns with cut-out, M-shaped handles (which may also have belonged to the earliest burial); two tripod bowls; cups; a pilgrim's flask; and various sizes of bronze cauldrons and bowls. Two small hollow terra-cotta statuettes of seated women, originally covered with a layer of gold foil, imitate East Greek scent bottles in the form of human beings. A great many more pottery vessels (probably of bucchero) than the three painted ones preserved in the British Museum seem to have formed part of the original find.

JEWELRY A large quantity of fine gold jewelry in European and American museums was originally found in the necropolises of Vulci, but their precise provenance and context are usually unknown. Among them is a particularly striking type of large disc earring, enhanced with concentric patterns of granulation, filigree, and glass paste (FIG. 138). Such earrings are represented in the tomb-paintings of the later sixth century at Tarquinia, for instance, in the Tomb of the Jugglers (*Tomba dei Giocolieri*), the Tomb of Hunting and Fishing (*Tomba della Caccia e Pesca*), and the Tomb of the Lionesses (*Tomba delle Leonesse*). The disc earring is originally a Lydian type of jewelry; it became fashionable in Etruria with the strong East Greek influence prevailing in the second half of the sixth century.

Valise-shaped earrings (It. *a bauletto*), probably also made at Vulci, found a large distribution (FIG. 139). Elaborate gold-chain necklaces with multiple pendants of diverse forms (floral elements, sirens, Acheloös, satyrs); gold fibulae enriched with decorative animal figures (lions, sphinxes) of stamped gold; hairpins; and bracelets and gold rings with oval bezels, the cartouche engraved or embossed with figures or embellished with carved gemstones or scarabs—all testify to the high technical competence of the local jewelers and to their patrons' exquisite taste.

The art of carving precious stones into intaglio seals, scarabs, and pendants flourished at Vulci and Tarquinia from the last decades of the sixth century and was probably taught in workshops set up by East Greek masters.

Etruscan ladies stored their jewelry in wooden caskets covered with ivory plaques carved in low relief with a variety of themes, such as banquets, dances, hunting scenes (FIG. 140), and wild and domestic animals—all familiar aristocratic subjects. At first stylistically related to the vase-paintings of the Pontic school, these remarkably fine relief plaques eventually became hackneyed in their themes and poor in their execution.

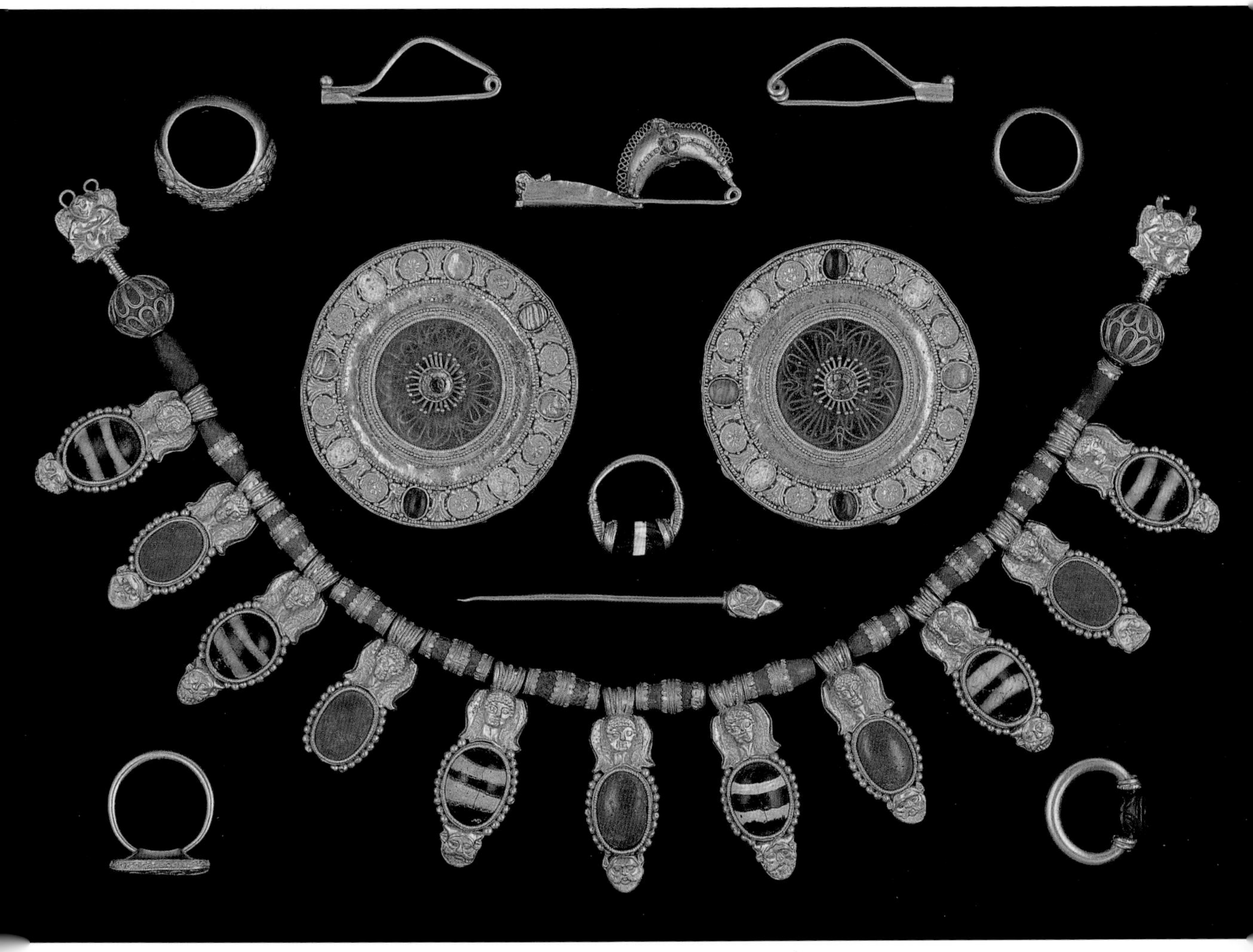

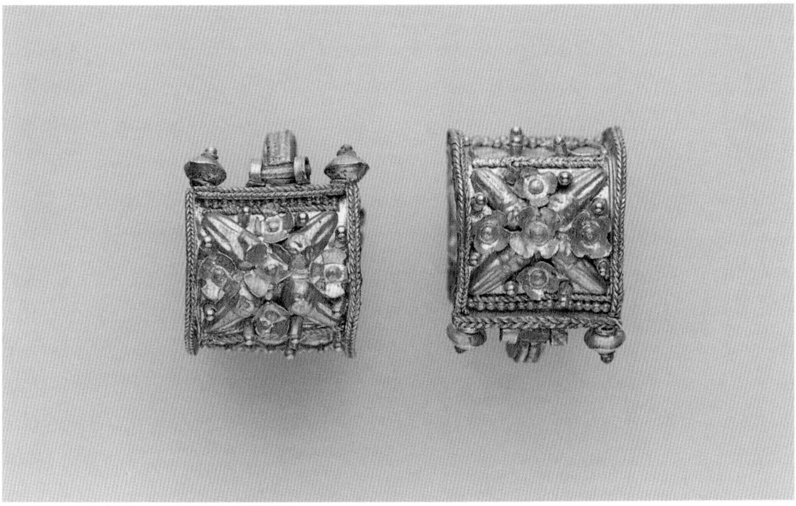

Fig. 138 Assembly of jewelry: disc earrings, necklace (L. 36 cm), fibulae, rings, and hairpin. From Vulci. First half of sixth century B.C. Gold, glass paste, and semiprecious stones. New York, The Metropolitan Museum of Art, Harris Brisbane Dick fund, 1940, inv. 40.11.7–.18.

Fig. 139 Pair of *bauletto* earrings. From Vulci. Third quarter of sixth century B.C. Sheet gold, granulation, and plaited wire. H. 1.6 and 1.7 cm. Hamburg, Museum für Kunst und Gewerbe 1967/2.

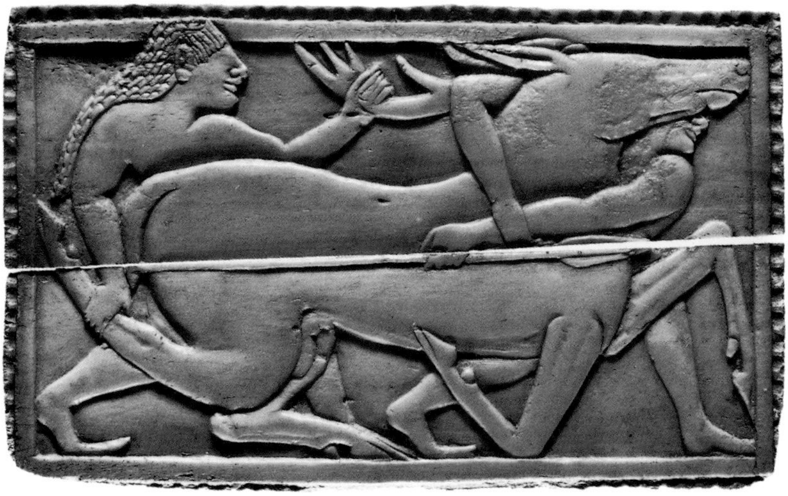

Fig. 140 Relief plaque with two hunters and a stag. From a casket in a tomb at Orvieto. Second half of sixth century B.C. Ivory. Florence, Museo Archeologico.

BRONZEWORKING The region of Vulci produced fine bronzes as early as the Villanovan period, and this tradition had continued. Important examples of Orientalizing bronzeworking were found in the Tomb of the Bronze Chariot, a chamber tomb in the Osteria necropolis containing a chariot of embossed sheet bronze as well as numerous other bronze objects and pottery dated to 680–670 B.C.

The strong East Greek influence noticeable in Vulcian stone sculpture from the middle of the sixth century onward can also be traced in bronze works. A particularly interesting piece is a large fragmentary bronze statuette of a nude standing youth with a wavy mass of long hair hanging over his back (Orbetello, Antiquarium 924). This kouros, headless, armless, and without his lower legs, is still 30 cm high and must originally have been 50 cm tall. Cast solid, it weighs about 11 kg. Such exceptional size and weight have suggested that this may have been a conspicuous votive gift, if not a cult statue. It was discovered in 1959 at Selvanera near the lagoon of Lake Burano in the territory of Vulci. In style the kouros is closely related to East Greek, particularly Samian and Milesian, sculpture, and it points to an undoubted connection between Greek bronze workshops from Asia Minor and the area of Vulci.

During the Archaic period the city's bronze workshops created a veritable industry. They manufactured not only chariots, weapons, armor, and vessels, all finely decorated, but also cast utensils ornamented with elaborate figures in the round of mythical beings, demons, fighting animals, and vegetal motifs. Outstanding in their quality and imaginative design, such Vulcian tripod stands (FIG. 141), candelabra, incense burners (FIG. 142), mirrors, and banqueting vessels were commissioned for practical and ceremonial use by the local aristocratic families, but they were also widely exported abroad and have been found as far apart as the Athenian Acropolis, Olympia, Magna Graecia, and the tombs of Celtic chieftains in Central and western Europe. Ancient sources tell us that Athenian connoisseurs praised Etruscan gold cups as the best of their kind, "but also their bronzes of every sort for the decoration and service of houses" (Ath. 1.28b).

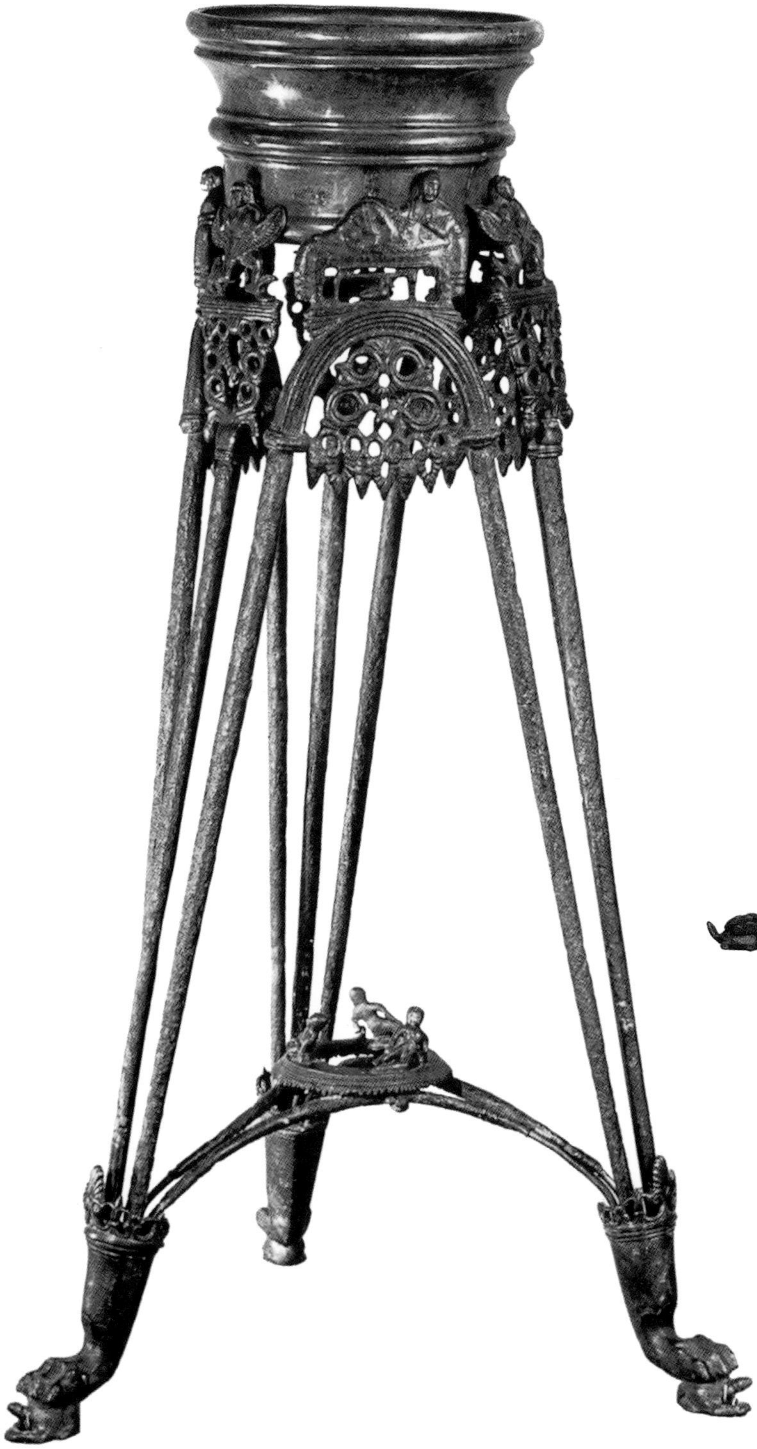

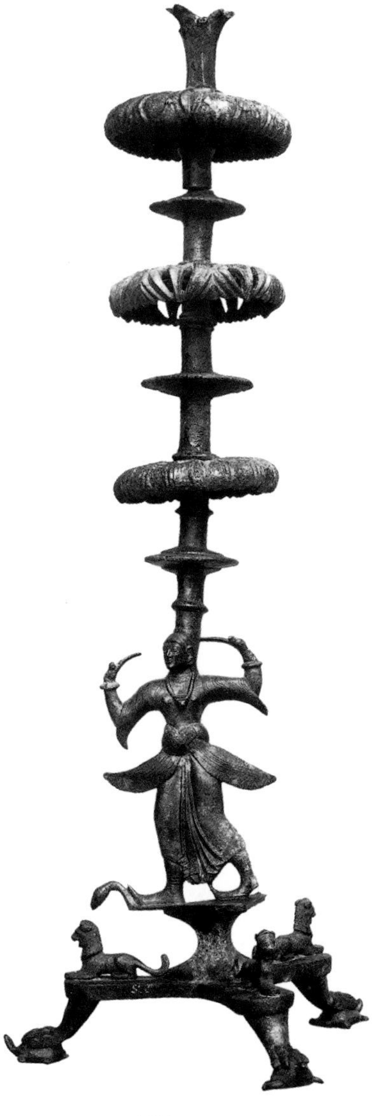

LEFT

Fig. 141 Tripod stand with figured decorations of diners on couches. From Vulci. Early fifth century B.C. Cast bronze. H. 64 cm. Karlsruhe, Badisches Landesmuseum F 203.

ABOVE

Fig. 142 Incense burner with a shaft supported by a dancing girl. Probably from Vulci. Early fifth century B.C. Cast bronze. H. 45 cm. London, The British Museum GR 48.6-19.11

THE TOMB OF THE WARRIOR The rich Tomb 47 in the Osteria necropolis of Vulci is called the Tomb of the Warrior (*Tomba del Guerriero*) because of the bronze panoply of the dead commander buried in it. It consisted of a helmet of Negau type with a crest holder in the form of two youths—perhaps the Dioscuri—each reining in a winged horse, and two heads of the river god Acheloös marking the center front and back of the helmet; furthermore there were greaves, an exceptionally large round shield, a sword with an iron scabbard, two spears with iron heads, and two tongue-shaped bronze plates with repoussé decoration of volutes and palmettes, surmounted by rectangular plaques showing Achilles ambushing Troilos at the fountain; these probably came from the armband of a shield. A bronze banqueting service comprised a large stamnos, two beaked jugs, two smaller jugs with circular mouths, two ladles, a sieve, an incense stand, and a shallow bowl with small figures of lions on the rim.

Besides such bronze objects of local manufacture, the tomb contained a large number of fine imported Attic vases, among them a so-called Panathenaic amphora, an oil-filled amphora awarded as a prize to the victor in one of the athletic games of the Panathenaic festival in Athens. This range of Attic pottery can be dated between 550 and 510 and indicates that the owner of the tomb was buried in the last decade of the sixth century. His military equipment and the numerous banqueting vessels deposited with him show that he belonged to the warrior aristocracy of Vulci, who, like the aristocracy elsewhere in Etruria, in this tangible way defined their social and political status as war leaders and givers of banquets.

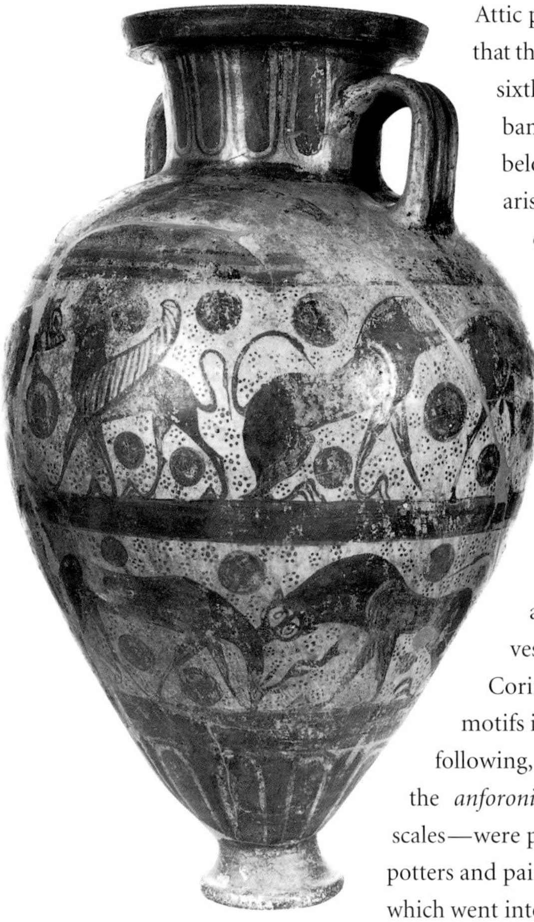

Fig. 143 Amphora by the Painter of the Bearded Sphinx. From the Osteria necropolis, Vulci. Last third of seventh century B.C. Painted pottery. H. 82 cm. Rome, Museo Etrusco di Villa Giulia 82547.

VASE-PAINTING In chapter 2 we drew attention to the development of important Late Orientalizing workshops for vase-painting in Vulci under the stimulus of corinthianizing and East Greek masters, such as the Painter of the Bearded Sphinx (FIG. 143) and the Swallow Painter (see p. 111). The former initiated the Etrusco-Corinthian style of vase-painting about 630 and produced numerous, often large-scale vessels with a decoration of animal friezes, using Corinthian black-figure technique mixed with East Greek motifs introduced by the Swallow Painter. He had a large local following, and such workshops also operated in Cerveteri (where the *anforoni squamati*—large amphorae with a decoration of scales—were produced). The third generation of Etrusco-Corinthian potters and painters started a mass production of this ware about 580, which went into decline during the next generation (ca. 560–540).

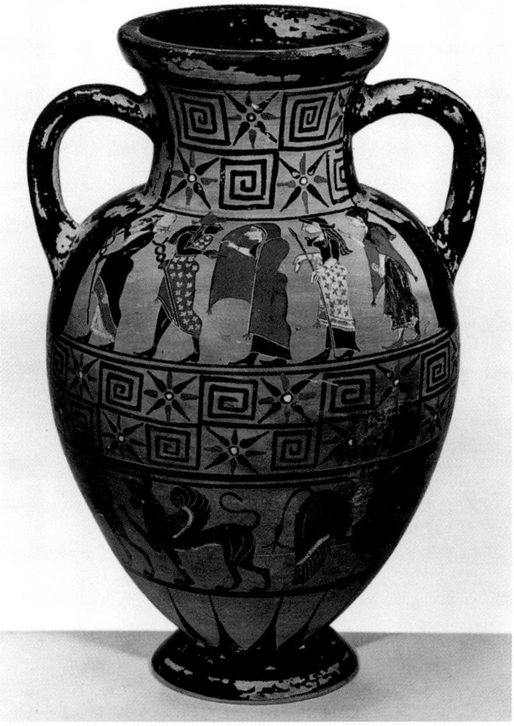

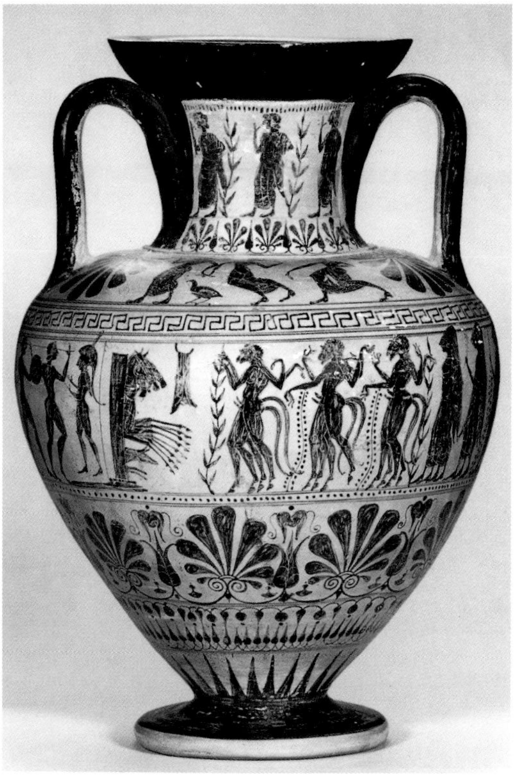

From the second quarter of the sixth century an ever-increasing mass of fine Greek, mainly Attic, painted pottery reached Etruria through the emporia on the Tyrrhenian coast, providing a vast repertory of Greek myths in pictorial form. A fresh wave of Ionian Greek models brought by immigrant East Greek masters from Asia Minor inspired the Paris Painter—the Vulcian artist of the Pontic amphorae, a considerable group of black-figured vases painted between 550 and 520. They share with the Tyrrhenian amphorae (Attic works produced almost exclusively for the Etruscan market) a decorative scheme on the neck and belly of the vessel of ornamental friezes, which frame the main figured frieze; this often shows a Greek mythological theme, such as the Judgment of Paris on a fine amphora by the Paris Painter (FIG. 144). At least five different vase-painters, conventionally named after subjects on their most representative works, followed the tradition of the Paris Painter.

One of the most prolific local Vulcian black-figure vase-painters, whose activity spanned the last two decades of the sixth century and perhaps the beginning of the fifth, is called the Micali Painter. About two hundred vases by him have been excavated from tombs at Vulci; he seems to have worked mainly for the funerary needs of a less wealthy class than the opulent aristocrats, who preferred imported works of Greek manufacture. The motifs represented by the Micali Painter are predominantly connected with ceremonies and dances and with death

ABOVE LEFT
Fig. 144 Pontic amphora with the Judgment of Paris. Name vase of the Paris Painter. From Vulci. 550–540 B.C. Painted pottery. H. 35 cm. Munich, Staatliche Antikensammlungen und Glyptothek 837.

ABOVE RIGHT
Fig. 145 Black-figured neck-amphora by the Micali Painter with representations of funerary games and dancing satyrs. From Vulci. About 500 B.C. Painted pottery. H. 47.5 cm. London, The British Museum B 64.

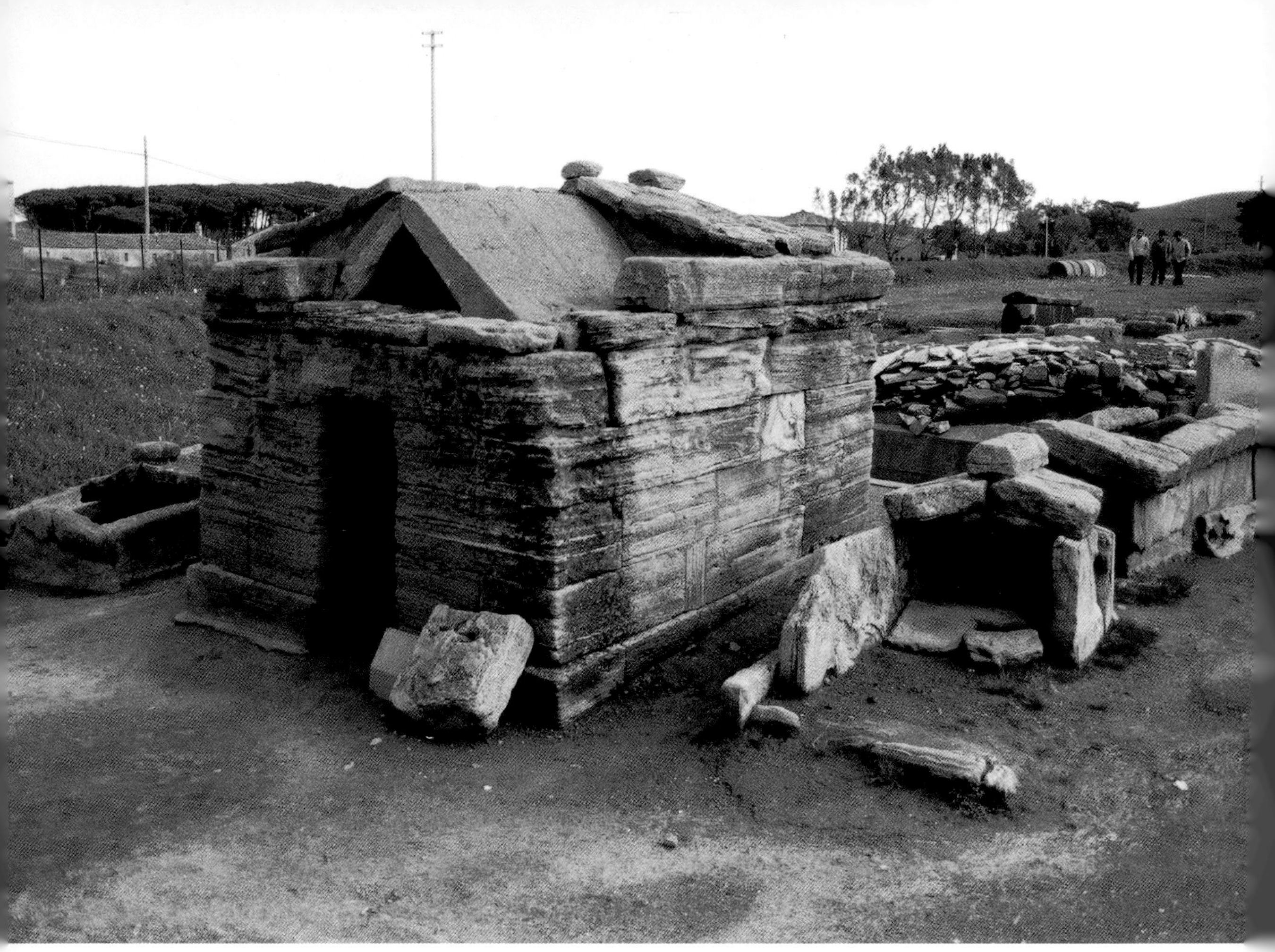

Fig. 146 View of stone-built *aedicula* tomb. Tomb of the Bronze Statuette of the Offering Bearer, Casone necropolis, Populonia. 530–500 B.C.

rituals as well as with mythical creatures, such as sirens, sphinxes, centaurs, and satyrs, who symbolize the transition from this life to another existence (FIG. 145). Carved in stone, similar transcendental and apotropaic beings were also placed in front of or on top of tombs (see FIGS. 133, 134), and they appear in tomb-paintings as well (see FIGS. 181, 185).

Populonia

At Populonia a new type of tomb (the *aedicula*) in the form of a small house or temple of ashlar blocks made its appearance in the middle of the sixth century (FIG. 146). The ridge roof of stone slabs was adorned with terra-cotta or stone antefixes and acroteria, of which fragments have survived. The painted terra-cotta antefixes show a close relationship with models found at Tarquinia, whereas the stone ones can be compared with East Greek, in particular Samian and Milesian, examples. *Aedicula* tombs contained one chamber only; they were used in some cases over several generations (e.g., the Tomb of the Bronze Statuette of the Offering Bearer [*Tomba del Bronzetto di Offerente*] from the second half of the sixth to the mid-fifth century). Further *aedicula* tombs have survived near San Cerbone; these and the one just mentioned in the Casone necropolis were probably erected for aristocratic families. They were surrounded by simpler and more numerous *cassone* tombs—box- or sarcophagus-shaped, stone-built graves, also surmounted by volute-shaped acroteria of East Greek inspiration; these were perhaps the burials of a new middle class. In the Casone necropolis, *cassone* tombs flanked two roads in an orderly alignment. In their uniformity and relative simplicity they may be indicative of an economic leveling of the local society. A more general distribution of wealth among the inhabitants seems to have resulted from new metallurgical activities, transferred from the island of Elba to Populonia itself.

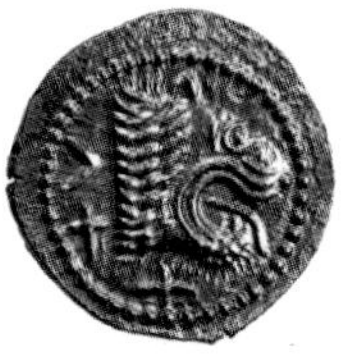

Fig. 147 Etruscan coin with lion's head and value mark 25. Probably from Populonia. Late sixth–fifth century B.C. Gold. Diam. 1.3 cm. London, The British Museum, Department of Coins, Lloyd 10.

The earliest known series of Etruscan gold coins, marked with the head of a lion and tentatively dated to the end of the sixth or the fifth century, were probably issued at Populonia (FIG. 147). Their value appears to be based on East Greek ponderal systems—presumably those of Phokaia or Massalia—which apply worth to coins based on their weight.

The main industry of Populonia in the past had been the production of bronze from the copper and tin ores mined in the hills of the Campigliese (Val Fucinaia) and the Catena Metallifera; but from the second half of the sixth century, the smelting of Elban iron became prevalent here, as shown by the remains of smelting furnaces with iron slag and workshops and workmen's quarters on the slopes of the Poggio della Porcareccia and Campo Sei. Locally discovered fragments of pottery inscribed with single names and dating from the sixth to the early third century show that their owners were slaves and a number of them foreigners. The export of pig iron remained one of the enduring sources of Populonia's wealth. The Etruscan name for Populonia was Fufluna, derived from the name of Fufluns, the Etruscan god of wine. This may be indicative of a period when vine-growing was important here. Pliny records as a curious fact that a statue of Zeus at Populonia was carved from a single vine (*NH* 14.1).

Vetulonia

After the prodigious richness of Vetulonia evident in its aristocratic tombs of the seventh century, the city appears to have declined somewhat during the sixth, a change perhaps caused by the rise of neighboring Roselle. Marsiliana d'Albegna, to the south of Roselle, and other smaller settlements in the Albegna valley seem to have been abandoned under pressure from Vulci. Another possible reason for Vetulonia's seeming loss of importance is the silting up of the ancient lagoon, the Lacus Prilius, on which the city's harbor must originally have been situated, probably near the present Castiglione della Pescaia. The resulting reduction in Vetulonia's far-flung export of metalwork, based on the copper mines of the Massetano, may have contributed to the waning of its former prosperity; but, as recent excavations have proved, there can be no question of Vetulonia having ceased to exist in the Archaic period. The imposing sixth-century city walls alone contradict this earlier theory, and a number of flourishing small settlements seem to have sprung up in the surrounding territory during the late seventh and sixth centuries. One such is the group of houses identified by their rectangular plans with rubble foun-

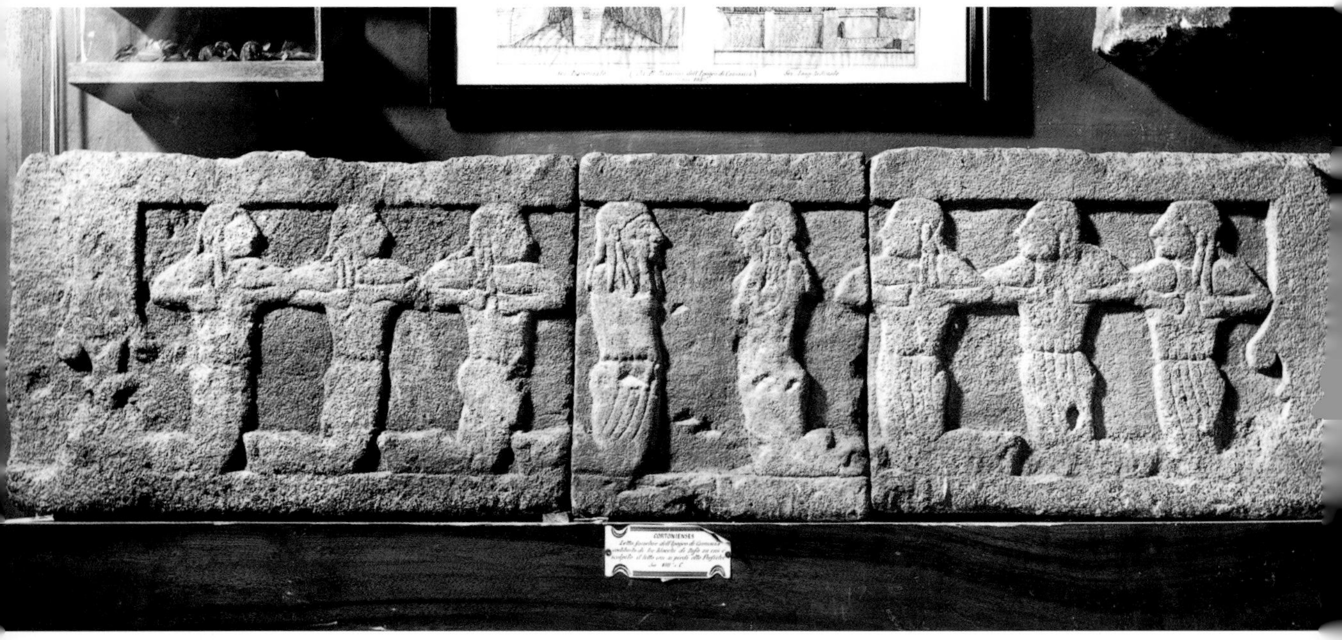

Fig. 148 Relief with mourning women, from the front of a funerary bed. Camucia tumulus, Cortona. Third quarter of sixth century B.C. Tufo. Florence, Museo Archeologico.

dations and a small necropolis at the Lago di Accesa near Massa Marittima; the houses served a small community dependent on Vetulonia and engaged in the extraction of metal ores and smelting.

Cortona

At Cortona three big tumuli (two *del Sodo* in the north and the *Melone di Camucia* in the south) dominated the roads in the plain below the hill on which the future city arose. Here the manifestations of aristocratic power and self-representation persisted during the sixth century and took on a special local note in the rich sculptural decoration attached to one of these grave mounds. Recent excavations have revealed a large altar platform abutting the eastern side of the drum of the Tumulus 2 of the Sodo. The complex chamber tomb inside the tumulus, accessible by a long dromos from the southwest, was oriented toward this external altar. A flight of stairs led up to the platform, which could be seen and approached from the town; here sacrifices and ritual acts must have been carried out. The steps were flanked by parapets, each decorated on top by three large, finely carved acroterial slabs in the form of two addorsed volutes linked by a horizontal strap and surmounted by a palmette. At the front end of each parapet was a large group carved in the round representing a kneeling man in a short pleated and belted tunic. With one hand he grasps the mane and sinks his dagger into the belly of a huge crouching female sphinx or lioness clutching him between her paws. The struggle between the large mythical beasts and the smaller human beings seems unequal, but the symbolism of the scene is probably that inevitable death, represented by the beast, is ultimately overcome by the aristocrat, who will be heroized.

The crowning anthemia on the parapet recall the decoration of Ionian Greek altars, such as that of Poseidon at Cape Monodendri near Didyma on the west coast of Asia Minor; the costume of the heroes and the massively rounded forms of the figures are likewise of Ionian inspiration. The sculptures, which are unfortunately badly damaged, are so far unique; they were presumably meant to glorify visibly and in perpetuity the noble family to whom the tumulus belonged.

From the richly furnished Tomb A in the nearby *Melone di Camucia* tumulus comes the front panel of a funerary bed composed of three slabs of tufa carved in low relief. The elegantly fretted legs and the horizontal stretcher of the bed frame a group of eight kneeling women in close-fitting, pleated and belted Ionic tunics (FIG. 148). They face each other beating their breasts in mourning; the two innermost wailing women seem to be lacerating their cheeks in ceremonial fashion. The keening that went on around the bed of the deceased before burial is here eternalized in sculpture. Dated to the third quarter of the sixth century, the relief has stylistic affinities with the earliest Chiusine reliefs on funerary cippi (see pp. 243ff.).

Perugia

Perugia, in the Umbrian territory adjoining Etruria to the east, became a flourishing Etruscan city as late as the sixth century. In the surrounding countryside excavations of two rich aristocratic chamber tombs (at San Valentino di Marsciano and Castel San Mariano) show the ability of landowning chiefs of clans to commission very elaborate tomb furnishings. These two chamber tombs each yielded a wealth of elaborately embossed bronze objects as well as cast bronzes strongly influenced by Ionian prototypes. Among the finest of the repoussé reliefs are the remains of a lady's carriage and of parade chariots (from Castel San Mariano) and three big figured bronze stands with their cauldrons preserved (the Loeb tripods in Munich from Marsciano). Reliefs in silver and electrum from Castel San Mariano in the British Museum were originally nailed to a wooden object (British Museum, *Catalogue of the Silver Plate* [London, 1921], nos. 2–4). These two tomb groups are now sadly scattered, with pieces also in Perugia, Berlin, and Paris.

Most of the contents of a chieftain's tumulus tomb in the *Colle del Capitano* near Monteleone di Spoleto, however, were kept together and are now in the Metropolitan Museum in New York. The main piece, an extremely well-preserved ceremonial chariot, had on the parapet of the box a complex decoration in repoussé sheet bronze, incised and inlaid with ivory, representing scenes from the myth of Achilles (FIGS. 149a, b). The three relief panels on the front and sides of the box are linked by the frontal figures of two nude, long-haired youths standing on lions. The work has recently been ascribed to an artist trained by an East Greek active in Vulci in the mid-sixth century. The sumptuous bronze vessels and other funerary gifts of the buried couple included two Attic Little-Master cups, which suggest a date of 550–525 for the interment. This Sabine chief probably had the

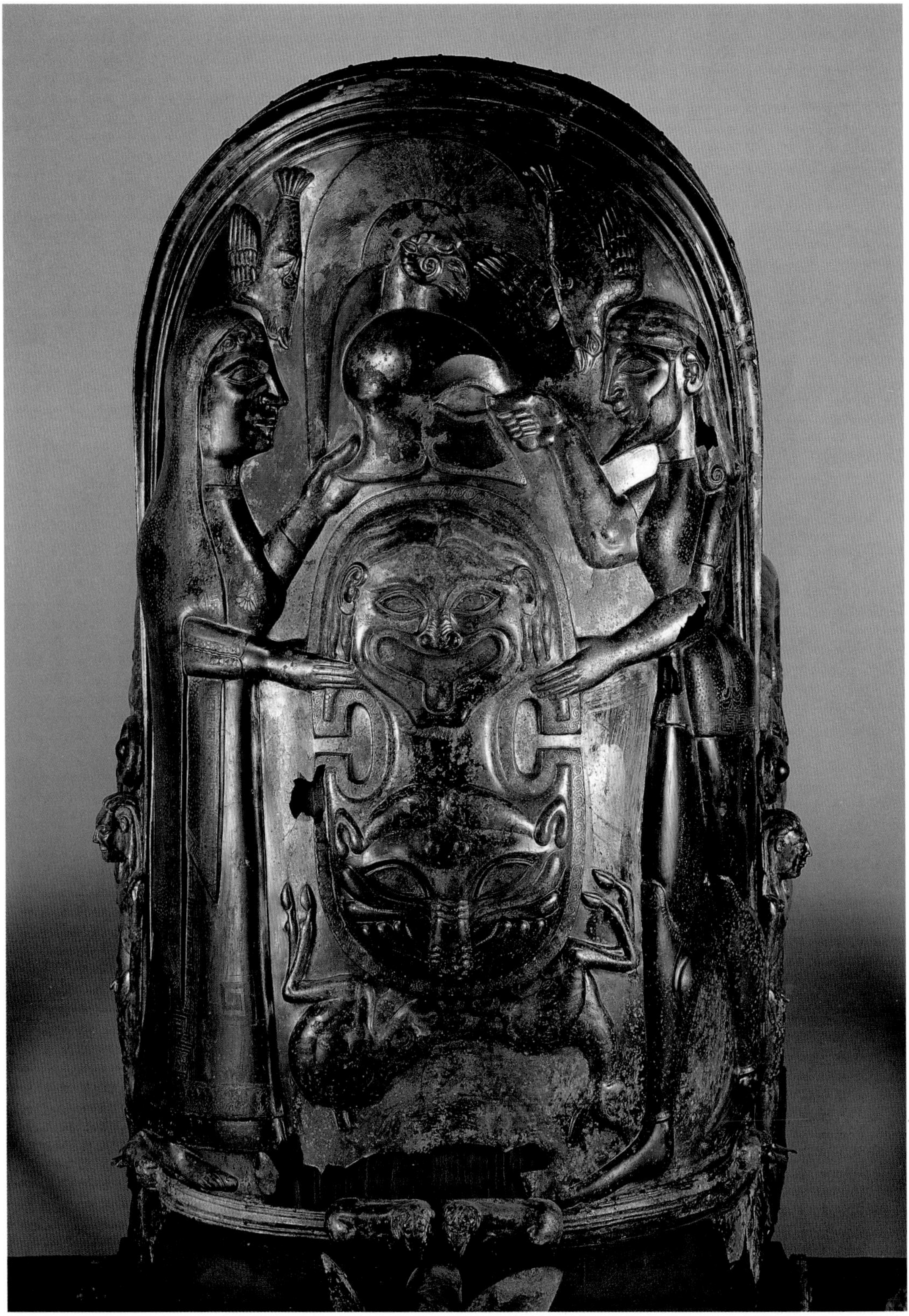

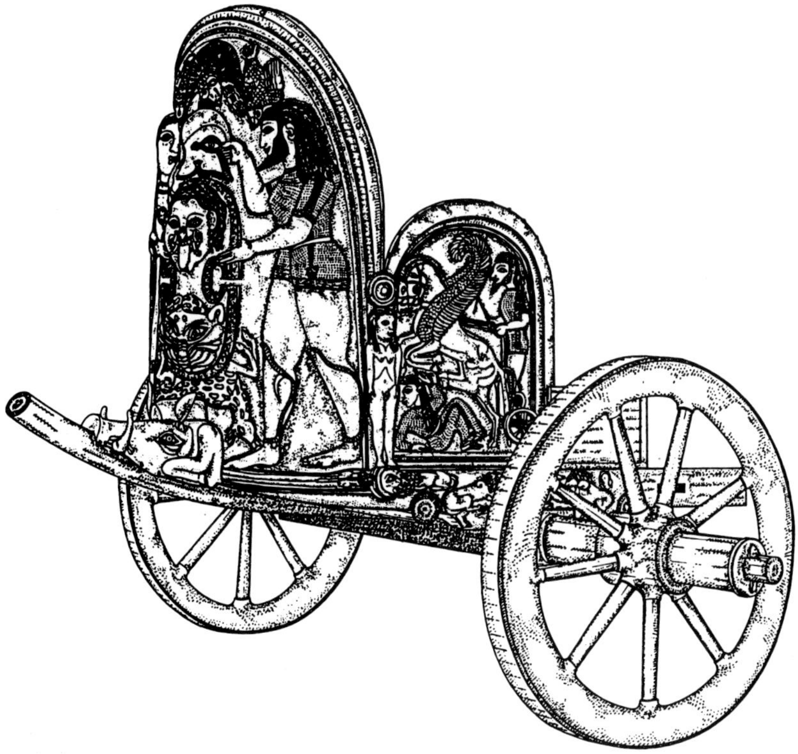

vehicle made to display his high social position and heroic warrior qualities, likening himself to the heroes of the *Iliad.*

Chiusi

In the region of Chiusi, the traditional burial in Canopic urns placed inside large terra-cotta containers was gradually replaced by burial in rock-carved chamber tombs with several chambers opening off a central one. In the Late Archaic period a number of these (at Chiusi and Sarteano) were adorned with wall-paintings, some of whose themes echo those of the more competently painted tombs of Tarquinia (see FIGS. 188, 191).

The earliest such chamber tombs contained the later examples of the Canopic urns; inhumation was practiced alongside cremation. From the first half of the sixth century the funerary sculpture in *pietra fetida*—the local fine-grained limestone with a strong sulphur odor—came into its own and remained on a remarkably high level for several centuries. We have already mentioned sculptures of this type from the Molinello tumulus near Asciano and from Podere Casalta near Lucignano (see FIG. 93), but Chiusi itself and surrounding necropolises in the neighborhood (Chianciano, Città della Pieve, Sarteano) yielded by far the largest quantity of these various types of ash containers and tomb markers, and there can be little doubt that they were carved in local Chiusine workshops.

OPPOSITE

Fig. 149a Parade chariot with relief decoration. From Monteleone di Spoleto. Third quarter of sixth century B.C. Embossed sheet bronze inlaid with ivory. H. of front panel 1.31 m. New York, The Metropolitan Museum of Art, Rogers Fund, 1903, inv. 03.23.1.

ABOVE

Fig. 149b Reconstruction of front and side panels of chariot, figure 149a.

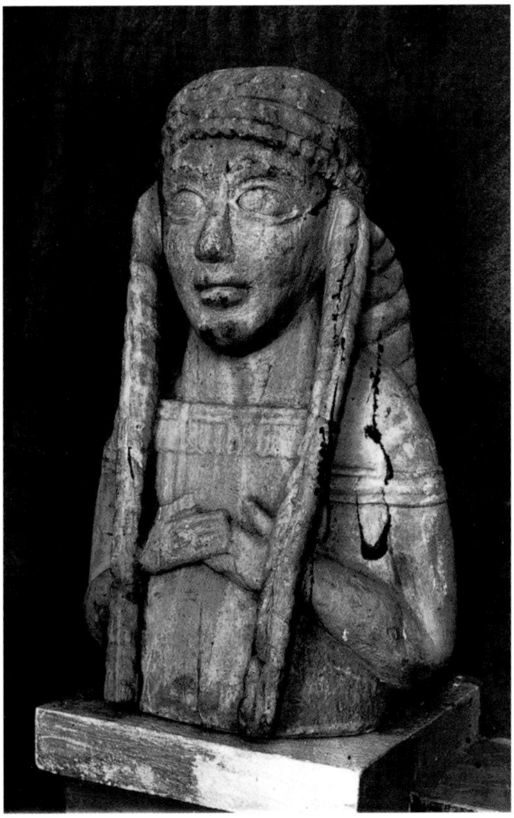

Fig. 150 Bust of a woman. From Chiusi. First half of sixth century B.C. Limestone. Florence, Museo Archeologico 2258.

Several more or less identical busts of women, whose lower body may have consisted of featureless stone drums, seem to have stood as tomb markers, "guardians," or wailing women outside tomb chambers of the first half of the sixth century (FIG. 150). They are dressed in short-sleeved chitons with decorated borders; their flat hands are placed one on top of the other on their chests. Their faces are characterized by large, thickly rimmed almond-shaped eyes and wide, low foreheads overhung by a double beaded fringe; two tresses of hair fall forward over the shoulders and flexed arms, while the mass of hair hangs down the back. Their gesture recalls that of the female statue from the Pietrera tumulus at Vetulonia (see FIG. 65).

Particularly impressive are the funerary statues representing a monumentalization of the same original idea that had inspired the creation of the Canopic urns. They take the form of standing or enthroned men and women, partially hollowed out to receive the ashes of the deceased, whom they probably represent in a heroized state. The earliest surviving seated statues, from the third quarter of the sixth century, represent men. In their massive, blocklike shape these statues are clearly indebted to East Greek, particularly Milesian, models, such as the sculptures from Didyma in the British Museum. No seated female statue earlier than the middle of the fifth century has come down to us, after which date they become more frequent and appear on sarcophagi and ash urns as well; we shall discuss these sculptures below.

The chamber tombs in which such statues were deposited also contained a variety of carved-stone bases, supporting cippi, and relief-decorated and painted ash urns and sarcophagi, but the circumstances of their discovery during the nineteenth century were rarely reliably reported.

The earliest phase of Chiusine funerary sculpture was influenced by late Daidalic, probably Peloponnesian, prototypes, but in the second half of the sixth century Ionian models predominated, particularly on the reliefs of the cippi and ash urns. Later on Attic vase-paintings served as inspiration. The representations on many of the reliefs can tell us a good deal about daily life, and we shall treat them separately. The style of apotropaic figures from the tombs, such as winged lions and sphinxes, seems to have followed the example of Vulcian funerary sculpture of the sixth century (see FIG. 134).

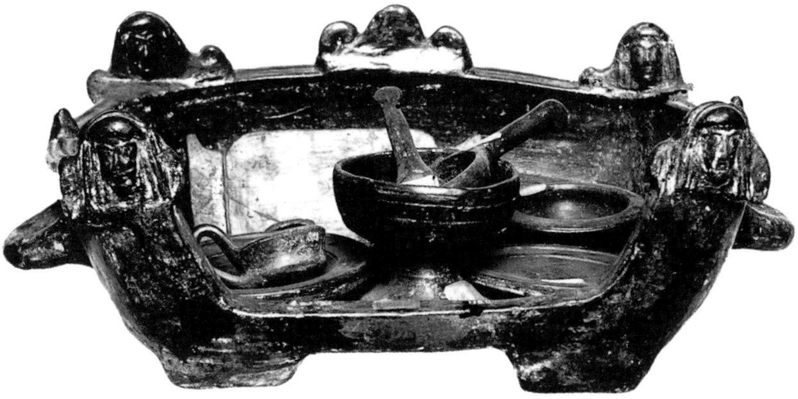

Fig. 151 Miniature funerary tray (It. *focolare*). Probably from Chiusi. About 550–500 B.C. Bucchero. L. of tray 41.7 cm. Florence, Museo Archeologico 3122–31.

During the Archaic period, the production of *bucchero pesante*, much of it destined for tombs, was an important industry in Chiusi, whence it was widely distributed elsewhere in Etruria. The fine, thin-walled *bucchero sottile*, originally made in Southern Etruria during the seventh century, was gradually replaced by thicker wares decorated with impressed friezes made with a cylindrical carved roller or with a rich relief decoration of female heads and added figures modeled in the round (FIG. 151). This type of bucchero was also manufactured in great quantities at Vulci, Tarquinia, and Orvieto and, in local variations, in Etruscan Campania. The production declined during the fifth century and was eventually replaced by other types of pottery, such as black-glazed wares.

THE EMPORIA

The gradual erosion of the power of the landowning aristocratic chiefs, in whose hands the production and distribution of goods had formerly been concentrated, coincided with the rise of a new form of commerce. Whereas foreigners, under the protection of local rulers, had been integrated into Etruscan society during the seventh century, in the course of the sixth and fifth centuries, they seem to have been excluded from the cities proper but allowed to frequent or to settle in emporia—trading enclaves—situated at the margins of the urban territory, usually where Etruscan port facilities already existed. Here the foreign craftsmen and merchants were protected by their own divinities in newly founded sanctuaries that guaranteed the conditions of their life and trade and gave asylum to fugitives and slaves.

We have mentioned emporia founded earlier by Phoenicians and Euboeans as well as by other Greeks. The most famous of the more recently established emporia was Naukratis, settled by Aiginetans and Ionians in the Nile Delta during the reign of the pharaoh Amasis (579–526 B.C.). Similar Greek trading posts grew up on the Tyrrhenian coast of Etruria during the early sixth century: Pyrgi, depending on Cerveteri; Regae on Vulci; and Gravisca on Tarquinia. A little later Adria and Spina were founded in the Po Delta on the Adriatic.

Gravisca

Excavations at Gravisca (near Porto Clementino), the harbor of Tarquinia, have provided much information on what nationalities visited this emporium and what divinities they worshiped. Excavations have revealed the remains of a number of Greek sanctuaries, of which the earliest, dating from the beginning of the sixth century, was dedicated to Aphrodite (Etr. *Turan*). The name of this goddess, *mi turuns*, incised on the lip of a Laconian krater tells us that both Greek and Etruscan mercantile families frequented the spot.

From the middle of the sixth century onward, the votive offerings at Gravisca became numerous, consisting, beside fine imported pottery, of amphorae, lamps, bronze and ivory statuettes, Oriental luxury goods and their imitations made at Naukratis, agricultural implements of iron, and pieces of stone anchors. Many of the gifts were inscribed by their dedicants, the majority in Ionian Greek dialect, indicating that they came mainly from Samos, Miletos, and Ephesos. A large influx of Laconian pottery occurred during the second and third quarters of the sixth century, and there are also many fragments of Corinthian wares. In the second half of the sixth century Attic vases came to the fore, at first black-figured and, later on and in lesser quantity, red-figured ware.

One significant votive gift was a collection of pigments used for painting, tangible proof that East Greek wall-painters, as well as vase-painters, were active in Etruria. Their influence is clearly recognizable in several of the tomb-paintings at Tarquinia and in painted terra-cotta panels from the walls of houses and tombs at Cerveteri.

Some of the names inscribed on objects dedicated in the sanctuary of Gravisca are found also at Naukratis, which shows that the emporia on the Tyrrhenian coast formed part of an extensive commercial network that involved some Lydians, but mainly Greeks from Asia Minor, the Dodecanese, Egypt, Corinth, and Aigina. The unusual name of one Pactyes recalls that of the Lydian appointed by the Persian king Cyrus to look after the treasure of the defeated king Kroisos at Sardis (Hdt. 1.153). The Persian conquest of Ionia and subsequently of Egypt closed the emporium of Naukratis in the Nile Delta and brought many foreign traders and craftsmen to the west.

Among the most striking votive objects discovered at Gravisca is part of a marble anchor bearing a dedicatory inscription to Aiginetan Apollo by one Sostratos. Perhaps he is the same Sostratos, son of Laodamas of Aigina, who is mentioned by Herodotos (4.152) as a merchant so rich that none could rival him, an active trader during the last quarter of the sixth century. The incised or painted Greek letters *SO* found on the underside of over a hundred Attic vases imported into Etruria are thought by some to be his monogram. Many of these vases were produced in the Athenian workshop of Nikosthenes, which catered particularly to the Etruscan market by adopting original Etruscan (bucchero) shapes.

Aiginetans were also responsible for the opening up of the Adriatic emporia already mentioned, which, in the following century, with Attic participation, flourished on trade with the Northern Etruscan regions of the Po valley, with Venetic peoples, and eventually with immigrant Celtic tribes, who had begun to cross the Alps, probably as early as the sixth century (Livy 5.33.4).

Returning to the emporium of Gravisca, we find that the divinities under whose protection the foreign merchants and craftsmen operated were predominantly great goddesses. We have already mentioned Aphrodite, protectress of navigation and safe landing; the goddess here seems to have been connected with the Laconian armed Aphrodite and with certain aspects of the Phoenician armed Astarte. A pair of Greek bronze votive statuettes of a helmeted and armed female divinity of the second quarter of the sixth century was discovered in the sanctuary of Aphrodite (inv. 72/10674 and 75/18896).

The other Greek goddesses venerated at Gravisca were Hera and Demeter. The first presided over marriage and the sexual life of women, the second, together with her daughter Kore, was the provider of corn and agricultural wealth. Under the name of Vei, Demeter was worshiped by the Etruscans. A minor male divinity was Adonis, the Oriental youth and lover of Aphrodite. His cult and ritual burial were practiced in a special garden enclosure adjoining the temple of Aphrodite. A single dedication mentions the goddess Aretume/Artemis.

Gravisca illustrates how closely interwoven the Archaic culture of the coastal cities of Southern Etruria had become with that of their Greek and other foreign trading partners. Etruscans, for their part, could dedicate objects in Greek sanctuaries in Greece, as shown by a fragmentary owner's inscription in Etruscan (*mi pl*[. . . *c* . . .] *minur*) under the base of a stemless Laconian cup fragment in Munich (inv. VK 86) that was excavated at the Temple of Aphaia on the island of Aigina.

The Greek frequentation of the port of Gravisca ceased about the time of the battle off Cumae in 474, but the harbor continued to serve the city of Tarquinia, and the sanctuaries of Gravisca were restructured and enlarged. Henceforth dedications were made purely in Etruscan to the goddesses Turan, Vei, and Uni, the Etruscan equivalents of Greek Aphrodite, Demeter, and Hera. At the beginning of the third century, the cults were abandoned, probably as a result of the Roman conquest.

Etruscan industrial production, in particular bronze and iron utensils and pottery, was distributed, besides by maritime trade, via interior land- and river routes to the Italic peoples of the peninsula. Warlike pastoral-agricultural nations inhabiting the Apennines and Abruzzi lived at a less advanced level than the urbanized Etruscans, for whom they provided a source of manpower for manual work and warfare. Their aristocrats accumulated Etruscan luxury goods in their own tombs, as shown by finds from Fabriano and Pitino di San Severino in the Marche, as well as from Capestrano, Alfedena, and Campovalano in the Abruzzi.

Pyrgi

Of the harbors of Cerveteri the one nearest the city was Alsium (It. Palo Laziale), another was Punicum (a name hinting at Punic frequentation), but the most important was to the north at Pyrgi (It. Santa Severa, at km 52 of the Via Aurelia). On the site of a Bronze Age village, this coastal settlement was founded at the end of the eighth century, urbanized about 600 B.C., and probably eventually became the base of the navy of Cerveteri. Its Greek name, *Pyrgoi* = the Towers, implies that the settlement was fortified. Servius (*Aen.* 10.184), the fourth-century-A.D. commentator on Vergil, calls it a fortified settlement (Lat. *castellum*) and the "metropolis" of the Etruscans. This reflects an ancient story, according to which the Etruscan nation was of Lydian origin. The Lydians, so Herodotos tells us (1.94), left their country because of famine and sailed from Asia Minor under Tyrrhenos, son of their king, Atys. Disembarking and settling in Italy, they henceforth called themselves Tyrrhenians after their leader. Having become Etruscans, they occupied the Pelasgian city of Agylla and changed her name to Caere (It. Cerveteri; Strabo 5.220).

The sanctuary of Pyrgi, which comprised several temples, lay directly south of the port and consisted of two different nuclei, all facing the sea. According to ancient Greek writers, the sanctuary was dedicated to the goddess Eileithyia, a helper in childbirth, and to Leukothea, a sea goddess; Apollo is also mentioned.

Excavations at Pyrgi, carried out since 1957, have led to spectacular discoveries that shed fresh light on the political and social conditions prevailing at Cerveteri at the end of the sixth century, as well as on historical and linguistic aspects.

THE SANCTUARY OF EILEITHYIA Oriented to the southwest, like the preexisting harbor settlement, the northern part of the sanctuary was erected on a large artificial platform surrounded by a rectangular enclosure, accessible through a main gate in its east wall. Here ended the 10-m-wide carriage road built in the first half of the sixth century that connected the town of Cerveteri with its main port. The seaward side of the enclosure wall (and presumably the altars that must have stood in front of the temples) has been eroded by the receding shoreline, while of the temples only the foundations have survived dismantling and subsequent ploughing.

TEMPLE B Some smaller, older shrines (fragments of their terra-cotta decoration of ca. 530–510 have been identified) lay somewhere in this area, but, about 510 an ambitious new building program replaced them with one of the largest known sanctuaries in Etruria (FIGS. 152a, b). The first structure erected was Temple B, dedicated to Uni/Astarte, with a sacred Area C to the left of its facade; the south-

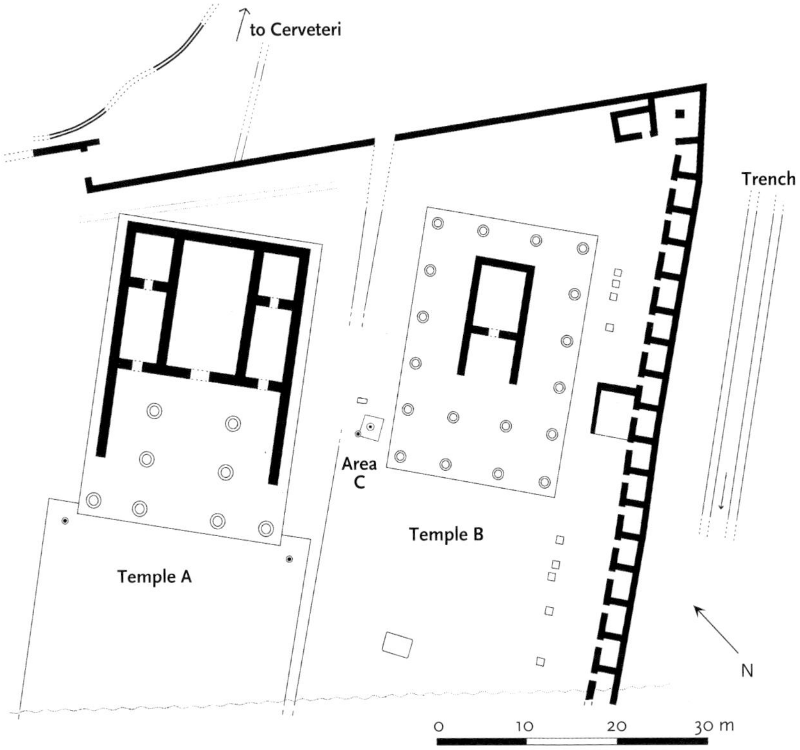

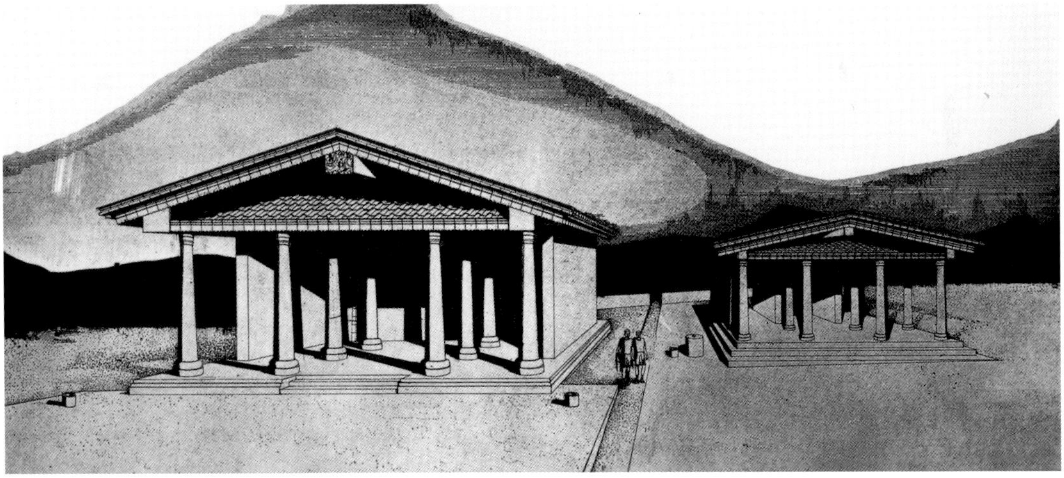

Fig. 152a Plan of Temples A and B at Pyrgi (Santa Severa).

Fig. 152b Reconstruction of Temples A and B at Pyrgi (Santa Severa). Drawing: Museo Etrusco di Villa Giulia.

ern enclosure wall consisted of a long row of small identical cells (perhaps once containing couches) with several altars in front of them.

The Greek-style Temple B was of a type with columns on all four sides (*peripteros*), four on the short sides, six on the long ones. The single *cella* for a cult statue was accessible through a deep porch with a second row of four columns and a *pronaos*. At the back of the temple there was only one row of columns with much less space between them and the *cella* wall. Built of tufa blocks brought from quarries at Cerveteri, the stuccoed walls and the Tuscan columns supported a wooden entablature. This and the tiled ridge roof were decorated with painted terra-cotta revetments; antefixes of heads of satyrs, maenads, and negroes; and with acroteria. Following Etruscan practice, the two pediments were open, with the front ends of the three main longitudinal supporting beams of the roof protected by figured terra-cotta panels representing scenes from the myth of Herakles.

AREA C In the sacred Area C to the left of Temple B stood a cylindrical tufa altar with a vertical conduit for liquid offerings that communicated with the soil below, an arrangement suggesting a cult for an underworld divinity. Next to this altar were a well and a trapezoidal monolithic altar. At the back of this the excavators discovered a low protective enclosure made of re-used terra-cotta *sima* blocks from Temple B that had been improvised here after the temple's destruction by the Romans about 270 B.C. Inside this sheltering enclosure were hidden three rectangular sheets of inscribed gold foil, rolled up; several large gold-covered nail heads, perhaps originally from the wooden door of the temple; and an inscribed bronze tablet. The whole cache was covered by a new pavement of the piazza, created from the rubble of Temple B after its destruction in 270.

THE INSCRIPTIONS Two of the longer gold-foil inscriptions, one in Etruscan, the other in Phoenician, were at first thought to be a bilingual text (like the Rosetta Stone); however, although they turned out to refer to the same events, the texts were not identical, and some of the details remain in dispute. The inscriptions commemorate the dedication of a holy place, sacred to a goddess called Uni in Etruscan and Astarte in Phoenician by one Thefarie Velianas, "king over Kisry" (Kisry being the Phoenician, C[a]isra the Etruscan for Lat. Caere/It. Cerveteri). This ruler, whose existence had so far been unknown to scholars, made his dedication "in the third year of his reign, in gratitude to the goddess, his protectress."

Thefarie Velianas may have been a tyrant, whose rise to power in Cerveteri was facilitated by a Carthaginian presence in the area; his gratitude to the Phoenician goddess for her protection could imply his dependence on his foreign allies for the maintenance of his position at Cerveteri. The shorter Etruscan text on the third gold plaque seems also to refer to the foundation of this new cult and the prescribed ritual for it.

It appears that the great goddess of the temple, Uni, was here assimilated to the armed Phoenician goddess of love and war, Astarte. From Phoenicia, Cyprus, and Carthage her cult had spread to the Carthaginian parts of Sicily, with an important sanctuary at Eryx and others in Numidia and on Sardinia. The fact that one of the longer texts is written in Phoenician, combined with the excavators' plausible interpretation of the row of identical cells beside the temple as destined for the Phoenician priestesses (Gr. *hierodoulai*) of Astarte, suggests that the new cult was introduced to Pyrgi with the support of the Carthaginians, who were

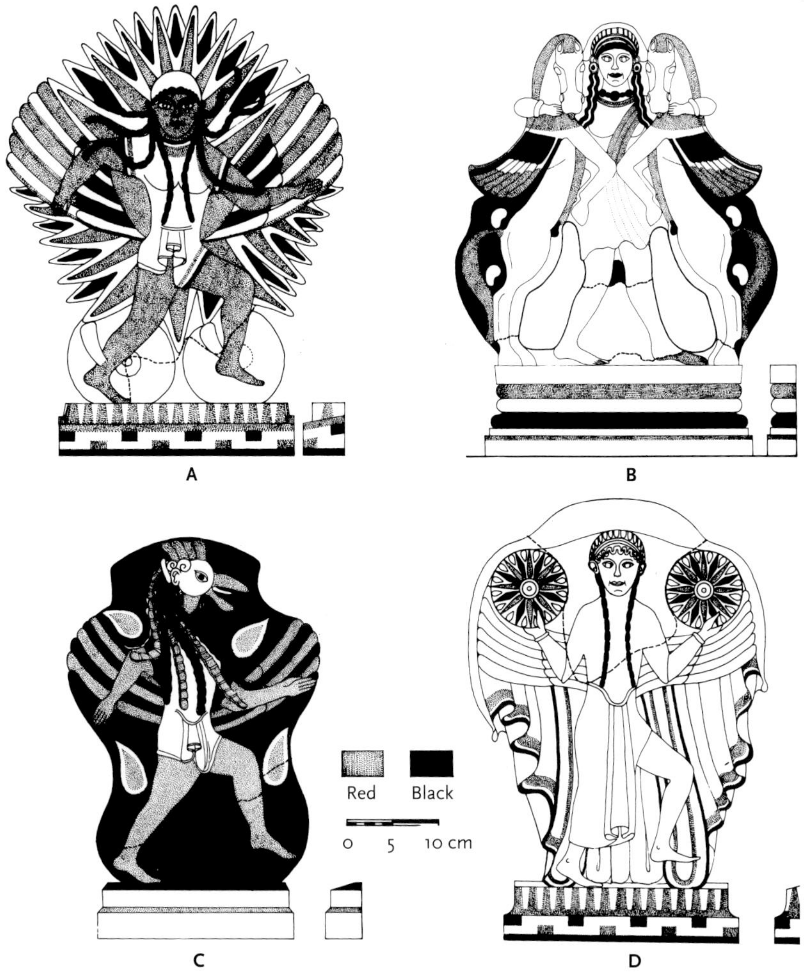

Fig. 153 Reconstructions of antefixes from row of cells on south side of Temple B at Pyrgi (Santa Severa). Late sixth century B.C. Drawings: Museo Etrusco di Villa Giulia.

allies of the Etruscans in the battle in the Sardinian Sea. The priestesses of Uni/Astarte probably practiced sacred prostitution, habitual in the cult of Astarte (Hdt. 1.93 and 1.199).

The front of the long row of cells was decorated with antefixes of six different and most unusual subjects, four of which can be reconstructed with certainty from many fragments (FIG. 153). The facade was oriented from sunrise to sunset, and the moldmade antefixes with the figures in movement from left to right were probably arranged along the edge of its roof in a logical sequence according to their subject. First came an antefix showing the sun god, Usil, rising from the sea (A); he is represented as a youth in a short tunic, rushing past disc-shaped waves, his body and head surrounded by a nimbus of rays. Preceding him is Dawn = Etruscan Thesan (Gr. Eos), a female figure in the short tunic of a charioteer and flanked by the two white horses of her team, whom she holds around the neck (B). Lucifer, the morning star, in the form of a winged man with the head of a cock, runs ahead of her, his beak opened in a crow, announcing the arrival of daylight (C); four drop shapes painted around him have been interpreted as dew-drops. A female figure in a widespread mantle holds two large, disc-shaped stars in front of its folds (D); she may be Astarte, the mistress of the morning and evening stars. The next antefix is badly preserved, but it seems to have represented an apotheosis of Herakles, the hero being flanked by a pair of horses like a master of horses (Gr. *potnios hippon*). The last end tile in the sequence is also preserved in fragments only, but it probably showed the epiphany of Leukothea/Astarte/Aphrodite rising from the waves. This extraordinary iconography has no precedents and was obviously created specifically for the sanctuary, showing astral divinities, the multifaceted great goddess, and Herakles.

The inscription on a fragmentary bronze tablet discovered together with the gold ones names the goddess Uni and her husband Tinia. He is the Etruscan equivalent of the Greek Zeus, husband of Hera. In several sanctuaries in Etruria (above all at Orvieto) Tinia was, however, worshiped as a chthonic, or, underworld divinity. The round altar communicating with the subsoil in the sacred Area C may therefore have been dedicated to Tinia in his chthonic aspect.

TEMPLE A There seems to have been a lull in the building activities at Pyrgi after the battle off Cumae in 474. In this fateful encounter at sea, a powerful Etruscan fleet was defeated by the Greeks of Cumae, who had called for assistance from the fleet of the Syracusian Greeks under Hieron the Elder of the Deinomenid family. This event marked the beginning of the decline of Etruscan sea power in the southern Tyrrhenian Sea. But, as if in defiance of her Greek enemies (the Deinomenids had fallen in 465, and Syracuse did not renew her hostilities until 454), the city of Cerveteri enlarged the sanctuary's enclosure about 470–460 and erected another, even bigger temple, Temple A, parallel with and just to the north of Temple B (see FIGS. 152a, b). This, in deliberate contrast to the earlier building, follows a non-Greek plan, whose proportions might be compared with the Tuscan temple, as described by Vitruvius. It was dedicated to Thesan/Leukothea.

The facade, which was symmetrically flanked by two wells, consisted of four columns of stuccoed tufa. Access to the body of the temple, which took up the entire width of the podium, was through a deep porch formed by an anta wall on each side and two rows of two columns between them. Three doors led into the interior, divided into a large oblong *cella* in the center and two smaller and narrower ones on each side of it. The walls were constructed of tufa blocks (the internal ones of mud brick), covered with a fine white stucco and painted with motifs in red. Entablature and roof were wooden, tiled, and decorated with mold-made, painted terra-cotta antefixes of heads of satyrs and maenads (made from the same molds as those used in temples at Cerveteri); the *sima* was decorated with a palmette-and-lotus chain, of which important parts have survived.

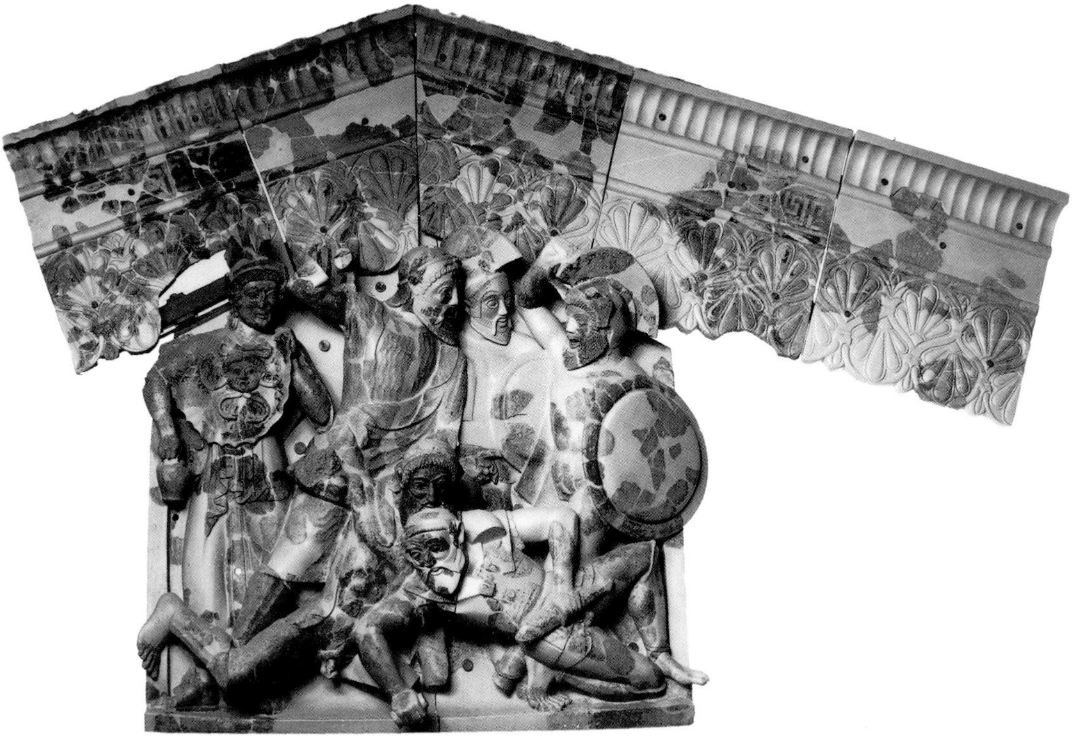

Fig. 154 Relief panel from apex of pediment at rear of Temple A at Pyrgi (Santa Severa). 470–460 B.C. Painted terra-cotta. Rome, Museo Etrusco di Villa Giulia.

Hand-modeled terra-cotta plaques in high relief were once nailed to the ends of the three main wood beams in both the open pediments. The plaques on the back of the temple, less exposed to the sea wind, remained in situ during the life of the building and were dismantled only when it was destroyed. The central one of these three plaques could be restored from innumerable fragments; it is an intricate six-figure composition combining several different episodes from the Greek myth of The Seven against Thebes (FIG. 154). This theme, which had inspired great epic and tragic writing in Greece, became very popular in Etruria. It is the story of the failed expedition led by the Argive king Adrastos against the city of Thebes, a generation before the Trojan War. Of the two lateral plaques only small fragments have survived; perhaps they showed the rest of the heroes who fell before the walls of Thebes, while the central plaque represented the hybris and the resulting tragic fate of the heroes Tydeus (who lost his chance at immortality) and Kapaneus (who was struck by a thunderbolt).

The upper left part of this panel is taken up by the imposing figure of the bearded Zeus, draped in chiton and mantle, striding to the right to hurl his thunderbolt against the rebellious Kapaneus. The latter is nude but wears a shield on his left arm and a crested helmet on his head. Staggering backward under the onslaught of Zeus, he still raises his right arm to strike. His fiercely aggressive face with bared teeth is turned defiantly toward the god, his destroyer, while his helmeted Theban adversary recedes between them.

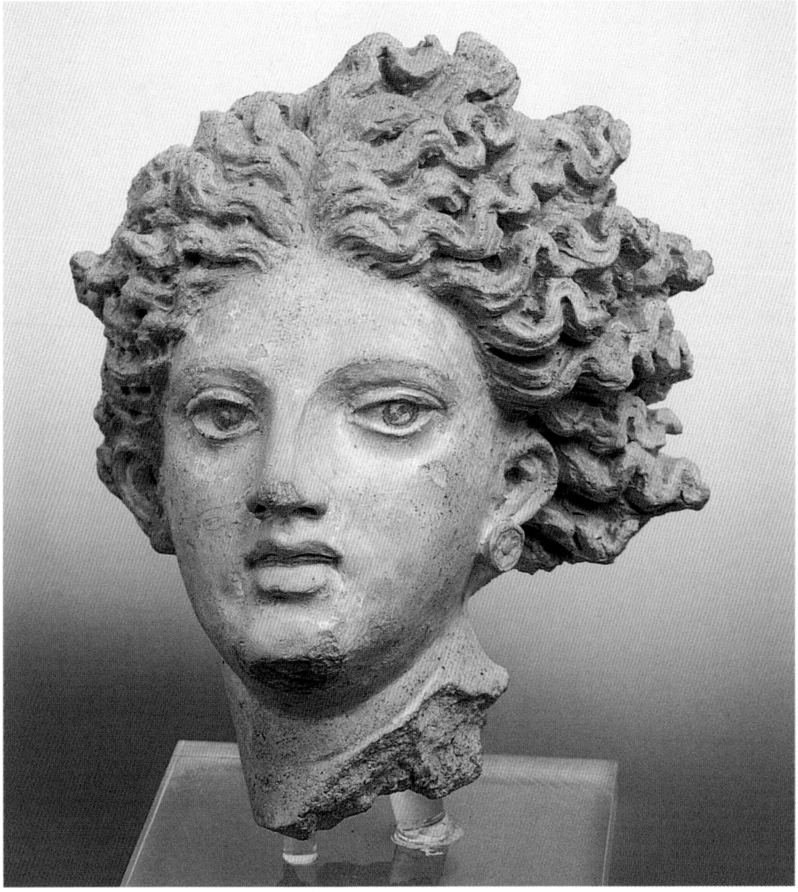

Fig. 155 High-relief head of a young woman (Leukothea?). From the front pediment of Temple A at Pyrgi (Santa Severa). Third quarter of fourth century B.C. Painted terra-cotta. Rome, Museo Etrusco di Villa Giulia.

To the left of Zeus, the goddess Athena with spread wings and wearing chiton, aegis, and helmet, moves to the right but hesitates at the sight of the gruesome scene at her feet. In her right hand she carries a small bottle containing the drug (Gr. *pharmakon*) of immortality (Gr. *athanasia*), which she had procured for her protégé Tydeus. His disgusting action makes her draw back. Tydeus, naked and without helmet, and Melanippos, in a cuirass, having wounded each other mortally, have collapsed in front of Zeus, with Tydeus bending down over the head of Melanippos and biting it. In the literary Greek sources, Tydeus ate the brain of Melanippos after his enemy's head had been lopped off.

This unusual version of the Theban myths and the incidents condensed here into a single scene must have been decided on by the Etruscan master modeler and his employers. The subject from Greek mythology was perhaps chosen because of the Theban origin of the story of the goddess Ino/Leukothea. The significance implied in this complex theme may be the condemnation of hybris and cruel and tyrannical acts, which the worshiper might well have connected with the recent rule of Thefarie Velianas. The positioning of this plaque at the apex of the rear pediment, where it would be visible to all entering the gate of the sanctuary's enclosure, was probably carefully calculated.

The relief panels on the left and right corners of the front pediment of Temple A (battle with Amazons?) were replaced toward the end of the fifth century, and hardly a trace of them survives. In the third quarter of the fourth century the central panel was renewed and, when the temple was finally dismantled, only a few fragments of this relief were buried in the two wells flanking the facade. Of its original four quietly standing figures only one, representing Herakles, is fairly well preserved: a three-quarter life-size youth, nude but for a sword belt passing over his left shoulder, his hair crowned with poplar leaves, he holds a cup in his left hand, while his right hand is placed on his hip. To the hero's right a young woman rested her right hand on a small pillar; only this and her beautiful head are preserved. She looked back over her left shoulder with an anxious expression, her lips slightly parted and her curls flying (FIG. 155). To her right, only a torso survives, apparently that of a boy. The style of the finely balanced, slim figure of Herakles and the agitated beauty of the goddess shows the Etruscan sculptor's profound understanding of Greek sculptural prototypes of the mid-fourth century.

The scene has been interpreted as the arrival in Italy of the persecuted Ino/Leukothea with her son Melikertes/Palaimon after their flight from Thebes. Having brought up Dionysos, her sister Semele's child by Zeus, Ino/Leukothea escaped from her husband, Athamas, who had been driven mad by Hera, and leaped into the sea with her son; but she was rescued and became a sea goddess. As such she was thought to protect sailors from shipwreck and drowning, while her nursing of the young Dionysos probably gave her the character of a protectress of small children (Gr. *kourotrophos*).

In addition to the divinities already mentioned as having been worshiped in the sanctuary, the name of the goddess Thesan (Gr. Eos; Lat. Aurora; Dawn) is preserved on a fragmentary inscription on bronze found in the neighborhood of Temple A. It records the dedication of an image of Thesan "in the sanctuary of Uni."

The wells flanking the facade of Temple A yielded further material. A votive terra-cotta head of a young woman wearing earrings of a type resembling grape clusters (It. *a grappolo*) and a necklace of disc-shaped beads stands out by its directness and simplicity (FIG. 156). Comparing this example of popular art by a local artisan of the first half of the third century with the head of "Leukothea," the sensitive work of a considerable Etruscan artist inspired by Late Classical Greek prototypes, we can appreciate the range of quality in the terra-cotta production of the region of Cerveteri.

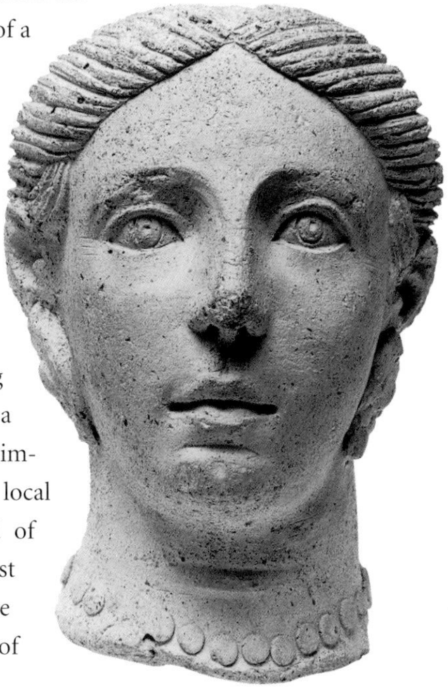

Fig. 156 Votive head of a young woman. From the well at the southern angle of Temple A at Pyrgi (Santa Severa). First half of third century B.C. Terra-cotta. Antiquarium of Pyrgi, Santa Severa.

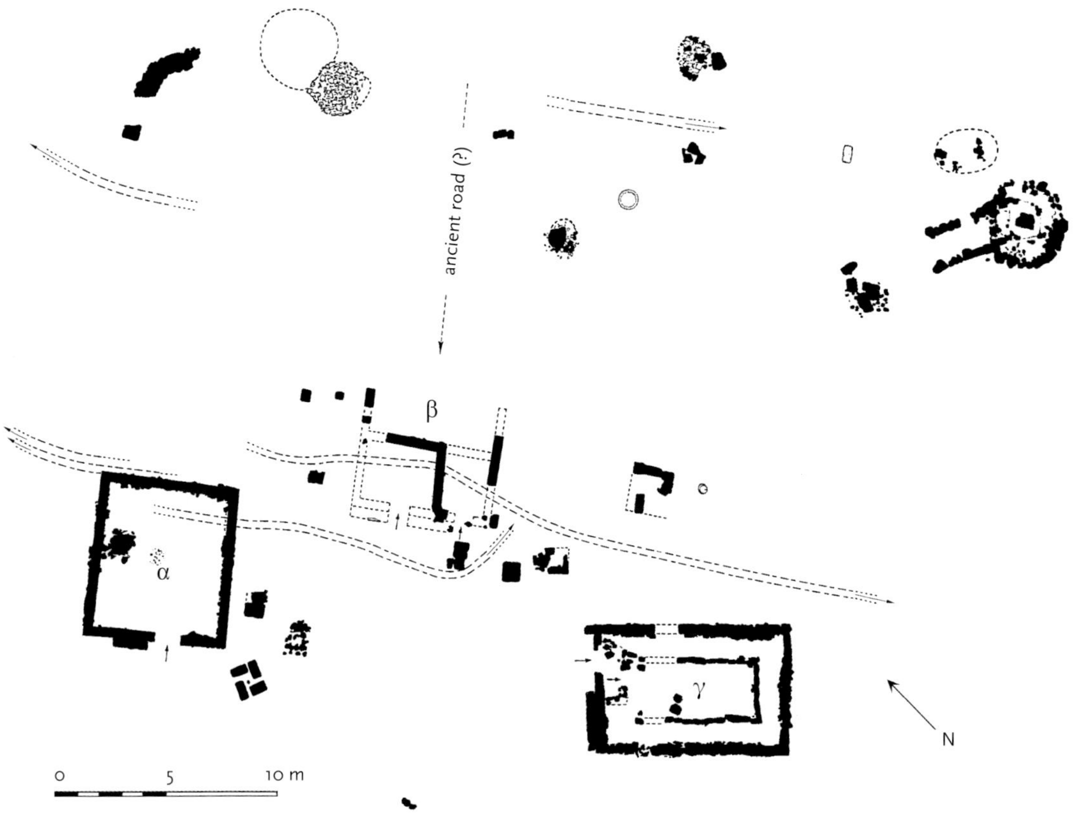

Fig. 157 Plan of sanctuary in southern area of Pyrgi (Santa Severa).

THE TREASURE OF THE SANCTUARY Nine Greek silver coins discovered in the trench where the back wall of Temple A had been dismantled are the only miserable remnants of the immense wealth carried off as booty during the raid on the sanctuary of Eileithyia at Pyrgi in 384 by Dionysios I of Syracuse (Strabo 5.226). The ancient sources mention that the loot included gold and silver coins as well as precious votive objects. Diodorus Siculus (15.14.3–4) speaks of one thousand talents' worth of loot, while Aelian (*VH* 1.20) relates that Dionysios robbed all the riches of Apollo and Leukothea and, after addressing a blasphemous after-dinner toast to the god, ordered that a silver table in front of Apollo be taken away.

The nine silver tetradrachms found were issues of Attica, Syracuse, Messana, and Leontinoi, indicating the nature of Pyrgi's trade connections. Since the recorded mass of treasure held at Pyrgi is unique among Etruscan temples, the excavators suggested that, like many Greek sanctuaries, that of Pyrgi may have functioned as a branch of the public treasury of Cerveteri, with which it had the closest political and economic links.

THE SOUTHERN SACRED AREA OF THE SANCTUARY OF PYRGI Excavations south of Temples A and B have revealed another sacred area separated from the temples by an ancient watercourse (FIG. 157). The discovery includes altars and remains of a rectangular edifice (γ) with a roof decorated with acroteria in the form of heads of Acheloös and rams, dating from the last quarter of the sixth century. Two further *aediculae* (α and β) were constructed after the sack of Pyrgi in 384. Of the many votive deposits found, the earliest, from the late sixth century, contained forty-two Attic black-figured vases as well as Corinthian and Ionic pottery. Other deposits yielded fragments of Attic red-figured vases; statuettes; arms; jewelry; big lead bars; as well as thin, perforated leaves of iron, presumably used as oracular lots. Votive inscriptions indicate that the cult was dedicated to the divinities Śuri and Cav(a)tha. Śuri was an Apollo of the underworld; he has been identified as an equivalent of the Faliscan *pater soranus*, the god of Mount Soracte, to whom a grotto filled with deadly pestilential vapors was sacred. The priests at his sanctuary, known as *hirpi sorani*, ritually imitated wolves. This relates Śuri/Apollo's nature to that of Aita/Hades or Veiovis/Dispater, gods of the underworld and death. In the Etruscan version Hades is represented in a wolf's cap as ruler of the underworld in the wall-paintings of the Tomb of the Underworld (*Tomba del'Orco*) in Tarquinia (p. 314).

The name Śuri found in association with the remains of sacred buildings in the southern area proves the existence of a sanctuary of Apollo at Pyrgi, as mentioned by Aelian (*VH* 1.20). Worshiped together with Śuri was Cav(a)tha, a solar goddess whose cult is attested in various Etruscan cities. She appears to have an underworld aspect as well and was connected with family cults.

THE MAIN GODS AT PYRGI Surveying the divinities named by ancient writers as well as in votive inscriptions from Pyrgi, we note the outstanding importance of goddesses with caring and saving aspects: Uni/Astarte, Ino/Leukothea, and Eileithyia were all mother goddesses who were supposed to help mortal women in childbirth and watch over the growth of young children, as well as save sailors. Thesan and Cav(a)tha brought light; the latter, however, who also had an underworld aspect, should perhaps be compared to the Greek goddess Kore.

Prominent, too, was Herakles, whose apotheosis and deeds as a savior were represented on Temples A and B and on the antefixes of the long row of cells. His close connections with Uni is documented elsewhere in Etruria. At Pyrgi and at Cerveteri a local tradition seems to have held Herakles to be a forefather of Tyrrhenos. Two recently found Latin inscriptions inform us that Herakles was here worshiped together with Jupiter.

The other male gods mentioned were connected with the underworld: Tinia, who was perhaps worshiped only at the circular, chthonic altar in the sacred Area C; and Śuri, whose sanctuary and altars were situated in the newly excavated sacred area to the south of the enclosure wall of the sanctuary.

It is perhaps not surprising that the main harbor sanctuary of one of the most important Etruscan coastal cities, visited by many different nationalities, should be the site of a conflation of various divinities and cults answering the perennial human needs of diverse worshipers. The complexity of Etruscan religious beliefs and the people's ability to absorb and transform foreign religious concepts and images and imbue them with a significance of their own manifest themselves in a very tangible way at Pyrgi.

Although the incursion of the Syracusians robbed the sanctuary of its fabulous wealth, the temples seem to have remained more or less intact, and Pyrgi flourished again as a result of the good relations Cerveteri then enjoyed with Rome. These deteriorated, however, during the invasion of Italy by Pyrrhus of Epiros, and the fatal event for the harbor settlement of Pyrgi and the temples was their destruction by the Romans about 280–270 B.C. After the dismantling of the temples, the remaining parts of their terra-cotta decoration and votive offerings were ritually buried. Some cult continued in the sanctuary, but the territory of Cerveteri was incorporated into the Roman state, and a maritime colony was founded at Pyrgi. The polygonal walls of the Roman *castrum* are partly preserved at the base of the castle of Santa Severa.

THE SANCTUARY OF PUNTA DELLA VIPERA

In the territory of Cerveteri, on the seashore 2 km north of Santa Marinella (ancient Punicum, the third harbor of Cerveteri), lay another sanctuary with a temple founded about 540–520 and dedicated to the goddess Menerva. The remains of the terra-cotta decoration of the building show that it was reconstructed in the middle of the fourth century, presumably because it had been destroyed in 384 by the Syracusan sack of this coastal area (see p. 182), and again in the second century, finally to be superseded by a Roman agricultural villa in the Augustan period.

Terra-cotta statuettes representing a helmeted goddess and inscriptions on vases indicate that Menerva was the presiding divinity of the sanctuary. A votive deposit contained offerings of Attic and Etruscan pottery, terra-cotta figurines, and metal objects dating from the late sixth century right through to the end of the sanctuary's existence. From the nature of the ex-votos—terra-cotta models of intestines, male and female genitalia, limbs, and swaddled babies—it emerges that Menerva was here worshiped as a healing goddess, a protectress of fertility, and perhaps an oracular divinity. A well on the east side of the temple contained an inscription covering both sides of a fragmentary rectangular strip of lead and a small perforated lead disc, also inscribed on both sides, perhaps an oracular lot (Lat. *sors*). A perforated stone altar communicating with the soil hints at an underworld aspect connected with the cult of Menerva. Such polyvalency of single divinities is a notable feature of Etruscan religious beliefs.

LA CASTELLINA DEL MARANGONE

North of Punta della Vipera (near Civitavecchia), on the left bank of the river Marangone, lies the walled hill of La Castellina. Settled from the Middle Bronze Age onward and surrounded by extensive necropolises, the site has yielded Euboean Geometric pottery sherds of the mid-eighth century. The metal-rich Tolfa and Allumiere Mountains, in the western foothills of which La Castellina is situated, attracted economic interest from an early period. Recent excavations on top of the hill have identified two adjacent Archaic buildings, presumably temples. The surface find of a small, exquisitely carved ivory head of a woman(?) dates from the mid-sixth century and may have adorned a piece of furniture (FIG. 158). A large cistern and a Tuscan stone capital were discovered in earlier explorations, as were fragments of architectural friezes in terra-cotta with female figures and flowered scrolls, probably dating from a Hellenistic sanctuary.

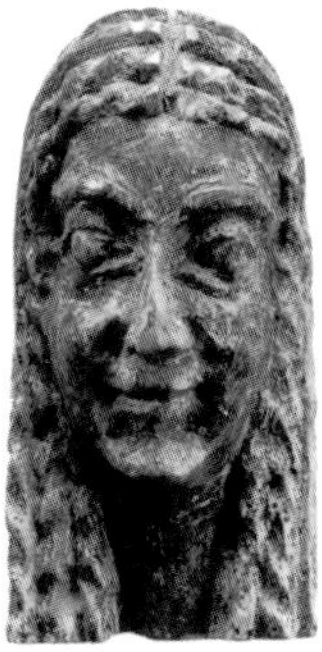

Fig. 158 Miniature head of a woman. From Castellina del Marangone. Mid-sixth century B.C. Ivory. H. 2.5 cm. Civitavecchia, Museo Nazionale Archeologico CAS 98.34031D1.

A GLIMPSE OF ARCHAIC ETRUSCAN HISTORY

A shaft of light illuminating the often confused and contradictory literary sources and legends on the early wars between Rome and the Etruscan cities is provided by the speech in the senate made by Emperor Claudius in A.D. 48. Part of it is preserved in a transcription on a bronze plaque found at Lyon (*CIL* 13.1668). Claudius says that there are two divergent traditions regarding the origins of King Servius Tullius (578–535): According to Roman sources, he was the son of an enslaved woman named Ocresia; but according to Etruscan sources, Servius Tullius was the faithful companion of the Etruscan chief Caelius Vibenna, whom he accompanied in every enterprise. After many events, Servius Tullius was driven from Etruria with the rest of the army of Caelius and occupied Mount Caelius in Rome, naming it after his erstwhile leader. Changing his own name—which in Etruscan had been Mastarna—to Servius Tullius, he became the ruler of Rome to the great benefit of the state. (The traditional time-span of the regal period at Rome [753–509] and the number of her kings are still a matter of an animated scholarly debate that need not concern us here.)

The single name Mastarna/Macstrna is thought to be based on the Latin word *magister* plus the Etruscan adjectival suffix *-na*. Some scholars have therefore assumed that the magistrature of *magister populi* existed as early as the mid-sixth century at Rome. Antipatrician constitutional reforms were, in fact, ascribed to Servius Tullius by Roman sources.

The brothers Caeles and Aulus Vibenna were famous heroes in Etruscan tradition and probably historical personalities.

Some two hundred years after these mid-sixth-century events, which Claudius referred to so learnedly in his speech, an Etruscan (Vulcian) version

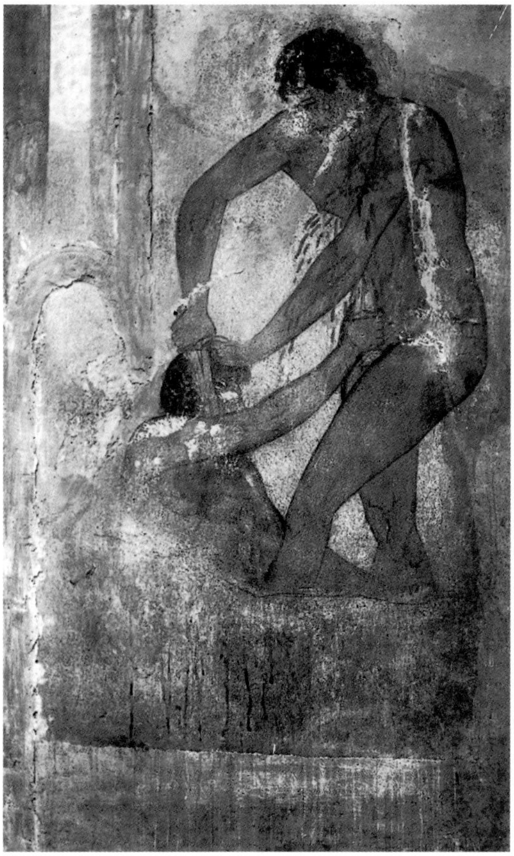

Fig. 159 Wall-painting showing Eteokles and Polyneikes killing each other. From the François Tomb, Ponte Rotto necropolis, Vulci. Second half of fourth century B.C. Rome, Galleria Albani e Collezione Archeologica.

of them was illustrated by the wall-paintings from the François Tomb (*Tomba François*) at Vulci. The two main scenes in the atrium of this complex chamber tomb depict episodes from Theban myth (FIG. 159) and the *Iliad* (the slaughter of the Trojan prisoners at the funeral of Patroklos) as well as a seemingly historical event. The latter shows naked men with swords killing unarmed, helpless opponents. The figures, identified by names inscribed beside them, include Macstrna (as he is here named) and the brothers Caile and Avle Vipinas. Macstrna frees the bound Caile Vipina, while Avle Vipinas and three other, probably Vulcian, heroes stab victims from Volsinii, Sovana(?), and Rome. The latter city is personified by a cowering figure (*Cneve Tarchunies Rumach* = Cnaeus Tarquinius of Rome), who is being dispatched by Marce Camitlnas. The identity of this Roman is a matter of debate. Some scholars take him to be Tarquinius Priscus, despite the fact that his traditional first name was Lucius; for others he represents one of the younger members of the family of Tarquinius Priscus, who resented the succession of Macstrna/Servius Tullius (with the help of Tanaquil) to the Roman throne. But nothing in the painting characterizes him as a king or anything other than one of a group of men, surprised and overcome by a band of armed companions. At any rate, the paintings undoubtedly celebrate a past victory of Vulcian heroes over enemies, including a Roman—a feat of valor—recalled at a time when Vulci was under threat from Rome.

Although we have no reliable historical sources of hostile encounters between armies or surprise ambushes led by the brothers Vibenna and Mastarna, there must have been many raids and wars by private armies under chiefs in search of land and cattle, which set clans or cities in Etruria and Lazio against each other. Aulus Vibenna, at least, is probably a historical personality, as indicated by the discovery in the Portonaccio sanctuary at Veii of a bucchero vase dated to the sixth century and inscribed with a dedication by one Avile Vipiiennas, the archaic Etruscan form of the name (see p. 205).

A sarcophagus of Chiusine manufacture from the early fifth century found in a tomb in the Sperandio necropolis of Perugia provides a striking illustration of a raid for cattle, booty, and prisoners carried out by the head of an aristocratic family (FIG. 160). The relief on the front panel of the sarcophagus shows the chief, followed by bound prisoners carrying possessions, returning from a successful raid. Two gesticulating women, their heads covered by their mantles, interrupt the

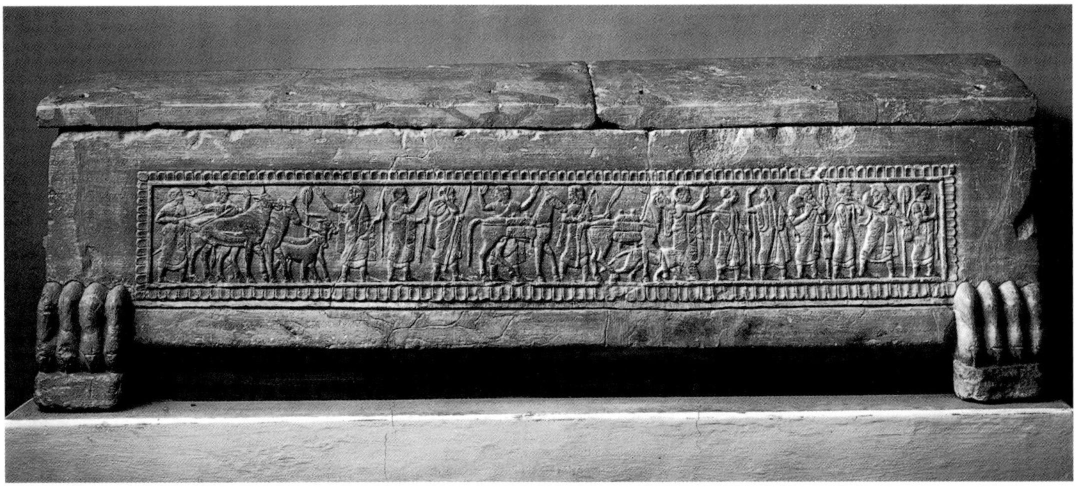

Fig. 160 Relief-decorated sarcophagus showing the return from a raid. From Sperandio necropolis, Perugia. First quarter of fifth century B.C. Limestone. H. 58 cm. Perugia, Museo Archeologico Nazionale dell'Umbria 195.

procession, which continues with three men and a dog beside two loaded mules. The end is brought up by further armed followers driving along two bulls and a goat. The other long side of the sarcophagus shows a symposium with three men on two couches, served by a nude cupbearer, thus coupling in the reliefs the two main activities of aristocratic men: warfare and feasting. The scene of the raid is unique among the usual themes for the decoration of Chiusine ash urns and may have been specially commissioned for a warrior chief (weapons and a helmet were found inside the sarcophagus), who probably led the migration of a family group into the territory of Perugia at the period of the greatest extension of the power of Chiusi.

The great increase in the Etruscan cities and in the emporia of traders, foreigners, and people in servile condition gradually eroded the cohesion of the old gentilicial system and led to the formation of groups not bound to aristocratic families by clients' ties but united by common political interests—a nascent plebs. This component of the population of the great cities was further increased by the destruction of minor settlements by their more powerful neighbors and the transplantation of the defeated inhabitants. Like Murlo and Acquarossa, smaller inland towns of Southern Etruria, such as San Giovenale, Blera, Tuscania, Castro, Poggio Buco, and Bisenzio, were thus depopulated.

NORTHWARD EXPANSION FROM ETRURIA

From Northern and inner Etruria groups of people set out to claim new land in the vast, less densely inhabited areas of the Po valley, repeating in a way the Villanovan migration. Archaeological activity has identified a number of new Etruscan cities, among them Marzabotto, San Polo d'Enza, Forcello near Mantua, and Spina. From inscriptions and archaeological evidence it seems that Orvieto and

Chiusi were involved in these colonial enterprises, as were, to a certain extent, Volterra and Fiesole. The populations of pre-existing transapennine centers, such as Bologna, were reinforced and their cities renovated. Bologna and Mantua are said to have been founded by Ocnus, son of Aulestes who was king of the Northern Etruscan-Umbrian city of Perugia (Servius 10.198). Although Ocnus is a mythical figure, his supposed provenance from Perugia suggests a remote memory of the origin of some of the early settlers.

This northward expansion was probably connected with a series of economic and political events that caused a crisis for the Etruscan control of the Tyrrhenian Sea and led to the growing importance of the Adriatic ports. While the emporia of Southern Etruria suffered a decline, the more northerly ports on the Tyrrhenian coast, such as Populonia, Pisa, and subsequently Genoa and Aleria on Corsica, remained or became prosperous, participating in the trade circuit that included Massalia and the southern coast of France.

Marzabotto

The city of Marzabotto was built at the beginning of the fifth century, probably to facilitate the greatly increased traffic across the Apennines to Bologna and the region of Modena, as well as to guard an important ford of the river Reno. Epigraphic evidence suggests that settlers from Etruscan cities of the Po valley, such as Felsina, also contributed to the population of the city, for among the inscriptions from Marzabotto, family names ending in *-alu* (e.g., *kraikalu*, *achalu*, *sualu*), typical of the Po region, are more numerous than those ending in *-na*, which are characteristic of Tyrrhenian Etruria.

Replacing a provisional settlement of early sixth-century huts, probably inhabited by local people, Marzabotto was reconstructed on a rigorously oriented, regular plan (FIG. 161). The city's Etruscan name is not known, but some think it was called Misa. Marzabotto was situated on a plateau north of a bend in the swift-flowing Reno, which has eroded about a quarter of the surface area of the town in the course of two and a half millennia.

The habitation quarters of Marzabotto were divided by a north–south main street (comparable to the Roman *decumanus*) and by three streets crossing it at right angles, all about 15 m wide. All these streets had drainage, a central driveway, and broad sidewalks for pedestrians. Stepping-stones across the middle part of the streets saved walkers from rainwater and mud in bad weather. There were a number of public wells in the streets. Minor streets, about 5 m wide and running parallel to the main north–south axis, further divided Marzabotto into long rectangular blocks (Lat. *insulae*, ca. 250 x 30 m). This layout seems to have been based on the measure of the Attic foot and mirrored Greek colonial town plans, such as those of Metapontum, Megara Hyblaea, and Selinus, which had long, narrow *insulae*. A large river pebble incised with a cross indicating the four quarters of the sky was found buried below street level at the central crossing point of the main

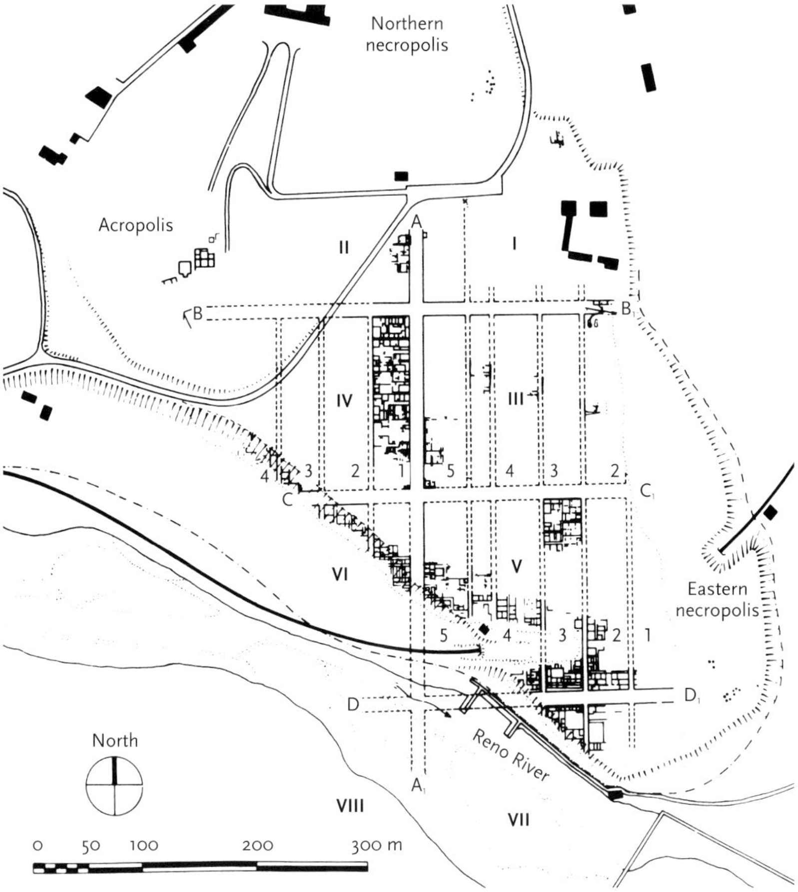

Fig. 161 General plan of the Etruscan city of Marzabotto. Early fifth century B.C.

street, strongly suggesting that this was the geometric center of Marzabotto; the layout of the city was measured in accordance with the sacred prescriptions, which projected the heavenly division of the sky onto the earth. Official land surveyors carried out this task, directed by priests.

The *insulae* were occupied both by houses and by industrial workshops, whose plans and sizes vary somewhat according to the area. Furnaces for pottery and tilemaking, as well as iron smithies and bronze foundries with smelting furnaces have been identified. One of the latter contained a mold for casting the head of a bronze statue of Late Archaic style as well as a mold for casting a bronze ingot marked with the sign of the *ramo secco*, the *aes signatum*. Evidence of bronzeworking from the sixth century preurban phase of Marzabotto suggests that this industry, which depended on large supplies of wood for furnaces, had a long tradition here and probably exported its products. Attic pottery reached the city from the harbor of Spina, while decorated bronzes, jewelry, and ivory carvings came over the passes of the Apennines from Southern Etruria. Marzabotto was an industrial and commercial town. Agricultural production seems to have been ruled out by the lack of arable space on the plateau.

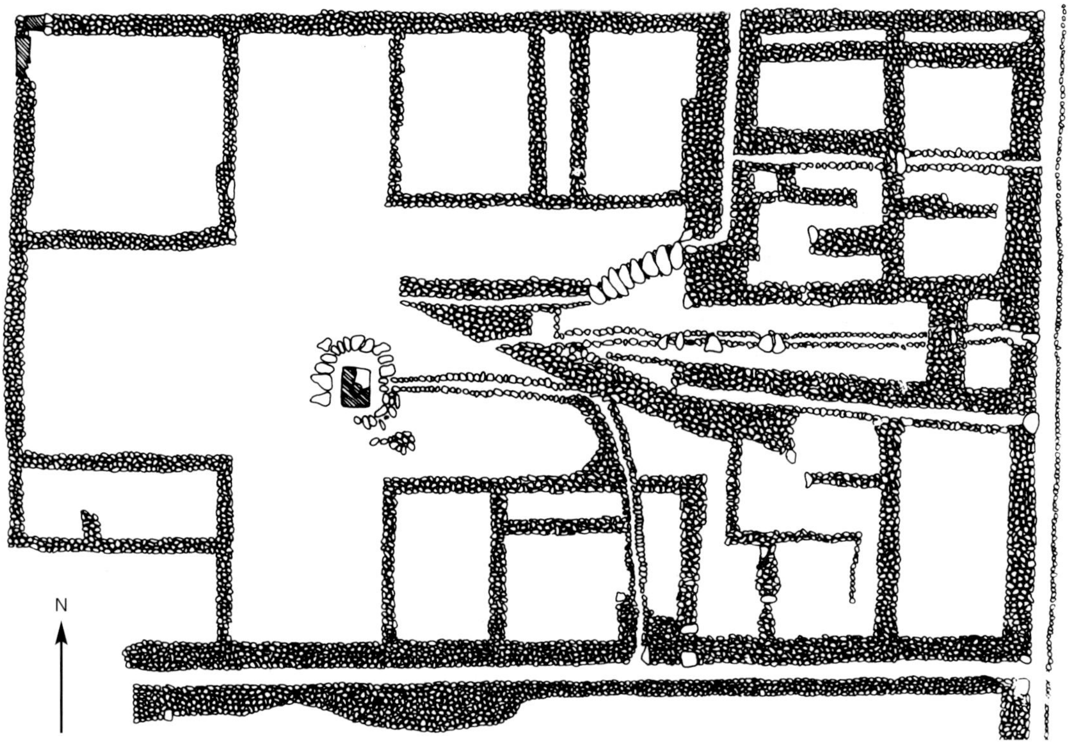

Fig. 162 Plan of a house in *insula* IV of Marzabotto. Early fifth century B.C.

The single-story houses faced the streets and often contained separate workshops and offices on that side (FIG. 162). The living quarters were reached by a narrow passage leading from the front door to an interior courtyard; this usually contained a well and drainage channels to collect rainwater running off the tiled slopes of the roofs. Opposite the entrance, on the far side of the courtyard, was a wide transverse corridor that communicated with a large central room at the rear, open toward the courtyard and flanked by smaller rooms; one of these probably served as kitchen. This arrangement is comparable to the three-roomed Archaic Etruscan transverse house type (see FIG. 118) and perhaps to the Roman atrium house with its *tablinum*, atrium, and alae.

The buildings were constructed on foundations of river pebbles with walls of wooden uprights packed with pressed and dried clay bricks. One particularly spacious house (in street D, *insula* V.2) with a wide door and stone posts has been interpreted as a public building. From the well in its courtyard was recovered a stone marked with a cross and inscribed with the words *mi lavtunies* = I belong to lavtunie, perhaps a re-used funerary cippus from the nearby eastern necropolis.

The uniformity of the comparatively modest domestic buildings and the utilitarian nature of the settlement point to a generally prosperous, but egalitarian society of colonial type.

The two necropolises of Marzabotto, to the east and north of the city, separated from it by gates, were not laid out in a regular way. Both cremation and inhu-

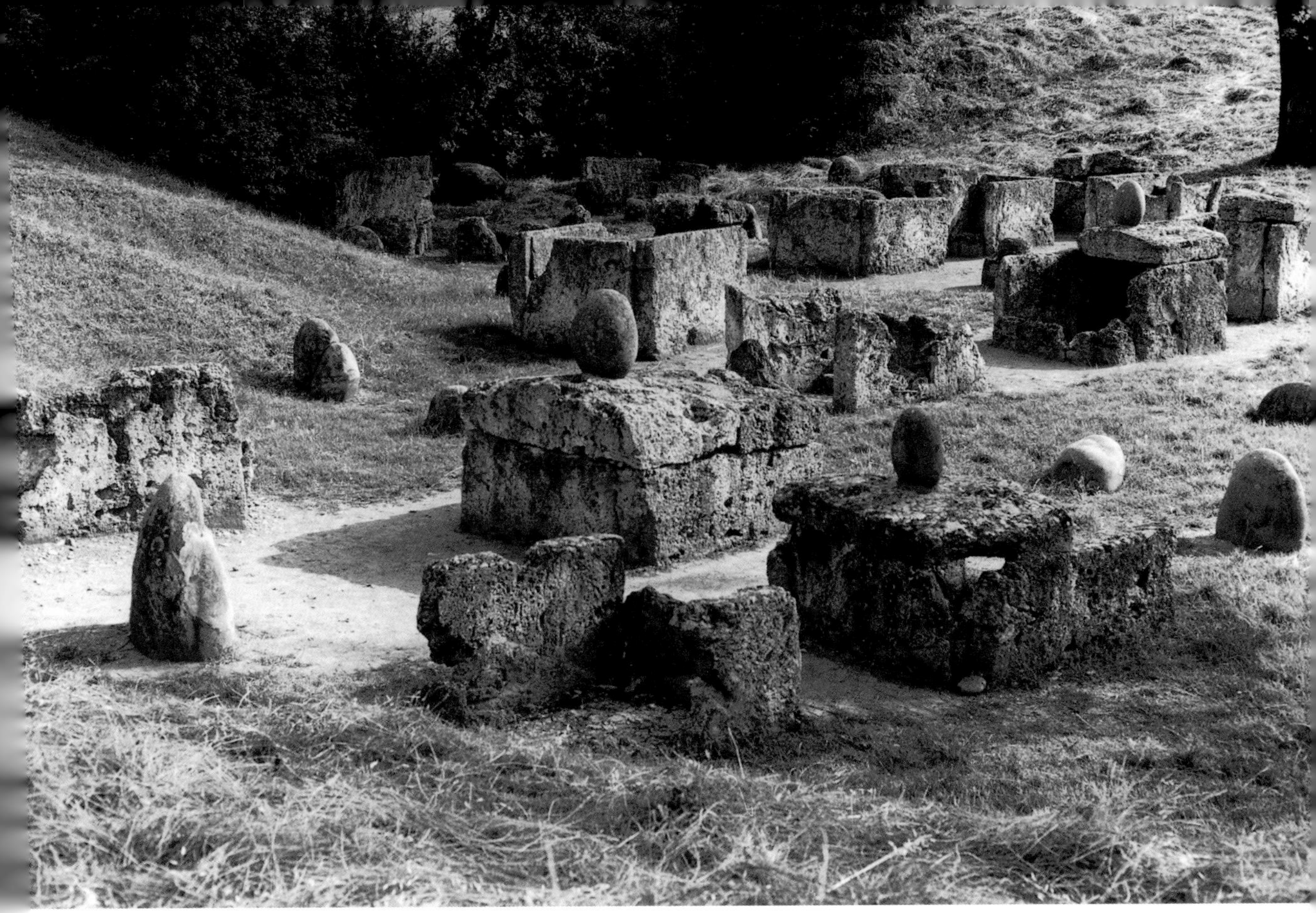

Fig. 163 View of the eastern necropolis, Marzabotto.

mation were practiced, either in trench graves or in small wells (It. *pozzetti*) sunk into the ground. Rectangular *cassone* tombs made of travertine slabs and covered by a flat or ridged lid also contained ashes (FIG. 163). Tomb markers took various forms: large river pebbles or marble cippi of onion shape, one carved in relief with prancing horsemen and a warrior, another with a square base with ram's heads at the corners (similar cippi are found in the region of Pisa and in the Arno valley). There were also columnar cippi and stelae carved from stone. Among the latter is one with an interesting representation in relief of a woman standing on a molded altar, which probably signifies her heroization (FIG. 164). Her left hand is placed on her hip and in her right hand she holds a cup to her lips. The figure is surmounted by a floral-and-volute ornament in relief. This and the stela's rounded top have stylistic connections with funerary monuments from Volterra and Fiesole.

Apart from the rare cinerary urns of bronze or pottery no spectacular grave goods seem to have been deposited in the tombs. But from the northern necropolis comes a fine bronze two-figure group of a helmeted warrior and a draped woman with a libation bowl that once surmounted a candelabrum; the subject was probably inspired by an Attic vase-painting. From a well in the town comes a small lid of an ivory box carved with a quadriga drawn by horses and panthers. It dates from the late seventh century and was perhaps brought from Southern Etruria as an heirloom. The broken-off head of a marble statuette of a Greek kouros, dated to about 500, was probably imported from Spina.

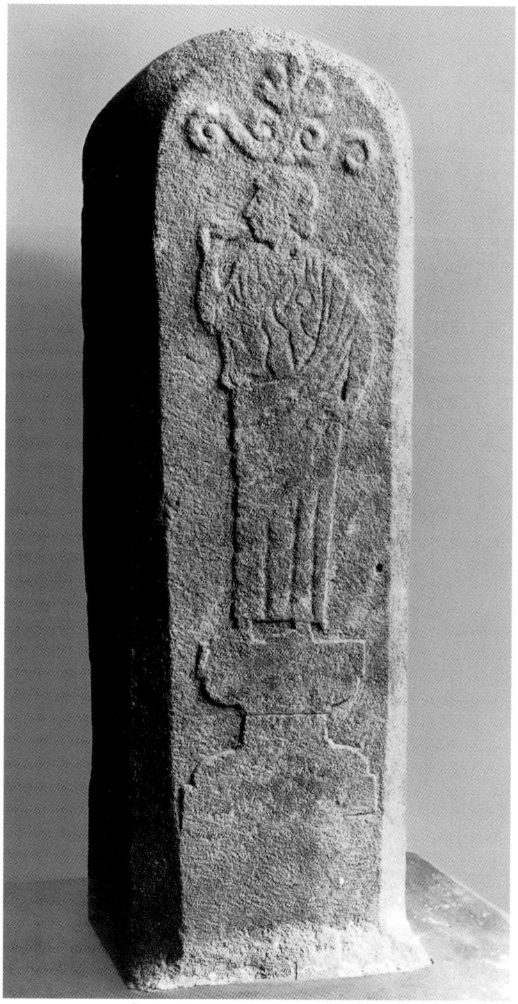

Fig. 164 Funerary stela with relief of a woman standing on an altar. From the eastern necropolis, Marzabotto. Mid-fifth century B.C. Sandstone. H. 1.52 m. Marzabotto, Museo Etrusco "Pompeo Aria" 441.

The sanctuaries of Marzabotto on the acropolis hill (Misanello) northwest of the city were all oriented in the same way, their facades facing south; they all date from the same period. Temple C had a triple *cella*, to judge by its surviving foundations, with a double row of four columns in front; of the superstructure only a few architectural terra-cottas are preserved, painted with geometric and vegetal motifs in three colors. Beside Temple C lay a monumental altar or precinct (D) with steps on the front leading up to the top of its richly molded podium. Another small, square structure (Y) once lay to the west on the highest point of the acropolis; it no longer survives but may have been a delimited area with good visibility whence augury took place (Lat. *auguraculum*). North of Temple C was a square podium (B), probably an altar, with steps leading up the front. Its center contained a deep pit (Lat. *mundus*) full of bones of oxen, goats, pigs, and deer—the remains of sacrifices to underworld divinities, probably connected with the foundation ritual of the city. Beside the podium were the scanty remains of another building (A), presumably a temple.

Outside the northeastern gate of the city lay a fountain sanctuary. In the early fifth century the area of the spring was walled and roofed, as suggested by a terra-cotta acroterion in the form of a seated male winged figure. The interior was paved with stone slabs and contained a well, a basin, and a water channel of travertine. A number of schematic bronze statuettes of worshipers and of anatomical parts as well as some Attic black-figured pottery of the second half of the sixth century were found nearby in a votive deposit. This suggests that a healing cult was connected with the spring, used as early as the preurban period of Marzabotto when the temples on the acropolis had not yet been built. In its fifth-century monumental form, the sanctuary probably mainly served the citizens and arriving travelers. Two further deposits on the acropolis also yielded a quantity of votive bronzes. These comparatively modest works were probably produced locally during the late sixth and fifth centuries.

The life span of Etruscan Marzabotto was only 150 years, for about 350 B.C. it fell to invading Celts. The conquerors settled in the partially destroyed city for about one hundred years, turning it into a sort of frontier post and burying their dead in abandoned houses and wells. But Marzabotto's well-preserved foundations give us invaluable insight into town planning and the forms of living of an Etruscan city founded *ex novo* in the Archaic period.

Spina

Known from ancient sources as an Adriatic harbor on the mouth of a southern branch of the Po, Spina was held to be both an Etruscan and a Greek city, founded by Pelasgians, or Thessalians, or by Diomedes. It was connected by lagoons and a canal both to the sea and to the more northerly harbor of Adria in the Veneto. Adria had been visited by Ionian Greeks since the first half of the sixth century. In the first century A.D. Pliny noted that the coastline had moved eastward, leaving Spina some distance from the sea (*NH* 3.120). Gradually submerged by the alluvial deposits of the river, the city's location was forgotten until drainage projects during the 1920s enabled archaeologists to identify its necropolises west of Comacchio. The site of the ancient city itself was revealed in the 1950s with the help of aerial photography.

Spina was founded about the same time as Marzabotto, but there is some evidence for earlier occupation in the form of fragments of Villanovan vessels and of two stelae of the type found at Bologna. For many decades only Spina's extensive and rich cemeteries, situated in the sand dunes of the ancient coastline in Valle Trebba and Valle Pega, have been explored; but more recent excavations at Motta della Girata have brought to light sparse remains of the ancient city and its harbor (about six hectares).

The city was built between 530 and 520 B.C. on a low triangular ridge at the confluence of an ancient arm of the Po and one of its tributaries. The swampy ground was strengthened with embankments of piling, reeds, and beaten clay, and the buildings were laid out according to an orthogonal plan with the main axis NNE to SSW. Served by waterways as well as streets, the settlement (like Venice later on) used boats and bridges for much of its traffic. At the intersection of two roads was found an oblong stone incised with a cross and the inscription *mi tular* = I (am) the boundary; it presumably marked the point from which the layout of the city had been planned.

The houses were built on wooden piles and frequently had to be reconstructed after inundations. The walls consisted of laths and pressed clay, with the upright posts, usually of oak, resting on wooden boards. The wooden roofs were covered by reeds (to avoid undue weight) or, in the Hellenistic period, by locally manufactured terra-cotta tiles. Workshop remains imply pottery and metalworking.

The necropolises, with both cremation and inhumation burials, occupied sandy dunes north and east of the city. The rich tombs were mainly trenches, sometimes lined with wooden boards and occasionally marked externally by river pebbles or by marble or limestone cippi. Some fine Greek marble urns with roof-shaped lids are exceptional. The nature of the shifting ground ruled out any durable funerary monuments. In contrast to the modest wooden houses of Spina,

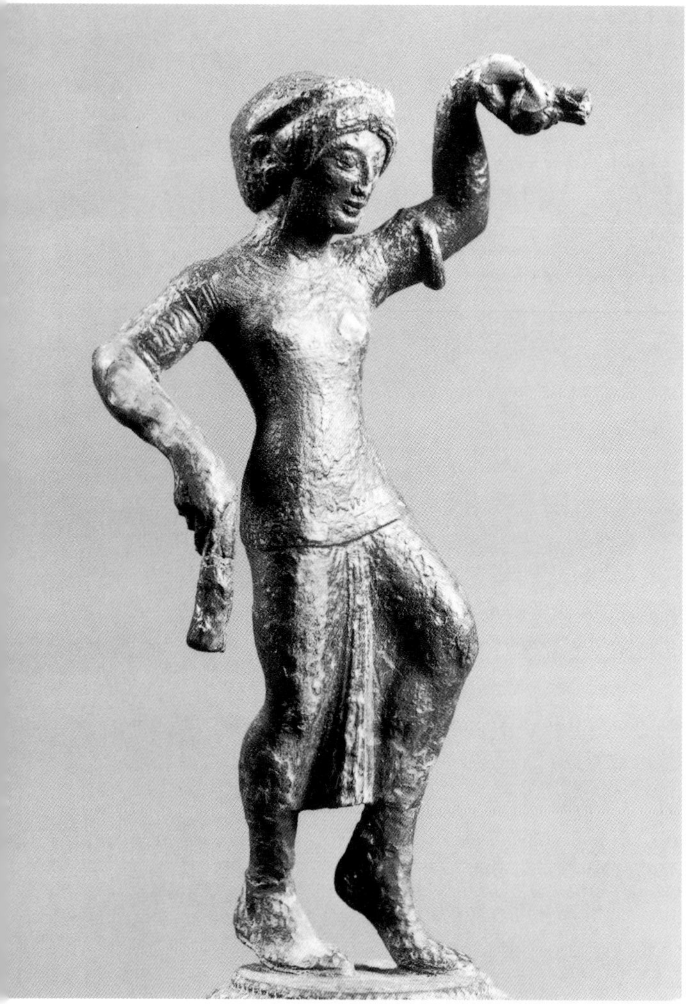

many tombs abounded in precious grave goods; conspicuous among them is the large number of splendid Attic painted pots and elaborate Etruscan bronze utensils and drinking services, ivory carvings, gold jewelry of both Etruscan and Greek manufacture, and amber necklaces. Some fibulae and bronze situlae are products of Palaeo-Venetic craftsmen and probably indicate intermarriage between Etruscan men and Venetic women. The contents of many tombs show the wealth of a population of various peoples (though predominantly Etruscan) between the end of the sixth and the fourth centuries. Banqueting vessels, candelabra, mirrors and other bronze objects (FIG. 165)—partly of Vulcian, partly of local manufacture—gaming pieces, and dice were found in both male and female tombs, and the sexes appear to have had equal economic importance. Weapons are rare in male tombs, but we can perhaps glimpse the ideal of the citizen-soldier in the numerous bronze statuettes of warriors arming that surmount candelabra; they are clearly inspired by prototypes on Attic painted pottery with the representation of hoplites. From the second quarter of the fourth century there are signs of a decline: deposition of metal banqueting vessels was replaced by pottery versions of the same shape. However, the lack of a comprehensive publication of the finds from the necropolises hampers a balanced evaluation of the evidence.

Fig. 165 Statuette of a dancing girl with castanets surmounting a utensil holder. From Tomb 228, Valle Trebba, Spina. First quarter of fifth century B.C. Cast bronze. H. of figure 11.1 cm. Ferrara, Museo Nazionale Archeologico 2898.

As attested by numerous inscriptions in the city as well as in the cemeteries, the Etruscan inhabitants seem to have come mainly from the northern cities (Perugia, Chiusi, Bologna) and, with a number of exceptions, did not belong to aristocratic families. Spina was a commercial foundation, whose riches, brought by trade, compensated for its insalubrious, marshy location.

The presence of a considerable number of Athenians is confirmed by inscriptions using the Ionic-Attic alphabet; some of these refer to the gods Hermes, Dionysos, and Apollo. Greek merchants obviously frequented Spina in large numbers, and the city was an important center for the exchange of imported luxury goods, including wine, and for agricultural and animal products from the fertile Po valley. This extensive river plain had been skillfully drained and, besides sustaining prolific herds and flocks, yielded a surplus of cereals, essential for the supply of Athens. Close contacts with Bologna/Felsina and Marzabotto via the Reno, with Mantua via the Po and Mincio, and with transalpine Europe via the Ticino placed Spina within a trade network that reached from Southern Etruria, the Greek islands, and Athens to Central Europe, across the Alps and via the Rhine and its tributaries. In those regions Celtic chieftains hoarded Etruscan bronze vessels and utensils, as well as Attic vases, while they consumed Greek wine and oil, transported first in amphorae by sea and river and finally by land in less fragile containers of wood or skin (large quantities of amphora fragments have been found at Spina and Mantua). Such was the wealth of the mercantile center of Spina that it was the only Etruscan city besides Cerveteri to erect a treasury in the sanctuary of Apollo at Delphi in Greece (Dion. Hal. 1.18.28; Plin. 3.120).

From the fourth century onward Spina's fortune slowly declined because of the increasingly difficult access to the sea, the coastline having been shifted eastward by the alluvial deposits of the Po. Added to this was the mounting pressure of Celtic tribes occupying the Po valley. It seems that between the fourth and third centuries Mantua, Spina, and Adria received many Etruscan refugees who had been driven from their own cities (Marzabotto, Bologna/Felsina) by the Gallic conquerors. From the ports Etruscan pirates appear to have made a living by preying on Greek merchant ships.

The opportunity of the Northern Etruscan cities to expand and settle their surplus population in these vast territories during the Archaic period probably helped to postpone the social tensions that in the great southern centers seem to have grown more acute.

Pisa

A separate northward expansion had taken place in Liguria, where the coastal regions under the cultural influence of Pisa, from Livorno to the upper Versilia, were occupied by many small Etruscan settlements.

Ongoing excavations at Pisa and San Piero a Grado have thrown new light on the growing importance of the Etruscan city and a harbor at the mouth of the Arno from the second half of the seventh century B.C. onward. Remains of smelting furnaces and iron slags (from Elban mines) have been discovered in both places, showing that they formed part of a vast Tyrrhenian maritime trade circuit radiating from Elba and Populonia. Pisa's favorable geographic position on the Arno and its natural wealth—wood suitable for shipbuilding, and marble quarries in the nearby mountains—placed it at the heart of a network of production and exchange. Locally made bucchero, roof tiles, pottery, and commercial amphorae were widely distributed along the coast of the Versilia, and, inland, in the valleys of the rivers Arno, Serchio, and Era. Remains of imported pottery from Southern Etruria, East Greek transport amphorae for wine and oil, as well as Ionian drinking cups point to the adoption by the Pisan aristocracy of Greek banqueting practices.

Excavation northeast of the Leaning Tower of Pisa has revealed vestiges of a circular mud-brick building from about 700 B.C. Above it was a structure from the end of the seventh century B.C. of rectangular plan with three internal subdivisions on foundations of stones of irregular size. The outer walls of this building were of trelliswork covered with a layer of waterproof clay and supported by wooden posts fixed in the ground. The roof was tiled with pan- and cover tiles and protected along the flanks by terra-cotta revetment plaques. A disc-shaped acroterion found in the neighborhood perhaps surmounted the gable. The plan recalls those of some houses at Acquarossa. It has been suggested that the older circular mud-brick building (comparable to that at Roselle) was perhaps the place of a family cult, while the rectangular one replacing it may have been a sanctuary devoted to institutionalized collective cults. Many fragments of fine imported Greek pottery from vessels for wine consumption along with local production and some ornaments, such as glass-paste beads and a carved amber pendant, seem to confirm the interpretation of the building as a sanctuary.

In the necropolises of Pisa cremation prevailed. From about 560 B.C. individual families seem to have occupied burial plots marked off by small globular marble cippi and separated from others by open spaces. The tombs, containing simple impasto ash urns and hardly any grave goods, were covered by small mounds of earth and clustered around one or two designated as particularly important by hemispherical or club-shaped marble tomb markers. The modesty or total absence of grave goods may be due to sumptuary regulations, such as those that seem to have existed at Rome and Veii. During the second half of the sixth century B.C., the ashes were frequently deposited in locally made or imported Attic and Laconian kraters or, more rarely, in finely carved kraters of local marble.

From the beginning of the sixth century B.C. tomb markers in the form of an inverted club came into use, apparently imitating in marble more perishable earlier types made of tree trunks, of which a few fragments have been identified in the necropolises. The club-shaped marble cippus became (with variations in detail) the most popular and widespread in the northwestern area of Etruria and remained in use until the Augustan era. During the late sixth and early fifth centuries a new type of marble cippus was introduced besides this: a pear or bulb shape placed on a square base with a ram's head at each corner or, more rarely, with rampant lions. These monuments show the influence of North Ionian, Milesian, and Samian models that also mark the funerary sculpture of Populonia and other towns in Northern Etruria. The marble for the cippi came from the Pisan mountains or the Apuan Alps. This points to a trade in unworked blocks, as well as to flourishing local Pisan schools of sculptors. Transport to the heart of the city was facilitated by a recently discovered harbor embankment of the fifth century B.C. at San Rossore.

The extent of Pisa's control over a large hinterland can be traced partly by the finds of typical funerary monuments, amphorae, domestic pottery, and bucchero, but it is more difficult to gain insight into the city's maritime traffic in the upper Tyrrhenian and the Gulf of Lion. However, in the second half of the sixth century an Etruscan settlement was founded on the castle hill of Genoa in an area inhabited by a Celto-Ligurian population. Though other Etruscan maritime cities, such as Cerveteri, may have been involved in this process of northern expansion connected with the battle in the Sardinian Sea, the material remains and funerary practice attested at Genoa seem to indicate a strong Pisan component.

In the eastern Languedoc an Etruscan trade settlement has recently been identified at Lattes near Montpellier on a hillside occupied until the middle of the sixth century by an indigenous population. Bucchero and impasto pottery as well as commercial amphorae found there are comparable to material from Genoa and Pisa. Several Etruscan inscriptions show characteristics that find parallels at Genoa indicating that some social integration of the local inhabitants with the newcomers seems to have taken place. Like Genoa, Lattes appears to have been exclusively a trade settlement, with no agricultural territory.

CAMPANIA AND THE AGER PICENTINUS

We know much less about the southward expansion into Campania and beyond, which took place at the same time as the northward expansion, and for the same reason—in search of land and new commercial bases. Numerous Etruscan inscriptions and other archaeological material have come to light at Capua (Lat. *Volturnum*), Nola, Suessula, Stabiae, Pompeii, Herculaneum, Vico Equense, Vietri, Fratte di Salerno, Pontecagnano, and Eboli. But in the northern part of the Sorrentine peninsula and the Sarno valley, which have also yielded quantities of Italic inscriptions, the proportion of Etruscan inscriptions is rather lower than in the Salernitan area. The whole Ager Picentinus, between the Sorrentine peninsula and the Sele River, with its center at Pontecagnano, was thoroughly etruscanized beginning in the Villanovan period; though here, too, a difference exists between Fratte and Pontecagnano, the former having produced a considerable number of inscriptions in the Greek alphabet of Paestum (Gr. *Poseidonia*) in addition to Etruscan ones. At Fratte the community seems to have been more mixed and devoted to maritime trade, favored by its position. The script used here connects the city with Tarquinia and Vulci, and its history was probably linked with these Etruscan coastal cities. From this area of the Gulf of Salerno Etruscan "pirates" probably attacked the Lipari Islands in earlier centuries; and here perhaps were the bases from which Etruscan ships set out toward the Straits of Messina in an ultimately failed bid to retain supremacy at sea in the lower Tyrrhenian during the first quarter of the fifth century. By the end of the century Fratte had come under the sway of the Samnites (an Italic people speaking Oscan).

Pontecagnano had shown a flourishing variant of the Villanovan civilization as early as the ninth century, and there are important aristocratic tombs of the Orientalizing period. The town's economic base was agricultural and its population more homogeneous. The Etruscan inscriptions, like those in Campania, show

Fig. 166 Inscribed tile. From a sanctuary at Santa Maria Capua Vetere. First half of fifth century B.C. Terra-cotta. H. 62 cm. Berlin, Staatliche Museen—Preußischer Kulturbesitz—Antikensammlung 30892.

affinity with the alphabets of Cerveteri and Veii. Pontecagnano managed longer than any other city of the region to preserve its language and identity, having survived a crisis at the end of the fifth century.

The Iron Age cemeteries of Capua go back to the second half of the ninth century, and occupation continues to the Roman period. The Etruscan population of the city may have been reinforced in several waves, but not until the sixth century does the city appear largely etruscanized. Capua was founded on a regular plan in the late seventh century and flourished in the following period. In 524, when Etruscans (perhaps driven from the Po valley by invading Gauls), allied to an Umbrian and Daunian army, attacked the Greeks of Cumae (Dion. Hal. 7.3.1–7.11.12), this city defended itself successfully in a battle in which a Cumaean aristocrat, Aristodemus, the son of Aristokrates, distinguished himself. By this action he gained the favor of the Cumaean demos opposed to the oligarchy. After the expulsion of the Tarquins from Rome in 509 and the establishment of a republic there, King Porsenna of Chiusi moved against Rome and probably occupied it for a while. In 504, Aristodemus, who may have given asylum to the exiled Tarquins at Cumae, intervened, leading a force of Cumaeans north to help the Latins near Aricia against the Etruscan forces of Porsenna, under the command of the king's son, Arruns. Arruns was killed and the Etruscan army beaten off by the allied Latins and Cumaeans. This military success emboldened Aristodemus to make himself tyrant of Cumae with the support of the lower social strata of the city. Some of the local Cumaean Greek aristocracy saved themselves from Aristodemus's tyranny by taking refuge in Etruscan Capua, where they bided their time until about 485–484, when Aristodemus and his family were killed by them with the help of Capuan aristocrats; the returned Greek exiles then reestablished themselves at Cumae.

Meanwhile, the aggressive northward thrust of the navy of Syracuse, as well as the ever-increasing westward pressure of Italic mountain tribes on the fertile Campanian regions under Etruscan control, led to the eventual decline and disappearance of the Etruscan element there, which had already suffered from the cutting of the land route connecting it with Etruria by the invading Volsci, who had settled in the Liris valley.

Suessula, Cumae, Nola, and Capua had for some time been infiltrated by Samnites . These newcomers, many of them probably mercenaries, finally gained possession of Capua in the mid-420s, slaughtering the aristocrats and taking over their wives and belongings. Nola fell in 423 and Cumae in 421, some of the inhabitants taking refuge in Greek Neapolis. Whereas in Campania Etruscan inscriptions ceased in the second half of the fifth century, at Pontecagnano Etruscan remnants continued to speak their language until the end of the fourth century.

The longest Etruscan inscription on durable material to have come down to us was incised before firing on a large (ca. 62 x 49 cm) terra-cotta tile found on the southwestern outskirts of Santa Maria Capua Vetere, in what was an extraurban Archaic necropolis/sanctuary of the ancient city (FIG. 166). Written alternately from right to left and (upside down) from left to right, the text seems to be a ritual calendar with prescriptions for sacrifices and offerings in the cults of several divinities. The inscription dates from about 470 and is distinguished by punctuation between the syllables. Written by a scribe whose signature at the end is only partially preserved (. . .]*ulis zichunce* = . . .]ulis has written), the badly worn text allows the identification of about three hundred words. It is likely that schools of priestly scribes attached to sanctuaries introduced this "learned" new system of syllabic division with one to three dots (placed above each other); previously all the words of an inscription had been run together in a continuous chain.

The artistic and industrial production in Campania during the period of Etruscan hegemony in the sixth and fifth centuries excelled in fine bronzework, such as hammered and engraved bronze vessels with cast figures, often of athletes

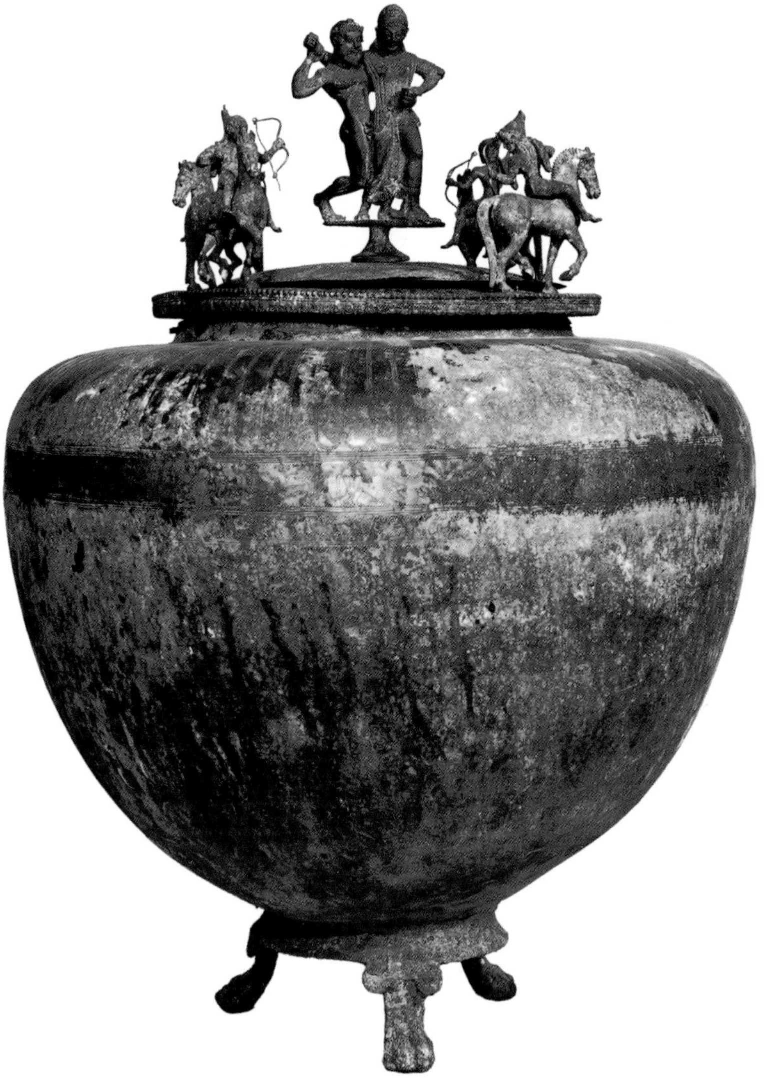

Fig. 167a Campanian ash urn with statuettes on lid and rim. From Capua. First quarter of fifth century B.C. Incised bronze sheet with cast-bronze adjuncts. H. 67 cm. London, The British Museum GR 55.8-16.1.

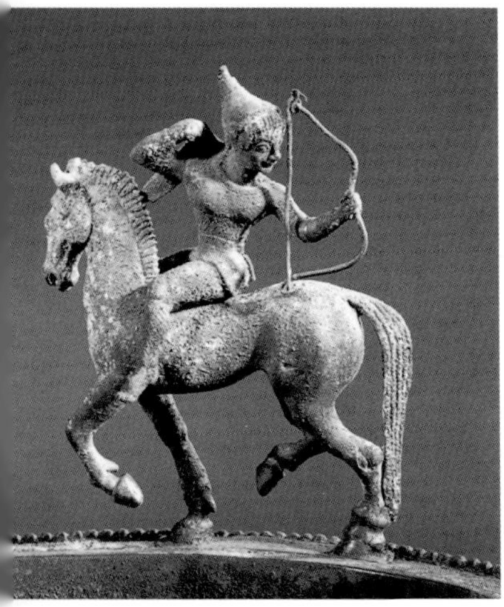

Fig. 167b Detail of Amazon from rim of ash urn, figure 167a.

and horsemen, decorating rim and lid; they were used as cinerary urns by aristocratic Capuan families (FIGS. 167a, b). Pottery (both painted and bucchero) was produced, as well as votive and architectural terra-cottas, the latter under strong influence from neighboring Greek Cumae. From the end of the the sixth century Attic models were reflected in the decoration of Campanian vase-painting, though the motifs are rarely mythological but repeat those found on contemporary Vulcian and Orvietan black-figured vases, such as animals, banquets, and games. From the late fifth century Greek Naples became the center of distribution of Attic red-figured vases into the non-Greek hinterland.

Here in Campania, as well as in the Etruscan heartland, the absorption of Greek civilization by the Etruscans had furthered its diffusion and assimilation among the Italic populations of the interior of Italy.

In Sicily, the center of the Mediterranean basin, many different peoples and interests were competing with each other. Greek colonists from Chalkis on Euboea controlled the Straits of Messina; other Greek colonies were spread along the island's north, east, and south coasts, while the Carthaginians had taken over the old Phoenician settlement on the small island of Motya near Trapani at the western tip of Sicily. From there and from Carthage itself on the African coast opposite, they were able to control the shipping routes passing south of Sicily. Other Carthaginian emporia were established on the northern Sicilian coast at Palermo and Solunto. On Sardinia they had occupied natural ports such as Bitia and Nora near Cagliari and Tharros near Oristano. Here, as in Sicily, the Carthaginians took over earlier Phoenician settlements.

The Etruscans' coastal points of support in the Gulf of Salerno were used for economic as well as military purposes. The main naval activities carried out from here were probably directed against the Lipari Islands, occupied by Greek settlers from Rhodes and Knidos who were able to interfere with Etruscan shipping in the southern Tyrrhenian Sea. Ancient sources as well as votive gifts dedicated by both sides in the sanctuary of Apollo in Delphi indicate that the fortunes of war varied, but the Etruscans' naval enterprises in the southern Tyrrhenian Sea ultimately ended in defeat.

In the western and northern Tyrrhenian and in the Gulf of Lion the situation had also changed considerably. As early as the second half of the seventh century the Samian seafarer Kolaios had reached Tartessos at the mouth of the Guadalquivir in southern Spain. About 600, the Phokaians—Ionian Greeks from western Asia Minor—had founded the colony of Massalia among the local Ligurian tribes. Long-distance sailors of great experience, the Phokaians were reported by Herodotos to have been the first Greeks to have reached Etruria, the Adriatic and, beyond the Pillars of Hercules (the Straits of Gibraltar), Tartessos, where they formed friendly relations with King Arganthonios, the ruler of this silver-rich region.

Massalia grew slowly, reaching considerable wealth by the end of the sixth century, when she was able to erect a treasury at Delphi. From Massalia luxury goods reached the interior of Gaul through native coastal and river trade routes up the Rhone and its tributaries. The best-known example is the treasure excavated in the Hallstadt-period princely tomb at Vix. Previously these northern Mediterranean shores had been the scene of sporadic activity of Etruscan merchants (p. 62).

The Battle in the Sardinian Sea

When, under siege from the Persian conquerors of Asia Minor, a part of the population of the Greek city of Phokaia decided about 545 to emigrate to the west, they sailed to Corsica. Here, on the east coast, they settled at the site of Aleria (ancient Alalia). The city had been founded twenty years earlier by other Phokaians, following a Delphic oracle (Hdt. 1.165.1). From Aleria the Phokaians began to raid the trade routes along the Tyrrhenian and Sardinian coasts used by both Etruscan and Carthaginian shipping. We know from Aristotle (*Pol.* 3.9.1280a.36) that the latter nations had reached accord on commercial matters, such as what goods could be imported, rights of residence, and nonaggression pacts. The piratical activities of the Phokaians seriously threatened the established safety of Etruscan sea traffic and Carthaginian plans of expansion in Sardinia and led to a military alliance between the two. It seems likely that it was individual Etruscan cities, rather than the whole nation, that formed alliances with Carthage.

About 540 a naval battle took place in the Sardinian Sea involving sixty Phokaian ships and an equal number of Etruscan and Carthaginian vessels; both sides suffered heavy losses. Herodotos tells us (1.167) that forty Greek ships were sunk and the rest, in which the survivors returned to Aleria, were badly damaged. The Phokaians who were taken ashore as prisoners by the men of Cerveteri were stoned to death, an outrage for which the offending Etruscan city suffered divine retribution in the form of a plague.

As a result of this sea battle the Phokaians abandoned Corsica, where Aleria now became an important Etruscan colonial settlement, extracting tribute from the indigenous population of the island in the form of slaves and natural products. Carthage meanwhile conquered Sardinia between 545 and 510.

An ivory plaque carved with a boar and inscribed on the back in Etruscan is an interesting document testifying to the friendly commercial relations that had existed between Etruria and Carthage. It was found in the necropolis of Ste. Monique at Carthage in Tunisia. The inscription describes the owner as Punic (*mi puinel*) and from Carthage (*karthazie*). Three small holes indicate that the plaque could be fitted together with a corresponding double and thus probably served as an identification for the bearer (Lat. *tessera hospitalis*), when he presented himself to a host on his travels. Similar inscribed plaques, found at Poggio Civitate and at Sant'Omobono in Rome, show the wide distribution of this custom.

The fugitive Phokaians first sailed to Reggio at the southern tip of the Italian peninsula and finally settled a new colony south of Paestum at Velia. Individual Phokaians, however, seem to have established themselves successfully in Etruria. Among these were two master vase-painters, who between 540 and 520 in a workshop in Cerveteri produced finely decorated water jars, the Caeretan hydriai. Their subjects are taken from Greek mythology, Homeric epic and hymns, and aristocratic life (FIG. 168).

According to Herodotos, the Caeretans were anxious to expiate their crime of killing the Phokaian prisoners and the resulting paralysis in men and beasts who passed the cursed spot. They sent a deputation to Delphi, where they had a treasury. The oracle advised them to honor the dead Greeks with a magnificent funerary ceremony and to institute recurring athletic and equestrian contests,

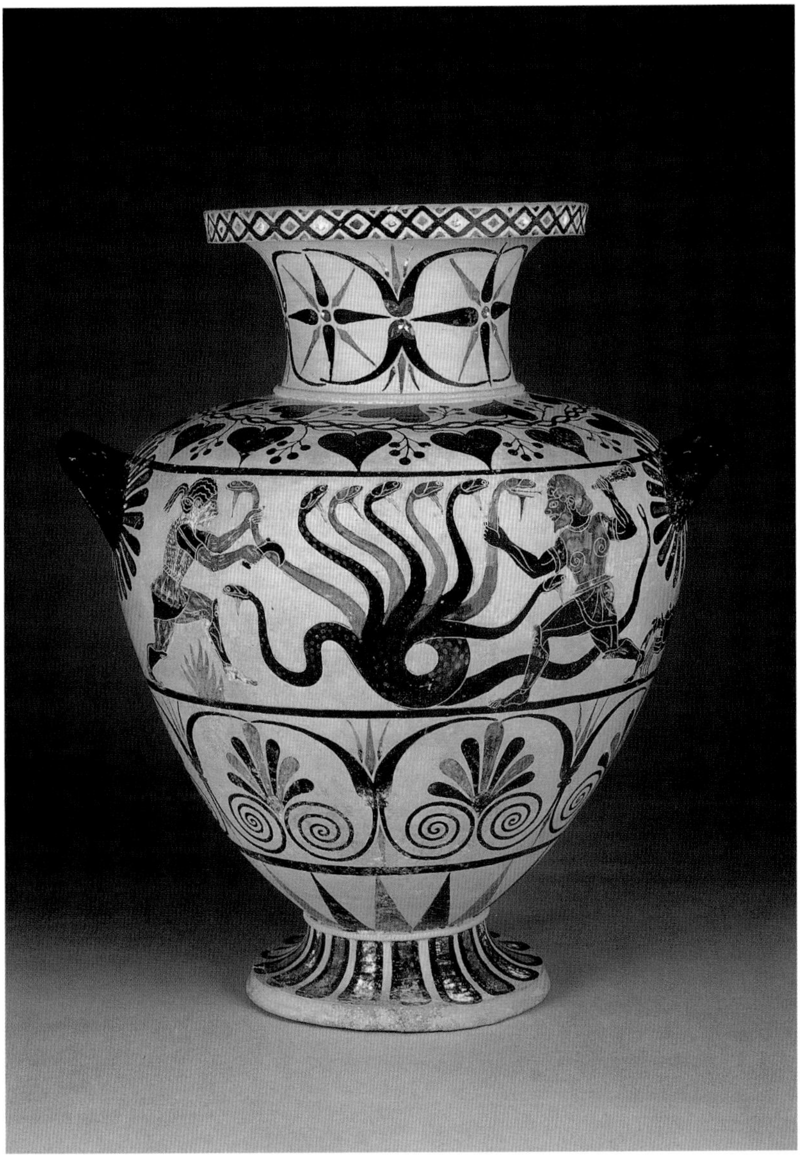

Fig. 168 Caeretan hydria with Herakles and the Hydra. Last quarter of sixth century B.C. Painted pottery. H. 44.6 cm. Malibu, J. Paul Getty Museum 83.AE.346.

which, so Herodotos tells us, continued to his day. A persuasive theory has identified a huge tumulus at Montetosto on the road from Pyrgi to Cerveteri (as well as a neighboring building) with the burial place of the slaughtered Greeks.

Developments in South Italy contributed to the gradual collapse of the existing network of political and trade connections. The Etruscans had long entertained friendly relations with the flourishing Greek city of Sybaris in Magna Graecia; but Sybaris was defeated and destroyed by her neighbor Crotone in 510 and was thus lost to Etruria as a trading partner. This and the events at Rome, Capua, and Cumae described above disrupted communications between Etruria and Campania.

VEII

History

Located 17 km northwest of Rome, Veii was the Etruscan city geographically closest to Rome and her rival from early on. The vast tufa plateau of the ancient city was probably never entirely occupied by habitation. Naturally defended by the valleys of the Fosso Piordo and the Fosso della Valchetta, Veii in the fifth century nevertheless erected a fortification consisting of an earth wall strengthened with tufa masonry and provided with numerous gates; some of these gave access to roads leading from the city to Rome, Cerveteri, Nepi-Tarquinia-Vulci, and Capena. In possession of the right bank of the Tiber and of the town of Fidenae on its left bank, Veii was able to exploit the salt pans at the mouth of the river and to control the traffic on this important waterway leading to central and Northern Etruria. Rome's conflicts with Veii are said to have begun as early as the time of Romulus and to have led to altogether fourteen wars (Dion. Hal. 2.55, 3.41). The expanding Rome certainly felt herself threatened by her powerful Etruscan neighbor, and Veii was the first city of Etruria to be defeated by Rome after prolonged warfare. For hardly any other Etruscan city do we have such a wealth of literary information, mainly from Livy. He tells us that Veii's tutelary deity was the goddess Juno Regina; archaeological finds have given us the names of other goddesses who had sanctuaries at Veii. As at Pyrgi, the most important divinities in Veii's pantheon were female.

Despite their early rivalry, close relations seem to have existed between Rome and Veii during the sixth century, when Rome was ruled by the Etruscan dynasty of the Tarquins. Ancient authors record that a famous Etruscan sculptor named Vulca was called from Veii to Rome to model the cult statue of Jupiter Capitolinus for his new temple (Plin. 35.157). The Tarquins also commissioned from Vulca an acroterial terra-cotta group of a quadriga for the roof of the Capitoline temple, and the building itself was constructed with the help of Etruscans (Livy 1.56.1).

Increased hostilities during the fifth century over the possession of Fidenae and the murder of four Roman ambassadors at the behest of the king of Veii, Lars Tolumnius, led to another war in the 430s, in which Aulus Cornelius Cossus killed the Etruscan king in single combat. Fidenae was captured by the Romans about 435. Veii had to ask for help against Rome from the other Etruscan cities at the reunion in the 420s in the federal sanctuary of the Fanum Voltumnae near Orvieto. However, military assistance was denied because Veii still was ruled by monarchs, while kings and tyrants seem to have been abolished in all the other cities of Etruria. Only Fidenae, Falerii, and Capena, all situated relatively close to Rome, offered to help Veii. The famous ten-years' siege of Veii began in 406; in later Roman literature the siege assumed almost mythical proportions, being compared with the siege of Troy and becoming surrounded with omens and miraculous events. Veii fell in 396, thanks to an underground passage tunneled by the

Romans, who emerged from it in the Temple of Juno Regina, taking the defenders by surprise. The general, M. Furius Camillus, sacked the city and transferred the statue of the goddess to Rome, where she continued to be worshiped in a new temple. He also sent a gold mixing bowl as a votive offer of thanks to the sanctuary of Apollo at Delphi. Veii's sanctuaries survived, as is proved by the mass of later terra-cotta votive gifts found in them, while her rich territories were distributed among Roman settlers.

The Sanctuaries

We have already discussed the early temple on the isolated outcrop south of the city area of Veii, the acropolis of Piazza d'Armi (see p. 127). This was divided by a ravine from the plateau of the city. The Temple of Juno Regina was probably situated opposite the acropolis, on the southernmost point of Veii itself, as suggested by Archaic sustaining walls and fragments of votive terra-cottas.

From the sixth century onward in the northern part of the walled city plateau at Campetti there seems to have been a popular sanctuary of the goddess Vei/Ceres. It has yielded quantities of votive terra-cotta figures of anatomical parts, heads, seated women with children, swaddled babies (see FIG. 284), and warriors. An interesting group representing the Trojan hero Aeneas carrying his aged father, Anchises, during his flight from the Sack of Troy has turned up in several examples in the city's sanctuaries, a tangible expression of the Roman settlers' perception of their remote Trojan ancestry.

THE TEMPLE AT PORTONACCIO The best-explored and best-preserved of the temples of Veii is that at Portonaccio, on the northwestern side of the tufa plateau outside the city walls. According to the votive inscriptions found here, the sanctuary was dedicated to the Etruscan goddess Men(e)rva (Gr. Athena; Lat. Minerva), who at this site may have had oracular and healing powers; she seems to have been associated with other female divinities, such as Turan (Gr. Aphrodite) and Aritimi (Gr. Artemis) and, on the evidence of terra-cotta sculptures, with Apollo and Herakles. Numerous Archaic inscriptions on vases found here indicate the nature of the cult and show that the dedicants came from all over central Italy. Among the names known to us are those of Avile Vipiiennas (*TLE* 35), probably the Vulcian friend of Mastarna/Servius Tullius; and those of Velthur and Karcuna Tulumnes, members of a famous Veientine royal family (*TLE* 36.38). The name Acvilna stems from Ischia di Castro, while Teithurna comes from Cerveteri.

On the Fosso Piordo side the sanctuary has been badly eroded by quarrying. The trapezoidal site was surrounded by an enclosure wall and flanked on the north by the road connecting it with Rome. As the inscriptions attest, the cult at Portonaccio went back to the early sixth century, but the surviving remains of buildings point to a first phase for the temple in the middle of the sixth century and a rebuilding at the end of the century (FIG. 169). This temple (A) was of Tuscan type;

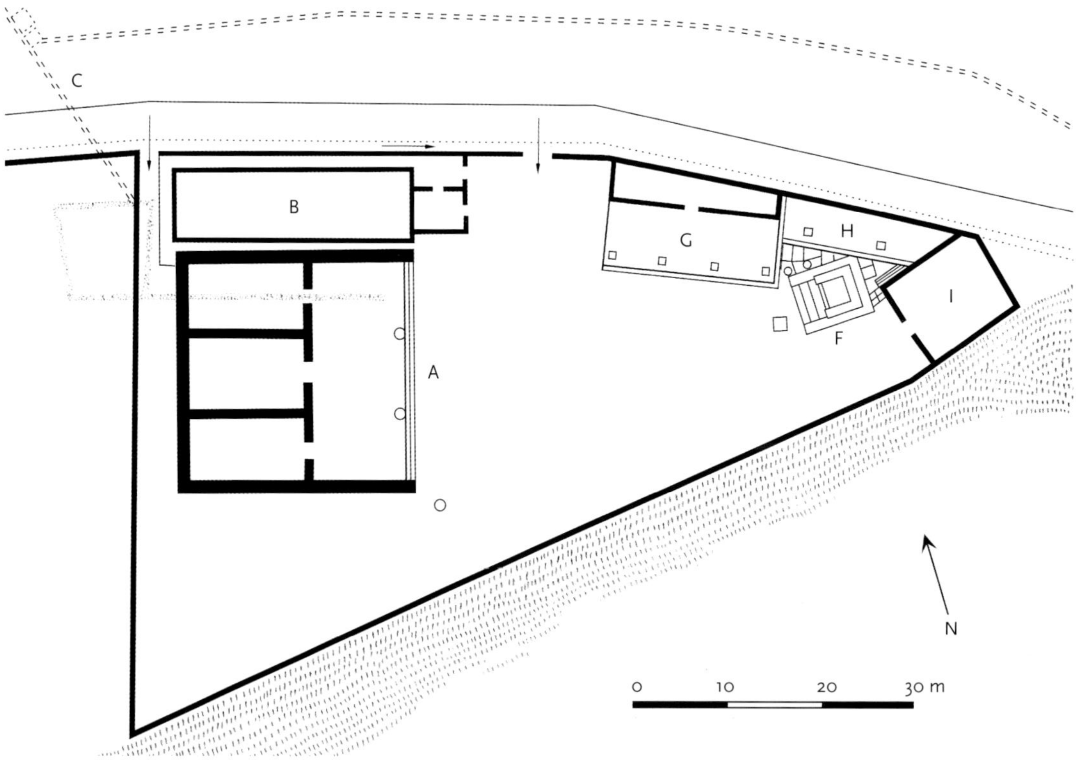

Fig. 169 Plan of foundations of the sanctuary of Portonaccio at Veii.

OPPOSITE
Fig. 170 Acroterial statue of Apollo. From the roof of the temple of Portonaccio, Veii. Late sixth century B.C. Painted terra-cotta. H. 1.81 m. Rome, Museo Etrusco di Villa Giulia 40702.

Fig. 171 Acroterial statue of Herakles and the Hind of Keryneia. From the roof of the temple of Portonaccio, Veii. Late sixth century B.C. Painted terra-cotta. H. 1.60 m. Rome, Museo Etrusco di Villa Giulia 40704.

its tufa-block foundation is almost square (18.50 m on each side). It once supported a low podium with steps at the front leading up to a deep *pronaos* with two columns crowned by Tuscan tufa capitals between anta walls. At the back, the temple probably had a triple *cella*, whose walls must also have been of tufa blocks. In the first half of the fifth century the internal walls were decorated with terra-cotta panels painted with mythological subjects and affixed with nails. Surviving fragments show Amazons brandishing lances, a female head, etc., clearly related in style to the contemporary tomb-paintings of Tarquinia and Chiusi.

Oriented toward the east, the temple faced a paved, triangular piazza. At its east end were a rectangular building (I), a winged altar (F), and two adjoining porticos (G, H). The foundations of the rectangular building yielded most of the votive inscriptions to Menerva and offerings that date its construction to the third quarter of the sixth century. In the angle between the altar and the porticos was a *bothros*, a sacred pit destined for libations to an underworld divinity, which were poured down the hollow center of an articulated column of four stone blocks joined by lead.

Parallel with the northern flank of the Portonaccio temple is a large rectangular pool (B), which probably served for purification or in a healing cult. Built of tufa blocks and lined with waterproof clay, it was fed by an underground channel from a nearby supply (C). Salutary waters were sometimes associated with Min-

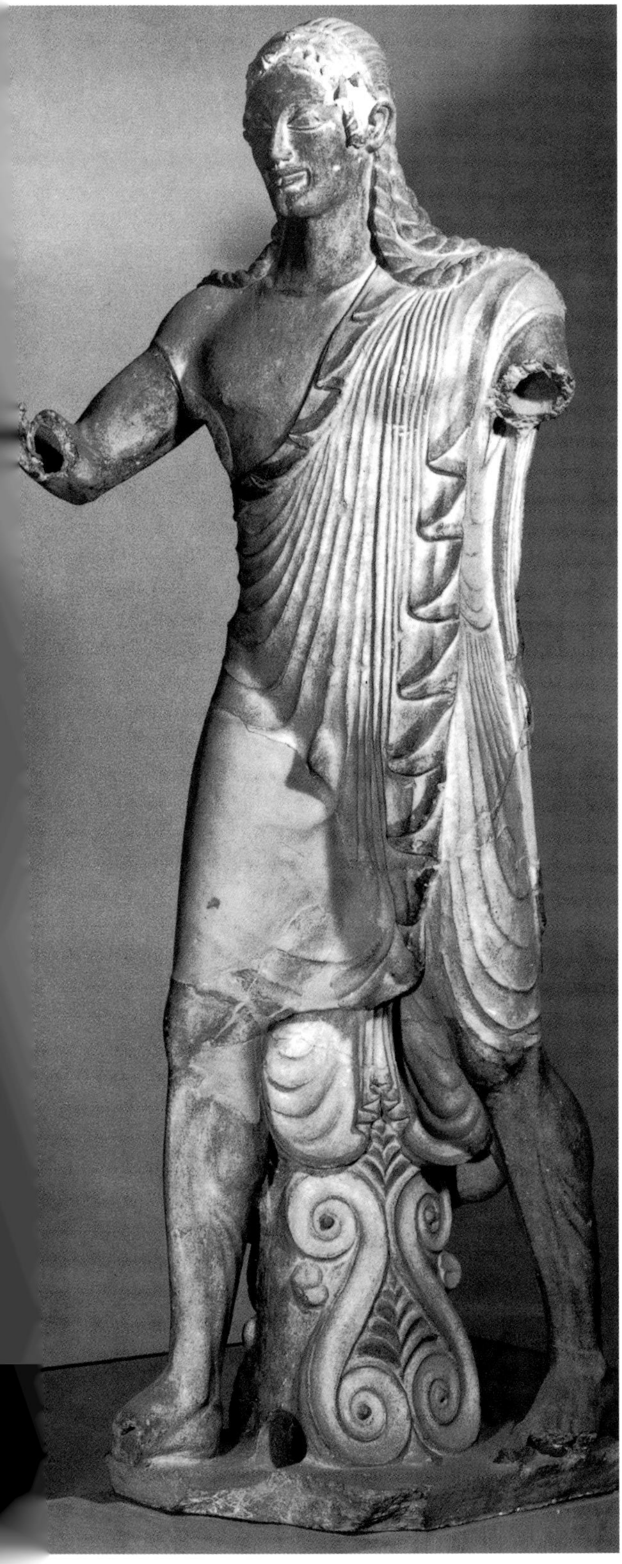

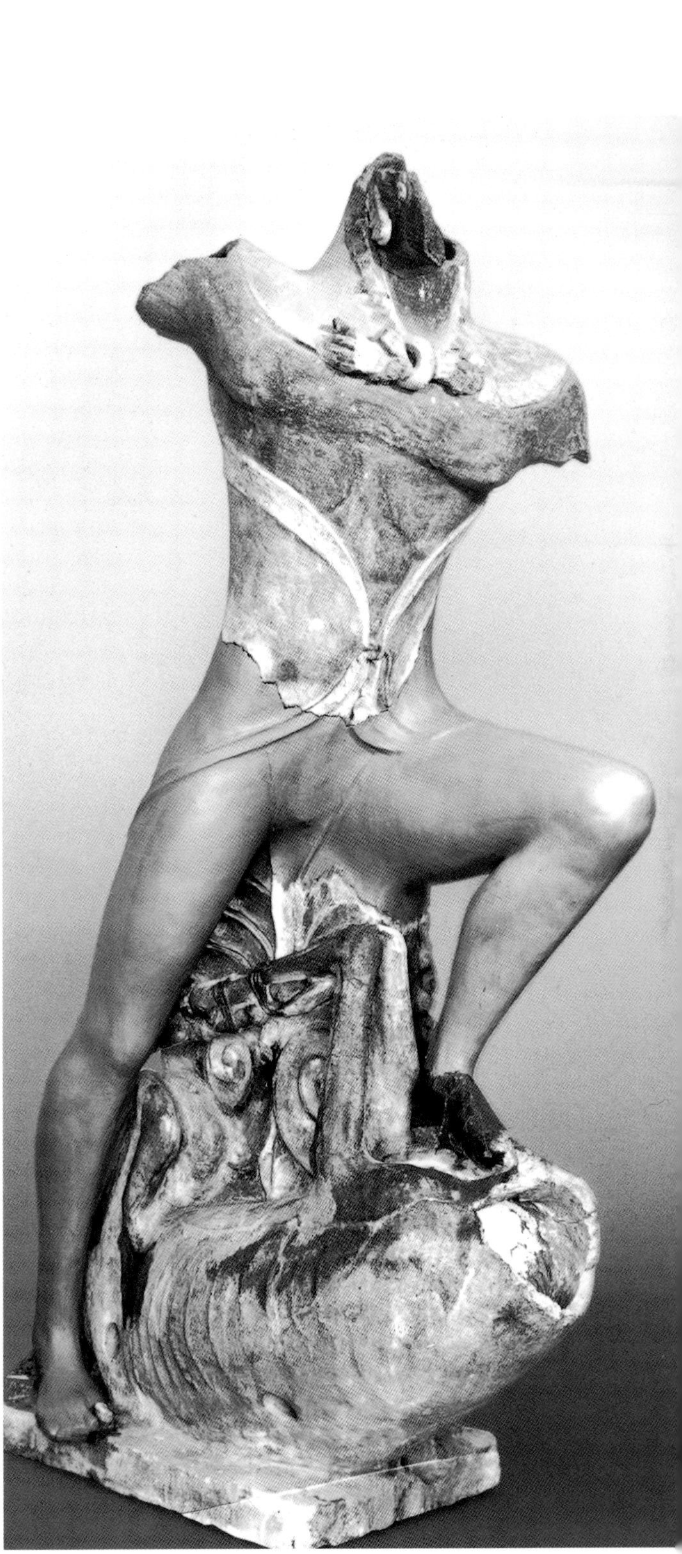

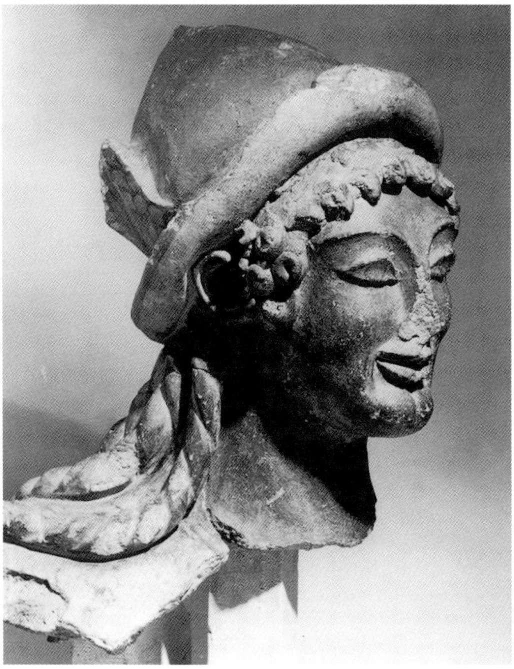

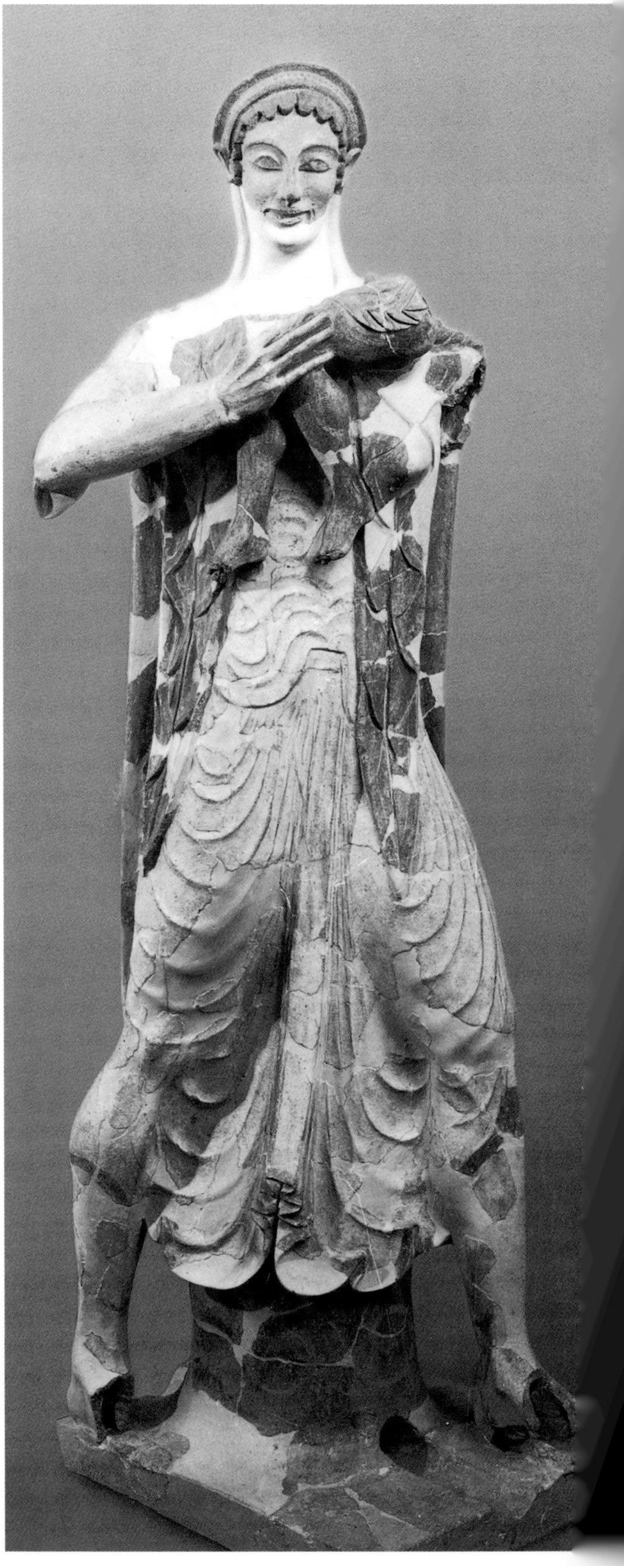

Fig. 172 Head of Hermes from an acroterial statue. From the roof of the temple of Portonaccio, Veii. Late sixth century B.C. Painted terra-cotta. H. 37 cm. Rome, Museo Etrusco di Villa Giulia 40778.

Fig. 173 Acroterial statue of a female figure (Leto?) carrying a child. From the roof of the temple of Portonaccio, Veii. Late sixth century B.C. Painted terra-cotta. H. 1.66 m. Rome, Museo Etrusco di Villa Giulia.

erva, but also with Apollo, who was held to send disease and death with his far-reaching arrows and yet be a purifier and healer. In Etruria Herakles was also often connected with springs.

What makes the Portonaccio temple outstandingly important from an artistic point of view is the wealth of its terra-cotta decoration. The wooden roof had terra-cotta revetments with a variety of exuberant floral ornament, some of it in openwork, while the antefixes consisted of heads of sileni, Acheloös, nymphs, and masks of Gorgons, all backed by a fluted shell shape. On high pedestals along the ridge of the roof was a row of over-life-size statues, all in lively movement and brightly painted. The statues represented the Greek myth of Apollo's fight with Herakles over the golden-horned Hind of Keryneia, sacred to the god's sister Artemis. Apollo, a powerful figure in a light chiton and elegantly pleated semicircular Etruscan mantle, strides forward with raised arms; he probably aimed his bow and arrow at his opponent (FIG. 170). His long hair falls in thick, ropelike strands over his shoulders and back. His face, with its almond-shaped eyes, finely arched brows, and slightly smiling mouth, reflects Ionian Greek models of the late sixth century; but the curved ridges defining the muscles and tendons of his calves and the long parallel loops and zigzags of the drapery folds have an abstract, ornamental quality that has nothing in common with the intense striving for the natural forms that characterized Attic sculpture of this period. The modeler of the statues was a highly accomplished artist with a strong sense for expressive outline and ornamental surface treatment.

Large parts of the statue of Herakles are missing (FIG. 171). The hero's neck and torso, covered with the lion's skin, are preserved, as well as the body of the trussed-up hind, which he straddles, placing his left foot on the animal's throat; he probably raised his club to threaten Apollo. Of Hermes, a bystander in this scene, only the gently smiling head has survived (FIG. 172). The messenger god's forehead and temples are framed by snail-shell curls, and he wears the winged hat that characterizes his swiftness.

The only preserved female figure is dressed in chiton and mantle, richly detailed with ornamental folds, and she wears a diadem on her wavy hair (FIG. 173). She is moving forward, carrying a small child on her left shoulder. She probably represents the goddess Leto, mother of the twins Apollo and Artemis, holding her infant son. This divine child may have been directing his arrows at the dragon Python; a fragment of a snakelike body was discovered. In Greek myth, this dragon had occupied the sacred site at Delphi before Apollo killed it and took over the fissure in the earth and the Castalian spring to make the oracle his own. The Delphic story was probably chosen for the decoration of the roof of the Portonaccio temple because the sanctuary was itself an oracular one.

Important fragments of an independent terra-cotta group of an armed Athena in helmet and cuirass standing next to Herakles were also found in the sanctuary. This group, which probably was a votive gift by one of the aristocrats who fre-

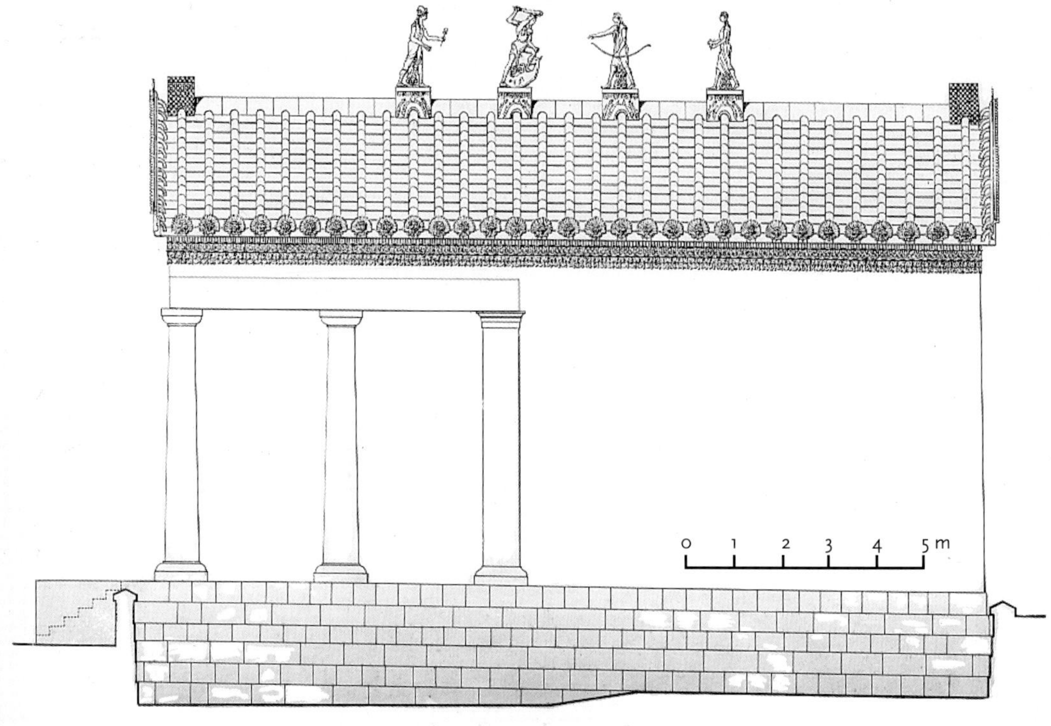

Fig. 174 Reconstruction of Archaic Etruscan temple based on remains of Portonaccio temple, Veii. Rome, Museo Etrusco di Villa Giulia.

quented the temple, must have stood in the open, most likely near the altar. The style, particularly of the statue of Herakles, with its sensitively modeled anatomical details, is quite different from the statues from the roof of the temple. Close parallels with Attic sculpture make it likely that this group was modeled about 500 or a little after by an Etruscan artist who was deeply influenced by such prototypes. Further terra-cotta fragments of votive statues from Portonaccio include that of a standing man, related in style to Samian sculptures.

The high artistic and technical quality of the terra-cotta sculptures at Portonaccio is such that the fame of the modelers from Veii, which ancient writers mention, is completely justified by the archaeological finds. The dramatic effect of the large divine figures placed along the ridge of the temple's roof and outlined against the sky must have been impressive (FIG. 174). Their size and positioning represent the perfection of a concept we first observed in the terra-cotta statues from the roofs of the "residence" at Poggio Civitate near Murlo (see FIG. 101).

Irrigation and drainage were specialities of Etruscan "hydraulic engineers." Like many other Etruscan sites, Veii on its steep-sided tufa plateau was surrounded by two rivers, so the city took great pains to keep its agricultural land from turning swampy. A network of underground *cuniculi* deflected surplus water and directed it where it was needed; one of these, between Fosso Formello and Fosso Piordo, is 600 m long. The Ponte Sodo conducts the river Valchetta (Cremera through an impressive natural rock tunnel that was skillfully enlarged and pro vided with holes in the roof to allow water to be drawn from above. Such hydraulic works were continued by the Roman settlers at Veii, as recently discovered *cuniculi* draining the area of the Portonaccio temple prove.

THE SANCTUARY OF JUNO CURITIS AT CELLE NEAR CIVITA CASTELLANA

North of Veii, about 55 km from Rome, lay the ancient capital of the Faliscans, named Falerii Veteres by the Romans, the modern Civita Castellana. Though the language spoken by the Faliscans was a dialect of Latin, the area, settled as early as the Bronze Age, was strongly influenced by the neighboring Etruscan civilization. Falerii Veteres may at one time have depended on Veii; it certainly supported Fidenae and Veii in their struggle with Rome during the later fifth and early fourth centuries (Livy 4.17–18, 21; 5.8–24), and Roman authors characterize the city as Etruscan (Plin. 3.51; Servius 7.607).

Situated on a tufa plateau flanked by two torrents flowing into the river Treia, Falerii Veteres had several suburban sanctuaries that lay outside the city. The most famous was that below the hill of Celle, dedicated to the goddess known as Juno Curitis (or Quiritis) to the Romans, for whom she was the goddess of the lance, a city goddess (Ov. *Am.* 3.13.35; *Fast.* 6.49).

The site, flanked by the Rio Maggiore and first excavated in 1886, has suffered much from erosion. But its earliest nucleus, which dates from the first half of the sixth century, could clearly be identified with the cult of a goddess who seems to have been connected with water. On a preserved platform of tufa blocks (4.80 x 9.60 m) once stood a small rectangular building containing the Archaic image of the divinity in local tufa; her head with remains of a wreath of bronze leaves has survived. Also discovered here were two statues of seated winged lions. At the back of this original sanctuary was a water basin fed by a stone runnel into which two *cuniculi* debouched.

In the second half of the fourth century a monumental temple was erected on a large terrace, at a right angle to the older building but respecting it. This huge new building (which recalls the contemporary Ara della Regina at Tarquinia) was decorated internally with a frieze of painted terra-cotta panels, of which fragments have survived. They show three-quarter life-size human figures in outline and without shading, set on a dark background, as well as floral elements. The precise form of the temple's superstructure is not certain, but it could have had a *pronaos* with two rows of four columns which would have allowed access to both its *cella* and the Archaic sanctuary.

It is perhaps not without significance that the new temple occupied an area that was used as a necropolis in the Late Bronze Age. As in other Etruscan cities (pp. 146f., 284), the extramural sanctuary of a goddess originally connected with water was located near an old necropolis.

CERVETERI

Archaic Architecture

Comparatively little is known as yet about the ancient city of Cerveteri, despite the fact that only about ten percent of the surface of Etruscan C(a)isra is overlaid by modern Cerveteri. The site is on a steep-sided tufa plateau of 150 hectares extending between the valleys of the Fosso della Mola and the Fosso Manganella. But recent surveys and explorative excavations in the area of the ancient city have provided fresh insight into the events that shaped Cerveteri at the end of the Archaic period and the new types of public buildings then being constructed.

The outcome of the battle in the Sardinian Sea about 540 B.C. illuminates Cerveteri's power at that period, as does her erection of the sanctuary at Pyrgi and of a treasury at Delphi. A corresponding building activity in the urban area of Cerveteri is attested by innumerable fragments of architectural terra-cottas from temples and houses discovered fortuitously or in (mainly clandestine) excavations in several parts on the city plateau. The style of these finely modeled, molded, and painted terra-cotta sculptures and revetments and of the recovered painted terra-cotta wall-panels is strongly marked by East Greek models; this imprint is also discernible in the Rome of the Etruscan kings, the Tarquins, where it traditionally reached its high point in the construction and embellishment of the Capitoline temple. Such "regal" activity seems to have been equaled in Cerveteri. The "king of C(a)isra," Thefarie Velianas, was involved in the ambitious building program of Temple B at Pyrgi and probably of other structures in Cerveteri itself, as visible signs of his tyrannical power. Excavations on the city plateau of Cerveteri suggest that his rule probably came to a violent end. It appears that soon after 480 the urban center of Cerveteri was destroyed and restructured, now to contain sacred as well as public buildings, all aligned in a rationally oriented layout comparable to the new spirit of urban planning in the necropolises. This grandiose reorganization of the city's center was perhaps the result of the public effort of a community no longer dominated by the individual will of a tyrant.

Ongoing excavations in the Vigna Parrocchiale have uncovered remains of the foundations of a building complex with triple rooms with a colonnaded front and, below it, earlier structures of the late seventh and sixth centuries. The disposition of the rooms apparently relate this building in type to the Archaic "residence" of Poggio Civitate/Murlo (see FIG. 94). This presumably aristocratic dwelling, decorated with painted terra-cotta antefixes and revetments of about 540, was deliberately destroyed around 480 to make way for other constructions.

A nearby large elliptical structure with a beaten earth floor was perhaps destined for public assemblies or spectacles. Oriented northwest to southeast, it measures ca. 20 x 35 m and is surrounded by a ring of ashlar masonry, probably once supporting stepped rows of wooden seating. It is tempting to see in this structure

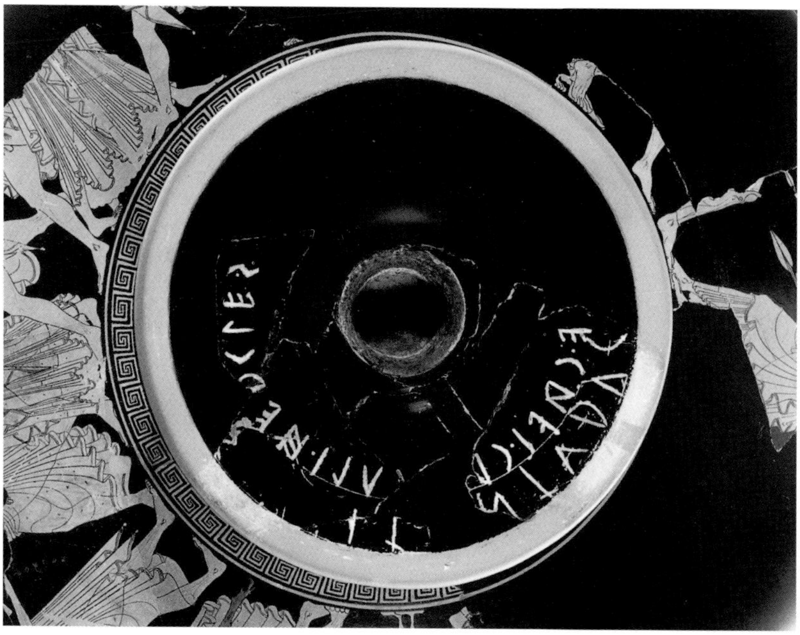

Fig. 175 Attic red-figured cup with incised Etruscan votive inscription to Hercle, under the foot. 500–490 B.C. Pottery. Diam. 46.6 cm. Rome, Museo Etrusco di Villa Giulia.

a building of comparable use to the Greek *ekklesiasteria* and Roman *comitia* of the late sixth and early fifth centuries, if not an early theater.

A second (ongoing) excavation at the southern edge of the city plateau has revealed the massive tufa foundations of two temples of late sixth-century date, as well as a vast cistern. Beside the foundations of one temple were discovered the remains of postholes, drainage channels, storage *pithoi*, and at least three skeletons buried in trenches; the latter point to the use of this part of the plateau as the necropolis of a village that may go back to the end of the Bronze Age. A lead weight with the inscription *Turms*, the Etruscan name of the god Hermes, has led to the suggestion that this divinity was the presiding god of the temple.

Unfortunately damaged and plundered by clandestine diggers over many years, the area of the second big temple here may have been a sanctuary of Herakles, as suggested by the recent discovery of several votive models of clubs and by the reputed findspot here of a large inscribed bronze club (now in an English private collection), as well as of an important Athenian red-figured cup of the early fifth century with a graffito under its foot (FIG. 175); both objects are dedicated to Hercle (*Herakles*). The big cistern by the temple has tentatively been associated with the Fons Herculis, the fountain of Hercules, mentioned by Livy (22.1).

Further northeast in the central part of the ancient city lay another large buildling, the Manganello temple, excavated earlier in the twentieth century. It had foundations of tufa blocks and was surrounded by numerous wells, a cistern, a water basin, drainage channels, and a furnace, probably for firing the terra-cottas

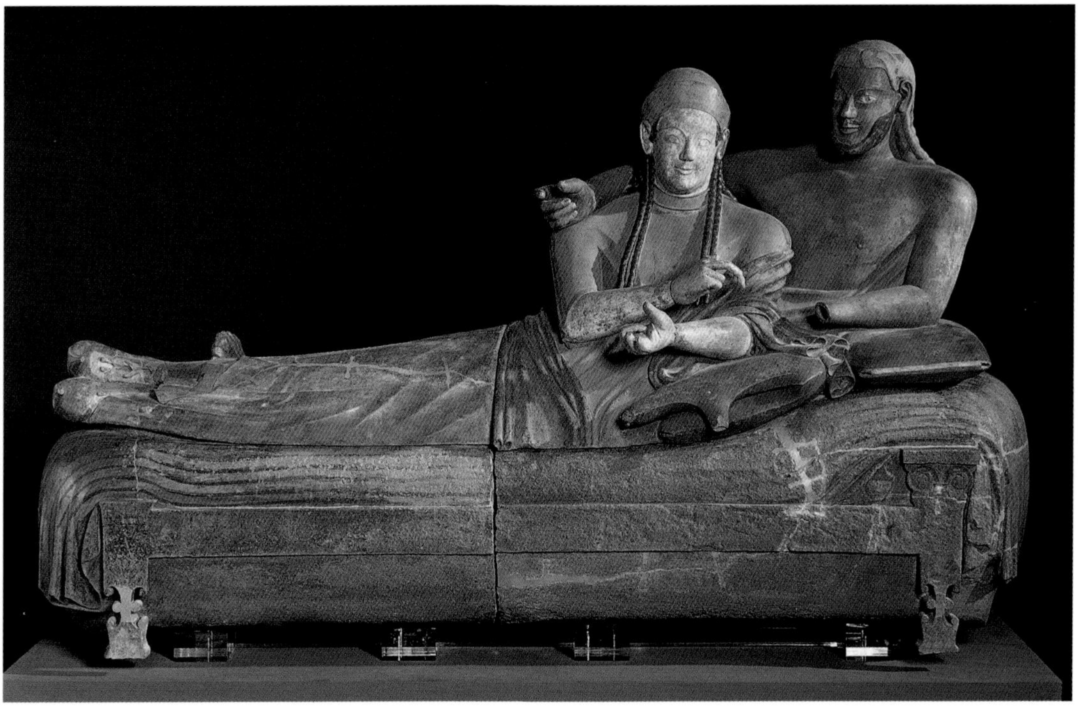

Fig. 176a Sarcophagus of a married couple. From the Banditaccia necropolis, Cerveteri. Ca. 530–520 B.C. Painted terra-cotta. L. 1.90 m. Paris, Musée du Louvre Cp 5194.

for the architectural decoration. Quantities of fragmentary antefixes and painted revetment plaques dating from Archaic to Hellenistic times were found in the neighborhood, as well as little terra-cotta altars (Lat. *arulae*) and sherds of vases with dedications to Hera written in Greek letters. Hera may have been the eponymous deity, but it has also been suggested that these votive inscriptions may be short for Hera(kles).

A large fragmentary acroterion of painted terra-cotta dating from the last quarter of the sixth century, now in Berlin, may have come from this temple. It shows a goddess in a long chiton and stiffly pleated mantle hurrying to the left above a curved supporting member in the form of antithetic horns and volutes representing waves. In her arms she carries a naked youth who clasps his arms around her neck. She may be Thesan, the Etruscan goddess of Dawn (Gr. Eos), who we know was worshiped at Pyrgi in association with Uni/Astarte.

Terra-cotta Sculpture

The art of modeling in clay and firing large-scale works had reached a high standard at Cerveteri by the second half of the sixth century. The Etruscans used clay for statues rather than stone—the favorite medium of Archaic Greek sculptors—partly because of the scarcity in central Italy of fine-grained hard stone that could take a high polish. (The marble of the Apuan Alps and of the Pisan mountains, though used locally for funerary cippi and statues, was not extensively exploited until the Roman period.) The funerary stone sculpture of Vulci, Chiusi,

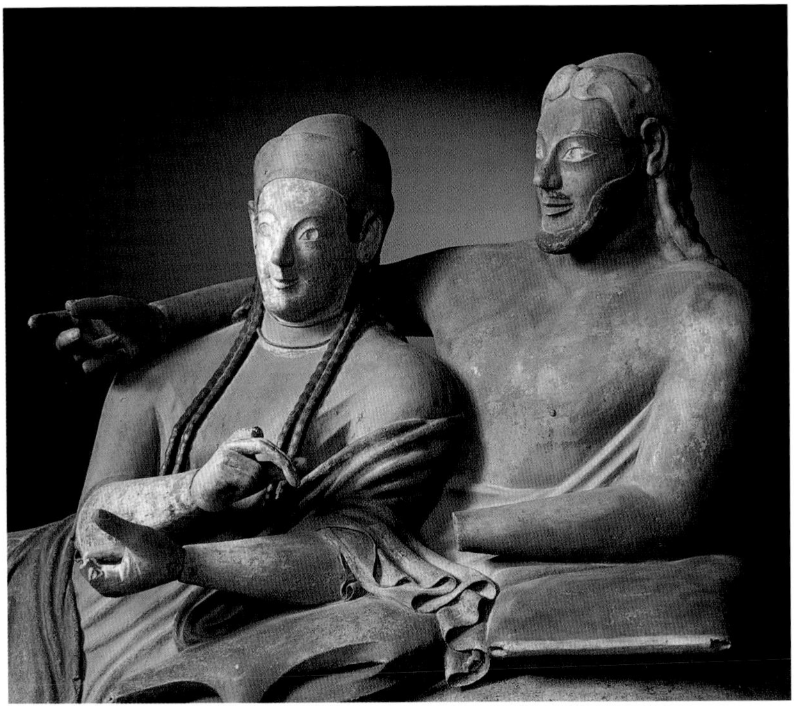

Fig. 176b Detail of sarcophagus, figure 176a.

Fiesole, and Volterra, for example, employed the local volcanic tufa, travertine, *nenfro*, or limestone, whose surface was often rough or friable and could not compare with the resilience and smoothness of marble. Applying paint to such surfaces was not easy. Highly levigated fired clay, on the other hand, permitted the depiction of the finest detail.

Two terra-cotta sarcophagi containing cremations are splendid examples of the art of modeling large-scale sculptures. Both were found in chamber tombs in tumuli in the Banditaccia necropolis of Cerveteri in the nineteenth century. They are now in the Louvre and in the Villa Giulia in Rome. If not made by the same master, the sarcophagi are certainly works of a single atelier (which probably also created a number of small ash urns representing the same subject).

The sarcophagus in the Louvre, found by the marchese Campana, is the better preserved, and recent cleaning has revealed much painted detail (FIG. 176a). The following description is therefore based on that sarcophagus. Both sarcophagi show a married couple, slightly over life size, reclining on a bed with a large overhanging mattress and striped cover. Heads and chests raised, they prop up their left elbows on cushions (hers in the form of a wineskin on the Louvre sarcophagus, FIG. 176b), the husband placing his right arm on his wife's shoulder, while she probably poured scented oil from a now-missing alabastron onto his left palm. His chest is bare and his lower body and legs are wrapped in an ample mantle draped in intricate folds that leave his naked feet visible. His long blond hair falls in a rippling mass over his shoulders, and he has a black beard and a painted mus-

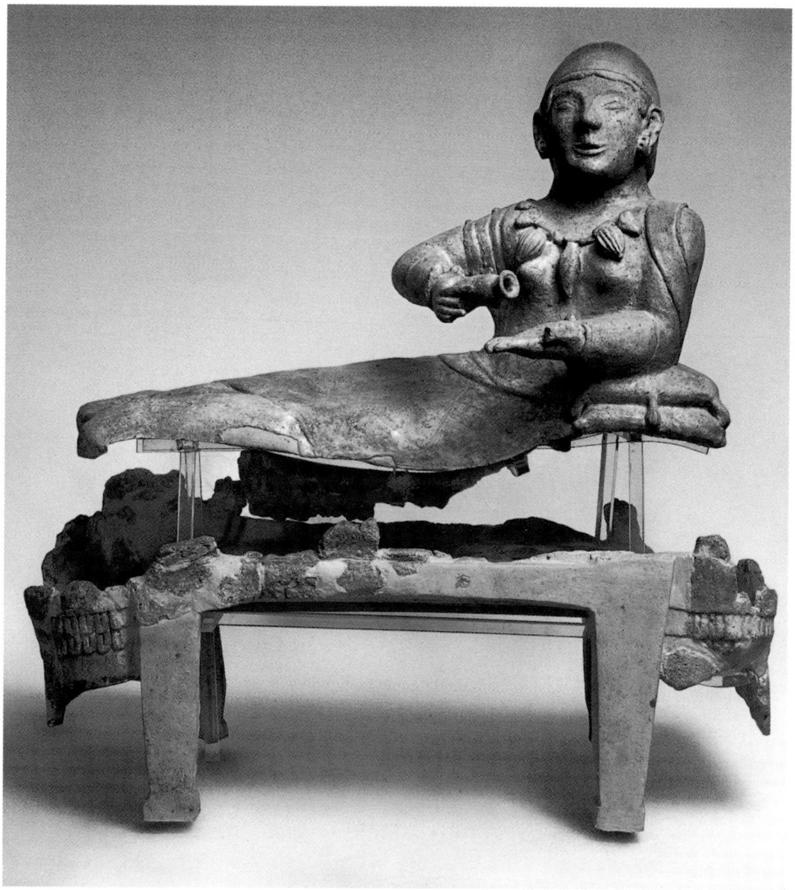

Fig. 177 Small ash urn with a woman pouring from an alabastron. From the Monte Abetone necropolis, Cerveteri. Ca. 540–530 B.C. Painted terra-cotta. H. 64 cm. Rome, Museo Etrusco di Villa Giulia 167.

tache. His skin is red, while hers is cream-colored, a convention universal in Etruscan painting to distinguish women, who led more sheltered indoor lives, from men, exposed to the sun in their outdoor pursuits.

She is dressed in a close-fitting orange chiton and a white-bordered mantle ending just above her feet, which are elegantly shod in laced red boots with upturned toes. She wears a broad collar around her neck, earrings (now missing), and a domed hat with a wide, upturned brim decorated with a pattern of antithetic volutes, from beneath which her long black tresses fall over her breasts and shoulders.

The couple's smooth oval faces have identical features with finely arched brows, long almond-shaped eyes whose irises were once inlaid in a different material, and slightly smiling mouths. In profile their noses and foreheads form a receding line, a type of face that was adopted by Etruscan artists in the second half of the sixth century from East Greek, in particular Northern Ionian, models.

The bed on which the couple reclines is also of Greek type with intricately fretted legs and a delicate painted decoration of lotus flowers and palmettes, which probably imitates wooden bedsteads inlaid with precious materials.

Bed and figures were modeled separately, forming, respectively, the box and lid of the sarcophagus. To facilitate the handling of such large and vulnerable pieces of clay, both these parts were divided across the middle in the leather-hard state before being fired.

The people who commissioned such an unusual and costly sarcophagus between 530 and 520 B.C. must have belonged to the aristocracy of Cerveteri. One cannot but be touched by the gentle and affectionate gestures of the couple; they must have held further small objects in their other, now-empty, half-closed hands, but the position of their fingers rules out that these were the drinking cups usually shown in banqueting scenes.

Wine and the funerary banquet may here be alluded to by the wineskin, used as cushion, but the main concern is the anointing, a rite for the dead sometimes represented on the reliefs of the Archaic ash urns of Chiusi, where women with alabastra perform this act on a draped corpse lying on a bedstead. That the couples on the Campana sarcophagus in the Louvre and on the sarcophagus in the Villa Giulia were indeed applying scented oil is suggested by a small ash urn of the same date and manufacture, also preserved in the Louvre (Cp 5193), on which the alabastron in the woman's right hand is intact, while in her left hand she holds a pomegranate, a symbol of death and rebirth. A comparable small ash urn from the Monte Abetone necropolis at Cerveteri shows a single reclining woman pouring oil from an alabastron onto her left palm (FIG. 177).

Such representations of husband and wife lovingly concerned with each other are unparalleled in contemporary Greek art and give expression to the profoundly different attitude toward women prevalent in Etruria.

Modestly sized ash urns show that more economical versions of this theme were manufactured at Cerveteri for the less well off. Even in these small works, the spirit of marital tenderness and the companionship in death of equal partners is very marked.

Although it was usual at Cerveteri during the Archaic period to deposit the bodies on the stone benches of the chamber tombs, the sarcophagi and urns just discussed prove that cremation was also practiced.

Painted Wall-Panels

A number of terra-cotta wall-panels painted with ornamental patterns and figures have been discovered in chamber tombs of Cerveteri during the last century; they are now in the British Museum and in the Louvre. That such panels were used to decorate the interior walls of temples and probably of aristocratic residences as well, is suggested by the many fragments that have turned up in excavations on the city plateau. Others with mythological subjects and scenes from daily life have recently appeared on the art market and may also come from the city itself rather than from the necropolises.

Five panels in the British Museum, named after their finders, the Boccanera brothers, were discovered in a tomb in the Banditaccia necropolis. Frame between

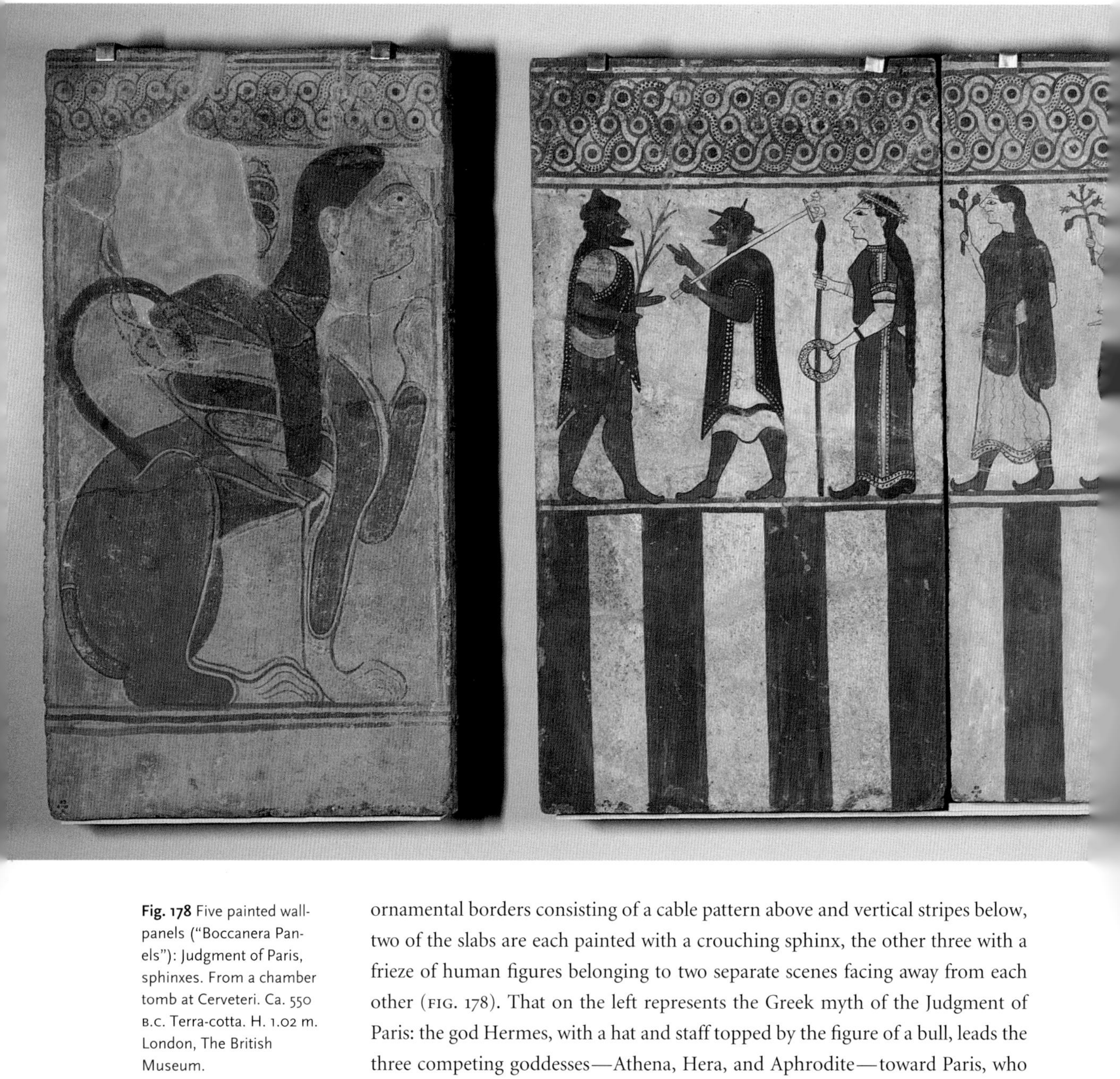

Fig. 178 Five painted wall-panels ("Boccanera Panels"): Judgment of Paris, sphinxes. From a chamber tomb at Cerveteri. Ca. 550 B.C. Terra-cotta. H. 1.02 m. London, The British Museum.

ornamental borders consisting of a cable pattern above and vertical stripes below, two of the slabs are each painted with a crouching sphinx, the other three with a frieze of human figures belonging to two separate scenes facing away from each other (FIG. 178). That on the left represents the Greek myth of the Judgment of Paris: the god Hermes, with a hat and staff topped by the figure of a bull, leads the three competing goddesses—Athena, Hera, and Aphrodite—toward Paris, who will judge them in a beauty contest. The physical attractions of the winning goddess, Aphrodite, are underlined by her particularly prominent breasts and her shapely legs, which she displays by having taken off her chiton and carrying it over her arm. Athena, characterized by a lance, and Hera are more modestly attired.

Turning their backs on this scene is a procession of women, three of them veiled and carrying a toilet box and alabastra, perhaps to adorn the leading figure on the right, who has exceptionally luxuriant wavy hair and seems to be winding

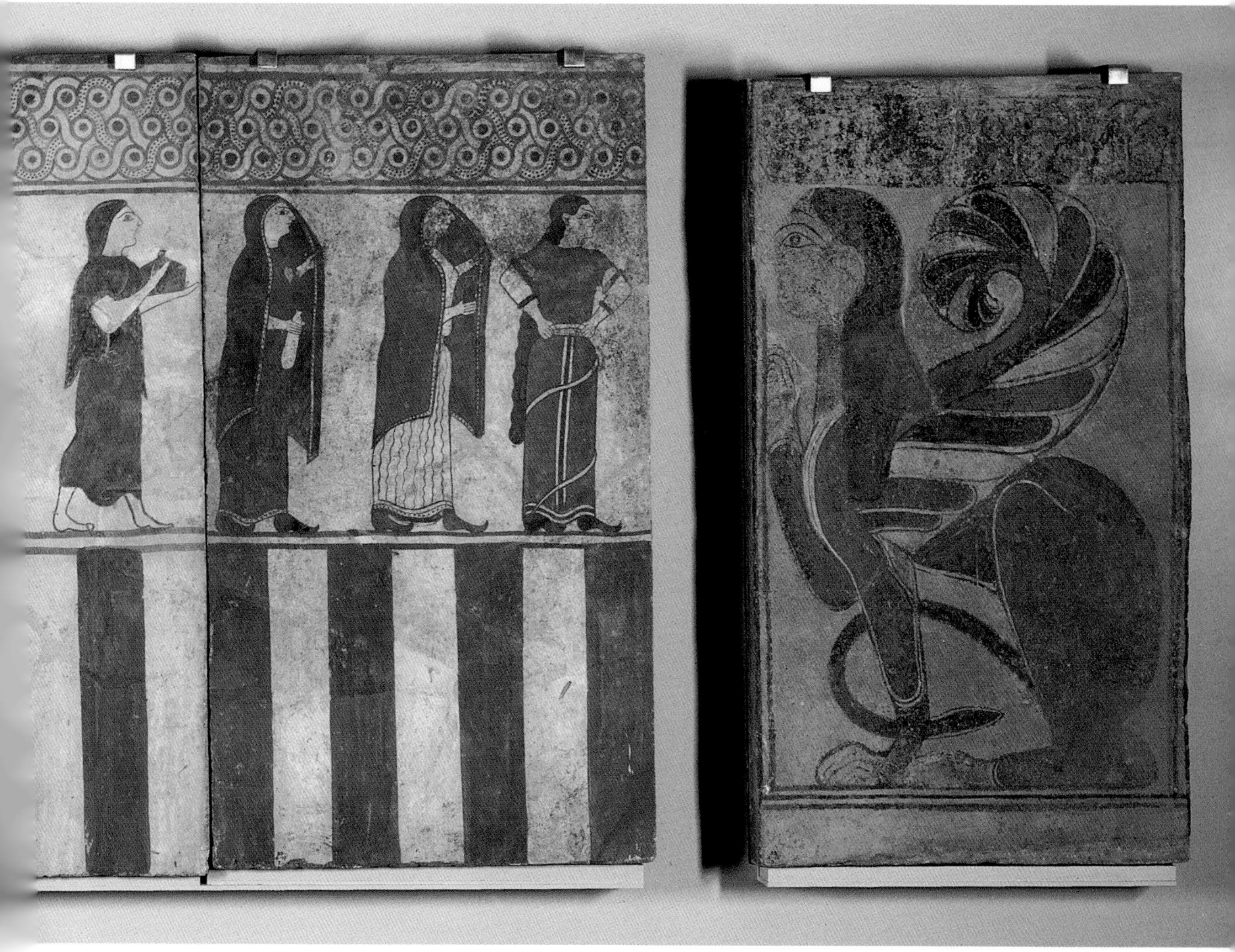

a long belt around her waist (falsely identified by some as a snake); she may be Helen, Paris's reward and the cause of the Trojan War.

The paintings combine stylistic features of Corinthian tradition with a strong Ionian, particularly Chiote inspiration.

A set of much-restored painted terra-cotta panels in the Louvre, likewise found in a tomb in the Banditaccia necropolis and partly cut at the top edge (which suggests their reuse), includes one with a cult scene. Framed by a border of different-colored stripes above and below, a short-haired youth stands in profile to the right (FIG. 179). He wears a brief, close-fitting tunic and boots with upturned points. He places his left hand on an altar with a burning fire while raising his right hand, with the top of the fingers bent, in front of his mouth and nose. The altar is a richly molded structure of ashlar masonry, its oblong blocks distinguished from each other by alternating colors. Beside the fire on the surface of the altar is a colum-

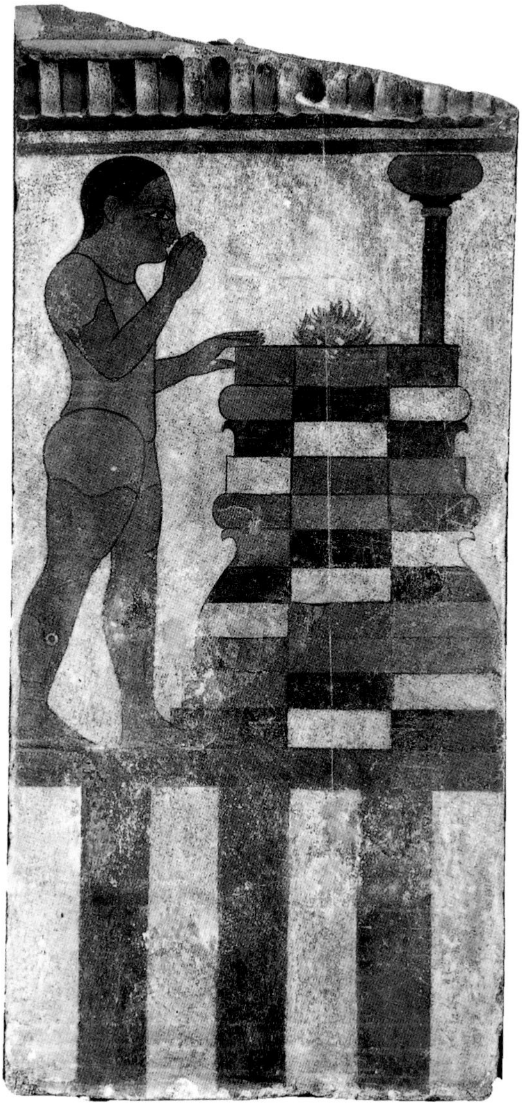

Fig. 179 Painted wall-panel: youth before an altar ("Campana Panel"). From the Banditaccia necropolis, Cerveteri. Third quarter of sixth century B.C. H. 1.24 m. Paris, Musée du Louvre Cp 6626.

nar support with a large shallow cauldron on top. The complex shape of the altar and its beak-shaped moldings recall those on cube tombs of the second half of the sixth century. The shorn hair of the youth may be a sign of mourning, and the burning fire denotes a sacrifice; the cauldron on a support could be a votive offering in a sanctuary or part of its furnishings.

TARQUINIA

The Ara della Regina Temple

We have discussed above the earliest sanctuary of Tarquinia on the city plateau, the Pian di Civita. Another temple, so far the largest known in Etruria, is the Ara della Regina, situated on the summit of the eastern height of Tarquinia in the neighborhood of the forum (FIG. 180). Flanked by roads on the long north and south sides, it was erected on an impressive platform of ashlar blocks of limestone measuring 77 x 34 m, much of which has survived. The remains of a sixth-century temple on this site were presumably covered by this platform. Fragments of its relief-decorated terra-cotta revetments represent a warrior mounting a chariot and a standing warrior in a tunic holding a lance. In the southeastern corner of the platform were a differently oriented altar and a small precinct, obviously important sacred spots of an earlier date, whose substance was thus religiously preserved. Further structures of the Archaic period have been identified in recent excavations to the east of the platform.

The new temple, constructed in the first half of the fourth century, was set well back on the platform. Of Tuscan type with a *cella* between alae and side walls prolonged to the front, it had a deep *pronaos* with four Ionic-Italic columns, accessible on the east by a ramp flanked by steps. At a later stage, probably during the third century, the *cella* was divided into three compartments at the back. The temple's painted terra-cotta revetments and relief decoration seem to be inspired by models of late fifth-century date, such as the Temple of the Belvedere at Orvieto/Volsinii. A fine revetment plaque from one of the beam ends in the pediment of the temple, decorated in high relief with a pair of winged horses from a biga, as well as the fragmentary figure of a goddess in a patterned dress are now in the Museo Nazionale Archeologico of Tarquinia. It is possible that the temple

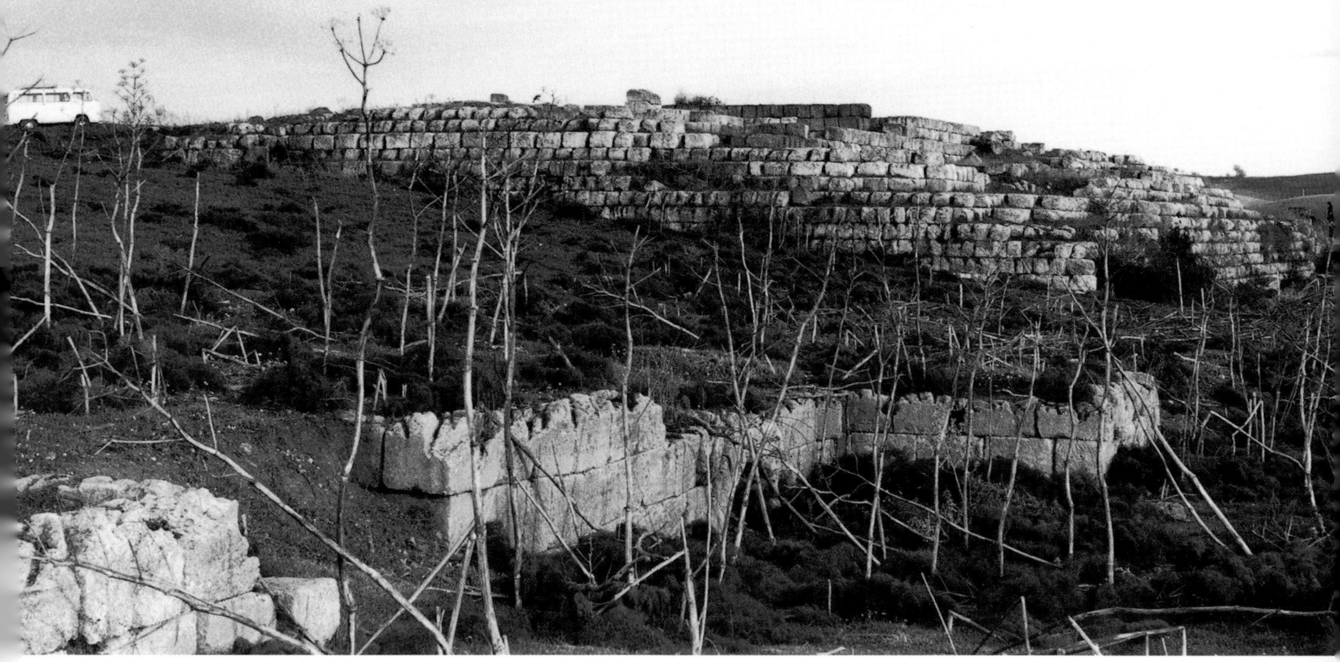

Fig. 180 View of platform of Ara della Regina temple on Pian di Civita at Tarquinia. First half of fourth century B.C.

was dedicated to Artemis, for among the few votive objects found was a fragmentary bronze rod inscribed with her name and the gold-covered bronze blade of a lance. The construction of such a huge temple in the fourth century is a sign of the renewed prosperity of Tarquinia, as is the grandiose circuit of the city walls.

Among the votive inscriptions found on the city plateau are the names of a number of other divinities: Śuri, Selvans, Culsans, and Thufltha.

Archaic Tomb-Painting

The most important wall-paintings in tombs of the Orientalizing period were found at Veii (see FIG. 72) and Cerveteri, but there outlines and colors, applied directly on the smoothed tufa walls, have suffered irreparable decay. The colors employed were black, yellow, red, and white, while blue and green appeared only rarely.

During the Archaic period Tarquinia became the prime center of tomb-painting and, thanks to the use of a more durable technique and a wider range of colors, the decoration on the rock walls here is better preserved, though today increasingly menaced by exposure. Of the more than six thousand tombs identified in the Monterozzi necropolis, only about two hundred were distinguished by painting, an indication that only the wealthiest families could afford such luxury.

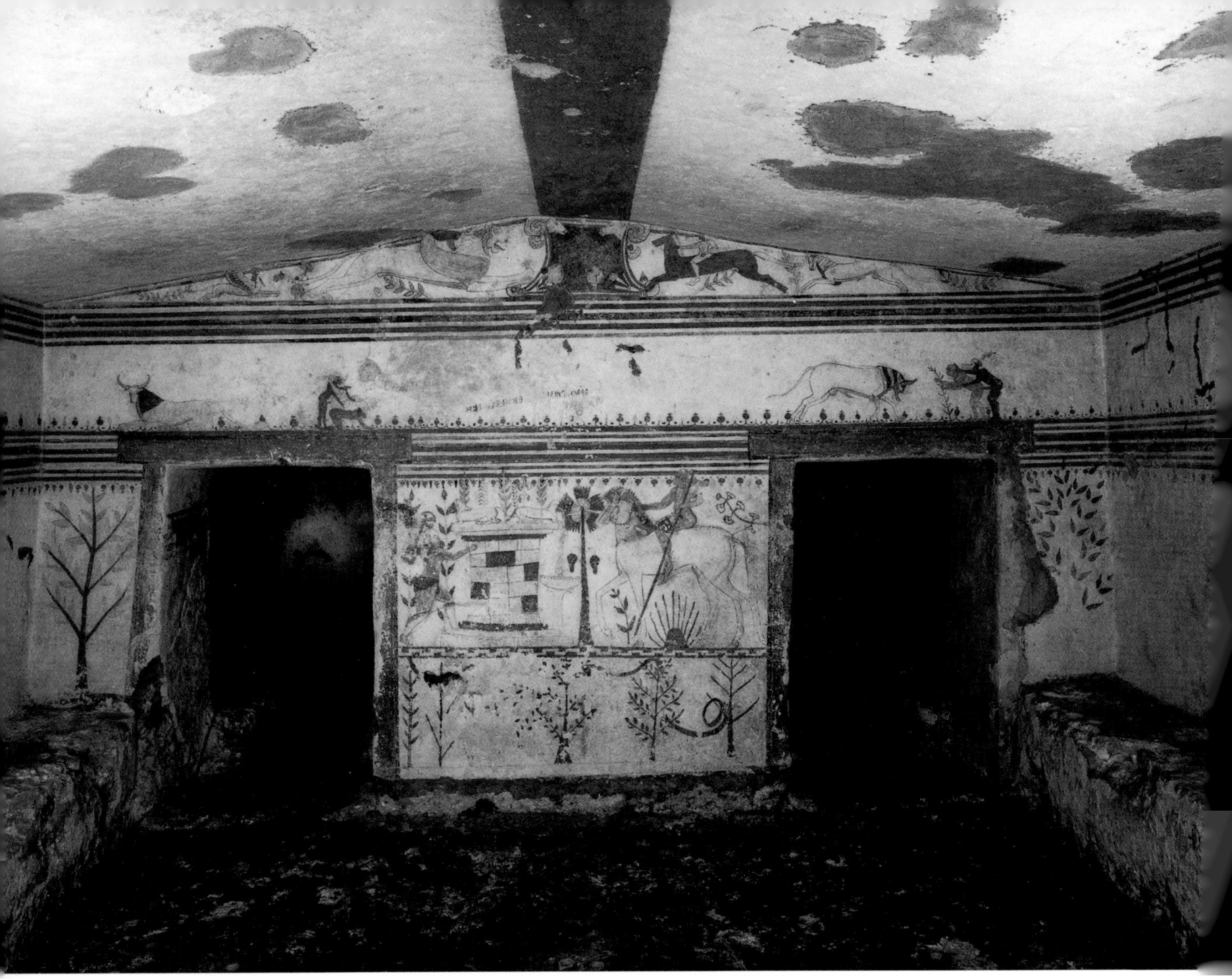

Fig. 181 Wall-painting: Achilles ambushes Troilos. From the main chamber of the Tomb of the Bulls, Tarquinia. Ca. 540–530 B.C.

The earliest of the tombs, dating from the end of the seventh to the mid-sixth century, are small rectangular rock-cut chambers with shallow ridge roofs, whose architectural features, imitating those of real wooden houses, are picked out by simple bands of paint. From about 550 onward, real or mythical animals arranged in heraldic schemes were painted flanking the king post, the central support of the pediments; such creatures probably have an apotropaic and transcendental significance. Other motifs that appear in the triangular space of the pediments are drinking parties in which the participants recline on mattresses on the ground in the open air or, more rarely, on wooden beds. After about 530, the entire walls of the tomb chambers were painted with figured scenes and occasionally with false doors, which perhaps symbolized the entrance into the other world.

THE TOMB OF THE BULLS One of the oldest and largest of the Archaic painted tombs and the only one with representations securely based on Greek myths, is the Tomb of the Bulls (*Tomba dei Tori*). It has a wide anteroom with two parallel tomb chambers opening off it in the rear wall. The space between their doors shows Achilles ambushing the young Trojan prince Troilos (FIG. 181), a story that was adopted in Etruria as early as the late seventh century, probably because of its sacrificial implications. Achilles in a crested helmet, loincloth, and greaves, hides behind a fountain set among exotic trees. Instead of a sword he holds a single-edged sacrificial knife, which hints at the slaughter of his youthful victim. The tall, molded base of the fountain resembles the altar seen on the Campana Panel in the Louvre (see FIG. 179) and reinforces the atmosphere of sacrifice. One of the two carved lions on top of the base spouts water into a shallow basin on a stand. The unsuspecting Troilos, nude but for pointed boots, rides up to the fountain where he will meet his fate.

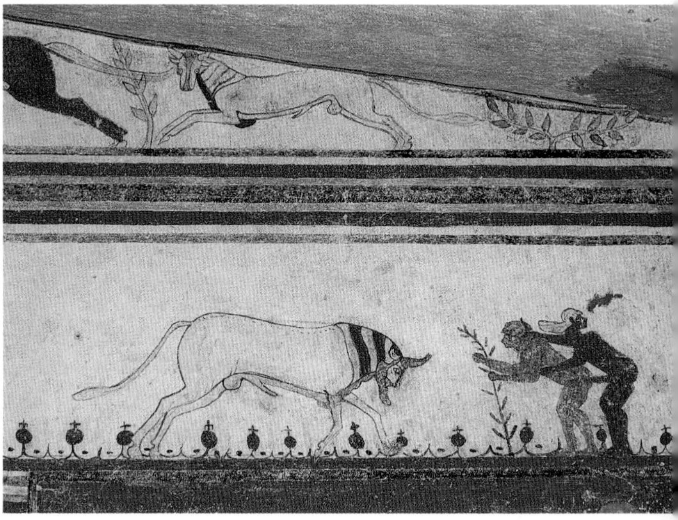

Fig. 182 Wall-painting: detail of erotic symplegma and bull. From the Tomb of the Bulls, Tarquinia. Ca. 540–530 B.C.

In the frieze above this scene (just above the doors leading into the tomb chambers) appear two erotic symplegmata and two bulls (FIG. 182). The animal on the left reclines and has turned its head to face the spectator. Next comes a group of a man entering a woman who lies on the back of another man, supporting himself on his hands and knees. On the right a bull with a human face (Acheloös?) charges a standing homosexual couple, the passive youth holding on to a shrub for support. Sexually aroused bulls and erotic activity are clearly life-affirming subjects. Compared with the frequency of representations of lovemaking, both hetero- and homosexual, in Greek vase-painting, erotic scenes are relatively rare in Etruria and, in tombs, may have an apotropaic or revivifying significance. It is presumably intentional that these particular scenes in the Tomb of the Bulls frame the name of the tomb's owner, Aranth Spurianas, inscribed on the wall. Perhaps he belonged to the same aristocratic family as the donor of a carved ivory relief in the form of a lion, incised with this name, *Araz silqetenas spurianas*, discovered in the sanctuary of Fortuna/Mater Matuta at Sant'Omobono in Rome (*CIE* 8602).

In the pediments of the outer chamber of the tomb are further interesting representations. On the main wall is a rider in Oriental costume who faces the Chimaira, followed by a sphinx. This depicts another Greek myth, that of Bellerophon overcoming the Chimaira, the Lycian monster composed of a lion, a goat, and a snake, a subject that was to receive its most monumental treatment in Etruria in the fourth century (see FIG. 246). The dromos wall of the outer chamber shows a youth riding on a *hippocamp* toward an island, perhaps an allusion to the dead's journey across the sea to the beyond.

Painted about 540–530, the frescoes of the Tomb of the Bulls are strongly marked by Ionian influence and resemble to some extent the style of Etruscan black-figured vases, in particular those of the Pontic group (see FIG. 144). But the wall-painter was unused to large-scale work, as shown by the many erratic lines in the preliminary drawing, particularly of the horse's head.

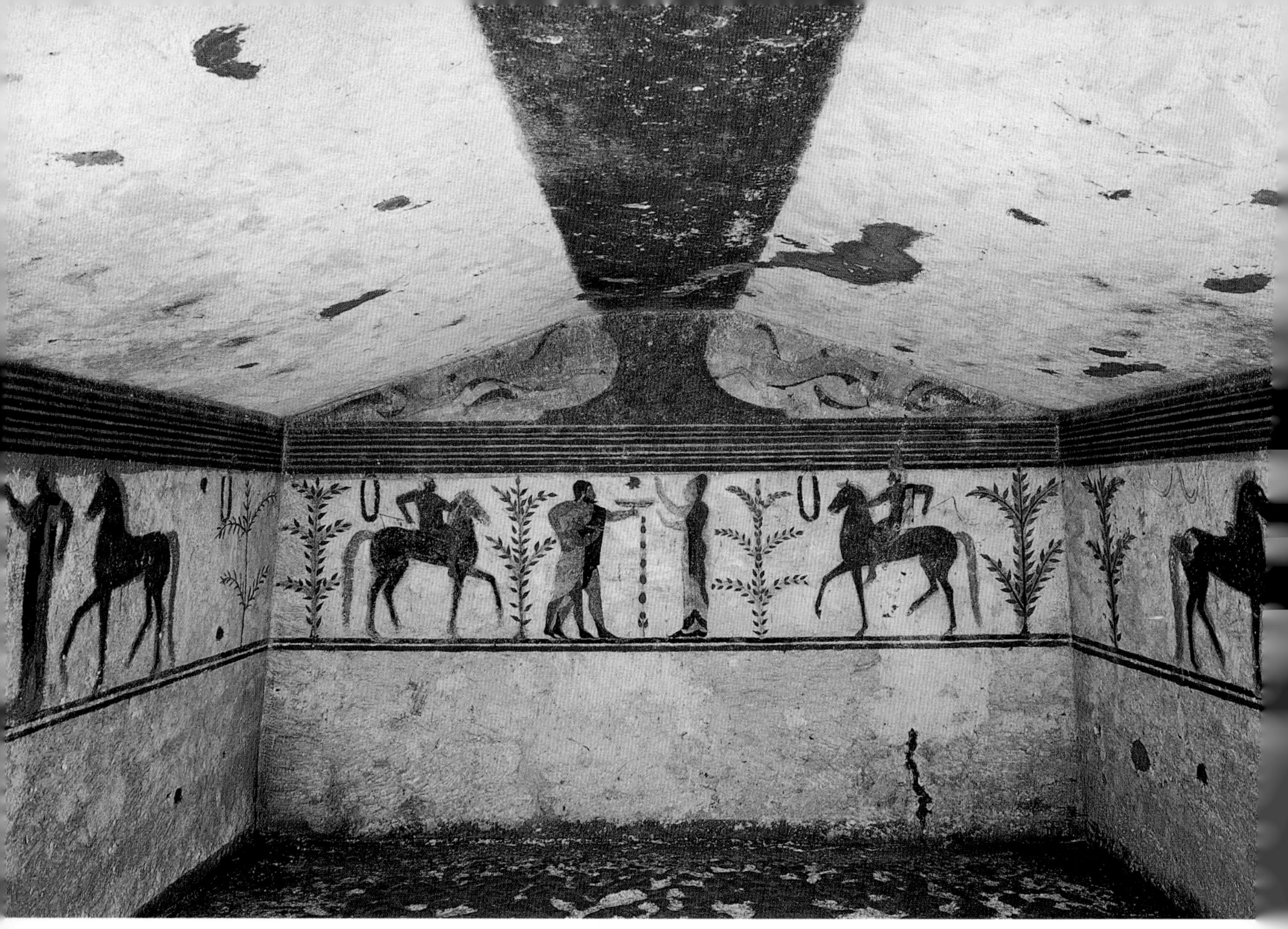

Fig. 183 Wall-painting: woman greeting man and boy, framed by horsemen. From the back wall of the Tomb of the Baron, Tarquinia. Late sixth century B.C.

THE TOMB OF THE BARON More harmonious and balanced is the decoration of the Tomb of the Baron (*Tomba del Barone*, named after Baron Kestner, who discovered it in 1827). The single chamber is painted with tall, symmetrically arranged figures with a strong silhouette effect, which is due to an undercoat of gray pigment. On the back wall, framed by laurel bushes, a stately woman in a clinging chiton and mantle covering her tall headdress raises both hands in blessing or greeting (FIG. 183). She is approached by a dark-haired, bearded man holding out a cup in his left hand and clasping in his right arm a fair boy, who plays the auloi; both wear the short semicircular Etruscan mantle (*tebenna*) and pointed ankle-high boots. From either side a young blond horseman in mantle and boots rides up to this central scene. On the left wall, the same(?) horsemen, dismounted, holding their horses and, raising one arm in adoration or greeting, frame the same(?) draped woman, who holds out her veil with her right hand. On the right wall, two dismounted horsemen, again holding a black and a red horse, face each other, each raising a wreath in one hand. Clearly, the most important figure is the woman engaged in a solemn scene of leave-taking or blessing. The other figures may be the dead woman's husband and sons who pay their respects to the departing wife and mother. Divergent interpretations make her a priestess, a heroine, or even a goddess; the horsemen are thought by some to represent the Dioscuri. We cannot be certain. The symmetrical grouping and the style of the figures are

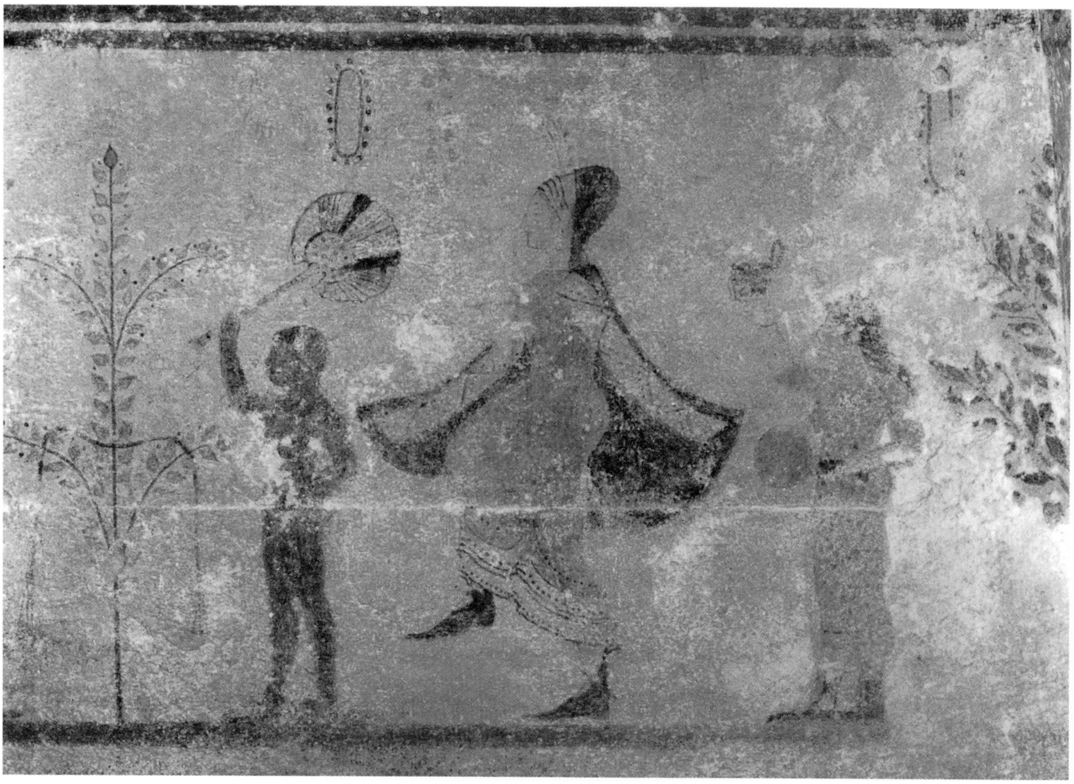

obviously closely related to North Ionian Greek black-figure vase-painting (Clazomenian sarcophagi and the Ricci hydria in the Villa Giulia), and some scholars have attributed the frescos to an Ionian painter. This beautiful work was created in the last decade of the sixth century.

Fig. 184 Wall-painting: woman with boy fan-bearer and servant girl. From the Cardarelli Tomb, Tarquinia. Late sixth century B.C.

THE CARDARELLI TOMB Named after a Tarquinian poet, this tomb (*Tomba Cardarelli*) dates from the same period as the Tomb of the Baron. Like it, one wall (on the left) is decorated with an elegant lady dressed in a semitransparent, bordered chiton; a mantle covering her tall, wreathed headdress; and pointed red boots (FIG. 184). She raises one foot in a stately dance movement, which makes her mantle fly out from her shoulders. A servant girl in a dotted dress and boots follows her, holding up a cup in her right hand and a circular bronze mirror with a handle in her left. The lady is preceded by a nude boy who waves a long-handled, multicolored fan in his right hand. Facing this group is a man in a loincloth and sandals; he dances with his right hand raised while holding out a large painted wine cup in his left hand, a red fillet draped over his arm. In front of him moves a wreathed boy flute player dressed in chiton, short mantle, and elaborately laced boots. On the right wall dances another man in loincloth, sandals, and wreath, while a second man opposite him in checked loincloth plays *kottabos* (a game in which one flings the dregs of wine from a cup at a target so as to dislodge it).

Between them are two nude and wreathed boys, one a musician playing the *barbiton*, a lyrelike string instrument, the other a cupbearer with an embossed-metal wine jug and a ladle in his left hand.

The entrance to the tomb is flanked by two potbellied, nude boxers, who raise their hands in a ritualized aggressive gesture; their position here beside the door may have apotropaic significance, rather than allude to funerary games and boxing contests. On either side of the painted false door on the rear wall stands a musician in a short, checkered and fringed jerkin and boots; the one on the left plays a kithara, the other a flute. A large krater with volute handles stands at the feet of the kithara player, and fillet-hung trees divide the groups of figures.

Though less solemn in spirit and less perfect in design than the Tomb of the Baron, the subject of the left wall of the Cardarelli Tomb may also honor a lady who is here represented dancing, accompanied by her young servants and toasted by a man who is probably her husband. The archaeological details make the tomb particularly interesting. We know that fans were status symbols (see pp. 37, 105) and that from the later part of the sixth century onward engraved bronze mirrors belonged to the equipment of a well-to-do woman; both are represented here. The Greek game of *kottabos* was introduced in Etruria together with banqueting. The large krater beside the false door presumably refers to the funerary banquet, as do the cups held by two of the men. Music played an important part in Etruscan life, accompanying activities and occasions as diverse as feasting, dancing, funerals and other ceremonies, hunting, sports such as boxing, and even the flogging of slaves. Musicians and entertainers, both male and female, often wear vividly patterned jerkins, such as those shown in this tomb. In Etruria they seem to be garments worn only by professional performers.

THE TOMB OF THE LIONESSES This tomb (*Tomba delle Leonesse*) is, somewhat misleadingly, named after the two female panthers with enormous dugs that flank the king post in the pediment of the rear wall of the chamber. The checkered ceiling, perhaps representing the material of a tent, is seemingly supported by six painted Tuscan columns. Above a dado in the form of dark waves with leaping dolphins and flying birds is a fine frieze of pendant lotus flowers and palmettes below a strip of green leaves. Above this, on each side wall, are two large figures of reclining draped men (not lying on couches but leaning on cushions on the ground). On the right wall, one of them holds a drinking cup in his left hand while raising an egg, a symbol of life, in his right one. On the left wall, one of the wreathed men points with a laurel branch toward the small pale figure, drawn in outline only, of a boy performing on a low pedestal holding auloi and a ring(?).

The paintings on the rear wall center on a huge volute-krater of bronze wreathed with ivy, a plant connected with Fufluns/Dionysos, the god of wine; a bronze ladle with a handle ending in a duck's head is suspended beside the krater (FIG. 185). It is flanked by a kithara player, whose music accompanies three

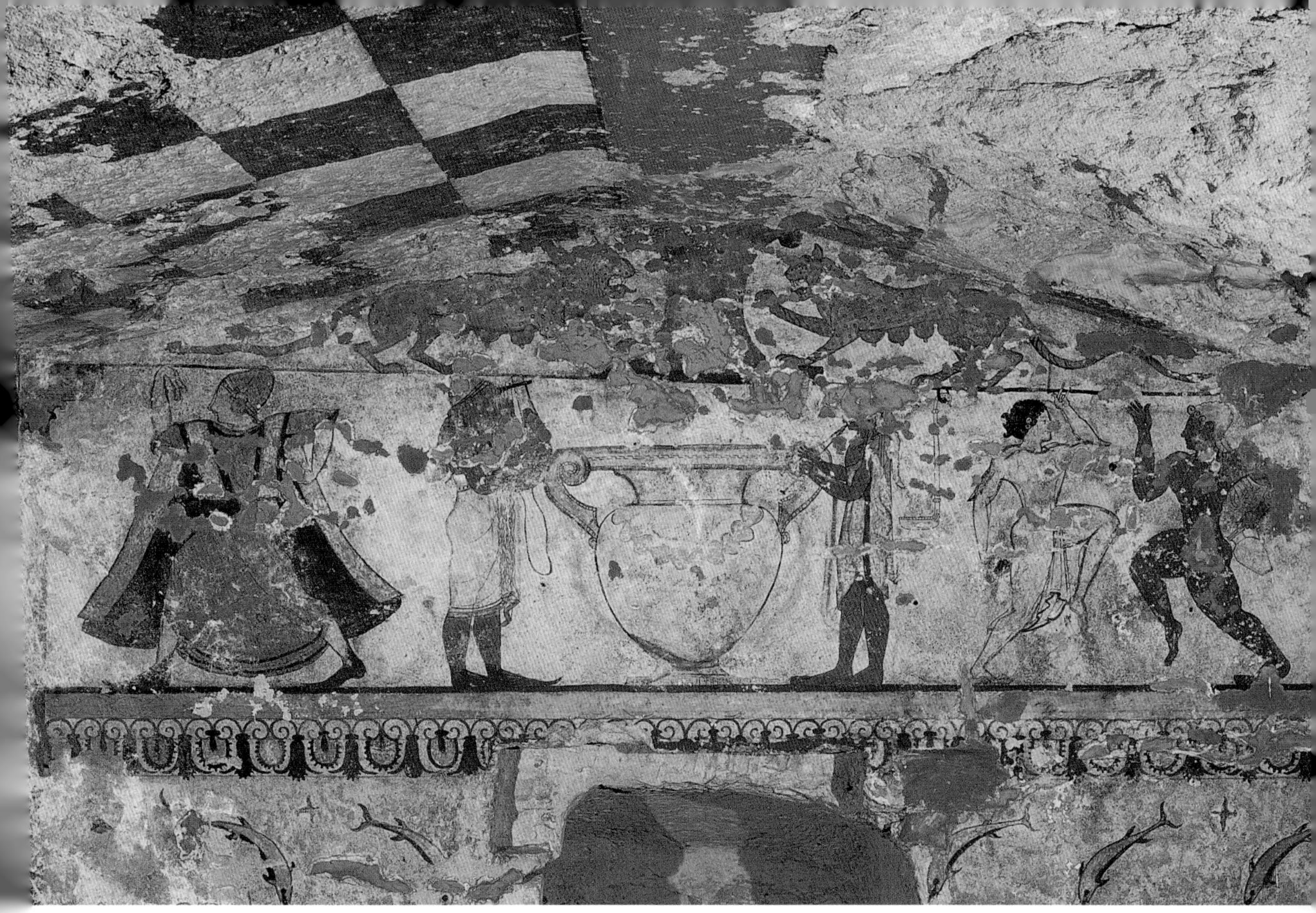

dancers: on the left side, a lady, perhaps the mistress of the tomb, dressed in the usual light chiton, woolen mantle, pointed shoes, and conical headdress (*tutulus*) strides solemnly to left, elbows and hands bent like an Indonesian temple dancer. On the right, a dark-haired girl wearing only a transparent chiton leaps in joyful partnership with a naked blond cupbearer opposite her. She has a castanet in her right hand and raises her left in a gesture to ward off the evil eye (still used in Italy today). He holds a pale metal jug in his left hand, and on the floor beside him stands a spouted black jug. Mistress and servants are clearly distinguished by dress and manner of dancing, the latter abandoned in Dionysiac frenzy, the former seemingly engaged in a stately dance of lament. Her husband may be the man reclining on the right side wall who alone holds a cup and an egg; he is probably the deceased in whose honor the banquet takes place. The niche in the back wall beneath the painted krater probably once contained his ash urn. Remains of two dancers are preserved on the entrance wall. The tomb was painted about 530/520 by an artist strongly influenced by East Greek models, if not by a Greek immigrant.

Fig. 185 Wall-painting: krater framed by musicians and dancers. From the back wall of the Tomb of the Lionesses, Tarquinia. Last quarter of sixth century B.C.

A motif increasingly used for the walls of the tombs as time went on was that of the banquet, male and female participants reclining on dining couches and attended by usually nude boy cupbearers, musicians, and female servants in simple dresses. The scenes of feasting on the ground are exclusively drinking parties, a fashion introduced from Ionia.

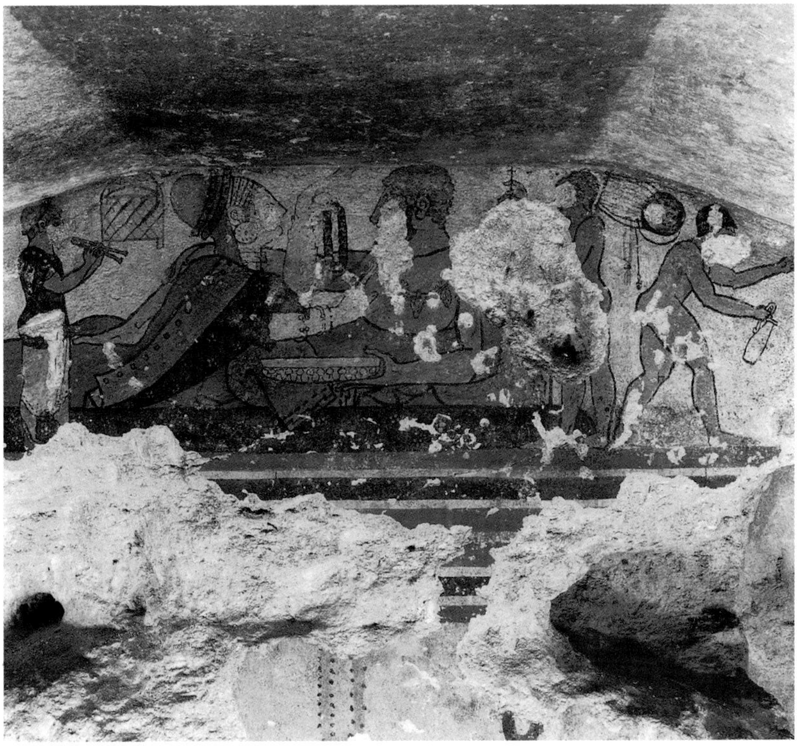

Fig. 186 Wall-painting: banqueting couple, girls, and servants. From the pediment of the Tomb of Hunting and Fishing, Tarquinia. Ca. 530–520 B.C.

THE TOMB OF HUNTING AND FISHING The most lively and beautiful of such representations is found in the pediment of the second tomb chamber of this tomb (*Tomba della Caccia e Pesca*, FIG. 186). An elegantly dressed and bejeweled lady wears her hair tied up high, covered by a veil and wreathed. She lies on her stomach on a mattress and, looking at her husband, hands him a wreath. Facing her, he places his right hand tenderly on her shoulder and his right leg on her back, while holding an embossed metal phiale in his left hand with the elbow supported on a cushion. He wears a mantle wrapped around his lower body and on his bare chest a gold necklace with pendants in the form of ram's heads. A lyre with a sound box made from a tortoiseshell and a plectrum attached to it by a string hangs from the wall, hinting at his musical accomplishment. On the wife's side this is balanced by a container for toilet instruments (Lat. *cista*), decorated with a lattice pattern, which is suspended above her. The couple are surrounded by two attentive girls in simple dresses (probably daughters), making wreaths; an aulos player; and two nude cupbearers, one dipping a stick into a scent bottle, the other bending to fill his jug from a large amphora that stands with other banqueting vessels within a thick packing of foliage, indicating that this is an outdoor scene.

Below this pediment the walls are painted with a seascape enlivened by leaping dolphins and countless birds flying and settling on the waves (FIG. 187). Youths in boats are fishing, and on multicolored rocks hunters armed with slings take aim at birds, while one boy dives into the sea.

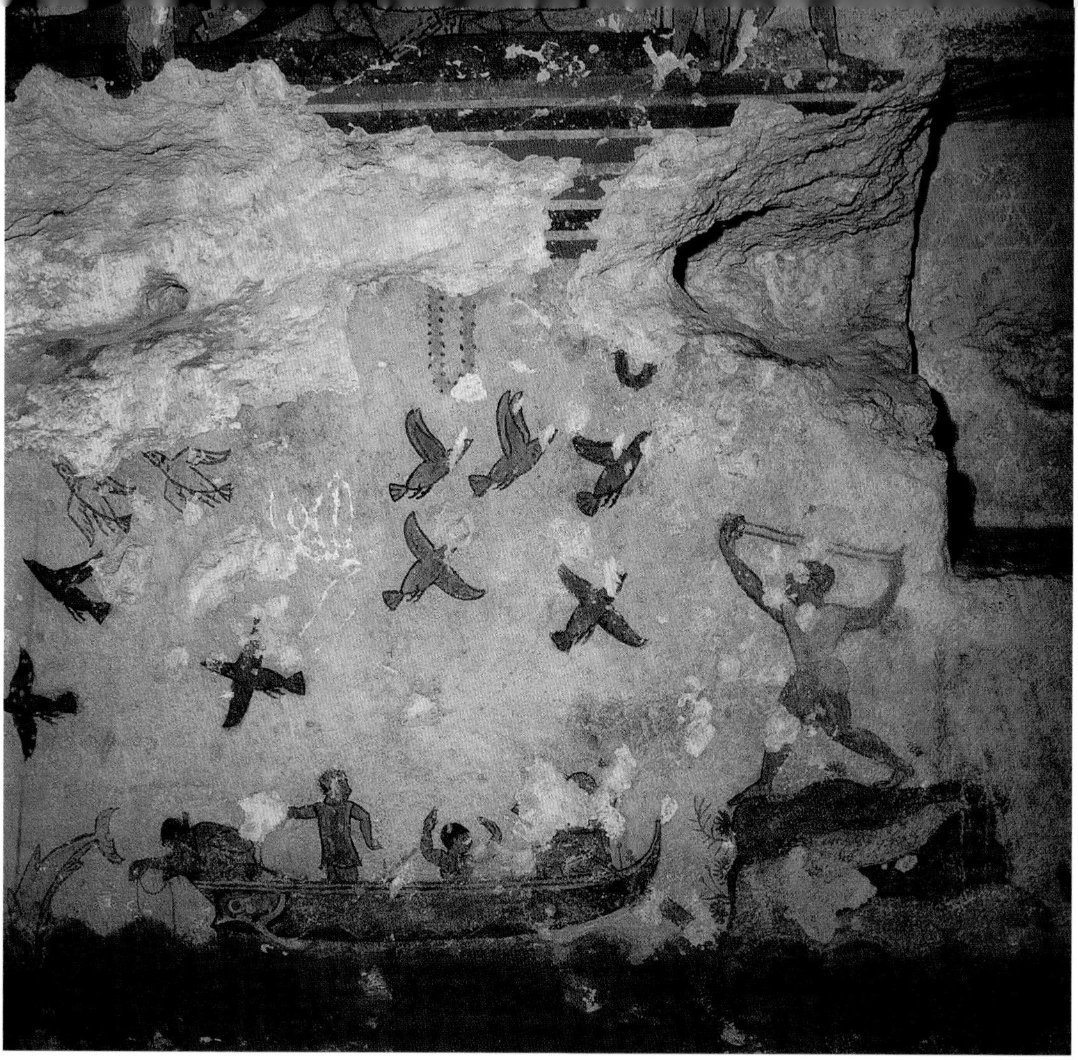

Fig. 187 Wall-painting: seascape and rocky shore. From the Tomb of Hunting and Fishing, Tarquinia. Ca. 530–520 B.C.

In the first chamber of this tomb the pediment represents the return from a hunting expedition, with two horsemen in the center accompanied by their dogs and servants carrying the quarry. The figures move through a forest of varied trees. On the walls below, small but sturdy figures of male dancers, dressed in loincloths, leap and gesture between slim laurel bushes hung with fillets, a mirror, baskets, and wreaths.

It has been suggested that these dancers are performing a religious rite in a laurel grove sacred to Apollo. But like similarly attired dancers in other Tarquinian tombs (Cardarelli Tomb, Tomb of the Dead Man [*Tomba del Morto*], Tomb of the Inscriptions [*Tomba delle Iscrizioni*], and Tomb of the Bacchantes [*Tomba dei Baccanti*]) disporting themselves between such trees, their enthusiasm must be inspired by Fufluns/Dionysos, the god of wine, rather than by Apollo. Dionysiac religiosity, which flourished in Attica in the sixth century, was also being introduced into Etruscan tomb contexts. This interpretation is confirmed by the representation of satyrs with drinking horns reclining in the gable of the entrance wall, mythical figures belonging to the cortege of Dionysos. The Tomb of Hunting and Fishing is unique in its exquisite feeling for nature and the activities of human beings blending with it. The figure of the boy diving from the rocks into

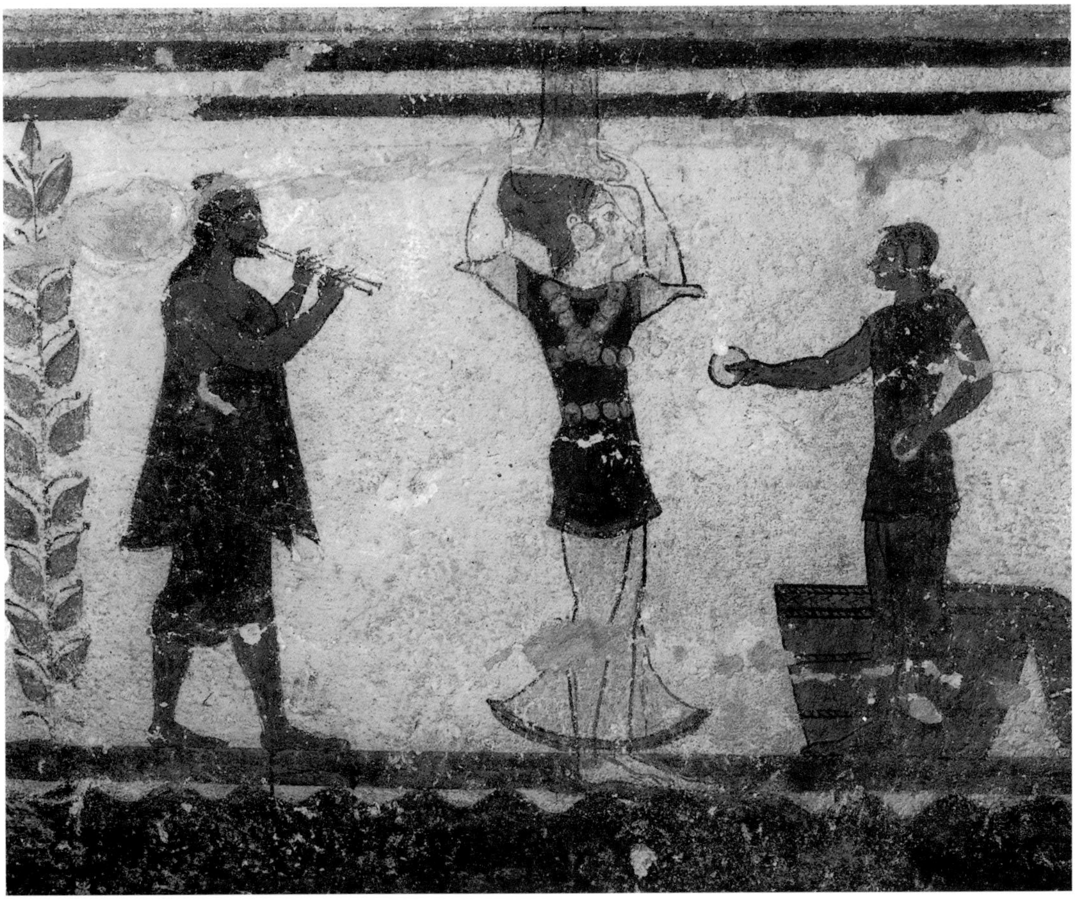

Fig. 188 Wall-painting: girl dancing with incense burner on her head. From the back wall of the Tomb of the Jugglers, Tarquinia. Late sixth century B.C.

the sea has been compared with that of a youth diving from a pedestal painted on the inside of a tomb at Paestum, a subject of possibly transcendental significance. The banqueting and hunting scenes in the pediments are well-known motifs celebrating aristocratic pleasures and privileges (cf. the friezes from Murlo, FIGS. 102, 105), but here, in the funerary context, the banquet may have a more esoteric meaning. The tenderness husband and wife express for each other in their gestures is typically Etruscan and recalls in spirit the terra-cotta sarcophagi from Cerveteri (see FIGS. 176a, b).

THE TOMB OF THE JUGGLERS This tomb (*Tomba dei Giocolieri*) is named after figures painted on its rear wall, which is divided by four slim laurel trees (FIG. 188). On the left are two small nude boys, facing right and drawn in outline only; their pale color may be meant to convey their tender age (cf. the small figure in the Tomb of the Lionesses, p. 226). One sits on the ground, the other stands on a low podium holding a wreath. A nude young man standing to the right of them looks with a gesture of amazement at the central scene, where a girl juggler performs a balancing act, accompanied by a draped flute player. She wears a transparent chiton with short sleeves and over it a sleeveless red jerkin with a belt of metal(?) discs, similar discs forming cross-straps passing over her shoulders; her head is covered by a tall red cap. On this she steadies with both raised hands a bronze incense burner, whose top bowl with the burning incense protrudes into the banded frieze above. The hem of her chiton flies out in a way that shows that she is whirling around. A youth in a short tunic stands in front of her holding out two pale disc-shaped objects that he has probably taken from the two large baskets beside him, whose lids are leaning against them. On the right sits a bearded, draped spectator on a folding stool; he holds a tall staff, a sign of dignity, and may thus be the deceased in whose honor the performance takes place. It is possible that the boy juggler with the discs is attempting to aim them, in a kind of *kottabos* game, at the top of the incense burner to extinguish the flame. With slight variations in the positions of the performers, the same juggling scene occurs in a rather lifeless fresco painted a little later in the Tomb of the Monkey in Chiusi by a copyist using cartoons.

On the right wall, four female dancers with long flowing hair, wearing jewelry, brightly colored chitons, bordered mantles, and pointed boots, step out and gesture in a hieratic fashion to the music of a draped syrinx (panpipe) player standing in the center. On the left wall, two nude youths, one of them armed with a throwing stick (Gr. *lagobolon*) used for hunting hares, move to the left, followed by a bent old man in a mantle, who holds out a stout knotty stick and grasps another boy by the wrist. A singular scene of difficult interpretation follows: a pair of birds fly toward a (palm?) tree behind which crouches a naked man excreting. The name *Aranth Heracanasa* = Aranth, the servant of Heracanas, is written across the tree trunk. This is thought to be the name of the crouching man, who has tentatively been identified as the painter of the tomb; his drastic scatological action is probably of apotropaic nature. On the entrance wall another unicum in Etruscan painting is badly preserved: a camellike animal (perhaps two actors disguised under a skin) flanks the door.

In its style the Tomb of the Jugglers is close to the Tomb of the Lionesses, with strong North Ionian, presumably Phokaian influence; its date is about 510. The dancing ladies with their solidly built limbs resemble some of the female figures on the painted water jugs known as Caeretan hydriai.

THE TOMB OF THE AUGURS Perhaps the most striking example of large-scale figure painting in Tarquinia is that of the Tomb of the Augurs (*Tomba degli Auguri*), which has been ascribed to an Ionian artist active about 520. He has represented purely Etruscan subjects, which are of the greatest interest for our understanding of what ceremonies were performed in honor of the dead.

On the rear wall is a massive painted false door flanked by two draped men solemnly raising one hand and placing the other on their heads in gestures combining salute and mourning. They are designated by inscriptions (*apas tanasar* and *tanasar*).

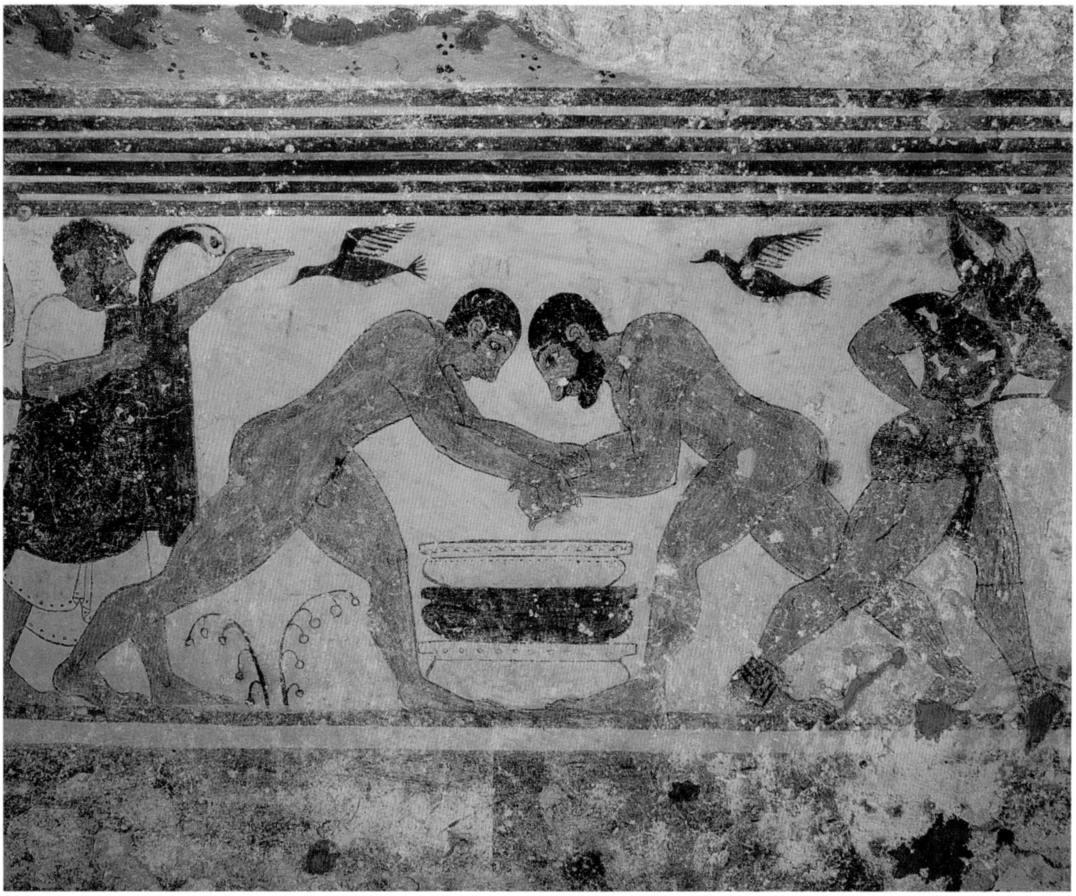

Fig. 189 Wall-painting: wrestling match with onlooker. From the right-hand wall of the Tomb of the Augurs, Tarquinia. Ca. 520 B.C.

On the right wall, a bearded man wearing a purple cloak and pointed boots turns back toward the door in similar gestures (inscription: *tevarath*). His importance is underlined by a boy servant beside him, dressed in a short dotted tunic and carrying the folding chair that we know to be a symbol of power. Another small boy, wrapped in a black cloak, crouches on the ground, asleep or mourning. To the right of this group, another draped man (also *tevarath*) holds a curved staff, either the augural staff known as *lituus* or a staff of command used by umpires in games (FIG. 189). He seems to supervise a wrestling match between two big nude men who have come to grips, bent over three large nesting metal basins representing the prizes for the victors in the funeral games. The wrestlers are named Teitu and Latithe, single names suggesting that they are slaves. A couple of birds fly above them toward the augur, whose figure has given the conventional name to the tomb.

Next comes a singularly attired figure wearing a bearded mask and a pointed hat, a black-and-white fringed jerkin, and a red loincloth; he holds a large black dog by a long leash (FIG. 190). This ferocious animal bites the legs of a man, already bleeding and wearing only a loincloth, while his head is wrapped up in a cloth so that he is unable to see to defend himself effectively with a club. The name of his

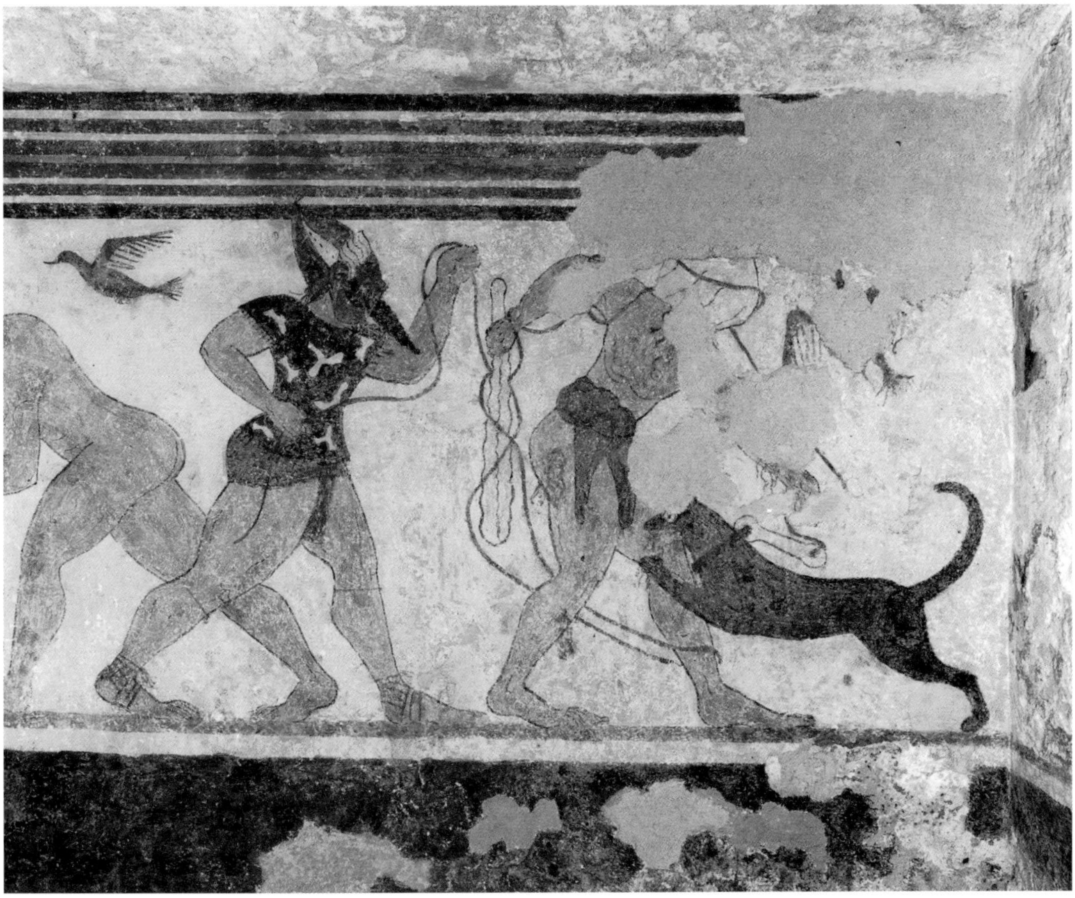

masked tormentor is Phersu (Lat. *persona* = masked actor, is derived from this Etruscan word). The same cruel scene is depicted in the Tomb of the Olympic Games (*Tomba delle Olimpiadi*). The masked Phersu character running or dancing also appears in the Tomb of the Pulcinella (*Tomba del Pulcinella*) and in the Tomb of the Cock (*Tomba del Gallo*) in Tarquinia.

Fig. 190 Wall-painting: Phersu with victim attacked by dog. From the right-hand wall of the Tomb of the Augurs, Tarquinia. Ca. 520 B.C.

On the left wall of the Tomb of the Augurs another Phersu is running to the right while looking back mockingly over his shoulders. Next to him two nude boxers accompanied by a flute player fight over a prize in the form of a large cauldron, and the last figure is a nude sprinter.

On the walls flanking the entrance are two, now largely effaced, masked figures involved in a dangerous game of strength with a long cord that ties them both by the neck and threatens to strangle either of them. The main subject of the paintings is the funerary games held for an important personage, which obviously included the ritual shedding of blood. The blindfolded man mauled by the dog incited by Phersu may have been a substitute for an older habit of slaughtering prisoners of war (cf. p. 306) or criminals in honor of a dead hero, a custom that survived into Roman times in the gladiatorial games. No woman is represented in this tomb.

THE TOMB OF THE WHIPPING This tomb (*Tomba della Fustigazione*), likewise with large-scale figures and dating from the end of the ionizing phase, about 490, is distinguished by having a false door painted in the center of three of its walls. The real entrance door is flanked by two boxers reminiscent of those in the Cardarelli Tomb. On the right wall, on each side of the false door, is an erotic scene, which—like those in the Tomb of the Bulls—may have an apotropaic, life-affirming significance. Much damaged, the scene to the right of the door shows a woman, dressed only in a *tutulus*, bending and holding on to the hips of a bearded, naked man who faces her with a smile. From behind the woman is approached by a youth who places one hand on her buttock and raises the other with a whip above her back. On the opposite side of the door another nude woman in a *tutulus* embraces a young man amorously, while a bearded man tries to penetrate her from behind. On the left and rear walls the false doors are flanked by musicians, dancers with drinking cups, and a tall painted amphora—subjects that give a Dionysiac flavor to the decoration. It has been suggested that, like the ritual whipping of women during the ancient Roman festival of the Lupercalia, the beating of the woman here could represent a fertility rite. However, the prevailing atmosphere in this tomb is one of Dionysiac revelry recalling komast scenes on Greek vases.

THE TOMB OF THE BIGAS The paintings of the *Tomba delle Bighe*, named after the two-horse chariots represented in the upper frieze of its single chamber, are now preserved in the Museo Nazionale Archeologico of Tarquinia. The two superposed friezes that covered the walls and pediments of the tomb are very damaged, but copies of them made shortly after their discovery in 1827 enable us to reconstruct the rich variety of themes they illustrate.

The taller frieze below shows on the rear wall a symposium with low tables in front of three dining couches, each occupied by a pair of wreathed and draped young men attended by cupbearers and a flute player. In the pediment above is a big krater flanked by cupbearers and reclining figures of drinkers. On the right wall, the scene continues with a table with amphorae and a jug—the vessels for the party (Gr. *kylikeion*). All the rest of the frieze was taken up with large-scale figures of male and female dancers and musicians stepping out in expressive attitudes between slim trees. The elegant, transparent linen chitons of the women and their variously draped, shawllike mantles enhance the decorative effect and clearly reveal their anatomy.

Even more remarkable is the smaller upper frieze with representations of athletic games and chariot races watched by a crowd of spectators seated on wooden stands (FIG. 191). The nude bodies of the athletes are shown in complex movements, including bold foreshortening and rear- and three-quarter views. The charioteers wear the customary Etruscan short tunics. The knees of one of them are bandaged with leather straps; all have seized their goads and the reins, the ends of which are tied around the driver's waist.

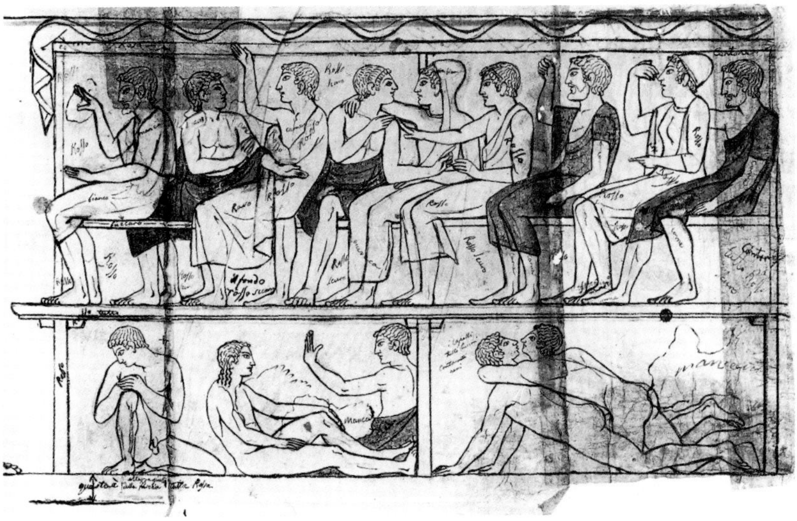

Fig. 191 Watercolor of wall-painting: spectators at games. From the left-hand wall of the Tomb of the Bigas, Tarquinia. Ca. 480 B.C. Tarquinia, Museo Nazionale Archeologico.

Between the groups of youthful athletes and acrobats stand older men draped in mantles and holding gnarled, forked staffs; they are the trainers and supervisors of the games. The flanking tribunes for the aristocratic families watching the performances are raised from the ground on posts and sheltered from the sun by canvas awnings. The spectators are seated on long wooden benches, the men wrapped in cloaks and the women wearing chitons, mantles, and *tutuli*. Some converse with each other in easy familiarity, gesticulate, point, and wave to the competitors, while others embrace their neighbors or sit lost in thought. In the confined space below the seating space, a crowd of youths in the nude, presumably slaves, amuse themselves in their own way, watching, disputing, and even making love.

The liveliness and variety of activity and movement in these extraordinary scenes owe much to depictions of the palaestra and the symposium on Attic red-figured vases, which were imported in large quantities into Etruria during the Late Archaic and Early Classical periods. Such prototypes suggest that the tomb was painted about 480. The aristocratic crowd of spectators composed of husbands, wives, and other members of the family at a public performance is, however, purely Etruscan.

THE TOMB OF THE TRICLINIUM The paintings from this single-chamber tomb (*Tomba del Triclinio*) have likewise been removed to the Museo Nazionale Archeologico of Tarquinia to prevent further deterioration; the understanding of the details is helped by watercolor copies made shortly after the discovery of the tomb in 1830. The name of the tomb comes from the three banqueting couches painted above a dado of red waves and black and red lines on the back wall. Three-legged low tables covered with vessels were placed in front of the first two couches, under which a cat stalks a cock and a partridge. A nude young cupbearer with a wine jug and sieve stands in the center, and behind him and the banqueters a woman in a

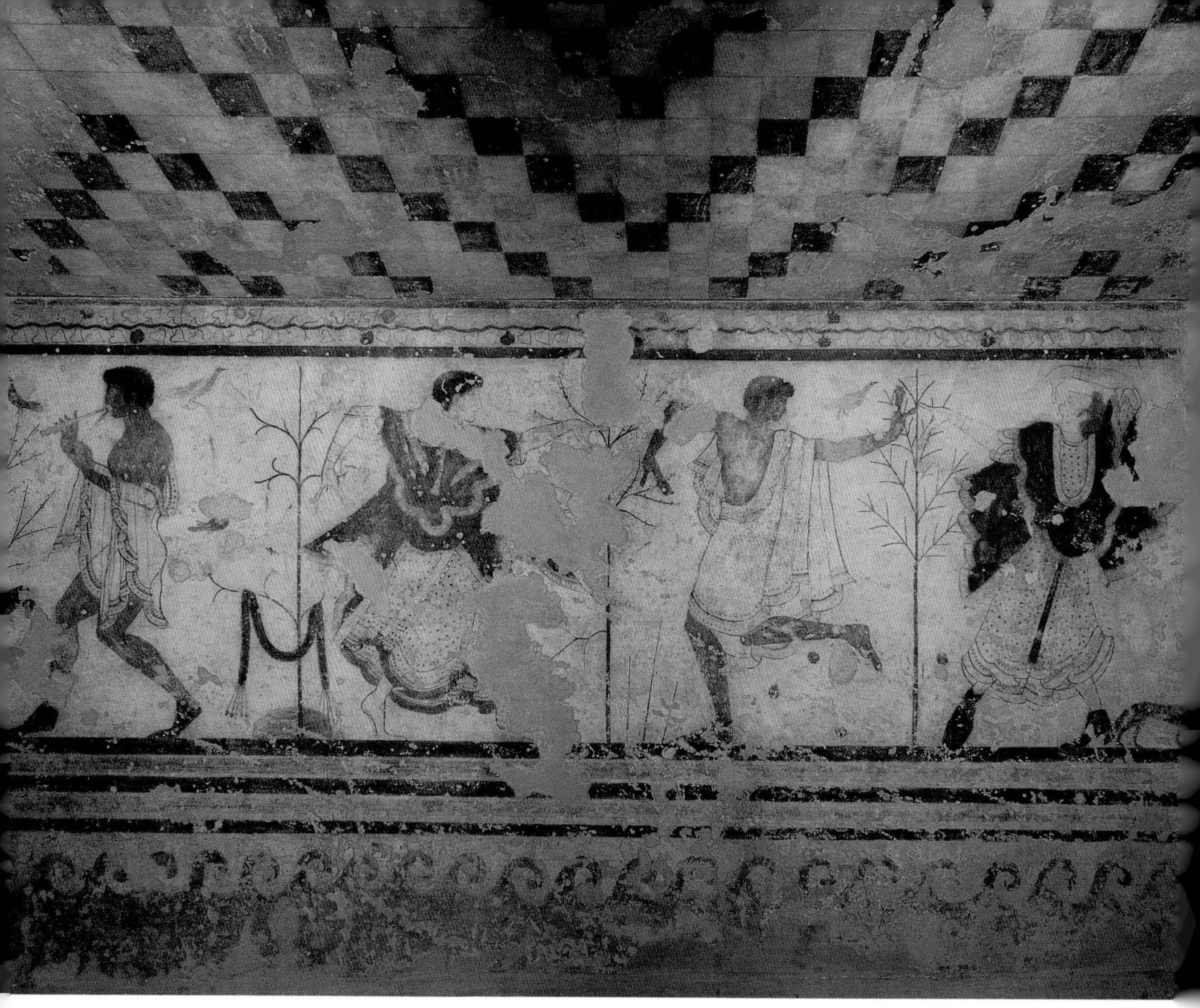

Fig. 192 Wall-painting: dancers and musicians. From the Tomb of the Triclinium, Tarquinia. Ca. 470 B.C. Tarquinia, Museo Nazionale Archeologico.

pale, flowered chiton and bluish mantle holds a large alabaster scent bottle. The side walls show wreathed dancers and musicians between a variety of slim trees and shrubs enlivened by birds, felines, a hare, a fox, and a squirrel. Men and women alternate in an elegant and subtle rhythmic dance, accompanied by the sounds of auloi, *barbiton*, and castanets (FIG. 192). The intricate movements of the performers' bodies are clearly revealed thanks to the transparency of their light clothes, which are enhanced by small overall patterns and richly bordered mantles.

Flanking the door on the entrance wall were two youthful horsemen in short cloaks, each descending from his bridleless mount with a lance in one hand, holding onto the mane with the other. They may represent the Dioscuri, the half divine, half human twin sons of Zeus, saviors and mediators between this world and the next. In the angles of the pediment above are panthers.

The opposite pediment shows two nude youths leaning on large kraters and reaching for the ivy corymbs and leaves decorating the king post as well as the ridge plank of the roof. These are Dionysiac symbols, reinforcing the impression that the ecstatic dancers on the walls are divinely inspired in their celebration of a

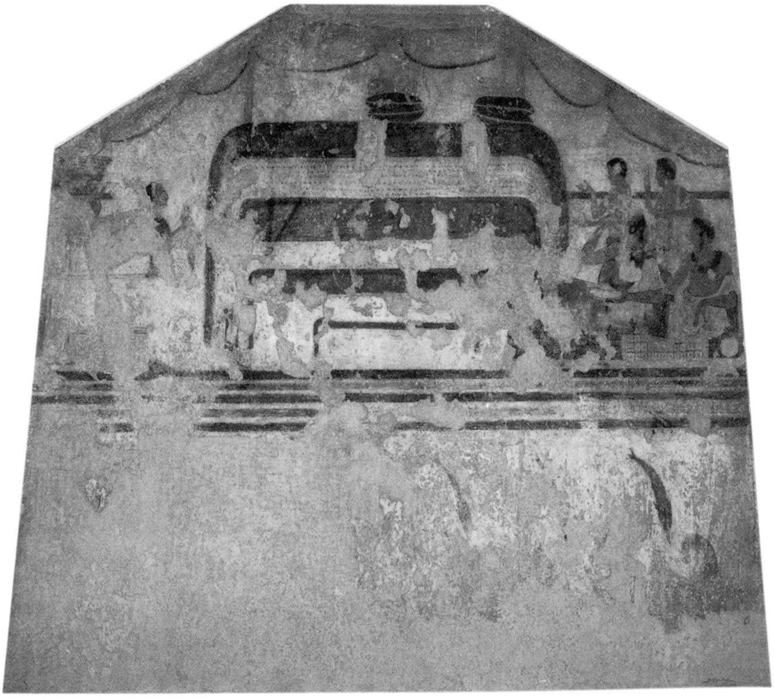

Fig. 193 Wall-painting: bed and banqueters. From the Tomb of the Funerary Bed, Tarquinia. Ca. 460 B.C.

rite for the deceased and/or for the divine twins, Kastor and Pollux. The style and type of the figures are closely related to Attic vase-painting of the first decades of the fifth century and indicate a date for this splendid tomb of about 470.

Only two of the painted tombs of Tarquinia, the Tomb of the Dying (*Tomba del Morente*, no longer preserved) and the Tomb of the Dead Man, represented the owners of the tomb on their deathbed, laid out and mourned over by relatives, but the subject is frequently shown on carved Chiusine cippi and urns (see FIG. 199) and surely reflects actual ceremonies. In the tombs we have just discussed, the deceased men or women may perhaps be identified with one of the people depicted, seemingly alive, or we must imagine the dead already beyond the symbolic false doors so often shown.

In the somewhat later Tomb of the Funerary Bed (*Tomba del Letto Funebre*), named after the funerary bed represented on the rear wall under a tent (FIG. 193), we recognize the symbolic presence of either a dead aristocratic couple, who are being honored by a commemorative banquet and games, or a divine pair, such as the Dioscuri. On this huge bed are two pale mantles and two conical, wreathed objects (perhaps funerary cippi), each supported on double cushions. These clothes and cippi stand for the deceased and/or for the divine twins, Kastor and Pollux, who are supposed to be present at the banquet held in their honor (Lat. *lectisternium*). An unusual glimpse of affectionate relations between two servants appears on the right-hand wall, where a young man in a loincloth turns back toward a woman wearing chiton, short mantle, and *tutulus* and gently strokes her

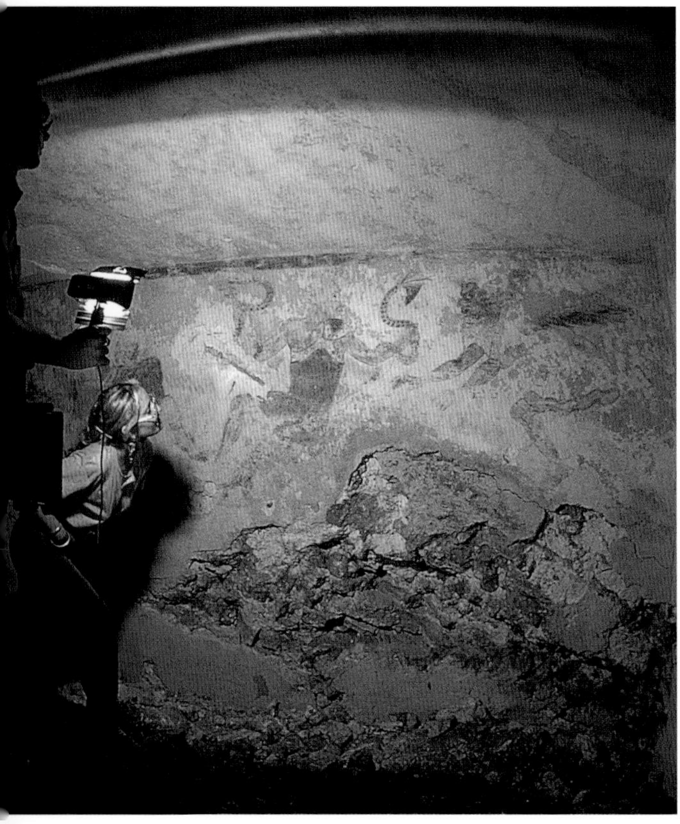

Fig. 194 Wall-painting: demons. From the Tomb of the Blue Demons, Tarquinia. 420–400 B.C.

face. The tomb, which dates from about 460, belongs to the following, sub-Archaic phase of Tarquinian tomb-painting. Its style shows the influence of imported Attic red-figured vases.

THE TOMB OF THE BLUE DEMONS A chamber tomb from the end of the fifth century B.C. was opened near Tarquinia in 1985. It has been named the Tomb of the Blue Demons (*Tomba dei Demoni Azzurri*) after the blue- and black-skinned demons depicted in the underworld scenes on the right wall (FIG. 194). Here the traditional representations of hunting and a funerary banquet of four to five couples on couches (on the central one the wife strokes her husband's face affectionately) is combined with new themes: the departure of the deceased on a chariot, accompanied by musicians, and a scene set in the underworld. The latter is presumably influenced by Attic pictorial and literary models of Hades of the middle of the fifth century. On the left side of the right wall a boat on the waters of the underworld river is steered by the Greek ferryman of the dead, Charon (Etr. Charu); from the prow hangs a ribbon. On the shore a draped woman holding a branch and placing her left hand on the head of a boy in front of her moves to the right. They face and greet another woman, flanked by two demons, one seemingly leading her forward and the other holding her back around her waist. On a hillside to the right of them two bigger demons—one seated on a rock and brandishing two snakes, the other rushing forward with bared teeth, piercing eyes, and raptorlike claws extended—combine elements of Greek invention with purely Etruscan features.

The scene has been interpreted as the arrival in the underworld of a dead woman who is being met in this grim setting by predeceased relations. Recently a more esoteric meaning has been claimed for the meeting between the two veiled women and the boy, linking it to the Eleusinian divinities and their mysteries, but this interpretation is based on the mistaken view that the woman by the shore holds stalks of grain or pomegranates.

In any case, the notion of the underworld as a desolate place whose entrance is supervised by horrid beings contrasts sharply with the happier vision suggested by earlier tomb-paintings and hints at a change in attitude toward life in the beyond. There may be complex reasons for this shift in perception, difficult for us to understand in the absence of any Etruscan literary sources. The penetration of Greek ideas into Etruscan religious beliefs may have played a part, as may, at least in the

Southern Etruscan cities most affected by the economic decline, an increased awareness of the transitoriness of human fortune. A need for the possibility of salvation and of the individual's blissful existence after death led to the adoption of Greek Orphic, Pythagorean, and perhaps Eleusinian ideas. It certainly favored the introduction of Dionysiac doctrines recognizable in the Bacchic iconography of painted tombs and vases and carved sarcophagi.

Another new element in the paintings of the Tomb of the Blue Demons (and subsequently on sarcophagus reliefs) is the appearance of individual members of the family, either those already dead, who are shown awaiting the arrival of the recently deceased relation, or the still living, who see the dead person off on the journey to the underworld with demons in waiting. Increasingly such scenes are accompanied by inscriptions naming important members of the family and their social rank and deeds, which points to the upper social strata's growing need for self-representation. The theme of the aristocratic hero's departure in a chariot, long known from Archaic terra-cotta friezes on temples and residences, here signifies the journey to the beyond.

The custom of painting the underground tomb chambers of the well-to-do continued with variations in quantity and quality at Tarquinia until the late third century B.C. Tarquinian models were used by copyists in the areas of Chiusi and Sarteano during the fifth century. We shall be discussing some of the later Tarquinian tombs in the following chapters.

It is worth remembering that these frescoes, of which those painted during the Archaic period are often of outstanding artistry, were never seen by the public. Their purpose was purely funerary, and they were probably meant to reintegrate the deceased into the circle of the still-living family, who were depicted with him, commemorating him in banquets and games and, by the proper rites, ensuring his heroization and transubstantiation. In the almost total absence of Etruscan religious literature, however, we must remain constantly aware that any modern interpretation of these frescoes is bound to be incomplete and often influenced by our views of the better-documented Greek ideas of death and the beyond.

Bronze Mirrors

In the wall-paintings of the Cardarelli Tomb we noticed the representation of a circular bronze mirror held by a maid behind her mistress (see FIG. 184). Such mirrors, often engraved with a figure scene on the reverse, became common from the last decades of the sixth century. They formed part of the possessions of well-to-do ladies, and we know from inscriptions on some of the mirrors that the Etruscan word for mirror was *malena* or *malstria* (e.g., *TLE* 695: *mi malena larthia puruhenas* = I am the mirror of Larthi Puruhena; and *TLE* 752: *tite cale:atial:turce malstria:cver* = Tite Cale to his mother gave this mirror as a gift). The subjects incised on the mirrors frequently refer to the world of women; their interpretation is therefore easier than that of the tomb frescoes, to which they are occasion-

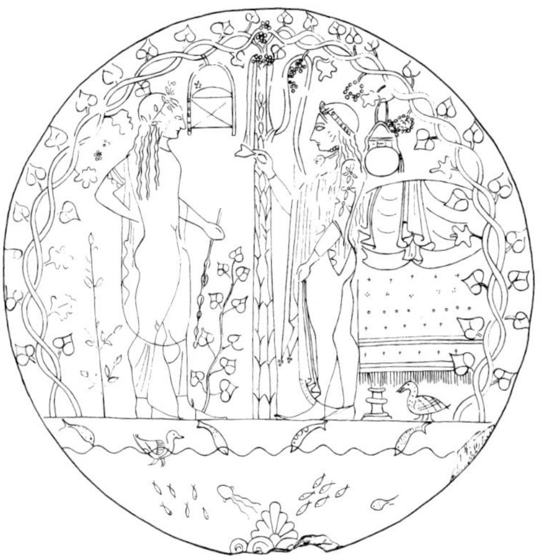

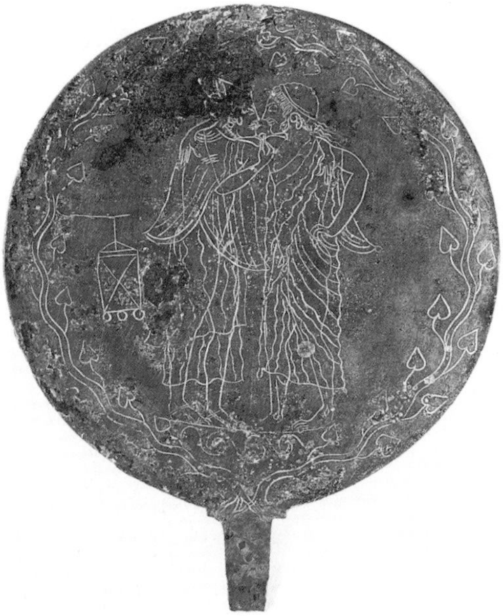

Fig. 195 Engraved mirror with young couple. From Tarquinia. Late sixth century B.C. Bronze. Diam. 13.6 cm. Berlin, Staatliche Museen—Preußischer Kulturbesitz—Antikensammlung Fr 32.

Fig. 196 Engraved mirror with couple embracing. Late sixth century B.C. Bronze. Rome, Museo Etrusco di Villa Giulia 51164.

ally related in style. But the majority of the scenes on mirrors are mythological, mostly inspired by Greek myths, yet often with characteristic Etruscan additions and alterations.

Several mirrors from Tarquinian tombs have been attributed to local workshops. One of the finest was found in 1830 (probably in the Tomb of the Bacchantes); it is now in Berlin (FIG. 195). The lower part of the disc, set off by a horizontal line, shows the surface of the sea with leaping dolphins, a duck, and diving fish. The main scene is framed by a bower of twisted ivy and vines supported by a central pillar sheathed by leaves. On the left stands a long-haired, wreathed and draped young man holding a cane. He faces an elegantly dressed and bejeweled young woman, who welcomes him with a flower in her raised right hand. Behind her is their bed with a thick fringed and patterned mattress and a mantle draped over it. The intimate setting is indicated by a *cista* and an aryballos suspended from the branches above.

A mirror in the Villa Giulia in Rome shows an embracing couple in transparent drapery (FIG. 196). Below their feet are crests of waves, and the scene is framed by an ivy wreath. Beside the woman a *cista* is suspended; this again hints at the private domestic setting in which the lovemaking takes place. On a mirror from Tarquinia in London a wreath of myrtle or laurel frames a group of three people standing above an exergue decorated with a vine, a crouching silenus, and a dog (FIG. 197). On the left of the main scene a fantastic tree with fanlike tiers of flowers and pendant fruits serves as a perch for a pigeon. In the center stands a woman in a transparent dress who seems to adjust with her right hand a veil draped over her *tutulus*. A bearded man in a mantle gesticulates in front of her; behind her stands a draped young man holding a branch in his left hand and eloquently raising his right index finger. This may perhaps represent part of a wedding ceremony with the father of the bride handing her over to the bridegroom. The style of the figures strongly recalls that of the frescoes in the Tomb of the Baron (see FIG. 183), while the exotic tree has parallels in the grove of the first room of the Tomb of Hunting and Fishing and of the tree beside the fountain in the Tomb of the Bulls (see FIG. 181).

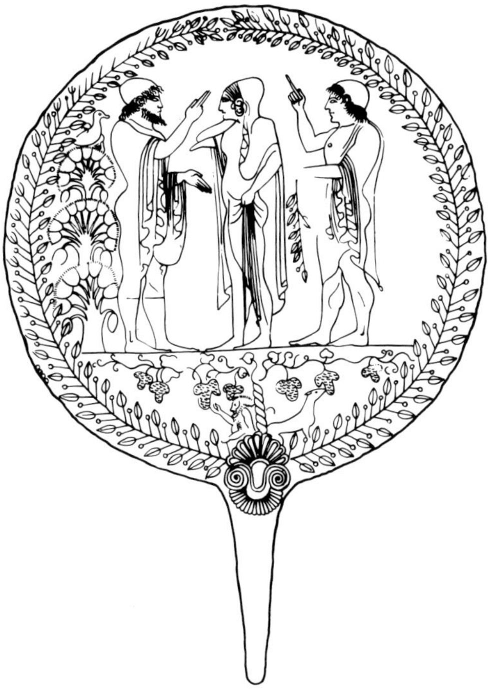

Fig. 197 Engraved mirror with a woman between two men. From Tarquinia. Late sixth century B.C. Bronze. Diam. 12.4 cm. London, The British Museum GR 1814.7-4.915 = *CSE* Great Britain 1.1, no. 16.

Apart from such domestic scenes depicting the life of women, the main subjects chosen for the decoration of mirrors were mythological, the figures often accompanied by inscriptions giving their names. Usually divinities of the Greek pantheon or heroes of Greek myth are represented; they are recognizable either by their attributes or by the names inscribed beside them, which give the Etruscan form of their Greek equivalents. Of the approximately three thousand surviving mirrors made between about 540 and 200 B.C., about half have engraved decoration, and about three hundred are inscribed with names. The earliest inscriptions appear about 490; a number of them name the owner, or the donor, the majority of them female; such inscriptions are testimony to the literacy of Etruscan aristocratic women. In some cases men seem to have owned mirrors; in the Hellenistic Tomb of the Ceicna Family (*Tomba dei Ceicna*) at Castiglione sul Lago, for example, the urns excavated from the chamber were exclusively male, yet among the grave goods was a mirror of third-to-second-century date engraved with two youths facing each other in short tunics and Phrygian caps; they probably represent the Dioscuri (Vatican, Museo Gregoriano Etrusco 16262). However, most mirrors were probably made as gifts for women, presumably as wedding presents.

Fine tang mirrors were produced in many Etruscan cities. Besides Tarquinia, there must have been workshops in Vulci, Orvieto, Bolsena, Chiusi, Perugia, and surroundings, the sites where the greatest number of mirrors were found. Occasionally particularly luxurious specimens were cast with relief decoration and inlaid with silver, such as the mirror in the British Museum with an Etruscan myth (FIG. 198): Herecele (Herakles) abducting Mlacuch; it was probably made in a workshop at Vulci. Two other fine mirrors in the same rare technique have come from the Vulci region: one with a relief of Eos and Kephalos (Vatican, Museo Gregoriano Etrusco 12241) and one with Minerva, Herakles, and Iolaos (Paris, Cabinet des Médailles 1288).

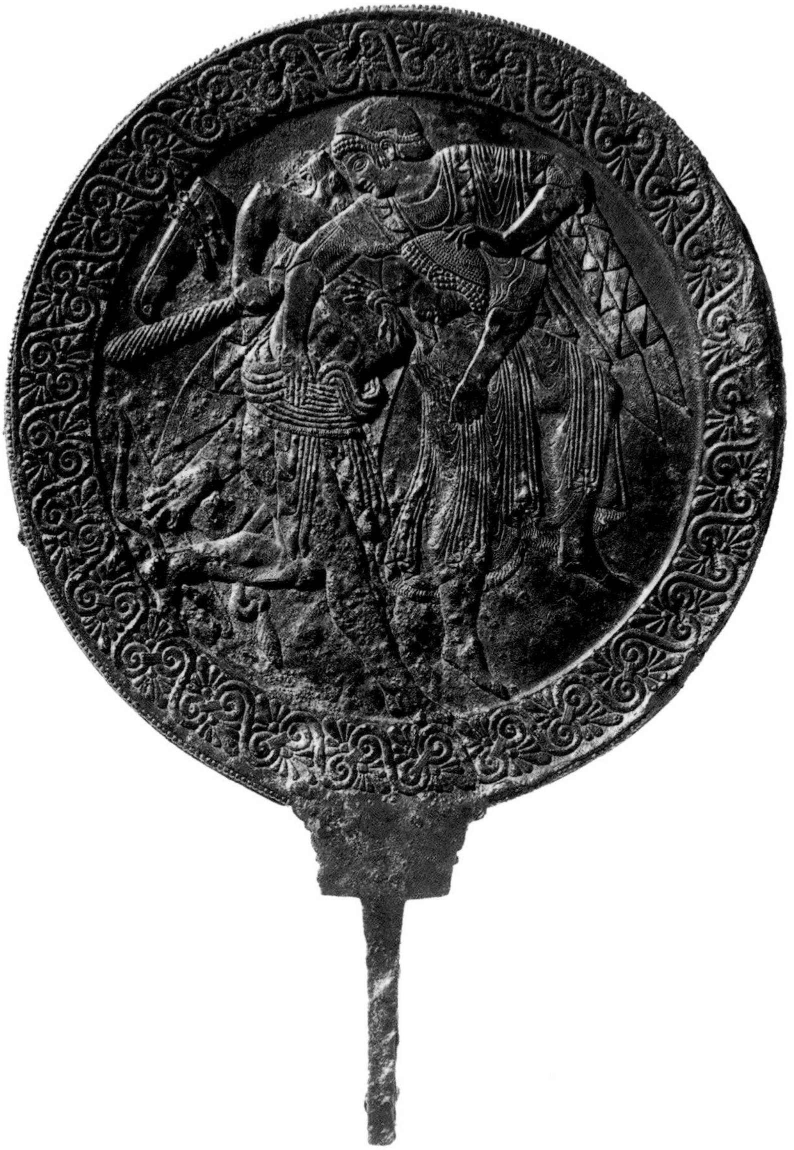

Fig. 198 Relief-decorated mirror with Herecele abducting Mlacuch. First quarter of fifth century B.C. Bronze inlaid with silver. Diam. 18 cm. London, The British Museum GR 1772.3-4.74 = *CSE* Great Britain 1.1, no. 20.

Archaic and Classical mirrors were cast with a tang that was fitted into a handle made of ivory, bone, or wood and sometimes decorated with carved and painted reliefs; few of these handles have survived, however, because of the perishable nature of their material. This type of mirror remained in use until about 300 B.C. Another large group of mirrors was cast in one with an elaborate bronze handle that usually ends in the head of a ram or a hind. The production of these mirrors begins in the first half of the fourth century and, in inner and Northern Etruria, lasts until the second century.

From about 400 B.C. onward mirrors were cast from an alloy containing a higher proportion of tin than used previously. Such a composition ensured a lighter color of the metal and therefore a clearer reflection, as well as greater hardness and thus resistance to scratches and corrosion—particularly important for the highly polished mirror surface.

A mirror with cover was developed in Greece in the fourth century and introduced to Etruria. It was particularly effective in protecting the polished mirror, while at the same time reflecting light. These mirrors consisted of two hinged valves, the lower being the mirror itself with its convex polished surface, the upper being a lid with a slightly concave inner surface, which closed over the mirror disc without touching it, its rim fitting into a groove around the outer edge of the disc. The inside of the lid might be polished or silvered to reflect light onto the face of the person using the mirror. The lid's outer surface was usually decorated with cut-out bronze-relief figures that had been worked in repoussé and chased, and whose back had then been filled with lead to give the reliefs strength and attach them to the background. Etruscan covered mirrors were similar in construction, but instead of being worked freehand in repoussé, the reliefs on top of the lids consisted of a circular sheet of bronze that was hammered into a matrix. This resulted not only in duplication of many scenes but also in the rather coarser and thicker forms of the figures. The themes represented on the Etruscan mirror lids include mythological subjects, particularly from the circle of Aphrodite and Dionysos, but also incidents from the *Iliad* and *Odyssey*. Where the provenance of such mirrors is known, they come mainly from Southern Etruria (Tarquinia, Cerveteri, Tuscania, Vulci), and they were probably made there.

Yet another type of covered mirror of the Hellenistic period, with the circular bronze disc set in a rectangular wooden lidded box, is represented on a number of ash urns from Volterra, where they are depicted in the hand of the deceased woman reclining on top of the lid.

Many handle mirrors found in tombs have had the polished surface intentionally made useless by incising across it the inscription *suthina* = pertaining to the tomb, funerary.

FUNERARY ART IN NORTHERN ETRURIA

Chiusi

Much of the subject matter represented on the reliefs carved on the ash chests, cippi, and sarcophagi of Chiusi can be compared with that of the painted tombs of Tarquinia and of Chiusi itself, but a number of scenes are peculiar to Chiusi and deserve special mention, in particular with regard to the role played by women.

Among the earliest relief-decorated fragments are those of a stepped circular funerary monument (an altar?) from Poggio Gaiella, a gigantic tumulus containing numerous tombs of different periods. Some of the carved fragments (striding warriors and galloping horsemen) were excavated in the 1960s and are in Chiusi;

others, from the former Casuccini collection, are preserved in the Museo Archeologico Regionale in Palermo. Of the latter, one (inv. 8450) shows a dance of lamentation by a chorus of women holding each other by the hands and following a draped musician to the right. One woman, looking to the left and slightly raising both open hands sideways, appears to be at the center of the (circular?) chain of her companions, trying to break out. They all wear long belted dresses and short capes covering their shoulders and breasts. A similar upper garment is worn by the female figures from the seventh-century temple of Prinias in Crete and by the Greek statuette found at Auxerre (see FIG. 66); this sub-Daidalic fashion, probably mediated through Magna Graecia, lingered on in Etruria well into the sixth century. That these women are mourners is suggested by other fragments of the same circular monument that show the battle over a fallen helmeted warrior and a file of marching warriors piped along by a draped auloi player. The dance probably took place before or during the lying in state of the fallen hero; a fragment of his funerary bed with a woman standing by its head is preserved. There is also a fragment with a wrestling match between two nude athletes watched by arbiters, probably a scene from funerary games. A number of these figured scenes are carved with a lotus-and-palmette frieze. This unique funerary monument probably dates from the second quarter of the sixth century.

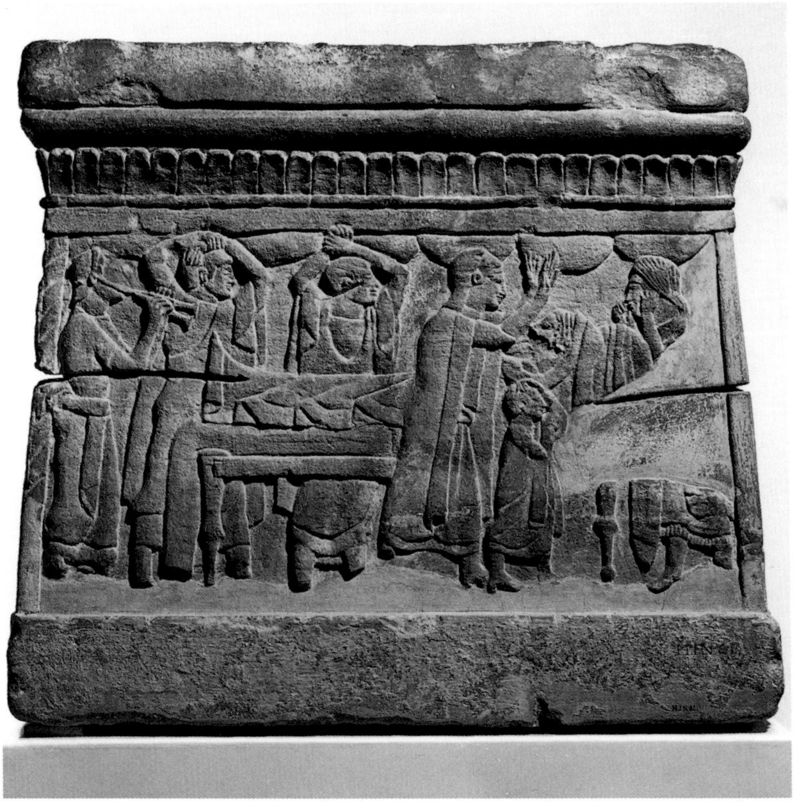

Fig. 199 Relief on a cippus base: lament for a dead woman. From Chiusi. First quarter of fifth century B.C. *Pietra fetida*. H. 47 cm. Copenhagen, Ny Carlsberg Glyptotek H 205.

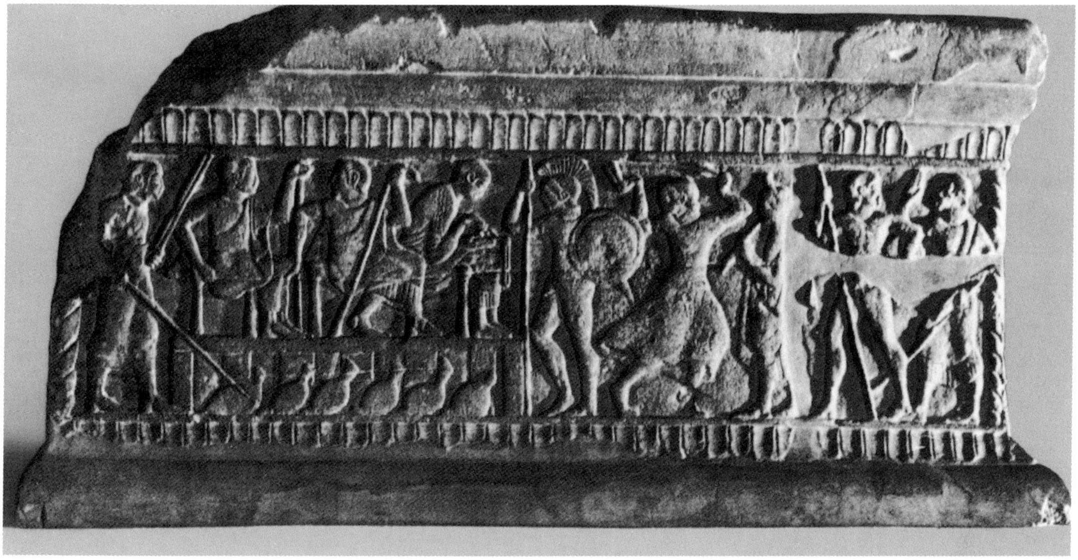

On a cippus in Copenhagen a dead woman is lying in state under a canvas canopy that is rolled up and tied at intervals to hang in swaglike semicircles from the molding at the top of the panel (FIG. 199). Other representations show that this part of the funerary ceremony appears to have taken place in a tent rather than inside a house. The deceased woman lies on a bed with turned legs, her head propped up high, and the hair covered by a veil. In front of the bed stand a child, his left hand raised to his head in a gesture of mourning, and a woman who lifts both hands in lament. At the head of the bed another woman is lacerating her cheeks. Two men behind the foot of the bed rest their arms on top of their heads, seizing one wrist with the other hand. On the left of the scene stands an auloi player with his instrument tied to his head by a halterlike leather mouth band. This is clearly a family mourning a wife and mother. Children are very rarely represented in Archaic art and are characterized merely by their small size, as diminutive adults rather than with chubby, childish proportions.

Fig. 200 Relief on a cippus base: judges of game seated on a tribune. From Chiusi. Early fifth century B.C. *Pietra fetida*. H. 39.5 cm. Palermo, Museo Archeologico Regionale NI 8385.

Athletic games and chariot races in honor of the dead appear both on Chiusine reliefs and on the walls of Tarquinian tombs. A base from Chiusi, however, may represent a public event (FIG. 200); this is suggested by the two magistrates or judges and a scribe sitting on a wooden stand, underneath which are displayed six wineskins—the prizes for the winners in the games. The scribe bends over his tablet to write down the names of the victors. In front of the tribune stand some of the participants: a nude helmeted warrior with greaves, lance, and shield who competed in the armed dance; a dancing girl whirling around, castanets held high and dressed in the typical transparent chiton and jerkin; an auloi player; a nude athlete with a spear; and, framing the scene on either side, an arbiter with the staff of office. On an adjoining side of the base is a triga race in front of a row of tufted trees.

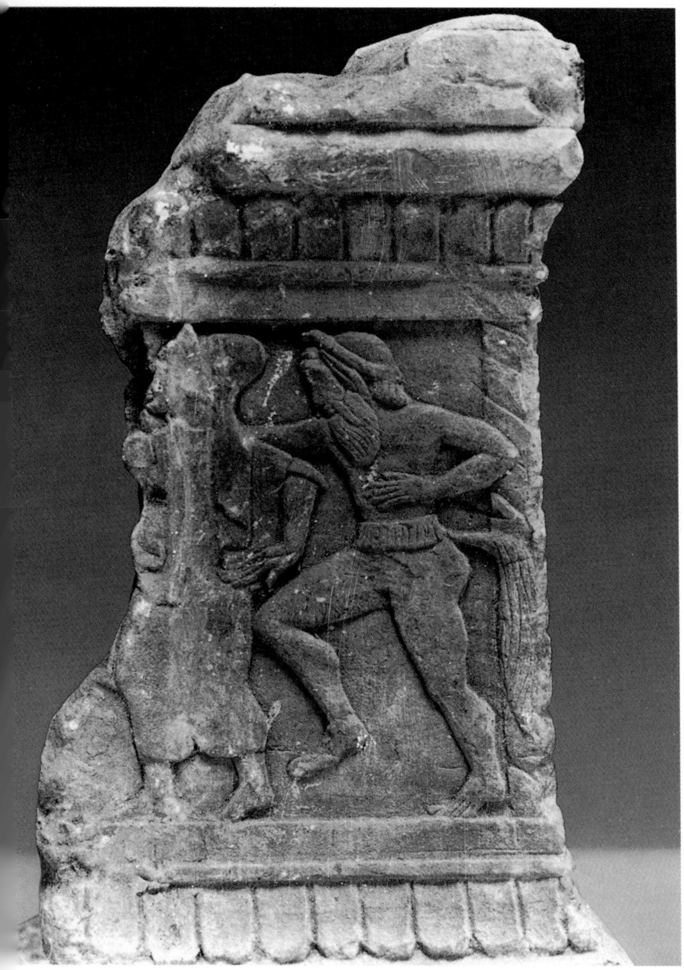

Fig. 201 Fragmentary relief on a cippus base: dance of a woman and a man disguised as a satyr. From Chiusi. Early fifth century B.C. *Pietra fetida.* H. 48 cm. Chiusi, Museo Archeologico Nazionale 2284.

More unusual, probably scenic, performances are represented on a base in Copenhagen (see FIG. 202) and on a fragment in Chiusi (FIG. 201). The latter shows a dancing man disguised as a satyr with a bearded mask and horse's ears as well as a horsetail attached to the back of his wide belt. He follows a dancing woman, whose *tutulus* is draped with a part of her mantle and crowned by a tall diadem. This form of headdress seems to be worn by women impersonating maenads on other reliefs with masked satyrs. The scene probably shows an apotropaic purificatory dance performed in connection with funerary rites. Livy tells us (7.2) that in 364, when a plague had broken out in Rome, mimes (Lat. *ludiones*) were brought from Etruria to perform dances, accompanied by flutes, during the games instituted to appease the wrath of the gods. The actions of these Etruscan mimes were held to be efficacious in such a calamity. (We know that the Latin word for actor, *histrio*, is derived from the Etruscan *ister.*)

The base in Copenhagen shows a different scene (FIG. 202). Two masked men in pointed hats, cloaks, and winged boots are whirling axes above their heads and chasing after two women who are hurrying to the right. One of the women carries on her head a tray with bread or cakes, while the other, looking back at the pursuers, carefully balances a large drinking cup in front of her. The scene has been convincingly interpreted as a mimic reenactment of an episode in the Greek myth of the Argonauts: the life of the blind seer, King Phineus, was threatened by starvation until he was rescued by Zetes and Kalais, the sons of the god of the wind, Boreas. Phineus had been punished by the gods with blindness and with daily visitation by the Harpies, rapacious females who snatched away all food and drink set before him. In exchange for Phineus's revealing to the Argonauts how to reach their goal, the two brothers pursued and killed the Harpies, thus saving Phineus's life. By reenacting this mythical salvation of essential food supplies, the Etruscan actors disguised as the Boreads and the women representing the Harpies probably symbolically ensured the eternal nourishment of the deceased. Again we note how the Greek model is subtly altered to serve a specific Etruscan interpretation. Such scenes prove the existence, at least from the later part of the sixth century, of scenic performances in Etruria in a funerary context in which women were participants.

Mime performances were not confined to Chiusi, as demonstrated by a black-figured neck-amphora by the Micali Painter (see FIG. 145), an artist active at Vulci from about 520 to 500 and in contact with the wall-painters of Tarquinia. On the body of the vase, which may well have been commissioned for a funerary rite, the painter has shown in abbreviated form all the events connected with games in honor of the dead. Here we meet again the chorus of satyrs or sileni; the pairs of women (maenads?) with tall, draped headdresses; nude boys dancing with castanets; and judges or trainers overseeing the athletics, boxing, and chariot racing. The latter competition is depicted in cunning shorthand by simply showing the heads and front legs of the horses appearing behind the goalpost. In addition there are a boy climbing a pole, and two bearded (masked?) characters, one of them a dwarf or child, who may be actors.

Such elaborately staged funerary games and performances were not reserved for aristocratic men. Women, too, appear to have received these honors. In the wall-paintings of the Tomb of the Monkey at Chiusi (named after the monkey depicted in a lopped tree on the rear wall of the tomb chamber), a red-robed, veiled lady, probably the tomb's founder, sits under a parasol on a stool with lion's feet, her feet on a footstool decorated with apotropaic eyes. She watches the jugglers and dancers, athletes, boxers, wrestlers, horsemen, and chariots, whose activities are painted on the walls around her. The scene directly in front of her—a girl dancer whirling around while balancing an incense burner on her head and accompanied by an aulos player beside a large basket—recalls the earlier fresco of the same subject in the Tomb of the Jugglers at Tarquinia (see FIG. 188) and shows that there must have been patterns that could be copied. The use of a template is suggested by the figures of the two boxers facing each other, one seen from behind, the other from the front, with identical but reversed outlines. These paintings date from the end of the Archaic period, about 480–470 B.C.

Other subjects of funerary nature appear most frequently on the reliefs of Chiusine cippi. Banquets with the participation of both sexes, accompanied by music, are frequently shown; they probably represent the feast in honor of the dead. But there are also scenes of daily life in which women play the major part: on another face of the cippus in Copenhagen is a group of women, two of them seated opposite each other and three standing and framing them, all engaged in examining pieces of cloth or mantles (FIG. 203). The two seated ladies may be the mothers of a bridal pair.

A seemingly similar scene is shown on a cippus in the Museo Barracco in Rome (FIG. 204). Here the two seated persons are a young man with shoulder-

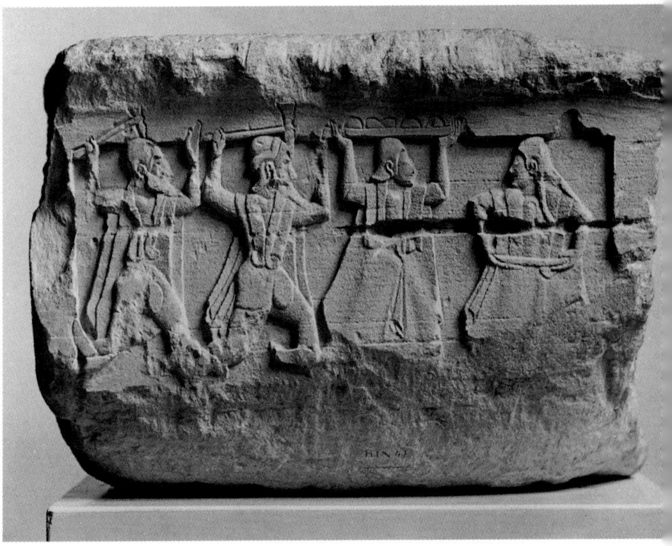

Fig. 202 Relief on a cippus base: actors performing. From Chiusi. Last quarter of sixth century B.C. *Pietra fetida*. H. 37 cm. Copenhagen, Ny Carlsberg Glyptotek H 204.

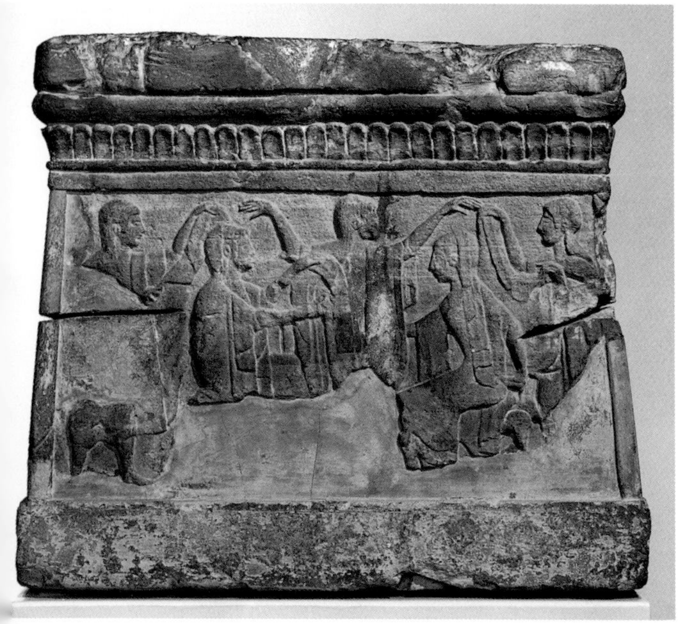

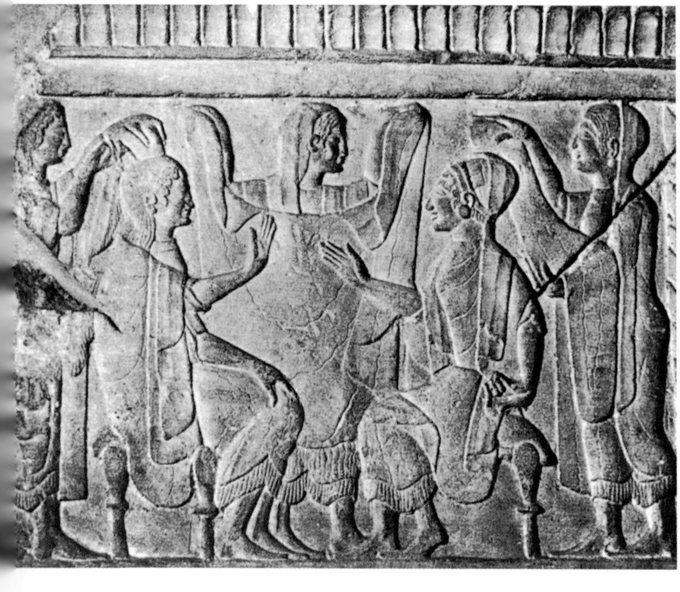

Fig. 203 Relief on the other side of cippus base, figure 199: women examining pieces of cloth.

Fig. 204 Relief on a cippus base: marriage ceremony(?). From Chiusi. Ca. 490–480 B.C. *Pietra fetida*. H. 40 cm. Rome, Museo Barracco 201.

length hair and a woman with her hair done up in a *tutulus* and covered by a veil. They look at each other and have each raised a hand toward the other. All three standing women behind them wear veils over their hair, and each holds up a piece of cloth or a mantle. This may be a young couple being shown the trousseau.

It seems that in one part of a wedding ceremony the bride and bridegroom were covered with a single mantle. A fragmentary relief carved on one long side of a house-shaped ash urn in Chiusi (Museo Archeologico Nazionale 2260) probably shows this part of the rite: on the right side two wreathed men hold up a fringed mantle horizontally, covering with it the heads and shoulders of three people standing beneath it. The central figure, seen from the front and entirely wrapped in a mantle, is likely to be the bride; she is flanked on either side by a man in profile who holds her arm; presumably they are the bridegroom and the girl's father. To the left of this group are three men: a wreathed auloi player, a man holding a branch and dressed in the pointed headdress of the priest who does divination (Lat. *haruspex*), and a third man who is wreathed and carries a branch. The presence of the priest, the wreaths, and the branches indicates that this is a solemn religious ceremony.

Tomb-paintings and funerary reliefs from Chiusi have given us insights into the rituals and clothing in this part of inner Etruria. By looking at a number of funerary monuments from further sites in Northern Etruria, we shall note that different forms of monuments prevailed there, and other customs were observed, a confirmation of the strongly regional character of Etruscan civilization.

Volterra

At Volterra stable economic conditions based on agricultural and mineral wealth appear to have permitted the continuity of the established social order. In the city and in the rural regions surrounding it a particular type of grave stela was developed during the sixth century for the monumental tombs of eminent aristocratic men, showing them in their social aspect of warrior or priest. We have first noticed this practice at Vetulonia, where the armed and helmeted figure of Avele Feluske

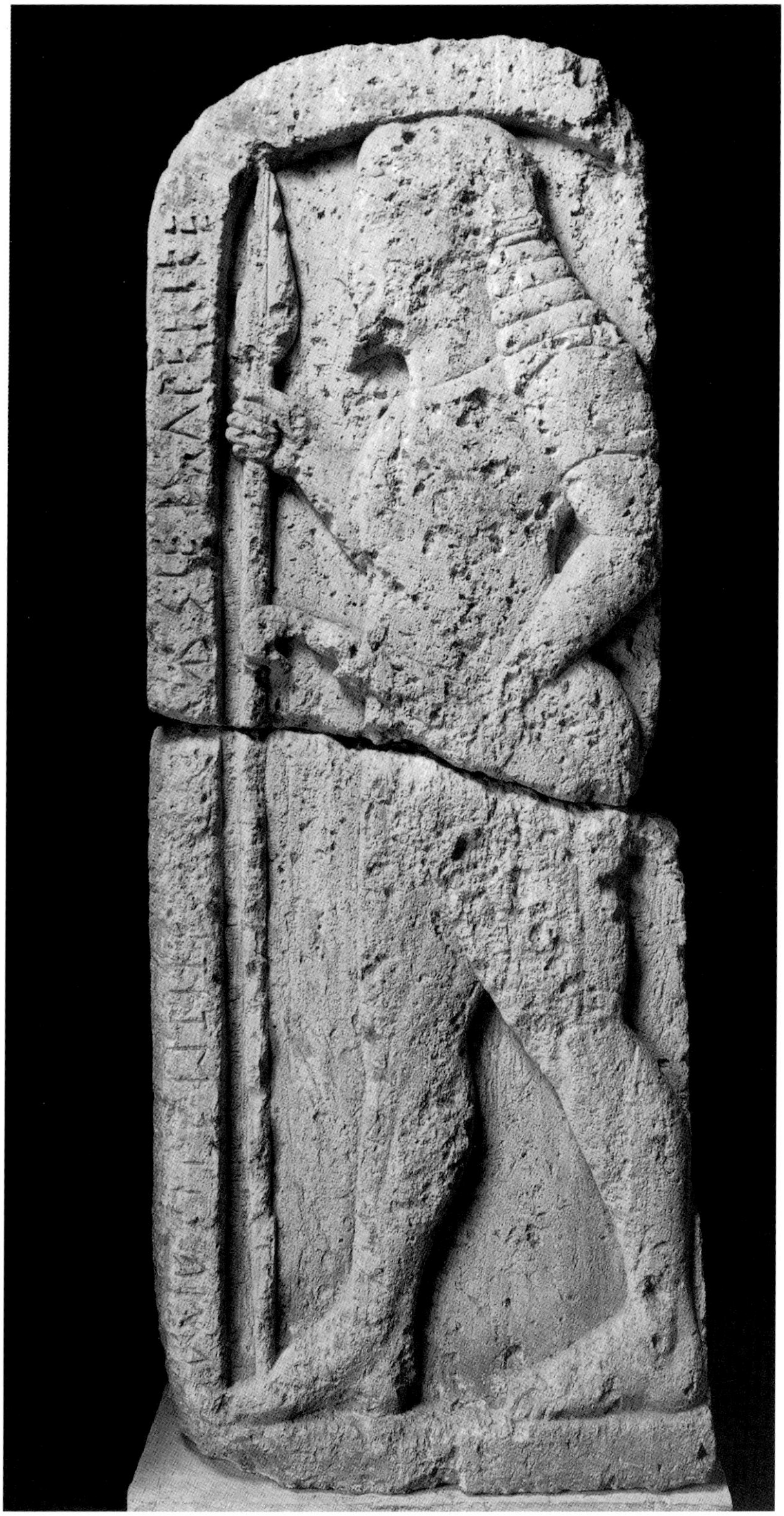

Fig. 205 Inscribed funerary stela of Avile Tite. From Volterra. Third quarter of sixth century B.C. *Nenfro.* H. 1.72 m. Volterra, Museo Etrusco Guarnacci.

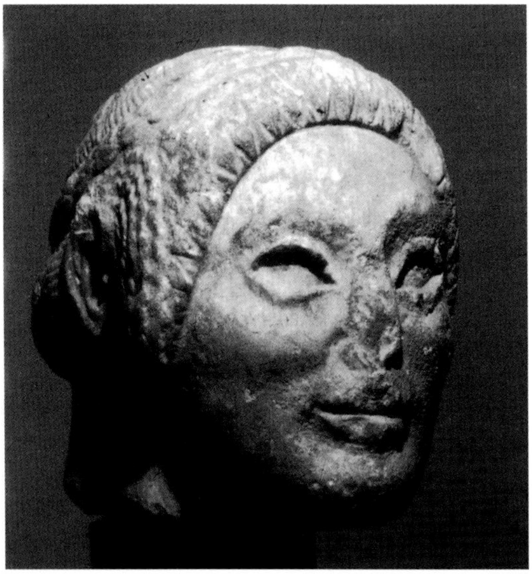

Fig. 206 Head of a cult statue (Apollo?). From Volterra. Ca. 500–480 B.C. Marble. H. 31.5 cm. Volterra, Museo Etrusco Guarnacci, Lorenzini collection.

was engraved on a rectangular stela (see FIG. 67). A fine Volterran stela of the third quarter of the sixth century is distinguished by being oblong with a rounded top; the figure of the deceased aristocrat is carved in low relief within a frame on which his name, Avile Tite, is inscribed together with the (damaged) name of the dedicator (FIG. 205). A bearded man with long, horizontally furrowed hair and dressed in a short tunic, Avile Tite walks in profile to the left, holding a spear in his right and a sword with a curved handle in his left hand. His massive, muscular body betrays East Greek prototypes.

A unique over-life-size marble head of Late Archaic date (ca. 500–480) from the Lorenzini collection may be part of a cult statue of a youthful god (FIG. 206). The round face with eyebrows carved in relief and almond-shaped eyes (once inlaid) has a slightly smiling mouth; it is framed by stylized locks carved in series of triangles, dressed at the back around a fillet, and crowned by a wreath. The artist was clearly inspired by heads of Greek kouros figures, but the vigorous, swelling features and the abstract, geometric treatment of the hair at the front are characteristic of the Etruscan interpretation of a Greek model.

Fiesole

Toward the end of the sixth century, stone stelae and cippi carved in low relief appeared as tomb markers in the area north of the Arno, from Pistoia and Artimino in the west to Londa in the east and Sant'Agata in the north, with the majority centered on the Fiesole region. So far, forty-one such monuments have been discovered. The inspiration for them may have come from Volterra, and particularly Pisa, where there must have been workshops using the local marble for funerary monuments. Some decorative elements derived from Chiusine models can also be identified, but there is no doubt that an independent school of sculpture flourished in the middle Arno region, imbued with the prevailing East Greek flavor.

A stela from Sant'Agata in the Mugello, now in the Museo Archeologico of Florence, shows a stocky, helmeted, and booted warrior holding a spear and a small round shield in profile to left. The sunken field of the rectangular stela is framed by the tongue pattern that frequently adorns the moldings of Chiusine monuments, and its horizontal top ends in a stylized palmette.

Also in the Museo Archeologico in Florence is a trapezoidal stela carved with two superposed fields showing a horseman below and a banquet above (FIG. 207). In this relief a bearded man reclines on a couch and turns toward his wife who, rather than sharing it with him, sits decorously upright on a chair at the head end.

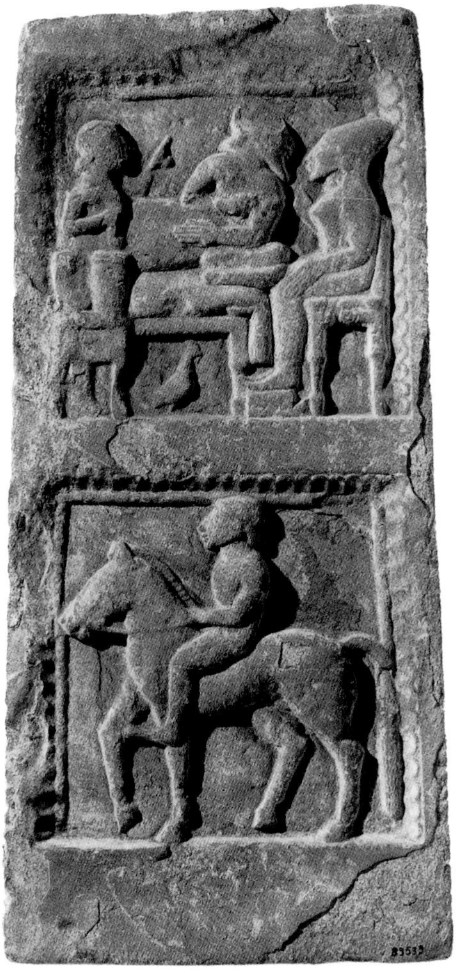

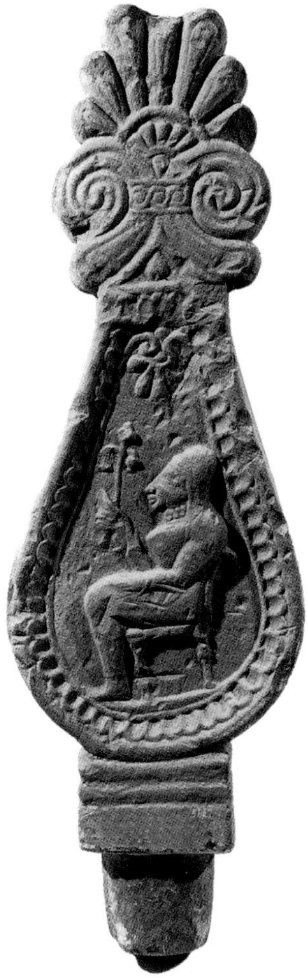

Fig. 207 Funerary stela with reliefs of banqueting and a horseman. Late sixth century B.C. Limestone. Florence, Museo Archeologico 87846.

Fig. 208 Funerary stela with relief of enthroned woman. From Londa. Last quarter of sixth century B.C. Limestone. H. 1.04 m. Florence, Museo Archeologico 5862.

A servant at the foot of the couch stands behind two stamnoi and holds a juglet and wine strainer. The seated lady contrasts with the custom observed in Southern Etruria and Chiusi and may represent a survival of the older fashion of both sexes sitting up while drinking and dining (pp. 93f., 111); but it is also possible that an Ionian custom is shown here. The same custom appears just once at Tarquinia, in the pediment of the Bartoccini Tomb (*Tomba Bartoccini*). There the owner of the tomb is depicted lying alone on his bed; turning toward his wife, who sits behind him on a throne, he lays his hand on her shoulder.

A stela from Londa was erected in honor of a lady who is represented enthroned on one face of the pear-shaped main part of the monument, a veil draped over her *tutulus* and a flowered branch in her right hand (FIG. 208); on the other face of the monument is carved a watchful sphinx with one paw raised. The stela is surmounted by volutes and a palmette; its unusual shape recalls the circular or horseshoe form of the grave stelae that became the characteristic monuments of the necropolises of Bologna in the fifth century (see FIGS. 247, 248).

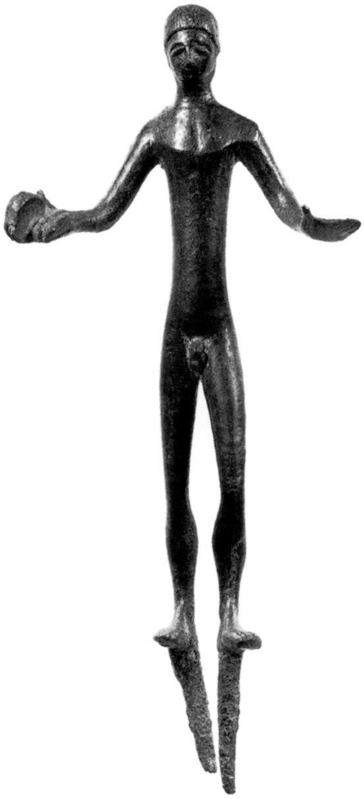

Fig. 209 Youth from of a group of votive statuettes. From Fiesole. Early fifth century B.C. Cast bronze. H. 15.5 cm. Oxford, Ashmolean Museum 1977.235.

The main Etruscan sanctuary of Fiesole was situated in the hollow on the northern slope of the hill; a cult seems to have existed here as early as the seventh century, as indicated by the discovery of two male and one female bronze votive figurines of nudes in the Geometric tradition. The remains of a Late Archaic temple were identified in 1902 under the successor buildings of Late Classical, Hellenistic, and Roman dates at this site. The fragments of a block carved with the statue of a recumbent lion and with a frieze of lotus, palmettes, and spirals of Northern Ionian inspiration dating from the late sixth century are probably connected with this earliest temple; they were found in 1900 beneath the steps of the Roman temple and have been recognized as the crowning elements of a monumental altar. Stylistically these fragments are related to some of the Fiesole stelae and cippi and confirm the existence of local sculpture workshops. Bronze ex-votos of anatomical parts at this oldest temple suggest that it was dedicated to a healing divinity, perhaps Menerva. A votive deposit found in the third-century temple included a small bronze statuette of an owl, the bird sacred to Minerva, which would support this identification of the sanctuary's presiding divinity.

Votive Bronze Statuettes

Forty-four Archaic votive bronze statuettes, some of them still affixed to their stone bases, were found on the grounds of Villa Marchi on the southern slope of Fiesole, the site of a small sacred building of rectangular ground plan. The statuettes—women in long, clinging sleeved chitons and pointed headdresses as well as slim nude youths (FIG. 209)—mostly stand with their arms raised sideways and often hold pomegranates, flowers, and some round objects (perhaps cakes or cheeses). It has been suggested that they were dedicated to an underworld divinity. The bronzes were in all probability cast on the spot, for some rejects and slags from smelting metal ore have been discovered together with them.

At Arezzo a deposit of 180 bronzes was excavated in 1869 near one of the ancient city gates and named after a nearby fountain, Fonte Veneziana. The dedicants here probably were the inhabitants of the Etruscan city, who made their offerings to a healing divinity, though sanctuaries were often near places needing special protection, such as gates. Besides numerous statuettes of men and women, modeled on the nude kouroi and draped korai of Ionian Greek votive sculpture, the Fonte Veneziana yielded small anatomical ex-votos of human heads, eyes, and legs, as well as domestic animals, a clear indication of the popular, sanative nature of the cult. The offerings seem to have been made during the years 530 – 480 and are fairly uniform in style, which suggests that local workshops produced these relatively modest offerings. Though we do not know the divinity to whom they were dedicated, it is clear from the large percentage of representations of female figures (all dressed in the clinging Ionic chiton, pointed boots, and conical Etruscan *tutulus*) that women were prominent donors.

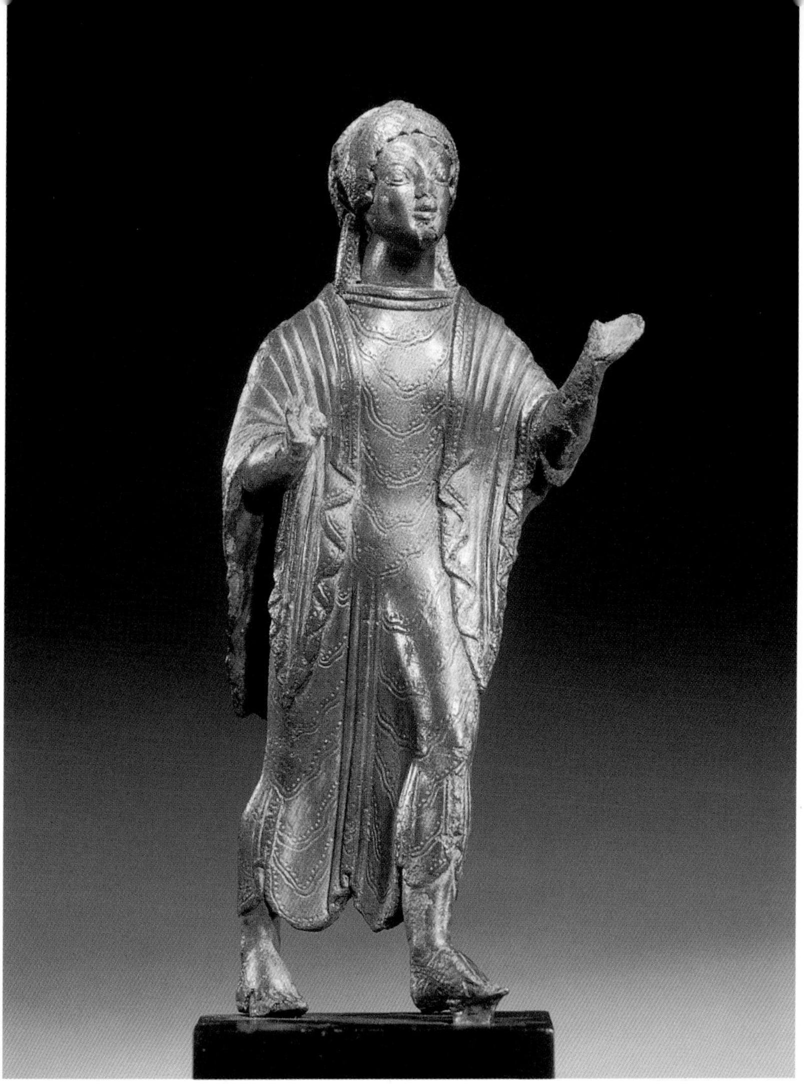

Fig. 210 Votive statuette of a wreathed woman with raised hands. From Lake Falterona. First quarter of fifth century B.C. Cast bronze. H. 14.3 cm. London, The British Museum GR 47.11-1.2.

Another important votive deposit was discovered in 1838 in a small mountain lake on the heights of Mount Falterona. More than five hundred bronze figurines; many pieces of raw, uncoined metal (Lat. *aes rude*); and some coins as well as iron and bronze arms were found in this lonely site. A cult appears to have been started here at the end of the sixth century, when the road across the Apennines from Northern Etruria to Romagna became important, and to have continued until the Hellenistic period. Again, the offerings seem to have been to a healing divinity, as attested by bronzes representing various human body parts. The main recipient of these ex-votos may have been Herakles, who was venerated in Etruria, often in association with springs. A particularly fine statuette of Herakles was among the bronzes recovered from the lake (BM *Bronze Cat.* 463). The number of statuettes of high quality is striking and includes representations of armed warriors and draped women. A wreathed woman in a short chiton of crinkly material, mantle, and sandals, walking with both hands raised in a gesture of prayer, is a telling example of the influence of Greek sculpture, increasingly engaged in the problems of showing the human body in movement (FIG. 210).

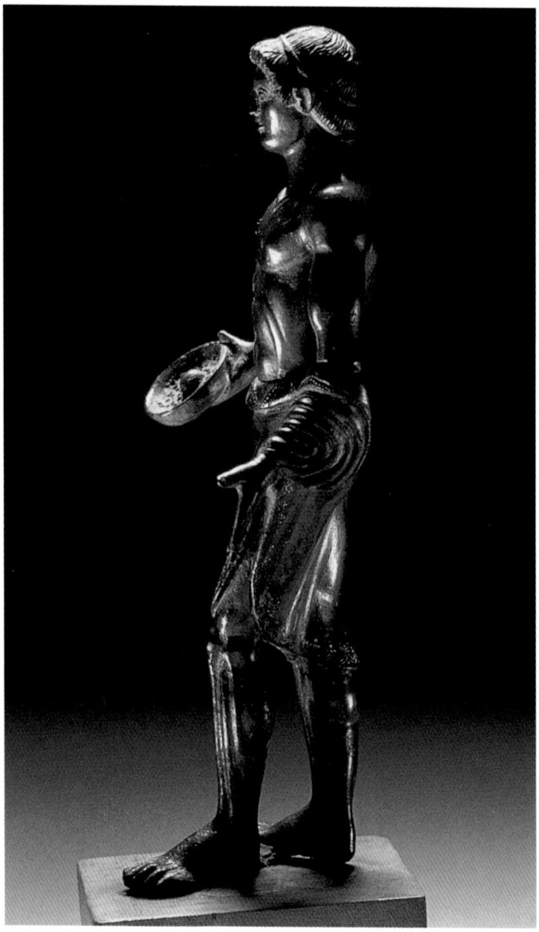

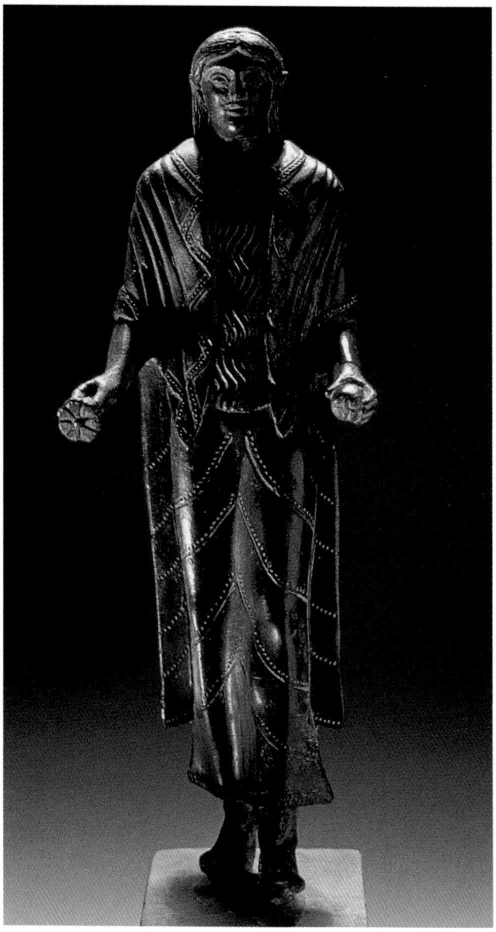

Fig. 211 Votive statuette of a young man. From Monte Acuto Ragazza. Ca. 480–460 B.C. Cast bronze. H. 22.2 cm. Bologna, Museo Civico Archeologico 27820.

Fig. 212 Votive statuette of a young woman. From Monte Acuto Ragazza. Ca. 480–460 B.C. Cast bronze. H. 22.3 cm. Bologna, Museo Civico Archeologico 27816.

A cult place was explored in 1882 at Monte Acuto Ragazza on a ridge road between the Reno and Setta valleys that connected the region of Fiesole with Marzabotto. Of the fourteen votive bronzes of human figures found there, a couple of statuettes originally mounted on a stone support in the open-air sanctuary are of particularly high quality (FIGS. 211, 212). A young man, draped around the waist in the short Etruscan semicircular cloak, pours a libation from a shallow omphalos bowl, while a young woman wearing chiton, rectangular mantle, and shoes holds out a flower and a pomegranate as offerings. Their serious faces reflect those of Greek kouroi and korai of the Severe Style, but the abstract, linear treatment of the drapery folds is characteristic of Northern Etruria. The statuettes were modeled by the same hand. In their similar size and solemn action they show that the couple who commissioned them were thought of as equals.

A beautifully modeled bronze votive group shows a draped couple standing each with an arm around the other's back while the man caresses the woman's breast (FIG. 213); they probably represent Tinia and Uni, the divine couple who correspond to the Greek Zeus and Hera. The man's long, flowing hair, crowned by a half-diadem, and his pointed beard and mustache suggest this identification. His consort, dressed in an elegantly pleated mantle and chiton, likewise wears a diadem and decorously complies with his lovemaking, while pulling up her chiton with her left hand. The nail holes in the corners of the square base show that the group was originally fastened to a support in a sanctuary. We do not know the provenance of this unique votive gift; it was probably made in Vulci.

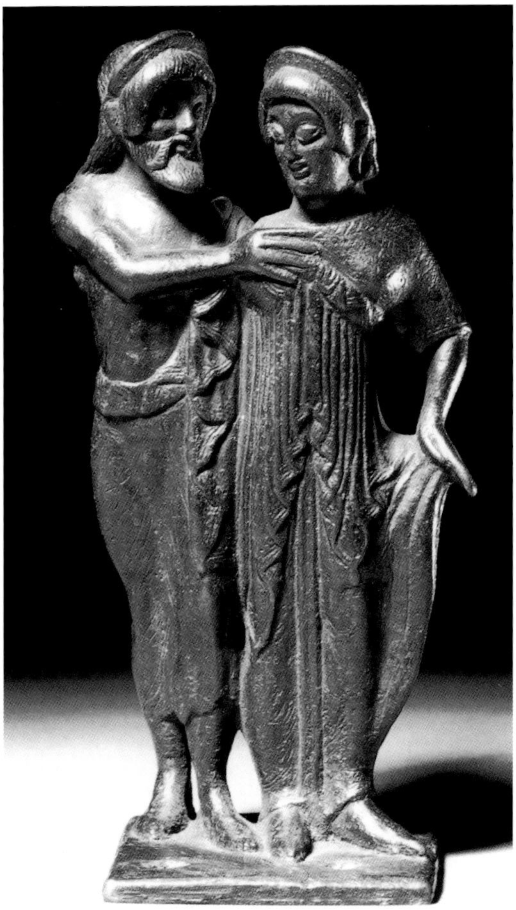

Fig. 213 Votive group of couple embracing (Tinia and Uni?). First quarter of fifth century B.C. Cast bronze. H. 11 cm. London, The British Museum GR 1824.4-53.11.

CONCLUSIONS

In summing up the evidence from the monuments of the Archaic period about the status of women, we can conclude that it confirms and amplifies what we learned from the preceding centuries: It is obvious that (upper-class) Etruscan women and wives were regarded with affection and tenderness, and that they were accorded the same honors in life and death as their consorts. They rode in carriages and moved about freely, participating in banquets with their husbands and being seen in public as spectators of games, seated on wooden tribunes (in the Tomb of the Bigas at Tarquinia, see FIG. 191), or as performers in rituals and theatrical displays (see FIGS. 201, 202). Such outdoor activities, depicted on wall-paintings and funerary reliefs, complemented those of the domestic sphere.

As a rule, during the Archaic period all women—whether wives and other female members of the family or slave girls—are shown fully dressed; dancing girls and female acrobats and musicians usually wear a characteristic costume consisting of a light chiton and a jerkin of thicker material, sometimes with cross-straps of (metal?) discs. Exceptional examples of nudity are two bronze utensils consisting partly of the figure of a nude girl. The first is the handle of a bronze shovel for burning incense, which is formed as a girl on whose nude body a votive inscription (*mi selvansl smucinthiunaitula*) identifies it as belonging to the god Selvans, the divinity of the woods and protector of the fields and boundaries (FIG. 214). The other utensil is an incense burner shaped as a three-legged table on which a girl acrobat balances on her head the stem for a (missing) incense bowl (FIG. 215). That she represents an entertainer at a banquet is suggested by a matching incense burner in Berlin (Fr. 693), which shows a nude youth dancing with castanets on an identical table.

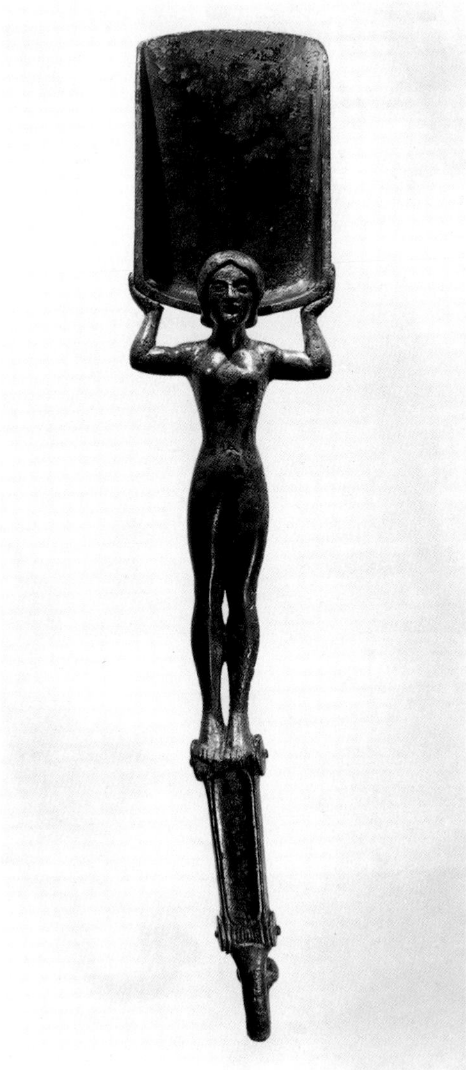

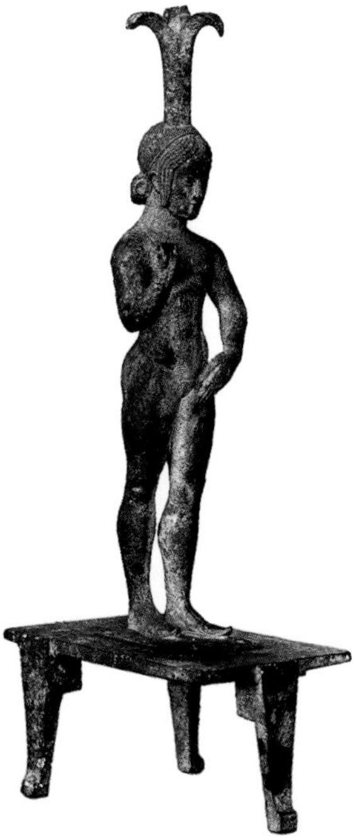

Fig. 214 Shovel with handle in the form of a nude girl. Second quarter of fifth century B.C. Cast bronze. L. 32.7 cm. Private collection.

Fig. 215 Incense burner in the form of a girl acrobat on a table. From Chiusi. Ca. 480–460 B.C. Cast bronze. H. 17.5 cm. London, The British Museum GR 68.5-20.51.

Female nudity is thus rare in Etruria in the Archaic period and, when represented, appears in a ritual or apotropaic context (cf. pp. 147 and 234), or it may indicate that the woman is a victim of violence or exposure (see FIG. 128). The archaeological evidence thus massively contradicts the notorious defamatory passages of the fourth-century-B.C. Greek historians Theopompos and Timaeus (quoted in Ath. 12.517d–518a) about Etruscan morals:

> He [Theopompos] says in the forty-third book that the women of the Tyrrhenians [i.e., Etruscans] are common property; they take great care of their bodies and they exercise in the nude, often together with men, sometimes by themselves, because they don't consider it shameful to

show themselves in that state. At table they lie down not with their own husbands but with the first to come of the other participants and they even drink toasts to whomsoever they wish. What is more, they drink a great deal and they are very beautiful to look at. The Tyrrhenians bring up all the children born not knowing who is the father of each. These children live in the same fashion as their foster-fathers, spending most of their time in drinking-bouts and in indiscriminate intercourse. To make love in public is not considered shameful by the Tyrrhenians, for that, too, is the habit of the country. And far from regarding such a thing as shameful, if the master of the house is engaged in making love and someone asks to see him, they say: "he is doing so and so," naming the act quite impudently. When they have parties, either with friends or with their families, they behave as follows: having finished drinking and feeling inclined for sleep, they make the servants bring in—with the torches still alight—sometimes prostitutes, sometimes beautiful boys, sometimes their own wives; once they have taken their pleasure with these, they make strong young men come and sleep with them. They make love and disport themselves, occasionally within view of each other, but more often they surround their beds with screens, made of interwoven branches over which they spread their mantles. Although they certainly have much intercourse with women, boys and young men please them even more. The latter are really good-looking in their country, because they go in for soft living and for having their body-hair removed . . . The Tyrrhenians have many establishments with specialists for depilation, just as we have barbers. When they go there, they let themselves be done, not minding being seen, even by passers-by.

Athenaeus also quotes (1.23d) the remark of Aristotle that the Etruscans eat with their wives, reclining at table with them under the same blanket, and that Etruscan slaves are very beautiful and better dressed than is usual with slaves, while he cites (4.153d) Timaeus's assertion that slave girls wait on the men naked.

The motivation and honesty of historians such as Theopompos and Timaeus were suspect already in antiquity, and their inherent anti-Etruscan bias has been shown up and explained by many modern scholars. Greek wives, particularly at Athens during the Classical period, did not participate in the feasts of their husbands, whereas courtesans did, and Greek writers therefore may have mistaken the liberty and equality enjoyed by married Etruscan ladies for licentiousness. But we need only recall the tender, decorous representations of Etruscan married couples in their aristocratic tombs and the careful recording of the names of fathers and mothers in funerary inscriptions to see the full absurdity and maliciousness of Theopompos's statements about the promiscuity of Etruscan women and their disregard for the paternity of their children. The translation of an epitaph from Tarquinia (*TLE* 888) may stand as an example: "Arnthi Metli was the wife of Larth Spitu, she lived sixty-four years and gave birth to three sons."

Male cupbearers, it is true, are frequently depicted in the nude in banquets, a custom adopted from Greece, as attested by numerous Attic vase-paintings, and therefore hardly a just cause for adverse comment on Etruscan morals by a Greek. The naked slave girls, whom Timaeus accused the Etruscans of employing, are conspicuously absent from the painted banqueting scenes, where female servants usually appear soberly dressed. Etruscan representations of homosexual lovemaking (in the Tomb of the Bulls [see FIG. 181] and the Tomb of the Bigas in Tarquinia [see FIG. 191], in the latter tomb among the slaves) cannot be taken as proof of a generally established sexual preference among the Etruscans. In view of the prevailing homosexual ethos in Classical Greece, Theopompos's disapproving moral tone strikes one as pure hypocrisy.

Another commonplace found in ancient literature is that of *tryphe*, the luxurious "soft living" and "gluttony" ascribed to the Etruscans. The critics lumped the Etruscans with the citizens of Miletos in Asia Minor and of Sybaris in Magna Graecia because of their love of pleasure. Timaeus reports (in Ath. 12.517d) that "the Sybarites wore mantles made from Milesian wool and from this sprang the friendship between the two cities. Among all the peoples of Italy, the Sybarites liked the Etruscans best, and among the Orientals they had a preference for the Ionians, because they were like them addicted to softness." The disapproval by poorer and therefore more austere Greeks of the opulence displayed by richer and more fortunate Greek and Etruscan cities was based on a mixture of jealousy, envy, and prejudice against different "barbarian" customs. A further, much-repeated commonplace that went back to Aristotle (Fr. 60, Rose, *Fragmenta Selecta*) was that of particular Etruscan cruelty. Etruscan pirates were said to tie their prisoners to rotting corpses. The misdeeds of Tyrrhenian pirates figured also in the *Homeric Hymn to Dionysos*, a fact that points to the long-standing rivalry at sea between Greeks and Etruscans.

Later Greek writers, such as the philosopher Poseidonios of Apamea (ca. 135–51 B.C.), whose works were excerpted by Diodorus Siculus during the second half of the first century B.C., were less biased. The Etruscans' former supremacy at sea and their rule over the larger part of Italy, their useful warlike inventions—such as the Tyrrhenian war trumpet for the organization of land forces—are mentioned in a fair-minded way by Diodorus Siculus (5.40), who explains the nation's present loss of glory partly by the ease of living, owing to the fertility of the Etruscan soil.

Even after romanization, the habit survived in certain areas of Etruria of mentioning in funerary inscriptions the name of the mother of a deceased person beside that of the father. Throughout Etruscan history, however, it was usually the case that a bride married into the family of her husband and was buried in his tomb or in that of his gens. Children received the patronym, whereas the matronym—a sign of the special consideration granted to Etruscan women in their society—appeared in a secondary position. Though the mention of the matronym distinguishes Etruscan women from their Greek and Roman sisters, it does not imply that Etruscan society was matriarchal, as has sometimes been assumed in the past. The existence of strictly agnatic tombs (such as that of the Cutu family at Perugia) in which only males descended directly from a common ancestor were buried, shows the supreme importance attached to filiation.

The continuing importance of goddesses in Etruscan religious belief during the Archaic period is clear. The ancient cult places and subsequently built big temples dedicated to them are eloquent proof of this fact. Their nature as divinities of fertility, nurturing, healing, but also of death and rebirth is attested by countless votive gifts and inscriptions and by images deposited in tombs or found in sanctuaries located in necropolises. Divine couples played a role in the Etruscan pantheon, as can be inferred from a number of representations that perhaps are meant for Tinia and Uni and hint at their sacred union. We recall the scene on a stone relief from Tarquinia (see FIG. 129) and the votive bronze group in the British Museum (see FIG. 213), as well as the frontal heads of a bearded god and a young goddess on terra-cotta antefixes(?) from the Cannicella sanctuary at Orvieto, who may represent Aita and Phersipnai.

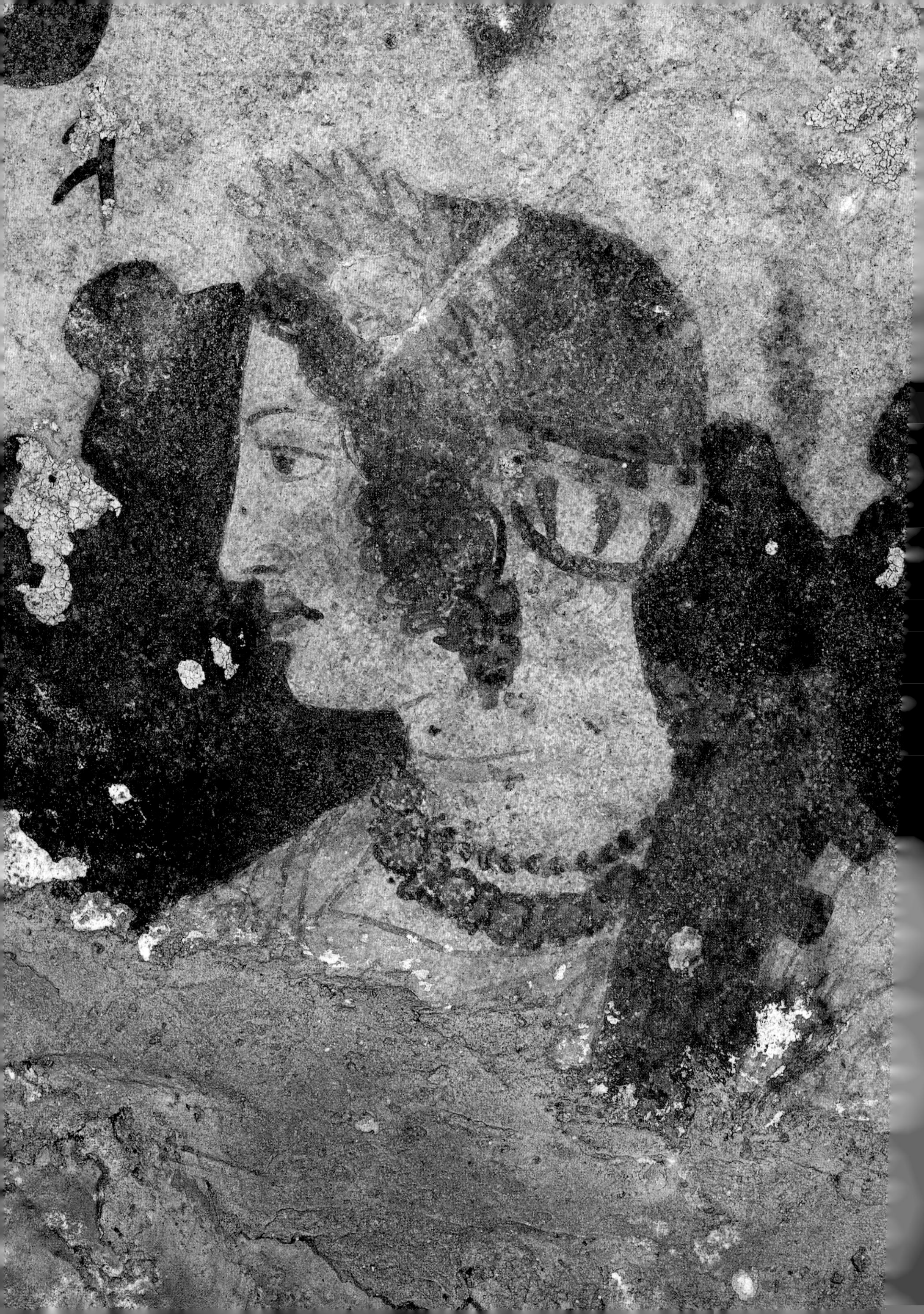

IV

Crisis and Renewal

The Fifth and Fourth Centuries

Detail of wall-painting: head of Velia, wife of Arnth Velcha, from figure 251.

RETRENCHMENT IN THE SOUTH

The rising power of Syracuse, culminating in the disastrous Etruscan defeat in the sea battle off Cumae in 474 B.C. (Diod. Sic. 11.51; Pind. 1.72), meant that the Etruscans gradually lost control over the shipping routes in the southern Tyrrhenian Sea. Eventually this affected the prosperity of the coastal cities—Cerveteri, Tarquinia, and Vulci in particular. The Carthaginians' ambition to expand their influence over Sicily had earlier been dealt a decisive blow by the Syracusan ruler Gelon (485–478). Allied with Theron, the Greek tyrant of Akragas (It. Agrigento), Gelon had defeated the Carthaginians under Hamilkar in the battle of Himera in 480 and reduced the Carthaginian sphere to the extreme western end of Sicily. The menace of barbarian invaders was traditionally held to have been overcome by the two great Greek victories in 480 B.C.—that of the Sicilians over the Carthaginians and that of the Athenians over the Persians in the naval battle off Salamis, which ended the Persians' attempt to conquer mainland Greece.

Gelon's victories enabled his successors to extend Syracusan rule both over all of eastern Sicily and over the territory of Anaxilas of Rhegion (It. Reggio) on the Italian mainland, thus gaining control over the Straits of Messina. Gelon's brother and successor, Hieron of Syracuse (478–467), pushed even further north toward Campania and sided with the Cumaeans in their conflict with the Etruscans in 474 (see p. xxx). Tangible testimony to the Etruscans' rout in this sea battle are three captured helmets dedicated by the Syracusan Greeks in the sanctuary of Zeus at Olympia. One of the two Etruscan helmets of the Negau type has a dedication with

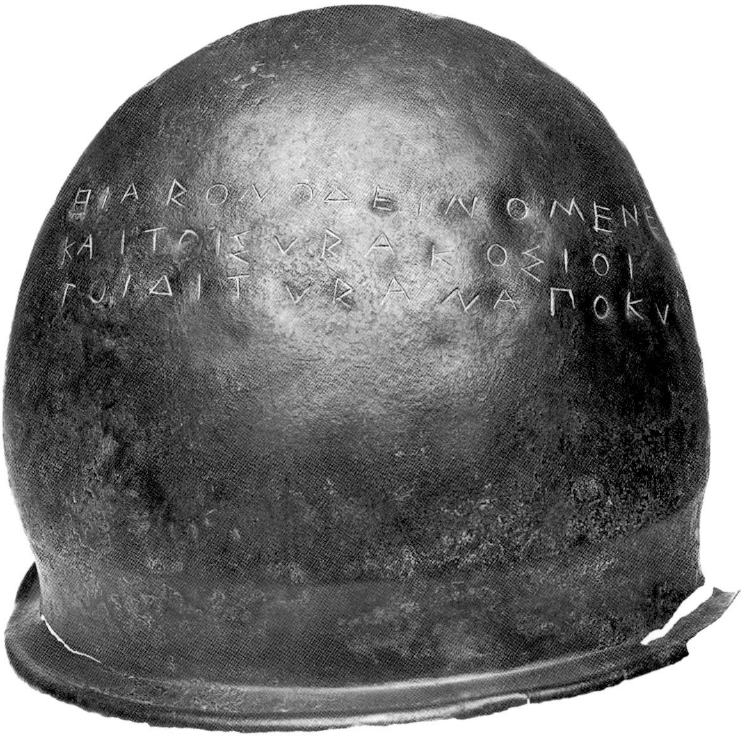

Fig. 216 Inscribed helmet of Negau type. From Olympia. Early fifth century B.C. Hammered bronze. H. 20 cm. London, The British Museum, BM *Bronze Cat.* 250.

three lines that tells us that Hieron, the son of Deinomenos, and the Syracusans gave (the helmet) to Zeus for the victory over the Tyrrhenians at Cumae (FIG. 216). The third helmet, of Corinthian type, bears a similar inscription.

To consolidate his influence in the Gulf of Naples, Hieron installed a Syracusan garrison on the island of Ischia. Despite the fall of the Deinomenid tyranny in 465, Syracuse again became active against the Etruscans in 453 by attacking the mineral-rich northern Tyrrhenian coastal areas as well as Elba and Corsica, ostensibly to suppress Etruscan "piracy," but more probably for economic reasons. The success of these naval raids by Syracuse testifies to weakened Etruscan power at sea, so ominously heralded by the defeat at Cumae twenty years earlier.

When, in 413, the Etruscans responded to Athens's appeal for help in her ill-fated expedition against their common enemy Syracuse, the Etruscan naval force sent to contribute to the siege of the Sicilian city consisted of only three ships (Thuc. 6.88.6).

In the first quarter of the fourth century, Dionysios I, tyrant of Syracuse (ca. 430–367), extended his rule over much of Magna Graecia and gained influence in the Tyrrhenian Sea (see p. 182 for the sack of Pyrgi) and in the Adriatic by colonizing the islands of Issa and Hvar on the Dalmatian side and controlling Ancona and Adria on the Italian shore. This Syracusan competition must have impinged on Athenian trade with the emporia in the Po valley, while Dionysios's attempted collaboration with the Gaulish invaders constituted a threat to Etruria.

The Economic and Artistic Consequences

The complex series of events that had disrupted the Archaic pattern of production, barter, and communication in the Mediterranean affected the Etruscan cities in different degrees. Particularly from the second half of the fifth century onward, the economic and social crisis in Southern Etruria was obvious. A number of events contributed to this crisis: the destruction of the trading partner Sybaris; the occupation of etruscanized Campania by Italic Samnites; and the upheavals in Lazio caused by the expansion of Umbro-Sabellian tribes into the coastal plains and by the expulsion of the Tarquins from Rome and the defeat of Porsenna's army at Aricia. But many of the inland cities—such as Civita Castellana (Lat. Falerii Veteres), Orvieto, and Chiusi, as well as Populonia, Pisa, Genoa, and Aleria on the northern Tyrrhenian coast and the harbors on the Adriatic coast and the cities of the Po valley—continued to flourish and even grow in importance.

An indication of the relative economic decline in Southern coastal Etruria is the decrease in the number of Attic vases found in the tombs there. The greatest number of banqueting vessels, particularly drinking cups, was imported there between ca. 500 and 475, but after the battle off Cumae the number dropped notably. The trading enclave of Gravisca near Tarquinia ceased to receive Greek merchants about the same time, and the flourishing commercial relations came to a halt.

Most of the sea trade will have consisted of cargoes of an impermanent nature, such as grain or metals, but the pottery that traveled with them has survived, and it provides a measure of the general diminution of commerce. The export of wine, for example, particularly from Cerveteri and Vulci, seems to have declined dramatically, as indicated by the drop in the number of Etruscan amphorae imported into Gaul.

Without the stimulus of close contact with Greek masters and models, the wall-paintings in the tombs of Tarquinia, for example, became repetitive in their themes and poorer in execution during the second half of the fifth century. Fewer grave goods were deposited, and their quality deteriorated, as did that of sculpture and bronzework. No great public buildings were erected, as the lack of architectural terra-cottas of that period indicates.

At Vulci we see an attempt to imitate the technique of Attic red-figured vase-painting by a painter—perhaps a Greek from Cumae or Reggio—who signed his name Arnth Praxias; he had a large following from about 480 onward (FIG. 217). But in this technique the red figures, instead of being

Fig. 217 Amphora in applied red-figure technique depicting Apollo carrying the infant Hermes, by Arnth Praxias. From Vulci. Second quarter of fifth century B.C. Pottery. H. 28 cm. Paris, Bibliothèque Nationale de France, Cabinet des Médailles 913.

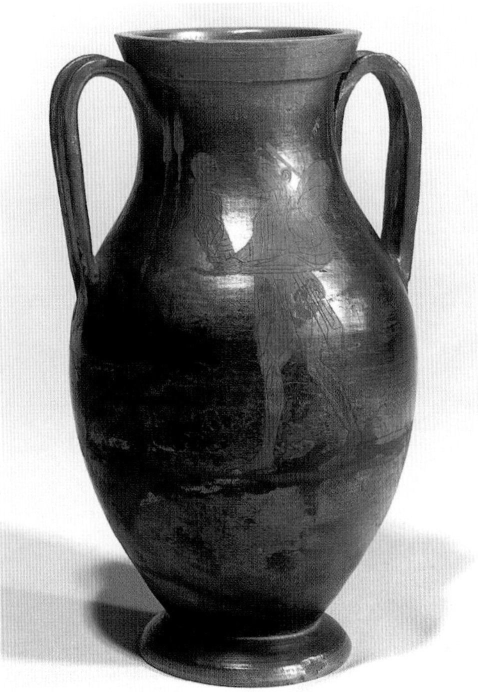

reserved in the black background, are painted on top of the solid black surface of the pot, their details incised through the red paint. The effect is far removed from the fluid and competent brush-drawn lines of red-figured Attic vases. It is possible that a branch of this workshop was active at Orvieto or Chiusi, where many of its products were found.

In Greece this period saw the flowering of Classical art after the bold experiments of the preceding generations of painters, sculptors, and architects. Etruria, however, seemed to languish, conservatively maintaining traditional formulae and only haphazardly responding to inspiration by foreign prototypes. An oddly eclectic and often archaizing style makes the exact dating of works created between ca. 470 and 350 somewhat difficult, particularly when they are found out of context.

At Orvieto and Chiusi the reduction in Attic pottery imports occurred only after the middle of the fifth century. The prosperity of these inland cities may be based on their agricultural productivity and the traffic across the Apennines and along the rivers Reno and Po to the Adriatic port of Spina.

CONTINUITY IN THE NORTH

At Spina the import of vases from Athens remained at a steady level between ca. 475 and 375, showing the sustained interest of the mainland Greeks in trade with this region. Finds in tombs of Bologna and Spina (and, beyond the Alps, in Central Europe) indicate that fine bronze vessels and utensils of Vulcian manufacture must have traveled north from central Etruria to the Po valley by the same trans-Apennine passes, at least during the first half of the fifth century.

Prosperity in Northern Cities

Populonia's acropolis was surrounded with impressive walls in the sixth century, while the fortifications linking the lower town and the port with the acropolis date from the fourth to the third century. Populonia owed its uninterrupted prosperity during this period largely to its mineral resources and the trade in Elban iron. The city does not seem to have suffered from the Syracusan incursions that affected other coastal areas of Etruria between 453 and 384, and no signs of crisis or retrenchment appear before the late second century. A special relationship with Athens is attested at Populonia by tombs that have yielded fragments and whole vases of fine Attic red-figured pottery. Outstanding among them are two hydriai by the Meidias Painter dating from 410–400 (Florence, Museo Archeologico 81947, 81948); they came from the trench tomb of a young noblewoman, rich in bronze utensils and jewelry. Particularly significant is a kylix tondo from the circle of the Penthesilea Painter; before firing, it was inscribed in the Southern Etruscan alphabet with the artist's signature: *metru menece* (*TLE* 370), his Greek name, Metron, having been etruscanized to Metru. He was perhaps an Etruscan craftsman working in Athens rather than a Greek in Populonia; we have no way of deciding this intriguing question.

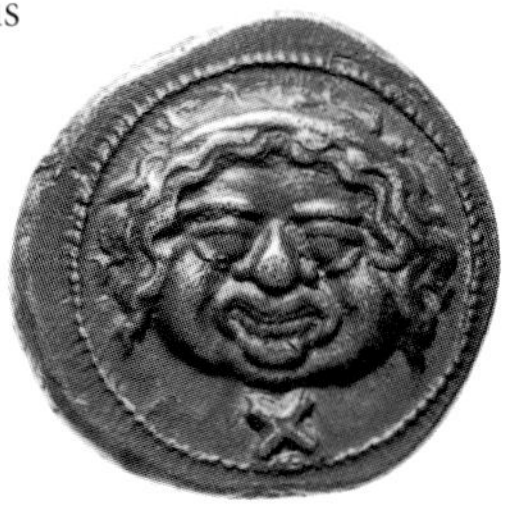

Splendid bronze banqueting utensils, some made in Southern Etruria, some of local manufacture, such as various types of situlae and candelabra, also attest to the continued wealth of the citizens.

A sure sign of the economic and entrepreneurial capacity of Populonia is the creation of coinage, a means of exchange whose value was guaranteed by the city. A number of gold coins with a lion's head (see FIG. 147) and silver coins with a Gorgoneion are presumed to have been struck by Populonia. A silver didrachm with the latter device and the value sign X, similar to that in figure 218, was excavated in 1981 in Prestino near Como in a level dated to the third quarter of the fifth century. This is not only the northernmost findspot of a coin believed issued by Populonia, but, so far, also the only securely dated archaeological context for such a coin. Recently a coin with a Gorgoneion has been discovered as far west as the area between Tarragona and the mouth of the river Ebro in Spain. A mixed hoard of silver coins found in 1868 near the walls of Volterra contained perhaps the oldest coins from Etruria; besides imported Phokaian types of the mid-sixth century B.C. and issues of Massalia, there were fifteen Etruscan pieces with a Gorgoneion and twenty-four with a Pegasos.

Fig. 218 Coin with Gorgoneion and value mark X, similar to coin excavated at Prestino. Probably struck at Populonia. Third quarter of fifth century B.C. Silver (Type Sambon 35). Weight 7.95 g. Oxford, Ashmolean Museum 7.

A series of bronze coins with a head of Minerva on the obverse and an owl, a crescent, stars, two small globes, and the legend *Pupluna* (Populonia) on the reverse has been dated to the late fourth–third century through associated material in excavated tombs of Populonia. At this period it is likely that the need to pay troops led many Etruscan cities to issue coins.

Vetulonia, by contrast with Populonia, seems to have suffered a decline in the second half of the fifth century, as indicated by the scarcity of finds from that period. The discovery in a ditch near the walls of the acropolis (Mura dell'Arce) at Vetulonia of about 125 bronze helmets of Negau type, distorted, battered, and incised with the word *haspnaś* (presumably a family name), suggests that they belonged to the members of a single clan. Dated to the early fifth century, these helmets may be testimony of events that recall the private war against Veii of the clan of the Fabii, an aristocratic Roman family (see below).

In the second half of the sixth century stone walls had been built around the acropolis of Roselle. The city, like Populonia, continued to prosper, probably at the expense of her neighbor Vetulonia. However, in the late fourth and early third centuries the walls of Vetulonia were repaired, and the city seems to have had an economic revival. To this period belong coins with the inscription *vatl*.

TRADE RELATIONS WITH MASSALIA

How closely Massalia was involved with the shipping and trading circuit of Northern Etruria, Corsica, and the south of France is strikingly documented by two inscriptions, in Ionian Greek and in Etruscan, preserved on a lead tablet found at Pech Maho, an ancient Iberian settlement on the coast of Languedoc. The Greek text, dating from the second quarter of the fifth century, reused a tablet already inscribed in Etruscan. In the latter appear the personal names of two individuals, *Venel* and *Utavu*, who were involved in a business deal at *Mataliai*, that is, at Massalia. The script resembles the few Etruscan inscriptions of the first half of the fifth century that have been excavated at Aleria on Corsica. This Etruscan "colonial" city, which had replaced the original Phokaian settlement, was ideally situated to carry on trade, not only with Etruria proper, but also with Liguria, Massalia, and other Greek colonies on the south coast of France and with Iberian settlements, such as Pech Maho. During the fifth and fourth centuries Aleria seems to have flourished on agricultural and mineral resources, including iron production. The Phokaian Greek scribe, perhaps using this lead tablet because the Etruscan text on it could be disregarded, recorded a complex transaction about the acquisition of a boat at Emporion (modern Ampurias, a colony of Massalia on the Spanish coast north of Barcelona) by two Greek merchants, one named Kyprios the other Heron of Ios. Witnesses to the complicated agreement were a number of persons with Iberian names, such as Basigerros, Bleruas, etc. The ethnic diversity of the participants and the sophisticated business agreements contracted by them make the tablet of Pech Maho one of the most fascinating documents of the commercial activities in the northern Tyrrhenian after the battle off Cumae.

SOCIAL TENSIONS

While the economic decline in the Southern Etruscan cities can, to some extent, be measured, it is much more difficult to trace the social and political changes that took place there during this period. We have noted the increasing wealth and importance of the population of the great Etruscan centers, evident from the more egalitarian form of their tombs during the sixth century. This as well as the large number of funerary inscriptions giving a personal and a family name shows that the size of this "middle class" in individual Etruscan cities was comparable to the demos of the Greek city states. Such a development must have led to tensions between the expanding urban population and the old aristocratic ruling class of landowners and entrepreneurs with its monarchic system of government. It is likely that the emergence of "tyrants" in a number of Greek colonial cities in South Italy and Sicily was mirrored by similar events in Etruria. Greek tyrannies, such as that of the Deinomenids of Syracuse, of Anaxilas of Rhegion, and Aristodemus of

Cumae, may be compared with that of the "ruler" of Cerveteri, Thefarie Velianas, whose name and building activities have been revealed by excavations at Pyrgi and the inscriptions found there.

DEVELOPMENTS IN ROME

Similar developments are seen in Rome, where King Servius Tullius was credited with the introduction of a new census system, a national register for taxation and military service that divided the people into new tribes and assigned them to one of five classes according to their wealth. This replaced the older gentilicial system of the *curiae*, which had implied regional divisions and aristocratic clan loyalties. The object of this reform was probably to ensure that the *centuries*—the levy units of the newly assessed army—represented a mixture of the whole community by comprising soldiers from all the tribes. The subsequent rule of Lucius Tarquinius Superbus, the last king of Rome, was a typical populist tyrannical monarchy. It ended with an aristocratic coup, which brought about the Tarquins' expulsion from Rome and the eventual establishment of a republic. In this confused situation, the city seems to have suffered the incursion of another Etruscan king, Lars Porsenna of Chiusi (Tac. *Hist.* 3.72; Plin. 34.139), who, having established his reign over a large area of inner Etruria, decided to intervene in Lazio and descended the Tiber valley. An army led by his son Arruns was decisively defeated by joint Latin and Cumaean forces in the battle of Aricia in 504 B.C.

From the names of some of the consuls from patrician families (the Larcii, Aquilii, Veturii, Tarquitii, Volumnii, etc.) it seems that a substantial Etruscan aristocratic element remained in Rome for a long time. They and the majority of the ancient Roman aristocratic families, whose power had been restricted by the Servian reforms, were soon trying to reassert their original authority in the city. The social struggle between this conservative class, jealous of its old prerogatives, and the *populus*, intent on political-military innovations that offered hope for the aspirations of the entire urban community, was to occupy much of the next centuries.

An exceptional late example of the Archaic gentilicial Roman conception of warfare was the private war (*bellum privatum*), traditionally fought by the aristocratic Roman clan of the Fabii against Veii about 480. In the course of the struggle between Veii and Rome, in which both tried to gain possession of bridgeheads occupied by the enemy on "their" side of the Tiber, Rome aimed at controlling Fidenae on the left bank, while Veii occupied a fort on the Janiculum Hill on the right bank of the river. To counteract this menace to their city (and probably to their own land), the 306 members of the clan of the Fabii, accompanied by their clients, mounted a frontier post on the river Cremera and engaged the Veientines in a series of skirmishes and cattle raids. The enterprise ended in the semilegendary battle in which the whole Roman clan, except one boy, was killed by the Etruscans (Livy 2.50.1–11; Dion. Hal. 9.19.1–22.6).

Veii herself had retained a monarchical government. Lars Tolumnius, the king of Veii, was killed in single combat by Aulus Cornelius Cossus in the course of the Veientine War of 437–435, which secured Fidenae for Rome. The rule of kings in many of the other Etruscan cities was becoming anachronistic by the late fifth century and may have led to Veii's isolation in her final struggle with Rome (406–396). The rule of an Etruscan *lucumo*, who in all probability exercised princely as well as priestly power, had given way to oligarchic government by colleges of magistrates elected for a limited period.

A ray of light is thrown on this (occasionally violent) process of change by a Latin inscription set up in Tarquinia in the first century A.D. by a descendant of Aulus Spurinna, son of Velthur. This (fragmentary) eulogy mentions that Aulus, who was *praetor* three times, deposed Orgolnius, king of Cerveteri, probably during the conflict between Tarquinia and Rome in 358–351.

The aristocratic families of the big cities, who shared these magistracies among themselves, seem also to have been in charge of a reorganization of the vast tracts of land that had been denuded of minor rural settlements during the Late Archaic period. The wealth-creating "middle classes" of merchants and manufacturers in the great cities probably lost importance in this new political climate of oligarchic reassertion, while a large class of agricultural serfs worked for the *domini* in control of the resettled rural areas.

AN OUTLINE OF ETRUSCAN RELIGION

During the Archaic period we could observe in the representations of Etruscan divinities an increasing assimilation to the Greek Olympian gods. By the fifth century B.C. this process was well advanced, and the identification of such divine beings and mythological figures and their iconographic dependence on Greek prototypes is often facilitated by inscriptions giving the Etruscan version of the Greek names of the gods and heroes represented. Such inscriptions are found most frequently on engraved mirrors, but also on wall-paintings in tombs, on painted pottery and, as votive texts, incised on bronze statuettes. It is, however, impossible to reconstruct a coherent and complete Etruscan pantheon from such incomplete evidence, for religious beliefs were formed by different local traditions and changed over time.

However strongly the outward form of Etruscan religion was visually indebted to Greek models, in character it differed profoundly from that of both the Greeks and the Romans. Ancient authors were aware of this difference, and there was a widespread view that the Etruscans were a "nation devoted beyond all others to religious rites (and all the more because it excelled in the art of observing them)" (Livy

NAMES OF ETRUSCAN DIVINITIES AND THEIR GREEK AND ROMAN EQUIVALENTS.

ETRUSCAN	GREEK	ROMAN
Aita (god of underworld)	Hades	Pluto
Apulu/Aplu	Apollon	Apollo
Aritimi/Artumes/Aretume/Artemes	Artemis	Diana
Atunis	Adonis	
Calu[s] (divinity of death)		
Cavatha/Cavtha/Cath[a] (solar goddess with underworld aspect)		
Cel (mother goddess)	Ge	
Culśanś/Culsu (divinity of the gates)		Janus
Fufluns/Pacha	Dionysos	Bacchus
Hercle	Herakles	Hercules
Laran/Maris	Ares	Mars
Letham (underworld divinity)		
Mania (wife of Mantus)		
Mantus (underworld divinity)		
Men[e]rva	Athena	Minerva
Nethuns	Poseidon	Neptune
Nortia (goddess of destiny)		
Phersipnai	Persephone	Proserpina
Selvans (god of boundaries and fields)		Silvanus
Sethlans	Hephaistos	Vulcan
Śuri (solar god with underworld aspect)	Apollo	Pater Soranus
Thanur (goddess of birth)		
Thesan	Eos	Aurora
Thufltha (goddess)		
Tin/Tinia/Tina	Zeus	Jupiter
Tinas Clenar	the Dioscuri	
Tivr/Tiur (divinity of the moon)		
Turan	Aphrodite	Venus
Turms (messenger god)	Hermes	Mercury
Uni	Hera	Juno
Usil (sun god)		
Vei	Demeter	Ceres
Veiovis/Veiove		Dispater
Veltha/Veltune/Voltumna (national god of Etruria and god of vegetation)		Vertumnus/Vortumnus

5.1.6), and that Etruria was the "begetter and mother of superstitions" (Arn. 7.26). Seneca described how the Etruscan conception of man's relationship with the gods and with the signs they send differed from Roman conceptions:

> This is the difference between us and the Etruscans, who have consummate skill in interpreting lightning: we think that because clouds collide, lightning is emitted; they believe that clouds collide in order that lightning may be emitted. Since they attribute everything to divine agency, they are of the opinion that things do not reveal the future because they have occurred, but that they occur because they are meant to reveal the future. (*Q. nat.* 2.32.2)

In Graeco-Roman religion man stood at center stage in his pragmatic dealings with the gods, which, in Rome, assumed quasi-juridical, concrete forms. For practical reasons the Romans had recognized the importance of certain Etruscan religious usages and incorporated them into their own rituals. In proposing the religious laws of his ideal state, Cicero said that, if the senate so decreed, prodigies and portents had to be submitted to Etruscan *haruspices*, and Etruria should teach the *disciplina etrusca* to the leading men (*Leg.* 2.9.21).

As far as we can tell, the Etruscans themselves seem to have regarded their divinities as overwhelming powers who completely dominated man's every activity and imposed inescapable temporal limits on his and the nation's existence. It was the religious duty of the priests to discover the will of the gods, to interpret it, and, by scrupulous adherence to prescribed norms and sacrifices, to conform to it.

In contrast to the religion of the Greeks and Romans, that of the Etruscans was a revealed religion. The miraculous and wise infant Tages had imparted the *disciplina etrusca* to eminent aristocrats at Tarquinia, who wrote down his teachings, known as *libri tagetici*. Another prophetic being, a nymph by the name of Vegoia or Begoe, was held to be the author of books on the interpretation of lightnings, but she was also concerned with the confines of land and the inviolability of boundary stones.

The books of the *disciplina etrusca* have not come down to us. Only fragments of translations or compendiums of them have been transmitted, usually characterized by misunderstandings and distortions of the original elements of Etruscan beliefs and rituals.

The Etruscan religious writings were divided into several groups: the *libri haruspicini*, which dealt with the *haruspices*' art of inspecting the intestines of sacrificial animals for oracular purposes; the books of lightning (*libri fulgurales*), which contained the doctrine of the interpretation of lightning; and the books of rituals (*libri rituales*), a large collection of prescriptions for the modalities of cults, the founding of sanctuaries and cities, the division of fields and properties, and the system of ordering civic and military affairs, as well as special texts about the division of time and the limits set for the length of the life of individual human beings and for entire nations; the beyond and the rites for salvation in the new life after death were treated in the books of the underworld (*libri acherontici*), while the interpretation of omens and miraculous events came under portents (*ostentaria*).

Etruscan Texts

Surviving original Etruscan texts are extremely scarce. We have already mentioned the one incised on a large terra-cotta tile from Capua, found just outside the city in a necropolis area among terra-cotta fragments of a sacred building of the late sixth century (see FIG. 166). This tile has been recognized as a ritual calendar with prescriptions for the periodic cult of a number of deities, among whom Letham, presumably an underworld divinity, is mentioned particularly often; perhaps the sanctuary was dedicated to him. Also named are Calu, a god of the nether regions; Thanur, a goddess connected with births; and Larun and other divinities unknown elsewhere in Etruria. A separate sanctuary of Uni is mentioned, perhaps the large site at Santa Maria Capua Vetere north of Naples known as the Fondo Patturelli, where innumerable statues and statuettes of seated mothers with babies have been found.

The second Etruscan religious text that has partially survived was written in neat columns with black and red ink on a piece of linen that originally formed a linen "book" (*liber linteus*), folded concertina fashion. It once served as a liturgical calendar with prescriptions for certain public ceremonies and for sacrifices to be made on given dates to specific gods. Among these are Nethuns (Neptune), Veive, Cath(a), and Crapsti; wine (Etr. *vinum*) is mentioned, presumably for libation. The meaning of many of the approximately twelve hundred words preserved is still in doubt, but the number of repetitions reduces the number of different words to about five hundred. Written during the third or second century, the piece of linen was subsequently cut into strips and reused for wrapping the mummy of a woman in Egypt. The circumstances of this reuse are unknown, but it probably took place in the Ptolemaic or Roman period, destroying considerable portions of the text (five strips survived and could be joined up again). Despite this loss, it is the longest Etruscan inscription to have come down to us; it may be classified among the *libri rituales*.

The mummy was brought from Egypt in 1848/1849 and donated to the museum of Zagreb in 1862. The linen was preserved due to the dry climate of Egypt, while similar "books," of which there must have been many, have not survived in Italy. We see them in sculpture, however: a carefully folded rectangular parcel, obviously representing a soft, pliable material with a painted inscription on it, is carved next to the head of a reclining dignitary on the lid of a sarcophagus (FIG. 219). It was discovered in the Tomb of the Sarcophagi (*Tomba dei Sarcofagi*) in the Banditaccia necropolis of Cerveteri and dates from about the second quarter of the fourth century. Another example may be two pieces of folded material

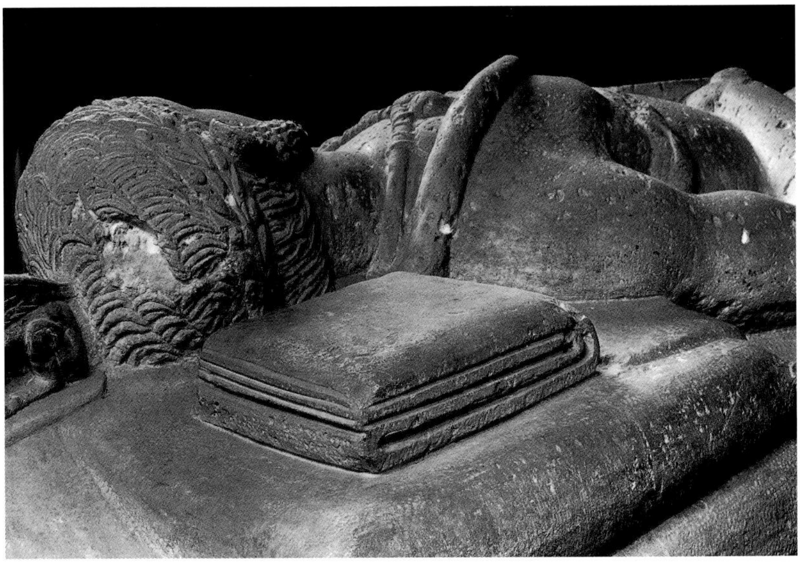

Fig. 219 Detail of the lid of a sarcophagus showing a linen book beside the head of the deceased. From Cerveteri. Second quarter of fourth century B.C. Painted Circeo marble. Vatican, Museo Gregoriano Etrusco 14949.

on top of a wooden chest represented among the reliefs of molded stucco in the Tomb of the Reliefs (*Tomba dei Rilievi*), a chamber tomb in Cerveteri dated to the third quarter of the fourth century. A further example is provided by a fragmentary sarcophagus from Chiusi in the Museum in Berlin (inv. E 33), on which the deceased is represented on his bed with his arm around a woman sitting next to him; beside her lies a neat pile of folded linen.

The prescriptive nature of the texts of the Capua tile and of the Zagreb mummy wrapping as well as the formulaic repetition of certain sentences reinforce the impression of a scrupulous concern with the correct performance of essential ritual acts. This preoccupation with the meticulous observance of cults may lie behind the judgments of later writers, mentioned above, on the particular religiousness of the Etruscans.

Groups of Divinities and Demons

However precise the prescriptions in the largely lost Etruscan cult texts may have been, the nature of the original Etruscan divinities seems to have been somewhat vague as far as their number, sex, and appearance was concerned. Perhaps divinity was at first thought of as numinous powers that manifested themselves in different forms, and the amorphousness of this conception was modified only under the strong influence of the Greeks' anthropomorphic images of their Olympic gods. Space forbids a detailed discussion here of these well-known Etruscan great gods, identifiable by their assimilation to their Greek and Roman counterparts; but uniquely Etruscan divinities and demons, as well as special religious practices will be dealt with here.

The Etruscan pantheon remains distinguished from that of the Greeks by a number of groups of divinities and of male and female spirits whose nature is not easily defined. Among the rather mysterious colleges of divinities—whose names and numbers are unknown, though referred to obscurely by ancient writers on native Etruscan traditions—are the higher gods shrouded in mystery (*dii superiores* or *involuti*), who adjudicated on when Tinia was to hurl the third and most dreaded of his thunderbolts, that of destruction. Also mentioned are the twelve complices (*dii consentes*), equally advisers of the supreme god and known to be pitiless; other casters of lightning are the Nine Gods (*novensiles*). All these groups were perhaps considered gods of fate. Besides there were the tutelary gods (*penates*), categorized into divinities of sky, water, earth, and human souls.

The texts on the *liber linteus* in Zagreb and on a lead tablet from Magliano refer to an undefined group of divinities called *eiser* or *aiser*, to whom certain sacrifices are due. Pairs of gods appear in the couples who rule the underworld, such as Aita and Phersipnai and Mantus and Mania. Twin gods like the Greek Dioscuri are also known in the Etruscan pantheon, as attested by a votive inscription by one Venel Atelinas to *tinas cliniiaras* = to the sons of Zeus (*TLE* 156; on a kylix by Oltos, found at Tarquinia). The messenger god Turms seems to have had two manifestations, one subordinate to the divinity of the sky, Tinia, the other to Aita, the ruler of the dead. Of uncertain sex, Veltha/Veltune/Voltumna was an ambivalent supernatural being. This divinity may be concerned with vegetation or may become a god of war or the Etruscan national god (*deus Etruriae princeps*, Varro 5.46).

The goddess Thufltha is named in two compartments of the Piacenza bronze liver (see p. 277), associated with Tinia. We know of no representations of Thufltha, but a number of votive inscriptions show that she was worshiped in the Hellenistic period. The finest of the votive bronzes dedicated to her is a statuette of a standing nude boy holding a goose, found together with an incense burner at Montecchio and now in the museum of Leiden. The statuette is inscribed by a lady, Velia Fanacna, to Thufltha (*CIE* 446). On the incense burner is the inscription *A(vle) Vel(u)s Cus(us) Thuplthas alpan turce* = Avle Cusus, son of Vel, gave [this] to Thupltha as a welcome gift (*CIE* 4457). Both men and women made dedications to the goddess, but we do not know what her competence was.

The existence of the Etruscan goddess Nortia with a sanctuary at Volsinii (probably modern Orvieto) is known to us only through Roman sources (Cincius Alimentus, cited in Livy 7.3.7). A nail was annually hammered into her temple for the purpose of counting the years. This same ritual practice, Livy tells us (7.3.5), took place yearly on the Ides of September, the anniversary of the Capitoline temple; in the *cella* dedicated to Minerva the chief magistrate (*praetor maximus*) hammered in the annual nail (*clavus annalis*). The sanctuary of Nortia has not yet been identified. We may surmise that she was a goddess of destiny, given the Etruscans' preoccupation with the passage of time and of predetermined ages (*saecula*). The nails may have been the visible reminder of the inevitability of fate and the foreseeable end of the Etruscan nation. According to the *libri rituales*, the life time

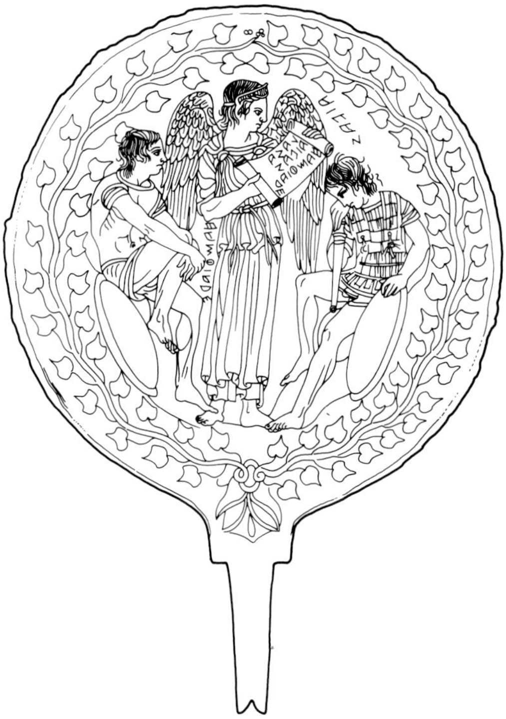

Fig. 220 Mirror with named figures of Lasa, Hamphiare, and Aivas. First half of fourth century B.C. Cast bronze. Diam. 16.5 cm. London, The British Museum GR 1847.9-9.4.

of the Etruscan nation was limited to a span of ten *saecula* of varying lengths, like the ages of human beings.

Indeterminacy also characterizes a whole host of spirits, both male and female, who appear, often unnamed, in a variety of contexts from the Late Archaic period onward. One group of youthful female spirits who are frequently shown winged, bejeweled, and either dressed or in the nude has been identified: the name Lasa is occasionally inscribed beside such figures, who are found in the company of both gods and men, most often in the circle of Turan, holding an alabastron, a hairpin, a wreath, or a mirror. These graceful beings have been likened to the Greek nymphs, and Lasa is perhaps likewise a generic term. A more ominous winged Lasa appears on a fourth-century mirror in the British Museum (FIG. 220). Dressed in a chiton and unrolling a scroll, she stands between two seated young warriors, whose attitudes express despondency. The names Hamphiare = Amphiaraos and Aivas = Ajax are written next to them and also inscribed on the scroll beneath the name of Lasa. Both heroes suffered an untimely death, and the suggestion that the Lasa on the mirror is meant to have announced their fate to them does not seem unjustified. The name Lasa also occurs in conjunction with various other names, such as Lasa Racuneta, Lasa Thimrae, Lasa Vecuvia, etc. Exceptionally, a male winged figure is called Lasa Sitmica (on the mirror *Etruskische Spiegel*, vol. 1, pl. 115).

Another type of female spirit, first represented in the Late Archaic period, is called Vanth. These beings are usually dressed in a chiton and often have wings. As messengers of death or escorters to the beyond (like the Greek Hermes Psychopompos), they may quietly guide or accompany human beings, or they may carry dead bodies. A related but iconographically more recent category of Vanth with attributes such as a torch, a snake, a sword, or a scroll and wearing a short, belted chiton with crossed straps as well as boots is present in Hellenistic tomb-paintings (FIG. 221) and carved in battle scenes or in the sacrifice of prisoners and other human victims on ash urns from Chiusi and Volterra; typologically these beings recall the Greek Furies, though their faces are usually fair.

A similarly dressed female demon, leaning on a large key, is named Vanth on a sarcophagus from Chiusi (in Palermo) belonging to the lady Hasti Afunei. The reliefs on the box represent the deceased taking leave of the members of her family. The door of the underworld is guarded by Vanth with the key. From the gate emerges Culsu with a torch, which is probably another manifestation of Vanth,

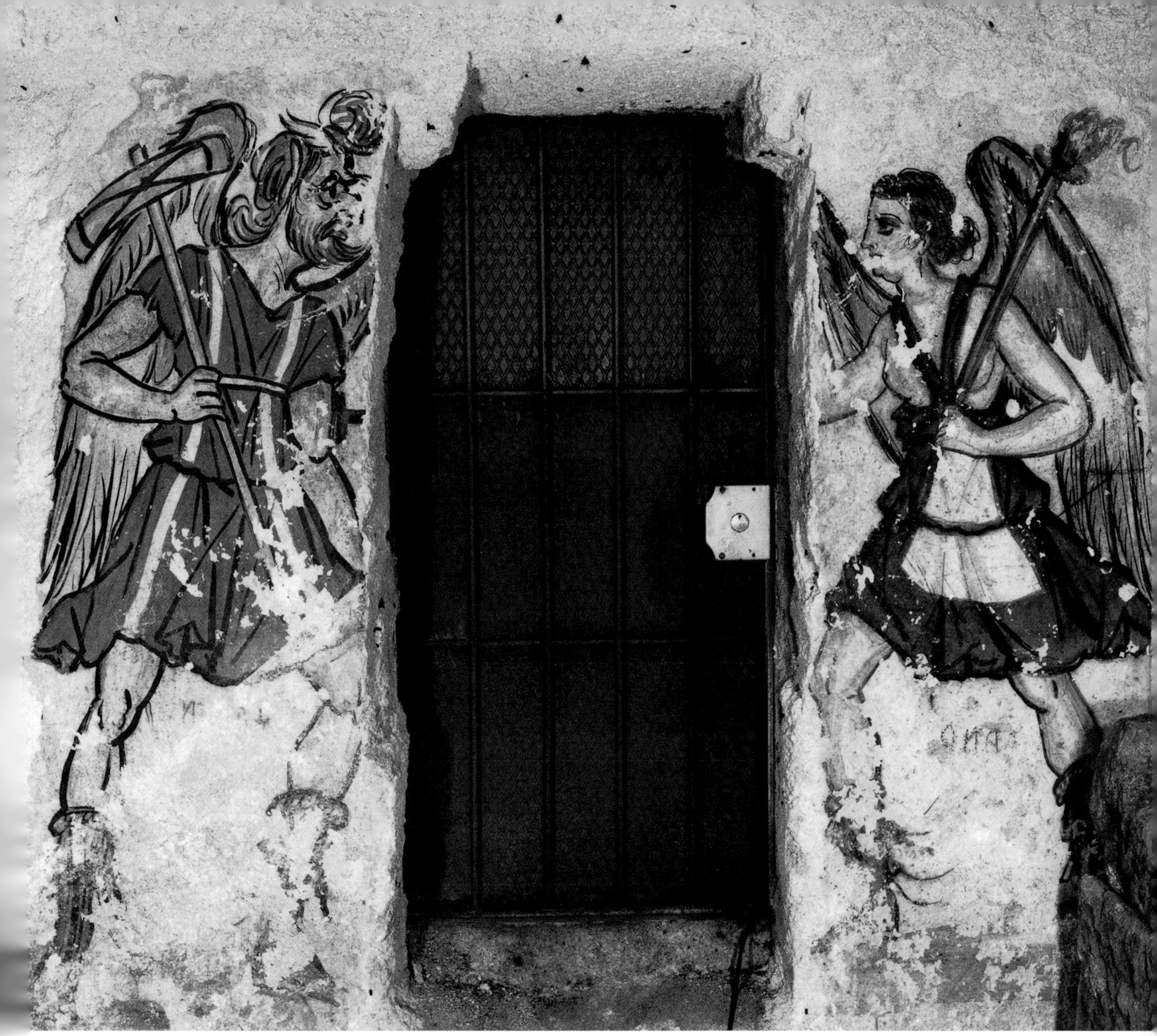

associated with the gate (FIG. 222). This growing diversity of the functions of Vanth in the passage of humans from life to the beyond may reflect the more complex religious beliefs that permeated Etruria from the late fifth century onward. A votive inscription to Vanth on a Vulcian aryballos of the second half of the seventh century, found at Marsiliana, suggests that Vanth was originally a (single) divinity.

Male demons connected with death and the journey to the beyond have a horrid aspect and, in eight cases, are named Charu(n). Although the name is derived from that of the Greek ferryman of the dead, Charon, Charu is only rarely represented carrying a rudder; his most frequent attribute is a big hammer and occasionally a key, indicating his role as keeper of the gate leading into the underworld (this is normally depicted arched like a city gate). Charu's hammer has convincingly been explained as the tool commonly used in antiquity to open a city gate, barred by a heavy, horizontally sliding piece of timber that was secured in position with metal bolts and keys. Charu's main task was to watch over the entrance to

Fig. 221 Wall-painting: Charun (left) and Vanth (right). From the entrance wall of the Tomb of the Anina Family, Fondo Scataglini, Tarquinia. End of fourth century B.C. H. of Charun 1.70 m, of Vanth 1.52 m.

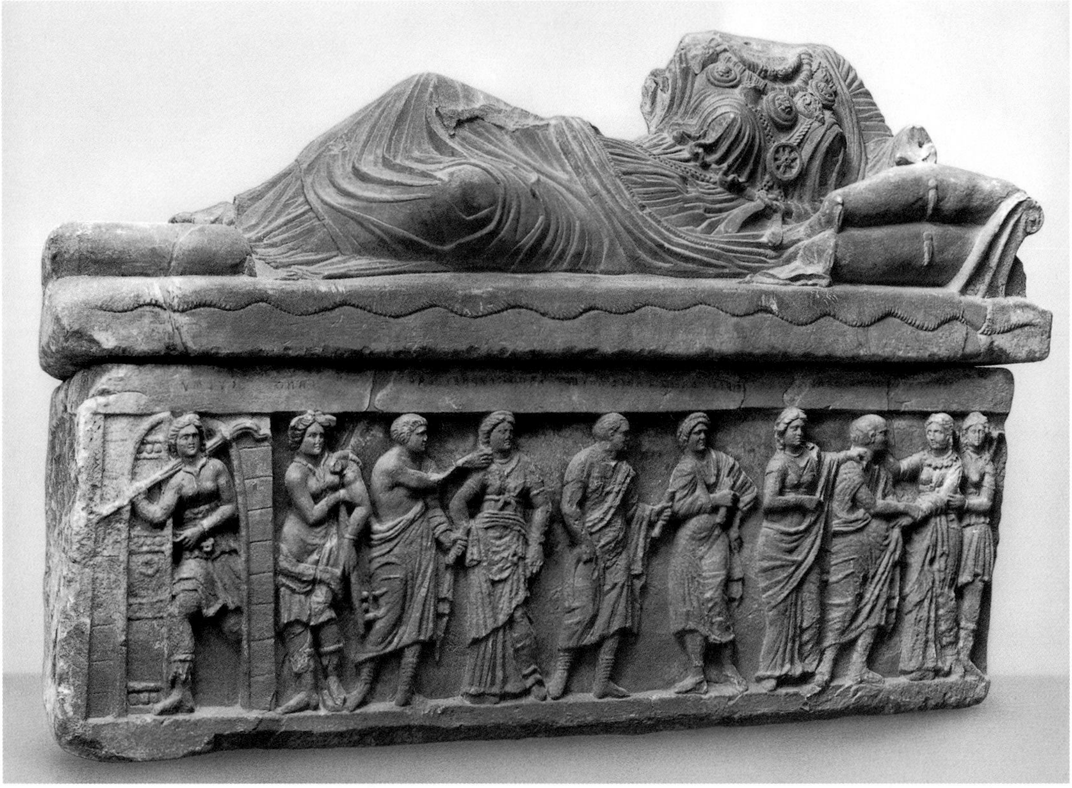

Fig. 222 Front of sarcophagus of Hasti Afunei showing leave-taking of the deceased, with the demon Culsu emerging from gate of underworld. From Colle Bonci Casuccini, near Chiusi. End of third century B.C. Alabaster. L. 2.00 m. Palermo, Museo Archeologico Regionale 24.

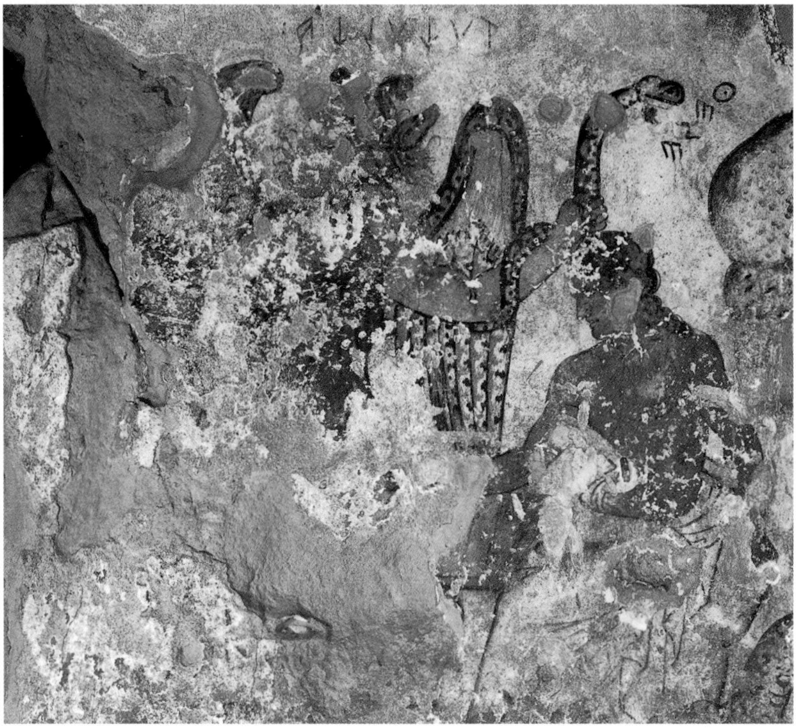

Fig. 223 Wall-painting: the demon Tuchulcha threatening These (Theseus). From the Tomb of the Underworld II, Tarquinia. Second half of fourth century B.C.

Hades, defend it (he sometimes holds a sword), and ensure that the deceased enter through it. Charu's face, though human, is made ugly by canine teeth and animal ears; he usually wears a short tunic and boots. In some Hellenistic tomb-paintings four or more figures of Charu are represented together, though with different epithets and attributes. Like Vanth, Charu's competences seem to have become diversified and led to the pluralization of what may at first have been a single divinity. An incised Etruscan votive inscription to Charu under the foot of a Greek cup attributed to the painter Oltos (Louvre F 126; *Corpus vasorum antiquorum*, Louvre 10, p. 3, pl. 1.5–8, from the Campana collection) attests to his veneration in the late sixth century.

A demon named Tuchulcha brandishing snakes is painted in the underworld scene in the chamber of the Tomb of the Underworld at Tarquinia from the second half of the fourth century (FIG. 223); he may be another manifestation of Charu. His beaklike nose and cadaverous, bluish complexion hint at death and decomposition, while his huge donkey's ears and wings recall some purely animal- or bird-shaped death demons of greater antiquity in Etruria.

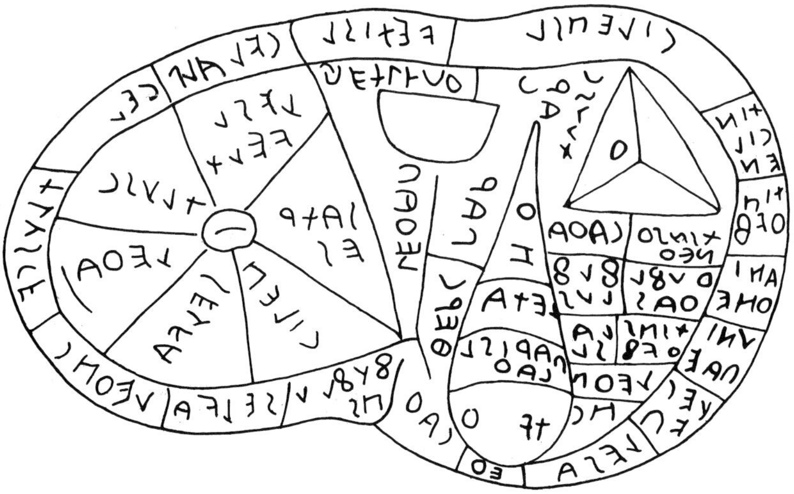

Fig. 224 Drawing of inscribed model of a sheep's liver. From Piacenza. Second half of second century B.C. Cast bronze. Piacenza, Museum.

The Bronze Liver from Piacenza and Etruscan Cosmology

Among the rare surviving written documents that can tell us something about Etruscan religiosity and cosmology is a life-size stylized bronze liver of a sheep found in 1877 near Piacenza and probably used for teaching purposes by Etruscan soothsayers (FIG. 224). Incised lines on the liver's visceral side subdivide its circumference into sixteen compartments; a further twenty-four irregularly shaped fields are marked out within this frame, all inscribed with the names of divinities. There are forty-two inscriptions in all, but only two names are on the convex side of the liver, *usil* = the sun, and *tivr* = the moon. All the names are those of purely Etruscan and Italic gods; absent are Greek gods, such as Apollo and Artemis, who appear in their Etruscan form *Aplu* and *Artumes/Aritimi* in other inscriptions, particularly in mythological scenes on mirrors. This unique liver model dates from the second half of the second century B.C., and the script used indicates that the writer came from Northern Etruria.

One of the main concerns of Etruscan priests was interpreting the will of the gods by inspecting the entrails of sheep, in particular the livers of sacrificial animals, and by observing lightning and other portents. The study of these signs and the prediction of the future from them (*haruspicina*) were the preserve of special Etruscan priests. Such practices of divination had precursors in Mesopotamia and Greece and were adopted by the Romans, who in addition (like the Umbrians) went in for the observation of the flight and behavior of birds (*auspicium*). Auspices connected with birds were also used by the Etruscans and will have belonged to that part of the *disciplina* concerned with prodigies (*ostenta*).

Cicero's *De divinatione* is the most important surviving Latin text on these subjects. Another useful source is the work of Martianus Capella, who wrote in the fifth century A.D. His *De nuptiis Philologiae et Mercurii* (1.41–61) preserves an Etruscan tradition about the division of the sky and of sacred space, though with later additions, omissions, and distortions. It seems that Etruscan cosmology imagined the dome of the sky as divided into four main sections, oriented on the cardinal points, and each subdivided into four parts. These sixteen celestial regions each had a divine inhabitant, whose precise location was reflected in the named compartments of the bronze liver; this small entity thus represented a complete vision of the world. In this system in which heaven and earth, macrocosm and microcosm, corresponded to each other, the orientation and division of heavenly and earthly space were matters of the utmost religious importance, not only for the observation and interpretation of omens, but also in such rites as the foundation of temples or cities and the layout of tombs, altars, etc.

It appears that the eastern, and particularly the northeastern sector of the sky was considered favorable, being the seat of the great celestial deities Tinia and Uni. The south was inhabited by terrestrial and nature gods, such as Cel (a mother/earth goddess), Fufluns, and Selvans. The region of the sunset, and especially the northwestern sector was the abode of the underworld divinities; signs from these parts were extremely inauspicious.

Haruspices *and Augurs*

The direction from which divine signs emanated in the sky was thus highly important for their interpretation by the priests. In the case of a thunderbolt, for example, the point of its celestial origin and the line of its retirement determined whether it was a good or a bad omen; the form and color of the lightning and the place and date where it struck were further means of determining the nature of the message it carried (Sen. 2.38–42). The same applied to the flight and behavior of birds.

The complex and detailed knowledge of the meaning of signs—who sent them; were they mere warnings, reminders, commands, or final judgments; what did they portend for the future; and what expiatory measures should be taken—was the preserve of particular male priests: the *haruspex* (Etr. *netsvis*) and the *fulguriator*, the interpreter of lightning (Etr. *trutnvt frontac* or *trutnvt*). The interpretation of both the entrails and the thunderbolts could be the office of a single person, as shown by the rare bilingual inscription on a cinerary urn found at Pesaro and dating from the Roman period: it gives the name of the deceased, L. Cafatius, and both his priestly titles in Etruscan and Latin (*TLE* 697).

The practice of the *fulguriator* included not only the explanation and expiation of lightning and attempts to avert it but also the ability to elicit thunderbolts by prayer and sacrifices so as to cause the elimination of enemies. Pliny (2.53.140) tells how a monster named Olta devastated the territory of Volsinii and was annihilated by a thunderbolt elicited by King Porsenna.

Such ancient usage was still known in Etruria as late as A.D. 408. A passage by the fifth-century-A.D. Greek historian Zosimos (5.41.1) describes how some Etruscans in Rome approached the prefect Pompeianus and offered to drive away with thunderstorm and lightning the besieging army of the Visigoth Alarich "by means of prayer and ceremonies in the manner of their fathers." Their offer, however, was dismissed, for the Etruscans insisted that they had to perform the customary rites publicly in the Forum and on the Capitol; since most people were Christians, no one dared to take part in such acts of ancestral worship.

A late fourth-century-B.C. bronze statuette of a *haruspex* in the Museo Gregoriano Etrusco of the Vatican (inv. 12040) shows how these priests were dressed: over a sleeved tunic reaching to the top of the boots is draped an irregularly shaped mantle with a thick, woolly-looking edge (most likely a sheepskin, worn inside-out), pinned on the chest with a large bow-fibula of Archaic type. The headgear consists of a cap with a tall conical peak and straps tied under the chin. He holds a liver in his left hand and a votive inscription is incised on his left leg: *tn turce Vel Sveitus* = Vel Sveitus gave this (*TLE* 736).

The ritual position for interpreting the liver is represented on two inscribed Etruscan bronze mirrors. On the first (FIG. 225), dated to the second half of the fourth century, we see a youth, *pava tarchies* = the boy from Tarquinia, or the son of Tarchon(?), draped in a mantle pinned with a large fibula and wearing the typical peaked sheepskin hat of the *haruspex*; with his left foot on a rock and supporting his left arm on his knee he leans forward toward the liver in his left hand, touching it with his right. Watching him thoughtfully is a bearded and draped man, who is likewise distinguished by a *galerus*, which hangs on the nape of his neck; his long staff is a sign of his dignity. Named *avl(e) tarchunus*, he is clearly related to Tarchon, the eponymous hero of Tarquinia, who originally learned the art of the *haruspicina* from the miraculous boy Tages. The older man supervises his young

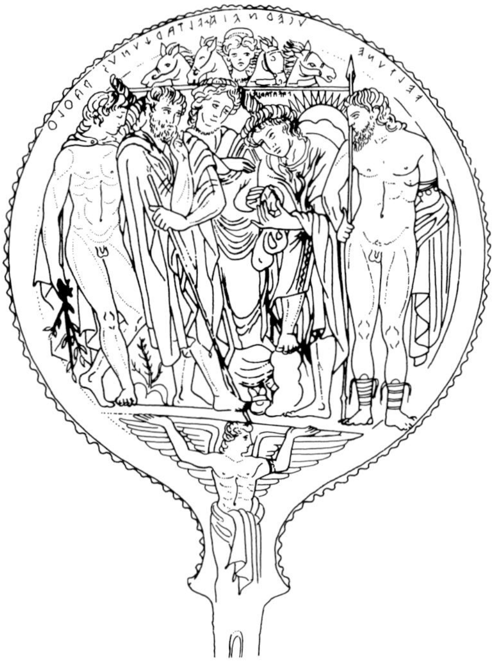

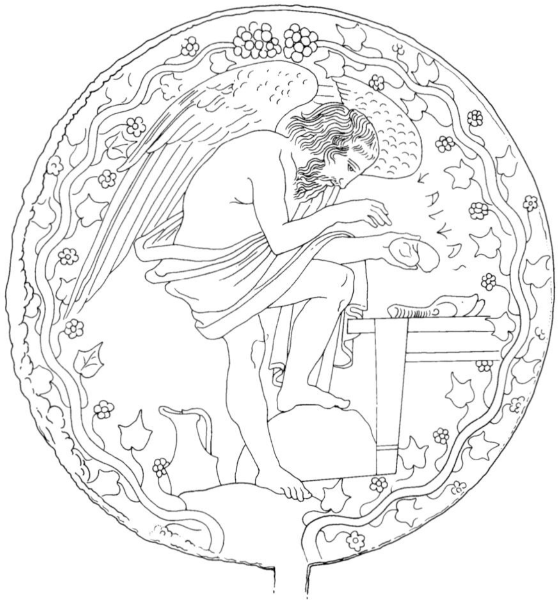

Fig. 225 Inscribed mirror showing the inspection of a liver. From Tuscania. Second half of fourth century B.C. Cast bronze. Diam. 12.3 cm. Florence, Museo Archeologico 77759.

Fig. 226 Inscribed mirror showing Khalkhas inspecting a liver. From Vulci. Ca. 400 B.C. Cast bronze. Diam. 14.8 cm. Vatican, Museo Gregoriano Etrusco 12240.

pupil's explanation of the liver in the presence of three bystanders. In the background a woman named *ucernei* may be his wife. On the left, a nude youth named *rathlth* with a mantle and a laurel twig has been identified as a mantic divinity in whose sanctuary the scene takes place. On the right a bearded man, *veltune*, nude but for boots and a mantle draped over his left arm circled by a bracelet with *bullae*, is armed with a spear. He is probably Voltumna/Velthumna, the national god of Etruria. The sun is rising in the background behind *pava tarchies*. Framed above by the heads of the goddess of Dawn (Thesan) and the four horses of her quadriga in the exergue and below by a winged underworld demon supporting the surface of the earth, the main scene thus assumes cosmic as well as a mythical, historical, and cultic significance, exalting the religious preeminence of Tarquinia.

A mirror from Vulci dated to ca. 400 B.C. shows a bearded and winged man draped in a mantle, again with his left foot on a rock and his left elbow supported on the knee, bending forward to inspect a liver in his left hand (FIG. 226). On a table in front of him lie other entrails, above which is inscribed his name, *khalkhas*. This is the Etruscan version of the Homeric diviner Kalchas, who accompanied the Greek army to Troy; he is here represented as a semidivine *haruspex*, harking back to the heroic age.

An *auspicium* is probably represented in a wall-painting of the middle of the fourth century in the François Tomb (FIG. 227). From the atrium, flanking a doorway, comes the stately figure of Vel Saties, an eminent member of the aristocratic family who owned the tomb. He is wreathed with laurel and wrapped in a purple mantle embroidered all over with figures of nude male dancers brandishing shields.

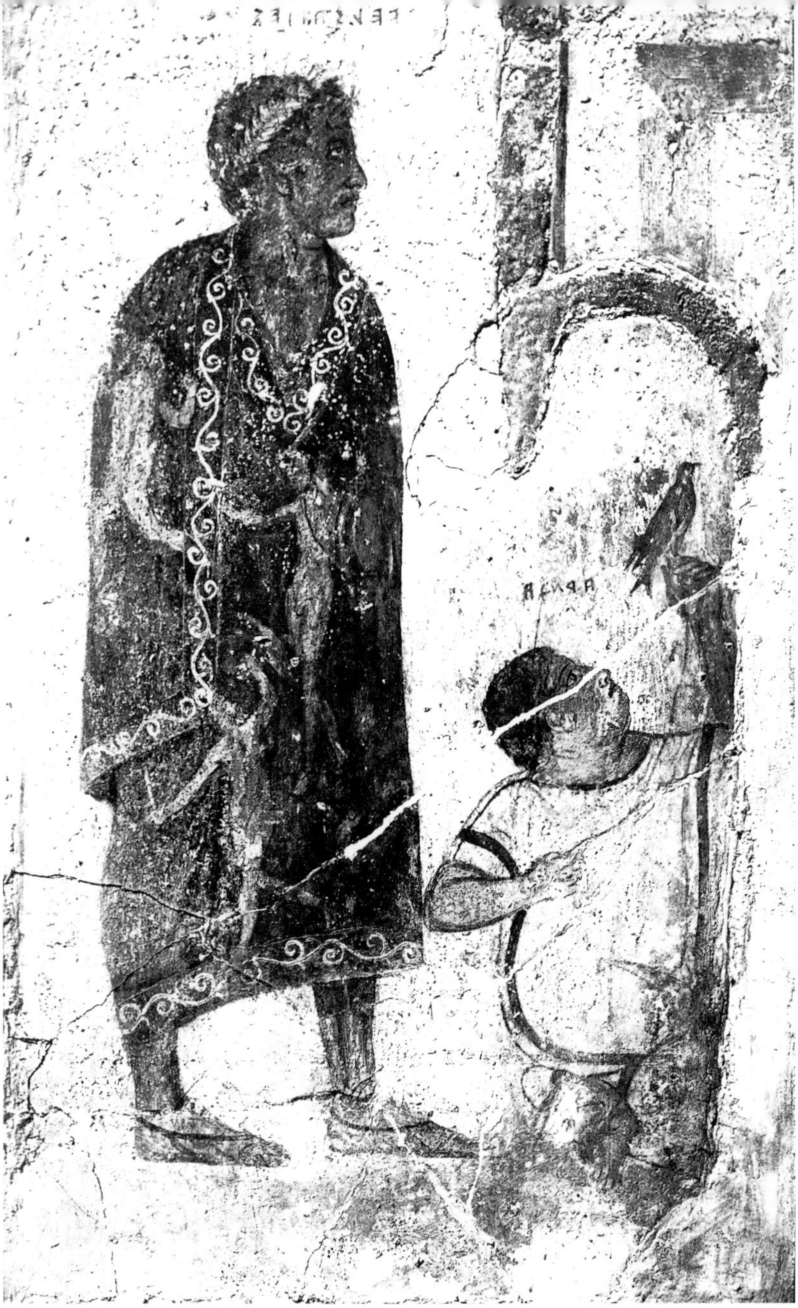

Fig. 227 Wall-painting: Vel Saties and Arnza with bird. From the François Tomb, Vulci. 350–330 B.C. Rome, Villa Albani.

He looks fixedly ahead at the space into which a small figure named *arnza* (little Arnth), who kneels at his feet, lifts a bird on a string perched on his left hand. Its small head, long wing tips, and forked tail suggest that it is a swallow. Vel Saties' splendid dress and solemn attitude express the ritual importance of his office of observing and interpreting the flight of the bird. A divergent interpretation sees in Arnza a child at play with a pet.

Aristocratic Etruscan women, too, were able to divine events from the flight of birds, as Livy tells us in the story of Tanaquil (1.34.8f.). During their decisive move from Tarquinia to Rome, Tanaquil and her husband, Lucumo, had arrived in their carriage at the Janiculum, when an eagle descended from the sky and snatched off Lucumo's cap, carried it up, and then swooped down once more to replace

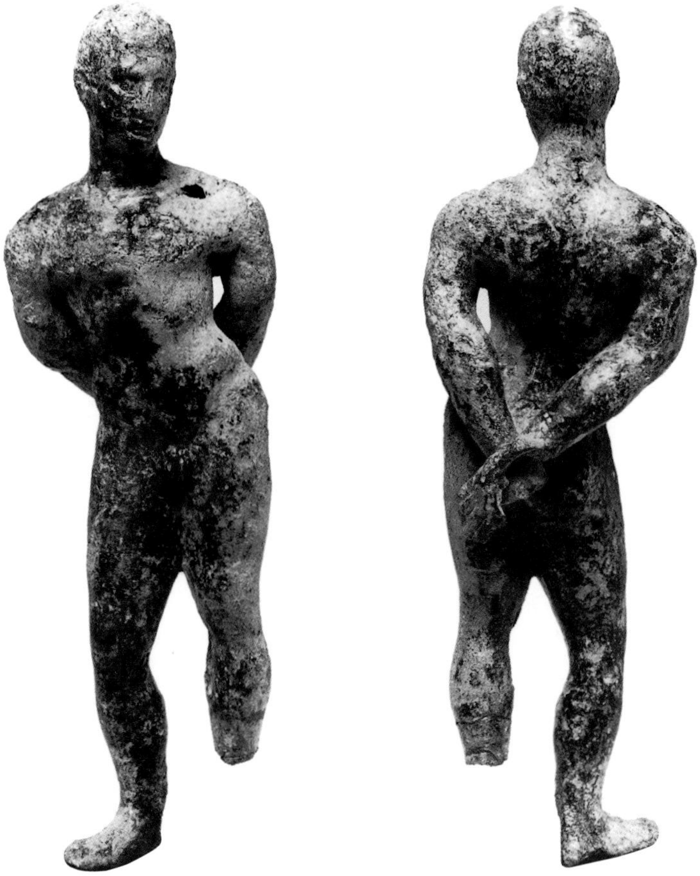

Fig. 228 Front and back of statuette of a man, with inscribed name. From Sovana. Late fourth–early third century B.C. Lead. Florence, Museo Archeologico.

it on Lucumo's head. Tanaquil, skilled in celestial prodigies, embraced her husband and joyfully predicted that the highest fortune awaited him in the city: the direction from which the bird was sent by the god and the fact that it had taken Lucumo's cap from the crown of his head indicated future greatness. They drove on into Rome where Lucumo changed his name to Lucius Tarquinius Priscus and eventually became king.

Magic and Curses

Lentil-shaped capsules called *bullae* in Latin were worn suspended around the neck by Roman and Etruscan children of noble families, but also by magistrates, the Roman victorious general (*triumphator*), and by images of some Etruscan gods. These amulets of gold were known as Etruscan gold (Lat. *Etruscum aurum*). A number of actual Etruscan *bullae*, occasionally finely decorated with figured scenes, have survived, while *bullae* are represented on countless votive terra-cotta statuettes of small children and on a few bronze statuettes of boys (see FIG. 285). *Bullae* probably often contained some charm or medicine believed to protect the wearer from evil.

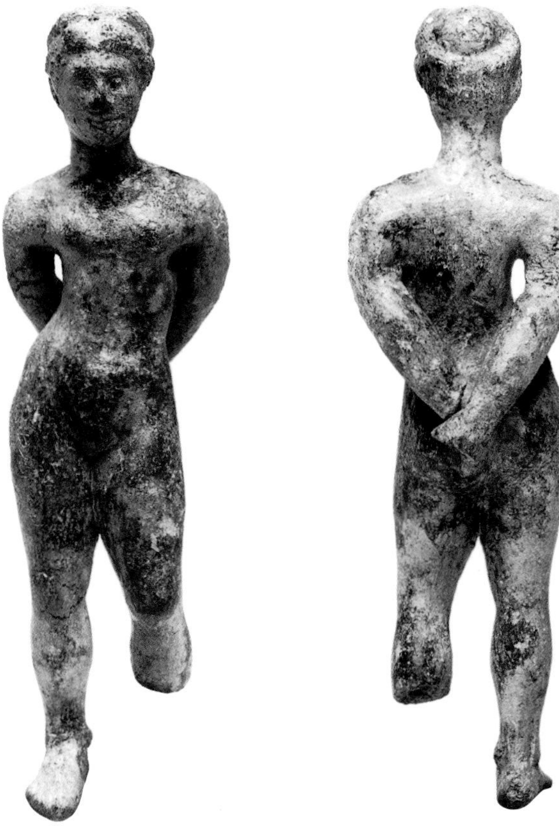

Fig. 229 Front and back of statuette of a woman, with inscribed name. From Sovana. Late fourth–early third century B.C. Lead. Florence, Museo Archeologico.

Intention to destroy an adversary or rival by magic formulae or actions is documented by a number of lead tablets inscribed with curses and by small lead statuettes. Two such cast-lead figures of a young man and young woman, both in the nude and with their hands behind their back as if tied, were discovered in 1908 in a tomb at Sovana (FIGS. 228, 229; *CIE* Suana 5234, 5235). Both their "Polyclitan" stance with one relaxed leg and their hairstyle suggest a date for their manufacture in the fourth–third century. The names incised on the thigh of the male are *zertur cecnas* = Sertorius Caecina, those on the young woman's are *velia satnea*. Perhaps the couple were engaged or married and had a jealous enemy who wished to destroy them. The old chamber tomb in which the statuettes had been placed in a corner contained only impasto, bucchero, and a few Etrusco-Corinthian pottery pieces of the early sixth century, but no material contemporary with the lead figures. They must have been secreted into this tomb several centuries after it was originally used. Deposition in a tomb of the images of hated persons must have been considered an efficacious way of ensuring their death. Incised lead tablets were often thrown into deep wells or places of ill omen thought to be connected with underworld divinities; and lead itself seems to have been so considered.

Female Worshipers and Priestesses

The evidence of inscriptions and votive figurines has shown that in their own right women dedicated objects in sanctuaries of various kinds. Bronze statuettes in the form of richly dressed ladies can often be identified by their gestures as representing the dedicants themselves rather than goddesses. Three fine fifth-century bronzes perfectly exemplify this type; all are dressed in a chiton of thin crinkly linen with a heavy, rectangular woolen mantle draped over the left shoulder and a half diadem on their neatly parted hair, rolled up at the back. Two of them have a tasseled ribbon hanging over the right shoulder, a fashion item (or sign of rank?) often found in the—otherwise Classical Greek—costume of aristocratic Etruscan ladies (and of some goddesses) during the fifth and fourth centuries.

The first statuette, which dates from the middle of the fifth century, comes from the votive deposit discovered in the fountain sanctuary of Fontanile di Legnisina in the necropolis east of the ancient city of Vulci. The sanctuary was dedicated to Uni and Vei, goddesses closely concerned with female sexuality, birth (numerous terra-cotta models of uteri were also found), and with the underworld and therefore situated in a necropolis area. The woman offers in her raised hands an egg and a pomegranate, objects symbolizing fertility, renewal, and survival in the beyond. It is likely that the statuette was made in a bronze workshop at Vulci.

Of unknown provenance, but probably likewise of Southern Etruscan manufacture, are two related statuettes in the British Museum, both dating from the last quarter of the fifth century. One of them (FIG. 230), distinguished by a necklace and the ribbon hanging from her shoulder, prays with both open hands raised sideways. The other (FIG. 231), whose eyes were originally inlaid, lifts with her right hand a bunch of flowers, while looking thoughtfully at her missing left hand, which probably held another offering.

Piety and aristocratic self-representation are skillfully blended in these votive statuettes. Nothing in the way they are dressed (except perhaps the ribbon?) allows us to decide whether these ladies were priestesses or worshipers. However, a Late Archaic bronze statuette from the eighteenth-century collection of the Comte de Caylus in the Bibliothèque Nationale de France in Paris (inv. B.B. 862) is clearly characterized by her peculiar costume as holding some priestly office. The large fibula pinning her long, shawllike mantle above her breasts connects her with the statuette of a *haruspex* discussed above. However, her mantle is not a sheepskin, but a smooth textile with a woven edge and tasseled triangular end hanging over her back. Under it she wears a sleeved chiton reaching down to her ankle boots; its center front is decorated with a wide vertical band, a feature also found on the dress of the large Etruscan bronze statuette of a girl from near Naples in the British Museum (BM *Bronze Cat.* 447), dated to the early fifth century. The hair of the priestess in Paris is covered with a clinging light veil placed low across her forehead and tied by a ribbon with a knot at the back of her head. She holds both her

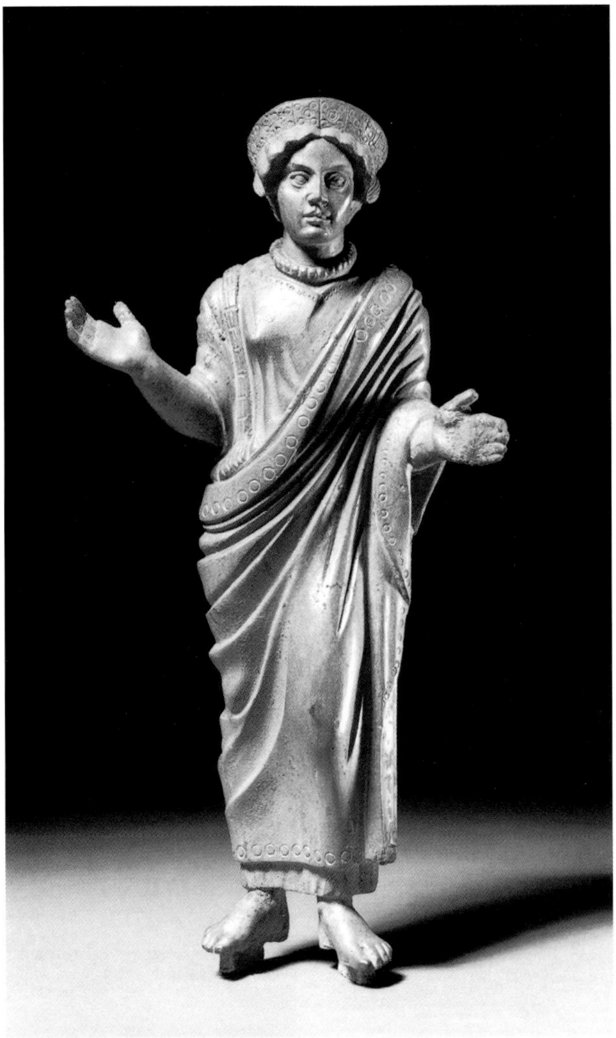
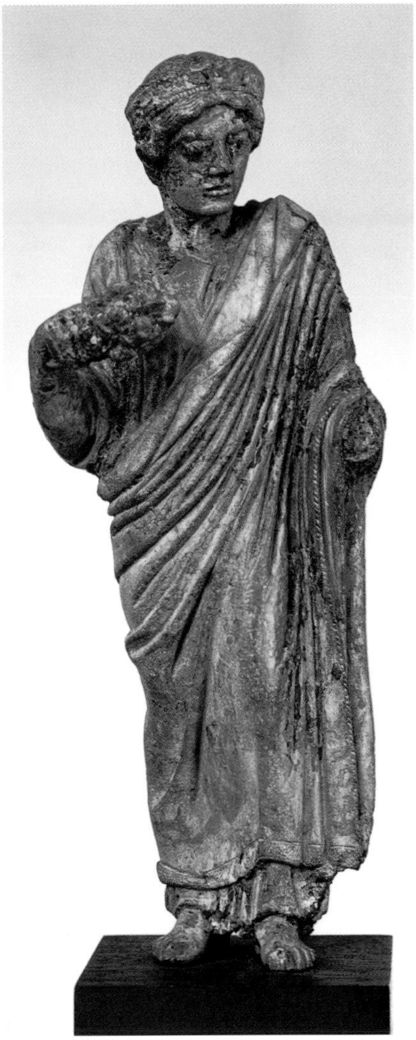

open hands forward in an attitude of prayer. The uniqueness of this costume does not rule out the authenticity of the statuette. Due to the lack of literary sources, we cannot tell what office she may have held.

The only Etruscan word identified in exclusively female funerary inscriptions from Vulci that could be interpreted as a priestly title is *hatrencu*. It occurs carved four times on stone fragments of funerary monuments from various Vulcian necropolises and at least five times in a multiple, rock-cut chamber tomb founded in the fourth century and known as the Tomb of the Inscriptions (*Tomba delle Iscrizioni*). The members of several families were buried in its six chambers, arranged asymmetrically off the four sides of a rectangular vestibule accessible by a dromos. Two of the ladies designated as *hatrencu* belonged to the Mura family, two to the Zimaru, and one to the Pruślna family. This latter aristocratic gens seems

Fig. 230 Votive statuette of a draped woman. Last quarter of fifth century B.C. Cast bronze. H. 14.1 cm. London, The British Museum GR 84.6-14.57.

Fig. 231 Votive statuette of a woman with a bunch of flowers. Last quarter of fifth century B.C. Cast bronze. H. 16.8 cm. London, The British Museum GR 84.6-14.58.

to have been the founding family. The tomb was used over several generations and contained the remains of many males of these families, as well as of female members without the title and also four burials with Latin inscriptions. Two of the five ladies distinguished as *hatrencu* were not laid to rest together with their husbands and children, as is usually the rule in Etruria for female burials in family tombs, nor with their original families, but in the company of women with a different family name but bearing the same title. Thus the *hatrencu* by the name of Pruślnai was buried together with a *hatrencu* of the Zimaru family in Chamber IV, rather than with her Pruślna relations in Chamber III, while a Zimaru *hatrencu* shared Chamber I with a Mura *hatrencu*. The collegial link between the women laid in the same chambers seems to have prevailed over the usual custom of joining husband and wife in death (though the colleagues may have been connected by marriage).

The meaning of the word *hatrencu* is still a matter of debate, but it has been persuasively argued that the title refers to the member of a college concerned with a female cult dedicated to the fertility of families and to marriage and perhaps comparable to the Roman college of matrons, devoted to the cult of the goddess Mater Matuta.

Only a few objects remained in the Tomb of the Inscriptions when it was discovered in 1957, but the social eminence of the occupants was underlined by the presence in Chamber II of twelve gold-covered nailheads that probably served to attach a gold tablet with an inscription (cf. Pyrgi, p. 176) and of a stone sarcophagus carved on all four sides with reliefs representing a battle between Greeks and Amazons, watched by winged demons of death. This theme of slaughter and death—here the opponents seem equally vulnerable, for they fight each other almost completely in the nude—appears frequently on sarcophagi from the second half of the fourth century onward. Although the theme is Greek, the Etruscan sculptor has interpreted it in an unmistakably central Italian way by adding the non-Greek figures of Charun and Vanth and by showing the Amazons in the nude.

The importance attached to marriage links between the most prominent aristocratic families of Vulci emerges from the fact that in their large and splendid chamber tombs the individual founding families often accommodated the dead of other aristocratic stock who had married into the family. Thus some members of the Mura family found their last resting place in the François Tomb, while a lady called Ramtha Viśnei (who may also have been a *hatrencu*, the letter *h* being preserved after her name) was probably married to a Pruślnas and was therefore buried in Chamber V of the Tomb of the Inscriptions. This suggests that noble families may have attempted to control certain offices and perhaps political power within a restricted circle of clans closely linked by marriage. In general we may assume that priestesses were probably ladies of high social standing. The evidence in the sanctuary at Pyrgi of a row of identical cells that were perhaps used by (Phoenician?) women serving as sacred prostitutes for Uni/Astarte, is unique in Etruria.

SARCOPHAGI AND FUNERARY SCULPTURE FROM SOUTHERN ETRURIA

Among the finest surviving sarcophagi of the fourth century are the two famous examples found in 1846 in the Ponte Rotto necropolis of Vulci (see FIGS. 232a–d, 233). On the lid of each, the married couple is carved in high relief, lying in loving embrace on their marital bed under the same cover. Ramtha Viśnai, the portly wife of Arnth Tetnies (*ramtha viśnai arntheal tetn*[*i*]*es puia*, *CIE* 5312, *TLE* 320), is dressed in a light chiton and wears disc-earrings and a bracelet; her hair is neatly braided and wound around her head (FIG. 232a). The husband is clean shaven, his short hair framing a heavy, middle-aged face. He is naked under the light cover (perhaps his mantle, the Etruscan *tebenna*), which is wrapped around both of them. Although they are represented together on the lid, it seems from the inscription carved on the front edge that Ramtha Viśnai alone occupied the sarcophagus. (We do not know from which tomb in the Ponte Rotto necropolis the sarcophagus came and what the relationship was between its occupant and the *hatrencu*(?) Ramtha Viśnei, whose name is preserved among the funerary inscriptions in Chamber v of the Tomb of the Inscriptions, see p. 286.)

The reliefs on the front of the box show that the Ramtha Viśnai on the sarcophagus was a lady of high social (and probably priestly) position (FIG. 232b). The draped couple stand united, she with her left hand on his shoulder, he clasping her right wrist. Shading her under what is probably a large umbrella, from which hangs a small situla, is a youth with a short cloak wrapped around his waist. He is followed on the left by three women, the first carrying a box on her head and an oinochoe, the second a splendid fan and a situla, the third a kithara. Umbrella and fan are ancient status symbols, while the objects carried by the attendants, such as the oinochoe and situla, as well as the box (containing incense?), may be connected with priestly duties of Ramtha Viśnai, rather than with her adornment. Her husband, Arnth Tetnies, is likewise shown with four attendants carrying the objects symbolizing his power as a high magistrate: the folding seat of ivory (*sella curulis*); rods and the curved staff or trumpet (*lituus*); an almost circular war trumpet; and finally the double pipes (auloi). The perfectly balanced composition emphasizes the couple's equal importance in their different spheres of duty.

In the reliefs on both the short sides of the sarcophagus, husband and wife again appear in comparably balanced scenes, which may allude to their departure for the underworld. Ramtha must be one of the two identically dressed and adorned women who sit side by side under an umbrella on a two-wheeled carriage drawn by two horses and driven by a coachman (FIG. 232c); in the background hovers a winged female death demon holding snakes. The similarity of the two ladies' appearance suggests that they may be colleagues, perhaps *hatrencus*. Arnth, for his part, is shown mounting a chariot with an attendant holding a *lituus* in the back-

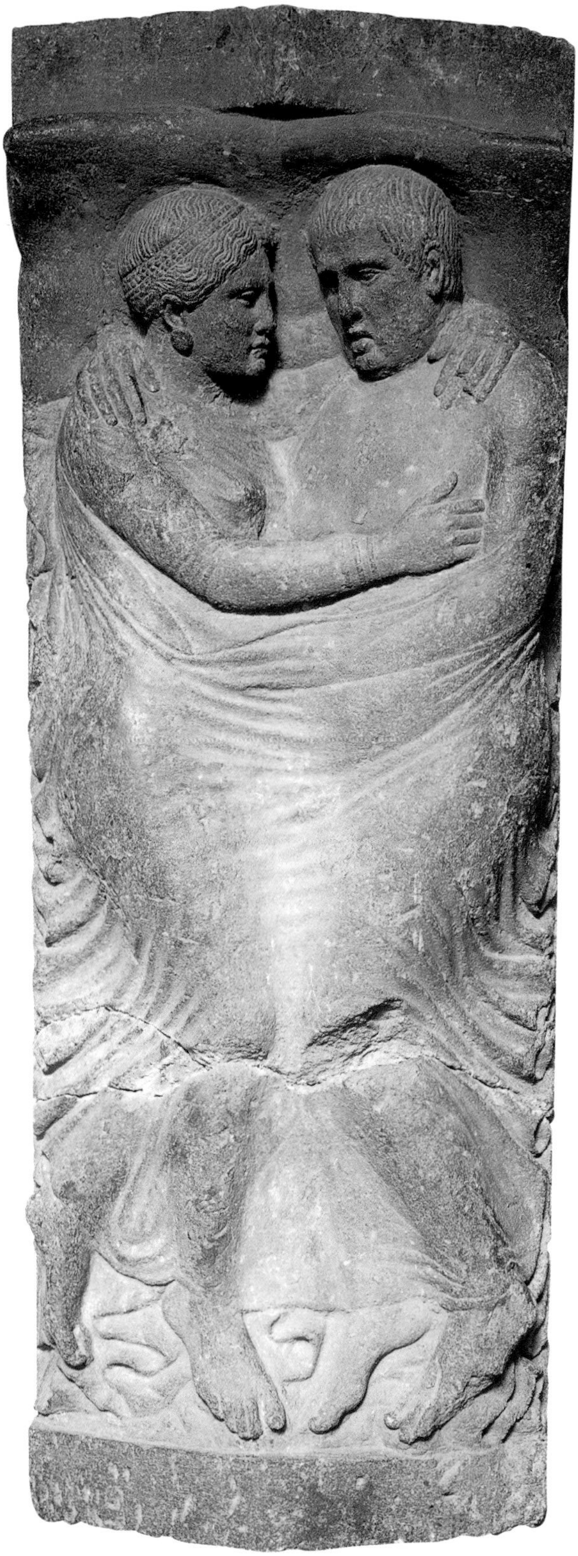

Fig. 232a Sarcophagus lid with the images of Ramtha Viśnai and Arnth Tetnies. From the Ponte Rotto necropolis, Vulci. Mid-fourth century B.C. Local marble. L. 2.18 m. Boston, Museum of Fine Arts, Gift of Mr. and Mrs. Cornelius C. Vermeule III, 1975.799.

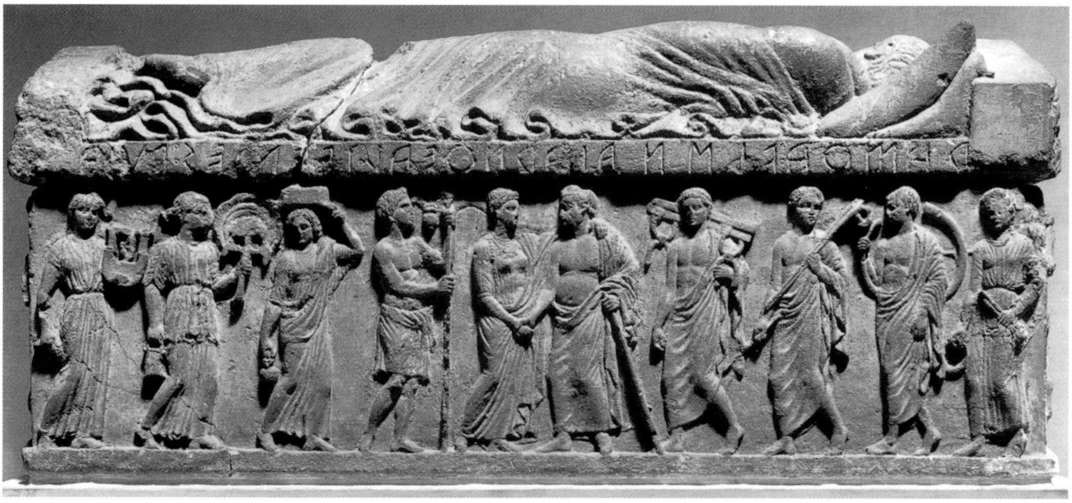

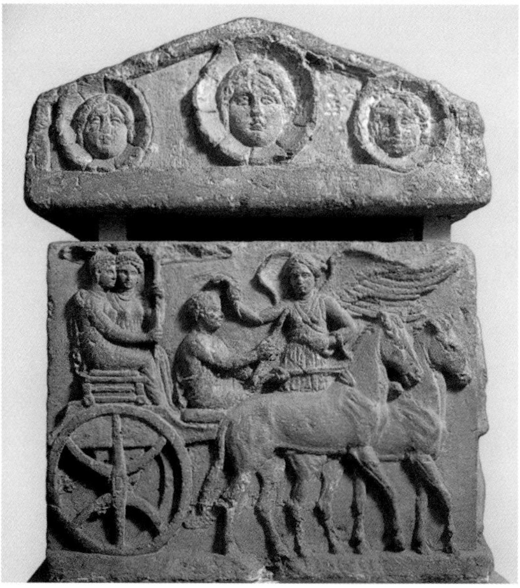

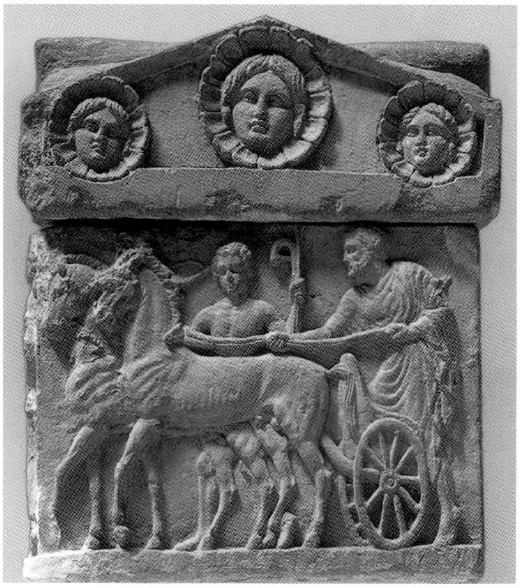

Fig. 232b Front of sarcophagus, figure 232a. The married couple surrounded by attendants.

Fig. 232c Short side of sarcophagus, figure 232a. Wife departing for the underworld.

Fig. 232d Short side of sarcophagus, figure 232a. Husband departing for the underworld.

ground (FIG. 232d). In the gables of the sarcophagus lid above both these side panels are carved three frontal female heads surrounded by flower petals, a motif that frequently occurs painted on South Italian funerary vases of the fourth century and may have a transcendental significance.

According to its inscriptions (*TLE* 321), the second sarcophagus in Boston belonged to Larth Tetnies—the son of Arnth Tetnies and Ramtha Viśnai—and to his wife, Thanchvil Tarnai (FIG. 233). The couple on the lid, both nude under the light cover draped over their legs, embrace and gaze intently at each other. The husband's hairstyle and beard and the wife's elegantly waved locks reflect Greek fashion; it has been suggested that the sculptor was a Greek, for, unusually for Etruria, the man is shown lying on the woman's right-hand side; also unusually, he wears

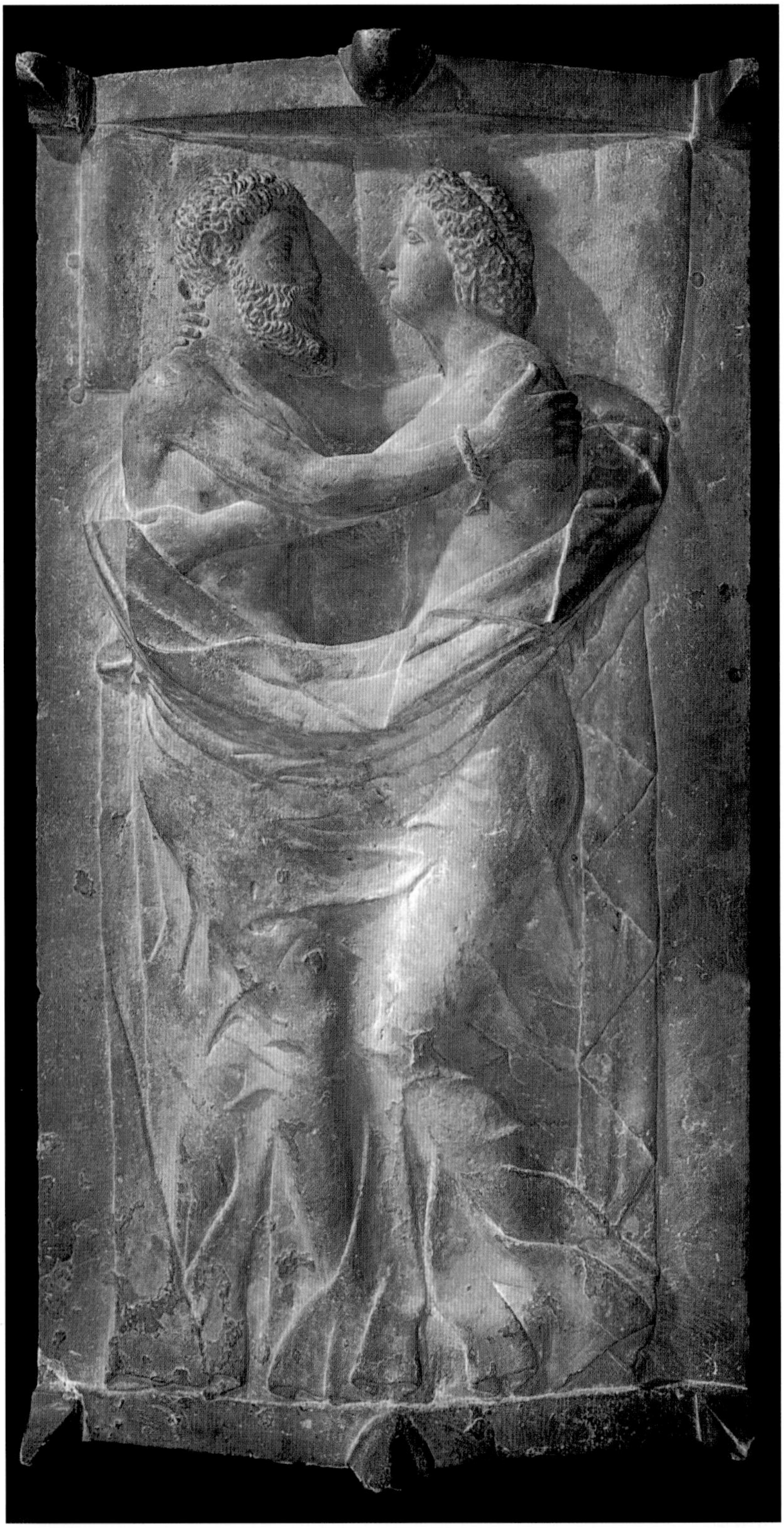

Fig. 233 Sarcophagus lid with the images of Larth Tetnies and Thanchvil Tarnai. From the Ponte Rotto necropolis, Vulci. Second half of fourth century B.C. Local marble. L. 2.13 m. Boston, Museum of Fine Arts, Gift of Mrs. Gardner Brewer, 86.145.

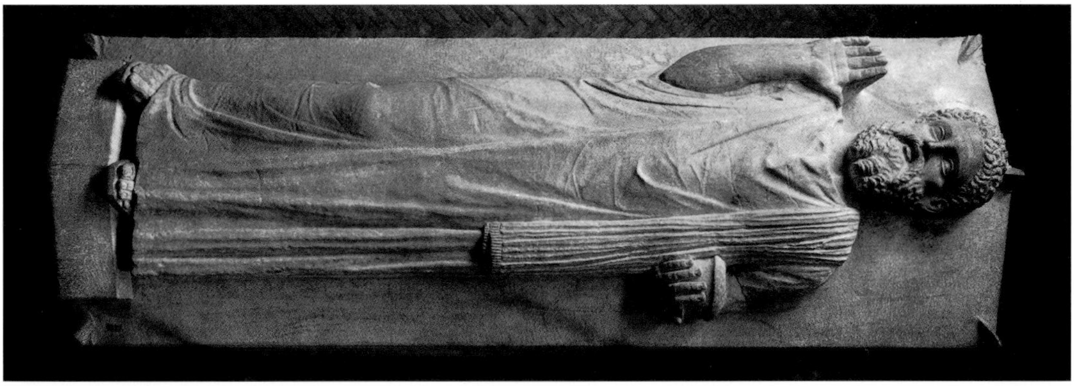

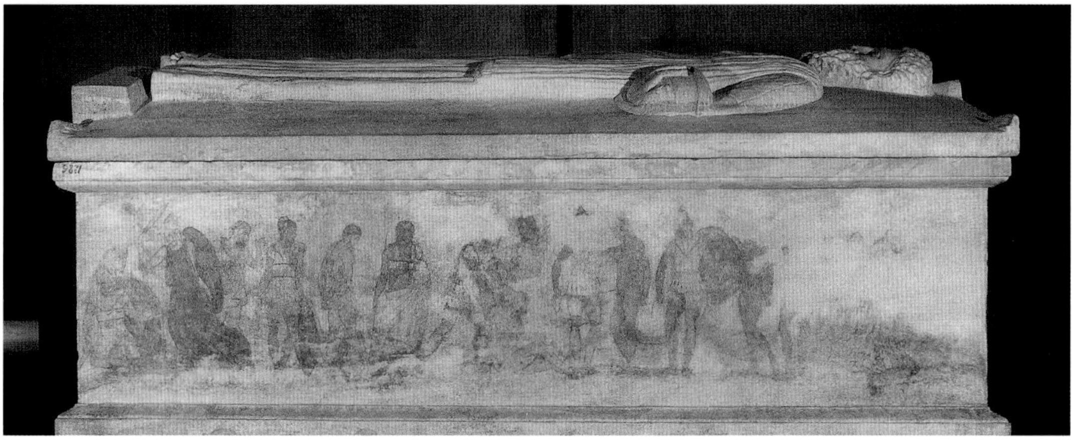

a bracelet on his right wrist. Greek, too, are the motifs on the box of the sarcophagus. On the long sides are carved two battle scenes, one representing Greeks fighting Amazons, the other horsemen attacking armed men on foot, while on the short sides further symbols of death appear: two griffins devouring a collapsed horse and two lions slaying a bull. These groups of animals are clearly related to the painted frieze decorating the atrium of the François Tomb (pp. 186, 280f.). Those paintings have been attributed to artists trained in Magna Graecia and working in the middle of the second half of the fourth century. The Greek models for the individual battle scenes on our sarcophagus are probably derived from a frieze on the Mausoleum of Halikarnassos. As on that gigantic funerary monument, the Amazons here are dressed in short, belted chitons.

The intimacy of the groups of the two couples of the Tetnie family on their marriage beds has no parallel in later funerary sculpture (except once at Chiusi, see FIG. 240), but it grants us a glimpse of the lasting marital affection that existed between couples of all ages, which was thought worth eternalizing.

Like Vulci, Tarquinia has yielded quantities of sculpted sarcophagi of high quality from the middle of the fourth century onward. After the decline of the fifth and early fourth centuries, the new large chamber tombs of aristocratic fam-

Fig. 234a Sarcophagus of the Priest. Lid. From the Tomb of the Partunu Family, Monterozzi necropolis, Tarquinia. Second half of fourth century B.C. Parian marble. L. 1.98 m. Tarquinia, Museo Nazionale Archeologico RC 9871.

Fig. 234b Front of the Sarcophagus of the Priest, figure 234a.

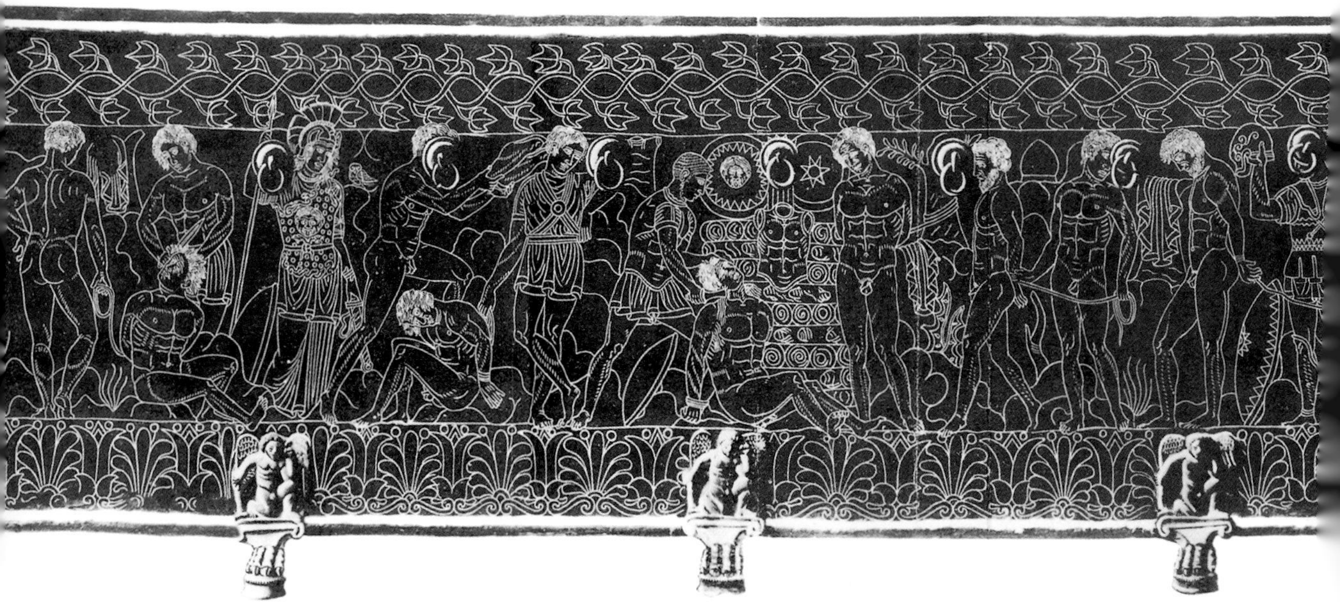

Fig. 235 Roll-out of decoration on an engraved *cista* showing the sacrifice of the Trojan prisoners. From Palestrina. Last quarter of fourth century B.C. Box and lid of hammered sheet bronze, feet cast bronze. H. 36 cm. London, The British Museum GR 59.8-16.1.

ilies were now often decorated with fine wall-paintings of fresh subjects and contained numerous sarcophagi, pointing to a strong political, economic, and cultural revival in both these cities.

An interesting example of the complex artistic impulses that reached central Italy during this period is the Sarcophagus of the Priest (*Sarcofago del Sacerdote*, FIGS. 234a, b). Found in 1876 with fourteen other sarcophagi in the chamber tomb of the Partunu family in the Monterozzi necropolis, Tarquinia, it stands out by being the only one carved from Parian marble, all the others being of local *nenfro* or polished white limestone.

The image lying on the lid is that of a bearded man in a long chiton and ritual stole; he holds a round box for incense in his left hand, raising his right in prayer or greeting. Two similar Parian marble sarcophagi have been excavated in the Punic necropolis of Ste. Monique near Carthage, and it seems likely that the specimen from Tarquinia was originally destined for the Carthaginian market, for the "priest" wears an earring in his left ear, a typically Punic male fashion that is unknown in Etruria. Paros has been identified as the center of production and export of such sarcophagi (and of others of purely architectural form). Once in Tarquinia, the box of the sarcophagus was painted in tempera technique on all four sides with (now very faded) scenes of battles between Greeks and Amazons and of the slaughter of the Trojan prisoners at the funeral of Patroklos. The Etruscan painter used traditional Greek figure schemata but added Etruscan death demons and gave the Amazons long chitons, which are unusual in Greek representations. The theme of the sacrifice of the Trojans by Achilles is found, with variations in

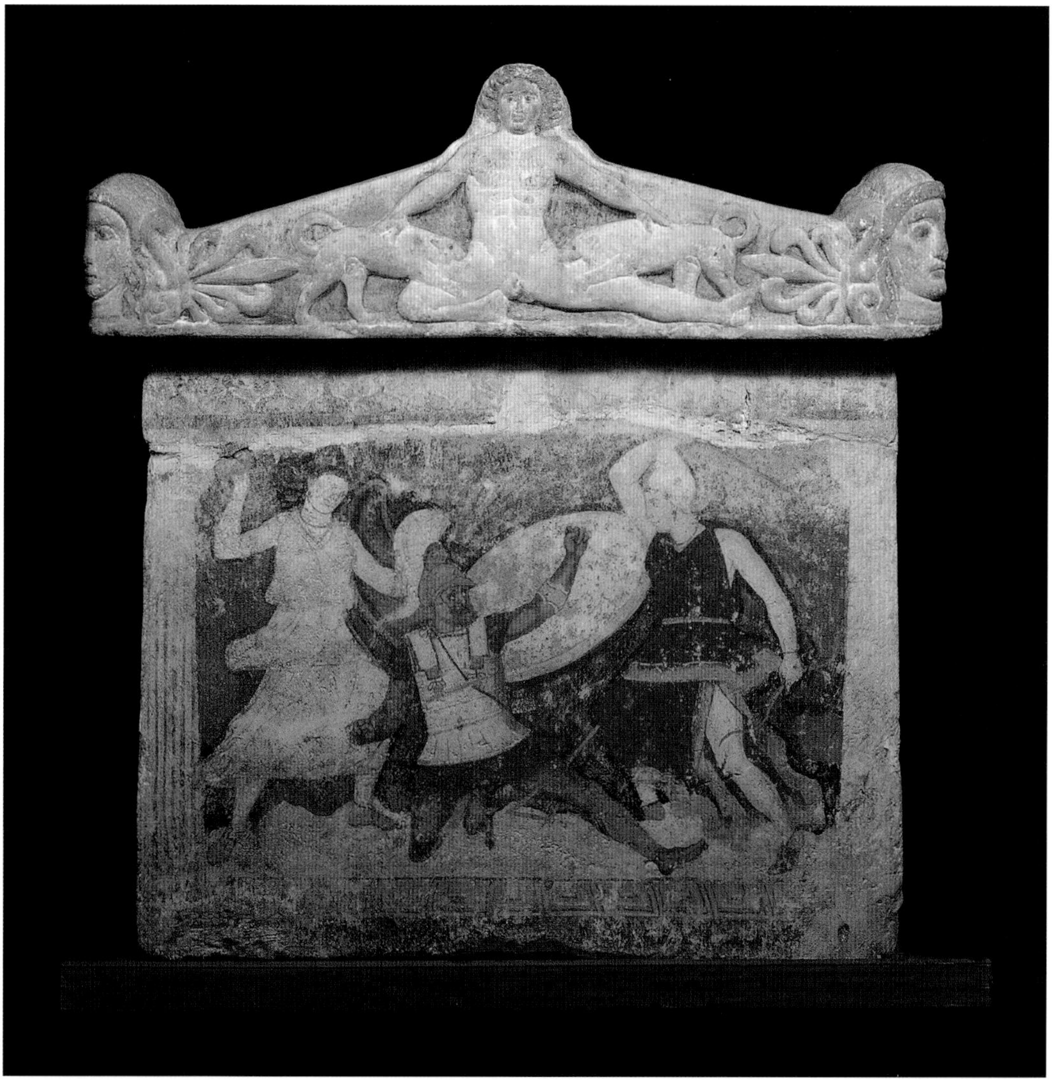

the number of figures and details, on five other central Italian monuments, the most notable of these being the wall-paintings in the François Tomb (p. 186) and a bronze *cista* from Palestrina (FIG. 235); they may all represent different adaptations of an original painting, created in the second half of the fourth century.

Another painted marble sarcophagus from Tarquinia is better preserved, and its paintings are of higher quality (FIG. 236). Their subject is likewise Amazons battling Greeks, but here the warlike women are fighting on horseback and on four-horse chariots, as well as on foot. Iconographical details of costume again show that the painter was an Etruscan who adapted Greek models. The figures, though still confined by contour lines, are given plastic volume by fine hatching, which conveys a chiaroscuro effect. This reflects pictorial developments that had taken place

Fig. 236 Short side of painted sarcophagus of Ramtha Huzcnai showing Amazonomachy. From Tarquinia. Third quarter of fourth century B.C. Marble. L. 1.94 m. Florence, Museo Archeologico.

in Greece. (According to Pliny 35.131, the Attic painter Nikias, son of Nikodemos, "painted women with particular care. He observed the light and shadows; and he aimed at making the paintings stand out from the panel as much as possible.")

The occupant of this painted Tarquinian sarcophagus in Florence was the lady Ramtha Huzcnai; her name and that of her descendant are inscribed on both the box and the lid (*TLE* 122): *ramtha:huzcnai:thui:cesu:ati:nacnva:larthial:ap(a)iatrus zileteraias* = Ramtha Huzcnai lies here, the mother *nacnva* (grandmother?) of Larth Apaiatrus, *zilc* of the *etera*. Larth Apaiatrus, the son (or grandson) who buried Ramtha, held the office of *zilc* of the *etera* (perhaps a magistrature concerned with organizations of juveniles). The gable ends of the lid of the sarcophagus are carved at the corners with female heads in the round and in the pediments with reliefs of the collapsing hunter Aktaion, attacked by two of his dogs.

Such scenes of battle, sacrificial bloodshed, and mythical death occur again and again on sarcophagi of both men and women from the second half of the fourth century onward and must be connected with Etruscan ritual ideas about the cult of the dead.

A further example of such themes appears on the limestone sarcophagus of another member of the Partunu family, Velthur (FIG. 237). The aged magnate lies, half turned toward the spectator and supported by cushions under his head and left shoulder, on a banqueting couch spread with a ragged-edged cover representing an animal's skin, an allusion to the Dionysiac cult. A mantle is wrapped around his legs, a wreath is on his head, and he holds a shallow libation vessel (*patera*) in his right hand. Recumbent lions and a female head are carved at one of the gabled

Fig. 237 Sarcophagus of Velthur Partunus. From Tarquinia. Last quarter of fourth century B.C. Limestone. L. 2.16 m. Tarquinia, Museo Nazionale Archeologico.

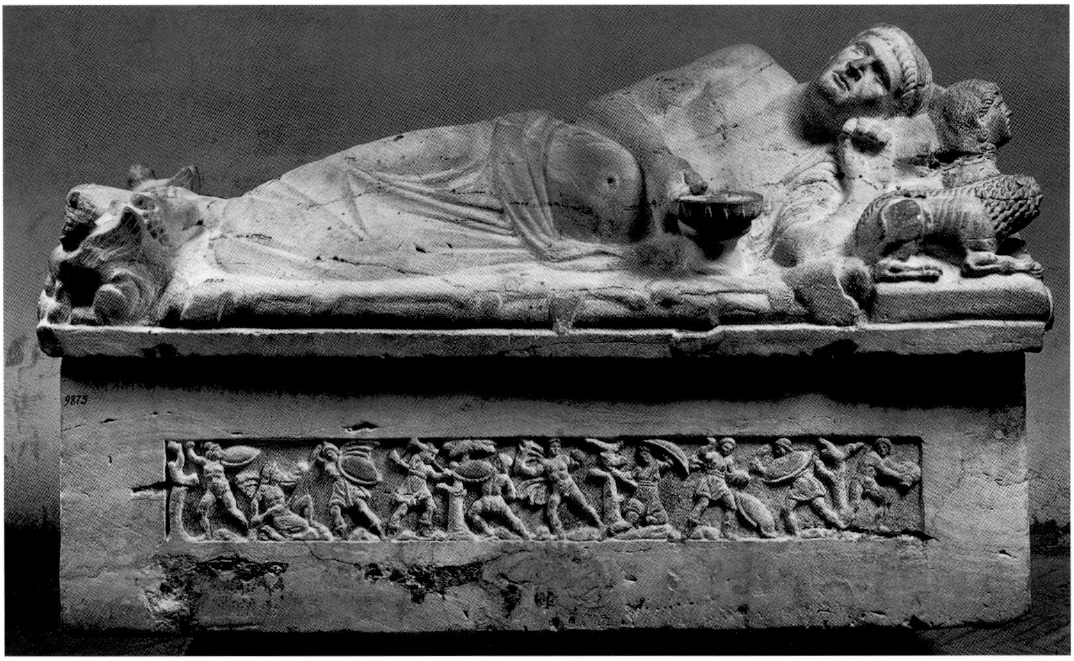

ends of the lid, two seated sphinxes frame a head of Acheloös at the other. The sunken panels of the box, which is modeled on a wooden chest, contain scenes in low relief (with paint remains) showing fights between Greeks and Amazons on the front and, on the back, a battle with centaurs interspersed with typically Etruscan demons. Uneven ground and a few tree trunks suggest a landscape setting, a new element reflecting developments in Greek art. Along the top of the box runs an inscription (*TLE* 126) giving the name and parentage of Velthur Partunus, as well as his age at death—eighty-two years. His father was Laris Partunus, the head of the family, and his mother Ramtha Cuclni. Velthur was a magistrate by the title of *zilch cechaneri*, perhaps a prominent office of limited duration. The sarcophagus dates from the end of the fourth century.

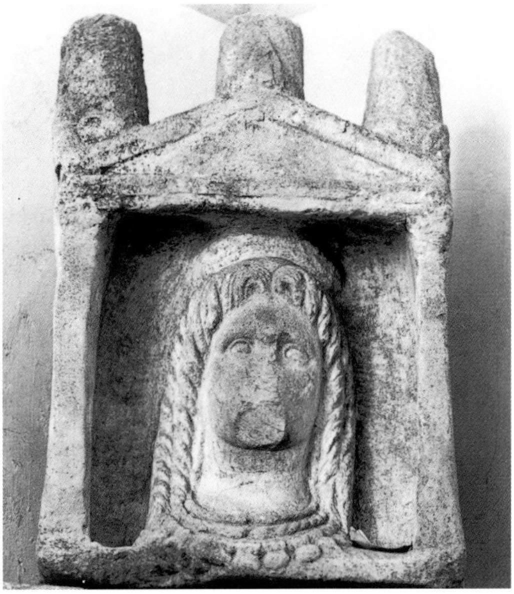

Fig. 238 Female head in a small shrine. End of fourth century B.C. *Nenfro.* Tarquinia, Museo Nazionale Archeologico.

Not only the sarcophagi inside Tarquinian tombs, but also the external part of some of the family sepulchres were decorated with sculpture at that period, but, owing to their exposure to the weather and vandalism, only a few examples of such figures in the round have survived. A now headless, almost life-size female statue of elongated proportions must have come from such a monumental tomb. The limestone statue, excavated in 1857 at Ripa Greppa, is now in the Museo Nazionale of Tarquinia. The woman stands on a square base with a fragmentary dedicatory inscription (*CIE* 5565) below her sandaled left foot. With her right leg relaxed and her left arm and body completely wrapped in a richly draped mantle over a chiton, she seizes the folds of the former with her right hand. Her face has deep-set eyes framed by shoulder-length tresses of wavy hair. Ostentatious jewelry underlines her high social position: a spiral bracelet ending in serpents' heads, two twisted torques, and a necklace with pendants of alternating heart- and *bulla* shape, the central one decorated with an embossed frontal bust of a woman. The statue was probably placed prominently above the entrance to a tomb, which she was the first to occupy.

Draped female statues standing within a small pillared shrine open on all sides (*aedicula*) are represented on a number of funerary vases from Magna Graecia of the second half of the fourth century; such prototypes may have inspired the Tarquinian artists who carved the statue from Ripa Greppa and also those Northern Etruscan sculptors responsible for funerary statues of draped women from the area of Volterra (see FIGS. 278, 279).

From a Tarquinian tomb excavated in 1888 comes an unusual *nenfro* stela in the form of a small temple with a pediment surmounted by three palmette-shaped acroteria and above by three column stumps (FIG. 238). Within this *aedicula* is

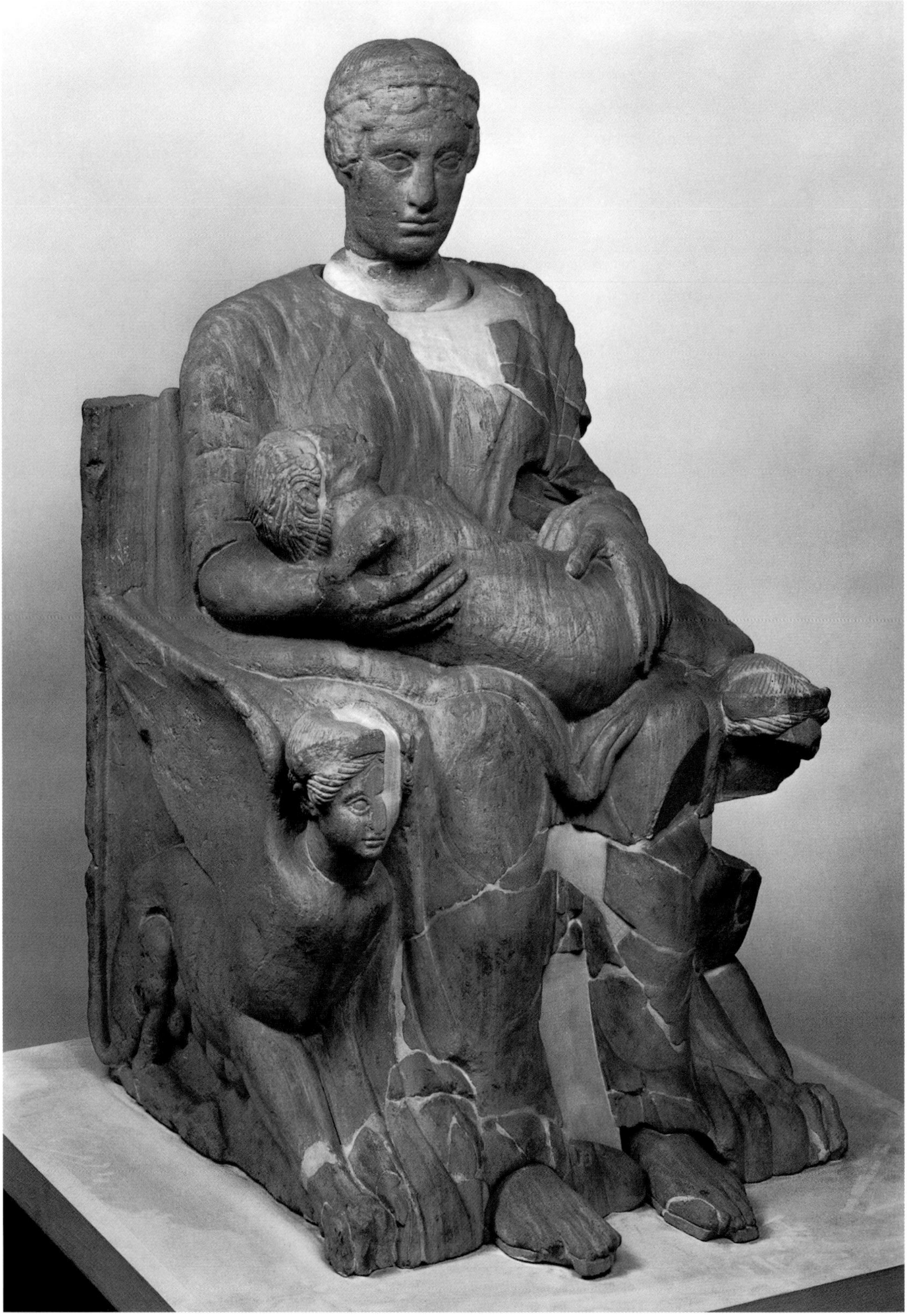

carved in high relief the frontal head of a woman, whose shoulder-length hair twisted into corkscrew curls frames a full face with small deep-set eyes. She, too, wears two torques and a necklace with *bulla* pendants in addition to earrings of inverted pyramid shape. From the grave goods found in the tomb, which included two Etruscan red-figured vases (stamnoi) of the end of the fourth century, it appears that the chamber with its sarcophagi and benches, hollowed by trenches for the deposition of the dead, was first in use at that period. Again, the prototypes for representing a female head within a small temple have been traced to South Italy, in particular Apulia and Taranto, where they signify the heroization of the dead women. It is, however, likely that Carthaginian cult stelae in the form of *naiskoi*, surmounted by obelisks, influenced this stela. It was probably set above the entrance door in the tomb's facade. More economical to carve than an entire statue, this stela may represent a lady who belonged to a less elevated social group of small or medium landowners.

CHIUSI: CINERARY STATUES, STONE SARCOPHAGI, AND ASH URNS

We have discussed above older examples of funerary sculpture particular to Chiusi. The local tradition of placing the burnt remains of the dead in a pottery or bronze container that took on increasingly realistic human form continued in the sixth century in cinerary statues carved from local stone. They represented the deceased in a heroized form and were hollowed out to contain his ashes. This tradition continued in the fifth and fourth centuries, its figurative repertoire enriched by new types. The comparatively rare older standing (see FIG. 93) or seated male statues were replaced by images of enthroned women and of men reclining on banqueting couches together with their wives (either reclining or sitting upright beside the husband). In some cases a female death demon, probably Vanth, is seated on the couch next to the deceased instead of his wife. Such monuments replaced the numerous relief-decorated ash urns, bases, cippi, and sarcophagi that had dominated Chiusine funerary art from ca. 570 to 450. They are found distributed over a wide area of the Chiusine territory and were probably commissioned by aristocratic landowners on their rural properties, whereas many of the relief-decorated cippi must have been produced for a large urban class buried in the vicinity of the city of Chiusi.

Among the most moving cinerary statues of the fifth century is that of a woman, found in 1846, enthroned on a chair flanked by crouching sphinxes, who holds on her lap a child wrapped in a cloth (FIG. 239). The mother wears a short-sleeved chiton; a mantle; and a diadem on her neatly parted, wavy hair, caught up at the back. Her head and feet were carved separately. The grave goods contained together with the ashes in the internal cavity included gold jewelry and an Attic female-head oinochoe from the second quarter of the fifth century. In her hieratic

Fig. 239 Ash urn in the form of a seated woman holding a baby. From La Pedata, Chianciano. Third quarter of fifth century B.C. Limestone. H. 90 cm. Florence, Museo Archeologico.

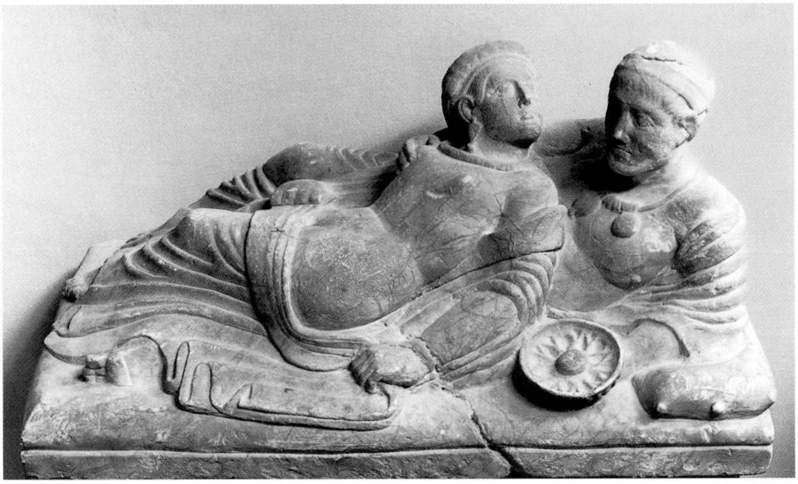

Fig. 240 Lid of ash urn with husband and wife. From Chiusi. Middle of fourth century B.C. Stone. Palermo, Museo Archeologico Regionale, Casuccini collection.

attitude and sternly beautiful face the mother reflects the Severe Style of Greek art of that period. Some scholars, however, pointing to the more advanced treatment of the child's hair, prefer to date the statue to the third quarter of the century. The sculpture shows undoubted stylistic relations with contemporary works in bronze and terra-cotta, many of which come from the region of Perugia, Orvieto, Veii, and Falerii and prove a strong influence of Greek Classical art, probably mediated from Magna Graecia via Rome and up the Tiber valley.

The cinerary statue in figure 239 is often referred to as Mater Matuta, identifying her with a mother goddess. The sphinxes of her throne (also found on other seated female funerary sculptures from Chiusi) are powerful demons watching over the dead, while the pomegranate held by some of these statues is a symbol of death and regeneration. However, the strong local tradition of depositing the ashes of the dead in a container that eternalized his or her image militates against such a definite identification with a divinity; it is possible, though, that the idea of a goddess of death and rebirth may have influenced the iconography of this group of female cinerary statues.

The apparent uncertainty about the exact date of this sculpture is characteristic for the larger part of Etruscan works of the fifth and fourth centuries. This span of time—the interval between the Late Archaic and the Hellenistic periods, during which Etruscan art responded only sporadically or with delay to such stimuli as it received from Greek models of the Classical period—has in German been labeled *Interimsperiode* (intermediate period).

The image of a seated mother holding or nursing one or more infants at her breasts occurs in countless small votive statuettes of terra-cotta from Etruscan sites and in larger stone sculptures, particularly from a sanctuary in the Fondo Patturelli in Campania. This existed, as attested by architectural terra-cottas, as early as the first half of the sixth century and was sacred to a mother goddess and minor divinities. The majority of the votive statues and statuettes of seated or standing women with babies found there date between the fourth and the first centuries. Such intimate scenes of motherhood are characteristic for central Italy but, with the exception of a few examples from Magna Graecia, hardly find counterparts in mainland Greek art.

During the middle years of the fourth century, the area of Chiusi displayed a kind of cultural eclecticism. Influence from Vulci (so prominent in the early Chiusine monumental sculpture, see p. 170) again became noticeable, particularly in the rare subject of a couple on their marital bed. The lid of a cinerary urn from Chiusi shows husband and wife leaning against each other, propped up on their left elbows (FIG. 240). Both wear only a mantle, that of the wife leaving most of her torso bare. The husband rests his right hand on her shoulder and breast, while she turns her diademed and bejeweled head back toward him. In his left hand he holds an embossed omphalos bowl. Front and side panels of the urn are carved with fighting animals and the characteristic cloud motif, hinting at the underworld. The figures of the seminude loving couple recall those of the Vulcian sarcophagi of the Tetnie family (see FIGS. 232a, 233), but their attitude is somewhat awkward and stiff, betraying a modest provincial artist.

ORVIETO: TEMPLES, ARCHITECTURAL TERRA-COTTAS, AND WORKS IN BRONZE

On the rock plateau of Orvieto—in all probability the site of Volsinii Veteres—stood a number of temples, as attested by the discovery of quantities of fragments of terra-cotta revetments and of votive inscriptions (p. 178). One temple, situated on the northeastern tip of the rock at the Belvedere, has been excavated in various campaigns since 1879 and partly restored. According to the inscription *tinia calusna* on a cup found with other votive gifts, the divinity to whom the sanctuary was dedicated was Tinia in his underworld aspect. The temple rose at the end of a walled enclosure, on a platform of tufa blocks accessible by a frontal flight of steps. The plan is that of a typical Etruscan temple, divided into three chambers behind a deep porch with two rows of four columns in front. The oldest fragments of the building's architectural decoration date from the beginning of the fifth century. They are few in number, but include molds for the manufacture of terra-cotta figures of Late Archaic style.

The most conspicuous group of fragments dates from the late fifth or early fourth century, a period of renewed architectural activity all over the city. Outstanding among the revetments of the Belvedere temple are the panels with figures in high relief that covered the ends of the beams of the ridge roof in the pediments. Most of them were found in a trench at the back of the building and therefore presumably decorated the rear gable. The themes represented by the preserved figures are still a matter of debate; they comprise divinities such as Artemis, Athena,

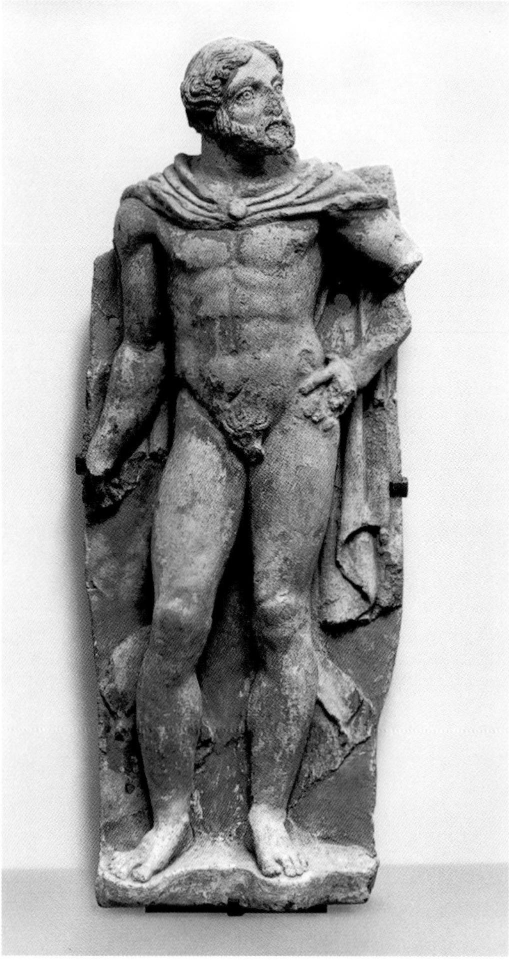

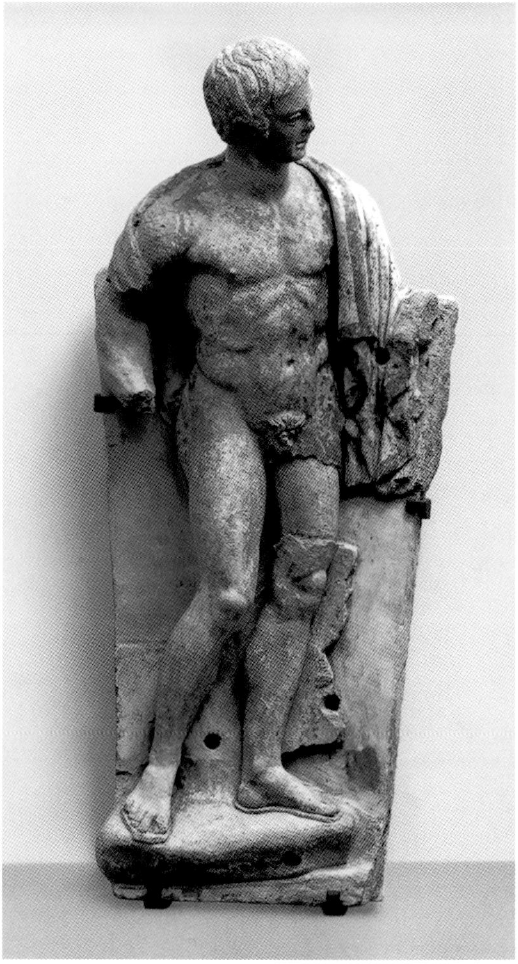

Fig. 241 Panel with figure of a bearded man in high relief. From the pediment of the Belvedere temple, Orvieto. Late fifth–early fourth century B.C. Terracotta. H. 85.1 cm. Orvieto, Museo "Claudio Faina" 2005.

Fig. 242 Panel with figure of a young man in high relief. From the pediment of the Belvedere temple, Orvieto. Late fifth–early fourth century B.C. Terracotta. H. 87 cm. Orvieto, Museo "Claudio Faina" 1377.

Hermes, and Herakles, as well as warriors wearing a cuirass, young and old lightly draped men (FIGS. 241, 242), and seated women, probably mythological personalities. The high quality and Classical style of these figures show that the modelers at Orvieto were strongly influenced by Greek prototypes of the school of Pheidias. Inspiration by Phidian works is noticeable also in splendid terra-cottas from a temple in Via San Leonardo and from the sanctuary in the Cannicella necropolis. In contrast to the southern coastal cities, the Tiber area of inner Etruria of which Orvieto and Civita Castellana were flourishing examples profited from continued connections with Greece and Magna Graecia.

In their style and technique the terra-cotta figures from the Belvedere temple, in particular the figure of a standing warrior in cuirass and mantle, are closely linked with the bronze statue known as the "Mars from Todi" (FIG. 243). This near life-size votive statue of a warrior in a cuirass, leaning on a lance and pouring a libation, is inscribed with the dedication of an Umbrian donor, *Ahal Trutitis*. Probably made

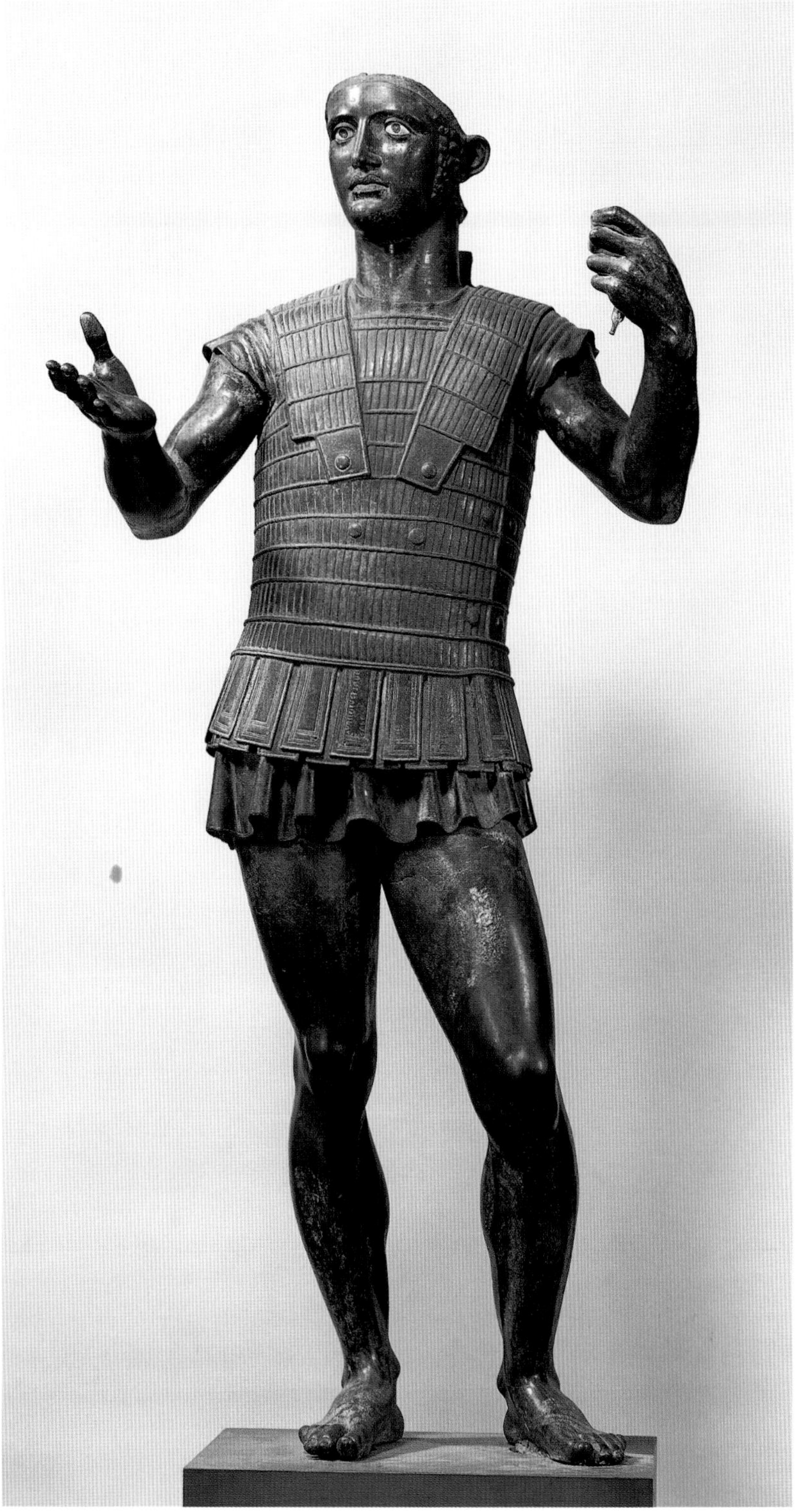

Fig. 243 Statue of Mars. From Todi. Late fifth–early fourth century B.C. Cast bronze. H. 1.42 m. Vatican, Museo Gregoriano Etrusco 693.

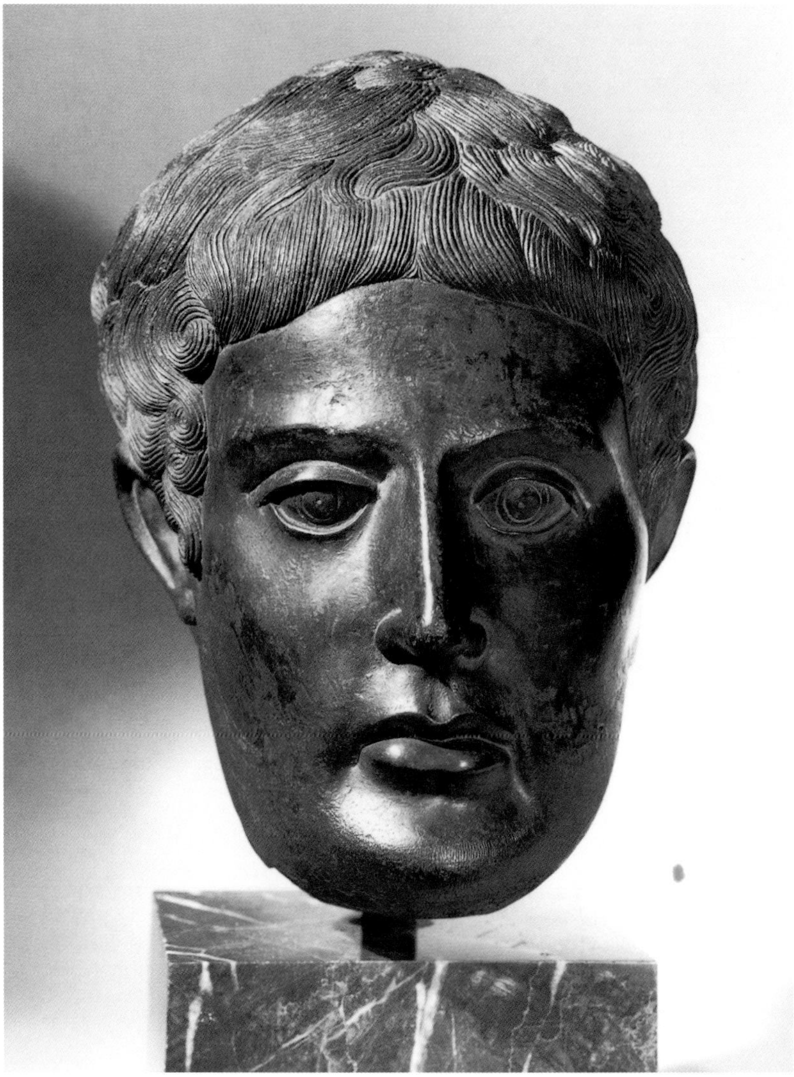

Fig. 244 Head of a statue of a young man. From Lake Bolsena. Second quarter of fourth century B.C. Cast bronze. H. 25 cm. London, The British Museum GR 1824.4-70.6.

in a workshop of Orvieto, the statue was discovered near Todi, ritually buried in a travertine-lined trench, apparently after having been struck by lightning.

A splendid life-size head from Lake Bolsena representing a young man with curly hair and a finely hatched first beard on cheeks and chin probably came from a large votive statue from Orvieto (FIG. 244); it has been dated to the second quarter of the fourth century. Stylistically it depends on models of the school of Polykleitos, as does a contemporary bronze jug in the form of the head of a young man with a *bulla* pendant in his curly hair from Gabii (Louvre *Bronze Cat.* 2955) and a similar jug in the Antikensammlungen in Munich (inv. 2573).

Apart from large bronze statues, Orvieto may have produced important bronze utensils, such as the situla found at Offida, now in the British Museum

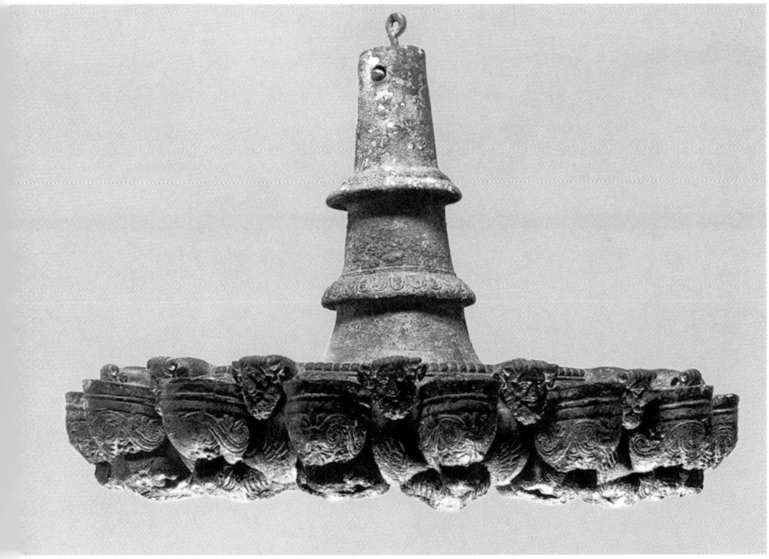

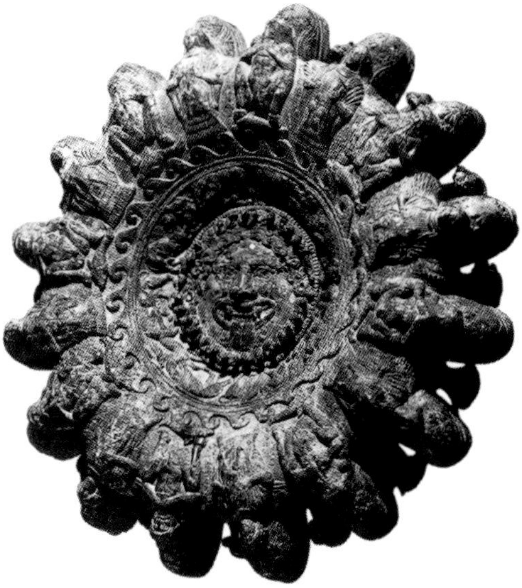

Fig. 245a Lamp with sixteen nozzles and relief decoration. From Fratta. Late fifth–early fourth century B.C. Cast bronze. Diam. 58 cm. Cortona, Museo dell'Accademia Etrusca.

Fig. 245b Angled view of lamp, figure 245a.

(BM *Bronze Cat.* 650), and a very large lamp discovered in 1840 at Fratta near Cortona (FIGS. 245a, b). The circular oil dish has sixteen radiating nozzles for individual wicks; the nozzles are decorated on their front and sides with double palmettes flanked by tied volutes; alternating on the underside of each nozzle are frontal figures of crouching sileni playing auloi and syrinx and draped and bejeweled sirens with spreading wings and bird's tails. From the interstices between the nozzles project sixteen identical bearded heads of the river god Acheloös. The central motif on the underside of the lamp is a mask of the Gorgon surrounded by two circular friezes: fighting animals and a wave pattern with leaping dolphins, all familiar from tomb decorations; here, however, a cosmic symbolism may be implied, as suggested by the division into sixteen parts (cf. pp. 277f.). It is likely that the lamp was originally made for a funerary setting and later reused, for a (damaged) inscribed bronze plaque with a votive inscription, dated on palaeographic grounds to the Hellenistic age, was found with the lamp and must be a later addition (*TLE* 646). It refers to the lamp as *thapna* = container (of oil) and mentions the gentilicial name of the Muśni family and the word *(t)inścvil* = belonging to Tinia, or perhaps, more generically, "sacred, divine." The difficulties of dating the lamp itself are typical of the eclectic works created between the Late Archaic and Hellenistic periods. The motifs chosen by the bronzeworker are borrowed from models that diverge widely in time and were composed in an over-rich decoration that left not a single inch devoid of reliefs. While the sileni and sirens hark back to models of the mid-fifth century, the Acheloös heads point to prototypes of the fourth. It has been suggested that the workshop where this massive lamp (weight: 57.7 kg) was made at the end of the fifth or beginning of the fourth century, was located at Orvieto and may have included bronzeworkers from Vulci.

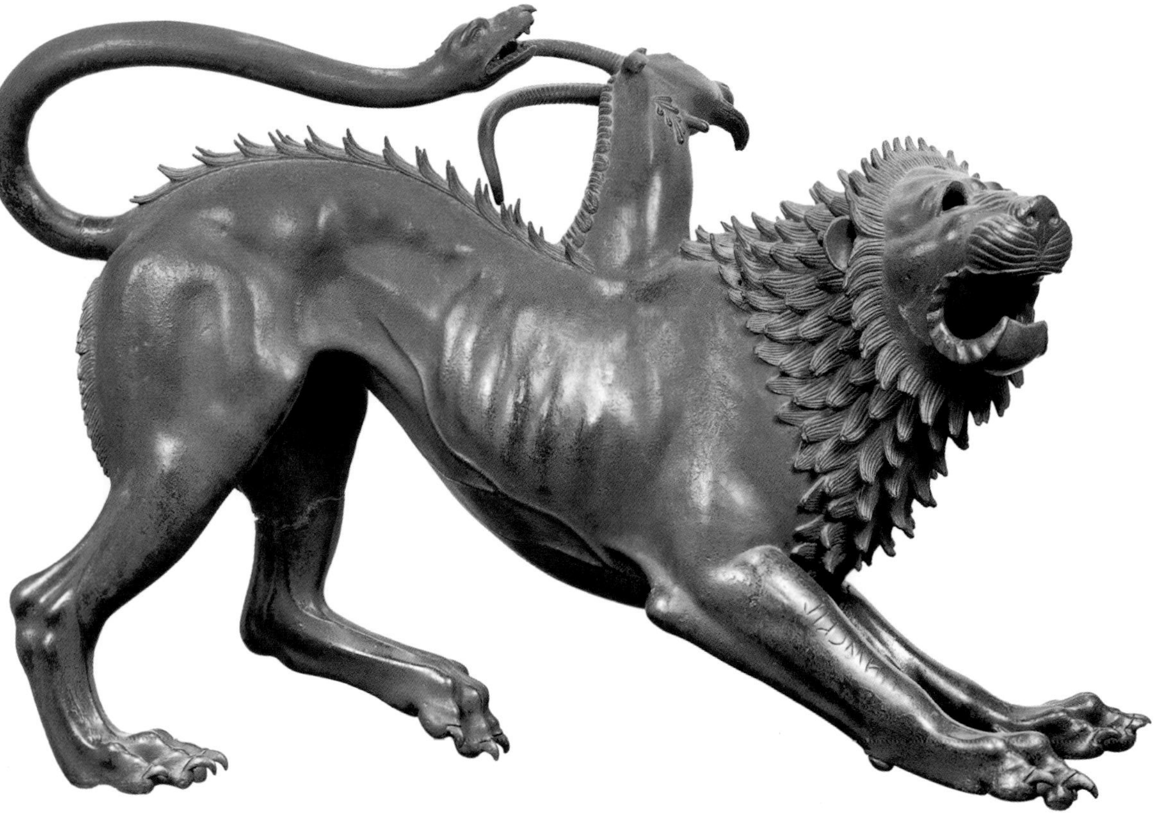

Fig. 246 Votive bronze statue of the Chimaira. From Arezzo. Late fifth–early fourth century B.C. Cast bronze. H. 80 cm. Florence, Museo Archeologico 69750.

Equally problematical is the date of a splendid large bronze statue of the Chimaira, a creature consisting of a lion, a goat's head, and a snake, which, according to Greek myth, was killed by the hero Bellerophon (FIG. 246). The statue must have formed part of a group, for the goat's head and the hindleg of the lion show bleeding wounds, which imply the original presence of the Chimaira's slayer, mounted on his winged horse, Pegasos. Only the monster has survived, however. It was discovered in 1553, together with numerous small votive statuettes of youths and animals, outside the Porta San Lorentino of Arezzo. The inscription, *tinścvil* (*TLE* 663), engraved in the wax model of the beast's right foreleg before casting, shows it was intended as a votive offering. The tensed, splendidly modeled body of the crouching Chimaira has been compared with that of the sphinxes flanking the throne of a Chiusine cinerary statue of a woman from Marciano in the Chiana valley (Berlin E 34), and the triangular tufts of mane radiating from the head of the Chimaira with those of lion's-head waterspouts from the temple of Metapontum in Magna Graecia. The Chimaira's fiercely aggressive, masklike head with the stylized tufts of mane and back hair goes back to sub-Archaic prototypes. The bronze was probably made in the late fifth or early fourth century.

THE GALLIC INCURSION

The valleys of the Chiana and the Tiber served as corridors for relatively easy cultural communication between inner Etruria, Rome, and South Italy. In 390 B.C., after crossing the Apennines, a marauding horde of Gauls from the Po valley used this route through Etruria to the outskirts of Rome. Here they defeated a hastily raised Roman army on the river Allia after half the Roman troops fled in terror to Veii. Under their leader Brennus the Gauls went on to sack the city of Rome and finally forced the surrender of the garrison defending the Capitol. Having exacted large quantities of gold from the vanquished, the Gauls withdrew.

There was a tradition that the Gauls were lured into Etruria by a promise of fruit and especially wine (Livy 5.32–35). A man named Arruns from Chiusi wanted to take revenge on Lucumo, who had seduced his wife and was too powerful to be punished except with the help of foreigners. It is said that to this end Arruns guided the Gauls across the Alps to Chiusi. Livy points out, however, that Gauls had crossed into northern Italy two hundred years before they attacked Chiusi and Rome, and Gallic armies had fought many battles with the peoples who lived between the Alps and the Apennines. He goes on to explain the great extent of Etruscan domination, which included the whole of the Po valley as far as the Alps, except the little corner where the Venetians lived. Placing the first arrival of the Gauls in northern Italy firmly within the reign of Tarquinius Priscus, Livy describes the successive migrations of different tribes during the following two centuries. First were the Insubres, who defeated the Etruscans on the Ticino and settled Milan; then followed the Cenomani, the Libui, the Salui, the Boii, the Lingones, and lastly the Senones, who by the beginning of the fourth century had taken over the land along the Adriatic as far as the river Esina. It seems that it was marauding Senones who attacked Chiusi and Rome.

Notices in Diodorus Siculus (14.117.6) and Strabo (5.2.3) that on their way back from the south the Gauls were defeated by an Etruscan army from Cerveteri in the (otherwise unknown) Trausian plain have been plausibly connected with the subsequent movements of these Gauls. In the service of Dionysios of Syracuse (who we know sacked the Caeretan harbor of Pyrgi in 384 B.C.), the Gallic mercenaries may have been intended by the Sicilian Greeks as a supplementary land army against Cerveteri, which was then on good terms with Rome. In the terrible days after the battle on the Allia, the routed Romans had sent the Vestal Virgins and the sacred objects of the nation to Cerveteri, where they were given refuge. A close friendship must have existed between the two cities in this period, which lasted throughout the Veientine War of 406–396 and found expression in the mutual granting of public hospitality (*hospitium publicum*) by the Romans and Caeretans to their repective citizens (Livy 5.50.3).

In that period Rome seems to have looked upon Cerveteri as a center of civilization, as suggested by a passage in Livy (9.36.3), who writes that young Roman aristocrats were regularly sent there to be schooled in Etruscan literature (*etruscae litterae*), just as in Livy's day they were trained in Greek.

Rome recovered quickly after the Gallic sack and soon resumed aggressive campaigns against Etruria. After the annexation of Veii the Romans allotted parts of its territory to their own citizens (Livy 5.30.8), granting citizenship to some of the Veientine survivors who had not been sold into slavery. Rome's next northward expansion was to occupy Sutri (Lat. Sutrium) and Nepi (Lat. Nepete) in 383 B.C., thus encroaching relentlessly on Southern Etruria.

Between 358 and 351 Tarquinia, their Faliscan allies, and Rome fought a war with appalling cruelties on both sides. In 356, the Tarquinians sacrificed 307 Roman prisoners of war in their forum (Livy 7.15.9–10), but the Romans retaliated later by publicly killing 358 aristocratic Tarquinian prisoners in their own forum. Having joined in hostilities against Rome, Cerveteri was obliged to accept a truce for one hundred years; shortly afterward (in 351 B.C.) the city may have been endowed with the status of *civitas sine suffragio*, a form of Roman citizenship. Tarquinia had to sue for peace in 351. She and Civita Castellana were given truces for forty years; the latter eventually became a subject ally of Rome.

During the peace between 351 and 311, when a final series of wars broke out between Rome, Etruria, and Gallic tribes, the Romans were preoccupied in the south, defeating the Volsci and the Samnites.

BOLOGNA: FUNERARY STELAE

The Northern Etruscan area of Bologna had from an early period developed tomb markers in the form of tall stone slabs decorated with paint and low reliefs. During the second half of the fifth century a large group of stelae assumed a characteristic circular or horseshoe shape, the front usually framed by a band of hatched triangles, a wave pattern, vine scrolls, or ivy leaves. The main surface could be carved with a single vegetal motif or with a figure of the deceased, or it could be subdivided into several superposed fields for a variety of scenes in relief. These also often cover the back of the stela, as well as its curved sides. The themes represented here are related to some extent to those painted on the walls of the subterranean tombs of Southern Etruria. Composite marine creatures, such as *hippocamps*, and chthonic ones, such as snakes, heraldically face or fight each other. Alluding to death and the world beyond the sea, they often fill the exergues above or below the main scenes on the stelae. New motifs appear, inspired on the one hand by Greek pictorial prototypes and on the other by contemporary historical events.

Thus we find on a stela in Bologna—below the fight between a huge snake and a *hippocamp*—a draped man, clearly the deceased, driving in a chariot drawn

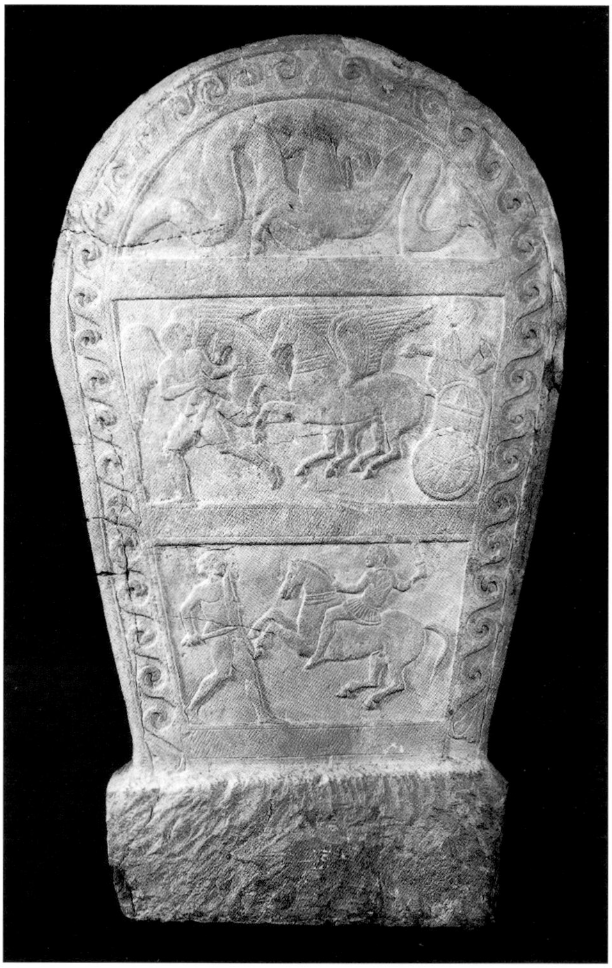

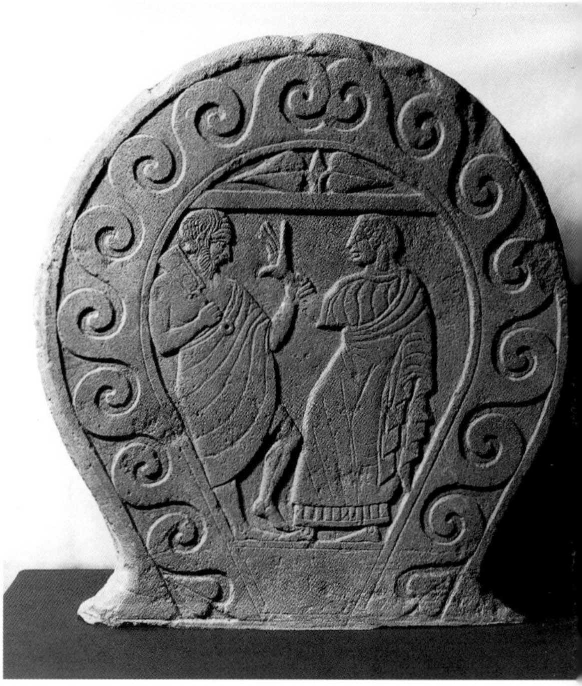

by winged horses and led by the running figure of a naked, winged youth (FIG. 247). The latter resembles Greek figures of Eros, the youthful god of love, or of death (*thanatos*), whose images were probably familiar to the Etruscans of the Po valley through Attic painted pottery. But the significance given to a borrowed Greek image is different in the Etruscan context. Here the winged youth has become a death demon, who hurries the deceased on his chariot journey to the other world. The winged horses hint at the eschatological nature of the journey. Directly below this allegoric scene appears a battle between a sword-brandishing horseman in cuirass and helmet and a huge naked warrior covering himself with a long shield, his sword at the ready. The form of his shield and his nudity characterize him as a Gaul; the scene may represent the last action of the Etruscan horseman whose grave the stela surmounted. He was perhaps killed in one of the many battles that the Etruscans of the Po valley fought against the invading Gallic tribes.

Another death demon frequently represented on stelae and also inspired by a Greek prototype is a bearded, ugly old man, occasionally winged, who holds a

Fig. 247 Funerary stela of a man carved with scenes in low relief. From the Certosa necropolis, Bologna. Late fifth century B.C. Sandstone. H. 1.80 m. Bologna, Museo Civico Archeologico.

Fig. 248 Funerary stela of a woman. From San Michele in Bosco. Late fifth century B.C. Sandstone. H. 84 cm. Bologna, Museo Civico Archeologico 17276.

paddlelike object in one hand and seizes the deceased with the other. On one such stela this mantle-clad demon roughly grasps the wrist of a richly draped and bejeweled woman to lead her off to the underworld (FIG. 248). The same subject appears on stela B from the Polisportivo at Bologna, but there the naked and winged demon gently guides the draped lady by the hand.

The paddle these demons hold as an attribute is derived from the occupational tool of Charon, the Greek ferryman of the dead, whose image appeared on many Attic white-ground funerary vases. Sitting in his boat, Charun is represented in the wall-paintings of the Tomb of the Blue Demons at Tarquinia (see FIG. 194), but here at Bologna he has been deprived of his watery context and serves as a hideous death demon, whose paddle remains the only connection with the original Greek model.

Greek satyrs, too, lent their animal ears and tails to Etruscan underworld demons on stelae, and they are shown seizing women in particular. Such satyrlike creatures may also be connected with the Dionysiac circle as in Greece and elsewhere in Etruria, as suggested by a gigantic satyr's head represented as the entrance to the underworld toward which the deceased proceed on a number of stelae.

Both male and female stelae, often inscribed, were carved for members of the local aristocracy. As a rule, the tombstones of men bear several superposed relief scenes, and the deceased are depicted in their main activities in life—as magistrates, warriors, or even as commander of a warship (Vel Keikna). Some men are shown receiving homage from a wife or family member, others on their way to the beyond in a biga, triga, or quadriga drawn by supernatural winged horses or felines. The stelae of women often have only a single scene on the main face, with the departure of the deceased lady guided by a demon. The production of these stelae seems to cease after the first half of the fourth century, when signs of a crisis are evident in the whole Po valley.

Of central importance for both the city and the necropolises of Bologna was a sanctuary situated in the elevated area of Villa Cassarini. Numerous molded travertine cippi that once supported votive offerings were discovered there. Bronze ex-votos included human devotees and two exceptional statuettes of divinities: a large figure of Herakles brandishing his club and with the lion's skin over his head and left arm, and an Apollo with his lyre, a work of modest size and quality. These votive bronzes date from the sixth to the fourth century.

TARQUINIA: ARISTOCRATIC TOMBS

During the respite from war with Rome in the second half of the fourth century, a series of especially grand underground aristocratic tombs with wall-paintings were created at Tarquinia, outstanding among them the Tomb of the Underworld and the Tomb of the Shields (*Tomba degli Scudi*), both in the Monterozzi necropolis. The latter is named after a row of shields painted in the rear burial chamber. The main room communicated with this and with two symmetrical lateral rooms through doors and windows. The wall space between these openings is painted with procession and banqueting scenes representing members of the Velcha family, who are identified by genealogical inscriptions.

The founder of the tomb, Larth Velcha, appears in a (much damaged) solemn cortege, escorted by horn and trumpet players, lictors, and a slave carrying a folding chair, all indicating his high dignity as a magistrate. He is further accompanied by male and female members of his family. Larth is depicted again, bearded, wreathed, and reclining on a banqueting couch with his wife, Velia Seitithi, sitting upright at the foot end according to the Greek fashion of not reclining together with her husband (FIG. 249). In front of their richly draped bed stands a serving table covered with fruit, cakes, and eggs. Velia hands Larth an egg while placing her other hand on his shoulder. Dressed in a semitransparent chiton and bordered mantle, she wears a gold diadem on her blond hair, which falls in corkscrew curls over her temples. Her other jewelry consists of necklace, bracelets, a ring, and earrings of grape-cluster type. On her feet are soft black leather ankle-high boots. The pretty slave girl standing beside her holding her mistress's fan wears similar boots, a long chiton, and earrings and bracelet; but her hair is cut short. This elegant attire of a mere servant and the sumptuously furnished couches and tables seem to illustrate perfectly Diodorus Siculus's description (5.40) of Etruscan banqueting habits with numerous slaves: "some of them [are] exceedingly handsome and dressed in a more costly way than befits their status." A long inscription above the dining couple is a eulogy of Larth Velcha (*TLE* 90).

His father, Velthur Velcha, with his wife Ravnthu Aprthnai, are represented in a similar manner on another couch (FIG. 250), Larth's mother with a simpler hairstyle and fewer jewels than her daughter-in-law. Velthur, the head of the family, holds an embossed metal drinking bowl and lays his right hand on his wife's shoulder; she responds by caressing him. A kithara- and an auloi player stand beside them.

This couple appear a second time, both looking more aged and probably imagined in a heroized state: they are enthroned on cushioned stools with footstools, Velthur holding a black scepter, while Ravnthu, with a didactic gesture, turns toward him and points him out as their venerable ancestor to their younger son, Vel, and their grandson. Further deceased relations are named in inscriptions, including a lady called Vethnai and members of the Aprthna and Camna families.

The style of beards worn by Larth and Velthur and the simple use of flat colors suggest that the paintings date to the third quarter of the fourth century. Some attempts seem to have been made to characterize the main protagonists' physiognomy, but the real purpose of the representation is to exalt the rank and offices of this important family, who intermarried with other aristocrats of Tarquinia. Recently fragments of the marble sarcophagus of Larth Velcha with his funerary

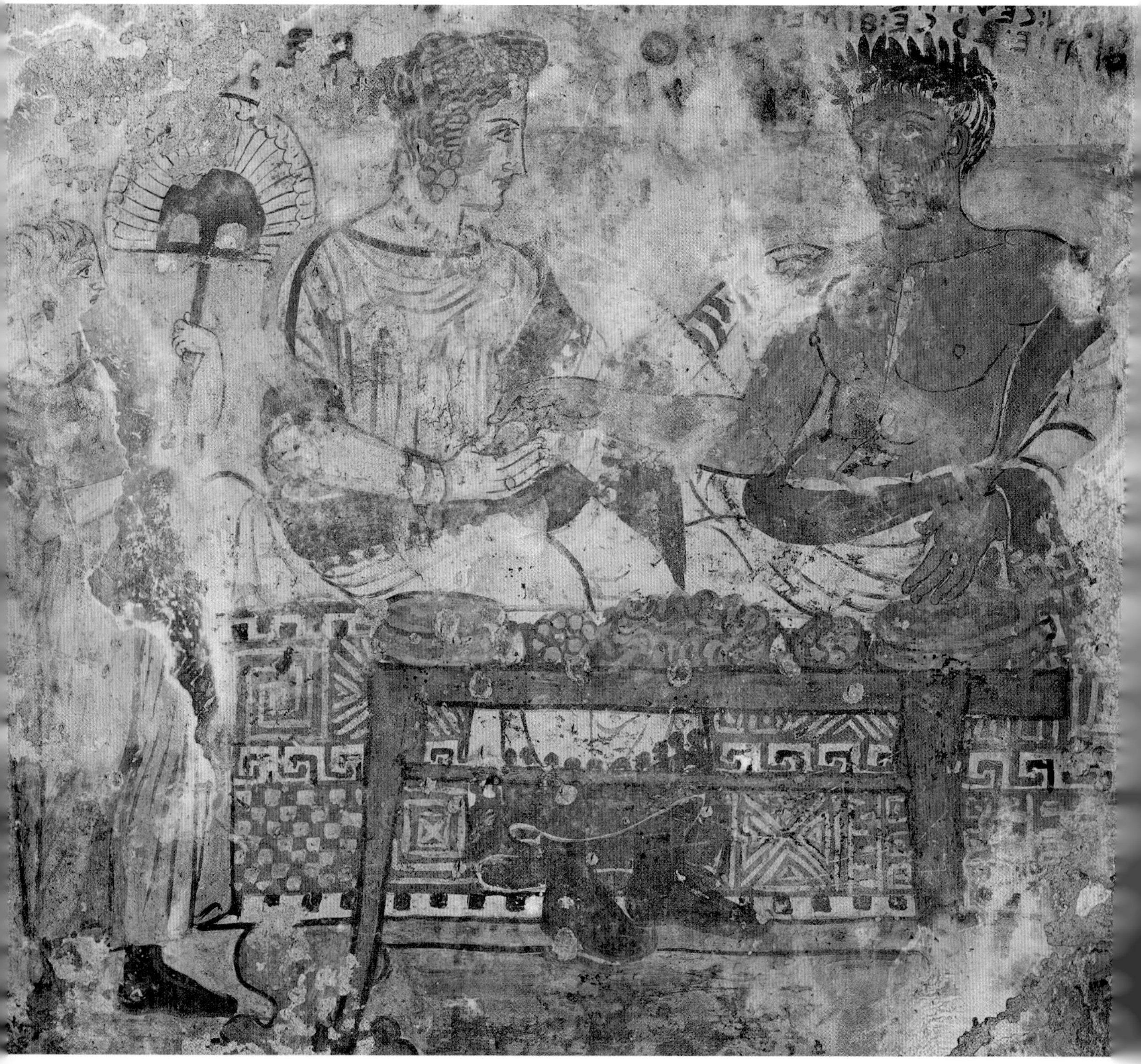

Fig. 249 Wall-painting: Larth Velcha and Velia Seitithi attended by a maid with a fan. From the Tomb of the Shields, Monterozzi necropolis, Tarquinia. Second half of fourth century B.C.

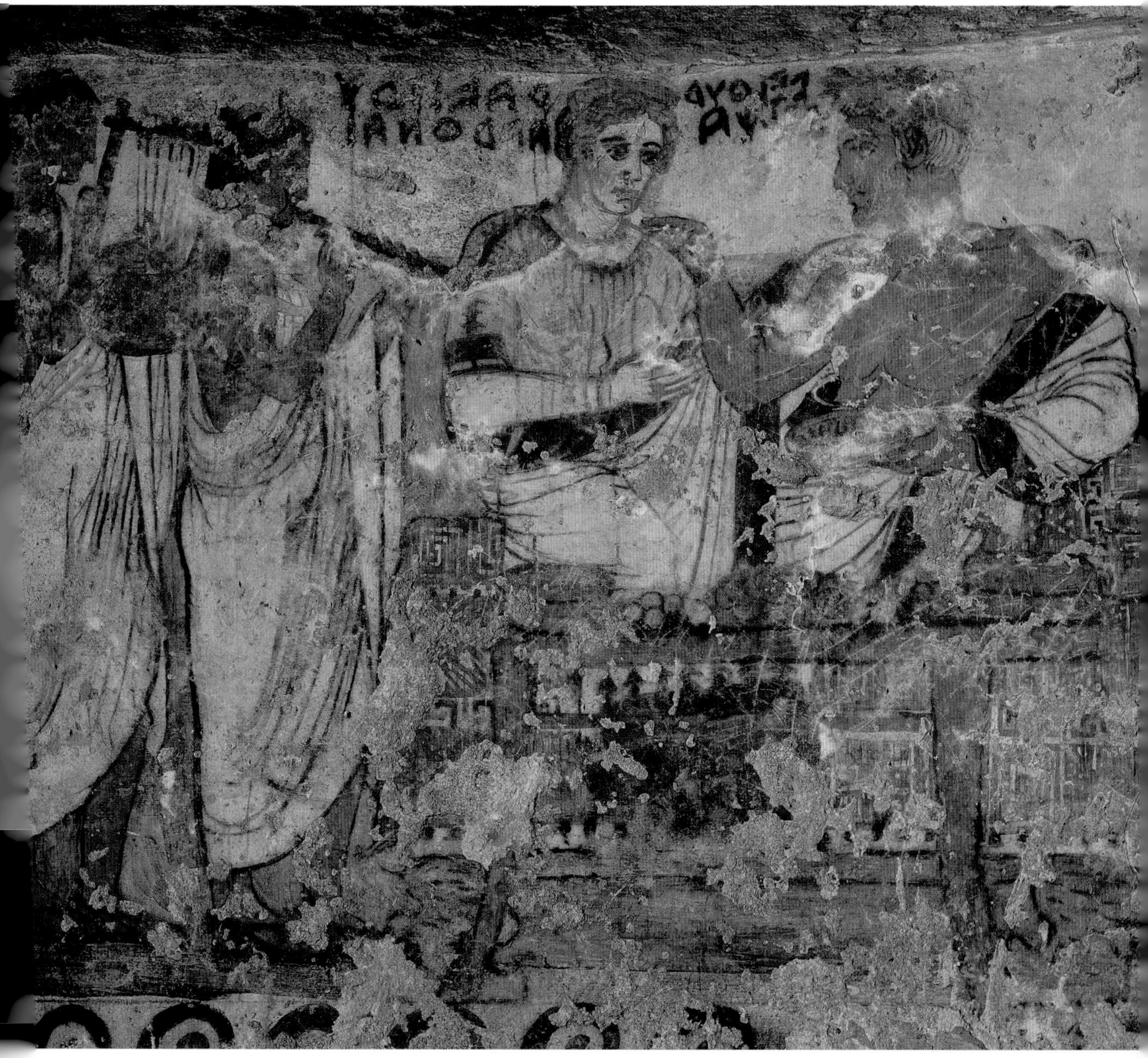

Fig. 250 Wall-painting: Velthur Velcha and Ravnthu Aprthnai attended by musicians. From the Tomb of the Shields, Monterozzi necropolis, Tarquinia. Second half of fourth century B.C.

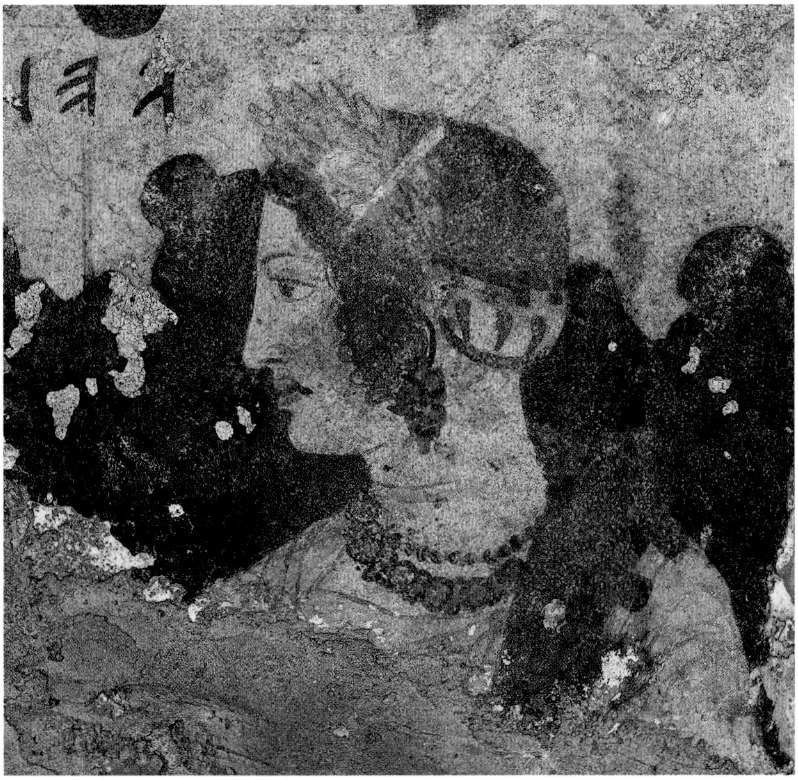

Fig. 251 Wall-painting: head of Velia, wife of Arnth Velcha. From the Tomb of the Underworld I, Monterozzi necropolis, Tarquinia. Second half of fourth century B.C.

inscription (*CIE* 5554) and of two further sarcophagi, all presumably removed from the rear burial chamber of the Tomb of the Shields, have been identified, built into the pavement of the medieval church of Santa Maria di Castello in Tarquinia.

The Tomb of the Underworld consists of two, originally unconnected, parallel chambers (named I and II), both with a rock-carved ridge roof and wall-paintings from the second half of the fourth century. In the first half of the third century these two chambers were connected at the back by a coffered passage (called III) and adapted for further burials. Where this restructuring had affected the left side of Tomb I, a fresh wall surface was prepared and painted with a cortege of figures, of which faint traces are preserved. Here the person presumably responsible for the alteration of the tomb is named in a newly identified inscription as *Murin*(. . .) *Larth* with the title of *zilath*.

The original main niche in the back wall of Tomb I was occupied by its fourth-century founder. Here, above a very damaged painted banqueting scene with three people on couches and a couple of children standing in front, a long inscription has partly survived, giving the founder's name as . . . (.)*urinas* (*TLE* 87). The missing initial letters of his family name had hitherto been restored as *sp*-. But the study of the recently discovered inscription on the left wall suggests that it should be read as *Murina* instead of *Spurina*. The older inscription on the back wall also gives his title as the highest magistrate of the city state (*zilath mechl rasnal* = Lat.

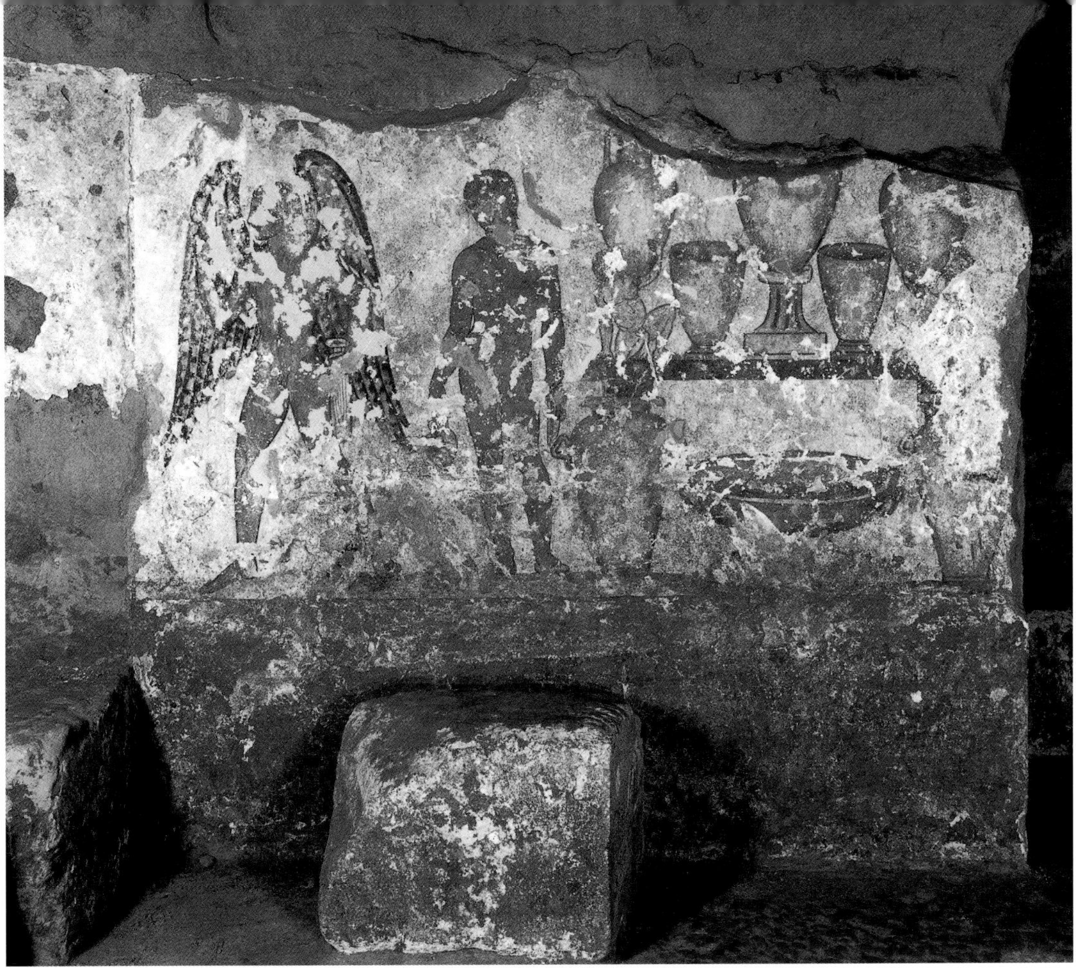

praetor rei publicae) and the name of a lady, (*R*)*avnthu* (*Th*)*efrinai*, presumably the grandmother of the children standing in front of the couch.

Further dead relations are depicted on the right-hand wall of Tomb I. Here the youthful lady Velia reclines beside her husband, Arnth Velcha (FIG. 251). Their couches, set against a dark, cloudlike background framed by sparse trees and surmounted by a continuous band of twisted vines, are imagined as being in the underworld. The presence of a threatening death demon confirms this location. Velia's chestnut hair is caught up in a patterned snood at the back and crowned by a laurel. Long corkscrew curls fall over her ears with grape-cluster earrings. She wears two strings of beads around her neck, at the base of which are painted "Venus rings"—flesh-colored folds indicated by darker ocher lines. Touches of pink on the eyelid, nostril, and cheek lend life to her severely beautiful profile.

On the walls of Tomb II are Etruscan interpretations of inscribed but badly preserved underworld scenes clearly inspired by Greek myth and epos, most probably episodes in the *Odyssey*. The banks of the underworld river are flanked by tall reeds. Here appear the shades of Teiresias (*hinthial teriasals*), Agamemnon (*Achmemrun*), and Ajax (*Avias*), dead heroes whom Odysseus came to consult about his future. Tiny insubstantial human figures (*eidola*), perhaps representing souls of Agamemnon's dead companions, flit about among the rushes. Other Greek heroes or sinners, such as Theseus (*These*) and Sisyphos (*Sispe*), are set

Fig. 252 Wall-painting: a banqueting table. From the Tomb of the Underworld II, Monterozzi necropolis, Tarquinia. Second half of fourth century B.C.

against a desolate rocky landscape and menaced by Etruscan demons, the hideous Tuchulcha, and by huge snakes. The rulers of the underworld, Aita, enthroned and wearing a wolf's-head cap, and Phersipnai, with a diadem of serpents, dominate the scene on the back wall of Tomb II, framed by a triple-headed dragon (Hydra?) and by the armed, three-headed Geryoneus (*Cerun*). All that survives of a banqueting scene in the beyond is a serving table set with splendid metal vessels and two nude boys, one of them winged and holding an alabastron (Eros/ Thanatos?), the other a cupbearer with a jug (FIG. 252).

On the rear wall of the connecting corridor (Tomb III) the blinding of the giant one-eyed Cyclop (*Cuclu*) Polyphemos by Odysseus (*Uthuste*) is badly preserved.

The paintings of the Tomb of the Underworld are of high quality. The artists active here, like the painters of the François Tomb in Vulci (see FIGS. 159, 227), the Golini Tomb (*Tomba Golini*) near Orvieto (see FIG. 260), and the sarcophagus of the Amazons from Tarquinia in Florence (see FIG. 236), were grappling with the new chiaroscuro technique developed by Greek painters on walls and panels. Such Greek pictorial prototypes were mediated to Etruria at this period through Magna Graecia, particularly Taranto and Campania. The growing importance of underworld scenes in tomb-paintings and on vases suggests knowledge not only of older Greek models, such as Polygnotos's painting of the underworld at Delphi (*nekyia*) and of funerary red-figured vases of Apulia showing the realm of Hades, but also of Orphic-Pythagorean ideas about the beyond. Both the Tomb of the Shields and the Tomb of the Underworld I and II are outstanding examples of the economic power and high social position of a self-conscious, closely related aristocracy of Southern Etruria in the second half of the fourth century. The Tomb of the Shields, in particular, emphasizes the role of the wife and ancestress as equal partner in maintaining the dignity of the family and the knowledge of the descent of the distinguished forebears of the family.

A section of the Tarquinian necropolis occupying an abandoned quarry on the height of the Monterozzi on the outskirts of the modern town and known as Fondo Scataglini is one of the rare systematically excavated parts of the cemeteries of the ancient city. The architecture of the 175 tombs (trenches, single and multiple chambers) and the grave goods found in them as well as the inscriptions and wall-paintings have recently been published in exemplary fashion.

Here we shall mention only the important Tomb 153, founded by Larth Anina at the end of the fourth century and in continuous use until the first century. The rock-cut, square chamber is surrounded on three sides by three stepped benches used for hollowing out pseudo-sarcophagi covered by separately carved lids, some in the form of shallow ridge roofs, as well as for the deposition of sarcophagi. The low ceiling was left unworked. The walls are only partially decorated with paintings, which do not conform to an overall plan but were applied in an episodic way after successive burials. To the earliest phase of the tomb belong the life-size figures of Charun with a hammer and Vanth with a burning torch, painted on either side of the entrance door (see FIG. 221). Striding forward in lively movement, the demons are competently sketched in rapid brushwork with shading and hatching on their wings and with highlights modeling their limbs. The artist was obviously familiar with the achievements of Greek Hellenistic painting techniques. The other frescoes on walls and benches are located mainly in the left half of the chamber and vary in execution. Painted on different levels, they include friezes of garlands and ribbons, *kymatia*, further underworld demons, a meeting between a woman and a youth, and long funerary inscriptions. Benches and sarcophagi were painted with geometric and textile patterns (towers with battlements, drapery), swags, and large rosettes—decorative themes familiar from grand tombs in Macedonia and Magna Graecia.

The effigies on the lids of the later sarcophagi of the Anina family are roughly sculpted and perfunctorily daubed with red. A single sarcophagus of a woman is of terra-cotta and belongs to the moldmade types found in Tuscania. Dating from the late third or early second century, it shows the deceased woman lying on a summarily modeled bed, whose decorative ends (*fulcra*) imitate real Greek prototypes with human heads and vegetal scrolls in relief.

The members of the Anina family do not seem to have been particularly distinguished, only one, Larth Aninas of the third generation, being described on his sarcophagus as a magistrate, *zilath* (inv. 153-S21). The family names of a number of the wives buried here are known from Northern Etruscan cities, Chiusi, Perugia, and Volterra. Apart from the sarcophagi, five inscribed and nine nameless cippi were found in the tomb, one of the latter taking the rare form of a female head rather than the more usual conical or columnar shape. In contrast to the use at Cerveteri, at Tarquinia the columnar cippus was used for marking both male and female burials.

CERVETERI: FAMILY TOMBS

From the middle of the fourth century, while the Romans concentrated on their military subjugation of Umbria and the Etruscan inland cities, Cerveteri, like Tarquinia, experienced a period of prosperity and renewed creativity. The Etruscans besieged Sutri in 311 B.C., and it took the Romans two successive years of campaigning to break the siege and continue their advance into the upper Tiber region. Battles forced the cities of Perugia, Cortona, and Arezzo to sue for peace, and truces were granted to them for thirty years. Livy's account of these wars (9.36.1–8) throws an interesting sidelight on the relations between Roman and Etruscan aristocrats at that time. The consul in charge of the campaign, Q. Fabius Maximus Rullianus, sent his brother to explore the dreaded and trackless Ciminian forests in Etruscan territory north of Sutri. The brother had been educated in Cerveteri, in

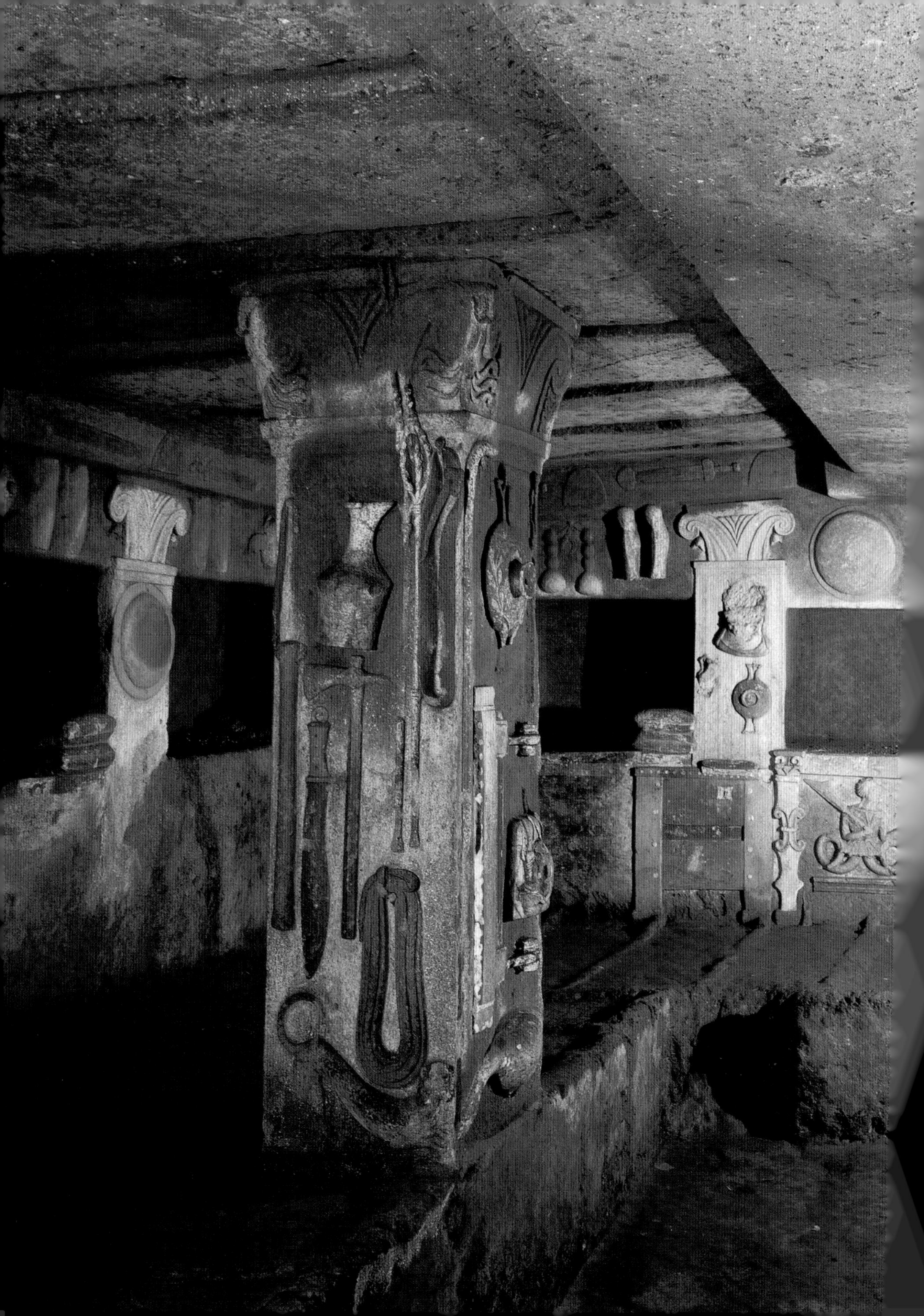

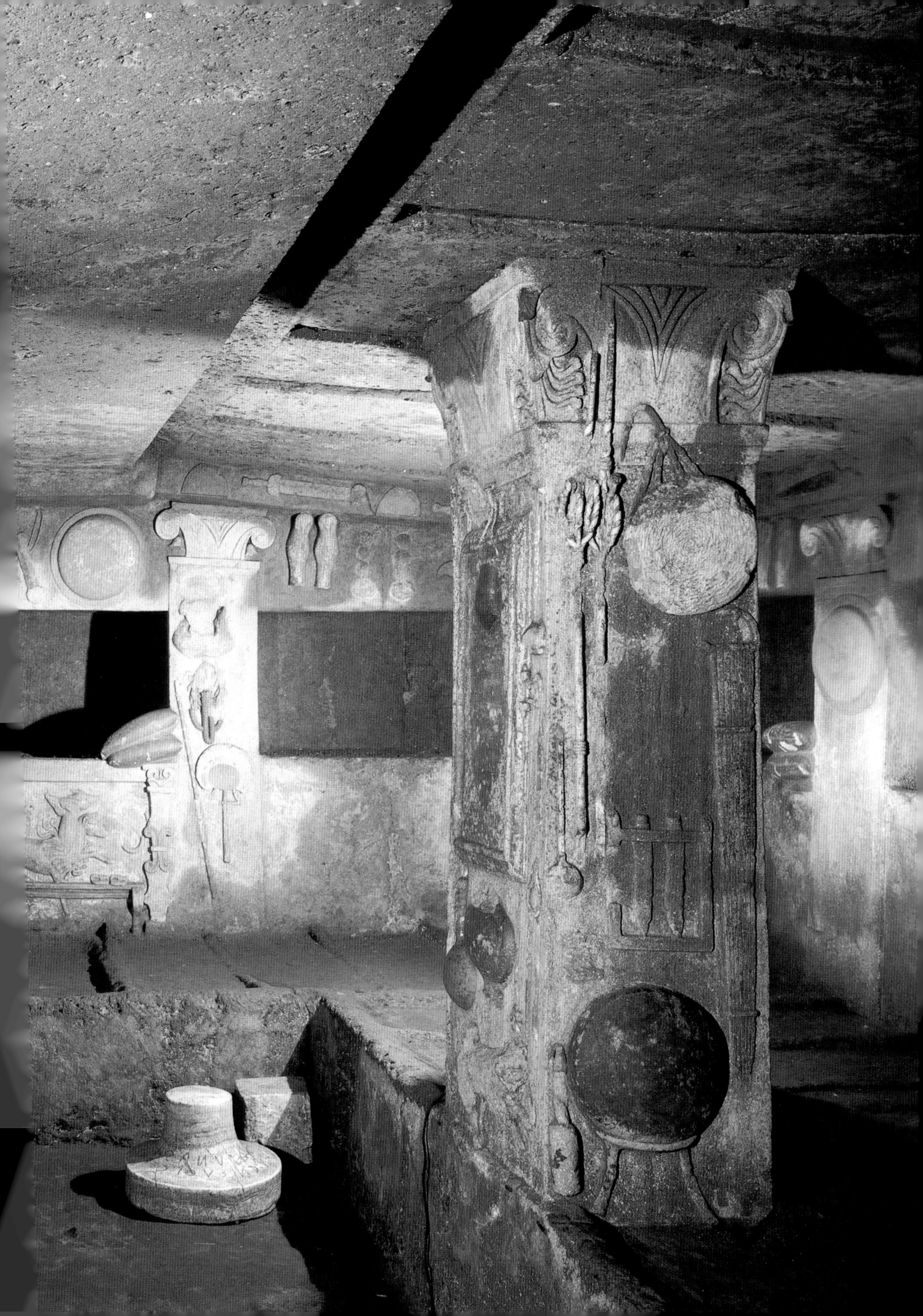

the house of family friends, and could therefore speak and write Etruscan well. He was accompanied only by a slave who had been brought up with him in Cerveteri.

The Caeretan family in which the two Romans were brought up may have been well-to-do aristocrats, such as the Matuna family, who had a splendid underground sepulchre carved for themselves in the tufa of the Banditaccia necropolis during the third quarter of the fourth century (FIG. 253). The Tomb of the Reliefs, as it is known from the unique and rich relief decoration in painted stucco that covers its walls and pilasters, resembles in its plan that of several other tombs created at that period in this necropolis—the tombs of the Tarchna and of the Tamsnie families, for example, and the Tomb of the Two Pilasters (*Tomba dei Due Pilastri*). The rectangular chamber of the Matuna sepulchre is reached by a steeply descending stepped dromos. All four sides of the tomb are surrounded by a bench, subdivided by low ledges into thirty-two spaces for the deposition of corpses. Above it, twelve oblong niches are carved into the walls, the central one in the rear wall being distinguished by its greater depth, which allowed the couple who founded the tomb to be laid there side by side on stucco pillows. The front of their last resting place is modeled like a bed with a footstool in front, on which stands a pair of sandals. The only allusion to death and the beyond in this domestic setting are the figures below the bed of Kerberos, the three-headed hound of Hades, next to a fishtailed underworld demon wielding a rudder and a serpent. Two much-damaged busts of divinities on the flanking pilasters presumably represent Aita and Phersipnai.

The surfaces of the walls and the two freestanding pilasters are modeled all over with every imaginable object of daily life: household utensils and vessels, bags, tools, ropes, a fan, wreaths, a gaming board, pets (such as a Maltese dog catching a lizard), ducks, geese, and, above all, the symbols of the power of the magistrate—the ivory folding chair, horns, and the *lituus*. Apart from holding high civic office, the members of the Matuna family were warlike and prepared to fight for their city. Twelve life-size representations of bronze helmets of "jockey-cap" type with cheek- and neck guards and other armor, weapons, and shields suspended as if from nails above and beside the niches show their warrior prowess. The helmet above the main niche is of Phrygian-cap type, indicating the leading position of the founder of the tomb. Inscriptions on the back walls of nine of the niches are now too faded to allow reliable readings. Analysis of the letters has suggested that the earliest inscriptions date from the last decades of the fourth century.

This tomb gives a very realistic impression of what the interior of an Etruscan house must have looked like: cupboards were unknown, so everything was hung up on walls. In other tombs surviving nails—and sometimes even the objects fallen from them—show that such was the normal form of tidy domestic storage. The only piece of furniture represented in the Tomb of the Reliefs is a locked wooden chest at the foot of the bed, probably for valuables. On top of it are pieces of folded material, perhaps "linen books," which we know were used for religious texts and probably for family records.

PREVIOUS PAGES
Fig. 253 Tomb of the Reliefs showing stucco decoration. Banditaccia necropolis, Cerveteri. Third quarter of fourth century B.C.

ETRUSCAN PAINTED POTTERY OF THE FOURTH AND THIRD CENTURIES

After massive importation of Attic painted pottery to Etruria during the sixth and fifth centuries, the supply virtually ceased toward the end of the fifth century. This has been explained in part by the defeat of Athens in the Peloponnesian War and the city's consequent economic decline. But the fact that Greek painting had reached a point where new challenges of color, chiaroscuro, and perspective were best realized on panels and walls may have had much to do with the waning interest in vase-painting, which offered limited possibilities for suggesting space.

To satisfy the continuing demand in Italy for Greek ceramics, new workshops were established in Magna Graecia and Etruria, at first under immigrant Attic potters and painters, some of whom had probably come to the west with the founders of Thurii (in 443 B.C.) and of Heraclea (in 432). A number settled in Lucania and at Taranto, where flourishing productions started. Other Greek craftsmen seem to have transferred themselves directly to the Faliscan capital Falerii, which (like Orvieto) became an important center for the communication between Southern Italy and inner and Northern Etruria, particularly after the fall of Veii. For two generations—from about 380 to 340—one of the workshops at Falerii produced large-scale red-figured vases with mythological subjects in the tradition of the Athenian Meidias Painter. Outstanding among the Faliscan artists is the Aurora Painter, named after a magnificent volute-krater from Civita Castellana decorated on one side with Eos/Aurora on a chariot, embraced by Kephalos, and on the other with Peleus subduing Thetis (FIG. 254). The shape and crisply painted moldings of the krater imitate metal prototypes; vases of this high quality were produced for a demanding local clientele.

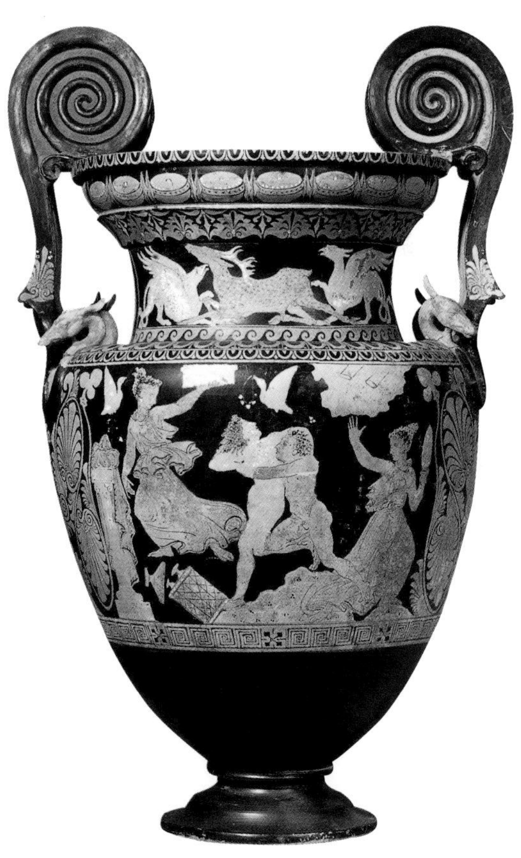

Fig. 254 Volute-krater by the Aurora Painter with Peleus wrestling with Thetis. From Civita Castellana. Second quarter of fourth century B.C. Painted pottery. H. 59.5 cm. Rome, Museo Etrusco di Villa Giulia 2491.

During the second and third quarters of the fourth century other Faliscan workshops specialized in smaller drinking vessels and in the technique of superposed colors. A cup with this type of decoration from a tomb at Falerii is signed *Sokra(tes)*, the shortened name of a Greek craftsman. Not only did these workshops produce for local markets but their pottery was widely distributed in an area stretching from Rome throughout most of inner and coastal Etruria. Workshops at Vulci likewise followed Attic red-figure traditions and from about 400 B.C. produced vases decorated in an eclectic style, often copying earlier

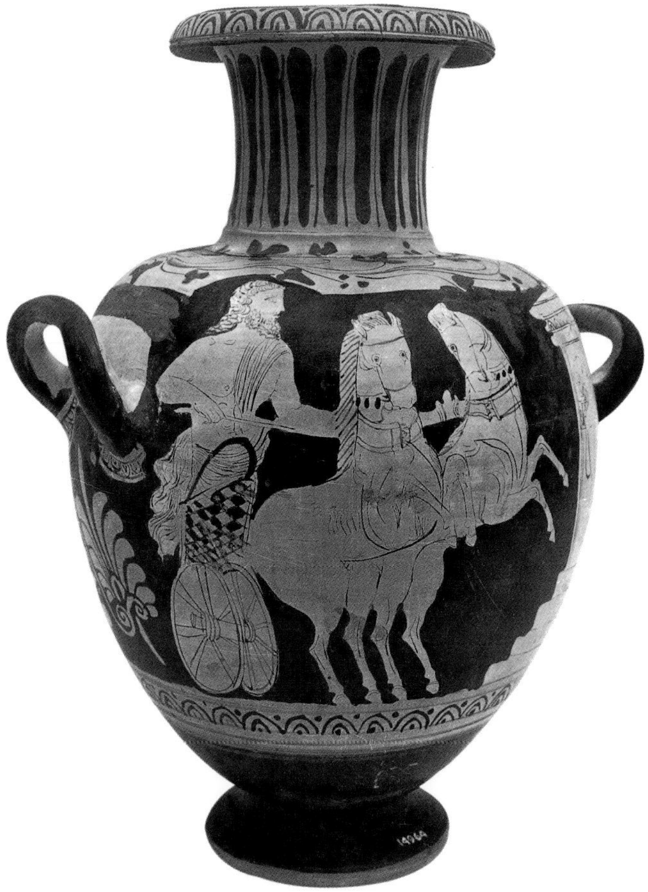

Fig. 255 Red-figured hydria with Hades(?) in a biga. From Vulci. 400–350 B.C. Painted pottery. H. 37 cm. Vatican, Museo Gregoriano Etrusco 14964.

Athenian models. In the works of the Perugia and Sommavilla Painters mythological and theatrical subjects predominate. The decoration of other vessels tended to indicate their use for funerary purposes. Such is the case with a hydria from Vulci (FIG. 255). On the belly of the vase the artist attempted boldly foreshortened figures by representing a bearded god (Aita?) on a biga with prancing horses driving up to what may be a circular funerary monument surmounted by a pinecone-shaped cippus. A nude youth with a paintbrush in his right hand and a small bowl of pigment in his left has put one foot on the stepped base of a building and stretches up to paint a decorative frieze on the molding. Cippi or *aediculae* of this form but surrounded by false columns occur in necropolises near Vulci and Sovana (p. 355, Tomb of the Silenus [*Tomba del Sileno*]). We cannot tell whether the underworld god is about to carry off the young painter himself, or whether his divine presence indicates that the unusual monument represents a tomb.

Both Faliscan and Vulcian workshops subsequently show the influence of South Italian Greek models from Campania and Apulia, particularly in their vegetal decoration.

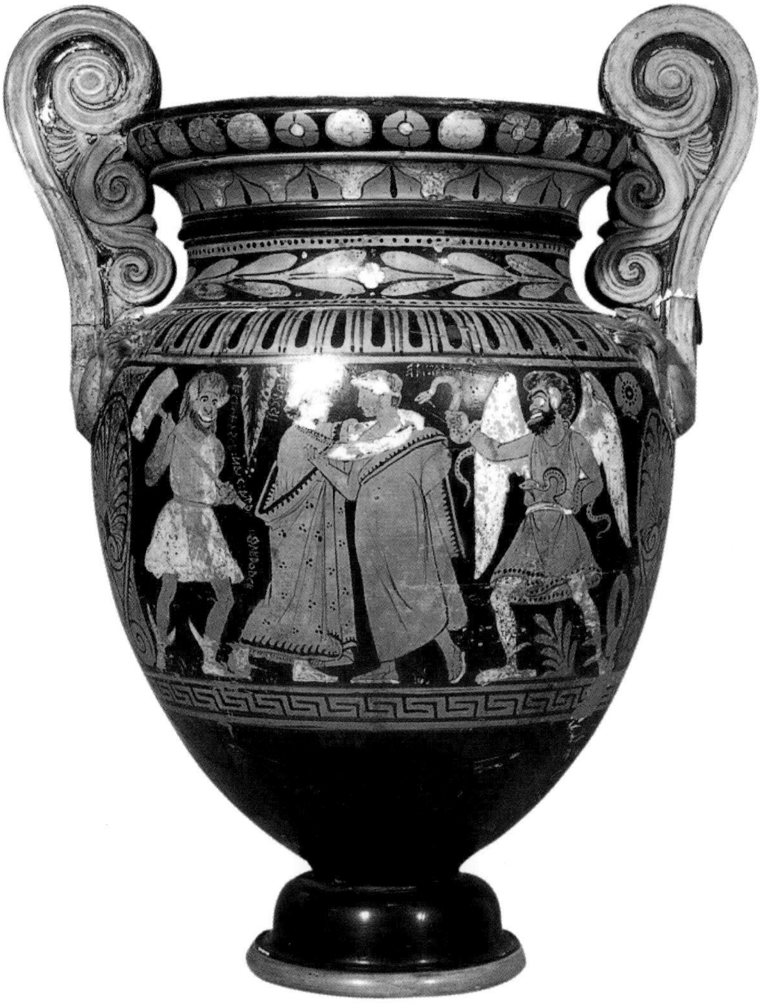

From about 340 some of the Faliscan production seems to have shifted from Falerii to Cerveteri, which became a veritable industrial center for painted pottery, though the quality reflects mass-production methods; other related workshops seem to have been established at Tarquinia. Generic Dionysiac themes with satyrs, maenads, and winged figures predominate in the repetitive decoration of this medium-sized pottery, which was widely exported.

Fig. 256 Red-figured volute-krater with Alkestis and Admetos. From Vulci. Second half of fourth century B.C. Painted pottery. H. 62 cm. Paris, Bibliothèque Nationale de France, Cabinet des Médailles 918.

During the second half of the fourth century an able artist at Vulci decorated large kraters and stamnoi with funerary subjects, some taken from Greek mythology and perhaps reflecting the influence of wall-painting (cf. the François Tomb, FIGS. 159, 227). On a red-figured krater found at Vulci overpainted with white and with Etruscan inscriptions we find the touching Greek story of Alkestis (Etr. *alcsti*), who embraces her husband, Admetos (*atmite*), after offering to die in his place (FIG. 256). The couple are framed by an Etruscan Charun with his hammer and by a demon with wings and raptor's feet holding snakes, both preparing to snatch away their victim to Acheron, referred to in the inscription (*TLE* 334). In Greek mythology Alkestis was saved from the underworld by the intervention of Herakles, a happy outcome that may have been familiar in Etruria, too. In any case, the story of a faithful and selfless wife was a suitably poignant theme for the decoration of a funerary vase, even if Alkestis's ultimate salvation is not alluded to here.

Beside Dionysiac and underworld scenes, battles of Amazons or centaurs and the slaughter of Trojan prisoners figure widely in the further Vulcian vase production of the last decades of the fourth century, subjects that were familiar from sarcophagi (see FIG. 236) and wall-paintings. Some of these masters seem to have operated also at Orvieto (the Painter of the Group of Vanth, the Painter of Settecamini, etc.). After 280 these workshops ceased production, presumably as the result of the Roman conquest.

In inner and Northern Etruria groups of potters and red-figure vase-painters were active both at Chiusi and at Volterra during the second half of the fourth century, creating a variety of vessels, some of them with plastic decoration such as askoi in the form of ducks. These vases bear erotic scenes of Greek mythology and others of female toilet or adornment (subjects often found on contemporary engraved bronze mirrors), as well as Dionysiac themes that hint at their eschatological significance.

Some column-kraters, known as *kelebai*, were used as ash urns. Probably made at Volterra, a number were distinguished by large-scale male and female heads in profile or three-quarter view, sketched with rapid brush strokes on the belly or neck of the vase (FIG. 257). The heads or busts might be taken for portraits of the deceased, but their generic quality and similarity with contemporary votive heads in terra-cotta militate against such an interpretation. The heads on the kraters only "stand for" the deceased, but are not true portraits. The fluidity of the design and hatched shading on the later *kelebai* show the artists' familiarity with Early Hellenistic pictorial achievements, a stylistic feature also noticeable in later Vulcian vase-painting. The tomb contexts in which a number of the Volterran column-kraters were discovered suggest that these vases were manufactured between the last decades of the fourth and the middle of the third century. Though produced and used mainly in the area of Volterra, the kraters were in demand as funerary vases elsewhere in Northern Etruria.

From the fourth to the first century the so-called black-glazed (more correctly black-painted) wares gradually replaced red-figured vases and those with decoration in superposed colors. Inspired by Attic prototypes of fifth- and fourth-century date, this fine, glossy-black banqueting and tableware with stamped and molded relief decoration was produced in several centers in Campania, Lazio, Rome, and Etruria and distributed all over the western Mediterranean. The shapes frequently imitate models in metal from Magna Graecia and Macedonia.

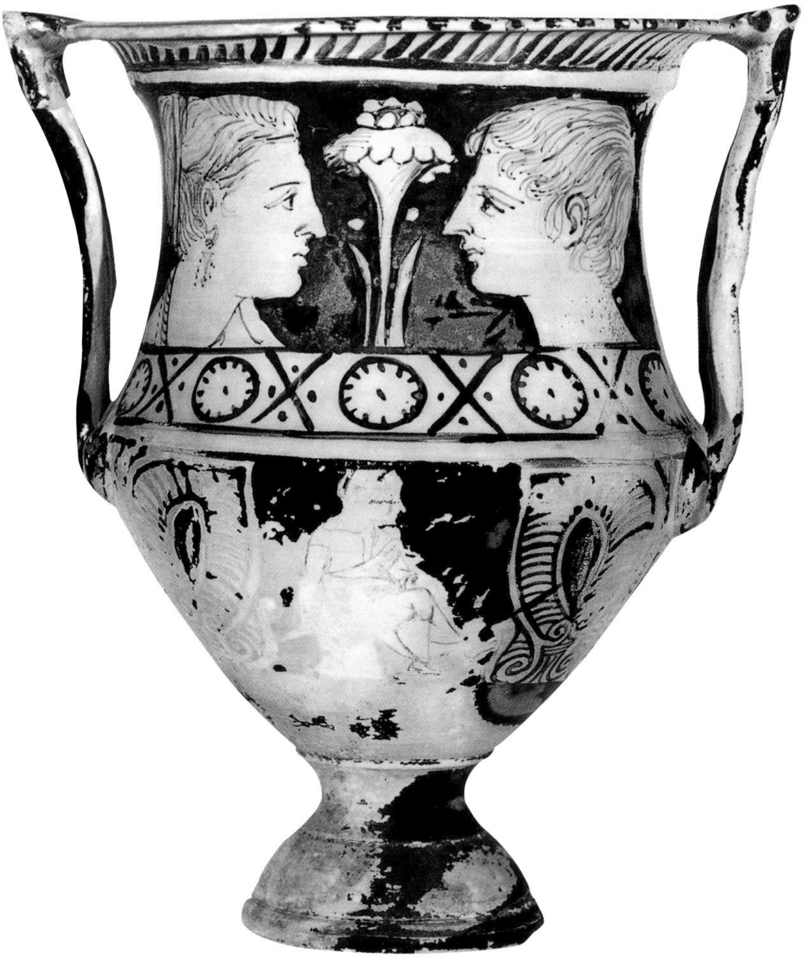

The highest quality of these wares was produced at Volterra; that was probably where Malacena ware was produced, so called after the site of the Tomb of the Calisna Sepu Family (*Tomba dei Calisna Sepu*) near Monteriggioni, where a large variety of vessels with this particularly fine, metallic blue-black glaze was found.

Another new type of pottery made for funerary use from the end of the fourth century onward was the *ceramica argentata*, a ware that aimed at imitating, in an economic way, precious embossed silver vessels. The "silvering" was achieved by dipping the fired clay pots into a bath of tin. This superficial silvery layer has often been worn away, but it must originally have looked quite shiny, and the moldmade figured relief decoration, obviously modeled after precious-metal prototypes, will have enhanced the illusion. The silvered vessels show affinities in their shapes and decoration with black-glazed wares.

The large size and technical excellence of late fourth- and third-century Volterran ceramics imitating metal vessels show that a demanding class of aristocrats continued to have banquets with elaborate tableware and vessels for wine

Fig. 257 Column-krater (*kelebe*). From the Tomb of the Calisna Sepu Family, at Monteriggioni. First half of third century B.C. Painted pottery. H. 38 cm. Berlin, Staatliche Museen—Preußischer Kulturbesitz—Antikensammlung V.I. 3988.

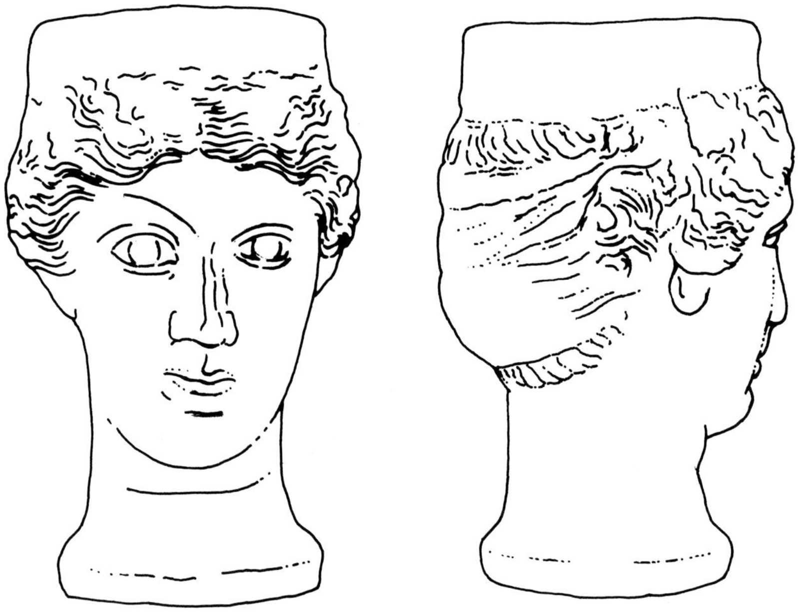

Fig. 258 Moldmade stand in the form of a female head. From Civita Castellana. Mid-fourth century B.C. Pottery dipped in tin (*ceramica argentata*). H. ca. 12 cm. Civita Castellana, Museo Archeologico dell'Agro Falisco, "sostegno" no. 3.

and to hold formal drinking parties as an expression of their social position in life as in death. Besides Volterra, mainly Orvieto and Bolsena, but also Falerii seem to have manufactured *ceramica argentata*.

In the Faliscan area some grave goods in silvered pottery from female burials in chamber tombs (at Civita Castellana and Corchiano) include objects found only in this region; they must have been made locally to satisfy a particular indigenous usage. The most important such object is probably of a ritual nature: a moldmade stand in the form of a woman's head surmounted by a low, cylindrical element resembling a headdress (*polos*) worn by several Greek goddesses (FIG. 258). These heads vary slightly in their hairstyle and jewelry, but their inspiration clearly goes back to South Italian and Sicilian models of the late fifth and early fourth centuries. They have been identified as representing Demeter, the goddess of agrarian fertility, who, through her daughter Persephone, was connected with the underworld. The deposition in a tomb of such a head may have symbolized the protection granted by the divinity to the deceased on her way to the beyond. Two tombs at Corchiano containing such heads seem to have been occupied exclusively by female burials, and it has been suggested that the women may have belonged to a religious association connected with Demeter (or her local equivalent).

A small figure of a draped woman standing on a capital made of *ceramica argentata* is connected with the female toilet. It dates to the late fourth or first half of the third century and is typical for women's grave goods in the Faliscan area. Moldmade in two halves, these little silvered figures originally formed the handles for a slim stick or pin fastened inside the capital, which could be inserted into an elongated scent bottle and used to apply the perfume. Such dipsticks, often represented on engraved mirrors in scenes of adornment, were usually made of bronze, but for funerary use the more economical silvered terra-cotta was preferred. Gilded terra-cotta for jewelry, decorative elements fastened to wooden sarcophagi, or other tomb furniture is known from the necropolises of Taranto, and this fashion spread from Magna Graecia to Lazio (Rome, Palestrina) and the Faliscan area.

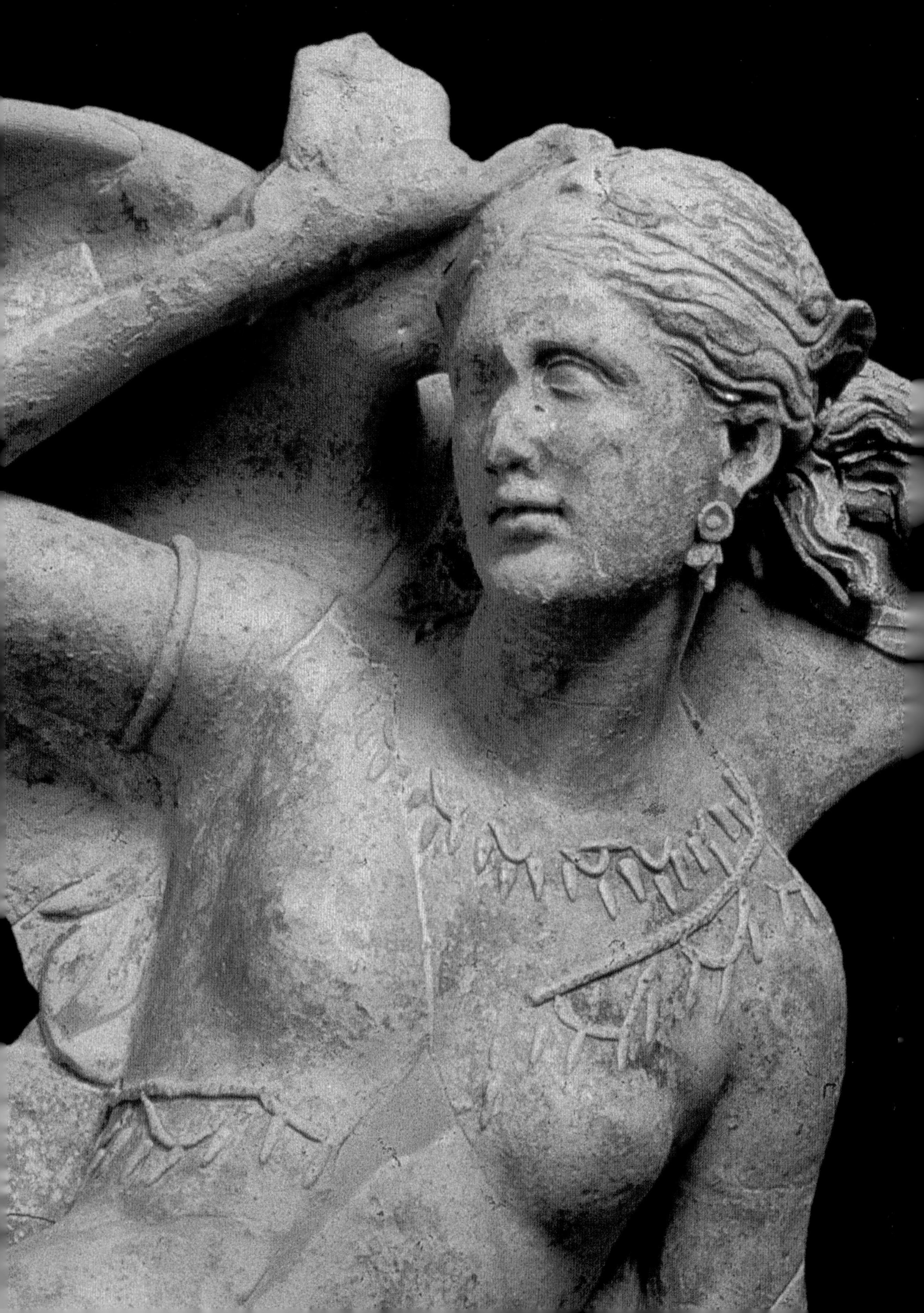

V

The Hellenistic Period

Third to First Century

ETRURIA'S ABSORPTION BY ROME

The Romans' ambition to conquer Italy necessitated continuous fights on several fronts, including annual campaigns against Etruria, Umbria, and the Samnites. The historical sources for this period are confused and contradictory, but the beginning of a new series of wars in Etruria in 311 B.C. (after a period of truces, see p. 306) is said to have been a siege of Sutri by all the Etruscans except the Arretines. After an initial defeat and two years' campaigning, the Romans were able to lift the siege, inflicting great losses on the Etruscans, and push northward into the upper Tiber region. They forced Perugia, Cortona, and Arezzo to sue for truces of thirty years. After breaking the truce in 310, the Perugians were defeated, and the consul Q. Fabius Maximus Rullianus celebrated a triumph. Another treaty of forty years' duration was made with Tarquinia. In 308 Decius Mures conquered fortified places of the people of Volsinii, terrifying all the other Etruscans into asking for a treaty (Livy 9.41.5–7).

For the year 307–306 we hear of the detachment of a number of Etruscan ships to help the tyrant Agathokles of Syracuse against the Carthaginians.

In 302 a popular rebellion broke out in Arezzo against the oppressive clan of the Cilnii, who were entertaining friendly relations with Rome. This attempt by the people of Arezzo to oust the family of local aristocrats, who were siding with the enemy, was successfully quelled by M. Valerius Maximus Corvus. There was also

Detail of relief of winged female spirit, from figure 270.

a Roman campaign against Roselle. After a brief peace in 300, the fight against the Faliscans was renewed in 298, and even Volterra in the north seems to have been subdued (Livy 10.12.8).

Despite recorded military successes, the Romans could not prevent the Samnites, Etruscans, Umbrians, and Gauls from forming a great coalition against Rome. After initial defeats the Romans won a hard-fought and decisive victory at Sentinum in Umbria in 295, in which huge numbers of the allied armies perished. The Romans also won battles against the Etruscans of Chiusi and Perugia. Before 294 the Romans carried on their campaigns only in the countryside and devastated it, while the Etruscans withdrew into their fortified towns. But that year Roman armies ravaged the territory of Volsinii and conquered the first Etruscan city, Roselle. Truces of forty years involving large reparations from the defeated were made with Volsinii, Perugia, and Arezzo.

In 293 the consul Spurius Carvilius Maximus besieged the Etruscan town of Troilum (whose location is unknown), permitting those inhabitants who were able to pay a large sum to leave before he attacked; the have-nots, who were left behind, suffered death or capture. He also extracted a fortune from the Faliscans in exchange for a treaty (Livy 10.46.10).

A fresh incursion by the Gauls in 284 tempted Orvieto to join them and besiege Arezzo, which had remained faithful to Rome. A Roman army sent to relieve the city was beaten by this Etruscan-Gallic alliance, but the next year the Romans inflicted a final defeat on the allies in the battle at Lake Vadimo (between Orte and Bomarzo) under P. Cornelius Dolabella. Further Roman triumphs over the Etruscans are recorded for 281 and 280, probably over Tarquinia and over Orvieto and Vulci, who all lost large parts of their territories. In 273 it was Cerveteri's turn to suffer defeat and confiscation of half her land. Vulci's loss of control over her coastal region was sealed with the founding of the colony of Cosa in the same year. Subsequent Roman colonies were founded at Fregenae, Alsium, and Pyrgi and, in 181, at Gravisca. For easy communication with and control of Etruria Rome built three great roads: Via Aurelia, Via Clodia, and Via Cassia.

The last battle against Gaulish tribes fought on Etruscan soil took place in 225 at Talamone on the Tyrrhenian coast (southwest of modern Grosseto). There the Etruscans fought as allies of Rome, and the consuls L. Aemilius Papus and C. Attilius Regulus led their combined troops to a decisive victory over the invaders.

The disunity between the individual Etruscan cities and their internal social tensions greatly contributed to their inability to defend themselves effectively against Roman belligerence. As shown by the rebellion at Arezzo with the restoration of the Cilnii and by the siege of Troilum, in inner and Northern Etruria Rome intervened in favor of the aristocratic oligarchies when they were threatened by the plebs. The division of Etruscan society by wealth is particularly obvious in the fate of Troilum, whose poorer inhabitants fell victim to Roman greed, which allowed 470 of the rich to bribe their way to safety, while the rest were left to perish.

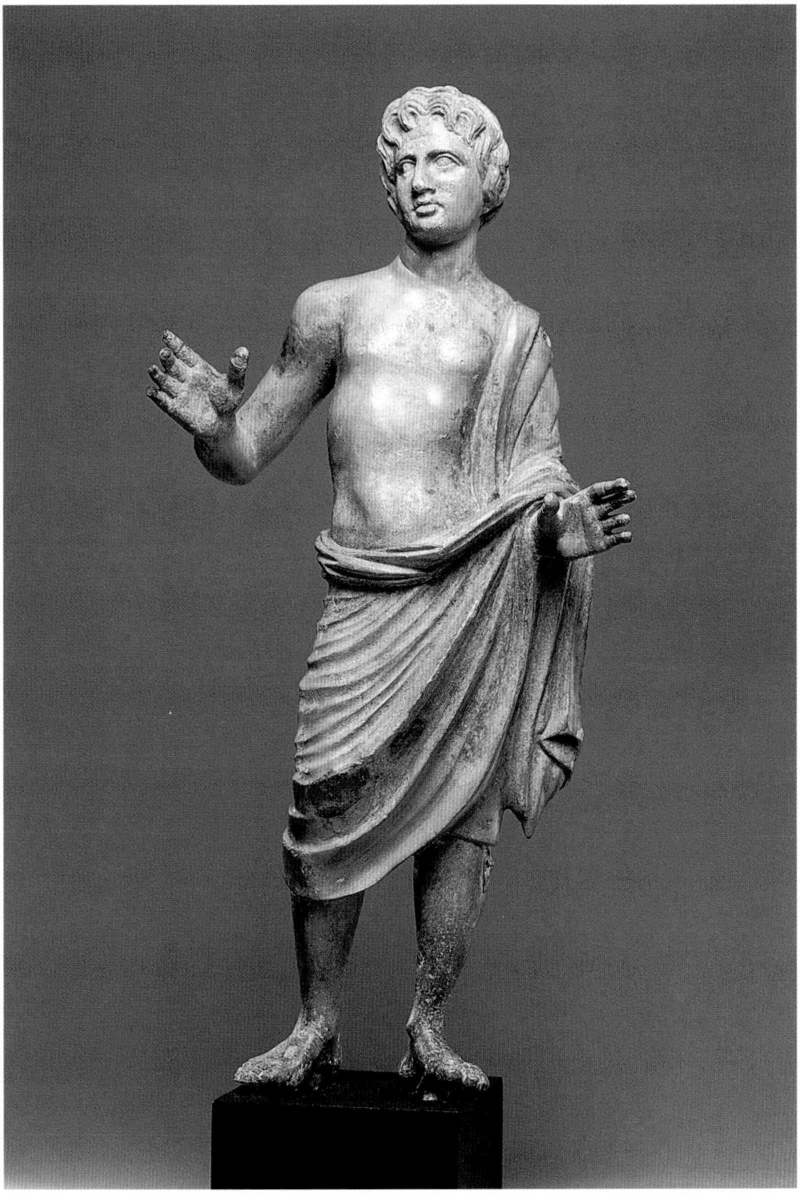

The case of Orvieto was especially complex and tragic (FIG. 259). The sources speak of a gradual process of emancipation of the slaves at Orvieto: at first their masters, who indulged in soft living, entrusted them with the military affairs; then the slaves achieved access to the administration and magistratures of the city, marriage to aristocratic women, and entry into the senate; and finally the former masters were oppressed by the manumitted slaves. It has been suggested that these stages of the slaves' rise to power might have developed between 295 and 280. By 265 the plight of the aristocrats and the rich had become such that they appealed to Rome for aid against their oppressors. A Roman army captured and sacked the

Fig. 259 Inscribed votive statuette of Vel Matunas. Said to be from Orvieto. Early third century B.C. Cast bronze. H. 31.6 cm. Malibu, J. Paul Getty Museum 96.AB.37.

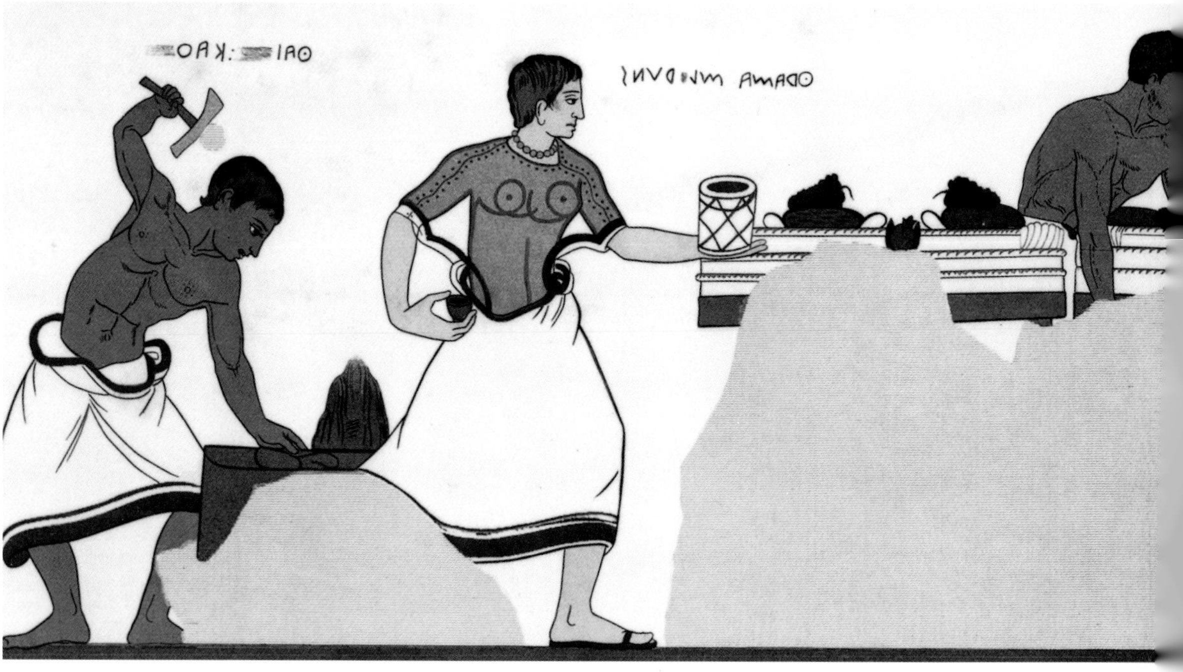

city in 264, killing the rebellious slaves or restoring them to their masters. The surviving population was transferred from the destroyed Volsinii (which was now known as *urbs vetus* = Orvieto) to Volsinii Novi/Bolsena on the northeastern shore of Lake Bolsena. A number of Volsinian families seem, however, to have preferred to move to the region of Chiusi and Perugia, where their names reemerge in third- and second-century inscriptions.

This destruction of one of the most powerful Etruscan cities, in whose territory the Fanum Voltumnae, the federal sanctuary, was situated, and its transplantation to a much less easily defendable site reveal the real purpose of the Roman campaign: domination and control of central and inner Etruria. According to Pliny (34.34), Metrodorus of Scepsis, who was a noted hater of Rome, maintained that Volsinii had been sacked for the sake of the two thousand statues that the Roman conquerors carried away from the city and its sanctuaries; the prospect of loot and reparations will certainly have played a part. The consul and Roman victor at Orvieto, M. Fulvius Flaccus, had himself represented in the dress of a victorious general (*triumphator*) in the Temple of Vortumnus on the Aventine Hill in Rome (Festus, p. 288 L), and it seems that he (like the earlier victor at Veii) "called" to Rome the great Etruscan god of Orvieto, Voltumna/Vortumnus, installing him in a temple there. Two votive statue bases with the consul's name inscribed and traces of the bronze statues they once supported have been excavated in the sanctuary of Fortuna and Mater Matuta at Rome. Further evidence of the abduction of statues from Volsinii may be the head of a life-size bronze statue of a youth found on an island in Lake Bolsena and now in the British Museum (see FIG. 244).

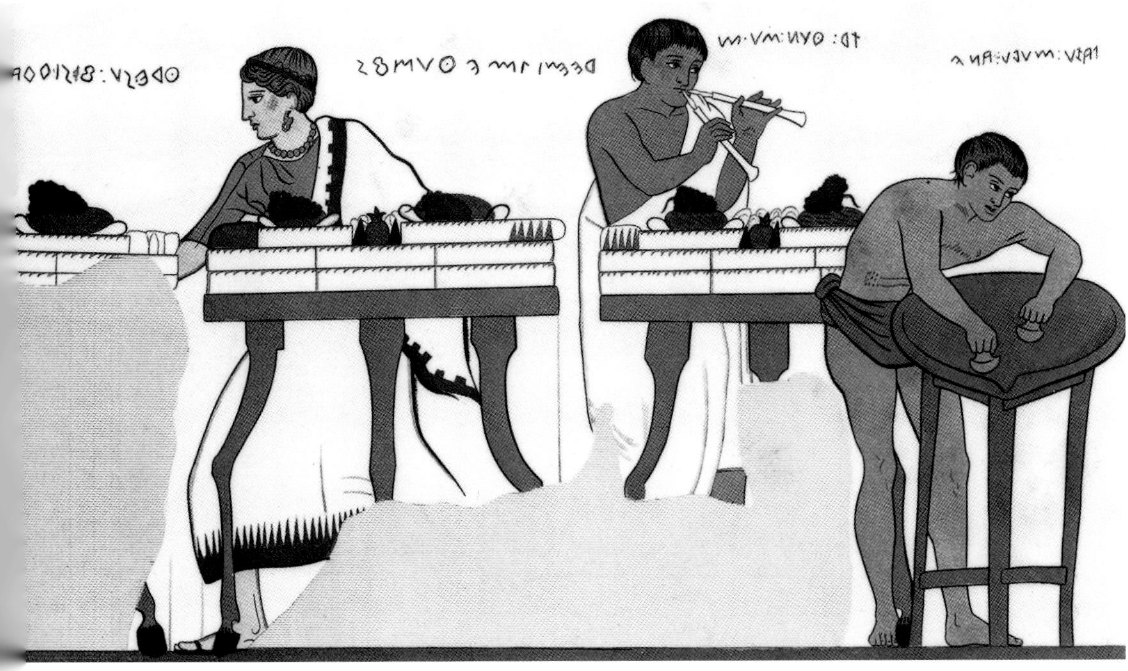

Fig. 260 Wall-painting from the left side of the Golini Tomb I, Settecamini, near Orvieto: slaves preparing a banquet. Third quarter of fourth century B.C. L. 5.21 m.

It is claimed by some scholars that hints of the rising power of the slaves at Volsinii are discernable in the frescoes of the Golini Tomb I at Settecamini near Orvieto, dated to about the third quarter of the fourth century. In the right-hand part of the tomb (divided from the left one by a spur wall projecting from the rear wall) five generations of the aristocratic Leinie family are shown at a banquet in the underworld, witnessing the arrival there of a further family member on a biga accompanied by a winged Vanth with a scroll in her hand. The divine couple Aita and Phersipnai preside over the feast, enthroned beside a table with banqueting vessels and an incense burner illuminated by two candelabra with lit candles—typically Etruscan bronze utensils. The entire left half of the tomb is, however, given over to representations of servants preparing the banquet, all with their names inscribed beside them. To the left of the entrance, suspended from hooks, are a butchered ox, partridges, a hare, a doe, and a couple of geese. Next a slave is cutting up meat on a block, followed by a row of four three-legged tables being set with food (pomegranates, grapes, etc.) by servants supervised by a female (FIG. 260); one of the slaves is pounding a substance in a large mortar to the sound of the auloi. Then comes a large oven at which two males are cooking food in pans; and finally there are three more slaves preparing the feast with a table set with different vessels.

The paintings (which have deteriorated badly and are now in the Museo Archeologico Nazionale, Orvieto) were copied shortly after their discovery in 1863. They give us a fascinating glimpse of the domestic arrangements, kitchen- and dining furniture, and cooking and banqueting vessels used in an aristocratic house-

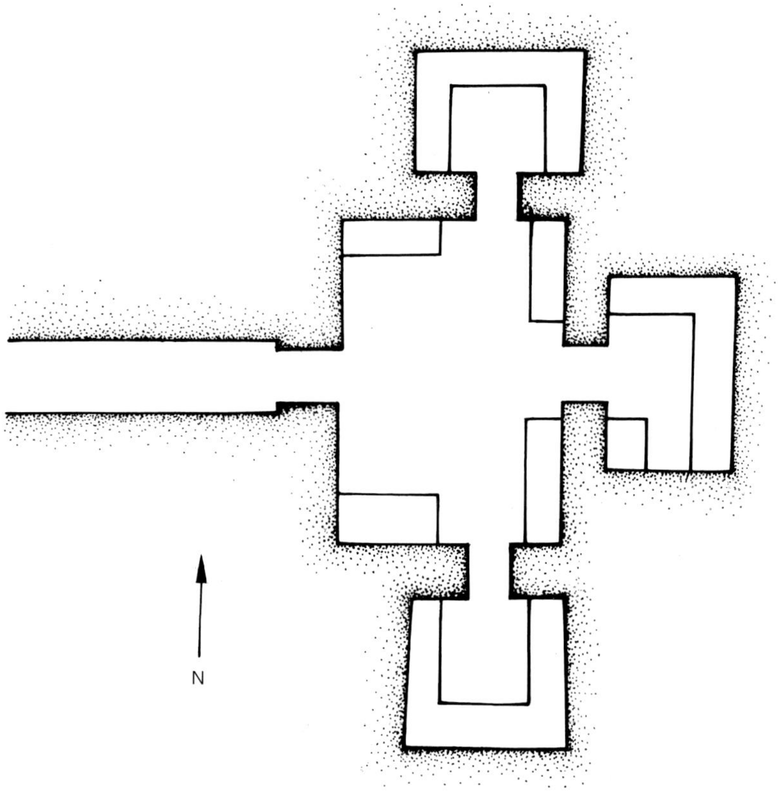

Fig. 261 Plan of the Tomb of the Monkey, Chiusi. Second half of sixth century B.C.

hold in the fourth century. The equal space granted to the representation of masters and servants is unique in Etruscan art and may be indicative of things to come. However, there is no doubt that the aristocracy was still in command and able to commission decoration of family tombs that emphasized the ancient lineage and high offices held by their members. The paintings are not of the same quality as some of the contemporary tomb frescoes at Tarquinia and Vulci; on epigraphic evidence they have been ascribed to Chiusine artists.

Next to the Golini Tomb I is another painted aristocratic chamber tomb of slightly later date named the Golini Tomb II, or Tomb of the Two Bigas (*Tomba Golini II, Tomba delle Due Bighe*), after the two two-horse chariots that flank the entrance; the driver of one of the bigas is wearing the typical hat of a *haruspex*. Above a bench for deposition of sarcophagi the walls were covered with frescoes of a commemorative banquet, gladiatorial games(?), and a procession of musicians, all badly preserved. A further painted family tomb, that of the Hescanas family (*Tomba degli Hescanas*), lies in the neighborhood at Porano.

These tombs at some distance from Orvieto show that, unlike the Archaic uniform egalitarian cemeteries close to the foot of the city plateau (pp. 145f.), the fourth-century burials of the aristocracy of Volsinii were situated on their estates in the surrounding territory. Military valor was still one of the distinguishing ideals of noble families at that period, as we see from the fine bronze panoply excavated in the Tomb of the Warrior (*Tomba del Guerriero*) at Settecamini (Florence, Museo Archeologico 70517–520). His grave goods consisted of a helmet of "jockey-cap" type with hinged cheek-guards, an anatomical cuirass, greaves, and a circular shield decorated on the circumference with a guilloche pattern.

A similar ideology is expressed in the stucco reliefs of armor and weapons in the Tomb of the Reliefs at Cerveteri and also in the frescoes of the Giglioli Tomb (*Tomba Giglioli*) at Tarquinia belonging to the Pinie family and dated to about 330. These decorations are the visible signs of the pervading consciousness among the leading families of the struggle against Rome.

The fate of Orvieto—destroyed and rebuilt in a less defensible location—was shared by the capital of the Faliscans, Falerii Veteres (It. Civita Castellana). After more than fifty years of treaties with Rome, the Faliscans rose up in arms at the end of the First Punic War in 241 B.C.; following a short siege, the city was captured and sacked and later reconstructed in the plain to the west as Falerii Novi. The cult of the city goddess, Minerva, was transferred to Rome to a temple on the Caelian Hill known as that of "the prisoner Minerva" (*Minerva capta*, Ov. *Fast.* 3.843). Like other Southern Etruscan cities, Falerii lost half its territory to the victors, who subsequently constructed the Via Amerina in this region.

CHIUSI: TOMBS

At Chiusi the funerary practice of cremation, which had been a predominant feature since the Villanovan period, remained so throughout the Hellenistic and Roman periods. But with the emergence of small chamber tombs at the end of the seventh century, inhumation began to appear alongside cremation, sometimes in the same tomb. Particularly after the end of the sixth century the practice of depositing the dead of the aristocracy in complex chamber tombs had increased considerably, only to diminish again in Hellenistic times. The Late and Sub-Archaic tomb chambers with wall-paintings often had coffered ceilings in imitation of wooden roof construction; corpses were placed on rock-carved beds, while incinerated remains were placed in relief-decorated ash urns or cinerary statues.

The plans of Chiusine tombs changed over time. The earliest were simple spaces carved from the rock or clay. But soon a type of chamber divided in two by a wall in the center, and sometimes lined and covered with limestone slabs, was constructed for aristocratic families (see the Pania necropolis, p. 110, and the tomb in the località Morelli, near Chianciano, p. 106).

From the second half of the sixth century the chamber tombs of the great families became more elaborate in plan, often with a dromos, a vestibule, and lateral and rear chambers surrounding the main room in a cross-shaped plan (Tombs of the Monkey [FIG. 261], the Lion [*Tomba del Leone*], the Hill [*Tomba del Colle*],

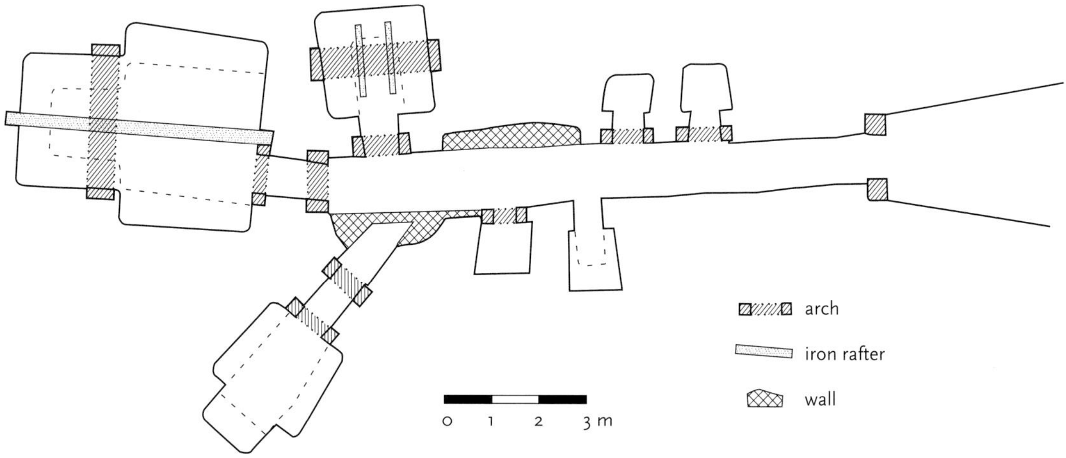

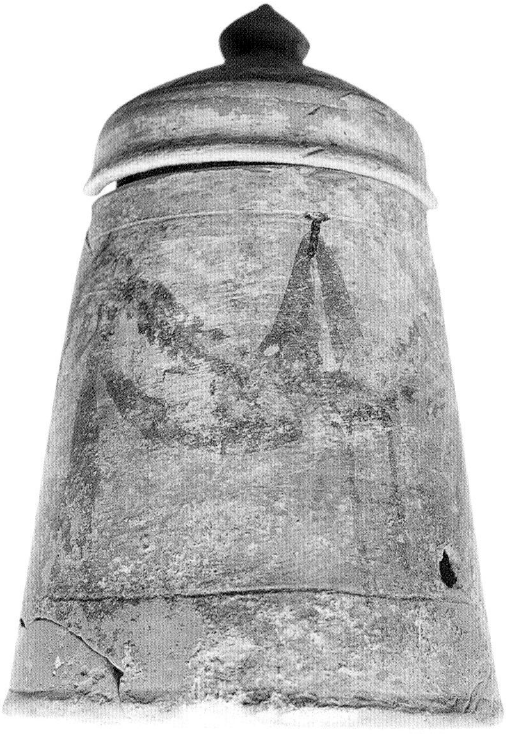

and the Hill of the Moro [*Tomba del Poggio al Moro*]). After the long period of economic and cultural flowering of Chiusi that began with the reign of King Porsenna and continued through the fifth and fourth centuries, even while the coastal cities of Southern Etruria declined, the later Chiusine chamber tombs became more simplified in plan, rectangular or cross-shaped with plain benches around the walls for urns and sarcophagi. In the Hellenistic period the entrance corridors of chamber tombs assumed increasing importance, in some cases reaching a length of 25 m. In the walls of these dromoi were carved numerous niches for the deposition of ash urns and sarcophagi. Large terra-cotta tiles that served to close the fronts of the niches were often inscribed with the names of the deceased. The Tomb of the Pellegrina (*Tomba della Pellegrina*, Poggio Renzo; FIG. 262) is an example of a tomb marking the transition between the older chamber tomb and this new development. The tomb's long corridor with many niches is flanked by two lateral chambers and ends in the main chamber, where both cremation and inhumation burials were found. Four generations of a family, the last dating to about 140/130, were laid to rest there.

Fig. 262 Plan of the Tomb of the Pellegrina, Poggio Renzo, Chiusi. Third century B.C.

Fig. 263 Bell-shaped ash urn painted with swags and ribbons. From Tomb 2, Mulin Canale at Sarteano. Second century B.C. Pottery. Sarteano, Museo Civico Archeologico.

In some instances the corridor itself became the tomb, consisting simply of a long dromos with numerous niches or cells but no chamber at all. From the inscriptions found on the urns (often bell-shaped and painted with swags and ribbons; FIG. 263) and on the tiles closing individual niches it appears that many of the deceased here belonged to a dependent class. Several such pure corridor tombs are

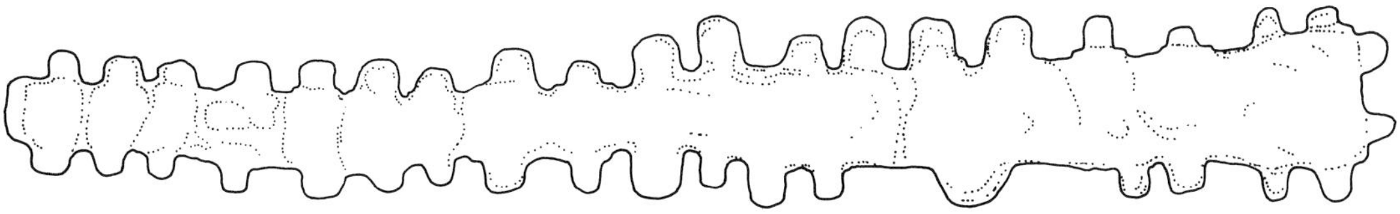

found in the northeastern part of the Chiusine territory near Lake Trasimene, as well as near Sarteano (Mulin Canale). At the latter site the dromos of Tomb 2 is open to the sky and has thirty-nine niches, a large number prefiguring the multiple rows of burial *loculi* in Roman columbaria (FIG. 264).

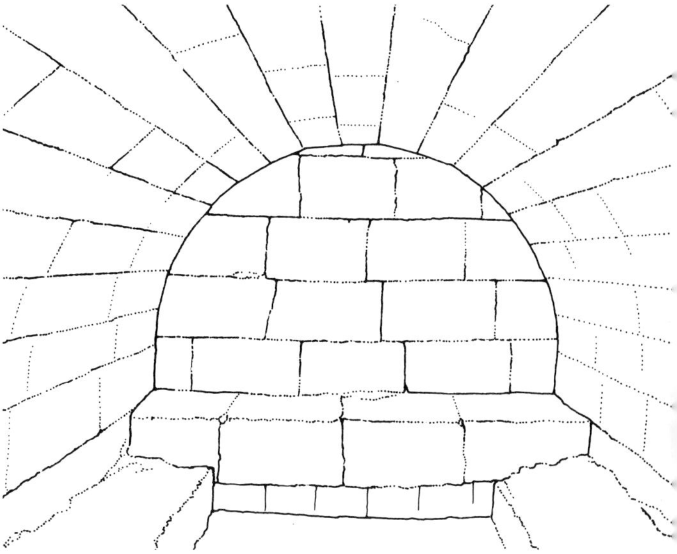

A completely different type of Hellenistic tomb with interior walls constructed of accurately cut rectangular blocks and a barrel vault constructed of wedge-shaped ones developed in Northern Etruria at Chiusi (Tomb of the Grand Duke [*Tomba del Granduca*], FIG. 265), Cortona (the Grotto of Pythagoras [*Tanella di Pitagora*]), and Perugia (Tomb of San Manno [*Tomba di San Manno*]). An isolated example is found in the south at Cerveteri (left-hand chamber of Tomb of the Charuns [*Tomba dei Caronti*], at Greppe Sant'Angelo) as early as the end of the fourth century. The models for such well-constructed, vaulted tombs were most probably the monumental tombs of Macedonia of the mid-fourth century, prototypes that were transmitted to Etruria via South Italy, where this kind of tomb is found in Calabria, Daunia, and Campania.

Fig. 264 Plan of corridor Tomb 2, Mulin Canale at Sarteano. Second century B.C.

Fig. 265 Interior view of the Tomb of the Grand Duke, Chiusi. Third century B.C.

Sarcophagi

The production of sarcophagi at Chiusi became important between the end of the fourth and the middle of the third century and soon rose to a considerable artistic level, so much so that it has been suggested that sculptors previously active at Tarquinia transferred their workshops to Chiusi, where a wealthy landowning aristocracy continued to be able to commission costly works, whereas at Tarquinia artistic activity declined as a result of the Roman conquest.

Besides numerous undecorated sarcophagi (found also at Vulci and Orvieto in this period), the earliest stage at Chiusi is represented by sarcophagi that show the deceased lying on the lid as if asleep, a type clearly derived from Tarquinian prototypes (pp. 288ff.). The box itself is often carved to represent a bed (*kline*) of the richly decorated wood-and-ivory type found in Early Hellenistic tombs in Greece.

The limestone sarcophagus of the lady Rav(nthu) Vetanei (Berlin, Antikenmuseum E 74) was found in the central position at the back of a chamber tomb belonging to the Velu family, with the plain sarcophagus of her husband, Arnth, placed on the left. Two generations of the family were buried here in either sarcophagi or urns.

Ravnthu, draped in a mantle covering her head and body, lies on a mattress and cushions, holding a fruit. Her youthful face with deep-set, open eyes is framed by shortish hair. The fretted legs of the bed are decorated with palmettes and volutes, the stretcher between them with rosettes and mythical winged sea panthers. In the space below, a male Skylla with wings, fishtail, and a stone in his raised right hand appears between two winged sea panthers with acanthus-leaf tails. The panthers must allude to Dionysos and hint at his mysteries. This fine sarcophagus is a work of the first quarter of the third century.

On later sarcophagi the deceased on the lid is shown half raised on cushions under the left elbow and turned toward the spectator. The men often hold a fluted omphalos bowl and wear the banqueter's wreath and a garland around the neck; the women are richly bejeweled, with a fan or a mirror, a bowl or a Bacchic cup. The front (only rarely the short sides) of the boxes are carved in relief, frequently representing battle scenes in which some of the opponents may be identified as Gallic warriors by their dress and the form of their long shields. This subject must have seemed relevant to aristocratic families who had been involved in the wars between Romans and Gauls, but the iconographic inspiration for such compositions came from Greece and Asia Minor. Delphi had been threatened by marauding Gauls, as had the Pergamene kingdom, and the victories gained over the invaders by King Attalos I (269–197) were celebrated by several famous monuments.

Battle scenes appear on both male and female sarcophagi, as do scenes of Greek mythological content, usually concerned with violent death (the slaughter of Troilos by Achilles, scenes from the Theban cycle, etc.) and often accompanied by Etruscan underworld demons.

During the early part of the second century the production of stone sarcophagi at Chiusi declined and was replaced by the more economical material of clay. The lesser material was no obstacle to artistic quality, however, as seen in two monumental terra-cotta sarcophagi, of Seianti Hanunia in the British Museum and of Larthia Seianti in Florence.

Seianti Hanunia Tlesnasa's sarcophagus was found in 1886 by itself in a small chamber tomb at Poggio Cantarello (FIG. 266a). From iron nails on the interior walls had hung five silver objects, one of which was still in position when the tomb was discovered (*Catalogue of the Silver Plate [Greek, Etruscan and Roman] in the British Museum*, nos. 21–25, pl. 4, lost since 1939). The disc of a silver-gilt mirror with a long handle terminating in a leaf was framed by a wave pattern; the metal was so thin that it could not have served for actual use but was made for funerary purposes only. Beside it were a globular scent bottle with a gilt band of wave pattern; a cylindrical lidded box decorated on the body with swags and ox skulls; an egg-

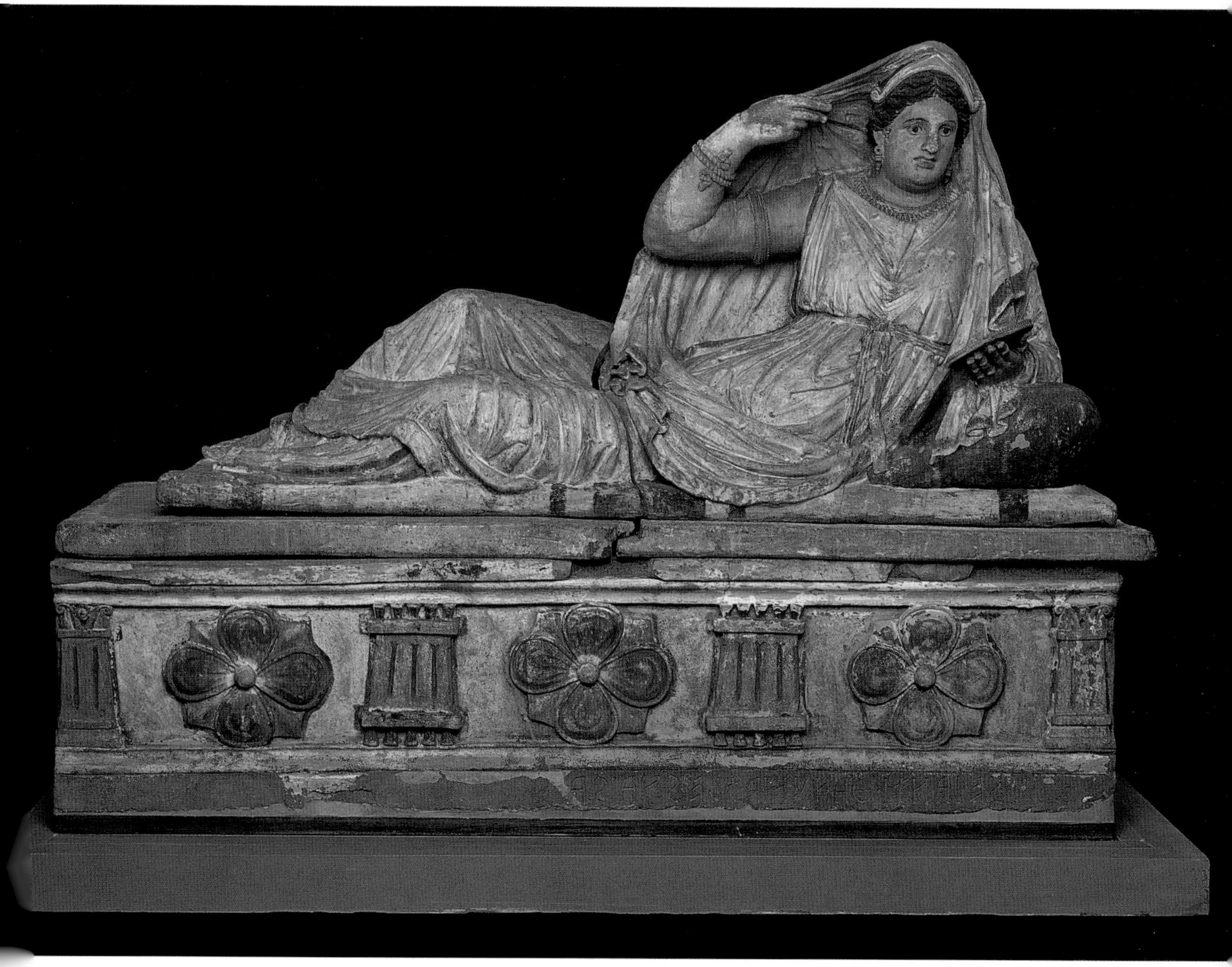

shaped situla with a flat, semicircular, movable handle; and a toilet instrument for scraping ointments from the body (strigil).

The box of the sarcophagus takes the form of an architectural pedestal with a frieze of alternating triglyphs and rosettes; it no longer suggests a banqueting couch. The lady's name was cut into the bottom ledge while the clay was still malleable. Seianti is the female form of what was originally a family name, derived from the name of a place, in this case probably the Umbrian town of Sentinum north of Perugia. Hanunia is a given name. The clan name of the Seiante family (her own) and that of the Tlesna family (her husband's) are familiar from other inscriptions from the Chiusi region. On the lid (made in two parts) her mature figure, dressed in a sleeveless, high-girt chiton and mantle, rests on a mattress and pillow. She holds a circular lidded mirror in her left hand while her right hand lifts the edge of the mantle draped over her head in a bridal gesture. Her full face with

Fig. 266a Sarcophagus of Seianti Hanunia Tlesnasa. From Poggio Cantarello, near Chiusi. First quarter of second century B.C. Painted terra-cotta. L. 1.83 m. London, The British Museum GR 1887.6-8.9.

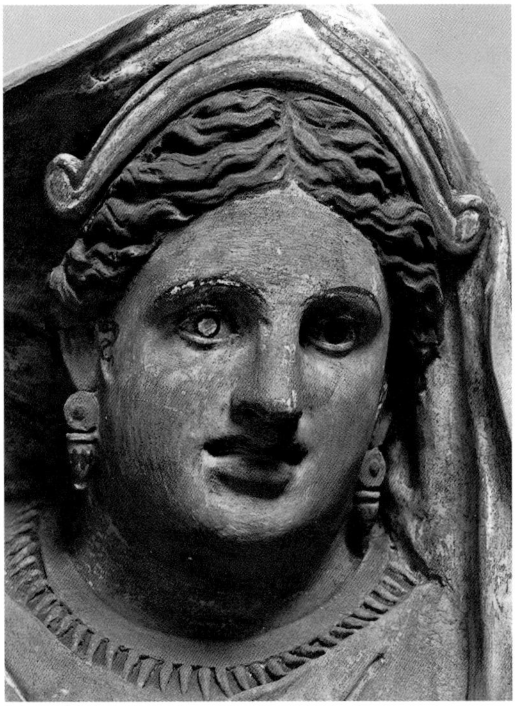

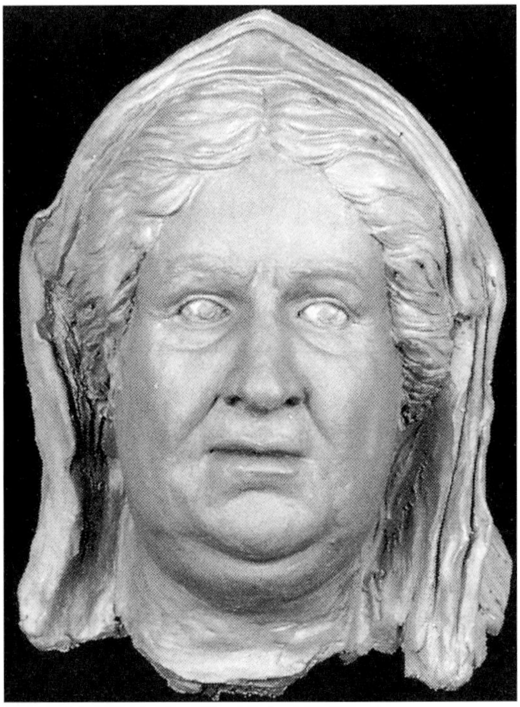

Fig. 266b Detail of Seianti Hanunia Tlesnasa, figure 266a.

Fig. 266c Forensic reconstruction of the head of Seianti Hanunia Tlesnasa, figure 266a.

a double chin is framed by centrally parted wavy hair; the head has an insipid, classicizing beauty often found in works of this period, with an almost straight profile line from the forehead to the tip of the nose and the slightly open lips. Her jewelry—tiara, earrings, necklace, two bracelets, and rings—are more restrained in design and size than the ostentatious torques, multiple necklaces with huge embossed *bullae* and pendants, and the crossed chains worn on earlier stone sarcophagi, for example, by the Chiusine lady Hasti Afunei (see FIG. 222). The effect of the skillfully modeled figure of Seianti Hanunia is heightened by the extensive remains of color over white slip: black, purple, brown, and pink on flesh, hair, eyes, and clothes; bluish green for the bronze mirror; and yellow for the gold jewelry.

By a lucky chance Seianti Hanunia's skeleton was preserved in the sarcophagus. The bones have recently been reinvestigated by a group of classical scholars, pathologists, and dental experts, whose conclusions provide fascinating and poignant glimpses of the physical life of this well-to-do, upper-class lady. She was 1.52 cm tall (almost 5 feet). A reconstruction has been made of her head based on her skull; it shows her as somewhat older looking than the blooming matron on the sarcophagus. Analyses of her bones and teeth indicate that she was fifty to fifty-five years old. She had probably been a horsewoman from childhood and had suffered a serious accident in early adulthood. She may have been trapped beneath a rearing horse or upset cart, which crushed and tore her right leg and pelvis, leading to arthritis in her hip joint, curvature of the spine, and increasingly restricted movement, discomfort, and pain in her hip and back as she advanced in age. The same accident may have led to the pathological deformation of her right lower jaw and its joint and to the early loss of some of her teeth there. Poor oral hygiene caused caries and chronic gum disease. She must have suffered many years of pain in her mouth and difficulty in eating. Less serious dental conditions were sometimes treated sucessfully in Etruscan patients, as suggested by finds from several tombs of false teeth joined with gold bridge bands.

The discrepancy in appearance between the reconstructed face of Seianti Hanunia and her idealized image on the sarcophagus is a salutary warning not to be too ready to see real portraits in the features of funerary sculpture of the Hellenistic period (FIGS. 266b, c, and cf. p. 368).

From the same workshop was commissioned the equally splendid, but probably slightly more recent terra-cotta sarcophagus of Larthia Seianti, which was discovered in 1877 at La Martinella near Chiusi in the Larcna family tomb (FIG. 267). A rich collection of toilet vessels and instruments of silver, glass, alabaster, and bronze surrounded the sarcophagus. Inside it was found a worn Roman coin, an uncial as (obverse: head of Janus; reverse: ship's prow to right), which has latterly been dated to between 189 and 180 B.C. The coin is likely to have been put there for payment to Charon, the ferryman of the dead. For us it is a useful *terminus post quem*: the burial cannot have taken place before the coin was minted, and it probably occurred shortly afterward, between 180 and 170.

The deceased is represented in the same attitude and dress as Seianti Hanunia, but her body is more elongated and her face less full. The box is decorated with an architectural frieze of alternating rosettes and paterae between triglyphs. Larthia Seianti's name was incised on the top ledge, but was subsequently plastered over and a barely decipherable name painted on it; this leads to some uncertainty about the identity of the person buried here. If she was Larthia Seianti, she belonged to the same clan as Seianti Hanunia.

The owner of the tomb and the only male buried there together with four females, was Laris Larcna Cencual. On the box of his plain, house-shaped sarcophagus was painted a bed with turned legs and a departure scene. The ashes of his first wife, Fasi Velui, were deposited in an urn. Larthia Seianti was probably his second wife. Seianzi Viliana, a flat recumbent figure, sunk, as it were, in a bathtublike terracotta sarcophagus (Berlin, Antikensammlung Sk. 1300), was first thought to be his third wife, but she has recently more convincingly been identified as a niece of the head of the family. The variety of types of burial and the different qualities of urns and sarcophagi deposited in a single tomb are instructive. Larthia Seianti's sarcophagus was by far the most splendid, and along with that of Seianti Hanunia it marks a last artistic high point in the production of Chiusine sarcophagi for aristocratic families.

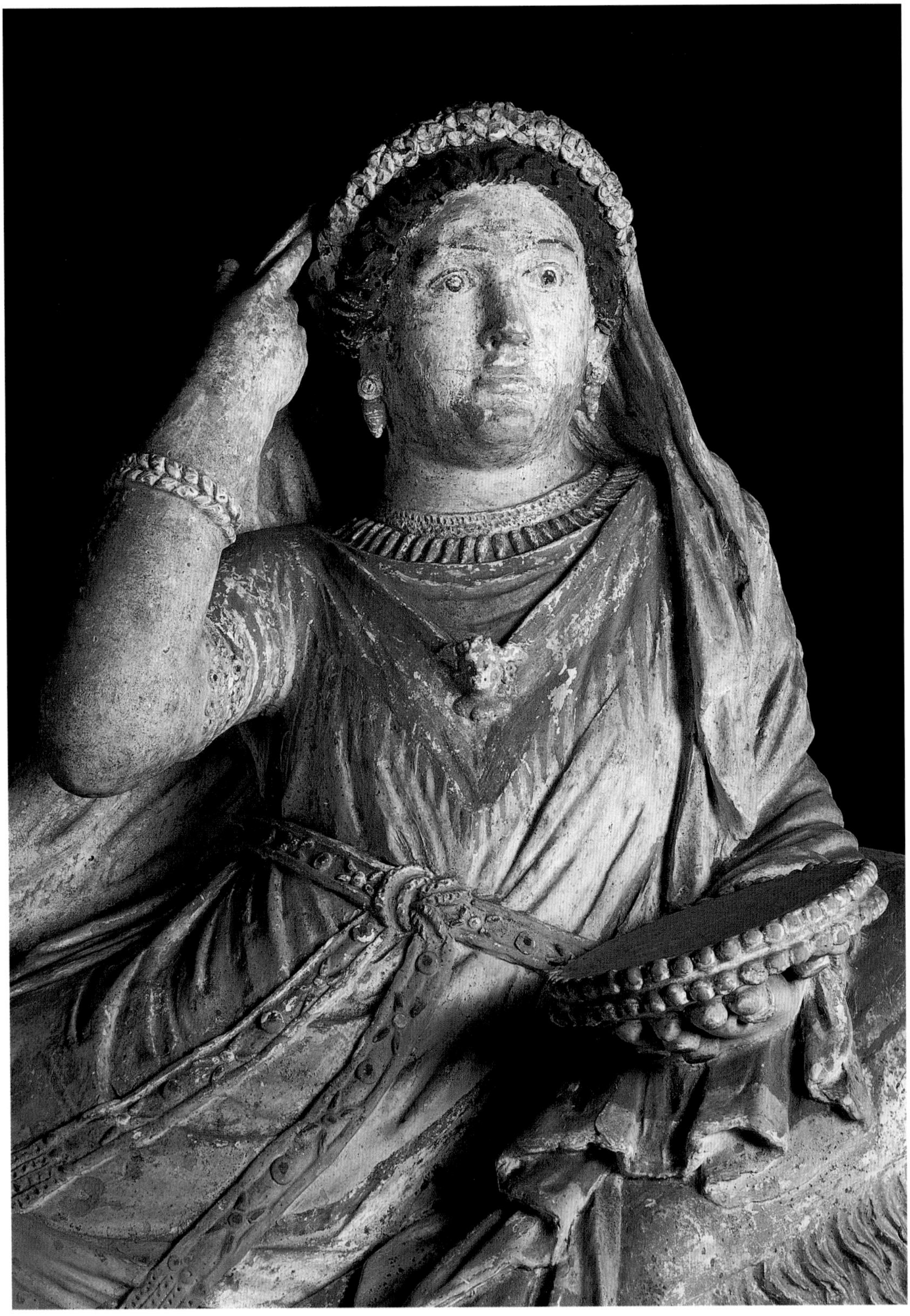

Ash Urns

Chiusine ash urns of the Hellenistic period were made either of local *pietra fetida*, alabaster (used particularly from the second half of the third century onward in a production showing close relations with works from Volterra, pp. 365ff.), or travertine (from the second century onward), or they were modeled in clay. Both stone and terra-cotta relief-decorated urns were originally painted in vivid colors, which, in the case of the former, have often faded completely.

During the second half of the second century and continuing into the first the vast majority of the small, once brightly painted terra-cotta ash urns found in Chiusi and its territory were mass-produced in molds, with a relief only on the front of the box and the figure of the deceased resting asleep or in a banqueting position on the lid. Such urns were made by a number of different workshops catering to a large social class of modest means, often former slaves, who worked and were buried in the rural areas belonging to the city's territory. The preferred subjects for the reliefs were again battle scenes of Greek inspiration, such as the sons of Oedipus—Eteokles and Polyneikes—killing each other in the presence of female demons, but also local myths, particularly one in which a hero wielding a plowshare (Echetlos?) fights his armed opponents; the latter theme may hint at the social struggles that took place in Northern Etruria. These often complex, interlocking figure compositions were inspired by sculptural prototypes from Asia Minor (Pergamon), Rhodes, and South Italy, transmitted via Rome. They are apparent also in the figured terra-cotta pediments of Hellenistic temples in Etruria (p. 345), finally mirrored in the molds of local artisans.

An urn in the British Museum with a closely knit battle of five warriors framed by pilasters on the front of the box shows particularly well-preserved colors over a white slip: yellow, brown, red, mauve, blue, and black (FIG. 268). Virtually identical scenes on a large number of urns show that these boxes were mass-produced in molds (e.g., Chiusi, Museo Archeologico 361 and 974; and Vatican, Museo Gregoriano Etrusco 14140). Above a dentil frieze is painted the name of a woman, Thana Ancarui Helasa; but on the lid rests the fine, hand-modeled figure of a young man dressed in a tunic and mantle, holding an omphalos bowl in his right hand. He turns his wreathed head upward and back over his left shoulder with a yearning expression. The fact

OPPOSITE
Fig. 267 Sarcophagus of Larthia Seianti. Detail of head. From the Tomb of the Larcna Family, La Martinella, near Chiusi. Ca. 180–170 B.C. Painted terra-cotta. H. 1.05 m. Florence, Museo Archeologico.

BELOW
Fig. 268 Ash urn with a reclining youth on the lid and a battle scene on the chest. From Chiusi. First half of second century B.C. Painted terra-cotta. H. 74.8 cm. London, The British Museum GR 1926.3-24.124.

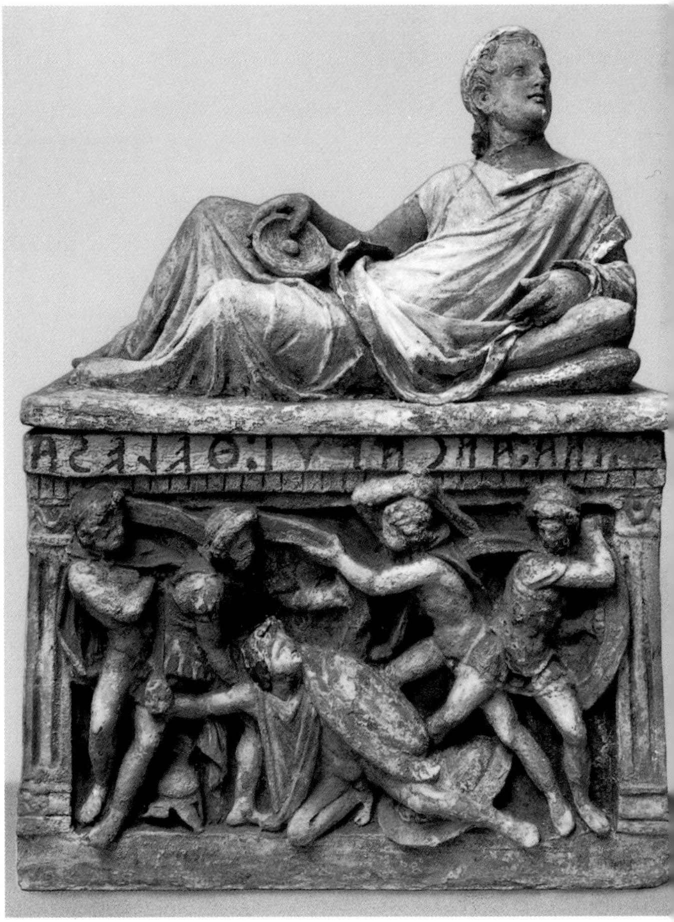

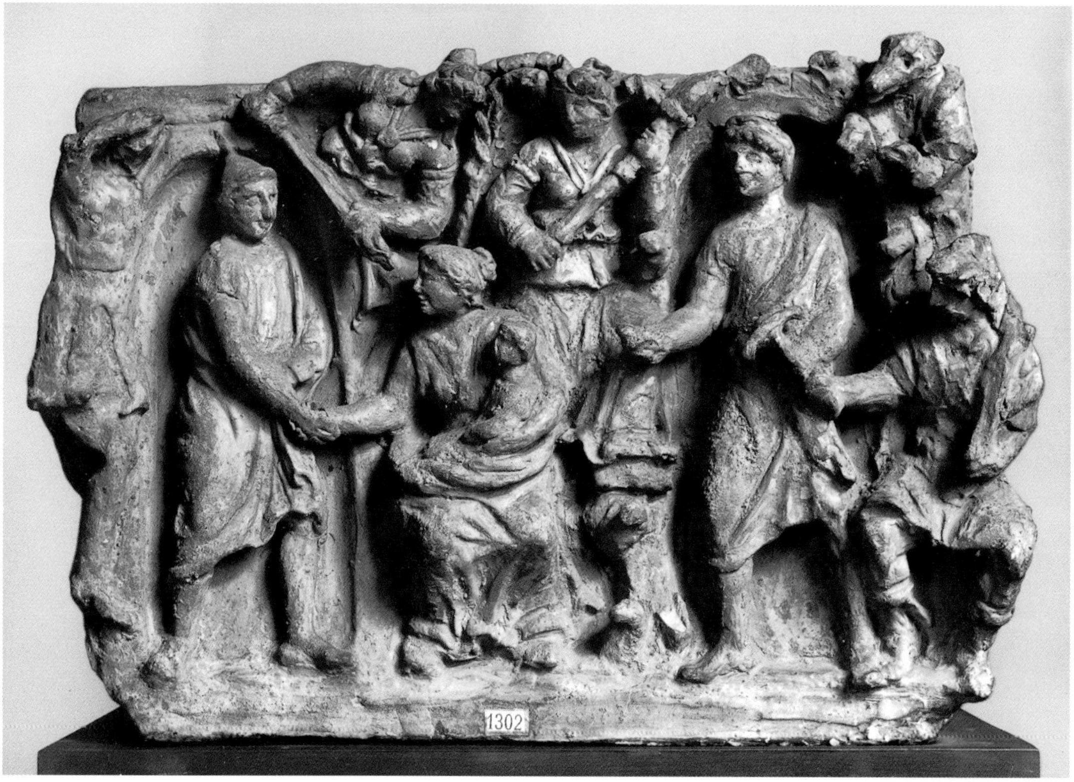

Fig. 269 Chest of an ash urn with a relief of a family framed by underworld demons. From Chiusi. 150–100 B.C. Painted terracotta. L. 62 cm. Berlin, Staatliche Museen—Preußischer Kulturbesitz—Antikensammlung SK 1302.

that this banqueter's upper body is not bare but decorously covered by a tunic with vertical purple stripes and a purple-bordered mantle may be connected with Roman legislation following the senatorial decree of 186 B.C. against bacchanalia. The size of the lid fits the box, but the mismatch between a female name and male image is probably due to exceptional circumstances at the time of burial or a mix-up with similar pieces after its discovery. The latter was a frequent hazard during early excavations.

The hand-modeled relief on the urn of an elderly man in Berlin is an unusual case (FIG. 269). In the center is seated a youthful wife; she cradles a baby in her left arm and joins hands with her husband, who is departing for the beyond. He stands under an archway on the left side of the box, wearing the costume of a *haruspex* with a peaked hat. From a similar arch on the right—the doorway to the underworld—emerges a tall figure with a fur cap, probably Aita, flanked by a seated Charun with an animal skin on his head and holding a hammer and a paddle; above him appears a demon with an animal's head. Two snake-haired Furies with torches threaten the young widow from behind, while a short-skirted, indistinct figure hovers beside the arch under which the departing priest stands. This poignant scene must have been specially commissioned by the family of the *haruspex*, rather than purchased from a workshop of serial productions.

Bronze and Terra-cotta Sculpture in Sanctuaries

To the west of Chiusi, the modern spa town of Chianciano Terme is the site of numerous thermal springs, some of which were the focus of healing sanctuaries at least as early as the beginning of the fifth century B.C. Immediately beside the spring named Sillene (near the spring called Acquasanta) remains of the square floor of a sanctuary were excavated in 1867 along with fragments of large-scale bronze sculptures (now in Florence, Museo Archeologico). The oldest of these belong to a fine, hollow-cast statue of a long-haired youth, perhaps Apollo. In the back of the head, above a fillet, was a large rectangular opening that must have served for the insertion into the head of some object (a lamp?). Only the exquisitely modeled and incised hair and the upper torso are preserved; they suggest a date for the statue about 480–470. Of an over-life-size statue there remain the left foot and the right hand.

Other fragments, probably of fourth-century date and also of high quality, belong to a bronze group of the moon goddess Selene in a biga. These sculptures were presumably the work of Chiusine masters and indicate that the sanctuary was of considerable importance. The cult at the healing spring was dedicated to Selene (and perhaps to an oracle of Apollo): a half-moon of sheet bronze (Florence, Museo Archeologico 76537) was found at the Sillene spring. A large votive half-moon of cast bronze found in the eighteenth century half-way between Chiusi and Cetona (Vatican, Museo Gregoriano Etrusco 11065, height 29.6 cm) is incised with a dedication to the Etruscan divinity of the moon, Tiur, in the Northern Etruscan script used at Chiusi in the late sixth century; it may originally have come from this sanctuary. The veneration of a lunar deity at salutary waters is not surprising, night and humidity being connected with the moon and vegetation. Selene was considered a healer of lunacy and epilepsy and was intimately linked with women and their monthly cycle. On the southern slope of the sanctuary were excavated three inhumation graves and the burial of a horse, probably a sacrificial victim.

The destruction of this temple, which perhaps consisted only of a roofed area (no remains of walls were discovered), may have been due to the Gallic incursion of 225 B.C., but the sanctuary continued to be frequented in Roman times and was superseded in the medieval period by a church dedicated to the archangel Michael.

The remains of a sacred edifice of the Hellenistic period were excavated not far south of Chianciano in 1986 at a locality called I Fucoli, near another thermal spring situated in the Astrone valley. The site—a piazza overlooking the valley between two hills—has been eroded by a landslide, and only a few architectural fragments of wood and stone survive (the base and drum of a column and numerous stone discs), but a large quantity of roof tiles and fragmentary terra-cotta figures in high relief were recovered; they once decorated the pediments and facings of the gables and eaves. All this temple debris as well as a number of votive gifts had been intentionally deposited on the piazza, probably after the destruc-

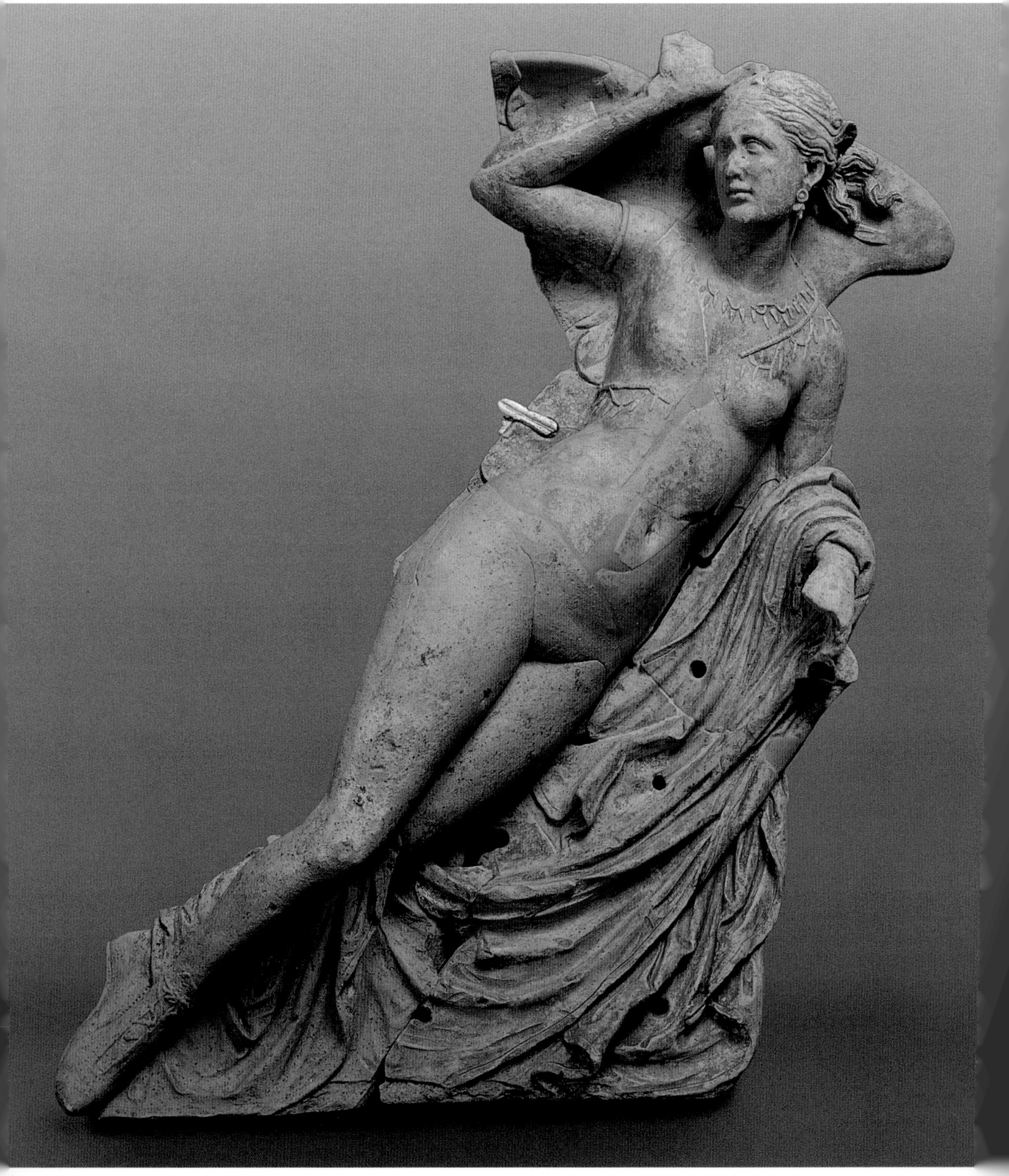

tion of the edifice. The style of these fragments shows that they were modeled by a number of different hands about the middle of the second century and strongly influenced by the art of Pergamon. The fragments from the pediment (recently reconstructed in the Museo Civico delle Acque at Chianciano) include an enthroned male figure and a seated male in Oriental dress in a rocky landscape with a large, garlanded wine krater; not incorporated are bearded heads, one with a Phrygian cap, another with a lion's skin (Herakles), as well as torsos and limbs of armed warriors. The *sima* was decorated with separately modeled figures forming a procession of small boys riding on dolphins and of draped sea nymphs (Nereids) sitting or leaning on marine monsters.

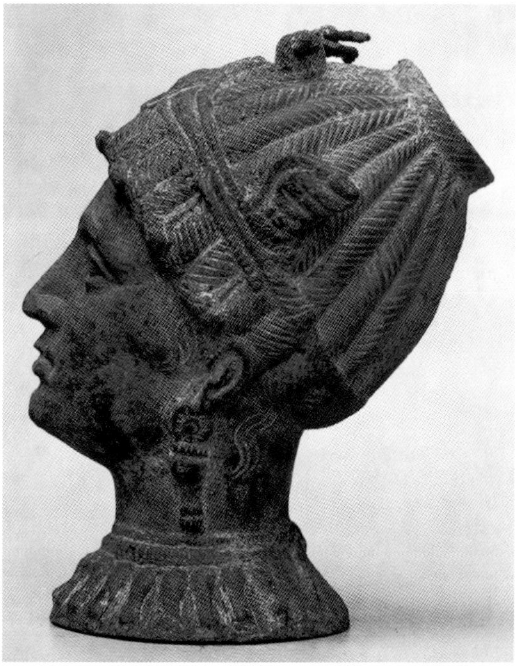

The best-preserved of all these terra-cottas is the right-hand acroterion of the raking *sima* (FIG. 270). Modeled in high relief, it shows the beautiful nude figure of a winged female spirit flying off diagonally to the right while looking back to the left with a frightened gesture of her raised right hand. In her lowered left hand she holds a Dionysiac drinking cup (kantharos); a large mantle trails from her left forearm over her leg. She wears elegant, laced ankle boots, a necklace and chain with pendants that crosses her chest obliquely, disc-earrings with pendants, and a diadem with small lateral wings on her wavy hair. Her full face with deep-set eyes, her jewelry and, above all, her winged diadem connect her typologically with a group of small portable Hellenistic bronze vessels in the form of female heads found in graves (FIG. 271). These bronze head-vases may have had some transcendental significance, the female head being occasionally joined back-to-back to a satyr's head, a clear reference to the Dionysiac circle. The kantharos carried by the acroterial figure is a strong hint that this winged beauty belongs to the same world.

In view of the fragmentation of the terra-cotta decoration of the temple's pediment, it is impossible to guess what the unifying iconographic theme was, though a Pergamene theme has been suggested, including Herakles, Laomedon, and Telephos. However, the scattered remains testify to the high level of artistic ability of Chiusine modelers of that period. It is significant that, following Roman custom, the gable was completely filled in with figured terra-cotta panels, whereas in earlier Etruscan temples only the ends of the three main roof beams in the open pediment were protected by revetment panels with modeled figures (see FIGS. 152b, 154). This new development is also found in other great Hellenistic temple gables in Etruria, such as those of Civitalba (Bologna, Museo Civico Archeologico), of Luni, and of Talamonaccio (both in Florence, Museo Archeologico).

OPPOSITE
Fig. 270 Relief of winged female spirit. Right-hand acroterion of raking *sima* of the temple at I Fucoli, near Chianciano Terme. Mid-second century B.C. Painted terra-cotta. H. ca. 1 m. Chianciano Terme, Museo Civico delle Acque.

ABOVE
Fig. 271 Portable vessel in the form of a female head with winged diadem. Late third–early second century B.C. Cast bronze. H. 10.6 cm. London, The British Museum, *Bronze Cat.* 759.

TUSCANIA: TOMBS AND SARCOPHAGI

At Tuscania in the hinterland of Tarquinia, the Archaic period had seen the development of unusual and impressive monumental tombs attesting to the wealth and wide cultural connections of the ruling families in control of important traffic routes from the coast to the interior. The political and economic crisis that struck the area at the end of this period seems to have affected Tuscania as well as other Southern Etruscan cities in the fifth century. However, the fourth century saw a remarkable revival of artistic productivity based on the agricultural wealth of a number of aristocratic families with close marriage links to Tarquinia. The prosperity of such local families as the Vipinana, the Curuna, the Treptie, the Statlane, etc., manifests itself in their rock tombs and the opulence of their sarcophagi and grave goods. Unlike Tarquinia, which suffered decline after the Roman conquest, Tuscania's fortune continued for almost two centuries, probably due to its geographical position in the interior and the construction of the Via Clodia, which connected Rome with northwestern Etruria.

In the necropolis of the Madonna dell'Olivo southwest of Tuscania, a series of chamber tombs carved side by side into the tufa banks has been excavated from 1967 onward. Three of them belonged to the Curuna family. Their contents are now in the Museo Archeologico of Tuscania.

Tomb I was founded about 340–330 for the heads of the family, Vel Curunas and his wife, who must have been deposited either without sarcophagi or in wooden coffins that have not survived. Subsequently the tomb chamber was tightly packed with eight sarcophagi of the three following generations, the last one dating from about 250–240. They all respected the space on the bench in the center of the rear wall and that to the right of the entrance, which were originally occupied by the founding couple.

As the tomb was robbed in antiquity, the grave goods were discovered in a broken and scattered state, but among the ceramic fragments were numerous examples of fine red-figured Faliscan and Etruscan vases, the earliest belonging to the second quarter of the fourth century; others came from vases with decoration in superposed colors and from black-glazed ware. Besides this fine painted pottery, there was plenty of common household ware and wine amphorae of Etruscan and "Graeco-Italic" type. The most splendid set of bronze banqueting vessels belonged to Vel Curunas and his wife; it had escaped the robbers, for it was hidden in a trench at the foot of the rear bench, with the sarcophagus of their son Arnth placed on top of it. Another cache of bronzes was found outside the tomb to the left of the dromos, where it had probably been dropped by the thieves. Outstanding among the numerous bronze vessels are a pair of situlae (FIG. 272) with handle attachments in the form of horses with fishtails (*hippocamps*); their rims are decorated with a vegetal frieze divided by a strip of silver from a lower frieze of leaping dolphins above a wave pattern, all in low relief.

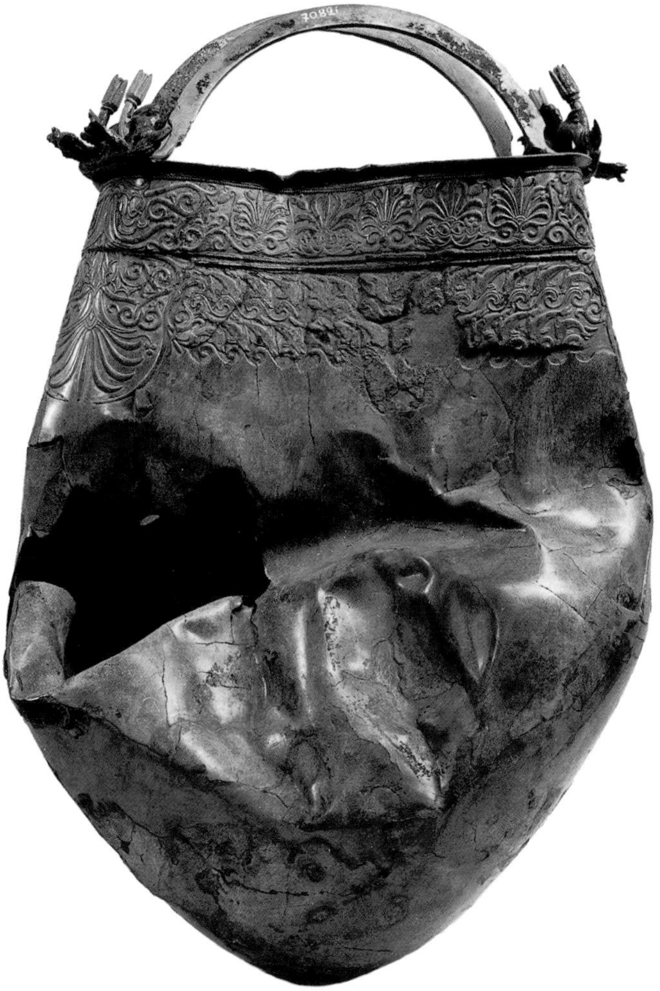

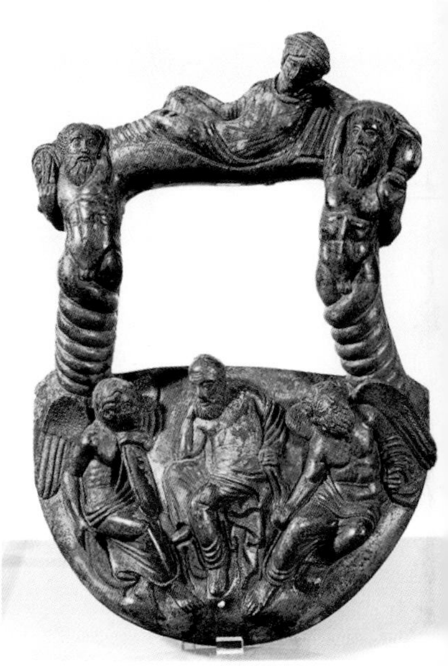

Equally fine is a large krater with a similar dolphin frieze and above it one of marine monsters, such as sea dragons and *hippocamps*, interspersed with fish and finished above with a tongue pattern. The two cast handles and the foot had been dismantled for burial and placed inside the vessel. Like the marine decoration with its allusions to the journey across the sea, the beautifully modeled handles with their attachment plates are composed of figures that have funerary significance (FIG. 273). Rising from the attachment plate to form the handle are two male underworld demons with twisted fishtails instead of legs; they support the reclining figure of a draped young woman, whose bent head rests in a melancholy attitude on her left hand; she probably represents the deceased. On the attachment plate below are three seated figures in high relief. A mourning elderly man is flanked on the left by a youthful winged demon holding a shield and on the right by an older demon who has turned away from him. The mourner might be the husband or father of the dead woman. It is perhaps not without significance that

Fig. 272 Two-handled situla with relief decoration (foot missing). From Tomb I of the Curuna Family, Tuscania. Ca. 350–325 B.C. Cast and hammered bronze. Total H. ca. 46 cm. Tuscania, Museo Nazionale 70821.

Fig. 273 Relief-decorated handle from a krater. From Tomb I of the Curuna Family, Tuscania. 350–325 B.C. Cast bronze. H. ca. 22 cm. Tuscania, Museo Archeologico 70820.

the most prominent feature of the handles of this krater is the women reclining in the position of banqueters (usual on sarcophagi). We have noted that women seem to have owned pottery kraters as early as the Orientalizing period (pp. 80, 96f.), and it may well be that this splendid bronze vessel was made specially for the wife of Vel Curunas. One of three fragmentary incised bronze *cistae* from the tomb presumably likewise belonged to her. These cylindrical, lidded boxes of sheet bronze originally had cast figured feet and handles. *Cistae* served as containers for ladies' toilet articles, such as combs, hairpins, scrapers, tweezers, scent bottles, and dipsticks. The center of manufacture of these characteristic utensils was Palestrina in Lazio, but the engraver of the oldest *cista* from the Curuna family tomb has made an important iconographical addition to the traditional figurative repertoire, probably at the request of the Etruscan aristocrats who commissioned the piece: Among the scenes of the life of Achilles appears a typically Etruscan winged male death demon in a short tunic with crossed straps on the chest.

Vel Curunas's name is incised on several of the minor bronze vessels, and his was the fine "jockey-cap" helmet dated to the last decades of the fourth century.

All but one of the stone sarcophagi of the descendants of the founders bear the images of the deceased on the lid, and a number have reliefs with battle scenes, funerary genii, or heraldically composed mythical marine creatures carved on the boxes. On some of them traces of the original paint are preserved. The oldest sarcophagi clearly were inspired by prototypes from Tarquinia, and the fact that the reliefs on some of the later ones were carved so as to be visible in their confined position suggests that itinerant craftsmen worked on the spot.

The external facade of Tomb I of the Curuna Family was originally decorated with sculpture, which has largely crumbled away. Remains of the drapery of a female statue in lively movement indicates the high quality of such funerary sculptures and show the influence of prototypes from Magna Graecia that we have noticed also at Tarquinia (see pp. 295f.). In the same bank of tufa lay two more chamber tombs belonging to other branches of the Curuna family (tombs II and III), and it looks as if certain areas of the necropolis had been allocated to related groups of families.

Though carved from the rock, a number of the aristocratic tombs of Tuscania had built facades of ashlar blocks with cornices and some sculptural decoration. Such seems to be the case of the monumental cube tomb of the Vipinana family (*Tomba dei Vipinana*) discovered in 1839 in the Carcarella necropolis by the Campanari family. These enthusiastic local excavators erected a copy of the tomb in their garden in Tuscania and filled it with some twenty-four recovered sarcophagi as well as numerous bronze and ceramic objects. Many of these objects were later sold to museums in Italy and abroad.

The tomb was in use from the late fourth to the first half of the second century. Perhaps from the carved decoration of the facade came the fine fragmentary high relief of a winged female spirit who in her right hand held a long object (a torch?) against her shoulder (Florence, Museo Archeologico 75842; conflicting early reports ascribe its origin either to Tuscania or to Vulci). She is dressed in a high-girt, sleeveless chiton, whose skirt she has pulled up and back, revealing her lower body in significant nudity. Her face is serious with deep-set eyes, and her striated hair falls in isolated tresses from behind her ears in which she wears rosette earrings. Her lower limbs are missing. The exposure of her pubic parts must be more than a mere apotropaic gesture. It has recently been suggested that the statue may have ended below in bird's legs and claws and that she was a siren—one of the erotic but sinister creatures whose lovely songs lured sailors to their death (Hom. *Od.* 12.39.184). In Sophokles (frag. 861 Pearson) the sirens sing the songs of Hades.

Further fragments of sculpture said to have come from the facade of the Tomb of the Vipinana Family include two lion's paws, one resting on the head of a man, the other on that of a ram. This motif, symbolizing the grimness of death, recurs in contemporary Celtic monuments from the south of France and was taken up in medieval church portals in Tuscany. A particularly fine complete example of such a funerary statue of a lion with its paw on a ram's head was discovered in the necropolis of Val Vidone; according to the inscription on the molded circular base it belonged to the tomb of Arnth Nevzna (Florence, Museo Archeologico 13922/78008).

In time the stone sarcophagi in Tuscania were replaced by the less costly moldmade and painted terra-cotta ones that seem to have been manufactured at first by a master modeler from Tarquinia and subsequently by several local workshops for about 150 years. The quality of these mass-produced works, manufactured with the help of numerous piece molds, deteriorated spectacularly, with the reclining figures of the deceased on the lids becoming more and more flattened and elongated. The ravages of the Hannibal wars in the early second century finally brought an end to this long artistic tradition.

SOUTHERN ETRURIA: ROCK TOMBS

During the Hellenistic period the interior of Southern Etruria with its deeply eroded canyonlike valleys of volcanic tufa saw the development of spectacular family tombs. These probably belonged to aristocrats who had established themselves as landowners in minor inland centers.

The most common type, carved from the perpendicular rock face, shows either a mere facade of a cube or a real half-cube, profiled with rich receding moldings along the flat top and provided with a central framed false "Doric" door on the front; the inconspicuous, roughly hollowed-out tomb chamber is situated underground below the foot of the rock (FIGS. 274, 275). On a stepped platform surmounting the cube, accessible by lateral steps, was a space for cippi of various forms, where cult ceremonies for the dead could be carried out as if on an altar. In these tombs the facade has assumed far greater symbolic importance than the undecorated tomb chamber beneath it. Inscriptions, such as *eca suthi* = this is the tomb of, followed by the name of the owners, were often carved on the front of the cubes (at Castel d'Asso and Norchia), and details of the facades were emphasized by stucco and paint. Such rock tombs were usually carved side by side (and occasionally in two superposed levels) along the steep flanks of the valleys surrounding the settlements on the plateaus; they seem to follow a rationally planned layout.

The main centers for this kind of funerary architecture were Blera, San Giuliano, Norchia, Castel d'Asso (west of Viterbo), and Sovana (near Pitigliano). In the southernmost of these sites—Blera and San Giuliano in the hinterland of the Tolfa Mountains—and in Tuscania interesting forms of rock tombs were created as early as the sixth century, but the flourishing of new types can be observed particularly at Norchia, Castel d'Asso, and Sovana beginning in Early Hellenistic times (late fourth to second century).

At Castel d'Asso—for example, in Tomb 75 (Large Tomb [*Tomba Grande*])—elaborate arrangements for the funeral banquet are found in the entirely rock-carved *sottofacciata* room. Stone benches within a projecting room with a sloping roof at the foot of the cubical tomb facade provide space for such rituals (see FIG. 274). The room communicated with the outside through three simple doors, while on its rear wall is a carved symbolic false door of Doric type with a molded frame. The actual tomb chamber in which the family's sarcophagi were deposited is a quite separate elongated underground space accessible by a descending dromos, the entrance of which is situated some distance from the facade at ground level. Occasionally such *sottofacciata* rooms were distinguished by an external portico.

In the Acqua Alta valley at Norchia two of the leading families had tombs designed in the form of temple facades with the rock face carved to simulate the front colonnade, entablature, and relief-decorated pediment of a real temple (FIG. 276). The pediments are carved with battle scenes. The columns above the podiums are now missing, but behind them, on the back wall of the porch of the left-hand temple tomb, are preserved the remains of a large frieze in relief, once stuccoed and painted. It shows a procession of the deceased led by a winged underworld demon, as well as suspended weapons, shields, and helmets, the latter symbols of the aristocratic valor of the tomb's owners. These themes recall those of the contemporary painted and relief-decorated underground family tombs of Tarquinia and Cerveteri (see FIG. 253). The prosperity of this local aristocracy must have been based on intensive agriculture and internal trade connections favored by the building of the Roman Via Clodia.

As early as the seventh century Sovana, a small settlement in the hinterland of Vulci, had profited from its position on the river Fiora, halfway between the metal-rich region of Monte Amiata and the coast. It flourished again during the Hellenistic period, after a decline during the economic crisis that lasted from the end of the sixth to the late fourth century. Surrounded by deep ravines, the city

Fig. 274 Isometric view of Tomb 75 (*Tomba Grande*), Castel d'Asso. Third century B.C.

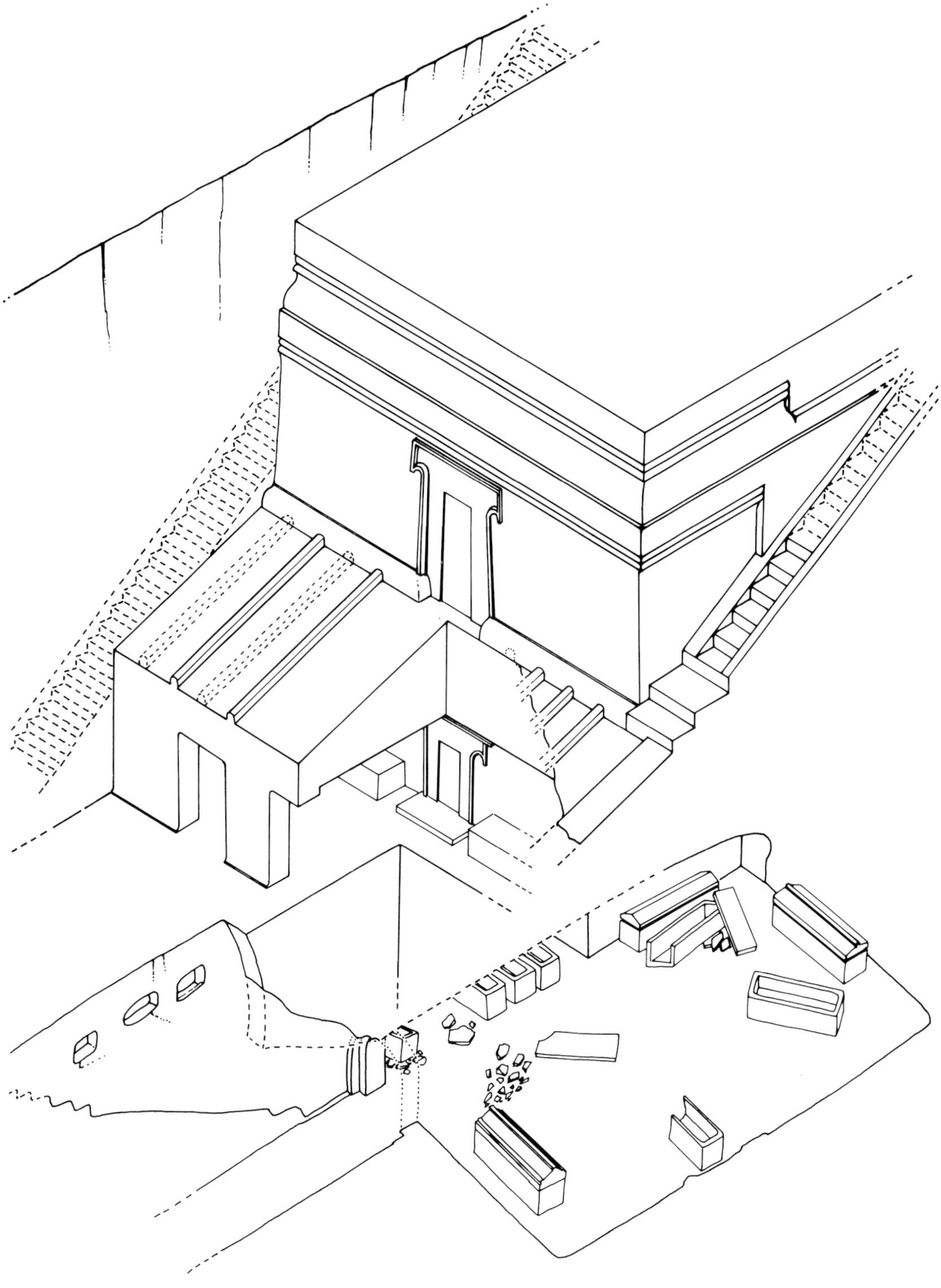

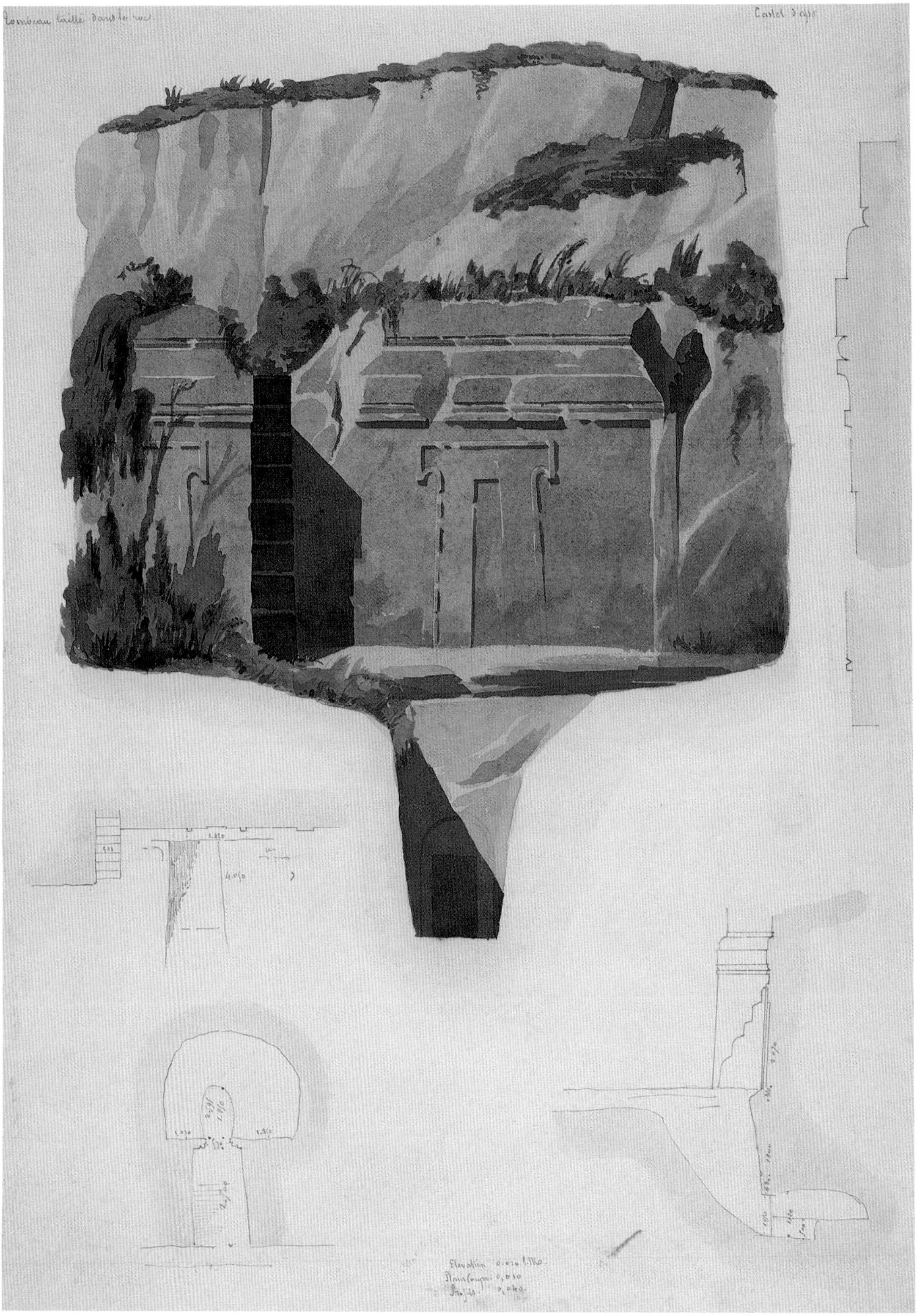
Tombeau taillé dans le roc.
Castel d'Asso

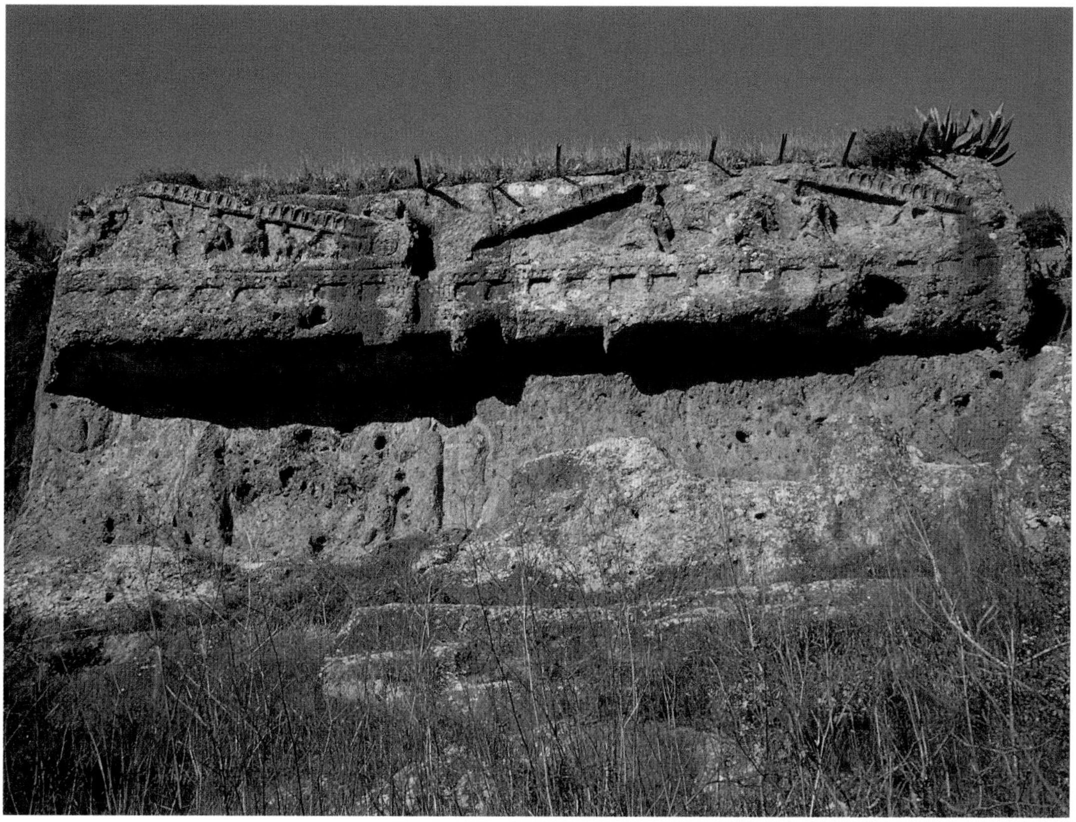

carved its monumental rock tombs along these during the third and second centuries, particularly in the valleys to the north- and southwest.

A variety of rock-tomb forms known from Norchia and Castel d'Asso is present at Sovana, though the cube tombs here lack the *sottofacciata* rooms of the more southerly sites, while their shape and decorative moldings show close affinities with smaller Vulcian funerary cippi of stone.

Aedicula tombs with reliefs in the pediments are represented by the Tomb of the Typhon (*Tomba del Tifone*) and the Tomb of the Siren (*Tomba della Sirena*). The latter's facade is carved in the center with a deep vaulted niche (perhaps representing the door of the underworld) containing a banqueting couch with the reclining figure of the deceased and the inscription with his name on the back wall. The niche was originally flanked by two bases with statues of winged female demons in short chitons and ankle boots who grasped tresses of their long hair in one hand, a sign of mourning. Above a Doric frieze, the pediment of the facade shows in low relief a frontal fishtailed Skylla with an arching veil above her. On either side a winged male figure escapes upward and away from her. The small burial chamber is underground, below the rock facade and reached by a dromos; it probably served for ash urns only.

The most spectacular of the tombs of Sovana is the Hildebrand Tomb (*Tomba*

OPPOSITE

Fig. 275 Tomb at Castel d'Asso. Watercolor and pencil drawing (1825–1833) by Simon Claude Constant-Dufeux. 33.4 x 23.5 cm.

ABOVE

Fig. 276 Facades of temple tombs in the Acqua Alta valley at Norchia. Third century B.C.

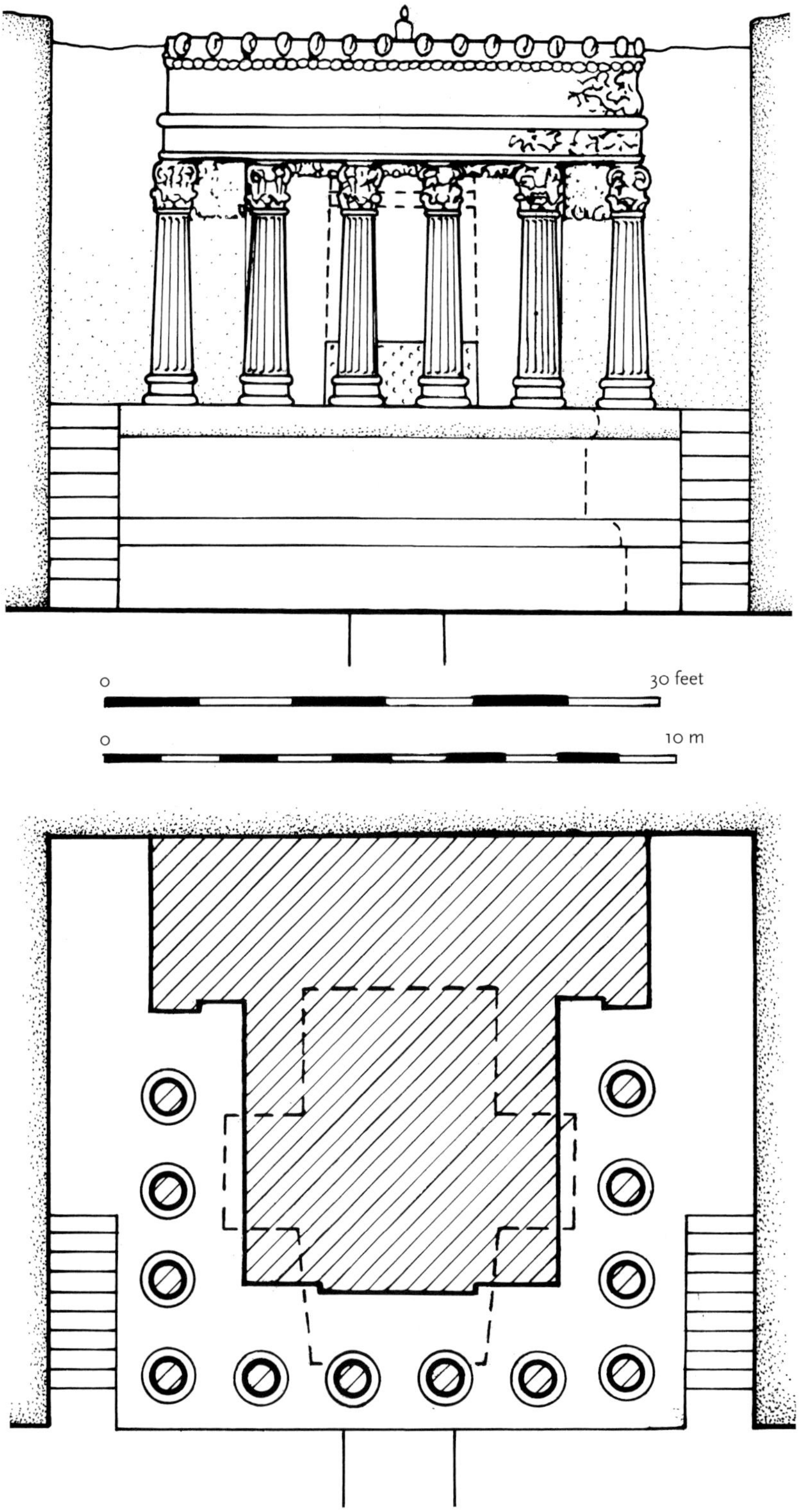

Fig. 277 Reconstruction of the Hildebrand Tomb, Poggio Felceto, near Sovana. Late third–early second century B.C.

Ildebranda, named after Pope Gregory VII, a native of Sovana, FIG. 277). Situated on the slope of Poggio Felceto, overlooking the hill of the town, it takes the form of a small temple on a high podium, flanked by lateral stairways. Except at the back, where it is still attached to the surrounding rock, its T-shaped cubic body was entirely carved from the tufa. Its front and sides were originally surrounded by twelve freestanding fluted columns (six on the facade, three on each side) with capitals decorated with volutes, leaves, and male and female heads. Carved in relief on the front wall was a false door with a low trellis. The ceilings within the colonnade were coffered, and the entablature bore a double relief frieze of griffins, plants, and vegetal motifs. Above this there seems to have been a gable on all three sides, suggesting an *aedicula* rather than a temple. This and the decorative features, heightened in their effect by stucco and paint, point to a strong influence from South Italy. The cross-shaped tomb chamber underneath the rock tomb contained only one bench for the deposition of the dead at the back. Implicit in this form of temple tomb is the heroization of the eminent person for whom it was carved during the third century.

A small, circular pseudoperipteral temple (diam. 2.52 m) is reproduced in the rock-carved Tomb of the Silenus at Monte Rosello (Sovana). Six half-columns on a podium surrounding the drum-shaped building originally carried a cornice and roof; the acroterial head of a silenus carved from tufa gave the tomb its name and hints at Dionysiac symbolism. The subterranean chamber was unviolated and yielded rich grave gifts of bronze vessels, utensils, mirrors, and ceramics, which allowed it to be dated to between the end of the third and the middle of the second century. Comparable in form to this circular tomb is a stone cippus from Vulci in the Vatican and the simple round temple painted on a red-figured vase (see FIG. 255).

FEMALE STATUES

We have already noted the widespread use during the sixth and fifth centuries of marble from the region of Pisa for funerary monuments in Northern Etruria (cippi of club, column, or onion shape and bases with ram's heads or rampant lions at the four corners, pp. 191–96). Five female marble statues from the third and second centuries have been discovered in an area comprising Volterra, Pisa, and Florence (San Miniato and San Martino alla Palma). They were probably carved for tombs and meant to represent the dead women. It has been plausibly suggested that these (relatively rare) funerary statues can be considered female equivalents of the column-shaped male tomb markers. A columnar tomb marker from San Martino alla Palma (Scandicci), richly carved on the shaft with five relief figures representing the departure of a warrior from two male relatives in the pres-

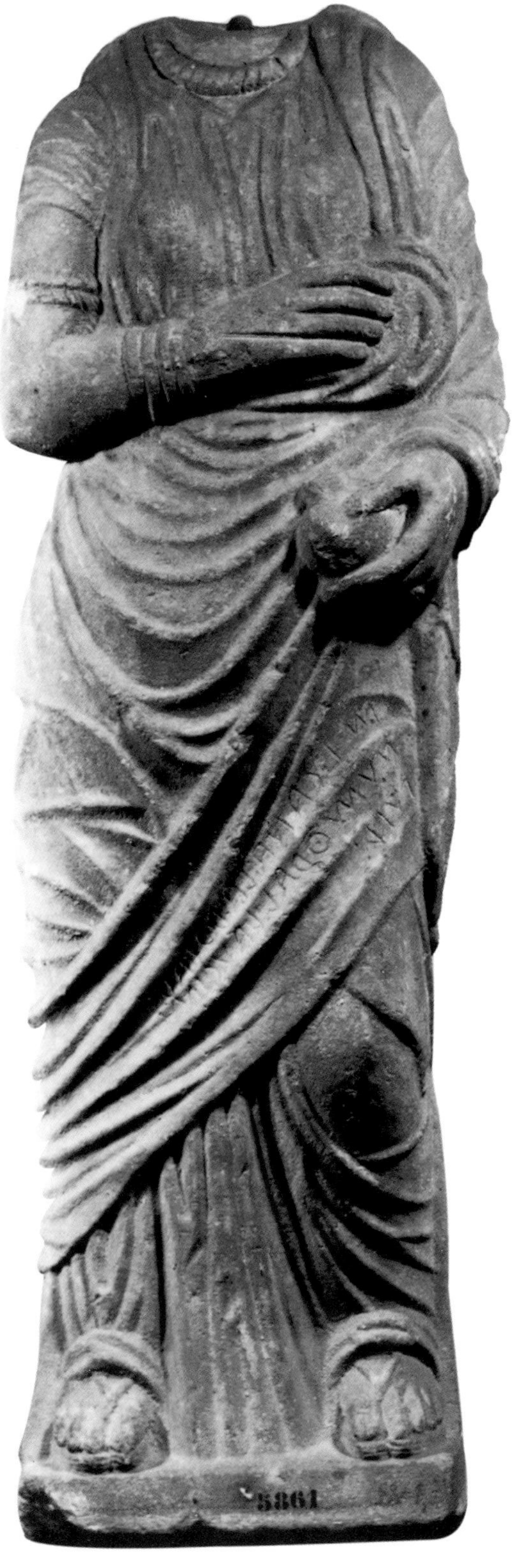

Fig. 278 Inscribed funerary statue of Larthia Numthrai. From San Martino alla Palma, near Scandicci. Late third century B.C. Italian marble. H. 1.37 m. Florence, Museo Archeologico 5861.

ence of two lictors, is inscribed with the name of the deceased, *Arnth Prastna*, the son of *Lauci* (*TLE* 681). From the same site comes the draped and bejeweled statue of a woman, *Larthia Numthrai*, wife of *Lauci* (*TLE* 682), who holds a pomegranate in her hand (FIG. 278). She seems to be the mother of Arnth Prastna. A relatively modest work inspired by Late Classical Greek prototypes, the statue has been dated on palaeographic grounds to the last decades of the third century.

Somewhat earlier (first half of third century) and of greater sculptural quality is a draped female statue found in the fifteenth century at Volterra (FIG. 279). It is known as the *kourotrophos Maffei*. A separate head, covered by a mantle, is carved from the same Italian marble and in all probability belonged to the statue originally. The woman, wrapped entirely in a mantle over a chiton, holds in her left arm a swaddled infant, half of whose head is missing. The woman's lower legs and feet are also missing. The damaged head of the statue shows a youthful face with widely spaced large eyes, level brows, and a few short locks of hair falling from under the edge of the mantle onto the forehead. A slanting votive inscription (*TLE* 397) is carved on the mantle covering her right arm and hand; it reads: *mi:cana:larthiaś:zanl: velchinei:śe*(*thra tur*)*ce* = I (am) the image (or gift) of Larthia Zan. Velchina Se(thra) gave me. It is not clear what the relationship between the two women was, but the dedication to the young woman suggests that the statue may have been set up by a close female relative, defining the deceased with her baby in her social role as a mother. There are stylistic affinities between this fine marble statue and certain funerary stone sculptures from Greek Taranto, while the stance and the mantle enveloping the arms and thrown over the left shoulder are motifs that go back to the school of Praxiteles of the second half of the fourth century.

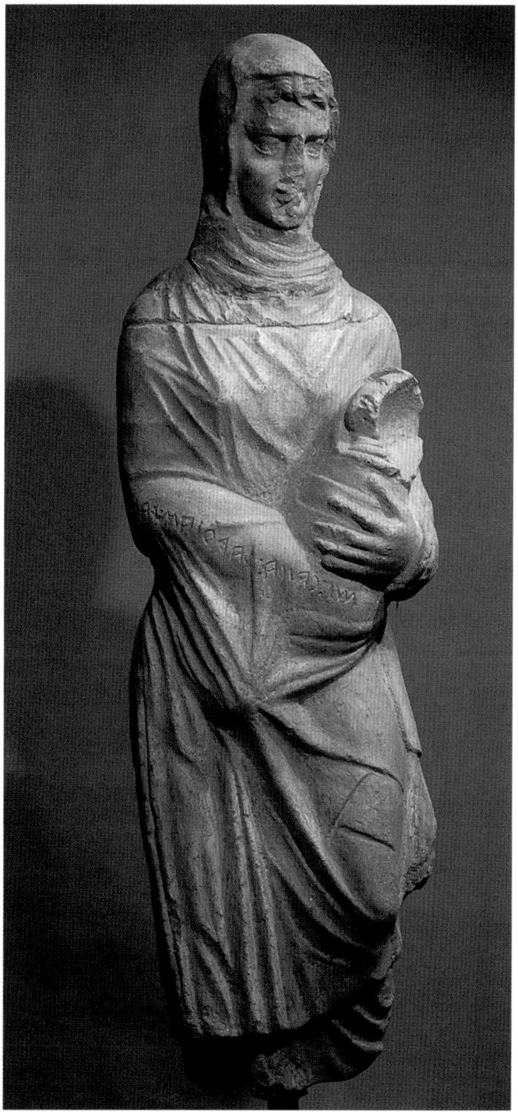

Fig. 279 Inscribed funerary statue of a woman holding a baby, the so-called *kourotrophos Maffei*. From Volterra. First half of third century B.C. Italian marble. Volterra, Museo Etrusco Guarnacci.

Marble funerary statues of this kind were presumably carved for women of well-to-do families at a period when Northern Etruria, particularly Volterra with its flourishing industries, enjoyed great economic prosperity.

There is great similarity in motif and style of a number of excellent votive bronze statuettes of young women, some found in Northern Etruscan sites (e.g., one from Montecchio near Cortona, now in Leiden, Rijksmuseum C.O. 30), oth-

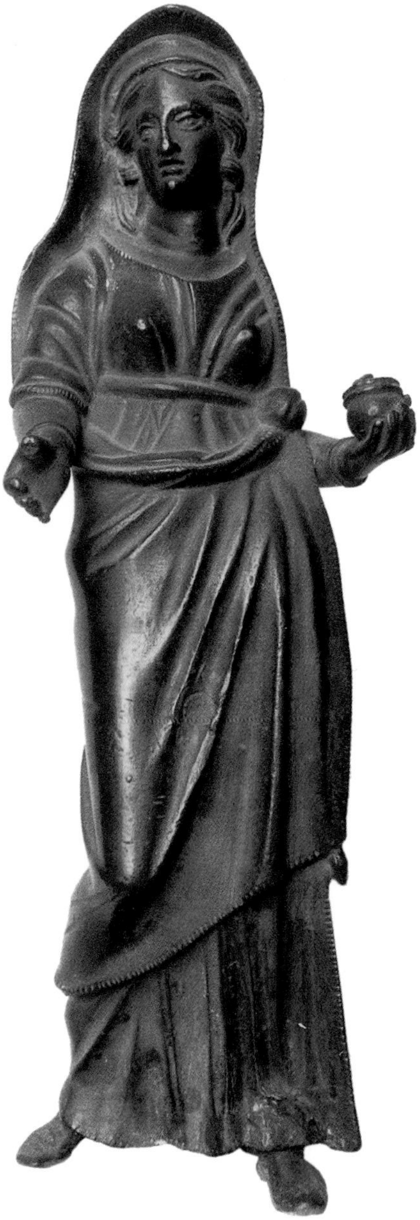

Fig. 280 Votive statuette of a woman with pyxis. Third century B.C. Cast bronze. H. 26 cm. Florence, Museo Archeologico 549.

ers, without provenance, in the Museo Archeologico of Florence (inv. 554, with inscription [*TLE* 739] by the dedicant Larce Lecni in letters of the type used in the Chiusi and Siena area; and inv. 549, FIG. 280). Their slim bodies are posed in a lively rhythm caused by the relaxation of one leg with the feet well apart and a strong turn of the head. The obliquely draped short mantle, tucked under the left arm or held by the left hand, goes over a sleeveless or short-sleeved chiton, girt high under the breasts. The proportions, the twist of the head, the hairstyle with short full locks rising above the forehead, and the far-away look of the eyes reflect Hellenistic ideals that were inspired by portraits of Alexander the Great.

A particularly fine statuette of over half life-size in the British Museum is said to have been found together with seven small statuettes of draped women and youths, each holding a libation bowl and an incense box, near the sanctuary of Diana Nemorensis on Lake Nemi south of Rome (FIG. 281). Unlike the small votive statuettes just mentioned, this girl had none of the usual offerings—such as a pyxis, pomegranate, or bird—in her lightly opened hands, held sideways. The attitude of her arms and now-empty hands suggests that she might have had a distaff tucked under her left elbow (where there is a small hole in the bronze for the insertion of a rod), while loosely grasping its wool-covered end with her fingers. A thread, presumably of bronze wire, might have passed from there across to her right hand, from which it would have hung down, weighted by the spindle. She gazes calmly into the distance without the lively turn of the head of the somewhat earlier statuettes in Florence and Leiden. Stance and drapery connect this fine statue with Southern Etruscan and Latin votive statuettes of the third century, but the cooler treatment of the face and folds points to a slightly later date. Her occupation hints at a new ideal for votive and honorary dedications of women. Except for a ribbon in her hair, a simple torque around her neck, and twisted bracelets, she wears no jewelry. Spinning and woolworking were the privilege of upper-class women in earlier periods of Etruscan civilization, the evidence being particularly strong for the Villanovan and early Orientalizing phases. None of the tomb-paintings or the sarcophagi of the Archaic and Classical times, how-

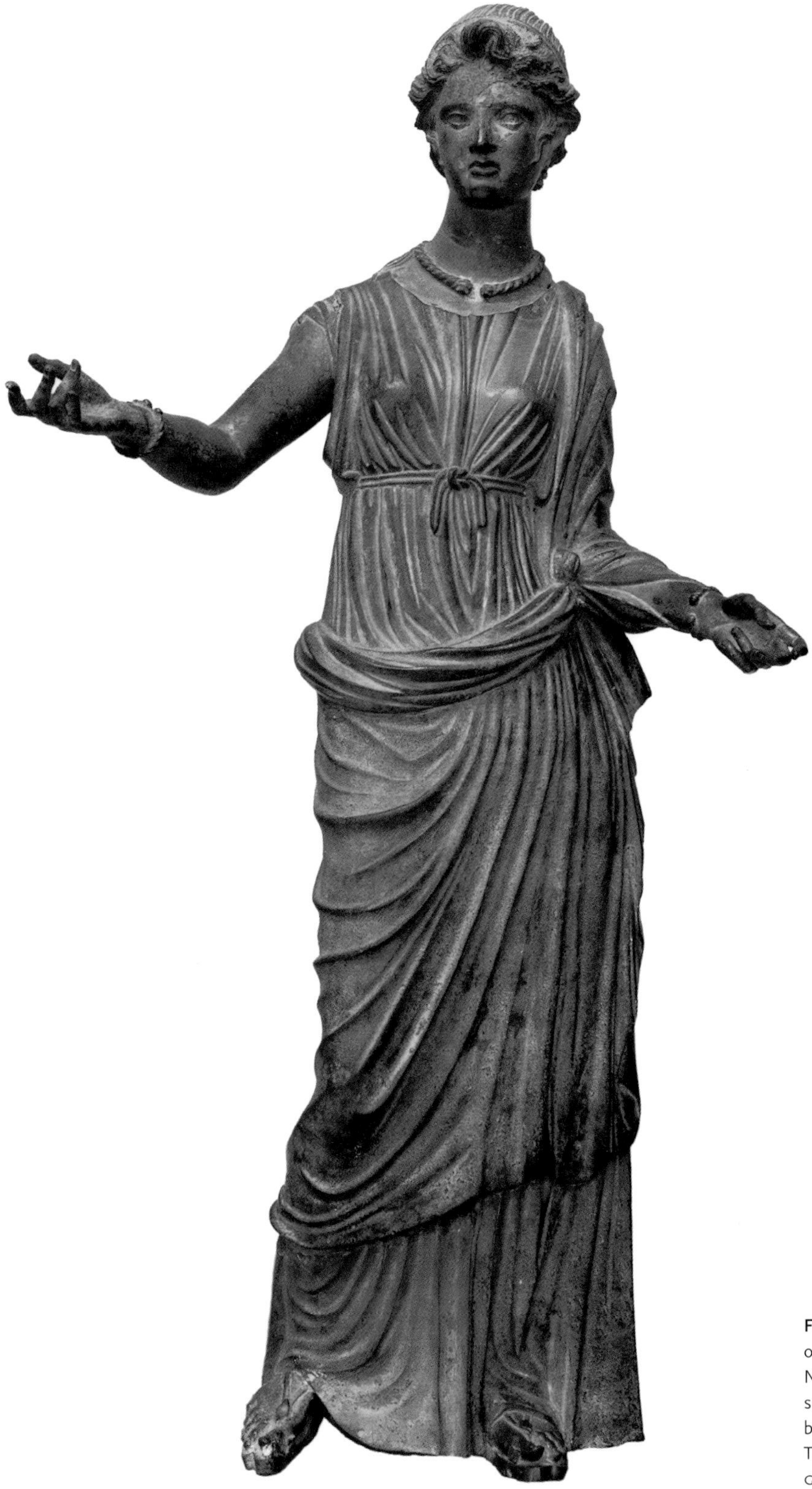

Fig. 281 Votive statuette of a girl. Probably from Lake Nemi. Late third–early second century B.C. Cast bronze. H. 97 cm. London, The British Museum GR 1920.6-12.1.

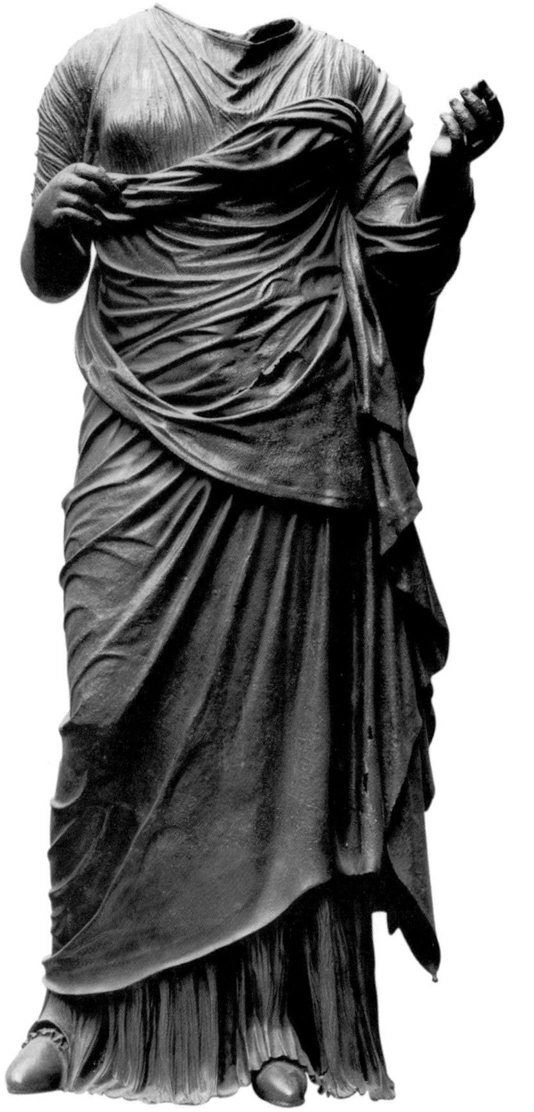

Fig. 282 Over life-size statue of a woman spinning. From Vulci. Third–second century B.C. Cast bronze. Munich, Staatliche Antikensammlungen und Glyptotek B 444.

ever, represent spinning ladies, so this aspect of female life seems to have lost some of its social implications at that period in Etruria. (Rare examples of fourth-century date are a small bronze statuette of Athena spinning [Florence, Museo Archeologico] and a mirror in Copenhagen [Ny Carlsberg Glyptotek, *CSE*, Denmark 1.26] engraved with a seated courting couple, the young woman holding distaff and spindle.) In Republican Rome meanwhile it remained the abiding stern ideal that the matron should look after the house and work with wool, as seen in funerary inscriptions such as that of Claudia: She served the house and worked wool (*domum servavit lanam fecit*; *CIL* 6.15346). It is perhaps no accident that the statue of the spinning young woman from Lake Nemi reflects ideals prevalent in Rome.

This same ethos seems to be expressed by a headless life-size bronze statue of a draped spinning woman found in 1835 in an exceptional context near the remains of a great temple on the city plateau of Vulci (FIG. 282). The type is based on a fourth-century Greek work, probably the statue of "the one who lets down the thread" (Gr. *katagousa*, i.e., the spinning woman), a bronze statue by Praxiteles known to us only from Pliny (34.69). The matronly body is dressed in a finely pleated chiton with half sleeves, fastened on shoulders and upper arms by a series of closely set, pointed, oval buttons or hooks of unique shape. A heavy, rectangular mantle is draped obliquely around her body, covering her left breast and wrapped around her left arm, whence it hangs in an overfold with a zigzag edge ending in a weighted corner. She wears pointed shoes and rings on the second and fourth fingers of her left hand. Its gesture clearly implies that it once held a distaff, while with her right hand she pulled the thread, rotating the spindle. Such an impressively large statue of a woman (her shoes, the extraordinary buttons of her chiton, and her rings rule out that she represents a goddess) must have been set up in a public place to honor some important personality engaged in the exemplary occupation of a lady. It is difficult to assign a date to this bronze, particularly in the absence of the head, whose hairstyle might have provided a clue. The probability is that the statue stood for some time on its travertine base near the steps leading up to the front of the great temple of Vulci. Subsequently struck by lightning, the bronze, its base, and the bronze crest from the helmet of a marble statue were buried according to Etruscan ritual (cf. the "Mars" from Todi, pp. 300ff.) between the enclosure wall of the temple and its front steps, in a box constructed of travertine slabs held together by lead. A Latin inscription on the slabs, which is dated on epigraphical grounds to the first century A.D., states the fact: struck by lightning (*fulg*[*ur c*]*onditum*). This inscription, however, dates only the burial of the statue, not its creation; it may well have been made in the Late Hellenistic period.

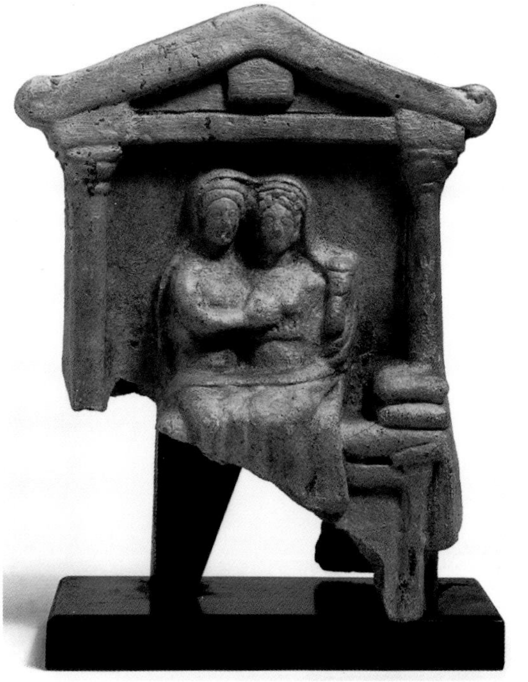

Fig. 283 Votive model of a couple sitting on a bed inside a house. Third century B.C. Terra-cotta. H. 21.7 cm. London, The British Museum GR 1982.3-2.58.

Couples, Mothers, Babies, and Small Children

A fourth–third-century terra-cotta model of a small, shrinelike house, sheltering under its pedimental roof a man and a woman sitting side by side on a bed, must be the votive offering from a young couple (FIG. 283). Each wears a wreath on the head, and she is dressed in a belted chiton. They are wrapped together in a single mantle, probably the husband's, which covers their hair, backs, and laps. The young woman raises its edge with her left hand in a bridal gesture, while the man has placed his right hand on her breast. Their marital bed is covered by a mattress and two pillows. This votive gift was presumably offered to a fertility divinity and symbolizes the idea that the family's house and the marital bed are at the heart of marriage; the couple's lovemaking signifies the continuity of their union and expectancy of offspring. A similar symbolism is seen in the emphasis in rock-carved family tombs on the central bed of the founding couple (see Tomb of the Reliefs, p. 318).

Parental concern for babies and their welfare is documented by innumerable small votive terra-cotta statuettes of mothers holding their infants in their arms or on their laps. These statuettes have turned up in Latial and Etruscan sanctuaries at Satricum, Cerveteri, Veii, Tarquinia, Vulci, and elsewhere from the late sixth to the first century B.C., while images of nursing mothers are relatively rare in Greece before the Hellenistic period. A fifth-century Etruscan example from Cerveteri in the British Museum (inv. GR 1922.4-12.27) shows the nursing mother sitting hieratically on a throne with a mantle covering her hair and both hands on the lap cradling the suckling baby.

The particular vulnerability of children of tender age prompted parents to deposit terra-cotta figures of swaddled babies with amuletic *bullae* in the hope that the presiding divinity of the sanctuary would protect and safeguard their offspring. The babies' smiling, chubby faces emerge from the tight swaddling clothes that cover the head and are wrapped around the body and arms, leaving only the toes

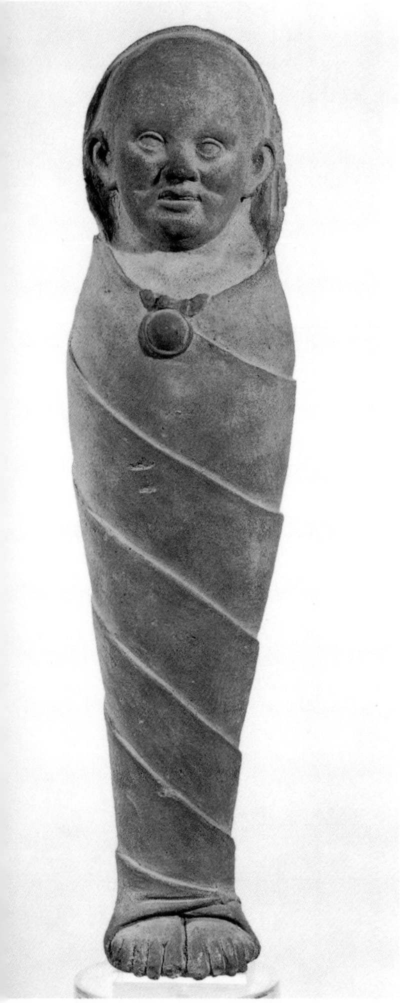

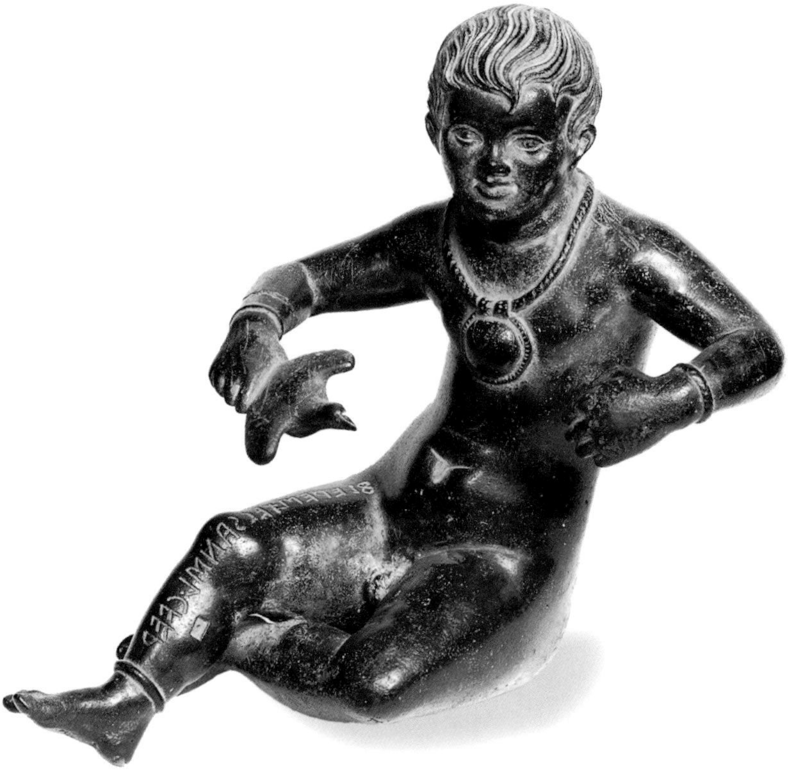

Fig. 284 Votive figure of a swaddled baby. From Veii. Third century B.C. Terra-cotta. Rome, Museo Etrusco di Villa Giulia.

Fig. 285 Inscribed votive statuette of a seated nude boy. From Lake Trasimene. Third century B.C. Cast bronze. H. 26 cm. Vatican, Museo Gregoriano Etrusco 12107.

free (FIG. 284). Children were breast-fed for a considerable time, as suggested by the bronze figure of a mother (forming the support of an incense burner in the Museo Nazionale of Tarquinia) who holds a remarkably tall swaddled infant to her breast.

Other terra-cotta votive figures represent seated or crouching small boys, some of them posed like Cypriote so-called temple boys with one bent knee horizontally on the ground, the other upright.

More costly than terra-cotta were votive gifts of bronze, and only a limited number of statuettes of young boys have survived. Bronze can be melted down easily and recast into some other form, a fate that befell most of the large bronze statues of antiquity and explains their comparative rarity. From Sanguineto on the northern shore of Lake Trasimene comes a bronze statuette of a seated nude boy with a *bulla* tied by a cord around his neck and a bracelet on each arm and one around the ankle (FIG. 285). His left foot is tucked under his right knee, and he leans back a little, trying to balance himself by raising both elbows. He holds a ball in his left hand and in his right a bird by its tail. His chubby face has an upturned nose, widely spaced eyes, and a small smiling mouth; softly waved hair falls on his forehead and temples. A votive inscription on his right leg reads: *flereś.tec. sanśl.cver* = sacred to Tec Sans (the father). This divinity seems to have been a protector of children, but he is also mentioned in the inscription (*TLE* 651) on the edge of the toga of the over-life-size bronze statue of Aule Meteli, the son of

Vel and Vesi, known as the "Arringatore," which was found in 1566 near Lake Trasimene (now Florence, Museo Archeologico). Tec Sans was venerated in the area northeast of the lake; it is possible that a number of small figures of boys in the Museo Archeologico of Perugia from a votive deposit at Colle Arsiccio near Magione were dedicated to this local god.

The bronze boy in the Vatican probably dates from the third century, for his hairstyle occurs on youthful male heads painted on Volterran red-figured vases (see FIG. 257), and his entire figure resembles that of a young boy supporting the shaft of an incense burner in the British Museum (BM *Bronze Cat.* 780) inscribed on the back with *thania lucini suthina*, which designates it as part of the grave gifts of this lady. Identical words are inscribed on bronze utensils now in the Villa Giulia (*CIE* 10854–860), which indicates that they originally came from the same third-century tomb above Bolsena.

LIFE EXPECTANCY

Based on the age at death mentioned on first-century funerary monuments at Volterra, a recent study has shown that both women and men were most likely to die between the ages of twenty and thirty, presumably in childbirth and war, respectively. More general investigations of the average life expectancies in Etruria (excluding those under twenty) point to a life span of forty-four years for women and forty-nine years for men in Southern Etruria, while at Volterra the figures are forty-eight for women and forty-six for men. A statistical analysis by gender of all surviving funerary monuments and inscriptions between 400/300 and the first century has shown that (with strong local variations) male burials and commemorations considerably outnumber those for females. The only exception is Tuscania, where the numbers are equal for the two sexes. The relatively smaller representation of women's burials is not confined to Etruria, but is general for all antiquity. The highest chances for commemoration fell to Etruscan women of the upper social strata who had lived long and left behind husbands or male descendants to bury and honor them.

VOLTERRA AND ITS TERRITORY

The Northern Etruscan area comprising Volterra and its territory showed a remarkable cultural homogeneity from the fourth to the first century. In the Late Classical period the city of Volterra had extended its existing Archaic stone walls to the impressive length of 7.28 km, enclosing an area of ca. 116 hectares, which was probably not entirely built up but included pastureland. The size of this circuit, however, points to a considerable increase in population and wealth. One of the

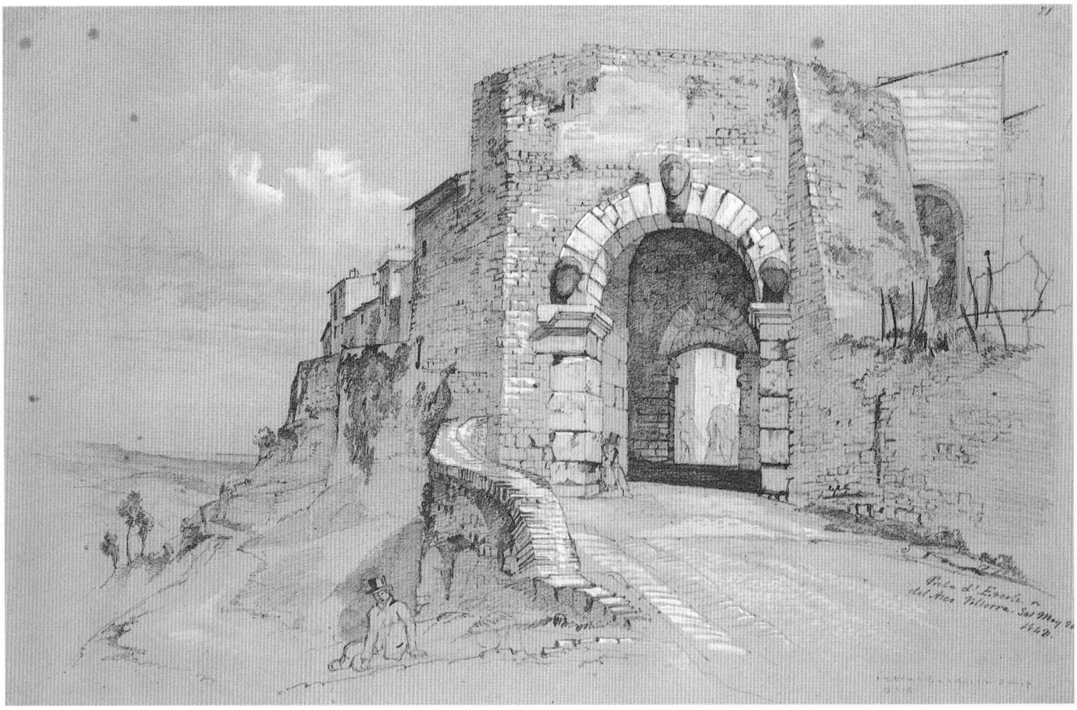

Fig. 286 S. J. Ainsley, *Porta all'Arco, Volterra*. Signed and dated May 20, 1843. Pencil on drab paper, heightened with white. 29.2 x 44.4 cm. London, The British Museum, Department of Prints and Drawings, cat. LB 64.

finest surviving parts of this longest of all Etruscan city walls is the Porta all'Arco; this vaulted gateway of ashlar masonry in a bastion on the south side of the city is guarded by three stone heads carved at the springs and crown of the arch (FIG. 286). These weathered sculptures probably represent tutelary divinities.

A series of potters' workshops in Volterra produced funerary vases decorated in red-figure and fine black-glazed tablewares, both of which found wide distribution. At the same time the mineral resources of the Cecina valley were exploited, while the enduring agricultural wealth of the territory rested firmly in the hands of the local aristocracy. The river Cecina ensured easy transport to the Tyrrhenian coast, and the Era River connected the city with the vast area of the Arno basin and its tributaries, such as the Elsa valley communicating with the region of Monteriggioni and Siena. The distribution in this region during the third century of Volterran cast-bronze coins with the double-headed image of the god Culśanś and of others with a club or a dolphin and the inscription *Velathri* shows the extent of the city's economic and political influence. Judging from funerary inscriptions, women from aristocratic families of Volterra seem to have contracted marriages with the landed gentry of outlying areas of the territory, such as Monteriggioni, Barberino, and Castiglioncello.

Local alabaster, quarried for the production of innumerable cinerary urns in the later Hellenistic period, was another wealth-producing natural resource for Volterra. From ca. 400 to 250, ash urns were carved predominantly from local tufa, but alabaster was increasingly used, and by the first century it had far surpassed tufa. The earliest urns take the form of house-shaped boxes, their lids that of ridge roofs with acroteria; subsequently the urns imitate wooden boxes, often resting on feline feet and with a relief decoration of fighting animals, mythical beings, and vegetal motifs (e.g., an urn in Volterra, Museo Guarnacci 45). From the end of the fourth century and throughout the third century the lids follow the types we know from sarcophagi and urns at Tarquinia, Chiusi, Tuscania, etc. The images of the dead at first recline as if resting on a bed (e.g., a lid with a nude woman under a mantle, Museo Guarnacci 193), then gradually raise themselves on their left elbows like banqueters, while holding objects and pulling up their knees and crossing their feet.

The boxes are carved with reliefs showing the journey into the beyond, soon adding more complex mythological scenes. Almost forty percent of the more than one thousand surviving urns are decorated with scenes from Greek mythology and drama, often connected with early death, abduction, or family tragedies. The quality of workmanship is uneven and suggests that several workshops operated under masters of different competence using a variety of pictorial models for the boxes. The artistic level of the image on the lid often diverges from that of the carving on the box and shows the dependence, in the same workshop, on totally different iconographical and stylistic sources. The heads of the deceased reflect the typology of the portraits of Hellenistic rulers of the third century. In the first quarter of the second century begins a series of very competently carved alabaster urns with dramatically composed scenes in high relief showing episodes from Greek myth (FIG. 287) and Attic tragedy, themes that were preferred by aristocrats imbued with Hellenistic culture and by artists familiar with the sculptural achievements of

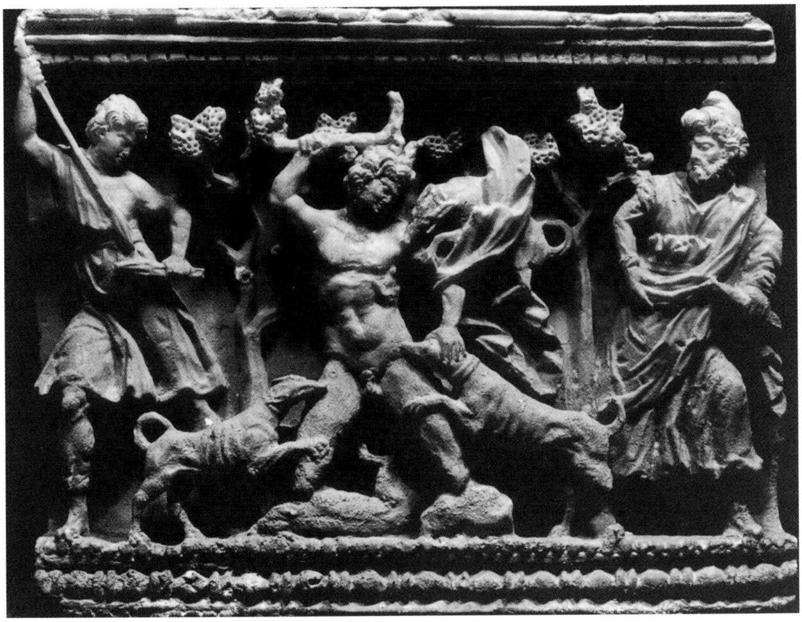

Fig. 287 Ash urn with a relief on the front showing the death of Aktaion. From Volterra. Second–first century B.C. Alabaster. H. 40 cm. Volterra, Museo Etrusco Guarnacci 356.

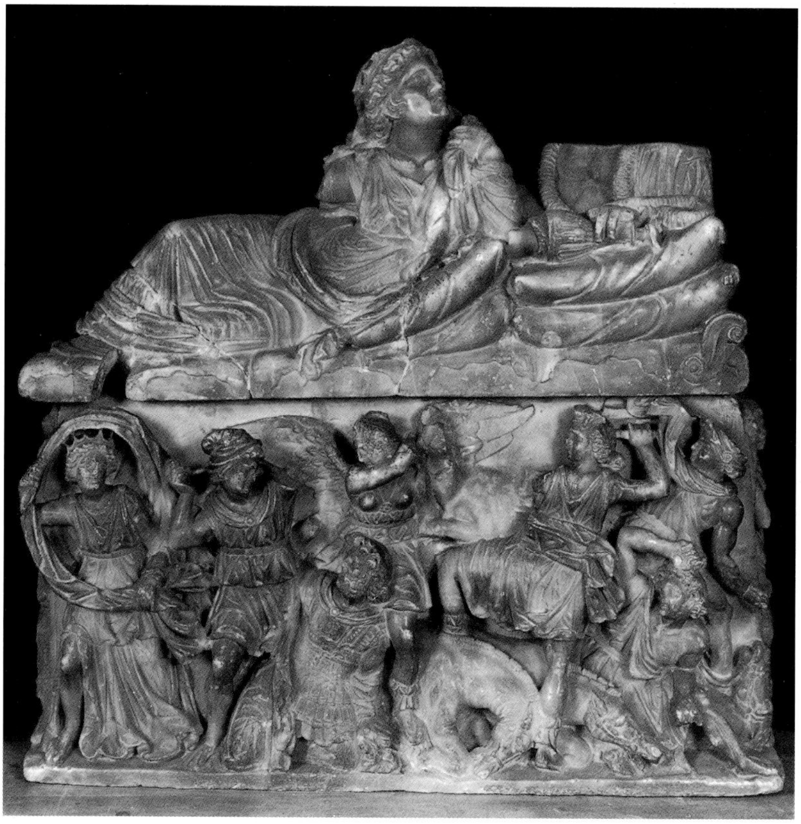

Fig. 288 Ash urn of married couple with a relief on the chest showing the murder of Oinomaos by Pelops. From Todi. First quarter of second century B.C. Alabaster. H. 83.5 cm. Vatican, Museo Gregoriano Etrusco 13887.

the schools of Pergamon and Rhodes; such models reached Northern Etruria as a result of the Roman conquests in the eastern Mediterranean.

The hands of several individual masters have been identified in the production of the second century, each named after an outstanding representation. One such urn is ascribed to the hand of the "Master of Oenomaus" (FIG. 288). On the lid rest a married couple on cushions and an animal skin spread over a bed with a volute-shaped head end. The man's head is missing; he holds a drinking-cup in his left hand and places his right one on his wife's right shoulder. She holds the edge of a mantle covering her head and turns back to gaze up at her husband. She wears a crown on her wavy locks and a torque around her neck. On the front of the box is carved the myth of the treacherous killing of the king of Pisa, Oinomaos, by Pelops, who aspired to the hand of Oinomaos's daughter Hippodameia. The bearded Oinomaos, thrown from his chariot because Pelops had tampered with the linchpin of a wheel, kneels beside his collapsed team of horses, trying to ward off the blows of the youthful Pelops, who wears a Phrygian cap. On the left the terrified Hippodameia flees, dressed in a chiton, torque, and crown similar to that of the wife on the lid; her mantle flutters in an arch over her head. Above the murder victim stands a winged female demon beating down on him, while a further menacing female in a short tunic and boots strides over the fallen horses. Behind

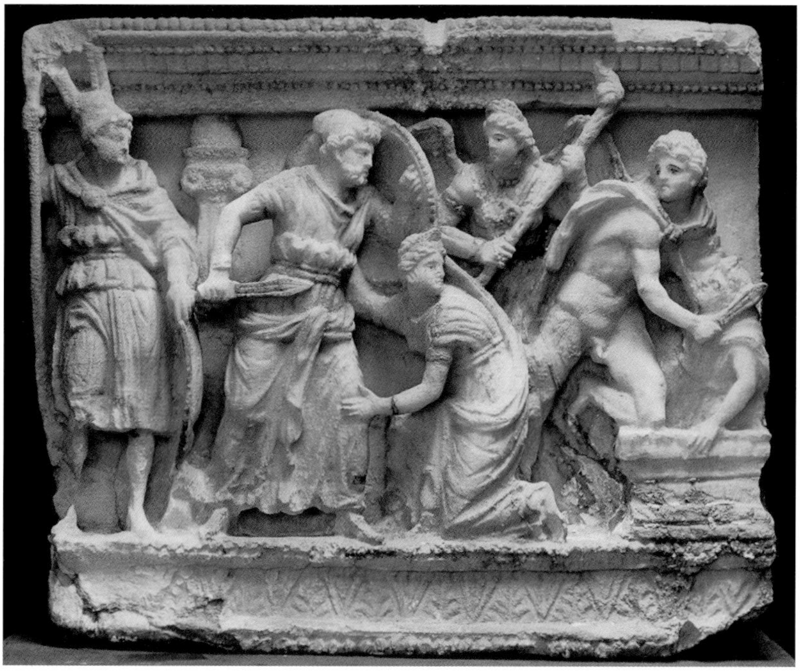

her cower two gesturing male figures. The two short sides of the box are each carved with a winged female demon.

Fig. 289 Chest of ash urn with relief showing Telephos threatening to kill the child Orestes. From Volterra. Mid-second century B.C. Alabaster. H. 48 cm. Volterra, Museo Etrusco Guarnacci 511.

The dramatic action is represented in a baroque composition, carved with great virtuosity, while the deceased couple, by the same hand, reinterprets a scheme created for sarcophagi of the Archaic period (p. 114). This itinerant artist, whose influence is also noticeable in the urn production of Perugia (p. 379), was followed at Volterra by the "Master of Myrtilus." Other artists of the second century have been named after particular characteristic decorative motifs (the "Master of the Small Paterae," the "Atelier of the Rosettes and Palmettes," etc.).

A particularly fine example of the middle of the second century is an alabaster urn carved with a scene inspired by a tragedy of Euripides (FIG. 289). Telephos, kneeling on an altar, threatens to kill his hostage, the child Orestes. While Agamemnon rushes to rescue his son, Klytaimnestra, the mother, tries to intercede. On the left stands Achilles, who will heal Telephos with his lance, and in the background hovers a winged female demon with a torch, signifying the inevitability of fate. The sculptural prototype for the scene is found on the small Telephos frieze on the Great Altar at Pergamon from western Asia Minor (Berlin, Pergamon Museum).

The images on the lids of the urns follow traditional schemes, the wreathed and garlanded men often holding banqueters' omphalos bowls or drinking horns ending in animal foreparts; eventually, perhaps as a result of Roman antisumptuary laws, the men wear a sober tunic rather than only a mantle that left the torso bare. The deceased men occasionally hold a diptych, a scroll or, in the rare case of a *haruspex* (Aule Lecu, Museo Guarnacci 136), a liver; the women grasp fans, mir-

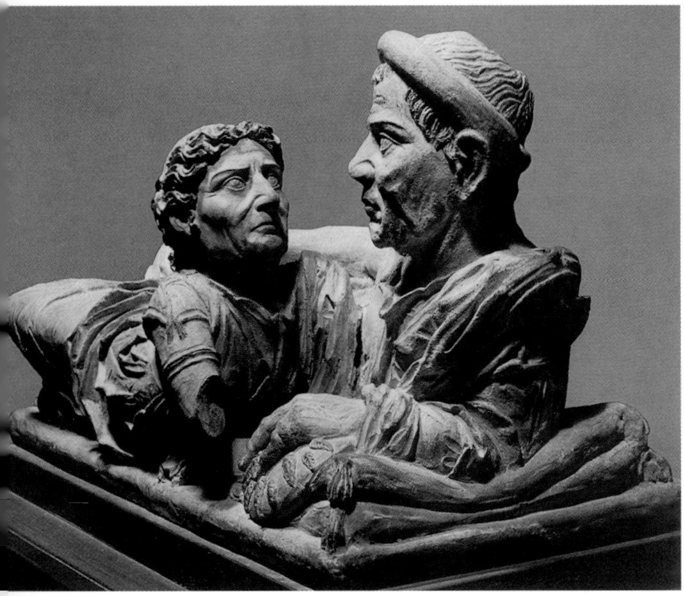

Fig. 290 Detail of the lid of an ash urn in the form of an old married couple. From Volterra. Late second–early first century B.C. Terra-cotta. H. 41 cm. Volterra, Museo Etrusco Guarnacci 613.

rors (often set in square, lidded boxes of wood that protect the surface of the bronze), and pomegranates.

Increasingly the proportional sizes of bodies and heads change in favor of the latter, and it is clear that the head has become the most important feature of the image of the dead. The faces, however, are not real portraits, but, as in vase-painting and votive terra-cotta sculpture (p. 322), generic images based on Hellenistic portrait types to which a few individual touches, such as furrows on the forehead, sunken cheeks, or receding hair, have been added to give an indication of the age of the occupant of the urn.

The most striking example of a realistic representation of old people is a married couple lying on a couch modeled in terra-cotta on what looks like the lid of an urn but may have been the urn itself (FIG. 290). The terra-cotta is hollow, and there is a large circular hole in the crown of each head (unnecessarily big for a vent for the escape of air during firing, but suitable for the insertion of ashes). Found in 1743 in a chamber tomb in the Ulimeto necropolis of Volterra, the terra-cotta was acquired by Mario Guarnacci, the founder of the eponymous local museum. The man, dressed in tunic and mantle and wearing a thick wreath on his receding hair, which is brushed forward over his forehead and temples, leans with his left elbow on two tasseled cushions, resting his left, veined and beringed hand on the back of a drinking bowl decorated with radiating leaves. His right hand rests on his right thigh. His brow and cheeks are marked with deep furrows, and he gazes into the distance past his wife's head; his irises and pupils are incised. Despite the man's seemingly individual features, his face can be paralleled on some other Volterran urns, thus proving that it is a generic type rather than a real portrait. Propped up on her left elbow, his wife lies on her stomach in front of him in an uncomfortably contorted position. She wears a sleeveless, high-girt tunic and a mantle wrapped around her left shoulder, lower body, and twisted legs. A grooved bracelet encircles her upper right arm; the forearm and hand, which were probably raised to caress his cheek, are missing. Her face, lifted toward her husband, appears in profile for the frontal spectator. Seen full on, it bears a grim expression of bitterness in strange contrast to her loving gesture. Her sunken cheeks, the mouth pulled down at the corners, the crow's-feet at the outer corners of the eyes, and the deeply creased brow bespeak a life full of care and disappointment. Yet her hair is elegantly waved and dressed from a central parting in loose backward locks gathered in a bun at the nape.

Clearly the woman in this "portrait of a marriage," as it has been called, is neither a caricature nor the representation of a death demon reclining beside the

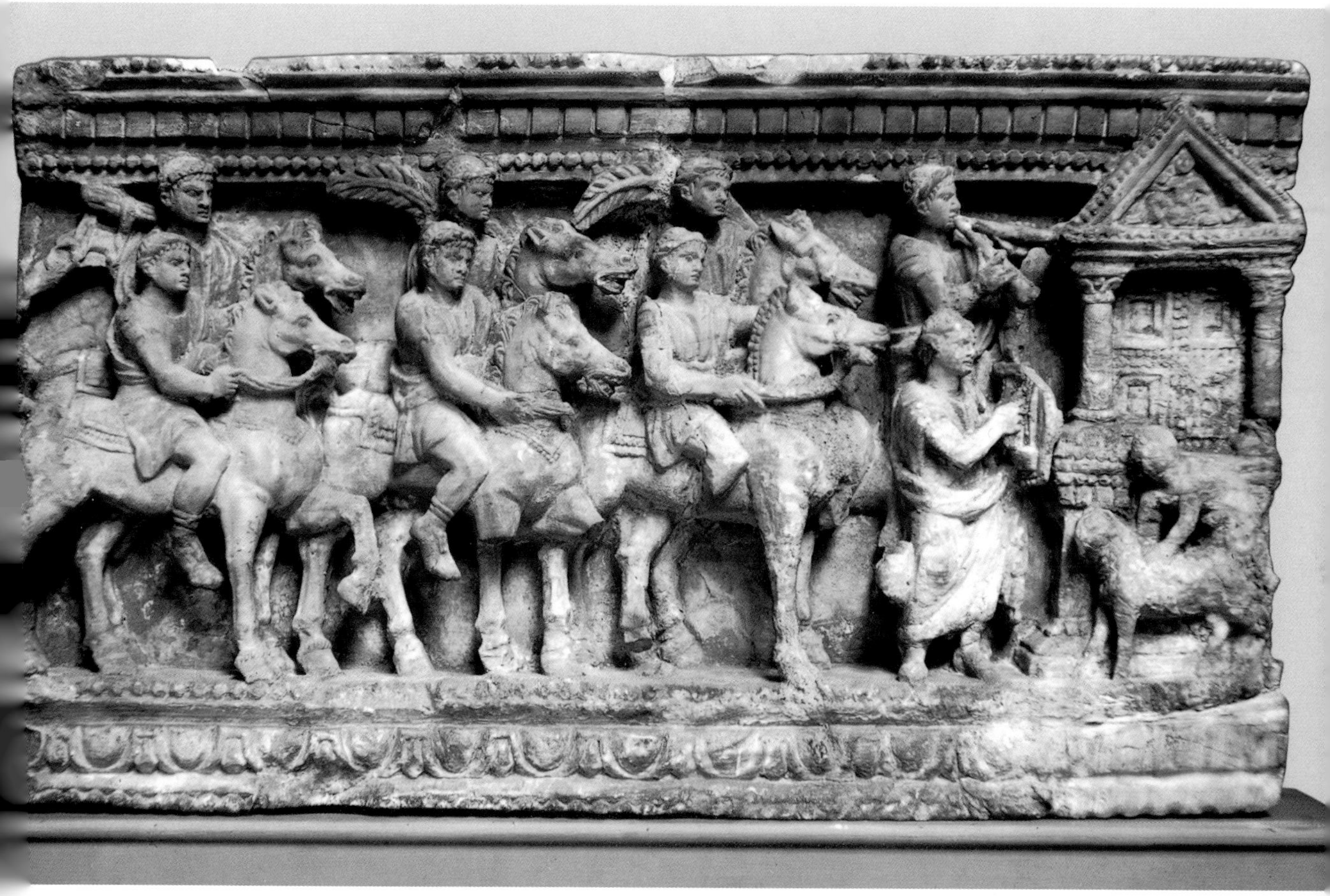

man, as has sometimes been thought. The urn must have been a special commission, for terra-cotta is a relatively rare material for urns at Volterra, and its choice was perhaps a deliberate attempt to go back to the ancient funerary use of it elsewhere (pp. 214ff.). The great care taken to depict old age suggests that the family of the deceased wished to give an ancestral look to the couple. The date of this striking cinerary urn is probably the late second or early first century.

Fig. 291 Front of an ash urn with a procession of horsemen. Late second–early first century B.C. Alabaster. H. 41 cm. London, The British Museum GR 1925.2-18.1.

Two alabaster urns represent a later stage in the production. The first (Volterra, Museo Guarnacci 135) was carved about the middle of the first century with scenes of Etruscan funerary beliefs and cult. It shows the deceased on his journey to the beyond. He lies in a mule-drawn covered wagon that is guided and followed by boys and men carrying an axe, a bag, a cup, and tablets(?)—probably members of his family and servants. The wagon is met by a horseman and a demon, unique in this kind of relief, who "frightens the horses" by raising two metal bowls; the reflecting light will make the horses shy, sending the wagon into the abyss.

An urn in the British Museum is carved with a procession of pairs of wreathed horsemen, three of whom in the back row carry palm branches on their shoulders (FIG. 291); the last one holds in addition a bundle of rods strapped around an axe:

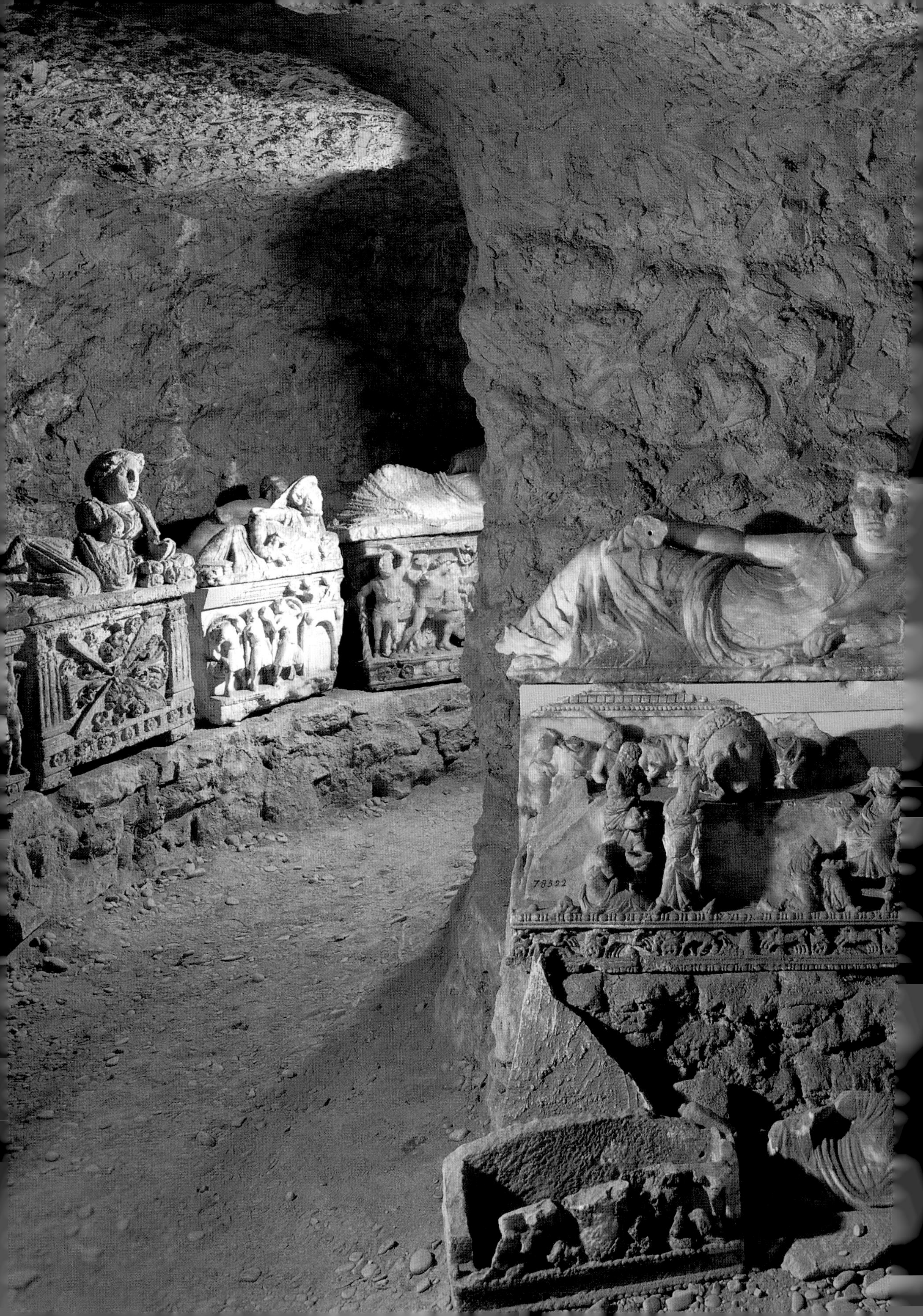
78522

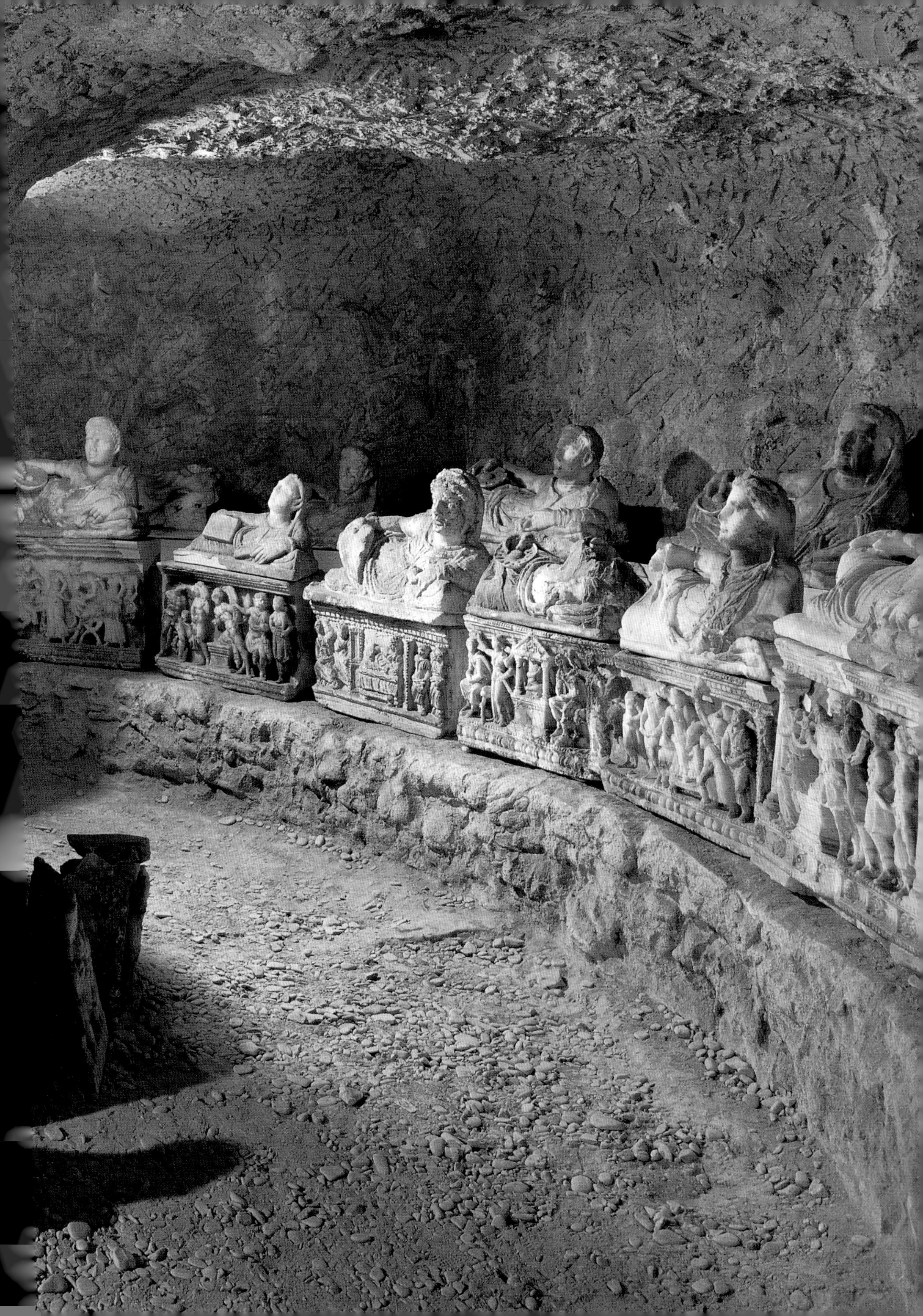

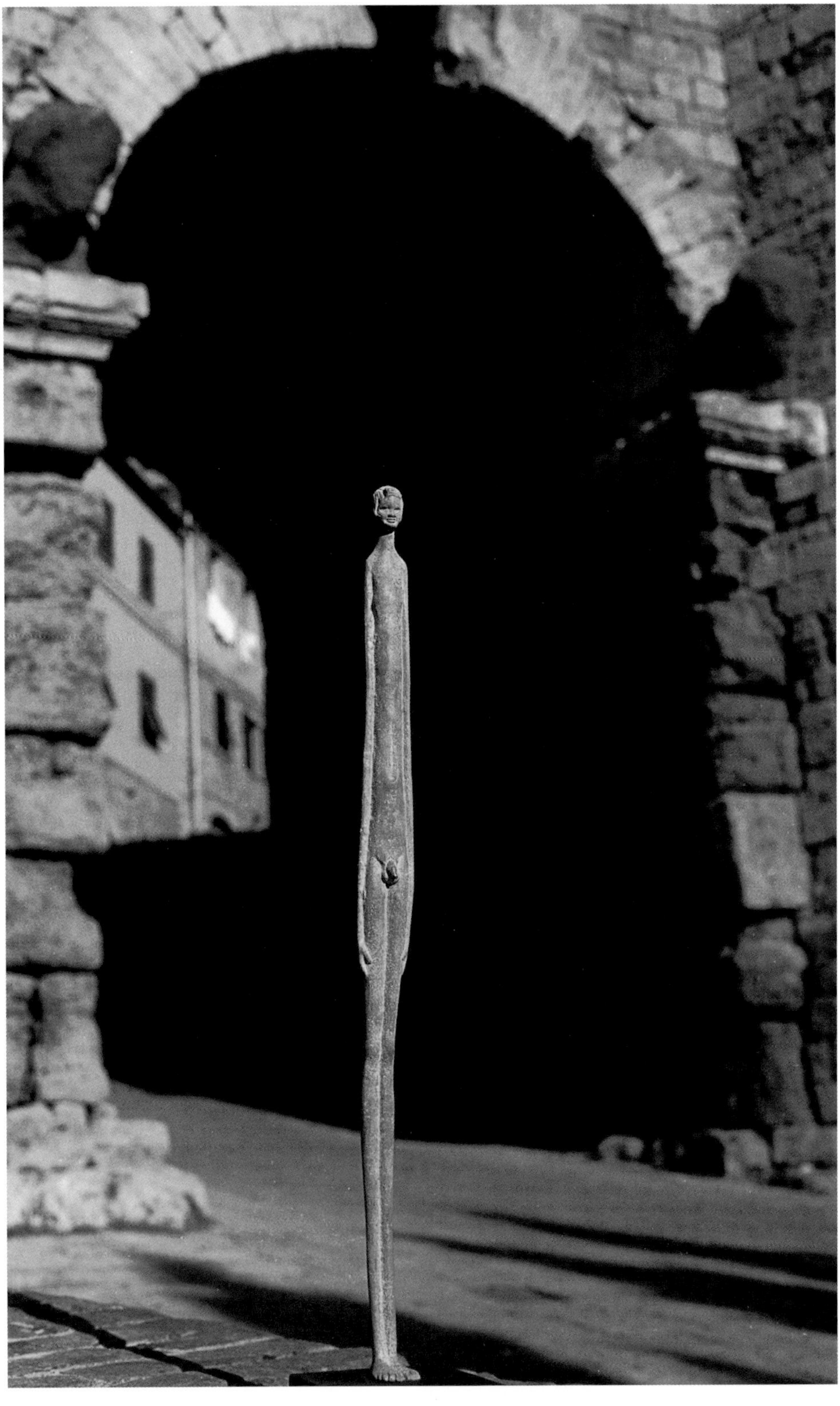

the fasces, symbol of Roman magisterial power. Guided by two toga-clad musicians, the riders approach a small columnar shrine on a high podium; its pediment depicts the frontal figure of a snake-legged underworld demon. This structure with an elaborately carved door is probably the funerary monument of a magistrate, visited for a commemorative ceremony that includes the sacrifice of a sheep. At the foot of the building a sacrificial attendant with bared torso bends over the victim.

In these works the dramatic effects of the older urn reliefs have been replaced by a sober, slightly wooden style, emphasized by the isocephalic alignment of the figures and the solemn subjects. The scene with the sacrifice follows iconographic models that were to become characteristic themes in the art of the Roman world.

The last Volterran urns date from Early Imperial times. Necropolises of the Hellenistic period that contained Volterran ash urns were situated at Badia, Portone, Ulimeto, and Poggio alle Croci. Chamber tombs, hollowed from the rock and reached by a dromos, were square or circular with benches for the deposition of urns along the walls; the circular chambers usually had a central, rock-carved support. Originally the tombs were surmounted by a tumulus and a cippus. One of the most impressive gentilicial tombs of this type from the Ulimeto necropolis is the Inghirami Tomb (*Tomba Inghirami*), which belonged to the Atia family. It contained fifty-three urns dating from the first half of the second to the middle of the first century. The tomb has been reconstructed in the garden of the Museo Archeologico in Florence (FIG. 292).

Votive bronzes of men and women seem to have been produced in the area of Volterra as early as the Orientalizing period. A local production is also well attested during the fourth to second century. Of particular interest is a group of comparatively modest works found in the neighborhood of the medieval fountain of Docciola, where in antiquity a small sanctuary dedicated to water divinities must have been situated. Besides a number of more familiar types of draped and veiled standing women there are statuettes of male water carriers, whose dress—a *perizoma* wrapped around the waist—suggests that they are servants. They each steady a widemouthed water vessel on one shoulder, balancing its weight with a slight inclination of the head and placing the free hand on the hip (Museo Guarnacci 1971/1 and 1971/2). Several examples of both types of statuettes show a tendency toward elongated bodies and disproportionally small heads, a curious stylistic feature that is found also in votive bronzes from other Etruscan regions (cf. the statuette from Brolio [see FIG. 110] and statuettes in the Villa Giulia in Rome, inv. 24474–80).

The most striking case of an abnormally long body combined with the minute head of a young boy is a statuette from Volterra known as "Evening Shadow" (*Ombra della Sera*, FIG. 293). The child's elongated, flat body with thin closed legs and arms pressed to the sides is modeled with sensitivity around the navel and sex. His snub-nosed head with sunken eyes, slightly smiling mouth, and soft curls falling sinuously over cheeks and forehead follow naturalistic prototypes. Face

PAGES 370–71
Fig. 292 Reconstruction of tomb in the garden of the Museo Archeologico, Florence. Inghirami Tomb, Ulimeto necropolis, Volterra. First half of second to middle of first century B.C.

OPPOSITE
Fig. 293 Votive statuette of a boy, the so-called *Ombra della Sera*. From Volterra. Third century B.C. Cast bronze. H. 57 cm. Volterra, Museo Etrusco Guarnacci 226.

and hairstyle recall those of two third-century votive offerings in the Museo Gregoriano Etrusco of the Vatican, both representing boys: a terra-cotta head (inv. 13761) and a bronze statuette (see FIG. 285). While they suggest a similar date for the Evening Shadow, the stylization of the latter's elongated flat body goes back to an older level of popular cult in Italy, documented by boardlike, wooden ex-votos and thin figurines cut from sheet metal, a formal tradition untouched by Classical and Hellenistic proportions.

Once Volterra had submitted to Rome (p. 328), the city and its territory suffered far less than other regions of Etruria, and their prosperity continued undiminished. The most important buildings of the Hellenistic period are two temples of the second century, aligned side by side on top of the ancient acropolis of Volterra, Piano di Castello. Temple A was built over an older cistern; part of its podium and wall have survived, but very little is preserved of Temple B. Beneath it were found terra-cotta fragments of an older temple of the early fifth century, whose *sima* was decorated with horsemen in relief. Parts of painted terra-cotta tiles with lotus-and-palmette motif were also discovered. These terra-cotta revetments show affinities with examples from Arezzo and Orvieto.

Of the Hellenistic temples fragments of a terra-cotta frieze with battle scenes survive, as well as the remains of fine and vigorously modeled figures in very high relief that may have decorated a small pediment that probably dates from the late third century.

While Hannibal's invasion of Italy in 218 bypassed Volterra, the Roman civil war between Marius and Sulla brought siege, starvation, and surrender to the city (82–80 B.C.), and Sulla confiscated Volterran territory for the settlement of a colony of Roman veterans. Only under Augustus are there signs of renewed prosperity, of which the most impressive evidence is the large Roman theater with a two-story stage building that has survived (and been partially reconstructed) in the Vallebuona area, below the medieval city wall on the north. On the steps of the theater are inscribed the names of well-known Volterran families—testimonials to the civic pride of a local aristocracy by now fully integrated into Roman society. A dedicatory inscription to Augustus names A. and S. Caecina as donors of the building. They were members of the ancient Ceicna family (in various spellings the name is also documented by funerary inscriptions at Orvieto, Orte, Castiglione del Lago, Tarquinia, and in Bologna as early as the fifth century B.C., see p. 308). The memory of the numerous Volterran Ceicna is preserved in the name of the river Cecina. Aulus Caecina was a friend of Cicero, who had defended Aulus's father in 69 B.C. in an inheritance case. Aulus was an orator and an expert in the *disciplina etrusca*, and both Pliny (2) and Seneca (2.3.9) used his works. One Caecina Albinus is recorded as late as A.D. 417 by the poet Cl. Rutilius Namatianus in his verse account of a journey to Gaul (*De reditu* 1.465–66), when he had to take refuge in the villa of his friend Caecina at Vada Volterrana.

The first mention of Perugia in classical sources refers to the war following the passage of the Roman army under Q. Fabius Maximus Rullianus through the Ciminian forest in 310 B.C. (Livy 9.37.11), in which Perugia was forced to ask for a truce. After Perugia broke the truce, a Roman garrison was placed there, but the city rebelled again and did not finally submit until after the defeat of the allied Etruscan, Italic, and Celtic armies by the Romans in the battle of Sentinum in 295. In his account of the events of 294 Livy names Orvieto, Perugia, and Arezzo as "three very powerful capital cities" of Etruria (10.37.5). After the defeat of Orvieto in 280, Perugia to some extent took over her role, and many families from Orvieto seem to have moved to Perugia. Faithful to Rome, the city and its economy flourished on agricultural wealth. Arezzo, which together with Cortona and Perugia had submitted to Rome (Livy 10.3.2), was soon convulsed by the popular rising against the aristocratic Cilnii clan, who were restored to their dominant position with Roman help. The main sources of wealth for the strategically situated city of Arezzo in the Hellenistic period were metal industry (see p. 304 and below), agriculture, and, from the first century, the manufacture of the red-glazed pottery with molded relief decoration known as Arretine ware.

After gaining control of the Po valley in the Second Punic War (218–201) and reinforcing his army with Gauls, Hannibal crossed the Apennines. Bypassing the Roman troops stationed at Arezzo, he lured them to an unfavorable position between Lake Trasimene and the mountains and completely annihilated them in 217. This left the road to Rome undefended and the capital in extreme danger of capture by the Carthaginians. Despite the devastating defeat of the Roman army on their soil and the ravages inflicted on their countryside by the enemy, the Etruscan cities did not defect to Hannibal, though the Romans suspected their loyalty. From 212 to 200 two Roman legions were stationed in Etruria. Arezzo in particular seems to have caused concern. The Romans took 120 hostages from the ruling families, whom they held responsible for the loyalty of the city. Seven of the leading Etruscan senators managed to excape with their children, and the Romans then confiscated and sold their property, probably assuming that they had sided with Hannibal. Evidence of an individual Etruscan's connection with Hannibal comes from the funerary inscription of one Larth Felsna (*TLE* 890) painted on the wall of Chamber Tomb IV in the Villa Tarantola area of the Tarquinian necropolis of Monterozzi. The four lines of text mention the age of Larth Felsna, who died at 106, and also the names of Hannibal (*hanipaluscle*) and Capua (*capue*). But the Etruscan cities kept their alliances with Rome, and some Etruscan troops even served as auxiliary cohorts in the Roman army.

Not being able to besiege Rome because of lack of bases of supply, Hannibal and his troops moved to Southern Italy, unsuccessfully trying to raise rebellion

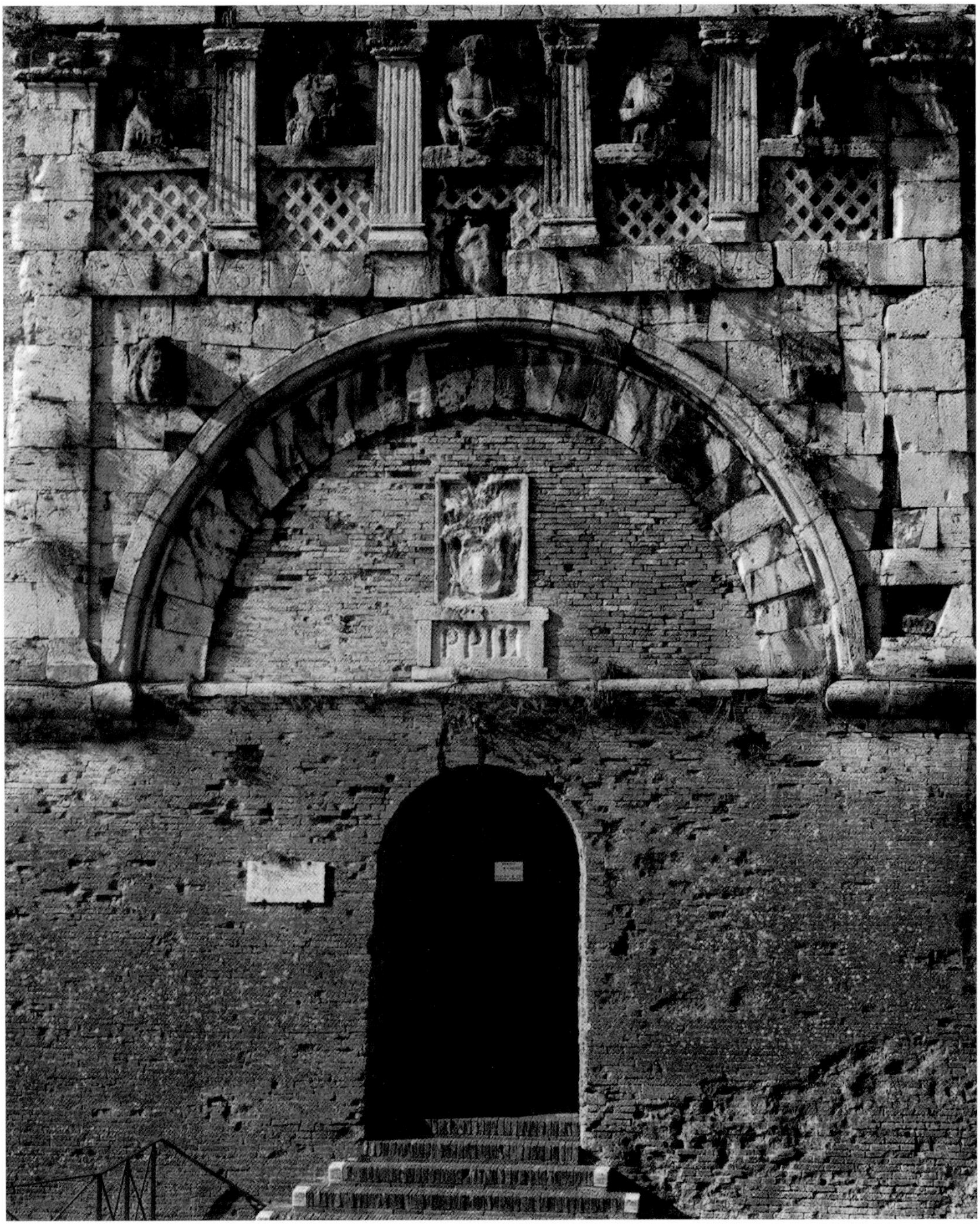

Fig. 294 Porta Marzia, Perugia. Zeus and the Dioscuri in high relief. Second century B.C.

there. In 216, however, he brilliantly defeated a large Roman army in an encircling battle at Cannae in Apulia, and as a result Capua and other towns in Campania went over to Hannibal; in 213 Taranto and other Greek cities in South Italy joined him. But stubborn Roman resistance, their reconquest of Capua, Syracuse, and Taranto, and the defeat of Hannibal's brother Hasdrubal on the river Metauro in

207 eventually forced the Carthaginians to leave Italy. Having held out in enemy country for sixteen years, Hannibal, undefeated, was recalled to Carthage in 203 to defend his city against the Roman attack. His army was finally defeated by Scipio Africanus in the battle of Zama in 202.

In 205 when Scipio had asked the Roman senate to carry the war into Africa but had been refused new levies, he appealed to the allied communities for contributions toward the building of a new fleet. When the senate agreed to let him take a volunteer army to Africa, the Etruscan cities were the first to promise him aid. Each supplied what they produced most of. Livy tells us that Cerveteri offered grain for the ships' crews, Populonia iron, Tarquinia sailcloth, and Volterra grain and timber for planks. Arezzo provided three thousand shields and helmets and fifty thousand pikes, javelins, and spears in addition to axes, shovels, sickles, basins, and hand mills to equip forty warships; she also contributed wheat. From Perugia, Chiusi, and Roselle came fir for building and large quantities of grain (Livy 28.45). These enormous contributions, though they may not have been entirely voluntarily supplied, show the economic wealth of the Etruscan cities, in particular the northern ones, at the end of the third century.

In 196 B.C. Etruscan slaves revolted against their masters, perhaps encouraged by the punishments meted out by the Romans to the nobles at Arezzo and other unnamed cities in 204 and 203. But the Roman praetor M. Acilius Glabrio suppressed the revolt, crucified some of the slaves taken prisoner, and returned others to their owners. This Roman system of supporting local aristocrats against their subjects and leaving the former to administer internal Etruscan affairs had functioned well and was certainly more economical than widespread Roman occupation and colonization.

The most impressive monument to the wealth and power of Perugia in the Hellenistic period is its 3-km-long wall enclosure, whose earliest phase seems to go back to the second half of the fourth century. Most of the existing rectangularly cut travertine masonry, however, probably dates from the later third century and was restored subsequently. Two splendid gateways stand out among a number of preserved ancient city gates, the Porta Marzia and the Arco di Augusto. Of the former only the upper part has survived, incorporated in the sixteenth century into the fortified bastion built by Antonio da Sangallo in the Rocca Paolina (FIG. 294). Like the Porta all'Arco at Volterra (see FIG. 286), the Porta Marzia arch was flanked and surmounted by three heads, probably representing tutelary deities, while the molded profile of the quoined arch resembles that of Falerii Novi, which dates from the second half of the second century. Above the arch of the Porta Marzia is a loggia in high relief, supported by pilasters and screened with latticed panels. Leaning over the parapet and separated by the pilasters into five spaces are three male figures flanked by the forepart of a horse on each side; the figures have been identified with Tinia and the Dioscuri. Two later Roman inscriptions carved above and below the loggia refer to the city as *Augusta Peru-*

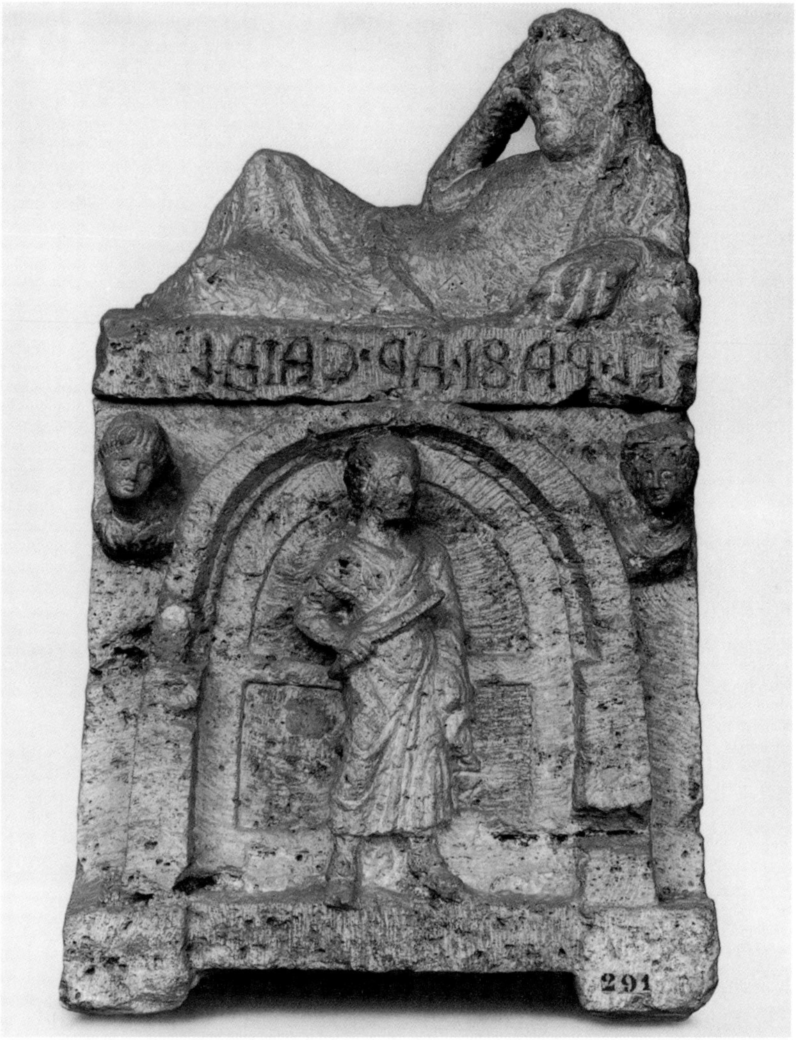

Fig. 295 Ash urn of Vel Rafi. From Perugia. Second century B.C. Travertine. Total H. 93 cm. Perugia, Museo Archeologico 26.291.

sia and *Colonia Vibia* (after the emperor Gaius Vibius Trebonianus Gallus, A.D. 251–253, who came from a Perugian family). The Arco di Augusto is set between two projecting towers of the Hellenistic walls and is decorated above the profiled arch with a frieze of round shields between Ionic pilasters. A (now blind) arch above this frieze dates from the Augustan period, as does the inscription *Augusta Perusia* carved on the lower one.

The carved and painted front of a travertine funerary urn with the summarily sculpted reclining figure of the deceased on the lid represents a barred doorway with a profiled arch flanked by two heads (FIG. 295). Before the door stands a draped elderly man holding a regularly notched ruler in his right hand. According to the inscription on the lid his name is Vel Rafi; it has been suggested that he probably was an architect responsible for building just such a gateway. The carefully marked ruler displayed by Vel Rafi forms the center of the composition and supports the interpretation that the gate behind him is his work rather than a representation of the entrance to the underworld.

Vast suburban cemeteries grew up on the slopes outside Perugia, and even the more distant countryside in the direction of Gubbio and Cortona must have been fairly densely settled by small rural communities in the Hellenistic period. Cremation was the predominant funerary rite. The cubic ash urns were usually carved from local travertine, whose roughness was smoothed by a plaster surface, which was brightly painted and occasionally gilded. Usually little of this original surface is preserved. The most common type of urn from the late fourth to the middle of the first century has a lid in the form of a ridge roof with heraldic or figure decoration in the gables and sometimes the funerary banquet on the front. A lid surmounted by the figure of the semirecumbent deceased is comparatively rare, but it is found between the end of the third and the second quarter of the first century. The boxes are usually carved with reliefs of generic battle scenes, more rarely with mythological subjects (such as the sacrifice of Iphigeneia and the murder of Klytaimnestra), and frequently with simple symbolic motifs (paterae, peltae, rosettes) of indifferent quality. From the surviving urns and their inscriptions it appears that there was a large class of citizens who were descended from serfs, as the term *lautni* beside the name makes clear, or from freed serfs who had adopted family names derived from original patrons' names.

After much social upheaval an accommodation seems to have been reached in the second century allowing the countryside around Perugia and elsewhere in Northern Etruria to be worked not only on behalf of the aristocracy but also by families of freedmen who had achieved a modest prosperity.

The spacious Hellenistic chamber tomb of the Volumnii (Etr. Velimna) is the best example of the wealth and power of noble families in Perugia. Carved into the local sandstone in the Palazzone necropolis on the southern slopes overlooking the Tiber valley, the underground tomb is reached by a steep staircase and a doorway originally closed by a travertine slab. It was probably begun in the third century. An inscription on the door jamb records the foundation of the tomb by Arnth and Larth Velimnas.

A large rectangular hall with a ridge roof imitating a wooden construction is flanked on each long side by two side chambers (FIG. 296). Its far end widens into a transept giving access to a central chamber containing the seven urns of several generations of the family, and to two lateral chambers, all three with coffered ceilings. This spatial arrangement owes something to the Etruscan atrium house with a *tablinum*, alae, and *cubicula*. The gable over the entrance to the atrium was carved in relief with a shield between dolphins, while that over the doorway into the *tablinum* bore a shield with the head of Gorgon flanked by two swords and two male busts, one a kithara player, the other a slave with a carrying stick. Beside the entrance are the remains of a relief of a winged demon. Fragments of two figured terra-cotta lamps and of foreparts of snakes set into the walls were found in the

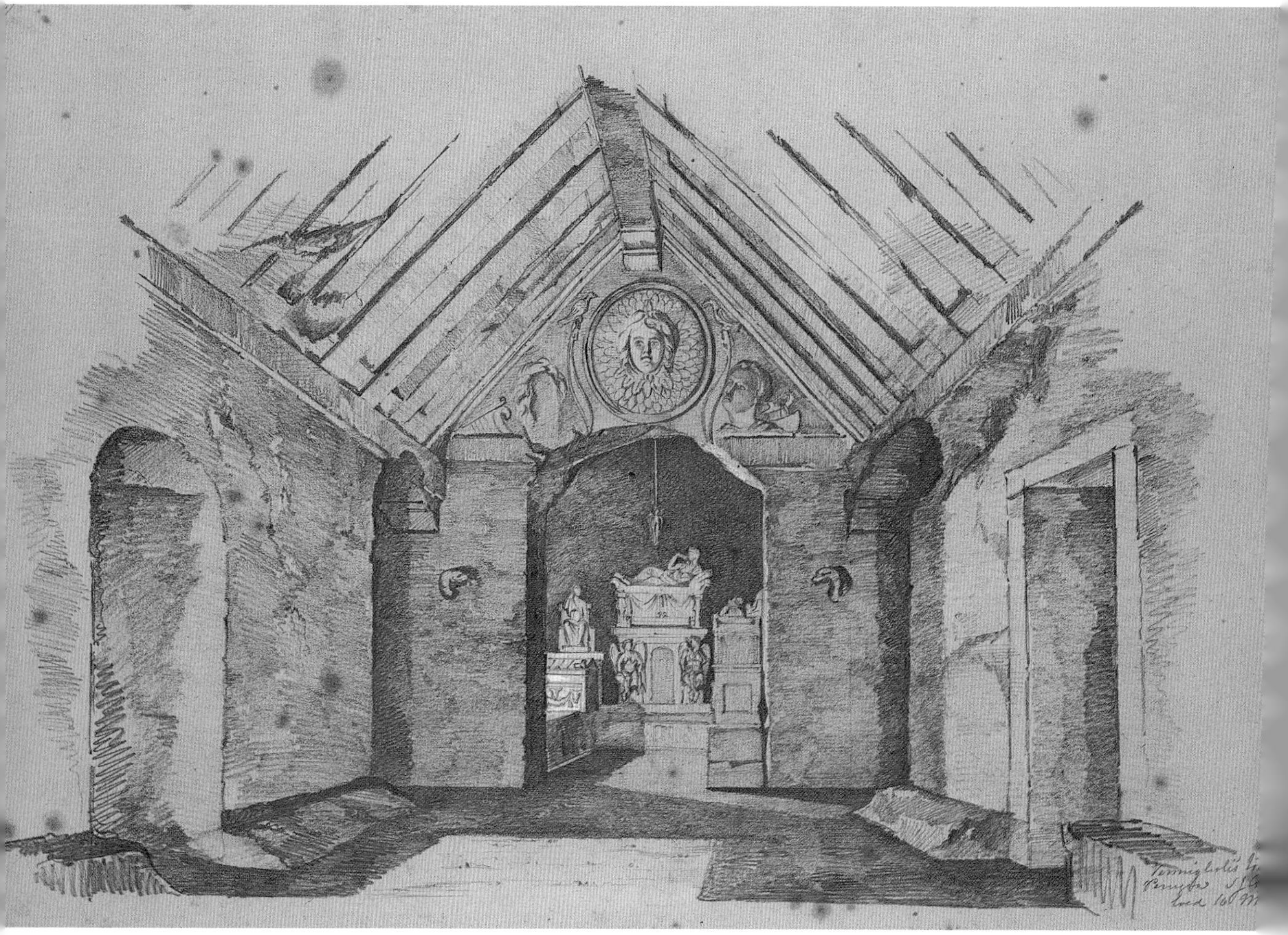

Fig. 296 S. J. Ainsley, *The Grotta de' Volunni near Perugia.* [Interior of the Tomb of the Volumnii, Palazzone necropolis, Perugia. Late third–early first century B.C.] Signed and dated May 10, 1843. Pencil on drab paper, heightened with white. 29.5 x 44.8 cm. London, The British Museum, Department of Prints and Drawings, cat. LB 62.

atrium. Other grave goods consisted of a Volterran krater (*kelebe*) painted in red-figure technique, a bronze helmet, a pair of greaves, a shield with a guilloche-and-animal frieze around the rim, as well as two bronze jugs and a *kottabos* stand decorated with bronze figurines. Shield, greaves, and helmet can be compared with those found in the Tomb of the Warrior at Settecamini near Orvieto and may represent the oldest objects in the tomb, probably heirlooms dating from the second half of the fourth century.

Of the urns standing on wall-benches in the *tablinum*, six are of travertine covered with fine stucco and originally painted, while the seventh is of marble and, being the youngest, differs in type and material. The stuccoed urns imitate wooden boxes with four round bosses on the front and the head of a female snake-wreathed demon in the central panel. The lids above the boxes are carved as draped dining couches on which the male members of the family recline on their elbows at a banquet. All are of the highest quality and so similar in style that they must have been

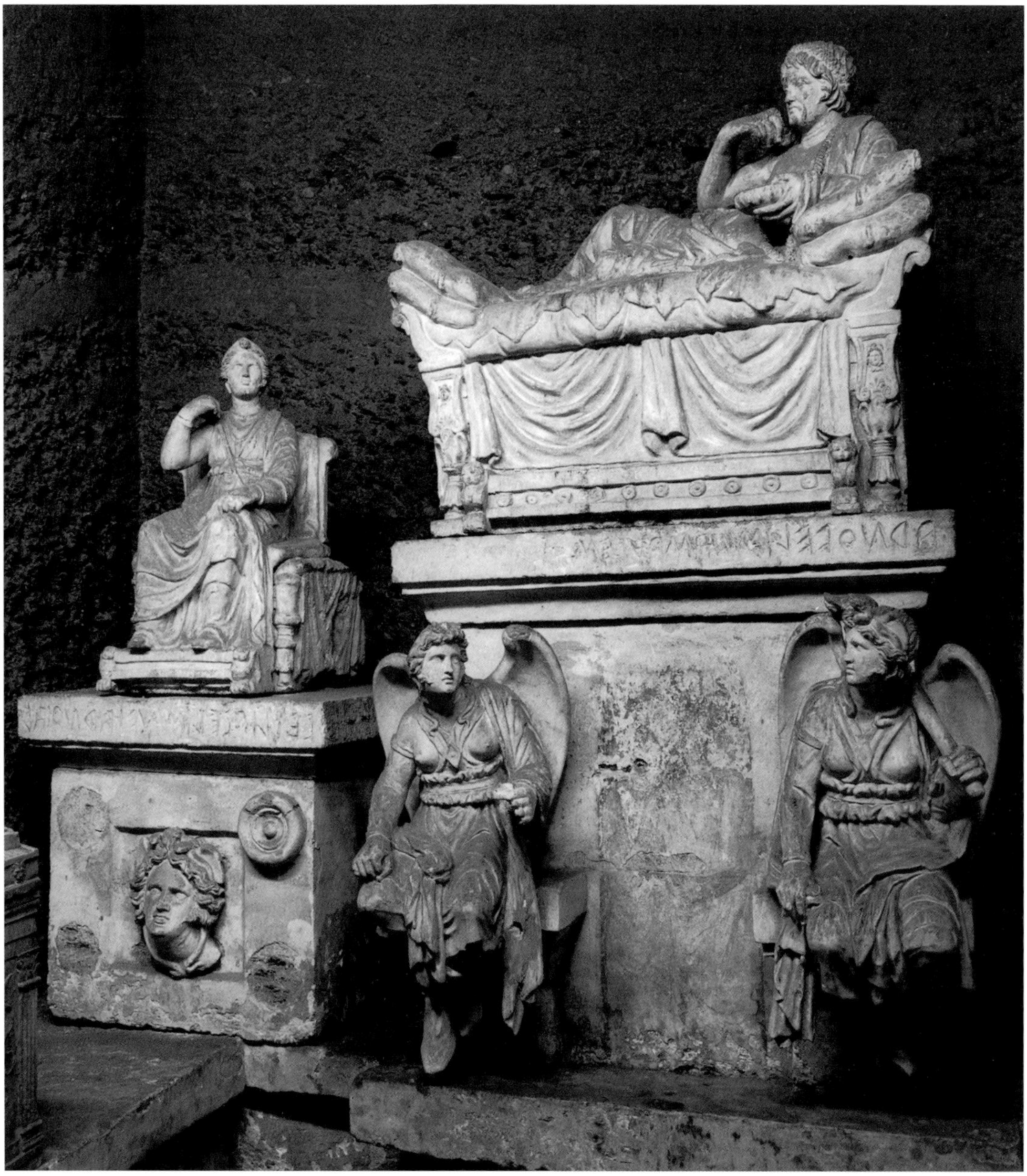

made in the same workshop, though that of the founder, Arnth Velimnas, is the largest and most splendid (FIG. 297). This urn, centrally placed, is further distinguished by two seated figures of winged, torch-holding female demons in high relief who guard the door to the underworld, which is painted in the center of the box. The colors have faded badly, but traces of togate male figures standing within and holding out their hands are still recognizable; they are presumably predeceased members of the family waiting to welcome the newcomer to Hades.

Fig. 297 Ash urns of Arnth Velimnas (*right*) and Veilia Velimnei (*left*). From the Tomb of the Volumnii, Palazzone necropolis, Perugia. Second century B.C. Travertine covered with painted stucco. Total H. 1.63 m (Arnth Velimnas) and 1.24 m (Veilia Velimnei).

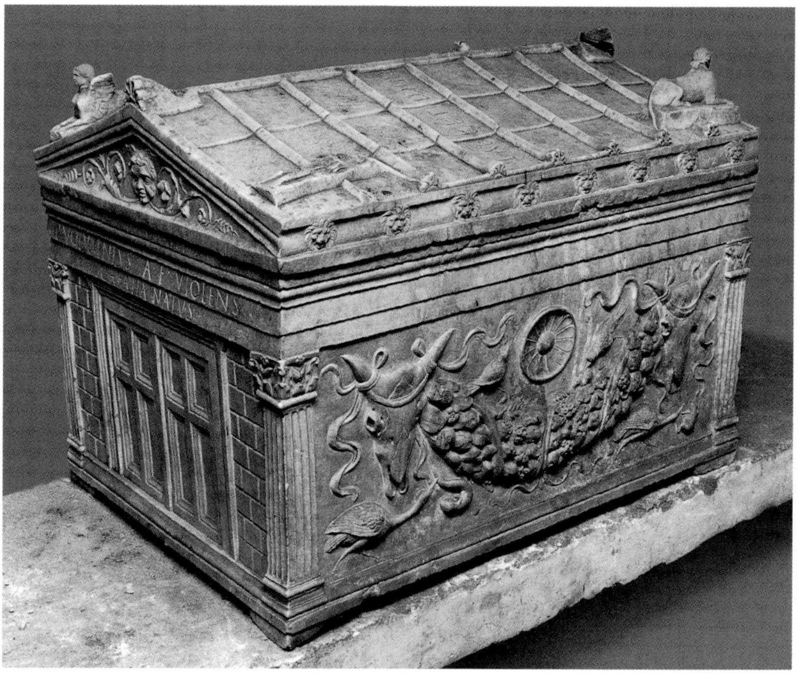

Fig. 298 Ash urn of Publius Volumnius Violens. From the Tomb of the Volumnii, Palazzone necropolis, Perugia. Early first century A.D. Marble.

All the urns are inscribed (*CIE* 3757–63), and only one belongs to a lady: *veilia velimnei arnthial*, Veilia Velimna, the (unmarried) daughter of the founder, Arnth (see FIG. 297). Unlike her male forebears and relations, she sits above her urn on a throne with a footstool, draped in chiton and mantle and wearing a half-diadem and earrings. She recalls the older scheme of seated women serving as cinerary statues that are found in the region of Chiusi in the fifth and fourth centuries (pp. 296f.). But the facial type of Veilia and of the men in the Velimna family (Thefri, Avle, Larth, Vel, and Arnth) as well as that of the female demons is inspired by Hellenistic prototypes of the third to second century.

The seventh urn in the tomb is of marble and belongs to a somewhat younger generation (FIG. 298): the name of its owner is inscribed on the box in both Etruscan and Latin. He is Publius Volumnius Violens, who, following Etruscan usage, gives the names of both his father (Aulus) and his mother (Cafatia). The urn takes the form of a house with a tiled ridge roof and acroteria of sphinxes. The front shows a double door between Corinthian pilasters, while both sides are carved in delicate relief with a swag hung from ox skulls with a patera above and birds below; on the back of the urn, under a fig tree, birds drink from a volute-krater next to a herm and a palm tree. The style of these fine reliefs dates the urn to the Early Imperial period and proves that the Tomb of the Volumnii was used by the family until the first century A.D.

A famous monument found in 1822 and now in the Museo Archeologico of Perugia is a tall, rectangular travertine block bearing the third-longest surviving

Etruscan inscription (*TLE* 570; FIG. 299). It was presumably a boundary stone, for the text deals with a legal contract between the Velthina and Afuna families concerning property. The lower third of the cippus is only roughly worked and must have been inserted into the ground. The inscription, which covers two sides of the block in regular letters, dates from the third to second century.

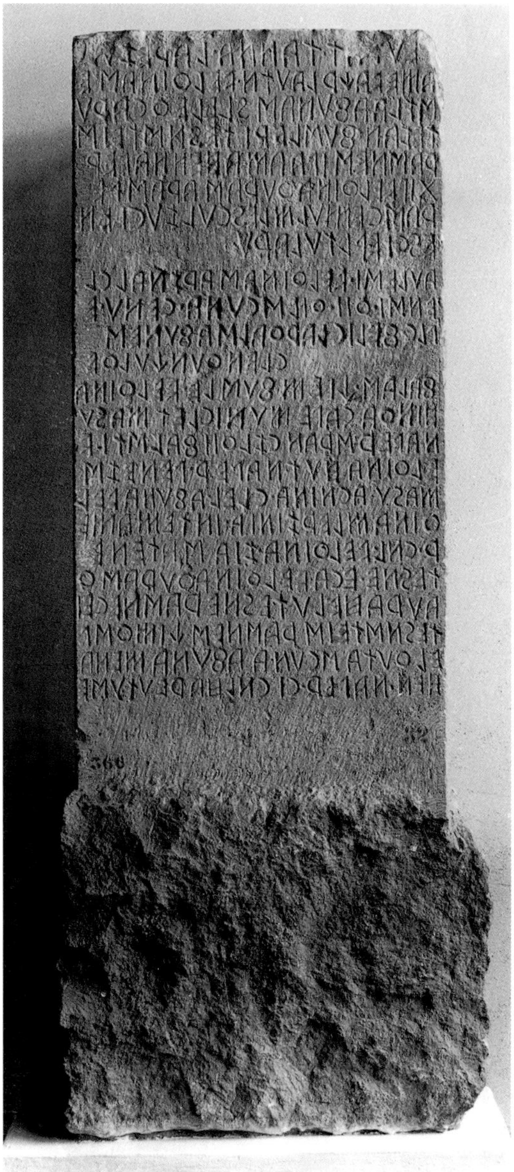

Fig. 299 Inscribed rectangular cippus from the vicinity of Perugia (*TLE* 570). Third–second century B.C. Travertine. Perugia, Museo Archeologico 366.

SOCIAL UNREST AND FINAL INTEGRATION

As a result of the romanization of Etruria and the inherently pro-Roman attitude characteristic of the local aristocracies, members of such families increasingly rose to become Roman senators. A Peperna from Perugia became consul in 130, and members of the Perugian Vibii and Volcacii joined the senatorial class. We have already mentioned the Roman connections of the Caecina of Volterra and of the Cilnii of Arezzo; the royal blood of the Cilnii flowed in the veins of Gaius Maecenas through his maternal ancestors. The Etruscan descent of this trusted friend and counselor of Augustus was exalted in the *Odes* of Horace and the *Elegies* of Propertius, whose patron he was.

In contrast to the economic conditions in Northern and inner Etruria (p. 379), in Southern coastal Etruria, where vast tracts of land from Cerveteri, Tarquinia, and Vulci had been turned into Roman colonies after their conquest, a system developed of large estates worked by foreign slave labor for a few rich landlords. In the mid-130s, when the *quaestor* Tiberius Sempronius Gracchus traveled through this coastal region on his return to Spain, he observed that the countryside had been almost totally abandoned by small free peasants and shepherds and was run on a servile agrarian system (Plut. *Vit. Ti. Gracch.* 8.9). Tiberius Gracchus's laws for social and economic reforms by redistribution of land for the alleviation of poverty are thought to stem from this experience. He was killed on the Capitoline by his political opponents, and the subsequent attempts of his brother Gaius Sempronius Gracchus to continue with the land distribution and other reform proposals to end exploitation ended in his own defeat and death.

In 91 Etruscans and Umbrians protested against the reformatory agrarian laws of Livius Drusus, which rivaled those of the Gracchi; they would have upset the existing economic order and the power of the local aristocracy. The conferment of full Roman franchise on the Italian allies, which Livius Drusus had also proposed, was opposed both in Etruria and by many parties in Rome itself.

From this unsettled period of threatened change and disaffection among the Etruscan allies comes a curious document. Preserved in a collection of Latin texts on land surveying (*gromatici veteres*), it is a fragment of the revelations of a prophetic Etruscan nymph, Vegoia, made to a certain Arruns Velthumnus of Chiusi. It has been suggested that this extract of the books of Vegoia was drafted in 91 B.C. as a propaganda pamphlet for the Etruscan popular revolt against the agrarian laws of Livius Drusus. (A less likely theory proposes that it dates from the time of the slave revolt at Volsinii.)

The message of the text is that socio-economic peace depends on the preservation of property boundaries instituted by Jupiter who, knowing the human greed for possession of land, insisted on defining these limits. The period of danger is the end of the eighth Etruscan century. The celestial and terrestrial order will be disturbed by those who move boundary stones for their own profit. The violators of the divine laws who enlarge their properties at the expense of others will be punished by the gods. If they are slaves, they will suffer harsher conditions. If they act in complicity with their masters, the houses and families of the latter will be extinguished. The guilty will suffer from illness and all sorts of debilities. Lightning, storms, and pests will devastate the land and the crops, and there will be much dissension among the people. The prophecy ends with the admonition: "Know that such punishments will follow when such crimes are committed. Therefore do not act in bad faith or with a treacherous tongue. Retain our teachings in your heart."

It is not without significance that the revelation purports to have been made to an Etruscan from Chiusi, that is to say, from an area of inner Northern Etruria, where, as we have seen also at Perugia, aristocratic owners of latifundia existed side-by-side with a numerous class of freedmen who worked their small holdings in the countryside. The latter may have feared that the more powerful *domini* would attempt to increase their own property and damage the adjoining ones, while the changes proposed by Livius Drusus would impinge on everyone.

The revolt against Rome of the Italian allies in 90 in fact hardly touched northern Italy, Etruria, and Umbria. But for Rome it brought the greatest peril since the wars against Hannibal. The Social, or, Italic War (90–88), fought by Rome's Italic allies against her predominance, was finally, after great losses on both sides, ended by political concessions: Rome granted citizenship to the enemy confederacy, having already conferred full Roman status on the Etruscans and Umbrians and on the Latin allies who had remained faithful.

In the subsequent civil war between the generals who had fought in the Social War—Marius and Sulla—the majority of the Etruscans in northern Italy sided with Marius. When Marius in 87 disembarqued at Talamone, he managed to recruit about six thousand Etruscans, mainly small landowners who probably felt economically threatened by the competition from large estates worked by slaves. Among his generals were also Etruscan aristocrats from the north: a Perugian, M. Peperna, and C. Carrinas from Volterra. This loyalty to the Marian side proved disastrous for much of Northern Etruria.

Between 83 and 82 ferocious battles were fought at Talamone, Populonia, Volterra, Arezzo, and Chiusi, and sieges, starvation, and Sulla's subsequent retaliatory acts against his opponents were devastating. Proscriptions, massacres, and confiscations of property and vast tracts of land assigned to soldiers discharged by Sulla profoundly altered the situation in Northern Etruria. Thousands of Sullan veterans were settled at Fiesole, Arezzo, Volterra, and Chiusi, displacing the previous owners of the land. In the neighborhood of Florence the dispossessed eventually rose against the new colonists and expelled them. This rebellion was supported in 77 by the consul M. Aemilius Lepidus, but collapsed with his defeat. However, in 62 the discontented who had been expropriated by the Sullan soldiers along with veterans who had failed to prosper joined the widespread conspiracy of L. Sergius Catilina. This ambitious and frustrated former lieutenant of Sulla, having demagogically championed the poor and disaffected, was frightened by Cicero into leaving Rome for Etruria. Here his rebel force was defeated by M. Petreius, the legate of the consul G. Antonius, and Catilina was killed at Pistoia. Other dispossessed Etruscans left Italy to settle in distant Africa, as attested by three boundary stones with Etruscan inscriptions found at Oued Miliane, south of Tunis.

Perugia, which had escaped the tragic fate of the Etruscan cities involved in the civil war, became a victim of the struggle between Octavius (the future emperor Augustus) and Mark Antony. In 41/40 Octavius besieged Mark Antony's brother Lucius in Perugia and starved the city into surrender. She was sacked and destroyed and, in a horrible echo of the cruelties perpetrated in the past (p. 202), Octavius had three hundred of the local aristocrats who had sided with his enemy slaughtered on the altar of Caesar. The territory of the city was greatly reduced, and a colony of Octavius's veterans was settled on the confiscated land. As emperor, Augustus later restored the city with the name *Augusta Perusia*.

The *haruspices*, still the guardians of the *disciplina etrusca*, saw this convulsed epoch as the tenth and final *saeculum* of the existence of Etruria. The Etruscan nation ceased to exist, for in the Augustan settlement of 27 B.C. Etruria became the seventh region of Roman Italy. In the Southern Etruscan coastal regions (e.g., at Cerveteri) Latin had already become increasingly common in funerary inscriptions from the late second century onward, and bilingual Roman decrees in Etruscan towns indicate the same date for the official introduction of the victors' language elsewhere. Although, as we saw in the last urn in the Tomb of the Volumnii in Perugia, Etruscan did continue to be used beside Latin by some aristocratic individuals until the first century A.D. (and probably for longer by the people in the remote countryside), it eventually disappeared.

In time the Augustan settlement brought peace to the war-torn lands of central Italy, and numerous new colonies were founded that ultimately contributed to reconciliation and growing prosperity.

In an attempt to revive ancient institutions for unifying purposes, Augustus reconstituted the Etruscan League, which of old had met for games and celebrations at the Fanum Voltumnae near Orvieto. The title of *praetor Etruriae* was reinstated; this probably corresponded to the Etruscan title *zilath mechl rasnal* known from a number of earlier funerary inscriptions. The religious festival at Orvieto survived until late antiquity, as shown by an inscription found at Spello with a decree by the emperor Constantine which refers to it: *Aput Volsiniis Tusciae* (*CIL* 11.5265).

In the forum near the main temple of Tarquinia, the Ara della Regina, were found fragments of inscribed marble slabs with the so-called *Elogia Tarquiniensia*. The slabs presumably originally faced statue bases on which, in the first century A.D., T. Vestricius Spurinna, in homage to three of his remote local ancestors, had their images put up. The texts recall their titles of *praetor* and their far-flung military exploits in the glorious days of Tarquinia's greatness before her submission. The genealogy and great deeds of such old Etruscan families had probably been inscribed in linen books and preserved. From the same area near the main temple of Tarquinia came fragments of a marble inscription with a list and eulogies of the *Ordo LX haruspicum*, the sixty priests who constituted the order. Although divination and augury seem to have degenerated in Late Republican Rome, the ancient priestly college of the *haruspices* was revived by the emperor Claudius in A.D. 47 (Tac. *Ann.* 11.15), and such priests continued to be consulted until the early fifth century A.D. (p. 279).

The high regard the Romans held for the religious traditions of the Etruscans is reflected in a passage in Diodorus Siculus written under Caesar and Augustus:

> Letters and the teaching about nature and the gods they [the Etruscans] also brought to greater perfection, and they elaborated the art of divination by thunder and lightning more than all other men; and it is for this reason that the people [i.e., the Romans] who rule practically the entire inhabited world show honor to these men even to this day and employ them as interpreters of the omens of Zeus as they appear in thunder and lightning. (*Bibliothēkē* 5.40)

Fig. 300 Throne with relief decoration, the so-called *Sedia Corsini*. From the vicinity of San Giovanni in Laterano, Rome. First century B.C. Marble. H. 82.5 cm. Rome, Palazzo Corsini 666.

Emperor Augustus entrusted the education of his grandsons to the renowned antiquarian and etruscologist Verrius Flaccus and made a confidant of Gaius Mae-

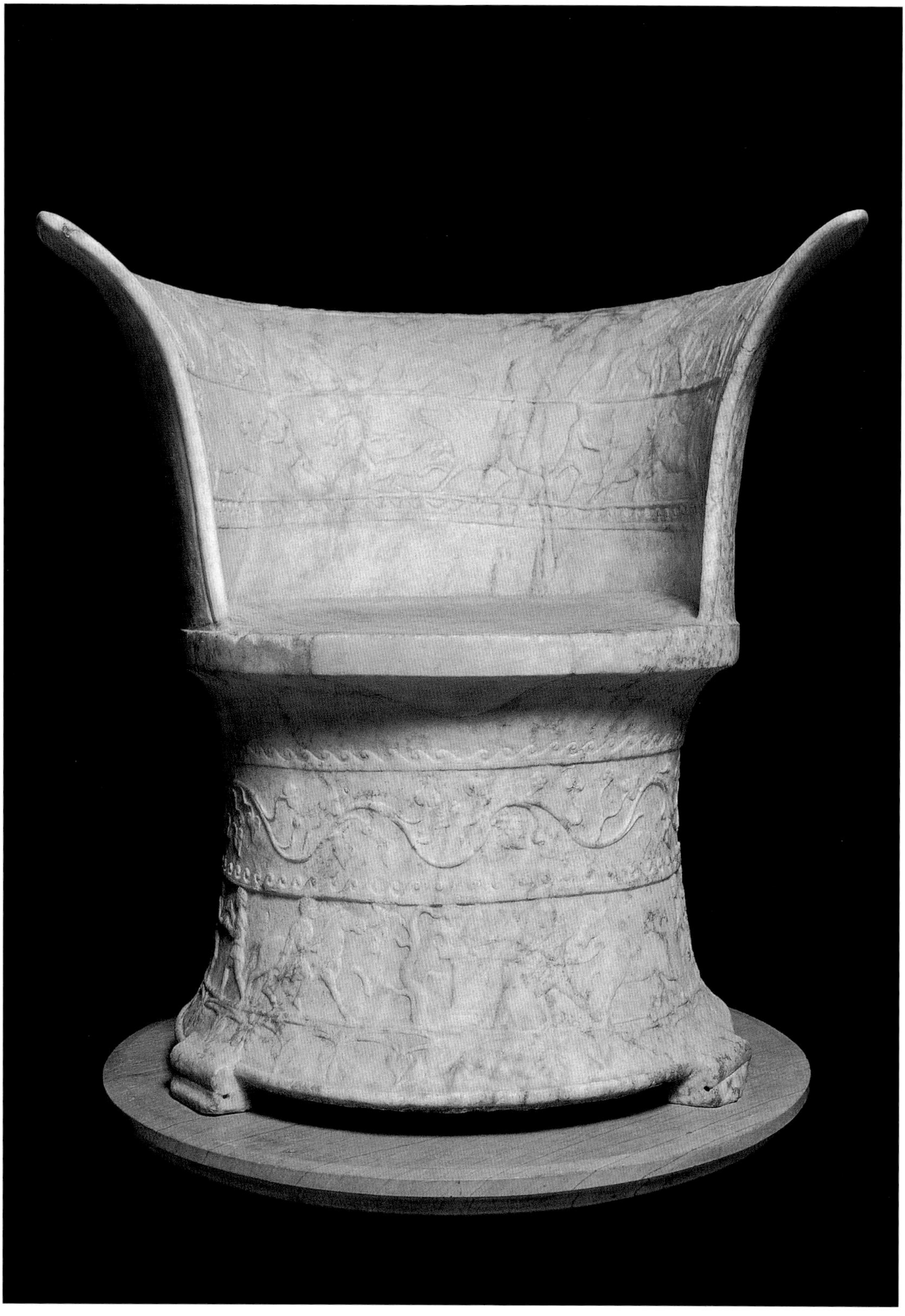

cenas, the scion of an ancient Etruscan family. Significantly, Augustus's monumental tomb was erected in the form of a tumulus on a circular base and marked by obelisks, an age-old type of funerary monument in central Italy.

Etruscan ladies, too, became influential in Rome's Early Imperial circles. Augustus's wife Livia had a friend named Urgulania, who was married (ca. 40 B.C.) to M. Plautius and enjoyed privileges normally granted only to members of the emperor's family (Tac. *Ann.* 2.34, 4.21–22). When summoned to court by L. Calpurnius Piso, Urgulania refused to attend. She felt herself so far above the law because of her friendship with Livia that she had herself carried in her litter to the Palatine instead. To oblige his mother, Livia, Tiberius went to support Urgulania; but, as Piso persisted, Livia finally ordered the sum demanded to be payed. Urgulania also disdainfully refused to appear as witness in a case being tried before the senate. A *praetor* had to be dispatched specially to take her testimony in her own house.

This haughty lady was descended from a noble Etruscan family at Cerveteri: in the second to first century B.C. the unusual name Urgulania is attested in the Banditaccia necropolis, Via delle Serpi, at Cerveteri, where a house-shaped urn bears the funerary inscription of a lady: *(T)ania Orculnia* (*CIE* 6187); the *Elogia Tarquiniensia* mention Orgolnius Velthume as a king of Cerveteri. Urgulania's son, M. Plautius Silvanus, was married to Lartia, also presumably an Etruscan lady, while their daughter (Urgulania's granddaughter), Plautia Urgulanilla, in A.D. 24 became the first wife of the future emperor Claudius. The Etruscan side of his wife's ancestry may well have contributed to Claudius's antiquarian and historical interests in the Etruscans. His twenty-volume work on the Etruscans is, unfortunately, lost to us, but a curious monument, connected with the Plautii, the noble family into which his wife's grandmother had married, has survived.

The Plautii Laterani had a splendid villa on the site of the great future church of San Giovanni in Laterano. It was here that the *Sedia Corsini* was discovered in 1732 (FIG. 300). This is a marble throne carved in low relief on its cylindrical base and curved backrest with a series of figured scenes and vegetal ornaments of neo-Attic inspiration typical for the Late Republican period. The shape of the throne imitates the age-old form of Etruscan thrones we first met in the wooden specimens from Verucchio (see FIG. 29a) and in numerous rock-carved examples in tombs. Hammered from sheet bronze or modeled in terra-cotta, they served as seats for ancestors or Canopic ash urns. From its earliest appearance this type of throne indicated the importance and dignity of its occupant. The *Sedia Corsini* is tangible testimony to the survival of the memory of such a traditional symbol of power in an ancient family connected with aristocratic Etruscan women.

The friezes on the throne represent a sacrifice at an altar by a tree, military parades, hunting, spectators and athletic games, and preparations for feasting, as well as a huge man putting his head into a pot or wellhead. They are all carved in a deliberately rustic style, which must have been meant to suggest ancient models.

The themes are largely those typical for aristocratic self-representation in Etruria. But, as has long been recognized, a number of these scenes, in particular some of the types of vessels and costumes and the sturdy style, have their prototypes in the relief decoration of hammered bronze situlae, products of the Iron Age art of northern Italy and the Alps (cf. p. 38), inspired by Etruscan models. Caesar's conquest of the Po valley and of Gaul had familiarized Rome with such ancient foreign artifacts and had added to the semantic repertoire of sculptors charged with giving expression to the new spirit of reconciling and unifying all those elements of Italian history that had contributed to its greatness. The aristocratic family who commissioned the throne (perhaps to serve in a family cult or for symbolic display rather than for real use, for which it is on the small side: height 82.5 cm, diam. of seat 49.5 cm) must have wished to show its regard for the ancestral manners and customs (*mores maiorum*), which, by this time, combined multiple traditions. Of these the Etruscan elements, as this book has attempted to show, were not the least, and some of them have left a lasting imprint on Western civilization.

Bibliography

The bibliography is divided into nine separate sections, each dealing with a single theme or a group of related subjects. The sections are: Etruscan Civilization and History, Early Italy, and the Eastern Mediterranean; Etruscan Language and Writing; Etruscan Art, Crafts, Coinage, and Architecture; Sites and Monuments; Exhibition Catalogues; Recent Museum Catalogues; Acts of Congresses, Study Meetings, and Seminars, Honorary and Memorial Volumes; Etruscan Religion; and Etruscan Women. This classification is designed to help readers find titles relevant to particular interests they may wish to explore in greater depth. All titles are given in full so that the subjects they deal with are clearly identifiable. Catalogues of exhibitions on Etruscan themes are listed chronologically from 1955, and acts of congresses, etc., from 1974.

ABBREVIATIONS:

BM *Bronze Cat.*
Walters, H. B. *Catalogue of the Bronzes, Greek, Roman, and Etruscan, in the Department of Greek and Roman Antiquities.* British Museum. London, 1899.

BM *Jewellery Cat.*
Marshall, F. H. *Catalogue of the Jewellery, Greek, Etruscan and Roman, in the Departments of Antiquities.* British Museum. London, 1911.

CIE *Corpus inscriptionum etruscarum.* Various places, 1893– .

CIL *Corpus inscriptionum latinarum.* Berlin, 1862– .

CSE *Corpus speculorum etruscorum.* Various places, 1981– .

ES Gerhard, E. *Etruskische Spiegel.* Vols. 1–4. Berlin, 1843–1867. Vol. 5, ed. A. Klügmann and G. Körte. Berlin, 1884–1897. Reprint (5 vols. in 4), Rome, 1960.

Louvre *Bronze Cat.*
De Ridder, A. *Les Bronzes antiques.* Musée du Louvre. 2 vols. Paris, 1913–1915.

RM *Mitteilungen des Deutschen Archäologischen Instituts, Römische Abteilung.*

SE *Studi Etruschi.*

TLE M. Pallottino. *Testimonia linguae etruscae,* 2nd edn. Florence, 1968.

Etruscan Civilization and History, Early Italy, and the Eastern Mediterranean

Aigner-Foresti, L. *Die Integration der Etrusker und das Weiterwirken etruskischen Kulturgutes im republikanischen und kaiserzeitlichen Rom.* Vienna, 1998.

Aubet, M. E. *The Phoenicians and the West: Politics, Colonies, and Trade.* Translated from the Spanish by M. Turton. Cambridge, 1993. Originally published as *Tiro y las colonias fenicias de Occidente.*

Barker, G., and T. Rasmussen. *The Etruscans.* Oxford, 1998.

Bartoloni, G. *La cultura villanoviana: All'inizio della storia etrusca.* Studi NIS archeologia 9. Rome, 1989.

Bianchi Bandinelli, R., and A. Giuliano. *Etruschi e italici prima del dominio di Roma.* Milan, 1973. Originally published as *Les Étrusques et l'Italie avant Rome* (Paris, 1973).

Boardman, J. *The Greeks Overseas: Their Early Colonies and Trade.* Rev. edn. London, 1999.

Boëthius, A. *Etruscan Culture, Land, and People.* New York, 1962.

Boitani, F., M. Cataldi, and M. Pasquinucci. *Etruscan Cities.* New York, 1975.

Bonfante, L. *Out of Etruria: Etruscan Influence North and South.* British Archaeological Reports, no. 103. Oxford, 1981.

———, ed. *Etruscan Life and Afterlife: A Handbook of Etruscan Studies.* Detroit, 1986.

Briquel, D. *Les Pélasges en Italie: Recherches sur l'histoire de la légende.* École française de Rome, 1984.

———. *L'Origine lydienne des Étrusques: Histoire de la doctrine dans l'antiquité.* École française de Rome, 1991.

Buchner, G., and D. Ridgway. *Pithekoussai.* Vol. 1, *La necropoli: Tombe 1–723 scavate dal 1952 al 1961.* Monumenti Antichi 55, serie monografica 4. Rome, 1993.

Camporeale, G. *La caccia in Etruria.* Rome, 1994.

Cerchiai, L. *I campani.* Milan, 1995.

Coldstream, J. N. *Geometric Greece.* New York, 1977.

Cornell, T. J. *The Beginnings of Rome: Italy and Rome from the Bronze Age to the Punic Wars c. 1000–263 B.C.* New York, 1995.

Cristofani, M. *Città e campagna nell'Etruria settentrionale.* Italy [Arezzo], 1976.

———. *The Etruscans: A New Investigation.* London, 1979.

———. *Gli etruschi del mare.* Archeologia 6. Milan, 1983.

———. *Etruschi e altre genti nell'Italia preromana: Mobilità in età arcaica.* Rome, 1996.

———, ed. *Dizionario della civiltà etrusca.* Florence, 1985.

———, ed. *Miscellanea etrusco-italica.* Vol. 1. Quaderni di archeologia etrusco-italica, no. 22. Rome, 1993.

———, ed. *Miscellanea etrusco-italica.* Vol. 2. Quaderni di archeologia etrusco-italica, no. 26. Rome, 1997.

Cristofani, M., and P. Bocci Pacini. *Gli etruschi in Maremma: Popolamento e attività produttive.* Milan, 1981.

Cunliffe, B. *The Ancient Celts.* New York, 1997.

Forte, M., and P. v. Eles, eds. *La pianura bolognese nel villanoviano: Insediamenti della prima età del ferro.* Florence, 1994.

Frederiksen, M. *Campania.* Edited by N. Purcell. [London], 1984.

Gras, M. *Trafics tyrrhénien archaïques.* [Rome], 1985.

Hall, J. F., ed. *Etruscan Italy: Etruscan Influences on the Civilizations of Italy from Antiquity to the Modern Era.* Provo, Utah, 1996.

Harris, W. V. *Rome in Etruria and Umbria.* Oxford, 1971.

Hase, F.-W. v. "Ägäische, griechische und vorderorientalische Einflüsse auf das tyrrhenische Mittelitalien." *Beiträge zur Urnenfelderzeit nördlich und südlich der Alpen.* Monografien/ Römisch-Germanisches Zentralmuseum 35: 239–86. Bonn, 1995.

Heurgon, J. *Daily Life of the Etruscans.* Translated from the French by J. Kirkup. New York, 1964.

Jannot, J.-R. "Musique et rang social dans l'Étrurie antique." In *Die Welt der Etrusker.* International Colloquium, October 24–26, 1988, ed. H. Heres and M. Kunze, pp. 43–51. Berlin, 1990.

———. "Les Navires étrusques, instruments d'une thalassocratie?" *Académie des Inscriptions et Belles-Lettres. Comptes rendus des séances de l'année* (July–October 1995): 743–78.

Kopke, G., and I. Tokumara. *Greece between East and West: 10th–8th Centuries B.C.* Papers of the meeting at the Institute of Fine Arts, New York University, March 15–16, 1990. Mainz, 1992.

Lambrechts, R. *Essai sur les magistratures des républiques étrusques.* Brussels, 1959.

Lemos, I. S., and M. R. Popham, comps. *Lefkandi III: The Toumba Cemetery: The Excavations of 1981, 1984, 1986 and 1992–1994.* British School at Athens, 1996.

Lo Schiavo, F. "Bronzi nuragici nelle tombe della prima età del Ferro di Pontecagnano." *La presenza etrusca nella Campania meridionale.* Atti delle giornate di studio, Salerno-Pontecagnano, November 16–18, 1990, pp. 61–82. Florence, 1994.

———. "Sardegna." *Enciclopedia dell'arte antica, classica e orientale.* Secondo Supplemento, 5: 141–60. Rome, 1994.

———. "Cyprus and Sardinia in the Mediterranean Trade Routes towards the West." *Cyprus and the Sea.* Proceedings of the International Symposium, Nicosia, September 25–26, 1993, pp. 45–59. Nicosia, 1995.

Macnamara, E. *Everyday Life of the Etruscans.* New York, 1987.

———. *The Etruscans.* London, 1990; Cambridge, Mass., 1991.

Massa-Pairault, F.-H. *La Cité des Étrusques.* Paris, 1996.

Menichetti, M. *Archeologia del potere: Re, immagini e miti a Roma e in Etruria in età arcaica.* Milan, 1994.

Nijboer, A. J. *From Household Production to Workshops: Archaeological Evidence for Economic Transformations, Pre-Monetary Exchange, and Urbanisation in Central Italy from 800 to 400 B.C.* Groningen, 1998.

Ogilvie, R. M. *Early Rome and the Etruscans.* London, 1976.

Origo Crea, B., ed. *Etruria Unveiled: The Drawings of Samuel James Ainsley in the British Museum = Etruria svelata: I disegni di Samuel James Ainsley nel British Museum.* Bilingual edn. With an introductory essay by M. Pallottino and a note by S. Haynes. Rome, 1984.

Osborne, R. *Greece in the Making, 1200–479 B.C.* New York, 1996.

Pallottino, M. *Saggi di antichità.* 3 vols. Rome, 1979.

———. *Etruskologie: Geschichte und Kultur der Etrusker.* Translated by S. Steingräber. Boston, 1988. Originally published as *Etruscologia* (Milan, 1984).

———. *A History of Earliest Italy.* Translated by M. Ryle and K. Soper. Ann Arbor, Michigan, 1991. Originally published as *Storia della prima Italia* (Milan, 1984).

———. *Origini e storia primitiva di Roma.* Milan, 1993.

———, ed. *Popoli e civiltà dell'Italia antica.* 6 vols. Rome, 1974–1984.

Peroni, R., ed. *Necropoli e usi funerari nell'età del ferro.* Archeologia: Materiali e problemi 5. Bari, 1981.

Popham, M., and I. Lemos. "A Euboean Warrior Trader." *Oxford Journal of Archaeology* 14 (1995): 151–57.

Potter, T. W. *The Changing Landscape of South Etruria.* New York, 1979.

Pugliese Carratelli, G., ed. *The Western Greeks: Classical Civilization in the Western Mediterranean.* London, 1996.

Rathje, A. "The Adoption of the Homeric Banquet in Central Italy in the Orientalizing Period." In *Sympotica: A Symposium on the Symposion*, ed. O. Murray, pp. 279–88. Oxford, 1990.

———. "Il banchetto in Italia Centrale: Quale stile di vita?" In *In vino veritas*, ed. O. Murray and M. Tecusan, pp. 167–75. London, 1995.

Ridgway, D. *The First Western Greeks*. New York, 1992.

Ridgway, D., and F. R. Ridgway, eds. *Italy before the Romans: The Iron Age, Orientalizing, and Etruscan Periods*. New York, 1979.

Säflund, G. *Etruscan Imagery: Symbol and Meaning*. Jonsered, 1993.

Serra Ridgway, F. R. "Etruscans, Greeks, Carthaginians: The Sanctuary at Pyrgi." In *Greek Colonists and Native Populations*. Proceedings of the First Australian Congress of Classical Archaeology, Sydney, July 9–14, 1985, ed. J.-P. Descoeudres, pp. 511–30. Oxford, 1990.

Sherratt, S., and A. Sherratt. "The Growth of Mediterranean Economy in the Early First Millennium B.C." *World Archaeology* 24.3 (1993): 361–78.

Sprenger, M., and G. Bartoloni. *The Etruscans: Their History, Art, and Architecture*. New York, 1983.

Stary, P. F. *Zur eisenzeitlichen Bewaffnung und Kampfesweise in Mittelitalien (ca. 9. bis 6. Jh. v. Chr.)*. Marburger Studien zur Vor- und Frühgeschichte 3. Mainz, 1981.

Steingräber, S. *Etrurien: Städte, Heiligtümer, Nekropolen*. Munich, 1981.

Swaddling, J., ed. *Italian Iron Age Artefacts in the British Museum*. Papers of the Sixth British Museum Classical Colloquium. London, 1985.

Swaddling, J., et al., eds. *Italy in Europe: Economic Relations 700 B.C.–A.D. 50*. British Museum Occasional Paper, no. 97. London, 1995.

Tandy, D. W. *Warriors into Traders: The Power of the Market in Early Greece*. Berkeley, 1997.

Thuillier, J.-P. *Les Jeux athlétiques dans la civilisation étrusque*. École française de Rome, fasc. 256. Rome, 1985.

Toms, J. "Some Aspects of the Villanovan Culture of Southern Etruria with Special Reference to Tarquinia." Ph.D. diss., Oxford University, 1994.

Torelli, M. *Elogia tarquiniensia*. Florence, 1975.

———. *Etruria*. Guide archeologiche Laterza. Rome, [1980].

———. *Storia degli etruschi*. Rome, 1981.

———. *La società etrusca: L'età arcaica, l'età classica*. Rome, 1987.

———. *Il rango, il rito e l'immagine: Alle origine della rappresentazione storica romana*. Milan, 1997.

Vacano, O. W. v. *The Etruscans in the Ancient World*. Translated by S. A. Ogilvie. Bloomington, Indiana, 1960. Originally published as *Die Etrusker in der Welt der Antike* (Hamburg, 1957).

Valvo, A. *La "profezia di Vegoia": Proprietà fondiaria e aruspiciana in Etruria nel I secolo a.C.* Rome, 1988.

Various authors. "Lazio arcaico e mondo greco: L'area sacra di S. Omobono." *La parola del passato* 32, no. 172 (1977): 9–128.

Various authors. *Rasenna: Storia e civiltà degli etruschi*. Milan, 1986.

Etruscan Language and Writing

Agostiniani, L. *Le "iscrizioni parlanti" dell'Italia antica*. Lingue e iscrizioni dell'Italia antica 3. Florence, 1982.

Atti del colloquio sul tema l'etrusco arcaico. Florence, October 4–5, 1974. Florence, 1976.

Bagnasco Gianni, G. *Oggetti iscritti di epoca orientalizzante in Etruria*. Florence, 1996.

Bonfante, G., and L. Bonfante. *Etruscan Language: An Introduction*. New York, 1983.

Bonfante, L. *Etruscan*. London, 1990.

Colonna, G. "Nomi etruschi di vasi." *Archeologia classica* 25/26 (1973/1974): 132–50.

———. "Nome, gentilizio e società." *SE* 45 (1977): 189–92.

———. "Greco more bibere: L'iscrizione della tomba 115 di Osteria dell'Osa." *Archeologia laziale*. Quaderni del centro di studio per l'archeologia etrusco-italica. Terzo incontro di studio del comitato per l'archeologia laziale, 3: 51–55. [Rome], 1980.

———. "L'etruschità della Campania meridionale alla luce delle iscrizioni." In *La presenza etrusca nella Campania meridionale*. Atti delle giornate di studio, Salerno, Pontecagnano, November 16–18, 1990, ed. P. Gastaldi and G. Maetzke, pp. 343–78. Florence, 1994.

Corpus inscriptionum etruscarum (= *CIE*). Various places, 1893– .

Cristofani, M. *Introduzione allo studio dell'etrusco*. Florence, 1973.

———. "Iscrizioni e beni suntuari." *Opus: International Journal for Social and Economic History of Antiquity* 3 (1984): 319–23.

———. "La formazione della scrittura in Etruria." *Annali della fondazione per il Museo "Claudio Faina"* 4 (1990), pp. 61–73.

De Simone, C. *Die griechischen Entlehungen im Etruskischen*. 2 vols. Wiesbaden, 1968–1970.

———. "Un nuovo gentilizio etrusco da Orvieto (Katacina) e la cronologia della penetrazione celtica (gallica) in Italia." *La parola del passato* 33 (1978): 370–95.

———. "L'ermeneutica etrusca oggi." In *Atti del secondo congresso internazionale etrusco*, Florence, May 26–June 2, 1985, ed. G. Maetzke et al., 3: 1307–20. Rome, 1989.

———. *Le iscrizioni etrusche dei cippi di Rubiera*. Archaeologica regiensia 6. Reggio Emilia, 1992.

———. "Le iscrizioni chiusine arcaiche." *La civiltà di Chiusi e del suo territorio*. Atti del XVII convegno di studi etruschi ed Italici, Chianciano Terme, May 28–June 1, 1989, pp. 25–38. Florence, 1993.

———. "I Tirreni a Lemnos: L'alfabeto." *SE* 60 (1994): 145–63.

———. *I Tirreni a Lemnos: Evidenza linguistica e tradizioni storiche*. Florence, 1996.

———. "I Tirreni a Lemnos: Paralipomena metodologici (nonche teorici)." *Ostraka* 6.1 (1997): 35–50.

Maggiani, A. "Appunti sulle magistrature etrusche." *SE* 62 (1996): 95–137.

Marchesini, S. *Studi onomastici e sociolinguistici sull'Etruria arcaica: Il caso di Caere*. Florence, 1997.

Morandi, M. "Novità sui Velcha di Tarquinia." *Archeologia classica* 47 (1995): 267–88.

Pallottino, M. *Testimonia linguae etruscae*. 2nd edn. (= *TLE*). Florence, 1968.

———. *La Langue étrusque: Problèmes et perspectives*. Translated from the Italian by J. Heurgon. Paris, 1978. Originally published as *La lingua degli Etruschi*.

———. "I documenti scritti e la lingua." In various authors, *Rasenna: Storia e civiltà degli Etruschi*, pp. 311–67. Milan, 1986.

———. "Lingua e letteratura degli etruschi." *SE* 61 (1996): 210–32.

Pandolfini Angeletti, M., and A. Prosdocimi. *Alfabetari e insegnamento della scrittura in Etruria e nell'Italia antica*. Florence, 1990.

Pfiffig, A. J. *Die etruskische Sprache: Versuch einer Gesamtdarstellung*. Graz, 1969.

Pirovano, C., ed. *Scrivere etrusco: Dalla leggenda alla conoscenza: Scrittura e letteratura nei massimi documenti della lingua etrusca*. Exh. cat., Perugia, Rocca Paolina, May–September 1985. Milan, 1985.

Rix, H. *Das etruskische Cognomen: Untersuchungen zu System, Morphologie und Verwendung der Personennamen auf den jüngeren Inschriften Nordetruriens*. Wiesbaden, 1963.

———. "Zum Ursprung des römisch-mittelitalischen Gentilnamensystems." In *Aufstieg und Niedergang der römischen Welt: Geschichte und Kultur Roms im Spiegel der neueren Forschung*, ed. H. Temporini and W. Haase, 1.2: 700–785. New York, 1972.

———. "Teonimi etruschi e teonimi italici." *Annali della fondazione per il Museo "Claudio Faina"* 5 (1998): 207–29.

———, **ed.** *Etruskische Texte: Editio minor*. 2 vols. Tübingen, 1991.

Sassatelli, G., ed. *Iscrizioni e graffiti della città etrusca di Marzabotto*. Studi e scavi, Università di Bologna, Istituto di archeologia 1. Bologna, [1994].

La scrittura nell'Etruria antica. Relazioni e communicazioni nel convegno del 1985. *Annali della fondazione per il Museo "Claudio Faina"* 4. Orvieto, 1990.

Thesaurus linguae etruscae. Vol. 1. Rome, 1978.

Etruscan Art, Crafts, Coinage, and Architecture

Andrén, A. *Architectural Terracottas from Etrusco-Italic Temples*. 2 vols. Skrifter utgivna av Svenska Institutet i Rom, no. 6. Lund, 1939–1940.

Bartoloni, G., et al. *Le urne a capanna rinvenute in Italia*. Rome, 1987.

Beazley, J. D. *Etruscan Vase-Painting*. Oxford, 1947.

Bentz, M. *Etruskische Votivbronzen des Hellenismus*. Florence, 1992.

Bianchi Bandinelli, R., and M. Torelli. *L'arte dell'antichità classica*. Vol. 2, *Etruria, Roma*. Turin, [1976].

Blanck, H. "Die Malereien des sogenannten Priester-Sarkophages in Tarquinia." In *Miscellanea archaeologica Tobias Dohrn dedicata*, ed. H. Blanck and S. Steingräber, pp. 11–22. Rome, 1982.

Boëthius, A., and J. B. Ward-Perkins. *Etruscan and Roman Architecture*. The Pelican History of Art. Harmondsworth, [1970].

Bonfante, L. *Etruscan Dress*. Baltimore, 1975.

Boosen, M. *Etruskische Meeresmischwesen: Untersuchungen zu Typologie und Bedeutung*. Rome, 1986.

Bordenache Battaglia, G., and A. Emiliozzi. *Le ciste prenestine*. 4 vols. Part 1.1–2. [Rome], 1979.

Bound, M. *The Giglio Wreck*. Athens, 1991.

Brendel, O. J. *Etruscan Art*. New Haven, 1995.

Catalli, F. *Monete etrusche*. Libreria dello Stato. Istituto Poligrafico e Zecca dello Stato. Rome, 1990.

Corpus speculorum etruscorum = *CSE* (*Belgique*, vol. 1, by R. Lambrechts [Rome, 1987]. *Bundesrepublik Deutschland*, vol. 1, by U. Höckmann [Munich, 1987]; vol. 2, by U. Liepmann [Munich, 1988]; vol. 3, by B. v. Freytag gen. Löringhoff [Munich, 1990]; vol. 4, by G. Zimmer [Munich, 1995]. *Città del Vaticano*, vol. 1, by R. Lambrechts [Rome, 1995]. *Deutsche Demokratische Republik*, no vol. no., fasc. 1–2, by G. Heres [Berlin, 1986–1987]. *Danmark*, vol. 1, fasc. 1, by H. Salskov Roberts [Odense, 1981]. *France*, vol. 1, fascs. 1–3, by D. Emmanuel-Rebuffat [Rome, 1988, 1991, and 1997]. *Great Britain*, vol. 1, by J. Swaddling [London, forthcoming]; vol. 2, by R. V. Nicholls [Cambridge, 1993]. *Hongrie, Tchécoslovaquie*, vol. 1, by J. G. Szilágyi and J. Bouzek [Rome, 1992]. *Italia*, vol. 1, fascs. 1–2, by G. Sassatelli [Rome, 1981]; vol. 2, fasc. 1, by A. Frascarelli [Rome, 1995]; vol. 3, fasc. 1, by G. Cateni [Rome, 1995]; vol. 4, by M. S. Pacetti [Rome, 1998]; vol. 5, by G. Barbieri [Rome, 1999]. *The Netherlands*, vol. 1, by L. Bouke van der Meer [Leiden, 1983]. *U.S.A.*, vols. 1–2, by R. De Puma [Rome, 1987, 1993]; vol. 3, by L. Bonfante [Rome, 1997].)

Cristofani, M. *Statue-cinerario chiusine di età classica*. Rome, 1975.

———. *L'arte degli etruschi: Produzione e consumo*. Turin, 1978.

———. *Miscellanea ceretana*. Rome, 1989.

Cristofani, M., and F. Boitani. *Strade degli etruschi: Vie e mezzi di comunicazione nell'antica Etruria*. Rome, 1985.

Cristofani, M., and M. Martelli, eds. *L'oro degli etruschi*. Novara, 1983.

Cristofani, M., et al. *I bronzi degli etruschi*. Novara, 1985.

———, "La ceramografia etrusca fra età tardo-classica ed ellenismo." *SE* 58 (1992–1993): 100–110.

Del Chiaro, M. A. *Etruscan Red-figured Vase-Painting at Caere*. Berkeley, 1974.

Dennis, G. *The Cities and Cemeteries of Etruria*. 2 vols. 1848. 3rd edn., London, 1883. Reprint, Rome, 1968.

De Ridder, A. *Les Bronzes antiques. Paris, Musée du Louvre*. 2 vols. Paris, 1913–1915.

Dohrn, T. *Die etruskische Kunst im Zeitalter der Klassik: Die Interimsperiode*. Mainz, 1982.

Egg, M. *Italische Helme: Studien zu den ältereisenzeitlichen Helmen Italiens und der Alpen*. 2 vols. Mainz, 1986.

Fischer-Graf, U. *Spiegelwerkstätten in Vulci*. Archäologische Forschungen 8. Berlin, 1980.

Formigli, E., ed. *Preziosi in oro: Avorio, osso e corno: Arte e tecniche degli artigiani etruschi*. Siena, 1995.

Geiger, A. *Prähistorische Bronzefunde*. Vol. 3.1, *Treibverzierte Bronzerundschilde der italischen Eisenzeit aus Italien und Griechenland*. Stuttgart, 1994.

Gempeler, R. D. *Die etruskischen Kanopen: Herstellung, Typologie, Entwicklungsgeschichte*. [Einsiedeln, 1973?].

Gentili, M. D. *I sarcofagi etruschi in terracotta di età recente*. Rome, 1994.

Gerhard, E. *Etruskische Spiegel*. Vols. 1–4. Berlin, 1843–1867. Vol. 5, ed. A. Klügmann and G. Körte. Berlin, 1884–1897. Reprint (5 vols. in 4), Rome, 1960.

Guzzo, P. G. *Le fibule in Etruria dal VI al I secolo*. Florence, 1972.

Hannestad, L. *The Paris Painter: An Etruscan Vase-Painter*. Copenhagen, 1974.

———. *The Followers of the Paris Painter*. Copenhagen, 1976.

Harari, M. *Il "gruppo clusium" della ceramografia etrusca*. Rome, 1980.

Hase, F.-W. v. *Die Trensen der Früheisenzeit in Italien*. Prähistorische Bronzefunde, Abt. 16, Bd. 1. Munich, 1969.

———. "Der archaische Handel Etruriens." *Hamburger Beiträge zur Archäologie* 15/17, 1988–1990 (1992): 347–64.

———. "The Ceremonial Jewellery from the Regolini-Galassi Tomb in Cerveteri: Some Ideas Concerning the Workshop in Prehistoric Gold in Europe." In *Prehistoric Gold in Europe: Mines, Metallurgy, and Manufacture*, ed. G. Morteani and J. P. Northover, pp. 533–59. Boston, 1995.

Haynes, S. *Etruscan Sculpture*. London, 1971.

———. *Etruscan Bronze Utensils*. Rev. edn. London, 1974.

———. *Etruscan Bronzes*. New York, 1985.

Haynes, S., and H. Menzel. "Etruskische Bronzekopfgefässe." *Jahrbuch des Römisch-Germanischen Zentralmuseums Mainz* 6 (1959): 110–27.

Herbig, R. *Die jüngeretruskischen Steinsarkophage*. Berlin, 1952.

Holliday, P. J. "'Celtomachia': The Representation of Battles with Gauls on Etruscan Funerary Urns." *Etruscan Studies* 1 (1994): 23–45.

Hus, A. *Recherches sur la statuaire en pierre étrusque archaïque*. Paris, 1961.

Jucker, I. "Bemerkungen zu einigen etruskischen Klappspiegeln." *RM* 95 (1988): 1–39.

———. "Die Geburt der Turan." *Quaderni ticinesi di numismatica e antichità classiche* 17 (1988): 101–23.

Jurgeit, F. *Le ciste prenestine*. Vol. 2, part 1, *"Cistenfüsse": Etruskische und Praenestiner Bronzewerkstätten*. [Rome], 1986.

Krauskopf, I. *Griechische Mythen in Etrurien: Der thebanische Sagenkreis und andere griechische Sagen in der etruskischen Kunst*. Mainz, 1974.

———. "Zur Datierung der etruskischen Löwenkopfmünzen." *RM* 90 (1983): 223–32.

———. "Zum Datum der Gorgoneia von Populonia." *Schweizerische Numismatische Rundschau* 64 (1985): 61–69.

Lambrechts, R. *Les Miroirs étrusques et prénestins des Musées Royaux d'Art et d'Histoire à Bruxelles*. Brussels, 1978.

Mangani, E. "Le fabbriche a figure rosse di Chiusi e Volterra." *SE* 58 (1992–1993): 115–43.

Martelli, M., ed. *La ceramica degli etruschi: La pittura vascolare.* Novara, 1987.

Mayer-Prokop, I. *Die gravierten etruskischen Griffspiegel archaischen Stils. RM*, Ergänzungsheft 13. Heidelberg, 1967.

Mertens-Horn, M. "Die archaischen Baufriese aus Metapont." *RM* 99 (1992): 1–122.

Michetti, L. M. "Figure femminili in ceramica argentata dall'agro falisco." *SE* 61 (1995): 103–38.

Micozzi, M. *"White on Red": Una produzione vascolare dell'orientalizzante etrusco.* Rome, 1994.

Naso, A. *La Tomba dei Denti di Lupo a Cerveteri.* Florence, 1991.

———. *Architetture dipinte: Decorazioni parietali non figurate nelle tombe a camera dell'Etruria meridionale (VII–V sec. a.C.).* Rome, 1996.

Nestler, G., and E. Formigli. *Etruskische Granulation: Eine antike Goldschmiedetechnik.* Siena, 1993.

Oleson, J. P. *The Sources of Innovation in Later Etruscan Tomb Design (ca. 350–100 B.C.).* Rome, 1982.

Pallottino, M. *Etruscan Painting.* Trans. M. E. Stanley and S. Gilbert. Geneva, [1952].

Pfister-Roesgen, G. *Die etruskischen Spiegel des 5. Jhs. v. Chr.* Bern, 1975.

Prayon, F. *Frühetruskische Grab- und Hausarchitektur. RM*, Ergänzungsheft 22. Heidelberg, 1975.

———. "Ostmediterrane Einflüsse auf den Beginn der Monumentalarchitektur in Etrurien." *Jahrbuch des Römisch-Germanischen Zentralmuseums* 37, 1990 (1997): 501–19.

Rasmussen, T. *Bucchero Pottery from Southern Etruria.* New York, 1979.

Rebuffat-Emmanuel, D. *Le Miroir étrusque d'après la collection du Cabinet des Médailles.* Rome, 1973.

Reusser, Ch. *Etruskische Kunst.* Basel, 1988.

Richardson, E. H. *Etruscan Votive Bronzes: Geometric, Orientalizing, Archaic.* 2 vols. Mainz, 1983.

Rizzo, M. A., ed. *Pittura etrusca al Museo di Villa Giulia.* Rome, 1989.

Shefton, B. B. "Der Stamnos." In *Das Kleinaspergle: Studien zu einem Fürstengrabhügel der frühen Latènezeit bei Stuttgart*, ed. W. Kimmig, pp. 104–52. Stuttgart, 1988.

Spivey, N. J. *The Micali Painter and His Followers.* New York, 1987.

———. *Etruscan Art.* New York, 1997.

Sprenger, M. *Die etruskische Plastik des v. Jahrhunderts v. Chr. und ihr Verhältnis zur griechischen Kunst.* Rome, 1972.

Steingräber, S. *Etruskische Möbel.* Rome, 1979.

———. "Zum Phänomen der etruskisch-italischen Votifköpfe." *RM* 87 (1980): 215–53.

———. "Überlegungen zu etruskischen Altären." In *Miscellanea archaeologica Tobias Dohrn dedicata*, ed. H. Blanck and S. Steingräber, pp. 103–16. Rome, 1982.

———. "Etruskische Monumentalcippi." *Archeologia classica* 43 (1991): 1079–1102.

Steingräber, S., D. Ridgway, and F. Serra Ridgway, eds. *Etruscan Painting: Catalogue raisonné of Etruscan Wall Paintings.* Translated from the German by M. Blair and from the Italian by B. Phillips. New York, 1986.

Strøm, I. *Problems Concerning the Origin and Early Development of the Etruscan Orientalizing Style.* 2 vols. Odense, 1971.

Szilágyi, J. G. *La ceramica etrusco-corinzia figurata.* Vol. 1, 630–580 *a.C.* Florence, 1992. Vol. 2, 590/580–550 *a.C.* Florence, 1998.

Thomson de Grummond, N., ed. *A Guide to Etruscan Mirrors.* Tallahassee, Florida, 1982.

Tuck, A. S. "The Etruscan Seated Banquet: Villanovan Ritual and Etruscan Iconography." *American Journal of Archaeology* 98 (1994): 617–28.

Turfa, J. "Anatomical Votives and Italian Medical Traditions." In *Murlo and the Etruscans: Art and Society in Ancient Etruria*, ed. R. De Puma and J. P. Small, pp. 224–40. Madison, Wisconsin, 1994.

Van der Meer, L. B. *Interpretatio etrusca: Greek Myths on Etruscan Mirrors.* Amsterdam, 1995.

Wiman, I. M. B. *Malstria-Malena: Metals and Motifs in Etruscan Mirror Craft.* Studies in Mediterranean Archaeology 91. Gothenburg, 1990.

Winter, N. A. "The Greek Backgrounds for Archaic Architectural Terracottas of Central Italy." In *Deliciae fictiles*, ed. E. Rystedt, C. Wikander, and Ö. Wikander, pp. 17–20. Stockholm, 1993.

Zazoff, P. *Etruskische Skarabäen.* Mainz, [1968].

Sites and Monuments

Acquarossa: Results of Excavations Conducted by the Swedish Institute of Classical Studies at Rome and the Soprintendenza alle antichità dell'Etruria meridionale. (Vol. 1, *The Painted Architectural Terracottas*, by C. Wikander [Stockholm, 1981]. Vol. 2.1, *Cooking and Cooking Stands in Italy 1400–400*, and vol. 2.2, *The Cooking Stands*, both by C. Scheffer [Stockholm, 1981 and 1982]. Vol. 3, *Zone A*, by M. B. Lundgren and L. Wendt [Stockholm, 1982]. Vol. 4, *Early Etruscan Akroteria from Acquarossa and Poggio Civitate [Murlo]*, by E. Rystedt [Stockholm, 1983]. Vol. 5.1, *The Head-Antefixes and Relief Plaques*, by M. Strandberg Olofson [Stockholm, 1984]. Vol. 6, *The Roof-Tiles*, by Ö. Wikander [Stockholm, 1986]. Vol. 7, *Trial Trenches, Tombs and Surface Finds*, various authors [Stockholm, 1994].)

Aurigemma, S. *La necropoli di Spina in Valle Trebba.* 2 vols. Rome, 1960–1965.

Barbieri, G. *Viterbo e il suo territorio.* Rome, 1991.

Bartoloni, G. "Populonium etruscorum quodam hoc tantum in litore: Aspetti e carattere di una comunità costiera nella prima età del ferro." *Archeologia classica* 43 (1991): 2–37.

Bartoloni, G., and M. P. Baglione. "Elementi scultorei decorativi nelle tombe tarquiniesi del primo ellenismo in Tarquinia." In *Tarquinia: Ricerche, scavi e prospettive.* Atti del convegno internazionale di studi La Lombardia per gli etruschi, Milan, June 24–25, 1986, ed. M. Bonghi Jovino and C. Chiaramonte Treré. Milan, 1987.

Bartoloni, G., and F. Delpino. *Veio.* Vol. 1, *Introduzione allo studio delle necropoli arcaiche di Veio: Il sepolcreto di Valle la Fata.* Rome, 1979.

Bianchi Bandinelli, R. "Clusium: Ricerche archeologiche e topografiche su Chiusi e il suo territorio en età etrusca." *Monumenti antichi* 30 (1925): 208–578.

———. *Sovana: Topografia ed arte, contributo alla conoscenza dell'architettura etrusca.* Florence, 1929.

Bietti Sestieri, A. M. *The Iron Age Community of Osteria dell'Osa: A Study of Socio-Political Development in Central Tyrrhenian Italy.* New York, 1992.

Blanck, H., and G. Proietti. *La tomba dei rilievi di Cerveteri.* Rome, 1986.

Blumhofer, M. *Etruskische Cippi: Untersuchungen am Beispiel von Cerveteri.* Cologne, 1993.

Bocci Pacini, P. "La stipe della Fonte Veneziana ad Arezzo." *SE* 48 (1980): 73–91.

Boitani, F. "Veio: Nuovi rinvenimenti nella necropoli di Monte Michele." *Archeologia nella Tuscia.* Primo incontro di studio sull'archeologia nella Tuscia, Viterbo 1980, pp. 95–103. Rome, 1982– .

Bonamici, M. "La Proserpina del Catajo, ritrovata." *Prospettiva* 81 (1996): 2–16.

Bonfante, L. "The Corsini Throne and the Man in the Pot." In *Coins, Culture and History in the Ancient World: Numismatic and Other Studies in Honor of Bluma L. Trell*, ed. L. Casson and M. Price, pp. 105–12. Detroit, 1981.

Bonghi Jovino, M., ed. *Gli etruschi di Tarquinia.* Modena, [1986].

Bonghi Jovino, M., and C. Chiaramonte Treré, eds. *Tarquinia: Testimonianze archeologiche e ricostruzione storica: Scavi sistematici nell'abitato: Campagne 1982–1988.* Rome, 1997.

Bothmer, D. v., and J. Heurgon. "An Etruscan Bronze in New York." *Monuments Piot* 61 (1977): 45–59.

Briguet, M.-F. *Le Sarcophage des époux de Cerveteri du Musée du Louvre.* Paris, 1988.

Bruni, S. *I lastroni a scale.* Rome, 1986.

———. "Di un nuovo specchio etrusco e delle officine tarquiniesi di età tardoarcaica." *Rassegna di archeologia* 9 (1990): 373–99.

———. "L'altare arcaico del tempio di Fiesole e la tradizione delle 'pietre fiesolane.'" *Archeologia classica* 46 (1994): 47–90.

———. *Pisa Etrusca: Anatomia di una città scomparsa.* Milan, 1998.

———. "Una 'pietra schema'. Contributo allo studio della statuaria etrusca di età arcaica dell'Etruria settentrionale." In *In Memoria di Enrico Paribeni*, vol. 1, ed. G. Capecchi et al., pp. 67–82. Rome, 1998.

———, ed. *Pisa, Piazza Dante: Uno spaccato della storia pisana: La campagna di scavo 1991.* Pisa, 1993.

Bruni, S., and F. Severini. "Problemi sulle presenze etrusche nella Toscana nord-occidentale: I dati delle necropoli di Pisa." *Aspetti della cultura di Volterra etrusca fra l'età del ferro e l'età ellenistica e contributi della ricerca antropologica alla conoscenza del popolo etrusco.* Atti del XIX convegno di studi etruschi ed italici, Volterra, October 15–19, 1995, pp. 559–96. Florence, 1997.

Buranelli, F. *La necropoli villanoviana "Le Rose" di Tarquinia.* [Rome], 1983.

———. *L'urna calabresi di Cerveteri.* Rome, 1985.

Camporeale, G. *La tomba del duce.* Florence, 1967.

———. *I commerci di Vetulonia in età orientalizzante.* [Florence, 1969].

———. *L'abitato dell'Accesa: Il quartiere B.* Rome, 1997.

Canciani, F., and F.-W. v. Hase. *La tomba Bernardini di Palestrina.* Latium vetus 2. Rome, 1979.

Carafa, P. "Organizzazione territoriale e risorse economiche nell'agro Volterraneo." *SE* 59 (1993): 109–21.

Carter, J. C. "The Tomb of the Siren." *American Journal of Archaeology* 78 (1974): 131–39.

Cataldi, M., and L. Ricciardi. *Tarquinia.* Guide territoriali dell'Etruria meridionale. Rome, 1993.

Christiansen, J. "En etruskisk Afrodite." *Meddelelser fra Ny Carlsberg Glyptotek*, 1988: 47–66.

Close-Brooks, J. "Considerazioni sulla cronologia delle facies arcaiche dell'Etruria." *SE* 35 (1967): 323–29.

Coen, A. *Complessi tombali di Cerveteri con urne cinerarie tardo-orientalizzanti.* Florence, 1991.

Colonna, G. "Novità sui culti di Pyrgi." *Rendiconti della Pontificia Accademia Romana di Archeologia* 57 (1984–1985): 57–88.

———. "Strutture teatroformi in Etruria." In *Spectacles sportifs et scéniques dans le monde étrusco-italique*. Actes de la table ronde organisée par l'équipe de recherches étrusco-italique de l'UMO 125 et l'École française de Rome, Rome, May 3–4, 1991. Collection de l'École française de Rome, fasc. 172, pp. 321–47. Rome, 1993.

———. "Altari e sacelli: L'area sud di Pyrgi dopo otto anni di ricerche." *Rendiconti della Pontificia Accademia Romana di Archeologia* 64 (1991–1992, 1994): 63–115.

———, ed. *L'altorilievo di Pyrgi: Dei ed eroi greci in Etruria*. Rome, 1996.

Colonna, G., et al. *Pyrgi: Scavi del santuario etrusco (1959–1967)*. 2 vols. Rome, [1972].

———. "Società e cultura a Volsinii." *Annali della fondazione per il Museo "Claudio Faina"* 2 (1985): 101–41.

———. "Il maestro dell'Ercole e della Minerva: Nuova luce sull'attività dell'officina Veiente." *Opuscula romana* 16.1 (1987): 7–41.

———. *Pyrgi: Scavi del santuario etrusco (1969–1971)*. Notizie degli scavi di antichità, II Supplemento al vol. 42–43 (1988–1989). Rome, 1992.

Colonna, G., and F.-W. v. Hase. "All'origine della statuaria etrusca: La tomba delle statue presso Ceri." *SE* 52 (1984): 13–59.

Colonna, G., B. Massabo, and L. Ricciardi. "Vulci II: Nuove scoperte nel santuario etrusco di Fontanile di Legnisina." *Bollettino d'arte* 73 (March–April 1988): 23–42.

Colonna, G., and P. Pelagatti. *Pyrgi: Il santuario etrusco e l'antiquarium*. Rome, 1990.

Colonna Di Paolo, E. *Necropoli rupestri del Viterbese*. Novara, 1978.

Colonna Di Paolo, E., and G. Colonna. *Castel d'Asso*. 2 vols. [Rome, 1970].

———. *Norchia I*. 2 vols. [n.p.], 1978.

Cristofani, M. "Nuovi dati per la storia urbana di Caere." *Bollettino d'arte* 71 (January–April 1986): 1–24.

———. "Mystai kai bakchoi: Riti di passaggio nei crateri volterrani." *Prospettiva* 80 (October 1995): 2–14.

———, ed. *Caere*. Vol. 3, *Lo scarico arcaico della vigna parrocchiale*. 2 vols. Rome, 1992–1993.

Cristofani, M., et al., eds. *Urne Volterrane*. Vol. 1, *I complessi tombali*. Florence, 1975.

———. *Urne Volterrane*. Vol. 2, *Il Museo Guarnacci*. Florence, 1977.

Cristofani, M., and G. Nardi. *Caere*. Vol. 1, *Il parco archeologico*. Rome, 1988.

D'Agostino, B. *Tombe "principesche" dell'orientalizzante antico da Pontecagnano*. Monumenti antichi 49, serie misc. 2.1. Rome, 1977.

D'Agostino, B., and P. Gastaldi. *Pontecagnano*. Vol. 2, *La necropoli del Picentino*. Part 1, *Le tombe della prima età del ferro*. Naples, 1988.

De Grummond, N. "Poggio Civitate: A Turning Point." *Etruscan Studies* 4 (1997): 23–40.

De Puma, R. D., and J. P. Small, eds. *Murlo and the Etruscans: Art and Society in Ancient Etruria*. Madison, Wisconsin, 1994.

D'Ercole, V., and F. Trucco. "Un luogo di culto all'aperto presso Vulci." *Bollettino di Archeologia* 13–15 (1992): 77–85.

Donati, L. *La casa dell'impluvium: Architettura etrusca a Roselle*. Rome, 1994.

Ducati, P. "Le pietre funerarie felsinee." *Monumenti antichi* 20 (1910): 362–727.

———. "Nuove stele funerarie felsinee." *Monumenti antichi* 39 (1943): 373–446.

Edlund-Berry, I. E. M., *The Seated and Standing Statue Akroteria from Poggio Civitate (Murlo)*. Rome, 1992.

Falchi, I. *Vetulonia e la sua necropoli antichissima*. Florence, 1891.

Fedeli, F., A. Galiberti, and A. Romualdi. *Populonia e il suo territorio: Profilo storico-archeologico*. Florence, 1993.

Feruglio, A. E. *Porano: Gli Etruschi*. Perugia, 1995.

Fiumi, E. *Volterra etrusca e romana*. I Monumenti antichi. Pisa, 1976.

Freytag gen. Löringhoff, B. v. *Das Giebelrelief von Telamon und seine Stellung innerhalb der Ikonographie der "Sieben gegen Theben."* Mainz, 1986.

Gentili, G. V. "Il Villanoviano Verucchiese nella Romagna orientale e il sepolcreto Moroni." *Studi e documenti di archeologia* 1: 1–30. Bologna, 1989.

Gerkan, A. v., and F. Messerschmidt. "Das Grab der Volumnier bei Perugia." *RM* 57 (1942): 122–235.

Gualandi, G. "Santuari e stipi votive dell'Etruria padana." *SE* 42 (1974): 37–68.

Haynes, S. "The Bronze Priests and Priestesses from Nemi." *RM* 67 (1960): 34–47.

———. "Ludiones Etruriae." In *Festschrift für Harald Keller*, ed. H. M. von Erffa and E. Herget, pp. 13–21. Darmstadt, 1963.

———. "Zwei archaisch-etruskische Bildwerke aus dem 'Isis-Grab' von Vulci." *Antike Plastik* 4 (1965): 13–24.

———. "Ein Etruskisches Parisurteil." *RM* 83 (1976): 227–31.

———. "The 'Isis-Tomb': Do Its Contents Form a Consistent Group?" In *La civiltà arcaica di Vulci e la sua espansione*. Atti del X convegno di studi etruschi ed italici, ed. A. Neppi Modona, pp. 17–29. Florence, 1977.

———. "The Bronze Bust from the 'Isis-Tomb' Reconsidered." *SE* 57 (1991): 3–9.

———. "Die Situla aus Offida." *RM* 98 (1991): 131–40.

———. "Thoughts on the Winged Female Figure in the Funerary Sculpture of Chiusi." In *La civiltà di Chiusi e del suo territorio*. Atti del XVII convegno di studi etruschi ed italici, Chianciano Terme, May 28–June 1, 1988, ed. G. Maetzke, pp. 297–309. Florence, 1993.

Hemelrijk, J. M. *Caeretan Hydriae*. 2 vols. Mainz, 1984.

Hencken, H. *Tarquinia, Villanovans, and Early Etruscans*. 2 vols. Cambridge, Mass., 1968.

Höckmann, U. *Die Bronzen aus dem Fürstengrab von Castel San Mariano bei Perugia*. Munich, 1982.

Hostetter, E. "A Bronze Handle from Spina." *RM* 85 (1978): 257–81.

———. *Bronzes from Spina*. Vol. 1. Mainz, 1986.

Jannot, J.-R. "Les Danseurs aux haches; ou, Le Ballet de Phinée: À propos d'un relief de Chiusi." *L'Italie préromaine et la Rome républicaine: Mélanges offerts à Jacques Heurgon*. Collection de l'École française de Rome, fasc. 27, pp. 471–85. Rome, 1976.

———. *Les Reliefs archaïques de Chiusi*. Rome, 1984.

———. "Remarques sur la 'situle' de Plikaśna." *Latomus* 51 (October–December 1992): 796–810.

Jehasse, J., and L. Jehasse. *La Nécropole préromaine d'Aléria (1960–1968)*. Paris, 1973.

Johannowsky. W. *Capua antica*. Naples, 1989.

Kearsley, R. A. *The Pendent Semi-Circle Skyphos: A Study of Its Development and Chronology and an Examination of It as Evidence for Euboean Activity at Al Mina*. London, 1989. See review: M. Popham and I. Lemos, "Kearsley, *The Pendant Semi-Circle Skyphos*," *Gnomon* 64 (1992): 152–55.

Mangani, E. "L'orientalizzante recente nella Valle del Ombrone." *Annali, Dipartamento di studi del mondo classico e del Mediterraneo antico. Sezione di archeologia e storia antica* 12 (Naples, 1990): 9–21.

———. "Castelnuovo Berardenga (Siena): Necropoli principesca in località Poggione, Tombe B e C (1983 e 1985)." *Notizie degli scavi di antichità* 92–93, 1990–1991 (1994): 5–86.

———. "Asciano: Le sculture tardo-orientalizzanti del Tumulo del Molinello." *SE* 56 (1991): 57–68.

———. "Castelnuovo Berardenga (Siena): L'orientalizzante recente in Etruria settentrionale: Tomba A della necropoli principesca del Poggione (1980)." *Notizie degli scavi di antichità* 42–43, 1988–1989 (1992): 5–84.

Martelli, M. "Documenti di arte orientalizzante da Chiusi." *SE* 41 (1973): 97–120.

Martinez-Pinna, J. "L'Oenochoe de Tragliatella: Considérations sur la société étrusque archaique." *SE* 40 (1995): 81–92.

Maule, Q. F., and H. R. W. Smith. *Votive Religion at Caere: Prolegomena*. University of California Publications in Classical Archaeology 4.1. Berkeley, 1959.

Meller Padovani, P. *Le stele villanoviane di Bologna*. Capo di Ponte (Brescia), 1977.

Michetti, L. M., and L. Ambrosini. "Sostegni a testa femminile in ceramica argentata: Analisi di una produzione falisca a destinazione funeraria." *Archeologia classica* 46 (1994): 109–68.

Minto, A. *Marsiliana d'Albegna*. Florence, [1921].

———. *Populonia: La necropoli arcaica*. Florence, 1922.

Morandi, M., and G. Colonna. "La gens titolare della tomba tarquiniese dell'Orco." *SE* 61 (1995 [1996]): 95–102.

Moretti, M., et al., eds. *I Curunas di Tuscania*. Rome, 1983.

Morigi Govi, C. "Il tintinnabulo della 'Tomba degli Ori' dell'Arsenale Militare di Bologna." *Archeologia classica* 23 (1971): 211–35.

Morigi Govi, C., and G. Sassatelli. "Il sepolcreto etrusco del Polisportivo di Bologna: Nuove stele funerarie." *Ocnus* 1 (1993): 103–24.

Naso, A., et al. *La Tomba dei Denti di Lupo a Cerveteri*. Florence, 1991.

Nielsen, M. "Cultural Orientations in Etruria in the Hellenistic Period: Greek Myths and Local Motifs on Volterran Urn Reliefs." *Acta Hyperborea* 5 (1993): 319–57.

Ortalli, J., and G. Bermond Montanari. "Il complesso monumentale protofelsineo di via Fondazza a Bologna." *SE* 54 (1986): 15–45.

Östenberg, C. E. *Case etrusche di Acquarossa*. [Rome], 1975.

Pairault-Massa, F. H. "La Romanisation du culte de Dionysos en Etrurie." *Mélanges de l'École française de Rome, Antiquités* 99.2 (1987): 573–94.

Pallottino, M. "Tarquinia." *Monumenti antichi* 36 (1937): 1–620.

———. *La scuola di Vulca*. Rome, 1945.

———. *The Necropolis of Cerveteri*. Translated from the Italian by M. E. Stanley. Rome, 1957.

Panichelli, S. "Sepolture bolognesi dell'VIII sec. a.C." In *Miscellanea protostorica*, ed. G. L. Carancini, pp. 187–409. Rome, 1990.

Paolucci, G. *Il territorio di Chianciano Terme: Dalla preistoria al medioevo*. Rome, 1987.

Pareti, L. *La tomba Regolini-Galassi del Museo Gregoriano Etrusco e la civiltà dell'Italia centrale nel sec. VII a.C.* Vatican City, 1947.

Paribeni, E. "La perplessità di Athena: Per una corretta lettura del frontone di Pyrgi." *Archeologia classica* 21 (1969): 53–57.

Pasquinucci, M. *Le kelebai volterrane.* Florence, 1968.

Phillips, K. M. *In the Hills of Tuscany: Recent Excavations at the Etruscan Site of Poggio Civitate (Murlo, Siena).* Philadelphia, 1993.

Pincelli, R., and C. Morigi Govi. *La necropoli villanoviana di San Vitale.* Bologna, 1975.

Pohl, I. *The Iron Age Necropolis of Sorbo at Cerveteri.* Stockholm, 1972.

Prayon, F. "Zum ursprünglichen Aussehen und zur Deutung des Kultraumes in der Tomba delle Cinque Sedie bei Cerveteri." *Marburger Winkelmann-Programm,* 1974: 1–15.

———. "Zur Datierung der frühetruskischen Sitzfiguren aus Cerveteri." *RM* 82 (1975): 165–79.

Proietti, G. *Cerveteri.* Rome, 1986.

Rastrelli, A., et al. *Le necropoli etrusche di Chianciano Terme.* Montepulciano, 1986.

Rebecchi, F., ed. *Spina e il delta padano.* Atti del convegno internazionale di studi "Spina, due civiltà a confronto," Ferrara, January 21, 1994. Rome, 1998.

———. *Spina e il delta padano: Riflessioni sul catalogo e sulla mostra ferrarese.* Rome, 1998.

Rendeli, M. *Città aperte: Ambiente e paesaggio rurale organizzato nell'Etruria meridionale costiera durante l'età orientalizzante e arcaica.* Rome, 1993.

———. *La necropoli del Ferrone.* Rome, 1996.

Riccioni, G., and M. T. Falconi Amorelli. *La tomba della panatenaica di Vulci.* Rome, 1968.

Riis, P. J. *Vulcientia vetustiora: A Study of Archaic Vulcian Bronzes.* Copenhagen, 1998.

Romualdi, A. *Guida archeologica di Populonia.* Rome, [s.a.].

———. "Un kouros di bronzo dalle vicinanze del lago di Burano: Aspetti della cultura vulcente in epoca arcaica." In *In Memoria di Enrico Paribeni,* vol. 1, ed. G. Capecchi et al., pp. 367–78. Rome, 1998.

———, **ed.** *Populonia in età ellenistica: I materiali dalle necropoli.* Atti del seminario, Florence, June 30, 1986. Florence, 1992.

Roncalli, F. *Le lastre dipinte di Cerveteri.* [Florence, 1965].

———. *Il Marte di Todi: Bronzistica etrusca ed ispirazione classica.* Memorie della Pontificia Accademia Romana di Archeologia, Series 3, 11.2. Vatican City, 1973.

Salvini, M. *Fiesole: Contributi alla ricerca delle origini.* Florence, 1990.

Sassatelli, G. *La città etrusca di Marzabotto.* Casalecchio di Reno, [1989].

———. "Verucchio: Centro etrusco di frontiera." *Ocnus* 4 (1996): 249–71.

Serra Ridgway, F. R. *I corredi del Fondo Scataglini a Tarquinia.* 2 vols. [Milan], 1996.

Serra Ridgway, F. R., and R. Linington. *Lo scavo nel Fondo Scataglini a Tarquinia.* 2 vols. Milan, 1997.

Sgubini Moretti, A. M., et al. *Vulci e il suo territorio.* Rome, 1993.

Small, J. P. "The Tragliatella Oinochoe." *RM* 93 (1986): 63–96.

Stary-Rimpau, J. S. *Die Bologneser Stelen des 7. bis 4. Jh. v. Chr.* 2 vols. Kleine Schriften aus dem Vorgeschichtlichen Seminar Marburg, herausgegeben von der Philipps-Universität Marburg, Heft 24. Marburg, 1988.

Steingräber, S. "Funerary Architecture in Chiusi." *Etruscan Studies* 2 (1995): 53–83.

———. "New Discoveries and Research in Southern Etruscan Rock Tombs." *Etruscan Studies* 3 (1996): 75–104.

Tamburini, P. *Un abitato villanoviano perilacustre: Il "Gran Carro" sul lago di Bolsena (1959–1985).* Rome, 1995.

Thimme, J. "Chiusiner Aschenkisten und Sarkophage der Hellenistischen Zeit." *SE* 23 (1954): 25–147.

Toms, J. "The Relative Chronology of the Villanovan Cemetery of Quattro Fontanili at Veii." *Annali, archeologia e storia antica,* Dipartimento di studi del mondo classico e del Mediterraneo antico, Istituto universitario orientale 8 (1986): 41–97.

———. "Symbolic Expression in Iron Age Tarquinia: The Case of the Biconical Urn." *Hamburger Beiträge zur Archäologie* 19/20 (1992/1993): 139–61.

———. "La prima ceramica geometrica a Veio." *Le necropoli arcaiche di Veio.* Giornata di studio in memoria di Massimo Pallottino, Rome, November 11, 1995, pp. 85–88. Rome, 1997.

Torcellan Vallone, M. "Cortona of the Principes." *Etruscan Studies* 2 (1995): 109–39.

Torelli, M. "Il santuario greco di Gravisca." *La parola del passato* 32 (1977): 398–458.

———. "La 'Sedia Corsini,' monumento della genealogia etrusca dei Plautii." In *Mélanges Pierre Lévêque,* ed. M.-M. Mactoux and E. Geny, 5: 335–67. Paris, 1990.

Uggeri, G., and S. Uggeri Patitucci. "Topografia e urbanistica di Spina." *SE* 42 (1974): 69–97.

Vacano, O. W. v. *Gli etruschi a Talamone: La baia di Talamone dalla preistoria ai giorni nostri.* Bologna, 1985.

Vagnetti, L. *Il deposito votivo di Campetti a Veio.* Florence, 1971.

Ward-Perkins, J. B. *Veii: The Historical Topography of the Ancient City*. Papers of the British School at Rome 29. London, 1961.

Weber-Lehmann, C. "Spätarchaische Gelagebilder in Tarquinia." *RM* 92 (1985): 19–44.

———. "Polyphem in der Unterwelt? Zur Tomba dell'Orco II in Tarquinia." *RM* 102 (1995): 71–100.

———. "Die sogenannte Vanth von Tuscania: Seirene Anasyromene." *Jahrbuch des Deutschen Archäologischen Instituts* 112 (1997): 191–246.

Wikander, C., and Ö. Wikander. "The Early Monumental Complex at Acquarossa." *Opuscula Romana* 18.11 (1990): 189–205.

Exhibition Catalogues

(listed in chronological order by date of exhibition)

Mostra dell'arte e della civiltà etrusca. Milan, Palazzo Reale, April–June 1955. Milan, [1955].

Mostra dell'Etruria padana e della città di Spina. Bologna, Palazzo dell'Archiginnasio, September 12–October 31, 1960. Bologna, [1960].

Mostra dell'arte delle situle dal Po al Danubio, VI–IV secolo a.C. Padua, Ljubljana, Vienna, 1961. Florence, 1961.

L'età del ferro nella Etruria marittima. [Grosseto, 1965?]

Teitz, R. S. *Masterpieces of Etruscan Art*. Worcester Art Museum, April 21–June 4, 1967. [Worcester, Mass., 1967.]

Arte e civiltà degli etruschi. Turin, Palazzo dell'Accademia delle scienze, June–September 1967. [Turin?, 1967].

Nuovi tesori dell'antica Tuscia. Viterbo, 1970.

Phillips, K. M. *Poggio Civitate (Murlo, Siena): Il santuario arcaico*. Florence and Siena, 1970. Florence, 1970.

Nuove letture di monumenti etruschi dopo il restauro. Florence, Museo Archeologico. Florence, 1971.

Gli etruschi: Nuove ricerche e scoperte. Milan, Castello Sforzesco, April–May 1973. Milan, 1973.

Nuove scoperte e acquisizioni nell'Etruria meridionale. Rome, Museo Nazionale Etrusco di Villa Giulia, 1975. Rome, 1975.

Aspects de l'art des Étrusques dans les collections du Louvre. Paris, Musée du Louvre. [s.l., s.a., 1976?].

Civiltà del Lazio primitivo. Rome, Palazzo delle Esposizioni, 1976. [Rome], 1976.

De Etrusken. Leiden, Rijksmuseum van Oudheden. The Hague, 1977.

Le Monde étrusque. Marseilles, Musée Borély, 1977–1978. Marseilles, 1977.

Roselle: Gli scavi e la mostra. Pisa, [1978].

I Galli e l'Italia. Rome, 1978. 2nd corrected edn., Rome, 1979.

La necropoli villanoviana di Cà dell'Orbo a Villanova di Castenaso: Problemi del popolamento dal IX. al VI. secolo a.C. Bologna, Museo Civico Archeologico, April 1979. Bologna, 1979.

Kunst und Kultur Sardiniens vom Neolithikum bis zum Ende der Nuraghenzeit, ed. J. Thimme. Karlsruhe, Badisches Landesmuseum, April 18–July 13, 1980. Karlsruhe, 1980.

Die Kelten in Mitteleuropa: Kultur, Kunst, Wirtschaft. Hallein, Keltenmuseum, May 1–September 30, 1980. Salzburg, 1980.

Gli etruschi e Cerveteri: Nuove acquisizioni delle civiche raccolte archeologiche: La prospezione archeologica nell'attività della Fondazione Lerici. Milan, Palazzo Reale, September 1980–January 1981. Milan, 1980.

Prima Italia: Arts Italiques du premier millénaire avant J.-C. Brussels, Musées royaux d'art et d'histoire, November 5, 1980–January 4, 1981. Brussels, 1980.

Kunst der Etrusker. Hamburg, Museum für Kunst und Gewerbe, August 13–October 2, 1981. Hamburg, [1981?].

Enea nel Lazio. Rome, Palazzo dei Conservatori, 1981. [Rome, 1981.]

Talamone: Il mito dei "Sette a Tebe." Florence, Museo Archeologico, February 14–October 3, 1982. Rome, 1982.

The Vatican Collections: The Papacy and Art. New York, The Metropolitan Museum of Art, February 26–June 12, 1983. New York, 1982.

Pittura etrusca a Orvieto: Le tombe di Settecamini e degli Hescanas a un secolo dalla scoperta. Rome, 1982.

Cento preziosi etruschi. Arezzo, 1984.

Civiltà degli etruschi. Florence, Museo Archeologico, May 16–October 20, 1985. Milan, 1985.

Artigianato artistico: L'Etruria settentrionale interna in età ellenistica. Volterra, Museo Guarnacci and other localities, May 18–October 20, 1985. Milan, 1985.

Santuari d'Etruria. Arezzo, Museo Archeologico "C. Cilnio Mecenate," May 19–October 20, 1985. Milan, 1985.

Case e palazzi d'Etruria. Siena, Spedale di Santa Maria della Scala, May 26–October 20, 1985. Milan, 1985.

L'Etruria mineraria. Portoferraio and other localities, 1985. Milan, 1985.

Architettura etrusca nel viterbese: Ricerche svedesi a San Giovenale e Acquarossa, 1956–1985. Viterbo, Museo Archeologico Nazionale, September 19, 1986. Rome, 1986.

Gli etruschi a nord del Po. 2 vols. Mantua, Palazzo Ducale, Galleria dell'Estivale, September 21, 1986–January 12, 1987. [Mantua, 1986–1987].

Schätze der Etrusker. Saarbrücken, Saarland Museum, October 19, 1986. [Saarbrücken, 1986].

Gli etruschi di Tarquinia. Milan, 1986. Modena, [1986].

Como fra etruschi e celti: La città preromana ed il suo ruolo commerciale. [Como], 1986.

Malerei der Etrusker in Zeichnungen des 19. Jahrhunderts: Dokumentation vor der Photographie aus dem Archiv des Deutschen Archäologischen Instituts in Rom. Cologne, Römisch-Germanisches Museum, January 17–April 5, 1987. Mainz, 1987.

La tomba François di Vulci. Vatican City, Braccio di Carlo Magno, March 20–May 17, 1987. Rome, 1987.

Etrusker in der Toskana: Etruskische Gräber der Frühzeit. Hamburg, Museum für Kunst und Gewerbe, June 18, 1987, and Malmö, Kunstmuseum Malmöhus, September 28–November 15, 1987. Florence, 1987.

L'alimentazione nel mondo antico. Viterbo, 1987. Rome, [1987].

La formazione della città in Emilia Romagna: Prime esperienze urbane attraverso le nuove scoperte archeologiche. 11th Biennale d'arte antica. Bologna, 1987.

Die Welt der Etrusker: Archäologische Denkmäler aus Museen der sozialistischen Länder. Staatliche Museen zu Berlin, Altes Museum, October 4–December 30, 1988. Berlin, 1988.

The Phoenicians. Under the scientific direction of S. Moscati. Includes a catalogue of the exhibition held in Venice in 1988. New York, 1988. Originally published as *I Fenici* (Milan, 1988).

Un artista etrusco e il suo mondo: Il pittore di Micali. Rome, Museo Nazionale Etrusco di Villa Giulia and other localities, 1988. Rome, 1988.

Dionysos: Mito e mistero, ed. F. Berti and C. Gasparri. Comacchio, Palazzo Bellini, May 7–December 17, 1989. Bologna, 1989.

La raccolta Giacinto Guglielmi. Vatican City, Palazzi Apostolici Vaticani, Stanze di San Pio V, May 23–July 29, 1989. Rome, 1989.

Etruscorum ante quam Ligurum: La Versilia tra VII e III secolo a.C., ed. E. Paribeni. Pietrasanta, Chiostro di S. Agostino, October–December, 1989. Pontedera, 1990.

Rubiera: "Principi" etruschi in Val di Secchia. Reggio Emilia, 1989.

La Chimera e il suo mito. Arezzo, Museo Archeologico Nazionale "Gaio Cilnio Mecenate," May 19–July 19, 1990. Italy: s.l., 1990.

La grande Roma dei Tarquini. Rome, Palazzo delle Esposizioni, June 12–September 30, 1990. Rome, 1990.

Die Phönizier im Zeitalter Homers. Hannover, Kestner-Museum, September 14–November 25, 1990. Mainz, 1990.

Fratte: Un insediamento etrusco-campano. Fratte, Museo Archeologico di Salerno. Modena, [1990].

Italy of the Etruscans. Translated from the German by A. Baker. Jerusalem, The Israel Museum, Weisbord Exhibition Pavilion, Summer 1991. Mainz, 1991.

Antichità dall'Umbria a New York. New York, Grey Art Gallery, September 9–November 2, 1991. Milan, 1991.

Les Étrusques et l'Europe. Paris, Grand Palais, September 15–December 14, 1992, and other localities (Milan 1992, Berlin 1993). Paris, [1992].

La Cortona dei principes. Cortona, Palazzo Casali. Cortona, 1992.

Spina: Storia di una città tra greci e etruschi. Ferrara, Castello Estense, September 26, 1993–May 15, 1994. Ferrara, 1993.

A Passion for Antiquities: Ancient Art from the Collection of Barbara and Lawrence Fleischman. Malibu, The J. Paul Getty Museum, October 13, 1994–January 15, 1995. Malibu, 1994.

Il dono delle Eliadi: Ambre e oreficerie dei principi etruschi di Verucchio. Verucchio, Museo Civico Archeologico. Rimini, 1994.

Alle origini di Firenze: Dalla preistoria alla città romana. Florence, Museo Firenze, June 25, 1996–January 19, 1997. Florence, [1996].

Carri da guerra e principi etruschi. Viterbo, Palazzo dei Papi, May 24–October 12, 1997. Rome, 1997.

Una donna di rango a Populonia: Tra la fine del quinto e gli inizi del quarto secolo a.C. Florence, Museo Archeologico, March 17–September 30, 1998. [Florence,] 1998.

Μαχη: *La battaglia del Mare Sardonio*. Oristano, Antiquarium Arborense, October 1998–March 1999. Oristano, 1998.

Le navi antiche di San Rossore. Pisa, Arsenali Medicei, June 25–August 6, 1999. Pisa, 1999.

Die Picener: Ein Volk Europas. Schirn Kunsthalle, Frankfurt, December 12, 1999–February 6, 2000. Rome, 1999.

Principi guerrieri: La necropoli etrusca di Casale Marittimo. Cecina, 1999. Milan, 1999.

Recent Museum Catalogues

ASCIANO, MUSEO CIVICO:
Mangani, E. *Museo Civico di Asciano: I materali da Poggio Pinci*. [Rome,] 1983.

BERKELEY, LOWIE MUSEUM OF ANTHROPOLOGY:
Nagy, H. *Votive Terracottas from the "Vignaccia," Cerveteri, in the Lowie Museum of Anthropology*. [Berkeley, 1988.]

BOLOGNA, MUSEO CIVICO ARCHEOLOGICO:
Morigi Govi, C., and D. Vitali, eds. *Il Museo Civico Archeologico di Bologna*. Bologna, 1982.

Tovoli, S. *Il sepolcreto villanoviano Benacci Caprara di Bologna*. Bologna, 1989.

BOLSENA:
Tamburini, P. *Un museo e il suo territorio: Il museo territoriale del Lago di Bolsena*. Vol. 1, *Dalle origini al periodo etrusco*. Bolsena, 1998.

CHIANCIANO TERME:
Paolucci, G., ed. *Museo Civico delle Acque Chianciano Terme*. [Siena,] 1997.

CIVITA CASTELLANA:
De Lucia Brolli, M. A. *L'Agro falisco*. Guide territoriali dell'Etruria meridionale. Rome, 1991.

COPENHAGEN, NY CARLSBERG GLYPTOTEK:
Moltesen, M., and M. Nielsen. *Etruria and Central Italy 450–300*. Copenhagen, 1996.

CORTONA, MUSEO DELL'ACCADEMIA ETRUSCA:
Cagianelli, C. "Bronzetti etruschi, italici e romani." *Accademia di Cortona, Annuario* 25 (1992): 9–169.

Bruschetti, P., et al. *Il museo dell'Accademia etrusca di Cortona*. 2nd edn. Cortona, 1996.

FLORENCE, MUSEO ARCHEOLOGICO NAZIONALE:
Romualdi, A. *Catalogo del deposito di Brolio in Val di Chiana*. Rome, 1981.

HANNOVER, KESTNER-MUSEUM:
Gercke, W. B. *Etruskische Kunst im Kestner-Museum Hannover*. Hannover, 1996.

KARLSRUHE, BADISCHES LANDESMUSEUM:
Jurgeit, F. *Die etruskischen und italischen Bronzen sowie Gegenstände aus Eisen, Blei und Leder im Badischen Landesmuseum Karlsruhe*. With a contribution by J. Riederer. Pisa, 1999.

MASSA MARITTIMA:
Camporeale, G., ed. *Museo archeologico*. Florence, 1992.

MURLO (SIENA):
Bruni, S., et al. *Antiquarium di Poggio Civitate*. Florence, 1988.

PARIS, BIBLIOTHÈQUE NATIONALE DE FRANCE:
Adam, A.-M. *Bronzes étrusques et italiques*. Paris, 1984.

PYRGI:
Pyrgi: Il santuario etrusco e l'Antiquarium. Rome, 1990.

ROME, MUSEO NAZIONALE ROMANO:
Helbig, W. *Führer durch die öffentlichen Sammlungen klassischer Altertümer in Rom*.[4] Vol. 3, *Museo Nazionale Romano. Museo Nazionale di Villa Giulia*. Tübingen, 1969.

ROME, VILLA GIULIA:
Proietti, G., ed. *Il Museo Nazionale Etrusco di Villa Giulia*. Rome, 1980.

Carducci, C. *Le antichità dei Falisci al Museo di Villa Giulia*. Rome, 1998.

SARTEANO (SIENA):
Minetti, A., ed. *Museo Civico Archeologico di Sarteano*. Siena, 1997.

TARQUINIA, MUSEO NAZIONALE:
Pianu, G. *Ceramiche etrusche a figure rosse*. Rome, 1980.

Comella, A. *Il deposito votivo presso l'Ara della Regina*. Rome, 1982.

Stopponi, S. *La tomba della "Scrofa nera."* Rome, 1983.

Bini, M. P., et al. *I bronzi etruschi e romani*. 2 vols. Archaeologica 114. Materiali del Museo Archeologico Nazionale di Tarquinia 13. Rome, 1992.

TUSCANIA, MUSEO ARCHEOLOGICO:
Sgubini Moretti, A. M. *Tuscania: Il Museo Archeologico*. Rome, 1991.

VATICAN, MUSEO GREGORIANO ETRUSCO:
Testa, A., and M. Sannibale. *Candelabri e thymiateria*. Rome, 1989.

Sannibale, M. *Le urne cinerarie di età ellenistica*. Rome, 1994.

Cagianelli, C., and M. Sannibale. *Bronzi a figura umana*. Rome, 1999.

Acts of Congresses, Study Meetings, and Seminars; Honorary and Memorial Volumes

(in chronological order by date of meeting)

Aspetti e problemi dell'Etruria interna. Atti del VIII convegno nazionale di studi etruschi ed italici, Orvieto, 1972. Florence, 1974.

La civiltà arcaica di Vulci e la sua espansione. Atti del X convegno nazionale di studi etruschi ed italici, Grosseto-Roselle-Vulci, 1975. Florence, 1977.

Caratteri dell'ellenismo nelle urne etrusche. Atti dell'incontro di studi, Università di Siena, April 28–30, 1976. Florence, 1977.

Este e la civiltà paleoveneta a cento anni dalle prime scoperte. Atti del XI convegno nazionale di studi etruschi ed italici, Este-Padova, June 27–July 1, 1976. Florence, 1980.

Die Göttin von Pyrgi. Akten des Kolloquiums zum Thema die Göttin von Pyrgi: Archäologische, linguistische und religionsgeschichtliche Aspekte, Tübingen, January 16–17, 1979. Florence, 1981.

L'Etruria mineraria. Atti del XII convegno di studi etruschi ed italici, Florence Populonia-Piombino, June 16–20, 1979. Florence, 1981.

Gli etruschi e Roma. Atti dell'incontro di studi in onore di Massimo Pallottino, Rome, December 11–13, 1979. Rome, 1981.

Die Aufnahme fremder Kultureinflüsse in Etrurien und das Problem des Retardierens in der etruskischen Kunst. Mannheim, February 8–10, 1980. Mannheim, 1981.

La Campania: Fra il VI e il III secolo a.C. Atti del XIV convegno di studi etruschi ed italici, Benevento, June 24–28, 1981. Galatina, 1992.

Coins, Culture and History in the Ancient World: Numismatic and Other Studies in Honor of Bluma L. Trell, ed. L. Casson and M. Price. Detroit, 1981.

Il commercio etrusco arcaico. Atti dell'incontro di studio, December 5–7, 1983. Rome, 1985.

Studi di antichità in onore di Guglielmo Maetzke. 3 vols. Rome, 1984.

Atti del secondo congresso internazionale etrusco, Florence, May 26–June 2, 1985, ed. G. Maetzke et al. 3 vols. Rome, 1989.

La formazione della città preromana in Emilia Romagna. Atti del convegno di studi, Bologna-Marzabotto, December 7–8, 1985. Bologna, 1988.

Populonia in età ellenistica: I materiali dalle necropoli. Atti del seminario, Florence, June 30, 1986. Florence, 1992.

Etruria e Lazio arcaico. Atti dell'incontro di studio, November 10–11, 1986. Rome, 1987 [i.e., 1988].

La Sardegna nel Mediterraneo tra il secondo e il primo millennio a.C. Atti del II convegno di studi "Un millennio di relazioni fra la Sardegna e i paesi del Mediterraneo," Selargius-Cagliari, November 27–30, 1986. Cagliari, 1986 [i.e., 1987].

La civiltà dei Falisci. Atti del XV convegno di studi etruschi ed italici, Civita Castellana, May 1987. Florence, 1990.

Crise et transformation des sociétés archaïques de l'Italie antique au ve siècle av. J.-C. Actes de la table ronde organisée par l'École française de Rome, Rome, November 19–21, 1987. Collection de l'École française de Rome, fasc. 137. Rome, 1990.

Les Princes celtes et la Mediterranée. Proceedings of a conference held November 25–27, 1987. Paris, 1988.

Die Welt der Etrusker. International colloquium, Berlin, October 24–26, 1988, ed. G. Heres and M. Kunze. Berlin, 1990.

La civiltà di Chiusi e del suo territorio. Atti del XVII convegno di studi etruschi ed italici, Chianciano Terme, May 1989. Florence 1993.

Etrusker nördlich von Etrurien: Etruskische Präsenz in Norditalien und nördlich der Alpen sowie ihre Einflüsse auf die einheimischen Kulturen. Akten des Symposions von Wien, Schloß Neuwaldegg, October 2–5, 1989, ed. L. Aigner-Foresti. 2 vols. Vienna, 1992.

Dionysos: Mito e mistero. Atti del convegno internazionale, Comacchio, November 3–5, 1989, ed. F. Berti. Ferrara, 1991.

Produzione artigianale ed esportazione nel mondo antico: Il bucchero etrusco. Acts of the international colloquium, Milan, May 10–11, 1990. Milan, 1993.

Tyrrhenoi philotechnoi. Proceedings of the meeting, Viterbo, October 13, 1990. Rome, 1994.

La presenza etrusca nella Campania meridionale. Atti delle giornate di studio, Salerno, Pontecagnano, November 16–18, 1990, ed. P. Gastaldi and G. Maetzke. Florence, 1994.

Deliciae fictiles. Proceedings of the First International Conference on Central Italic Terracottas at the Swedish Institute in Rome, December 10–12, 1990. Stockholm, 1993.

Gli etruschi maestri di idraulica. Convegno, Perugia, February 23–24, 1991, ed. M. Bergamini. Perugia, 1991.

Spectacles sportifs et scéniques dans le monde étrusco-italique. Actes de la table ronde organisée par l'équipe de recherches étrusco-italique de l'UMO 125 et l'École française de Rome, Rome, May 3–4, 1991. Collection de l'École française de Rome, fasc. 172. Rome, 1993.

Miscellanea etrusca ed italica in onore di Massimo Pallottino. 2 vols. Archeologia classica, no. 43. Rome, 1991.

Interactions in the Iron Age: Phoenicians, Greeks, and the Indigenous Peoples of the Western Mediterranean. International colloquium, Amsterdam, March 26–27, 1992. *Hamburger Beiträge zur Archäologie* 19/2 (1992/1993). Mainz, 1996.

Archäologische Untersuchungen zu den Beziehungen zwischen Altitalien und der Zone nordwärts der Alpen während der frühen Eisenzeit Alteuropas. Ergebnisse eines Kolloquiums, Regensburg, November 3–5, 1994. Regensburg, 1998.

Aspetti della cultura di Volterra etrusca fra l'età del ferro e l'età ellenistica e contributi della ricerca antropologica alla conoscenza del popolo etrusco. Atti del XIX convegno di studi etruschi ed italici, Volterra, October 15–19, 1995, ed. G. Maetzke and L. Tamagno Pernal. Florence, 1997.

Le necropoli archaiche di Veio. Giornata di studio in memoria di Massimo Pallottino, Rome, November 11, 1995. Rome, 1997.

Vaisselle métallique, vaisselle céramique: Production, usages et valeur en Etrurie. Revue des études anciennes 97.1–2 (1995).

Deliciae fictiles. Vol. 2. Proceedings of the Second International Conference on Archaic Architectural Terracottas from Italy, held at the Netherlands Institute in Rome, June 12–13, 1996. Amsterdam, 1997.

Dei ed eroi greci in Etruria: L'altorilievo di Pyrgi con i Sette contro Tebe. Colloquio internazionale, Rome, April 14–16, 1997. Forthcoming.

Accademia Etrusca di Cortona. Annuario 27 [in honor of Guglielmo Maetzke]. Cortona, 1997.

Der Orient und Etrurien: Zum Phänomen des "Orientalisierens" im westlichen Mittelmeerraum (10.–6. Jh. v. Chr.). International Colloquium, Tübingen 1997. Forthcoming.

From Huts to Houses: Transformation of Ancient Societies. International Seminar at the Swedish and Norwegian Institutes, Rome 1997. Forthcoming.

Etrusca et Italica: Scritti in ricordo di Massimo Pallottino. 2 vols. Pisa, 1997.

Studi in memoria di Enrico Paribeni. 2 vols. Rome, 1998.

Etruscan Religion

Colonna, G. *Bronzi votivi umbro-sabellici a figura umana.* Vol. 1. Florence, 1970.

———. "La dea etrusca Cel e i santuari del Trasimeno." *Rivista storica dell'antichità* 6–7 (1976–1977): 45–62.

———. "Riflessioni sul dionisismo in Etruria." In *Dionysos: Mito e mistero.* Atti del convegno internazionale, Comacchio, November 3–5, 1989, ed. F. Berti. Ferrara, 1991.

———. "L'Apollo di Pyrgi." In *Magna Grecia, Etruschi, Fenici.* Atti del 33. convegno di studi sulla Magna Grecia, Taranto, October 8–13, 1993, pp. 345–75. Taranto, 1996.

Cristofani, M. "Sul processo di antropomorfizzazione del panteon etrusco." *Quaderni del centro di studio per l'archeologia etrusco-italica* 22 (1993): 9–21.

———. *Tabula capuana: Un calendario festivo di età arcaica.* Florence, 1995.

Cristofani, M., and M. Martelli. "Fufluns Pachies: Sugli aspetti del culto di Bacco in Etruria." *SE* 46 (1978): 119–33.

Damgaard Andersen, H. "The Origin of Potnia Theron in Central Italy." *Hamburger Beiträge zur Archäologie* 19/20 (1992–1993): 73–113.

———. "The Etruscan Ancestral Cult: Its Origin and Development and the Importance of Anthropomorphization." *Analecta Romana Instituti Danici* 21 (1993): 7–66.

Edlund-Berry, I. E. M. "Gods and Places in Etruscan Religion." *Etruscan Studies* 1 (1994): 11–22.

Elliot, J. "The Etruscan Wolfman in Myth and Ritual." *Etruscan Studies* 2 (1995): 17–33.

Gaultier, F., and D. Briquel, eds. *Les Étrusques, les plus religieux des hommes: État de la recherche sur la religion étrusque.* Proceedings of the international colloquium, Paris, Grand Palais, November 17–19, 1992. Paris, 1997.

Hase, F.-W. v. "Présence étrusque et italique dans les sanctuaires grecs (VIIIe–VIIe siècle av. J.-C.)." In *Les Étrusques, les plus religieux des hommes,* ed. F. Gaultier and D. Briquel, pp. 293–323. Paris, 1997.

———. "Religiöse Ausdrucksformen in Etrurien." *Kult der Vorzeit in den Alpen: Opfergaben, Opferplätze, Opferbrauchtum.* Exh. Tiroler Landesmuseum Ferdinandeum. Innsbruck, 1997.

Herbig, R. *Götter und Dämonen der Etrusker.* Edited by E. Simon. 2nd edn., Mainz, 1965.

Jannot, J.-R. "Charu(n) et Vanth, divinités plurielles?" *Les Étrusques, les plus religieux des hommes,* ed. F. Gaultier and D. Briquel, pp. 139–66. Paris, 1997.

———. *Devins, dieux et démons: Regards sur la religion de l'Étrurie antique.* Paris, 1998.

Krauskopf, I. "Culśanś und Culśu." In *Beiträge zur altitalischen Geistesgeschichte.* Festschrift G. Radke zum 18. Februar 1984, ed. R. Altheim-Stiehl and M. Rosenbach, pp. 156–63. Münster, 1986.

———. *Todesdämonen und Totengötter im vorhellenistischen Etrurien: Kontinuität und Wandel.* Florence, 1987.

Maggiani, A. "Qualche osservazione sul fegato di Piacenza." *SE* 50 (1982): 53–88.

Meer, L. B. van der. *The Bronze Liver of Piacenza: Analysis of a Polytheistic Structure.* Amsterdam, 1987.

———. "Maris, Birth, Life and Death on Two Etruscan Mirrors." *Bulletin antieke beschaving* 63 (1988): 115–28.

———. "Etruscan *rites de passage.*" In *Stips votiva: Papers Presented to C. M. Stibbe,* ed. M. Gnade, pp. 119–23. Amsterdam, 1991.

Pallottino, M. "Deorum sedes." In idem, *Saggi di antichità,* 2: 779–90. Rome, 1979. Originally published in *Studi in onore di Aristide Calderini e Roberto Paribeni* (Milan, 1956–1957), 3: 223–34.

Pfiffig, A. J. *Religio etrusca.* Graz, 1975.

Rallo, A. *Lasa: Iconografia ed esegesi.* Florence, [1974].

Rendeli, M. "Anagoghe." *Prospettiva* 83–84 (July–October 1996): 10–29.

Ruyt, F. de. *Charun: Démon étrusque de la mort.* Études de philologie, d'archeologie et d'histoire anciennes 1. Rome, 1934.

Simon, E. *Schriften zur etruskischen und italischen Kunst und Religion.* Stuttgart, 1996.

Valentini, G. "Il motivo della 'Potnia Theron' su i vasi di bucchero." *SE* 37 (1969): 413–42.

Various authors. *Etrusca disciplina: I culti stranieri in Etruria.* Atti dei convegni IV e V. Annali della Fondazione per il Museo "Claudio Faina" 5 (1998).

Etruscan Women

(titles other than those listed in introduction)

Baglione, M. P. "Die Frau in Etrurien während der orientalisierenden Periode." In *Nachrichten aus der Zeit: Ein Streifzeug durch die Frauengeschichte des Altertums.* Frauenforschung 18, ed. E. Specht, pp. 177–93. Vienna, 1992.

Barber, E. J. W. *Prehistoric Textiles: The Development of Cloth in the Neolithic and Bronze Ages with Special Reference to the Aegean.* Princeton, 1991.

———. *Women's Work: The First 20.000 Years: Women, Cloth, and Society in Early Times.* New York, 1995.

Bonfante, L. "Etruscan Nudity." *Source: Notes in the History of Art* 12 (Winter 1993): 47–55.

Coldstream, N. "Mixed Marriages at the Frontiers of the Early Greek World." *Oxford Journal of Archaeology* 12 (1993): 89ff.

Haynes, S. "Muliebris certaminis laus: Bronze Documents of a Changing Ethos." In *Atti del secondo congresso internazionale etrusco*, Florence, May 26–June 2, 1985, ed. G. Maetzke et al., 3: 1395–1405. Rome, 1989.

Nielsen, M. "Women in the Late Etruscan Society: Practices of Commemoration and Social Stress." In *Fromhed og verdslighed i middelalder og renaissance: Festskrift til Thelma Jexlev*, ed. E. Waaben et al., pp. 192–202. [Odense], 1985.

———. "Sacerdotesse e associazioni cultuali femminili in Etruria: Testimonianze epigrafiche ed iconografiche." *Analecta Romana Instituti Danici* 19 (1990): 45–67.

———. "Portrait of a Marriage: The Old Etruscan Couple from Volterra in Ancient Portraiture: Image and Message." *Acta Hyperborea* 4 (1992): 89–141.

———. "Etruscan Women: A Cross-Cultural Perspective." In *Aspects of Women in Antiquity*. Proceedings of the First Nordic Symposium on Women's Lives in Antiquity, Gothenburg, June 12–15, 1997, ed. L. Larsson Lovén and A. Strömberg, pp. 69–80. Jonsered, 1998.

Prag, J., and R. Neave. *Making Faces: Using Forensic and Archaeological Evidence.* London, 1997. (For Seianti Hanunia, see pp. 172–200.)

Toms, J. "The Construction of Gender in Early Iron Age Etruria." In *Gender and Italian Archaeology*, ed. R. Whitehouse, pp. 157–79. London, 1998.

Illustration Credits

Negative numbers are given in parenthesis in italics for photographs from the Deutsches Archäologisches Institut, Rome, and from the Soprintendenza Archeologica per l'Etruria Meridionale.

© Copyright The British Museum, London: 14, 16, 36, 37, 38, 42 (drawing by M. Olive Miller), 80, 93, 115, 135, 136, 137, 142, 145, 147, 167a–b, 178, 197 (drawing by Susan Bird), 198, 210, 213, 215, 216, 220 (drawing by Susan Bird), 230, 231, 235, 244, 266a–b, 268, 271, 281, 283, 286, 291, 296.

© 1983, The Metropolitan Museum of Art, New York: 138.

© 1990, The Metropolitan Museum of Art, New York: 149a.

© 1999, Museum of Fine Arts, Boston: 232a–d, 233. All rights reserved.

© G. Dagli Orti, Paris: 29a.

© Louvre—RMN: 179.

© RMN—Chuzeville: 176a.

© RMN—Hervé Lewandowski: 47, 176b.

Alinari/Art Resource, New York: 49, 148.

Archivio Fotografico dei Musei Capitolini: 44, 79, 83a.

Archivio I.G.D.A., Milan: 25b, 35.

Art Resource, New York: 267.

Ashmolean Museum, Oxford: 209, 218.

Badisches Landesmuseum, Karlsruhe: 141.

Bibliothèque Nationale de France, Cabinet des Médailles, Paris: 217, 256.

Courtesy of Dr. Giulio Paolucci: 263.

Courtesy of Erik O. Nielsen. From Time-Life, *Etruscans: Italy's Lovers of Life* (Alexandria, Va., 1995), p. 79: 95.

Courtesy of Professor Cristiana Morigi Govi: 27, 211, 212.

Courtesy of Professor Friedhelm Prayon: 158.

Courtesy of Professor G. Colonna: 157.

Deutsches Archäologisches Institut, Rome: 3 (*81.230*), 48 (*72.900*), 51 (*72.894*), 69 (*71.2965*), 71 (*72.890*), 73 (*73.1562*), 74 (*73.1453*), 76 (*74.410*), 81 (*71.2971*), 82 (*78.666*), 87 (*80.445*), 126 (*80.4119*), 127 (*65.622*), 129 (*80.1848*), 130 (*78.754*), 132 (*68.1165*), 146 (*80.443*), 155 (*73.1258*), 156 (*81.2137*), 159 (*55.365*), 163 (*79.1203*), 164 (*1934.976*), 180 (*79.1303*), 181 (*81.4274*), 184 (*81.4226*), 186 (*82.615*), 188 (*83.1385*), 190 (*81.4251*), 191 (*79.960*), 193 (*82.2808*), 196 (*65.1065*), 201 (*1931.1207*), 221 (*82.565*), 222 (*71.578*), 223 (*82.629*), 226 (*56.312*, from *Museo Etrusco Gregoriano*, vol. 1 [Vatican, 1842], pl. CII), 227 (*63.790*), 234a (*79.1*), 238 (*31.2195*), 240 (*79.567*), 241 (*69.2407*), 242 (*69.2409*), 245a (*75.1836*), 245b (*75.1835*), 247 (*83.658*), 248 (*83.691*), 252 (*82.628*), 272 (*81.585*), 285 (*81.254*, courtesy of the Vatican Museums), 294 (*82.1552*), 295 (*82.1716*), 297 (*82.2041*), 298 (*82.2042*).

Erich Lessing/Art Resource, New York: 28a–b.

Fabio Fiaschi, Volterra: 7, 205, 289.

Getty Research Institute, Research Library 90-A33, Los Angeles: 275.

Giraudon/Art Resource, New York: 66.

Hirmer Fotoarchiv: 12, 39, 90, 91, 92, 133, 160, 236, 237, 239, 246, 254.

J. Paul Getty Museum, Malibu: 40, 168 (photos Ellen Rosenbery), 41, 175, 259 (photos Bruce White).

Johannes Felbermeyer archive, Getty Research Institute, Research Library 89.P.4, Los Angeles: 4, 8, 9, 11, 15, 24a–b, 50, 61, 62, 72, 77, 111a–b, 113, 114, 116, 125, 172, 206, 276, 278, 279, 287, 290, 293.

Museo Archeologico Nazionale, Orvieto: 128.

Museum für Kunst und Gewerbe, Hamburg: 139.

Nimatallah/Art Resource, New York: 102.

Ny Carlsberg Glyptotek, Copenhagen: 199, 202, 203.

O. Louis Mazzatenta/National Geographic Society Image Collection: 1, 124, 194.

Scala/Art Resource, New York: 46, 120, 165, 182, 183, 185, 189, 192, 243 (courtesy of the Vatican Museums), 249, 250, 251, 253, 292.

SEF/Art Resource, New York: 187.

Soprintendenza Archeologica dell'Emilia Romagna, by permission of the Ministero per i Beni Culturali e Ambientali: 30, 31, 32.

Soprintendenza Archeologica dell'Umbria, Perugia: 299.

Soprintendenza Archeologica di Roma: 2.

Soprintendenza Archeologica per l'Etruria Meridionale: 19 (*9118*), 20 (*3333*), 21a (*3603*), 21b (*3607*), 22 (*5370*), 23 (*1541*), 33 (*43293*), 34 (*35142*), 43 (*25493*), 75 (*33990*), 143 (*25023*), 152b (*27405*), 153 (*27028, 27029*), 154 (*189716*), 170 (*135596*), 171 (*5939*), 173 (*12318*), 174 (*6094*), 177 (*8195*), 234b, 273 (*24940*), 284 (*141284*).

Soprintendenza Archeologica per la Toscana—Florence: 10, 25a, 64, 65, 84, 88, 89, 96, 97, 98, 99, 100, 101, 107, 108, 109, 110, 112, 140, 150, 151, 207, 208, 228, 229, 270 (courtesy of Dr. Giulio Paolucci).

Soprintendenza Beni Artistici e Storici di Roma, Archivio Fotografico: 300.

Staatliche Antikensammlungen und Glyptothek, Munich: 144 (photo C. Moessner), 282 (photo Christa Koppermann).

Staatliche Museen zu Berlin—Preußischer Kulturbesitz—Antikensammlung: 166, 257 (photo Isolde Luckert), 269.

The University of Manchester: 266c.

Vatican Museums: 54, 55, 56, 57, 58, 59, 60, 219, 255, 288.

Drawings by Peggy Sanders: fig. 5, after Bartolini et al., *Le urne a capanna rinvenute in Italia*, fig. 39, no. 75; figs. 17, 18, after *Rasenna*, fig. 452; fig. 45, after Barker and Rasmussen, *The Etruscans*, fig. 30; fig. 67, after M. Pallottino, *The Etruscans* (Bloomington, 1975), fig. 30; fig. 117, after Rystedt, *Acquarossa*, vol. 4, pl. 1; fig. 118, after *Rasenna*, p. 514, pl. XV: 118; fig. 119, after Strandberg Olafsson, *Acquarossa*, vol. 5.1, fig. 49; figs. 121–23, after Strandberg Olafsson, *Acquarossa*, vol. 5.1, pp. 23, 24, and 26; fig. 152a, after G. Colonna, *L'altorelievo di Pyrgi* (Rome, 1996), fig. 7; fig. 169, after *Santuari d'Etruria* (1985), p. 100, fig. 5.1; fig. 225, after Pallottino, *Rendiconti Lincei*, ser. 6, vol. 6 (1930): 52, fig. 2; fig. 258, after L. Ambrosini, *Archeologia Classica* 46 (1994): p. 117, figs. 5a, b; fig. 262, after *Notizie degli Scavi*, 1931, p. 478; fig. 264, after Minetti, *Il Museo Civico Archeologico di Sarteano*, p. 98, fig. 104; fig. 265, after *Rasenna*, fig. 432; fig. 274, after Colonna di Paolo, *Castel d'Asso*, vol. 2: pl. CCCXLV.

Drawings by Patrick Finnerty: fig. 52, after F. Prayon, *Jahrbuch des Römisch-Germanischen Zentralmuseums* 37 (1990): 514, fig. 14; fig. 63, after G. Colonna, *SE* 41 (1973): pl. CXXIa, b; fig. 70, after Prayon, *RM* Ergänzungsheft 22 (1975): no. 12, fig. 12, plan 85; fig. 94, after Phillips, *In the Hills of Tuscany*, figs. 8 and 61; fig. 103, after T. N. Gantz, *RM* 81 (1974): fig. 1; fig. 104, after Mertens-Horn, *RM* 99 (1992): fig. 46; fig. 105, after J. P. Small, *SE* 39 (1971): fig. 1; fig. 106, after T. N. Gantz, *SE* 39 (1971): fig. 1; fig. 131, after A. M. Sgubini Moretti, *Bollettino di archeologia* 1 (1990–1991): fig. 12; fig. 224, after Barker and Rasmussen, *The Etruscans*, fig. 87; fig. 261, after Bianchi Bandinelli, "Clusium," p. 295, fig. 22; fig. 277, after Prayon, in Bonfante, *Etruscan Life and Afterlife*, p. 194, fig. V-37.

Reproduced, by permission, from books:

Fig. 6, from A. Rallo, ed., *Le donne in Etruria* (Rome, 1989), pl. XIII.1–6.

Fig. 13, from A. Minto, *Populonia* (Florence, 1943), fig. 23.

Fig. 26, from Bonghi Jovino and Chiaramonte Trerè, *Tarquinia: Testimonianze archeologiche e recostruzione storica*, pl. 125.

Fig. 29b, from Swaddling et al., eds., *Italy in Europe*, p. 175, fig. 5.

Fig. 53, from Colonna and v. Hase, *SE* 52 (1984): fig. 11.

Fig. 68, from Donati, *La casa dell'impluvium*, fig. 37.

Fig. 78, from Prayon, *Marburger Winckelmann-Programm*, 1974, fig. 2.

Fig. 83b, from W. Deecke, *Annali dell'Instituto di Corrispondenza Archeologica* 53 (1881): pls. L and M.

Fig. 85, from *Etrusker in der Toskana* (1987), p. 90. Courtesy of the Soprintendenza Archeologica di Firenze.

Fig. 86, from *Carri da guerra e principi etruschi* (1997), p. 167, fig. 3.

Fig. 149b, from *Carri da guerra e principi etruschi* (1997), p. 186, fig. 5.

Fig. 161, from Sassatelli, *La città etrusca di Marzabotto*, fig. 5.

Fig. 162, from Sassatelli, *La città etrusca di Marzabotto*, fig. 21.

Fig. 195, from *Corpus speculorum etruscorum*, Bundesrepublik Deutschland 4, fig. 16a.

Fig. 200, from Jannot, *Les Reliefs archaïques de Chiusi*, fig. 171.

Fig. 204, from Jannot, *Les Reliefs archaïques de Chiusi*, fig. 319.

Fig. 260, from G. Conestabile, *Pitture Murali* (Florence, 1865), pl. V.

Fig. 299, from D. Strong, *The Early Etruscans* (New York, 1968), p. 137.

Index

Note: Page numbers followed by letters *i* and *m* indicate illustrations and maps, respectively.

D

Q

R

S

T